LIBRARY
OKALOOSA-WALTON JUNIOR COLLEGE

D0810295

THE SCOTTISH NOVEL

From Smollett to Spark

THE

SCOTTISH
NOVEL

FROM
SMOLLETT
TO
SPARK

Francis Russell Hart

HARVARD UNIVERSITY PRESS
Cambridge, Massachusetts
1978

PR
8597
H37

Copyright © 1978 by Francis Russell Hart
All rights reserved
Printed in the United States of America

Library of Congress Cataloging in Publication Data

Hart, Francis Russell.
    The Scottish novel.

    Includes index.
    1. Scottish fiction—History and criticism.
2. English fiction—Scottish authors—History and
criticism. I. Title.
PR8597.H37   823′.03   77-20680
ISBN 0-674-79584-9

LIBRARY
OKALOOSA - WALTON JUNIOR · COLLEGE

In grateful memory of
Neil Gunn and Jane Duncan
and for their friends
Priscilla, Ruth, and
Russell Hart

66631

Preface

For two centuries the novel has served Western culture as a unique critical instrument. "In our phase of civility," Frank Kermode in *The Sense of an Ending* observes, as Lionel Trilling and others have observed before him, "the novel is the central form of literary art. It lends itself to explanations borrowed from any intellectual system of the universe which seems at the time satisfactory." However the novel's emergence may be accounted for or its dominant role assessed, its artistic and social importance cannot be doubted. And yet no comprehensive interpretive survey of Scotland's novelists has appeared. Why this neglect? There are several possible reasons.

For one, a distinctive feature of modern Scotland's literary establishment has been its hostility to, or relative lack of interest in, the novel as a form. Scotland's greatest modern poet, Hugh MacDiarmid, has frankly and influentially expressed the view that the novel is an inferior kind of literary expression, that "prose" is "non-creative." Critics have pronounced the judgment that the novel is "the most backward literary form in Scotland" (Edwin Morgan) and that there are "very few pieces of lasting value" in Scottish prose fiction (David Craig). Some have waited expectantly with Sydney Goodsir Smith in the conviction that "the novel should be the next citadel to fall," that what is needed is "one first-class novel in Scots . . . to prove that the thing can be done." Others have held to the gloomier prophecy of Edwin Muir that Scottish culture has long been too narrow, provincial, or uncentered to produce such a book. Meanwhile, Scottish literature's most illuminating recent theorists stand at opposite extremes: Kurt Wittig is excited by the imaginative peculiarities of a persistent Scottish tradition in all literary forms; David Craig is hostile to all who associate nationality with aesthetic value.

There are other possible reasons for the neglect. Literary education in the universities has been dominated until recently by a classical English curriculum, and academic studies of the "British novel" have found room for Scottish groups and movements only as provincial offshoots of English traditions. The inadequacy and irrelevance of such a perspective remain to be demonstrated. The demonstration, to be sure, is not made easier by the fact that the novelists themselves have often slighted or concealed linguistic or cultural nationality, or that when they have not done so, "cosmopolitan" readers have labeled them provincial. The Scottish novelist's problem of audience is a real one, no less so than the related problem of linguistic nationality. And there remains the haunting possibility that Scottish culture has features inimical to the novel, and that this situation may be not just inevitable but healthy.

Finally, there are reasonable uncertainties as to whether the novel has a distinctive Scottish tradition. This book's chronology begins with novelists of the 1760s and 1770s and ends with novelists of the 1960s and 1970s in whom a Scottish derivation or inspiration is not easily recognized. The problem of nationality in literature is complex, and this book is not dogged in its quest for the distinctive. But surely we can postulate that the novel as a form of historical and cultural representation must be significantly influenced or conditioned by the history and culture from which its practitioners come or within which they work.

This book seeks what general understanding of the novel in Scotland may be found in its historical development as well as in its development in history. I am reluctant to generalize when so much particular evidence must first be identified and interpreted. And I have included much evidence—fifty novelists and over two hundred novels—in the simple faith that such abundance may eventually lead to informed generalizations. I offer a few interpretations of my own in the concluding pages. This book is not an essay in criticism, but critical judgment must play a role in historical construction, and my own judgments will be acknowledged. Criticism of Scottish novelists has often seemed prejudicial or dogmatic; some who declare that there are few real achievements in Scotland's prose fiction seem uninformed about the books they ignore and unwilling to accord them serious attention. On the other hand, there is a danger that the interpreter of little-remembered works of art may founder in his own enthusiasms, but this is a risk I consider worth taking. If readers who find my enthusiasms indiscriminate will test them against the novels themselves, one of my main objectives will be won.

Certain limitations of my study should be acknowledged. Scotland's novel has developed in interplay with social and historical forces; yet my orientation as a literary historian holds me to the view that textual interpretation must largely precede the study of that interplay. Thus, while several chapters include perspectives in social history, such perspectives are limited. Another limitation: a major purpose here is to identify distinctive motifs and methods in the novel that are reflective of Scottish origins and experience; but to define them thoroughly would require a continuous comparison with novelists of other national literatures. Although I have occasionally made such comparisons, so abundant is the primary Scottish material that extensive comparative study must be postponed. For the same reason, I cannot undertake an intensive study of style, and this too is regrettable. Whether a Scottish fiction can be achieved without a national language has long been a controversial issue for Scotland's novelists. The use of Scots in the novel has been restricted, and several novelists have taken the issue of a native language as a cultural theme. The uses will be noted and the theme examined. But in general I have concentrated on nonlinguistic elements of narrative method and form.

I have not wanted to draw the outlines of my survey too sharply, for outlines are substantive interpretations, and in a large preliminary study such interpretations may seem premature. Yet the book must be shaped, and the obligation for shaping is mine. I have worked in large units and have proceeded for the most part chronologically, but within chronological frames I have spoken extensively of one novelist at a time. The beginnings of the novel in Scotland are traced in the distinct yet related modes of the Gothic novel and the novel of social history, the two joining in the example and influence of *Blackwood's Magazine* in its early days. The second section traces a sixty-year period, beginning with a handful of prodigious mid-Victorians, moving then to the despised (and misrepresented) figures for whose alleged parish idyllicism the derisive term "Kailyard" was coined, and closing with those in whom an anti-Kailyard impulse is dominant. The third section intervenes in chronology to consider the persistence of romance in Scottish fiction, while the fourth picks up with continuities and shifts in the novel of early modern Scotland and finishes with notes on the present generation. The final section gives separate attention to the novel of the Highlands, from late-Victorian Celticisms to the successors of Neil Gunn.

The list of novelists must seem at once overly ambitious and lamentably incomplete. Every knowledgeable reader can point to omissions. But it represents a beginning that may lead readers to seek out the novels themselves. They will discover as I have—and in their seeking begin to remedy—the unavailability of many of the novels. The Scottish novel suffers from a passive conspiracy of neglect.

This study was begun ten years ago in the hospitable Ross-shire homes of Neil Gunn, Jane Duncan, and Eric Linklater; none, alas, has lived to see its completion. It was greatly encouraged at the outset by Alexander Reid and by Reid's fine essays on modern novelists in *Scotland's Magazine*. Over the years many kind people have helped. Among critics and scholars, I should single out David Daiches, Ian Grimble, Ross Roy, Douglas Gifford, Ian Campbell, and George Bruce. My friends Meta and Ian Gilmour and Herschel Gower, who introduced me to Scotland, have been indispensable. Arlene Jacquette helped greatly with early research; the Guggenheim Foundation gave me the time to begin, while Dean Daisy Tagliacozzo of the University of Massachusetts arranged for the time to finish; the staff of the National Library of Scotland were always resourceful and kind. I am especially grateful to Susan Wallace, Sheila Stone, and Bunny Hart for discerning and rigorous editorial aid. My wife, Lorena, is as always my touchstone of taste and my tireless listener.

Francis Russell Hart
Hingham, Massachusetts
September 1977

Acknowledgments

Permission to quote from the following published materials has been kindly granted: Lewis Grassic Gibbon, *A Scots Quair* (Copyright 1946 by Ray Mitchell), by Schocken Books, Inc., and by Hutchinson Publishing Group, Ltd.; Lewis Grassic Gibbon, *Spartacus*, by Hutchinson Publishing Group, Ltd.; John Galt, *Annals of the Parish*, ed. J. Kinsley (1967), and John Galt, *The Entail*, ed. I. Gordon (1970), by the Oxford University Press; Douglas Young, *Scotland* (Copyright 1971 by Douglas Young), by Cassell & Collier Macmillan Publishers, Ltd.; *Whither Scotland*, ed. D. Glen, by Victor Gollancz, Ltd.; *Alastair MacLean Introduces Scotland*, ed. A. Dunnett, by Andre Deutsch, Ltd.; *Memoirs of a Modern Scotland*, ed. K. Miller, by Faber and Faber, Ltd.; William Power, *Literature and Oatmeal*, by Routledge and Kegan Paul, Ltd.; John Buchan, *Pilgrim's Way*, by Susan, Lady Tweedsmuir; Eric Linklater, *Fanfare for a Tin Hat, Juan in America*, and *Position at Noon*, by A. D. Peters & Co., Ltd.; Naomi Mitchison, *Return to the Fairy Hill*, by Thomas Y. Crowell Co., Inc.; Robin Jenkins, *The Changeling*, by Macdonald and Jane's Publishers, Ltd.; Derek Stanford, *Muriel Spark*, by Centaur Press, Ltd., Fontwell, England; Fionn Mac Colla, *The Albannach*, by Mary MacDonald; George Mackay Brown, *Magnus*, by George Mackay Brown and The Hogarth Press. For permission to include revised versions of my own published articles, grateful acknowledgment is made to the following: for "Limits of the Gothic: The Scottish Example," in *Studies in Eighteenth-Century Culture*, ed. H. Pagliaro (Cleveland: Case Western Reserve Press, 1973), to the American Society for Eighteenth-Century Studies; for "Beyond History and Tragedy: Neil Gunn's Early Fiction," in *Essays on Neil M. Gunn*, ed. D. Morrison (Thurso: Caithness Books, 1971), to David Morrison; for "The Hunter and the Circle: Neil Gunn's Fiction of Violence," in *Studies in Scottish Literature*, 1 (1963), and for "Jane Duncan's Friends and the Reachfar Story," in *Studies in Scottish Literature*, 6 (1969), to G. Ross Roy.

Contents

Introduction   1

BLACKWOODIAN BEGINNINGS:
GOTHIC ROMANCE AND PROVINCIAL MANNERS

1. Scottish Variations of the Gothic Novel   13
   Smollett, Scott, Hogg
2. John Galt   31
3. The Other Blackwoodians   53
   Moir, Ferrier, Lockhart, Wilson

THE SCOTTISH VICTORIANS:
IN AND OUT OF THE KAILYARD

4. Victorian Modes and Models   87
   Alexander's Johnny Gibb
5. Mid-Victorians   93
   Oliphant, MacDonald, Tytler
6. The Liberals in the Kailyard   114
   Crockett, Maclaren, Barrie
7. The Anti-Kailyard as Theological Furor   131
   Stevenson, Brown, Hay

THE PERSISTENCE OF ROMANCE

8. Romance after the Enlightenment 143
   Scott, Grant, Crockett

9. Stevenson, Munro, and Buchan 154

10. Mitchison and Later Romancers 182
    Tranter, Dunnett

THE NOVEL AND NATIONAL MYTH IN MODERN SCOTLAND

11. Contemporary Scotland in Fact and Myth 201

12. Novelists of the Modern Renaissance 207
    The Muirs, Blake, Mackenzie, Gibbon, Barke, Smith

13. Novelists of Survival 246
    Linklater and Jenkins

14. Kennaway, Spark, and After 287

THE NOVEL OF THE HIGHLANDS

15. The Tragedy of the Clearances 325
    Smith, Gunn, Mac Colla

16. Late Victorian Celticisms 336
    Black, "Fiona Macleod"

17. Neil Gunn 348

18. Highlands of the Humorists 374
    Munro, Mackenzie, Beckwith

19. Jane Duncan and George Mackay Brown 385

Retrospect: Notes for a Theory of Scottish Fiction 398
Notes 411
Index 431

THE SCOTTISH NOVEL

From Smollett to Spark

We are leaving the sphere of history and are about to enter that of mythology. Mythology is nothing more than history garbled; likewise history is mythology garbled and it is nothing more in all the history of man.
Muriel Spark, *The Abbess of Crewe*

Man is small, and, therefore, small is beautiful. To go for giantism is to go for self-destruction. And what is the cost of a reorientation? We might remind ourselves that to calculate the cost of survival is perverse.
E. F. Schumacher, *Small Is Beautiful*

"Have you time for a very short seminar, Gertrude, on how one treats of a paradox?"

"A paradox you live with," says Gertrude, and hangs up.
Muriel Spark, *The Abbess of Crewe*

Introduction

Centuries of social observers have told us of the distinctiveness of Scottish culture by invoking a peculiar national character. Put together, this heritage of tropes and stereotypes produces a logical absurdity. That grandly anomalous person the "typical Scot" is "a schizophrenic creature at once realistic and recklessly sentimental, scientific and soldierly, bibulous and kilted, teetotal and trousered, diligent, religious, liberal, warm-hearted, poetry-loving, devoted to law, learning, and mercantile enterprise, friendly, unassuming, living graciously, supine, dirty, fond of closing public houses unseasonably, violent and drunken, and addicted to casual homicide, too careful with money, generous, rash, disputatious, shy, loquacious, aggressive, refined, humane, zealous, hypocritical, adaptable, democratic, equalitarian, and peculiarly related to the Almighty."[1] He is also, we have been told for two centuries, disappearing, and with him a distinctive Scottish culture. But the myth survives. Its very persistence has become a notable cultural fact. Scots believe it, even as they jokingly display its anomalies; their sense of identity remains strongly typological, even as it is radically individual. Such a myth must affect the nature of the Scottish novel.

Related to the myth of national character is a long-lived passion for the local past, for the history of clan and family, burgh and parish. Local attachment can be found everywhere in Scottish history. Parish and burgh have been the settings for historic events and develop-

1

ments. Personal identity is closely associated in law and lore with place name and hereditary locale; Walter Scott perpetuated but did not invent the habit of memory that recalled a legend at every crossing or hillock. Political demographers have found that voting patterns in Scotland's largest cities remain parochial, suggesting that adaptation to urban life may have been as slow for Scottish people as it has long been feared in the Scottish novel.[2] At any rate, the endurance of local identity and national stereotype helps to explain the vigorous survival in Scotland of folk culture, legend, and traditional narrative. The Marxist critic Walter Benjamin has suggested that storytelling and the novel are mutually hostile.[3] If he is right, then the unusual strength of an oral storytelling tradition in Scottish culture must have been both an obstacle and a challenge to the formal development of the novel.

Local attachment has found its greatest cultural support in a fiercely independent, theologically passionate and disputatious church. Scottish survival has been tied to a national church from the fourteenth century Declaration of Arbroath, to the fierce martyrdoms of almost legendary seventeenth-century Covenanters, to the Great Disruption of 1843, and beyond. The specific cultural effects of Scottish Calvinism may be debated and deplored, but their importance is beyond question, whether one holds with T.S. Eliot that Scotland is a country ruined by religion or believes with historians such as Smout and Ferguson that the secularizing of the Calvinist tradition provided the psychological force behind Scottish industrial development, imperialist adventure, and even revolutionary socialism.[4] "A systematic Calvinist religion," as Smout puts it, "is itself so all-consuming in its demands."[5] And following the movement of royalty south and the parliamentary Union of 1707, the church, together with legal and educational institutions, remained as a bulwark of cultural distinctiveness. Church, law, and school—an aristocracy of professions—dominated life and letters; their influence has been both radical and conservative.

Every culture has its inner divisions or tensions, but those in Scotland seem peculiarly marked. The curious linguistic situation of the Lowlands—talking and feeling in Scots, thinking and writing in an artificial standard English—has produced what some have called a dissociation of sensibility.[6] It may be related to a deeply divided affinity for both fact and romance or what Kenneth Clark describes as "an extraordinary combination of realism and reckless sentimentalism" in

2

Scottish consciousness. This dissociation finds an emblem, a sign of terrific paradox for Muriel Spark, in the Edinburgh of classic civility with its towering black crag.[7] Moreover, the dual culture of Highland and Lowland Gael and Angle, its great cleft geologically etched, remains a potent dialectic in modern nationalist myth. And equal in force for many Scots has been a dual allegiance: a deep sense of identification with a small parochial home counterpointing an exhilarating kinship with the most remote, farflung corners of world commonwealth. One of Canada's pioneers, after all, was the greatest of Scotland's parish annalists, John Galt. To this catalogue of tensions early modern interpreters have added the metaphor of the "Caledonian antisyzygy," the taste for violent shifts of mood and perspective that for centuries is supposed to have expressed and possibly fostered such cultural divisions.[8]

Not all of these generalizations need be accepted to convince us that Scottish culture is distinctive enough to have produced substantial variations in the novel. But there is also the historical fact that the emergence of the novel in Scotland came at a later, and different, period than that of the novel in England. By the middle of the eighteenth century Daniel Defoe, Samuel Richardson, and Henry Fielding had established the novel as a major literary form in English. Imitators were numerous. Laurence Sterne was to follow shortly. But when, in 1769, the Scottish writer Henry Mackenzie was at work on *The Man of Feeling,* he observed that the novel was "a sort of composition which . . . the Scottish genius is remarkably deficient in." He could think of only two exceptions: Tobias Smollett and an unnamed "female author."[9] Mackenzie published three novels in the 1770s, then gave up the form, and it remained virtually invisible in Scotland until the turn of the century. The accounting for events that did not happen is always perilous and highly speculative. But what was happening in eighteenth-century Scottish culture has a bearing on the novel's late appearance. And the unique situation of Mackenzie warrants attention.

Scotland's cultural revival in the eighteenth century has sometimes been seen in terms of paradox and cultural schizophrenia. David Daiches's conception of the paradox, for instance, is that the Union of 1707 produced in the long run "forces which worked consciously for the improvement of agriculture and industry in Scotland, but those forces were bound up with elements that seemed at the same time to militate against a national culture."[10] And yet by ending political independence the Union had forced Scotland into greater cultural consciousness, awakened a defensive pride, and led to a revival of interest in her literary nationality.[11] But the literary past seemed almost exclusively poetical.

On the eve of the Union, Edinburgh printer James Watson began the revival of Scots poetry with the first volume of his *Choice Collection of Comic and Serious Scots Poems Both Ancient and Modern.* Allan Ramsay, wigmaker turned bookseller and poet, followed with broadsides of traditional poems and his own verse in Scots. His collection of *Ever Green* (1724) reintroduced the great medieval *makers* William Dunbar and Robert Henryson. His *Tea-Table Miscellany* (published between 1724 and 1737) included Scots songs and ballads, many of them "improved" into Augustan English. Emulator of Pope, Gay, and Prior, devoted Scottish antiquarian and patriot, Ramsay was indeed "a mixed and confused character"; "the dualism in Ramsay's life and character," says Daiches, "was deep-seated and corresponded to a dualism in the Scottish culture of his day."[12] What matters most for our purposes is that Ramsay encouraged many a Scottish gentleman to adapt or imitate traditional Scots songs. Thus, the literary rediscovery of Scots centered on poetry. It seemed inseparable from cultural nationhood. The poetry may well have been marked by revivalist condescension and nostalgia, by regional dialects used with mixed taste; it may have been what David Craig depreciates as "vernacular poetry and 'country wit.' "[13] The more remarkable, then, that such a revival climaxed in two poets as impressive as Robert Fergusson and Robert Burns, whose brief careers helped to confirm the association of poetry and cultural survival.

"It was too late," observes Daiches, "to do anything for Scots prose."[14] It had declined since the Reformation under the influence of England's Protestant Scottish allies, and by the end of the seventeenth century it had almost disappeared as a written language. The "polite culture" of the anglicizing eighteenth century demanded its total obliteration and chased away "Scotticisms" as barbaric remnants. The prose of what social historians still refer to as the Golden Age of Scottish culture had to be written in an artificial, "philosophical" English; the literati of Enlightenment Edinburgh had no workable written Scots and were mostly out of touch and ear with vernacular English. The author of *Mirror* no. 83 (1779-80) offers a pathetic account of "the Scarcity of Humourous Writers in Scotland":

> The old Scottish dialect is now banished from our books, and the English is substituted in its place. But though our books be written in English, our conversation is in Scotch . . .
> The circumstance of a Scottish author not writing his own natural dialect must have a considerable influence upon the nature of his literary productions. When he is employed in any grave dignified composition, when he writes history, politics, or poetry, the pains he must take to write, in a manner different from that in which he speaks, will not much affect his productions . . . But if a writer is to descend to common and ludicrous pictures of life . . . his language must be, as nearly as possible, that of common life, that of the bulk of the people; but a Scotsman who wishes to write English cannot easily do this.[15]

He cannot write prose in Scots, and the English he has acquired is unsuited to the novel.

Furthermore, the dominant literary interests of the time were remote from "common and ludicrous pictures of life." The honors list of the Scottish Enlightenment includes Hutcheson, Hume, and Smith in moral philosophy, Hume and Robertson in history, Hutton and Black in the sciences, the Monros and Hunters in medicine, Watt and McAdam in engineering, Ferguson in sociology, the Adams in architecture, Raeburn in painting, Kames and Blair in aesthetics. The creative energies of such an august and Augustan company were well spent without recourse to prose fiction. History came closest. "This is the historical age," exulted Hume, "and we are the historical people."[16] The same impulse that led to the histories of Hume, Robertson, and Smollett may also be seen in the growth of Scottish biography and autobiography and in the historical speculations of Scottish social theorists. The enthusiasm and controversy over the Burns phenomenon and the Ossianic effusions of Macpherson suggest the extent to which Scottish literary theory was a branch of historical inquiry when it was not a part of the "Philosophy of Mind." Not surprisingly, Sir Walter Scott's eventual turn to the novel was a late outgrowth of his antiquarian researches and reconstructions. And when John Galt did likewise, he was at pains to distinguish what he wrote from "the novel" and to characterize it as a kind of social history.

The literary arbiter of the Scottish Augustan company was Henry

Mackenzie. Like Scott after him, Mackenzie began as a poet and produced his best verse in imitation of old Scots ballads before discovering and practicing briefly what was clearly an alien form. In the mid-1760s he went to London to complete his legal training, notably in the one branch of Scottish law that was English, the Exchequer. While there he conceived the plan of *The Man of Feeling*, and he calls it "a real picture of my London adventures."[17] His letters suggest how strange the form felt. "You will find inclosed a very whimsical introduction to a very odd medley . . . I have seldom been in use to write any prose, except what consisted of observations (such as I could make) on men and matters. The way of introducing these by narrative, I have fallen into in some detached essays . . . [I] write now and then a chapter as I have leisure or inclination . . . I would have it as different from the entanglement of a novel as can be. Yet I would not be understood to undervalue that species of writing." To a friend he sends a similar apology: "You may perhaps, from the description, conclude it a novel; nevertheless it is perfectly different than that species of composition."[18]

The result, published in 1771, was *The Man of Feeling*. *The Monthly Review* saw it as "after the manner of Sterne" though at a "prodigious distance," abounding in "provincial and Scottish idioms." Even *The Scots Magazine* saw it as "after the manner" of Sterne. But *The Man of Feeling* differs in numerous ways from *A Sentimental Journey*, and the quality of its ambiguous sentimentality is only part of the difference. The fragmentary structure has nothing to do, in theme or comic effect, with Sterne's witty disjunctions and gaping innuendos. Harley, the hero, is nothing like Sterne's frenetic sensationalist, any more than he resembles the vain but amiable humorists of Oliver Goldsmith. Misremembered only for his dropping of tears, he is no Fool of Charity. His humor is bashfulness; his private feelings find little place in the social world. But he is not bashful about doing good or protecting the unfortunate. Seldom duped, he can be whimsical and sensible; for him as for his beloved Miss Walton "humanity was a feeling, not a principle"; he has prudence, a gently satiric understanding of fashionable society, and the ability to "ruminate on the folly of mankind." The susceptibility of Emily Atkins, the poor prostitute, is a dangerous excess of sensibility not evident in Harley. And in the notorious deathbed scene he is not killed by the sharing of love confessions; he is dying already when the scene takes place, ill with a fever contracted in acts of practical charity. Death is the end; but while *A Sentimental Journey* is a hectic, fortuitous flight from death, *The Man of Feeling* is an episodic pilgrimage home to mortality, monumental memory, and peace. In its calm melancholy and funereal frame, the book anticipates the late Victorian Ian Maclaren, but only by way of Scott's *Old Mortality* with its pathetic young wraith Peter Pattieson. Most interestingly, Harley's tears signal a sensibility that is unusual in its intense empathy. He becomes literally absorbed in the stories of misfortune he hears. "Let me," he says to old Edwards, "imprint the virtue of thy sufferings on my soul," as if there were a psychic power in the impersonation of suffering.[19]

Harley's world, after all, is a world of genuine misfortune. And in Mackenzie's other two novels the mixture of "high pathos" and "stark tragedy" (found by Wittig throughout Scottish poetic tradition) is more extreme.[20] *The Man of the World* (1773) is Richardsonian in plot and even more remote from the humor of Sterne and Goldsmith. The "man" is a libertine seducer, his obsessive object to seduce the daughter of his neighbor, a clergyman. Critics have seen him as a failed Lovelace. But Sindall has none of Lovelace's patrician complexity; he is motivated by powerful lust. And the sufferings of his victims are violent and extreme. The clergyman Annesley, sickened already by his son's "transportation" for armed robbery, dies when he learns his raped daughter is pregnant and has run away. She is tricked into supposing the rapist will marry her; when he forces an accomplice on her, she goes into premature labor, and the report that her infant is drowned kills her. Years later, the object of Sindall's lust is a young foundling who lives with him. She is barely saved from rape when Annesley's son, returned from exile, wounds Sindall fatally; and before he dies, a horrified penitent, he learns that he almost raped his own daughter.

The gentle man of feeling is also remote from *Julia de Roubigné* (1777), where the plot is equally grim and catastrophic, but fatality replaces the villainy of lust. Julia's proud father is saved from ruin by a benevolent but proud neighbor, Montauban. Julia marries him in gratitude, though she still secretly loves young Savillon, who is rumored to be married to another overseas. The report is false; Savillon returns to find her married and persuades her to grant a secret farewell meeting. Montauban suspects adultery and, half mad with jealousy, poisons her. Learning of her innocence, he poisons himself.

The similarities to Rousseau's *Julie* have often been noted; the echoes of *Othello* are conscious. *Julia de Roubigné* was considered Mackenzie's best novel,[21] and it suggests the direction in which Mackenzie's fiction is moving: toward the compact, grim tale of tragic fatality. To continue in this direction he gave up his position as chief of British novelists in the 1770s and turned to the short story, the "simple pathetic story" in which, Leigh Hunt wisely observed, he was excelled by no other British writer.[22]

Mackenzie's brief story of La Roche appeared in three of the *Mirror* papers two years after *Julia*. It centers once more on a father, a doomed daughter, a violent catastrophe. The father is a Swiss minister; a British philosopher (supposed to be founded on Hume) finds him seriously ill at a French inn, cares for him, and accompanies father and daughter home. Somewhat in love with the daughter, he corresponds with them, and upon returning later to visit, he hears that the daughter is about to marry a young soldier. He arrives for the wedding, only to find a funeral: the soldier has been killed by a friend in a duel; the daughter has died of heartbreak. The old father is sustained by a calm, deep piety that the sceptical philosopher laments he cannot share.

The scene is far from Scotland, but the elements and tensions of much later Scottish fiction are here already. The three stories—*The Man of the World, Julia*, and "La Roche"—are amply stored with sentimental piety. Yet the plot materials possess the grimmest sort of ballad-like intensity, tragic irony, sudden violence. The mixture anticipates novels to come: notably Scott's *Bride of Lammermoor* and *St. Ronan's Well* and John Gibson Lockhart's *Adam Blair* and *Matthew Wald*. Evident already is what Mackenzie himself as reviewer found to be a distinctively Scottish cultural conception at the heart of *Adam Blair*: the "sanctity of the clerical character."[23] In general, Mackenzie's mixture of pathos, violence, and irony anticipates Lockhart most clearly.

But after his brief, uneasy success as novelist in the 1770s, Mackenzie turned away to become the "Scottish Addison" of periodical writing in *The Mirror* (1779-80) and *The Lounger* (1785-86), the ardent but misguided patron of the "sublime" peasant Burns, the doyen of late Augustan Edinburgh. He lived into the age of Scott's *Waverley* and the Scottish novelists associated with *Blackwood's Magazine* as "ultimus Romanorum," Grand Old Man of Scottish letters. And when in 1814 "an unknown Admirer" dedicated *Waverley* to the "Scottish

Addison," the admirer "heartily" wished "that the task of tracing the
evanescent manners of his own country had employed the pen of the
only man in Scotland who could have done it justice—of him so distinguished in elegant literature, and whose sketches of Colonel Caustic
and Umphraville are perfectly blended with the finer traits of national
character."[24] (Scott is alluding to *Mirror* and *Lounger* figures in the
manner of de Coverley and the Man in Black.) But Scott's task came a
generation later than Mackenzie's fiction, and Mackenzie found the
form uncongenial. The question of why, in the 1770s, he did not become the first Scottish novelist in the mode of Scott, Galt, or Lockhart
is actually two questions: Why did he not think to record Scottish
manners? And why did he give up the novel to work in shorter narrative forms? The questions relate to Mackenzie himself, but also to the
novel's late arrival in Scotland.

Ian Watt and others have associated the rise of the novel in England
with early eighteenth-century socioeconomic individualism, with the
new psychologism of John Locke and other empiricists, with the
secularizing of spiritual autobiography, with the decorums of a newly
affluent bourgeoisie and the providential optimisms of a new religious
liberalism.[25] The novel in Scotland arose almost a century later in extremely different circumstances, the complex milieu of the late Enlightenment. This was a time of pioneering sociological thought, a
seedtime of speculative interest in man's societal evolution not from a
hypothetical contract but from primitive social impulses.[26] For some
this distinctive sociological emphasis is a reassertion of the societal
emphasis in Calvin. For the social historian T. C. Smout it proves the
inapplicability to Scotland of the Weber-Tawney thesis that a close
connection existed between Calvinism and the rise of economic
individualism—a thesis crucial to recent theories of the English novel.
In Scotland, says Smout, "the ethic of the kirk-session, with its strong
group discipline over moral behaviour, fitted in . . . perfectly with the
tradition of the guild and the burgh with their group discipline over
civic and economic behaviour."[27] Scotland's neo-Calvinism in this
period stressed the communal over the individual.

The late Enlightenment was a time of incredibly rapid socioeconomic change. "Scotland," notes Mitchison, "packed into about thirty
years . . . the economic growth that in England had spread itself over
three centuries."[28] Until Neilson's "hot blast" of 1828, the change was
predominantly agrarian—and this is of momentous import for the

forming of Scottish traditions in the novel. It was in the countryside that the shock was felt, in the glens that the terrible Clearances occurred in the name of improvement and progress, exploiting and shattering ancient fidelities. But this was a time, too, of burgh reform, exceeding in importance for Scotland the later 1832 reform of a remote British parliament.

The widespread religious revival of the period, which would later give Victorian England its evangelical earnestness, had other reverberations in Scotland. For it stirred a deep populist sentiment for parochial, hence local, self-determination, a sentiment climaxed by what Mitchison calls that "act of tremendous courage" and Ferguson cites as Scotland's "most momentous single event of the nineteenth century," the Great Disruption of 1843.[29] The religious revival carried with it an awakened fascination with the seventeenth century as an age of heroes and martyrs. Thus, religious revival strengthened nationalist sentiment in a time of perfervid European nationalism, when in many countries the repudiation of cosmopolitan enlightenment was focused against France and Napoleonic imperialism. Cultural importation from Spain and Germany played a substantial role in the awakening of romantic nationalism in Scotland, and three of the most influential of British "Germanizers" were Scots: Scott, Lockhart, and Thomas Carlyle. And the new sentiment had a peculiar ambivalence. Now, for the first time, three generations after the Union and two after Culloden, there grew a sophisticated malaise, even among legal and ecclesiastical leaders, over the assumptions of Unionist ideology, over the very survival of essential institutions: law, education, kirk. As N. T. Phillipson and J. A. Smith have shown, the task of allaying the malaise and perfecting a fictive Union fell to a generation newly sympathetic with the impulses of cultural nationalism.[30] A consequence was a deeply divided cultural identity among cultural leaders.

Finally, in literature and art this was a time of "romantic" revival, of the cult of visionary subjectivity, of memoir and confession, when literature turned inward to what Martin Price calls the "theatre of mind," an age of sensibility that turned into the age of revolutionary or Sadist sublimity and grotesque demonism we have come to call Gothic.[31] It is here that our survey opens.

Blackwoodian Beginnings:
Gothic Romance
and
Provincial Manners

1

Scottish Variations
of the
Gothic Novel

T he novel in Scotland began with various mixtures of mode— realistic and antirealistic, fantastic and antiquarian. On the one hand, novelists of the late eighteenth-century Gothic tendency in fiction followed an English example, modified to suit distinctive Scottish tastes and preoccupations. On the other, novelists of social realism transformed an established Augustan conception of "manners" into a historical and regional mode, which was later to transform the realism of English fiction in its turn. We can see both of these trends in Smollett and Scott; but because these two writers have received so much critical attention elsewhere—and because there are so many other (and relatively neglected) novelists to consider—I hope I may be excused for speaking of Smollett and Scott only briefly. Scott's younger contemporaries, conventionally called "Blackwoodians" because most of them wrote for that scandalous and often brilliant Edinburgh Tory magazine, deserve chief consideration here as the first identifiable generation of Scottish novelists.

The early novels in Scotland are undeniably associated with what we may cautiously call the Gothic tendency in fiction of the late eighteenth century. Recent years have seen several attempts to define the Gothic novel,[1] to distinguish what is essential from what is mere trapping, to separate serious from frivolous or popular Gothic, to insist on a hierarchy of generic elements, and to judge individual works according to their observance of such distinctions and priorities. My own view is that these efforts do not provide a fair critical approach to individual English novelists, let alone Scottish. We may learn something of the limits of generic definition, as well as something about the beginnings of a distinctive Scottish tradition in the novel, by viewing the novels of Smollett, Scott, and James Hogg—none of whom can be seen essentially as a Gothic novelist—in relation to a Gothic tendency. Smollett's variant of the tendency can be identified with the idea of the grotesque, Scott's with the idea of the historic, and Hogg's with the idea of the diabolic.

The Gothic tendency in the novel is normally seen to consist of five major elements, whichever predominates, however they are related: an antiquarian taste for what was taken to be the style or ornament of the late middle ages; an ambiguous taste for the preternatural, that is, a curious revival of the ghost story; a fascination with the mystery of human malevolence, perversity, sadism; a preference for the style or affective state called sublimity; and a shift of rhetorical aim away from the didactic and mimetic to the affective and expressive. A definition of genre or tendency cannot prematurely stipulate which emphasis is central, which element is mere trapping. What makes a novel in some sense Gothic is often closely related to what makes it interesting as a mixture of modes.

In his study of Smollett* Robert Spector quotes two modern critical judgments of *The Adventures of Ferdinand Count Fathom* that, taken together, make a revealing paradox.[2] Albrecht Strauss calls the book "a curious melange of incongruous fairy tale material and conventional claptrap," and this is accurate. Louis Martz sees Smollett turning away from the picaresque and "seeking new inspiration" in the horror tale, the fairy tale, Gothic, and fantastic narrative. This is true, too. The curious mixture and the new inspiration, however, should not conceal the degree to which Smollett is seeking new ways and matters for the expression of a vision he has had all along.

The conventional claptrap episodes have often been noted: the re-

---

*Smollett, Tobias George. Born in 1721, at Dalquhurn, Dunbartonshire, and died in 1771, near Leghorn, Italy. He attended Glasgow University, moved to London, and served as surgeon's mate in the Royal Navy. Unsuccessful as a physician, disappointed as a dramatist, he succeeded as author of five novels, notably *Roderick Random* (1748) and *Humphry Clinker* (1771). He was also an editor, travelwriter (see *Travels through France and Italy*, 1766), translator (*Don Quixote* and *Gil Blas*), and historian (*History of England*, 1757).

peated visits of Renaldo to Monimia's supposed tomb; the awesome appearance of her "phantom"; and the flight of Fathom from the tempest in the dark wood to the old woman's bloody hut, which Scott praises as a "tale of natural wonder which rises into the sublime; and, though often imitated, has never been surpassed, or perhaps equalled." Spector adds to this last the episode of Celinda's seduction, finds here "the materials later exploited by Ann Radcliffe," and cites them both as examples of Smollett's satiric treatment of the Gothic:

> Smollett never simply yields to the devices of supernatural terror; indeed, he ridicules them even as he uses them . . . Smollett presents not Gothic terror, but the natural turmoil of the mind and actual physical dangers . . . If this is an early use of the Gothic in the English novel, it is one that takes little advantage of supernatural elements to harry the imagination . . . In a way these two satiric attacks on the Gothic illusion serve to undercut the terror in the one genuinely Gothic portion of the novel when Renaldo comes to what he believes to be the grave of Monimia . . . It is all a language . . . to set doubts on the authenticity of the horror; and, while Smollett gets the most out of the new taste for terror, he does it clearly with the touch of the satirist.[3]

But this overlooks the way such episodes are related to other elements in the melange. Fathom's is the Hobbesian and mechanistic world of violent and gross physical needs, which Bruce rightly finds central to Smollett's vision.[4] It is a world of warring animals, where the central symbol of depravity is the spectacle, at once horrible and ludicrous, of the close and violent interdependence of mind and body. It is a world where terror and horror are the strongest emotions, where man, preternaturally sensitized by extreme fear, supposes himself in hell, responds in part with religious awe, and thus affirms the preternatural workings of conscience. In such a world, Gothic suppositions are no mere claptrap excrescences. Nor does Smollett merely parody. The terror is nonetheless real for its ludicrous aspect; it is an antisublimity that is true grotesque. We have not gone far in interpreting Smollett's Gothic tendency if we reject as irrelevant the preclassical mode Smollett reintroduced into British fiction: that vision of a monstrously perverse, fallen, but animated world; that powerful conflation of the terrible, the horrible, and the ludicrous which we call the grotesque. In Scottish Gothic, the grotesque plays an essential role.

The grotesque in Smollett is inseparable from another modality which some (Kurt Wittig, for example) would see as distinctively

Scottish, but which can also be identified with the later eighteenth century and its commitment to the theater of the mind, namely a radical and violent subjectivity of vision.[5] One recalls the multiple distortions of subjectivity in the epistolary method of *Humphry Clinker*. The grotesque and the radically distortive nature of subjectivity are theoretically linked by Smollett in a revealing passage in *Ferdinand Count Fathom*: "There is an affinity and short transition betwixt all the violent passions that agitate the human mind: They are all false perspectives, which though they magnify, yet perplex and render indistinct every object which they represent."[6] The mixture is no mere satiric undercutting of terror, but an express fascination with the violent and grotesque subjectivity of extreme emotional states.

Roderick Random's outrage and despair at the gross caprice of the world cause him to see that world through the double lenses of infernal horror and sadistic glee. What Sedlmayr calls the "secularization of Hell" in Goya, often a central vision in Gothic fiction, is nowhere more striking than in the infernal grotesque of Random's descents— into the cockpit, into the London ordinary:

> [I] found myself in the middle of a cook's shop, almost suffocated with the steams of boiled beef . . . While I stood in amaze, undetermined whether to sit down or walk upwards again, Strap, in his descent, missing one of the steps, tumbled headlong into this infernal ordinary, and overturned the cook . . . In her fall, she dashed the whole mess against the legs of a drummer . . . scalded him so miserably, that he started up, and danced up and down, uttering a volley of execrations, that made my hair stand on end . . . This poultice [of salt] was scarce laid on, when the drummer . . . broke forth into such a hideous yell, as made the whole company tremble . . . grinding his teeth at the same time with a most horrible grin.[7]

And the grotesque horror of the battle scene where Random lies stapled to the poop deck, blinded with blood and scattered brains, surely yields nothing in Gothic intensity to the gloomier scenes of charnel rape in *The Monk*. The effect is identical with what Kayser describes in Brueghel's secularizing of the infernal in Bosch: "the experience of the estranged world . . . the hellish torments, like the phantasmagoric, the ghostly, the sadistic, the obscene, the mechanical"—in short, "the terror inspired by the unfathomable, that is, the grotesque."[8] The revival of the grotesque is part of the Gothic tendency.

But it goes further than that in Smollett. The grotesque may be

16

grounded in a distinctive theology. The grotesque world reflects man's original and mysterious perverseness. Random's vision of subjective and sadistic violence may seem in part caused by the world's brutality, but this is clearly not the case in *Peregrine Pickle*. Pickle acts from what Poe will later call "a paradoxical something, which we may call *perverseness* . . . With certain minds, under certain conditions, it becomes absolutely irresistible. I am not more certain that I breathe, than that the assurance of the wrong or error of any action is often the one unconquerable *force* which impels us, and alone impels us to its prosecution . . . It is a radical, a primitive impulse—elementary."[9] Perry's "preposterous and unaccountable passion" is to "afflict and perplex" his fellow creatures. Nor is this perversity separable from his creative exuberance, the humorous power that makes him a hero. He is a mysterious hero, to be sure, pawn of an infatuation of fancy and will, in a monstrous, potentially tragic world of "humors," of inexplicable hostilities, of "fantastic and maimed characters" such as Commodore Trunnion (V. S. Pritchett's phrase), whose fantastic maiming excites Perry to new heights of sadistic creativity. The moral mystery of cruel perverseness is, I think, far more central to *Peregrine Pickle* than is its philosophical morality, wherein the hero systematically discovers the destructive consequences of unbridled imagination.[10] Perry is not a naif but a demonic scourge. He makes his world; it is his victim.

He torments his world not for its sordidness but for its solemnity, its conventional orders. His indefatigable intrigues have two essential effects: to expose the ludicrous in the solemn, and to invert or destroy the ordered reality of conventional society. The first gives the book its grotesqueness, the second its saturnalian humor. More often than judge or scourge, Perry is vice, demon, or lord of misrule. The example of Smollett's Perry suggests that we may have overlooked in the Gothic tendency a revival of saturnalian fantasy by overlooking its Scottish variations.

At any rate, here are two brief examples of the grotesque and the saturnalian in *Peregrine Pickle*.[11] Nights at inns are filled with diabolical terror, ludicrous raptures. Gay and fantastic, ominous and sinister, the world loses all rational shape, and humans become helpless puppets. Pallet the painter, amorously invading his Dulcinea's chamber, stumbles instead on the hiding Capuchin so that the painter having stript himself to the shirt, in groping about for his Dulcinea's bed, chanced to lay his hand upon the shaven crown of the father's head, which by a circular motion, the priest began to turn round in his grasp, like a ball in a socket . . . one of his fingers happened to slip into his mouth, and was immediately secured between the Capuchin's teeth, with as firm a fixure, as if it had been screwed in a blacksmith's vice . . . the unfortunate painter was found lying naked on the floor, in all the agony of horror and dismay.

This same unfortunate painter stalks about in female costume at a masquerade and is gazed at by the multitude "as a preternatural phaenomenon." Peregrine delights in manipulating such spectacles. His grotesque taste is a function of his perversity. But his even stronger delight is in disorder—as in the marvelous dinner episode, where the whole table is involved "in havock, ruin and confusion," and "before Pickle could accomplish his escape, he was sauced with the syrup of the dormouse pye, which went to pieces in the general wreck; and as for the Italian count, he was overwhelmed by the sow's stomach, which bursting in the fall, discharged its contents upon his leg and thigh, and scalded him so miserably, that he shrieked with anguish, and grinned with a most ghastly and horrible aspect." There is no sign here that the reader is to be morally concerned with imaginative excess. Rather, he is to share Perry's sadistic glee at monstrous disorder, and thus to recognize the "preposterous and unaccountable" fact of exuberant perverseness.

If the Gothic tendency in fiction of the late Enlightenment is to be restricted to ghost stories or to a modal unity of sublime awe, then Smollett's grotesque may be declared unrelated. But if it centers instead on the terror and horror aroused by the mysterious possibilities of alienation—perversity, monomania, diabolic possession—and on the power of such alienation to create and destroy, delude and fascinate, then *Peregrine Pickle* is pertinent indeed.

Although Sir Walter Scott does not use the word, Smollett's Gothic tendency was definitive for him. He stresses Smollett's sublimity, praises him as far above Fielding "in his power of exciting terror," refers to "the wild and ferocious Pickle" whose jokes resemble "those of a fiend in glee," and likens Smollett to Byron: "He was, like a pre-eminent poet of our own day, a searcher of dark bosoms, and loved to paint characters under the strong agitation of fierce and stormy passions. Hence misanthropes, gamblers, and duellists, are as common in his works, as robbers in those of Salvator Rosa, and are drawn, in most cases, with the same terrible truth and effect."[12]

The same Gothic inclination is evident in Scott.* But if Smollett is excluded from the Gothic for his grotesque antisublimity, Scott is excluded for assimilating such Gothic elements into a historical realism. Is the distinction between the Gothic and the historic as real or significant as their kinship? Is historicity as essential to Scott as numerous commentators suggest? If we allow for the characteristically Scottish setting or atmosphere of local history, we may find Scott at his best more significantly related to the Gothic tendency than to the historic and thus understand Gothic less reductively.

Recent Scott criticism has argued otherwise.[13] But I am increasingly impressed by earlier critics who saw Scott's historicism as dominantly aesthetic, his settings patterned on a macabre picturesque and conceived invariably, whatever the epochal surface, as timeless borderlands of romance where marvels jostle with human motives.[14] It is the same in *Waverley*, where eighteenth-century enlightenment is stunned by the ambience of "romance," or in the late Renaissance of *Nigel*, which Scott saw spatially as foothills where the marvelous in incident still mixes with the subtly natural in character, or in the decaying Middle Ages of *Durward*, where romance ventures into a perilous, anarchic borderland between cynical pragmatism and ferocious quixotry. In all three, the same barbarousness and the same civility interplay in chiaroscuro, and the picturesque aesthetic renders historical confrontation as a haunted landscape. I may be overstating the case for emphasis, but my suggestion is that Scott inclined more to use history in the service of romance than to assimilate romance to the interpretation of history.

To view Scott otherwise is to be faced with the following critical situation, seen in three juxtaposed critical propositions: *The Bride of*

*Scott, Sir Walter. Born in 1771, in Edinburgh, and died in 1832, at Abbotsford, near Melrose. The descendant of Borderers and the son of an Edinburgh solicitor Scott attended Edinburgh University, studied law, became Sheriff-Depute of Selkirkshire, and from 1806 served as Clerk of Session in Edinburgh. An enthusiastic folklorist, he edited *Minstrelsy of the Scottish Border* (1802-3); his verse romances brought fame and fortune—most notably *The Lay of the Last Minstrel* (1805), *Marmion* (1808), and *The Lady of the Lake* (1810). He edited and biographized Dryden and Swift. The twenty-seven novels later called the "Waverley Novels" commenced anonymously in 1814 with *Waverley*.

Lammermoor is certainly one of Scott's best novels; *The Bride* is one of the most complete and effective syntheses of Gothic elements; *The Bride* is not really a Gothic novel. If the best of a genre or an author must be atypical, then definition has lost its usefulness. But some will object that this evidence is unfairly limited, so let me add two other novels also cited as "best" and also taken as illustrative of Gothic derivations in Scott: *Old Mortality* and *Redgauntlet*. I do not deny that Scott is a very interesting and hugely influential interpreter of the historic in experience. I mean merely to suggest, in a shift of emphasis, that the archetypal recurrences are more basic than discriminations of temporal or cultural setting. The recurrences are centrally Gothic: the macabre-picturesque ambience already mentioned, the definitive character relationship, the hereditary curse.

The central relationship in what is generally identified as the Gothic novel is a mutual fascination between fatalistic innocence and sublimely willful evil.[15] The Gothic hero-villain alone is not definitive, and criticism that seeks moral interest in him alone mistakes the persistent Gothic characterology. Perilous innocence and demonic power are drawn to each other. Archetypally—some would say incestuously—akin, together they express or evoke the mysterious theodicy hinted at by even the most frivolously rationalized Gothic. As Anthony Winner puts it in a splendid essay on Hoffmann, "No one knows how the primal trespass comes about . . . We are paradoxically and unaccountably innocent and yet somehow guilty."[16] We yearn in fantasy for both the pastoral idyll and the godlike power. As readers of Gothic novels we identify not with individual characters but with the painful division or the grotesque bond of infatuation between them: Emily and Montoni, Antonia and Ambrosio, Caleb and Falkland, Monster and Frankenstein, Immalee and Melmoth, Cathy and Heathcliff—and some more mythic synthesists would add Christabel and Geraldine, Emanation and Spectre.

Such a bond is central in many Waverley novels. It is articulated, superficially at least, in terms of historical, cultural, or ideological division. The critical issue is whether the historic-cultural typology recently stressed in Scott's characterology has really displaced its antecedents in Gothic archetype or simply covered them up. The issue is not to be settled here in a few sentences. But having lengthily supported the earlier position elsewhere, I will briefly put the opposing case here.

The mutual fascinations in Scott are not really intercultural at all, and not between opposing epochs. They are the same in every age, and they are between moral and psychical poles: the meek but brave civility of moderation and the noble energy of monomania, the enlightened pragmatic and the barbaric idealistic, Sancho and Quixote. And in every age, says the ironic Stendhal, "the base Sancho Panza wins." At least on a conscious ideological level Scott evidently stood with Sancho and pragmatic civility. It is equally evident, as Scott sensed, that a semiconscious attraction to the charisma of the monomaniac, the demonic freedom of the antiempirical absolutist, reveals itself. Scott had a penchant for Gothic outlaws, humorous Jacobites, and fanatical Covenanters. That such figures are historicized into representative anachronisms sometimes seems little more than Scott's way of authenticating them—a familiarly Scottish way—and of saying that they are more ancient, more "given." What they really represent is a preenlightened persistence, a demonic element, in the human inheritance, to be sought out, exorcised, and not superficially denied or perilously overlooked. History itself is suspect. The absolutes of theological romance may be more basic.

Some such recognition is implicit in the quests and loyalties of Scott's protagonists, implicating them personally and irreversibly in the destinies of their demonic—that is, monomaniacal—counterparts. Henry Morton, barely known even as his legendary father's son, enters upon the destined path to his own identity, his birthright, by responding "helplessly" to the claim made in his father's name by the fanatical but compelling Burley. Morton suffers, but Burley is exorcised, dwindling at last into a mean devil at bay in a cave, a menace safely to be left behind. The tale of Wandering Willie sets a similar paradigm of exorcism for *Redgauntlet*. Steenie goes to hell and demands back his birthright from a satanic trickster-thief. Darsy Latimer likewise seeks his identity in a wild region dominated by his monomaniacal uncle; once more, the result is the exorcism, the comic diminution, of that demonic force. The exorcism in *The Bride of Lammermoor*, while tragically complex, is archetypally the same. The Master inherits a fanatical role he seeks to ignore, is fatefully attracted to a specious (because unstable, lifeless) innocence in Lucy Ashton. She is drawn for protection to his demonically divided inheritance. Trapped in his Gothic role, he simply disappears into the sands, as unreal at last as Caleb Balderstone's idolatrous illusion of a still noble house.

Idolatry and specious inheritance are closely linked in Scottish fiction. The role of the hereditary curse suggests as much. It is often the core of the protagonist's problem; it inheres in his disinheritance. Henry Morton lives in the ruins of his father's lost cause on the charity of his niggardly uncle. All that the Master has left are his name (hardly that), his ruined tower, and his quixotic fraud of a servant. Darsy Latimer has a friend, a fatalistic curiosity, and not even his own name. Superficially the cause of disinheritance is "history," but "history" simply stands in for the evil—the idolatrous monomania, the inhumanity—in the past, the barbarism of man's moral youth. The curse of the past in Scott's Gothic is transmitted not in historic process, but in the warped and despotic personality of the past's monomaniacal devotee, the parental figure who sacrifices humanity to a cruelly quixotic idea. Yet the interdependence of innocence and monomania is powerful, fateful. Scott's relation to the Gothic is definitive for all his Scottish preoccupation with local history and legend. The mixture is a variant of the Gothic, expressive of a distinctive culture.

The same can be said for James Hogg,* a third Gothic novelist in the early Scottish tradition. Least controversially yet most intriguingly Gothic, Hogg's *Private Memoirs and Confessions of a Justified Sinner* is a complex of diabolic possession, theological satire, and local legend.[17] Hogg's landscape could hardly be more remote from the vague medieval sublimities or inquisitorial dungeons of Walpole, Radcliffe, Maturin. Yet it is, even more than Scott's, a haunted locale, and it is haunted chiefly by the terror of the diabolical. This, too, can have many meanings and shapes, and Hogg's diabolic principle is significantly different from the repressed, sadistic sublimity of the Miltonic or "sensibility" Gothic. In Hogg, the terror of the diabolic is at once more primitive and more explicitly theological—a mixture we will come to recognize as definitively Scottish. Hogg has conflated a terrible theological monomania with a grotesque folk diabolism; the

Hogg, James. Born in 1770 at Ettrick, Selkirkshire, and died in 1835 at Eltrive, Yarrow. He was a self-educated shepherd, caricatured as the "Ettrick Shepherd" of the Noctes Ambrosianae in *Blackwood's Magazine*. He became Scott's friend (see *The Domestic Manners and Private Life of Sir Walter Scott*, 1834) and a leading member of the early *Blackwood's* group. He established himself as a poet with *The Queen's Wake* (1813); *Jacobite Relics of Scotland* (1819-21) includes his best lyrics. His collections of prose tales include *The Brownie of Bodsbeck and Other Tales* (1817), *Winter Evening Tales* (1820), and *Tales of the Wars of Montrose* (1835).

result is a tale of diabolic possession whose current appeal seems wider, more various, than the appeal of almost any other Gothic novel of its period. It derives not just from the horror Gothic of Godwin and Lewis, but from the newly imported macabre of Hoffmann as well. It bears significant likeness, in its treatment of the diabolic compact, to *Melmoth the Wanderer* and, in form, to its other immediate predecessor, *Frankenstein*. And yet, as Dorothy Bussy told André Gide, "This book is Scotch to its very marrow; no Englishman could possibly have written it."[18]

Gide's praise of the book centers on its conception of the diabolic. The devil, says Gide, is wholly believable in psychological terms without recourse to a simple supernaturalism; the end, which demands a more literal or naive credibility, is therefore weak. This is a major issue of interpretation in the book, and it is central to a conception of the Gothic as well: is the preternatural or the demonic to be consistently psychologized, naturalized, or is it to remain to some degree ontologically mysterious?[19] The example of Hogg forces one to the latter position, for the very nature and experience of diabolic possession demand that the devil have some sort of metaphysically separate existence. And Hogg carefully verifies such separateness through the senses, however puzzled, of numerous observers.

The relation of possession in Hogg to the more familiar psychologized diabolism of other Gothic novels is not simple. Edwin Eigner, writing of Hogg as an antecedent to Stevenson, stresses the discovery of the power of darkness as another power or side of the self.[20] For him, the discovery of one's shadowy double is essential to the moral shock that gives the Gothic its power: there was that *in me* that could love a murderer; part of *me* loved the spectacle of pain. Sometimes Hogg's sinner is sure that "I have two souls, which take possession of my bodily frame by turns," and the devil confirms the doctrine. But that is the point: the doctrine is diabolic and by no means the whole truth. In fact, it is crucial to diabolic possession in Hogg that possession is not mere "doubling"—that the self is possessed by an Other, that the story draws partly on the primitive fear of being bewitched, possessed, by the spirit or power of an Other, of being robbed of one's identity. The whole suspense of the struggle of Robert and Gil-Martin for Robert's soul hangs on the questions: Will Robert ultimately surrender his whole soul willingly to the Other and cease to be? When will human nature, as in *Melmoth*, relieve its torment by yielding to the ultimate horror? To identify this scourge of the proud and the damned too facilely with the German romantic doppelgänger is to ignore the more primordial fear of the metaphysical Other that robs one of oneself.

And yet Gil-Martin, whose reality is grounded throughout in folk diabolism, is highly sophisticated in his powers. What is most terrifying and bewildering about him (and terror and metaphysical bewilderment are inseparable in *The Sinner*) is his power of impersonation: "My countenance changes with my studies and sensations . . . It is a natural peculiarity in me, over which I have not full control. If I contemplate a man's features seriously, mine own gradually assume the very same appearance and character. And . . . by assuming his likeness I attain to the possession of his most secret thoughts.[21] Via impersonation comes possession, and possession is power over the mind, capturing one's ideas and transforming them so as to damn one. The conception of evil here in Hogg, as in Smollett and Scott, is distinctively Scottish. In the English Gothic, with its concern for political and clerical tyranny, the power is more apt to be vaguely political, even when implicitly sexual; the devil is a tyrant over the will. In the Scottish Gothic the conception appears to be more intellectual; the power derives from the awful corruption of theological doctrine, from intellectual pride and sophistry. The tempter is a monomaniacal sophist whose power derives not from a sublimity of will, but from a sublimity of idea—and suitably, the word "sublime" or "sublimity" in Hogg's *Sinner* is reserved to describe diabolic ideas: "There is a sublimity in his ideas, with which there is to me a mixture of terror . . . I was greatly revived, and felt my spirit rise above the sphere of vulgar conceptions and the restrained views of unregenerate men . . . the ruinous tendency of the tenets so sublimely inculcated."[22] The diabolic is the sublime power of theological doctrine impersonated by the devil.

But the diabolic in Hogg is a reality of folk legend and traditional Scottish culture as well. His novel is fixed in haunted locality. Localism is as essential to the book's credibility as its weird conflating of perspectives and its "swithering of modes" are to its rhetoric.[23] Hogg speaks as an enlightened and distanced sceptic; he also speaks from within his traditional culture as the transmitter of legendary truth. His characteristic apologia is the passage at the end of a tale called "The Bridal of Polmood":

Some may perhaps say, that this tale is ill-conceived, unnatural, and that the moral of it is not palpable; but let it be duly considered, that he who sits down to write a novel or romance—to produce something that is merely the creation of his own fancy, may be obliged to conform to certain rules and regulations; while he who transmits the traditions of his country to others, does wrong, if he do not transmit them as they are. He may be at liberty to tell them in his own way, but he ought by all means to conform to the incidents as handed down to him; because the greater part of these stories have their foundations in truth. That which is true cannot be unnatural, as the incidents may always be traced from their first principles—the passions and various prejudices of men; and from every important occurrence in human life a moral may with certainty be drawn.[24]

In tales and novels alike, Hogg alternates among three narrative voices and methods. He speaks as the traditional collector divided in allegiance to modern enlightenment and to the truth of the archaic local storyteller, for whom traditional materials are matters of fact, who has inherited them primarily in dramatic anecdotes, and who traces his knowledge to kin and heir of participants. He speaks, on occasion, through dramatic narrators of the Galt sort—parochial memoirists who tell their adventures with faith in their general import and in their manifestation of providence. Or he speaks by wholly dramatic means through the expository dialogue of the ballad. Whichever he employs, he is experimenting with perspectives of local immediacy; and from such perspectives, time is less historic than legendary—the violent, often preternatural past of legend—while place is intensely, yet matter-of-factly, localized by name and topography. The result is closer to Galt than to Scott, yet different from both.

The Brownie of Bodsbeck (1817) provides an interesting counterpart to *Old Mortality* (1816) as well as to Galt's *Ringan Gilhaize* (1823). Its protagonist Walter Laidlaw is a curious analogue to Scott's Henry Morton; both are religious moderates who become involved with the Covenanters, during the "killing time," largely through the force and ruthlessness of Clavers. Hogg's Clavers is as distinct from Scott's romantic cavalier as Galt's is; yet he remains the brutal and capricious figure of local legends, legends recounting his raid through "the vales of Esk and Annan." "The narrator of this tale confesses that he has taken this account of his raid . . . solely from tradition . . . but these traditions are descended from such a source, and by such a line, as amounts with him to veracity."[25] Hogg's is an attempt, as in Galt's *Ringan*, to do justice to the Covenanters by recounting their sufferings almost at first hand. His lack of narrative expertise results in an interesting confusion of point of view.

He wants evidently to speak in his own voice of the agonies and absurdities of the killing time, as one distanced and enlightened. Specifically, he treats with comic enlightenment the superstitions about a preternatural brownie who is actually a Covenanter in masquerade. He is offering historic truth to the curious but distanced modern reader. Yet he speaks as one in direct touch with the locale and its traditions; he has heard the descendants speak; he is closely acquainted with places that preserve local memories. Finally, he believes that Walter Laidlaw tells his own story best. In fact, he often reminds us that what is being narrated was preserved through Walter's repeated oral renditions: "as Walter was wont to relate the story himself, when any stranger came there on a winter evening, as long as he lived, it may haply be acceptable to the curious, and the lovers of rustic simplicity, to read it in his own words, although he drew it out to an inordinate length, and perhaps kept his own personal feelings and prowess too much in view for the fastidious or critical reader to approve."[26] Upon reaching the climax of Walter's trial in Edinburgh, he insists, "the conclusion of this trial must be given in Walter's own phrase"—and it is, in pages of broad Scots, dialogue and all, including Walter's mimicry of the dialect of his humorous Highland friend Sergeant Macpherson. The whole book might well have been done in Walter's own voice. But had it been so, Walter could not have told the mysterious, sophisticated story of his daughter Katharine, supposed to have entered into diabolical communion with the brownie; and Hogg could not have intervened in the voice of the amused modern.

The narrator describes his homecoming, with a condescending view of the sentimental rustic: "With all these delightful and exhilarating thoughts glowing in his breast, how could that wild and darksome road, or indeed any road, be tedious to our honest goodman? . . . He crossed the Meggat about eleven o'clock in the night, just as the waning moon began to peep over the hills to the southeast of the lake" (151). The topographical particularity is characteristic; the urbane narrator knows his country. Yet here he breaks off, for "such scenes and such adventures, are not worth a farthing, unless described and

related in the language of the country to which they are peculiar."
Walter takes over:

> I fand I was come again into the country o' the fairies an' the spirits
> . . . an' there was nae denying o' t; for when I saw the bit crookit
> moon come stealing o'er the kipps o' Bowerhope-Law, an' thraw her
> dead yellow light on the hills o' Meggat, I fand the very nature an'
> the heart within me changed. A' the hills on the tae side o' the loch
> war as dark as pitch, an' the tither side had that ill-hued colour on
> 't, as if they had been a' rowed in their winding sheets; an' then the
> shadow o' the moon it gaed bobbing an' quivering up the loch for-
> nent me, like a streek o' cauld fire. [152]

He meets a white shape on the road, yet remains humorously half-
sceptical—the moderate, somewhat enlightened protagonist, who is
still the local farmer of his time. Hogg's comic preternaturalism is thus
given dramatic reality—of a sort Burns, for example, never quite permits. "A' the stories that ever I heard about fairies in my life came
linkin into my mind ane after anither, and I almaist thought I was already on my road to the Fairyland, an' to be paid away to hell, like a
kane-cock, at the end o' seven years . . . Hout, thinks I, what need I be
sae feared? They'll never take away ane o' my size to be a fairy—Od, I
wad be the daftest-like fairy ever was seen" (153).

The narrator is not so remote from Walter as his language suggests.
In Hogg, the traditionary storyteller and the formal novelist are never
reconciled, except perhaps in *The Justified Sinner.* In texture and proportion, the short dramatic tales are invariably well-shaped; but Hogg
is unable to solve the problem of integrating them into the structural
decorums of the novel. The apology for including all the incidents of
Clavers' raids during the time Walter was his prisoner will often be repeated in kind in *The Three Perils of Man:* "It is necessary to mention
all these, as they were afterwards canvassed at Walter's trial, the account of which formed one of his winter evening tales as long as he
lived. Indeed, all such diffuse and miscellaneous matter as is contained
in this chapter, is a great incumbrance in the right onward progress of
a tale; but we have done with it, and shall now make haste to the end
of our narrative in a direct uninterrupted line."[27] Yet, in his uncertainty, this confused, would-be decorous narrator permits Hogg to
have his traditions both ways. He gives the tradition, apologizes for it,
recounts it in the character's own narrative, yet places himself where it

happened and indicates his own sense of its reality. "These minute traditions are generally founded on truth; yet though two generations have scarcely passed away since the date of this tale, tradition, in this instance, relates things impossible, else Clavers must indeed have been one of the infernals. Often has the present relator of this tale stood over the deep green marks of that courser's hoof, many of which remain on that hill, in awe and astonishment, to think that he was actually looking at the traces made by the devil's foot, or at least by a horse that once belonged to him" (79).

The Brownie of Bodsbeck is a tale of specific locales, and Hogg delights in local distinctions of dialect. His tales are filled with them.[28] Basil Lee recalls that when he went to America with a Highland lieutenant, "I could not speak English otherwise than in the broadest Border dialect, while he delivered himself in a broken Highland jargon." The "Love Adventures of Mr. George Cochrane" include a gypsy girl who speaks "in the true border twang," an "old wife of the same hamlet who spoke the border dialect in all its primitive broadness and vulgarity," and a Mary Park o' the Wolfcleuchhead, "who, having come from the head of Borthwick Water, did not speak with such a full border accent." *The Brownie* employs distinctive dialect narrators: Old Nanny mixes homely affection and covenant cant; Davie Tait produces a long prayer whose very language is to become local legend; John Hay, the shepherd, proves an impenetrable mystery to Clavers by virtue of the triumphant locality of his idioms and reflections. For Hogg local language is a force for the survival and integrity of local tradition; and thus, the integrity of his English narrator and of the structure that narrator seeks to impose becomes more problematical.

The same virtuosity of dialect fills *The Three Perils of Man* (1822). But the problem of formal integrity in this "comic, fantastic, and extravagant epic" is chiefly one of mode;[29] and the authenticity of the book's storehouse of local legend is compromised by its derivation from literary convention, whose very sophistication makes us aware of the book's formal disunities and disproportions. Douglas Gifford feels that disunity of plot structure is irrelevant. But the narrator himself more than once likens his effort to that of a waggoner laden with rich merchandise and forced to carry it part by part up a steep ascent. And the dramatic storytellers of the book's several interpolated tales are severe critics of each other:

"It is nae worth the name of a story that," said Tam Craik; "for, in the first place, it is a lang story; in the second place, it is a confused story; and, in the third place, it ends ower abruptly, and rather looks like half a dozen o' stories linkit to ane anither's tails."

"Master Michael Scott," said Gibbie, "and my friends, I again appeal to you all if this man has not fallen through his tale."[30]

Often it seems easy to turn such quips on Hogg himself; he invites them.

The framing romance is a courtly game of competing chivalric pledges, whose actual brutalities are often rendered in a grisly matter-of-fact style. The earl of Douglas vows to win Princess Margaret of Scotland by recapturing Roxburgh Castle from its English conqueror, Lord Musgrave, whose pledge to the Lady Jane Howard is to hold it until Christmas. These "two most beautiful ladies of England and Scotland" whimsically venture into the neighborhood in male disguise, and both are taken hostage; one appears to be executed, and Musgrave kills himself to save the other. An extravagant ethos of chivalric game combines with countless romance motifs of disguise, mistaken deaths, recognitions, metamorphoses, reunions, and restorations. Yet the plot is thinly historical and is allegedly taken from the manuscript of an old curate, recounted with the mock-romantic scepticism toward "the spirit of romance" characteristic of Scott. The siege plot takes up the first fifth and final quarter of this "most ambitious" of Hogg's novels. The long middle diverges from the siege plot to center on Sir Ringan Redhough, Warden of the Borders and supporter-rival of Douglas, and the prophecy that he will replace Douglas as lord of numerous Border baronies. Redhough sends an embassy to his kinsman, the grand warlock Michael Scott of Aikwood Castle, to learn his weird. The embassy, owing to Scott's magic contests with a mysterious friar and his struggle for power with his master the devil, is trapped on Scott's tower for several days, and engages in a competition of tales to determine who will be killed and eaten to save the rest. The competition is interwoven with the grotesque and farcical efforts of a rescue party. Ultimately, the ambassadors are made drunk by Scott and the devil and metamorphosed into cattle. The victory is celebrated by a visit from the king and queen, with chivalric games, knightings, and noble weddings. The book finishes with the awesome account of Michael Scott's climactic battles with the devil and his death.

Gifford praises "Hogg's courageous and epic attempt to work in the oral and popular tradition which had produced the ballads, folk-tales and legends." That he attempted to work in this tradition with frame and motif from chivalric romance makes for the work's intriguing peculiarity of mode, its "juxtaposition of romantic and realistic attitudes," its mingling—especially in the interpolated tales—of fabliau farce and demonic fantasy, its "unique blend of irony, racy humour, fantasy and romance."[31] Not surprisingly, Gifford is reminded of both Dunbar and Smollett. And such associations as these, in the face of such combinations, mixtures, and formal problems, vividly imply the unique difficulties of the early Scottish novelist in search of a distinctive form. But the virtuoso diabolism, at once sublime and grotesque, Gothic and folkloristic, is what reminds us of the more assured author of *The Justified Sinner:* this, and the extravagant orchestration of contrasting styles and personae, and the effort to integrate traditionary tales and tellers into the form and mode of historical romance.

How much was sacrificed to make the more constrained and subtle achievement of the later book? It seems plausible to numerous commentators that a more sophisticated talent, that of Lockhart, took a hand in fashioning *The Justified Sinner.* Do the short stories, to which Hogg turned after this, "merely illustrate," as Gifford feels, "how grievous a loss the Scottish novel had suffered?"[32] Or does Hogg's career in fiction, rather, illustrate the uncongeniality of the novel form to the fictional materials and impulses of Scottish tradition? The chapters that follow will suggest an answer. Meanwhile, the efforts of Hogg's great contemporary John Galt, who denied repeatedly that he was a novelist but seemed uncertain what term to prefer, point out additional complexities in the origins of the novel in Scotland. While Hogg sought to create novels that would encompass the Scottish Gothic and folkloristic revival of the late Enlightenment, Galt began with the "philosophical" interest in social history that marked the same epoch. Their strange kinship is suggested in the association of both authors with early *Blackwood's.*

2

John Galt

T he first generation of Scottish novelists, David Craig rightly
suggests, belonged to the "Blackwood milieu."[1] To label such
a milieu as "reactionary," its spirit "local" or "provincial," is
premature. Its nationalism was sometimes authentic, its romanticism
Germanic or Coleridgian, its radical Toryism the immediate ancestor
of the Fraserians and Thomas Carlyle. Blackwoodian reaction is the
manifestation of a Scottish counterenlightenment. And yet its concern
with the provincial is easily misinterpreted.

A fiction partly conceived around an idea of the provincial involves
complexities of attitude and duplicities of rhetoric perilous to control.
The novel of provincial life easily offends some, often appears to slip
into condescension, exploitation, stereotype, and distracting self-
consciousness. John Galt's achievement was to affirm the idea without
often falling prey to the dangers. Historical criticism owes him praise
as the novelist of manners who first gave fictive power—of a kind un-
paralleled, for example, in Edgeworth and Scott—to the provincial as
a major imaginative territory.

Galt,* writes Eric Linklater, traveled as widely as Smollett, "but as

*Galt, John. Born in 1779 at Irvine, Ayrshire, and died in 1839 at Greenock,
Renfrewshire. Having attended grammar school at Irvine, he worked as custom-
house clerk and studied law in London. Galt became Byron's fellow Mediterranean
traveler (see Life of Lord Byron, 1830), as well as a journalist, biographer, and
dramatist. His first literary success came with The Ayrshire Legatees (published in

a novelist he never moved from Ayrshire."[2] The complexity of this half-truth is not quickly understood. Galt's life and art together offer something of a paradigm of modern Scottish culture: both were formed in exile, emigration, and imperial adventure; both commemorate the persistence of local or provincial value through cosmopolitan character and experience.

The itinerant Pringle family of Ayrshire, their London letters and "ferlies" finished, return home by coach, and the community of Garnock gathers to welcome them. The image of locale serves to introduce Galt's world and his language.

> All the boys of Garnock assembled at the Braehead, which commands an extensive view of the Kilmarnock road, the only one from Glasgow that runs through the parish; the wives with their sucklings were seated on the large stones at their respective door-cheeks; while their cats were calmly reclining on the window soles. The lassie weans, like clustering bees, were mounted on the carts that stood before Thomas Birlpenny (the vintner)'s door, churming with anticipated delight; the old men took their stations on the dyke that encloses the side of the vintner's kail-yard; and "a batch of wabster lads," with green aprons and thin yellow faces, planted themselves at the gable of the malt-kin, where they were wont, when trade was better, to play at the hand-ball.

The image is broken at this point by a long elegiac parenthesis, sitting strangely in the vivid panorama of anticipation—

> (but, poor fellows! since the trade fell off, they have had no heart for the game, and the vintner's half-mutchkin stoups glitter in empty splendour unrequired, on the shelf below the brazen sconce above the bracepiece, amidst the idle pewter pepper-boxes, the bright copper tea-kettle, the coffee-pot that has never been in use, and lids of sauce-pans that have survived their principals—the wanted ornaments of every trig change-house kitchen).[3]

Finally, when the stage is set the stagecoach appears. And suddenly the novel's full image of social reality is evident. The London of episto-

---

Blackwood's in 1820); in addition to the seven novels discussed below, he competed with Scott .n historical fiction (see *The Spaewife*, 1823, and *Rothelan*, 1824) and wrote political novels, *The Member* (1832) and *The Radical* (1832). Failing in several commercial ventures, he worked strenuously as secretary and later Canadian superintendent of the Canada Company on the settlement of new lands, founding the town of Guelph, Ontario (see the fictional account in *Lawrie Todd*, 1830). He published an *Autobiography* (1833) and a *Literary Life* (1834).

lary report has been fragmentary, disturbingly abstract. The milieu of the letter-writing has been barely sketched; we have, instead, been shown the scenes where the letters were received and read aloud. The epistolary method of *Humphry Clinker* has been adapted and dramatically shifted—and with it the vision of cosmopolitan discovery and local attachment.

The method seems traditional enough in initial effect: familiar realities of the great world are seen anew through naive sensibilities. "It always afforded me great pleasure," Galt recalled, "to go a-lion-showing with strangers in London, and the zest of this kind of recreation was in proportion to the eccentricity of their characters."[4] Yet "eccentricity" will not do to describe the Ayrshire legatees. Young Andrew Pringle makes a distinction in London which Galt himself echoes in *The Provost* and *The Last of the Lairds*. "There was no eccentricity," observes Andrew, "but only that distinct and decided individuality which nature gives and no acquired habits can change" (125). Galt's complication of the traditional method—portraying the *read* letters as dramatic parts of provincial life—imbues his strangers with an individuality which London prohibits or destroys. The method constantly counterpoints the lively humanity of the Ayrshire parish with the bustling anonymity of the metropolis.

Andrew has begun in a rage of philosophic discrimination; he relishes the "flavour of the metropolitan style." His expressions of "metaphysical" delight at the "metropolitan character" are being read aloud at Miss Mally Glencairn's house in the Kirkgate of Irvine, when suddenly "one of the Clyde skippers" in attendance awakes with a snore and a groan from dreams of a fantastic fog. His companions declare the dream nicely suited to "what they had been hearing." For poor Andrew, in London, metaphysical enlightenment turns quickly to a "wilderness of mankind," a "painful conviction of insignificance, of nothingness," as he elbows his way "through the unknown multitude that flows between Charing Cross and the Royal Exchange." Individuality and community alike are lost. The scene of hilarious communal personality at Miss Mally Glencairn's stands in striking contrast: such is an essential irony in Galt's idea of the provincial.

Andrew, the naively enlightened protagonist undergoing disillusion with his own enlightenment, is a familiar figure in romance and novel of the counterenlightenment. He is aware of "our provincialism," of "the little personal peculiarities, so amusing to strangers," which are "painful when we see them in those whom we love and esteem." His good-natured respect for his father's innocence is condescending, but the irony is at the son's expense. While the father belongs with the amiable humorists of Goldsmith, Sterne, and Dickens, culture and nature have made him more than a humorist. He survives triumphantly by adjusting his experience of the great world to his provincial point of view. His provinciality is his character; his impervious innocence triumphs over the menacing depersonalization of the metropolis.

His innocence is carried further in his wife. Mrs. Pringle is often likened to the eccentric females of *Humphry Clinker*, and her epistolary vein is as original as anything concocted by Tabby Bramble or Win Jenkins. In her observations she seems narrow and trivial, yet in her limitedness there is nothing affected or selfish. Her characterization is not satiric, for there is no judgment implied. Mrs. Pringle's is the individuality of "nature," and in Galt nature fashions originals out of cultural restriction. Her very limitations make her valuable to her correspondents and vivid for us. The listeners at Miss Mally's agree that "Mrs Pringle gave a more full account of London than either father, son, or daughter." She is interested in the "partikylars" useful to seamstress Nanny Eydent in copying for parish occasions the fashions of the great. What could be more provincial? But there is more to it. In Galt a humane utilitarianism is the most direct access to reality, and Mrs. Pringle has it.

Her language defines her close, vital bond to the community receiving her report. But much of her stylistic eccentricity is communal in another way: phonetic spellings, run-on gossipy rhythms, and indiscriminate details derive from the fact that she is essentially nonliterate. Writing is not her metier; her letters, unlike the rest, are struggles to set down speech. Local or traditional character flourishes in oral narrative; the norm of provincial speech, for Galt, is oral. On this depends much of the stylistic humor of self-consciously *written* autobiography, as by Balwhidder in the *Annals* and Pawkie in *The Provost*. Mrs. Pringle's dominance as epistolary character is in her colloquial triumph over "metropolitan style." Style, like perspective, is a celebration of the real provinciality of human experience and communication.

The indestructible provinciality of the emigrant in *Andrew Wylie of That Ilk* (1822) is a variant of the same celebration. Galt's publisher imposed an artificial romance plot on the book, and the result is a mixture of "manners" realism and bourgeois fairy tale. The mixture is not unfitting, for in Wylie provinciality of character has become virtually a force of natural magic. Wylie is generically the Scottish *lad o pairts*, the shrewd, original rustic whose wit and humanity triumph over— and occasionally redeem—a supercilious cosmopolitan society. The folklorist would see in Wylie a Cinderella-hero, at first ugly, mean, narrow, a foolish original, and then miraculously something more. His chief interest, however, is evident in the earliest signs of his extraordinary character—his sensitivity to character in others, his humorous penetration. He was distinguished

> from all the lads of his own age, for the preference which he gave to the knacky conversation of old and original characters. It signified not to him, whether the parties, with whom he enjoyed his leisure, were deemed douce or daft; it was enough that their talk was cast in queer phrases, and their minds ran among the odds and ends of things. By this peculiar humour, he was preserved in his clachan simplicity; while he made, as he often afterwards said of himself, "his memory, like a wisdom-pock, a fouth of auld knick-knacketies —clues of experience and shapings of matter that might serve to clout the rents in the knees and elbows o' straits and difficulties."[5]

A loving knowledge of odd character is a wise humor, lodged in local experience and idiom, but applicable to the cosmopolitan world. Wylie the London lawyer can preserve his triumphant self only if he also remains the Ayrshire boy, bent ultimately on going home.

Such is Wylie's dream, and it is fixed in his language, which is the link with his human past, an index to his cultural versatility, and an emblem of the achieved double character that permits him to act as cultural mediator. The peasant boy, distantly in love with the laird's daughter, returns from exile a wealthy bourgeois prince, at ease with peer and peasant, and restores a decadent line into which he finally marries.

Wylie's character, too, has its fairy-tale aspect. In the aristocratic English world of social artifice "character" is surprising. Wylie's "eccentricity" is taken as a kind of genius; he becomes legendary, like George MacDonald's Sir Gibbie, the butt of jokes transformed into the hero of marvelous anecdote. His noble English friends wonder at the mystery of him, for they have lost the nature that makes him seem supernatural. He learns to play his whimsical originality as a mask, and becomes an ingenious private eye, his business chiefly to unmask artificial characters. He restores one noble marriage by teaching the wife that fashion has nothing to do with "the ties and charms which constitute the cement of society," and persuades her to act a part "more agreeable to her own original nature and character" (97). Her husband is redeemed through the talismanic force of Wylie's nature: "I have hitherto lived among machines . . . but this is a human being; it has brains, in which thought rises naturally as water wells from the ground, the wholesome element of temperance; it has a heart too; and in this little discourse has shown more of man than all the bearded bipeds I have ever met with" (73).

Wylie's adventures as shrewd prankster remind us of his immediate ancestor, Smollett's Peregrine Pickle. But the kinship suggests how far Galt has transformed satire into his own mixture of "manners" realism and traditional fable. The fable of the regenerative power of the "natural" in society climaxes as the transformed peasant prince restores a hereditary way of life. It is obviously fantastic, and its mythic potency may, as some allege, have fathered offensive stereotypes on later Scottish fiction. But Wylie shows in fabulous form the idea of the provincial central to Galt's more subtle and serious art.

Andrew Wylie celebrates the triumph of provincial character and community; Galt's best known book, *Annals of the Parish* (1821), laments their gradual extinction. The great world with its socioeconomic forces of change affects and is reflected on the provincial parish with its traditional sense of time, place, and person. The word "annals" suggests the uncertain, fluctuating control exercised by the bemused annalist, the minister Balwhidder. His aim is to set down a faithful record of his ministry (1760-1810) "to the end that I may bear witness to the work of a beneficent Providence, even in the narrow sphere of my parish."[6] In retrospect the aim is redefined: he has meant only "to testify to posterity anent the great changes that have happened in my day and generation—a period which all the best informed writers say, has not had its match in the history of the world, since the beginning of time" (201).

Balwhidder's view of time reflects his divided mind. From one of his wives he has learned the prudential view, the "value of flying time," yet his more fixed vision is antihistoric: the very marvels of his record testify that time is fallen; the "briefness of the chronicle" of a year "bears witness to the innocency of the time," and "quiet and good order" are the "Sabbaths of my ministry" (56-57). His hope is that all changes are providential improvements. Yet the pace of events, speeded by the growing entanglement of the parish with history (itself typical of "the times"), has the effect of destroying the very sense of wondrous particularity by which providence works. The weakness of Balwhidder's recent memory is more than individual old age. He is a type of local memory, of a way of life that preserved the memorable in tradition and is now fading away as his annals fade out. "The term clachan," he observes, "was beginning by this time to wear out of fashion; indeed the place itself was outgrowing the fitness of that title" (149). His most perceptive comment on his effort is this: "It is often to me very curious food for meditation, that as the parish increased in population, there should have been less cause for matter to record. Things that in former days would have occasioned great discourse and cogitation, are forgotten, with the day in which they happen; and there is no longer that searching into personalities which was so much in vogue during the first epoch of my ministry" (172). The traditional humorous sense of person, the source of Andrew Wylie's power, is dying.

The "kind of action presented" in the *Annals* has been identified as "a single typical event chosen for each year."[7] In fact, the selective process is more fluid and subtle than this. The record for 1795 will illustrate. The coming of a recruiting party opens the year with dreadful effect. The reader feels the "dunt that the first tap of the drum gied to my heart"; the sparely dialectal monosyllables convey empathic force. Local reaction was to marvel exceedingly "where these fearful portents and changes would stop." The second event comes on as equal in portentousness, "as it strangely and strikingly marked the rapid revolutions that were going on." This is the visit of "a gang of play-actors." Finally, two English Quakers and a Quaker lady preach in the same barn; Balwhidder attends and is pleased. Yet the year is unsatisfactory; the parish is losing its character—its simplicity, rigor, autonomy. The process shows itself in the interweaving of events great and small. The minister's enlightenment approves; his orthodoxy is apprehensive; his traditional humanity laments the cost. His ambiguous provinciality partakes of all three.

In Galt, provinciality is neither idyll nor absurdity. The parish, for Balwhidder, is the world in microcosm: "What happened in my parish was but a type and index to the rest of the world." In conventional mock-heroic, the pettiness of the great world is underlined satirically by juxtaposition with small or provincial counterparts. But Balwhid-

der's parish has the significance, as well, of small worlds in the historical novels of Scott. Provincial community is a microcosm, but it is
also a realm of humane values menaced by history. Can character and
community survive? Identity is restriction, personal and cultural;
identity is threatened, and as it fades the timeless elegiac question is
raised: can a gain be found in the loss?

Galt and Balwhidder do not sentimentalize the loss. The "natural
perversity of the human heart" is recognized and accepted, often with
amoral merriment. The death of daft Jenny Gaffaw is a grotesque
memento mori. The burning of the nabob's "scrimpet" sister Grizzy
warrants comparison with Crabbe and the grotesque of Smollett: "I
think to this hour, how I saw her at the window, how the fire came in
behind her, and claught her like a fiery Belzebub, and bore her into
perdition before our eyes. The next morning the atomy of the body
was found among the rubbish, with a piece of metal in what had been
each of its hands" (36). Nichol Snipe, the gamekeeper, is indicted for
fathering a bastard and forced to stand in kirk—a graceless reprobate,
for he "came with two coats, one buttoned behind him, and another
buttoned before him, and two wigs of my Lord's, lent him by the
valet-de-chamer . . . When I saw him from the pu'-pit, I said to him—
'Nichol, you must turn your face towards me!' At the which, he
turned round to be sure, but there he presented the same show as his
back. I was confounded, and did not know what to say, but cried out,
with a voice of anger—'Nichol, Nichol! if ye had been a' back, you
would nae hae been there this day' " (30).

The minister's virtuosity in local idiom is a power he shares with
Andrew Wylie. For cosmopolitan readers his mixture of languages is
an effective means of rhetorical accommodation as well as the expression of a complex outlook. His written style alternates between the
sustained formal rhythms of the moral historian and the run-on syntax
and dialectal particularity of the provincial raconteur. The mixture is
evident in a passage reminiscent of Galt's professed English model. We
may recall the pharisaical pranks of Goldsmith's Dr. Primrose during
Balwhidder's campaign against the luxury of tea: "Now it became very
rife, yet the commoner sort did not like to let it be known that they
were taking to the new luxury, especially the elderly women, who, for
that reason, had their ploys in out-houses and bye-places, just as the
witches lang syne had their sinful possets and galravitchings; and they
made their tea for common in the pint-stoup, and drank it out of caps

and luggies, for there were but few among them that had cups and saucers." Paradoxically, the new fad demands a cluster of dialectal references, a language it will help to displace. The self-consciously pensive man of God stumbles upon a "bike" of such new witches, and proudly scatters insects he can never in fact exorcise.

> Well do I remember one night in harvest, in this very year, as I was taking my twilight dawner aneath the hedge along the back side of Thomas Thorl's yard, meditating on the goodness of Providence, and looking at the sheafs of victual on the field—that I heard his wife, and two three other carlins, with their bohea in the inside of the hedge, and no doubt but it had a lacing of the conek, for they were all cracking like penguns. But I gave them a sign by a loud host, that Providence sees all, and it skailed the bike; for I heard them, like guilty creatures, whispering and gathering up their truck-pots and trenchers, and cowering away home. [13]

Whatever the ancestry, no one could confuse this with *The Vicar of Wakefield*. Balwhidder differs from Primrose in many ways. Both are "amiable humorists," but the term is misleading. Whether Goldsmith's vicar derives from Irish memory or English type, his satiric nature and function are plain: his vanity is a universal; his representativeness is moral. He is hero of a comic fable with echoes of Job, an entertaining mixture of self-righteousness, good humor, and benevolent blindness. Balwhidder is basically a cultural epitome rather than an ethical type. His limits of vision are historic and generic, and they constitute his identity as a superficially enlightened parish minister of the late eighteenth century in the West of Scotland, an individual perspective on provincial society between 1760 and 1810. Our comic interest is inseparable from his cultural particularity. But how will we interpret the limits of his "truth"? We can see his limited comprehension as simply a function of his naivete. We can see it as an index of his corruption, his complicity; after all, he prospers—he likes to prosper—and there is some truth, hidden from Balwhidder, in the heritors' view that he is avaricious. Or we can see his limits as the blindness of man in history, the blindness of any restrictive cultural identity. In every case we will be right. Primrose is chastened for his folly and rewarded for his constancy; his goods are restored many times over. What chastening or reward could history offer Balwhidder?

Judgment is equally problematic in *The Provost* (1822). For some readers this is Galt's masterpiece; Galt himself judged it a better book than the *Annals*. The Provost Pawkie that some see as a provincial stereotype is for George Kitchin "one of the great characters in our literature. His habitat could only be a Scottish burgh. He is not incredible. His mingling of rascality and concern for the public good is not improbable. In a chastened form he exists in numerous burghs today and exists strangely for the public benefit."[8] Ian Jack recognizes the "quintessentially Scots" quality of Pawkie's triumphant self-righteousness, and finds the book "an exercise in sustained irony that has few rivals in the language." In his own comment Galt insists characteristically on the truth of representation and on his dislike of "monsters and chimeras," of "the wild and wonderful." Questions of truth and typicality in *The Provost* call for close attention.

Apprehension of Pawkie and his provincial world is shaped by the function and interplay of his various motives as narrator. He is so patently and despotically "interested" in all he records, unlike the naive Balwhidder, that we cannot respond with any simple irony or rely on any fixed understanding with the author behind Pawkie's back. G. Armour Craig once said of *Jane Eyre:* "The power of the 'I' of this novel is secret, undisclosable, absolute . . . I know no other work that so effectively demonstrates the demon of the absolute."[9] Yet with Pawkie, as with poor little Jane, we find ourselves perplexed continually by the need for judgment. Pawkie is forever justifying himself, and we are the "posterity" to which he solemnly appeals for "unbiassed judgment" in favor of his "earnest and zealous public service" against the mean obstructionism and unkind suspicions of smaller men.

Pawkie hangs his apologetic effort on the issue of his public spiritedness. He claims to have joined the "reforming spirit abroad among men" and furthered the "main profit of improvement." He seeks judgment not as an individual but as an instrument of history. But while he persists in seeing himself as a historical type, his own individuality defies the impersonality he intends, and the personalities of others thrust themselves vividly into his record. His real lack of disinterestedness is essential to his truth: "these notandums have been indited" in a "free and faithful spirit," yet the freedom and fidelity are only real by virtue of being relative or provincial. Pawkie concedes as much, and the concession is the book's most interesting variation on the theme of the provincial—namely, the provinciality of time:

> Indeed, in thir notations, I have endeavoured, in a manner, to be governed by the spirit of the times in which the transactions hap-

pened; for I have lived long enough to remark that if we judge of past events by present motives, and do not try to enter into the spirit of the age when they took place, and to see them with the eyes with which they were really seen, we shall conceit many things to be of a bad and wicked character that were not thought so harshly of by those who witnessed them, nor even by those who, perhaps, suffered from them.[10]

Once more our judgments are disarmed. Yet once more Pawkie too is caught. For the principle repudiates his own claims of impersonal perspective and reminds us that Pawkie's provincial humanity is more real than the public typicality he claims.

His style is a formal, self-conscious English, individualized by an accidental counterpoint of local idiom and rhythm. The first chapter opens with a Johnsonian decorum akin to the opening of *Pride and Prejudice*:

> It must be allowed in the world that a man who has thrice reached the highest station of life in his line has a good right to set forth the particulars of the discretion and prudence by which he lifted himself so far above the ordinaries of his day and generation. Indeed, the generality of mankind may claim this as a duty . . . I have, therefore, well weighed the importance it may be of to posterity to know by what means I have thrice been made an instrument to represent the supreme power and authority of Majesty in the royal burgh of Gudetown. [5]

There are striking differences between Austen's irony and this. Austen's mock appeal to the generality of human understanding underlines the pettiness of feminine materialism warring for marriage. Galt's underlines the folly of seeing universal significance where a burghal provost claims it to be. But in both cases the provincial human truth behind the large public style is not to be slighted. At first reading, the smallness of Pawkie's affairs makes mock-heroic comment on his public pretensions; his manner seems Lilliputian in pomposity. At first reading, the mockery has its *Jonathan Wild* side: if this is really a type of the great man, then other great men are in fact pompous provincial despots. But provincial smallness, as elsewhere in Galt, outreaches in richness and humanity its initial mock-heroic potential. Pawkie's public life is actually made up of individual and local realities. His "digressions" and idiomatic lapses attest not just to his limits but also to a breadth of awareness and concern. His public impersonality is a mask for a humorous, often compassionate intuition.

It is this that makes the public official so true a provincial historian, so vivid a raconteur of affairs both grim and poignant, and abruptly farcical.

Consider the juxtaposing of Jean Gaisling's hanging for child-murder with the riot over the king's birthday bonfire, when "a dead cat came whizzing through the air like a comet, and gave me such a clash in the face that I was knocked down to the floor" (56). The scene of the drunken town drummer's mistaken fire alarm gives a brief glimpse of the provost as domestic person—"I heard the noise and rose; but while I was drawing on my stockings, in the chair at the bed-head, and telling Mrs. Pawkie to compose herself, for our houses were all insured" (167)—and an instance of his stylistic impressionism:

> The street was as throng as on a market-day, and every face in the moon-light was pale with fear. Men and lads were running with their coats, and carrying their breaches in their hands; wives and maidens were all asking questions at one another, and even lasses were fleeing to and fro, like water nymphs with urns, having stoups and pails in their hands. There was swearing and tearing of men, hoarse with the rage of impatience, at the Tolbooth, getting out the fire-engine from its stance under the stair; and loud and terrible afar off, and over all, came the peal of alarm from drunken Robin's drum. [47-48]

The rhythms are syntactically sure and refined, but the philosophic style is subordinated to the ludicrous personalities of parochial life. Bailie Pirlet, "who was naturally a gabby prick-me-dainty body, enlarged at great length, with all his well-dockit words, as if they were on chandler's pins" (161). Councilman Hirple was "a queer and quistical man, of a small stature of body, with an outshot breast, the which, I am inclined to think, was one of the main causes of our never promoting him into the ostensible magistracy; besides, his temper was exceedingly brittle, and in the debates anent the weightiest concerns of the public, he was apt to puff and fizz, and go off with a pluff of anger like a pioye" (130). Pirlet, bantered by M'Queerie, "like a bantam cock in a passion, stotted out of his chair with the spunk of a birslet pea" (162). Vivid dialectal images such as these—at which Galt is unequalled in Scots fiction—give an impressionistic animation to Pawkie's provincial world that utterly offsets his public impersonality.

In such passages, Galt's style offends some as "virtuoso," as exploitative in its use of a "skillful and slightly distorting or reducing humour" whereby Galt "nudges the reader to remind him that the local is rather absurd" and thus makes "fun and money of Scottish eccentricity."[11] The charge of exploitativeness is serious. In my view, while Galt's local realities are humorous, they are not absurd. And a distorting or reducing humor, as many have noted, is a traditional stylistic energy of Scots. In *The Provost*, at least, the style seems in character with Pawkie's vigorous provincial humanity. Most revealing is his account of the "windy yule," based on an event of Galt's Irvine boyhood: the storm at sea; ships foundering just off the coast; anxiety and suffering in the bereaved, and a subscription to alleviate their poverty. The force of Pawkie's account rests partly in his intense dramatic sympathy with the horror and dismay of the watchers. His compassion is a characteristic blend of public self-consciousness and particular feeling for the poorest orphans: "They were then sitting under the lea of a headstone, near their mother's grave, chittering and creeping closer and closer at every squall. Never was such an orphanlike sight seen" (123). His sympathetic penetration, a power shared with Wylie and Balwhidder,[12] is as genuine a part of Pawkie as his typological self-consciousness. His enjoyment of public authority has blinded him to the more traditional and humane sense in which he is "public." It is a sad irony that, unlike the elegiac Balwhidder, he is blind to the loss of values to which his own provincial vision bears vivid witness.

Galt was as much interested as Scott in the end of the past. The third of his "theoretical" histories, *The Last of the Lairds* (1826), closed this "series of fictions of manners" with the portrayal of a west country laird "about twenty years ago," the close of the epoch of Pawkie and Balwhidder.[13] Galt regretted that, for some forgotten reason, he changed his mode from autobiography to narrative—such are his own terms—"and in this respect it lost the appearance of truth of nature which is, in my opinion, the great charm of such works." Far from choosing autobiographers of provincial mind to exploit local absurdity, he chose them as mimetically indispensable. But simple truth of nature was evidently not enough. The characterization of the likely autobiographer here—Mailings of Auldbiggings, last of the lairds—cost him, Galt says, unique trouble. It was a character of "imbecility" and "selfish stupidity" and therefore would "not stand bringing out" or "endure much handling." Who, then, could narrate? Galt was significantly uneasy with the distancing device of judicial omniscience. For one thing, his art prohibited critical neutrality or the distortions of satire, and for another, his presbyterianism held to the essential mystery of personality and found folly or even blasphemy in pretensions of judgment and wisdom. The solution for *The Last of the Lairds* was a narrator at once in and out of the provincial society he describes. He is a familiar Blackwoodian persona, and his closest Victorian heirs are Trollope and early Eliot.

The narrator is an author himself, a man of some urbanity, free in speech of all traces of dialect. Yet at heart he is a provincial gossip, a good-hearted meddler. His cosmopolitanism is surface only, hence he provides one more statement of Galt's theme: the inescapable provinciality of human nature. An interested eyewitness with an eye for manners, he has many occasions for zestful place description, as in the Balzacian rendition of Mrs. Soorocks' cupboard, shelf by bulging shelf, for nearly five thousand words. But manners here differ from manners in the *Annals* and *The Provost:* this is a story of comic situation rather than historical reminiscence, and its narrator lacks a sense of history. Galt's favorite genre, memoir in colloquial character, must enter by another gate. The narrative is scenic; the scenic episodes are filled with long dialect speeches. The busy narrator must hear of some events at secondhand; hence, some speeches are long personal narratives in character, and Galt's norm of oral personal history is reinstated.

The later eighteenth century had discovered in memoir, diary, and anecdote the evocative power of recorded talk. The Scottish novel, beginning then, seems in its beginnings more markedly oral, more "talky," than English eighteenth-century fiction with its epic or confessional conventions. There are possible explanations for this in Scottish culture. The three dominant professional options left after the Union—preacher, pleader, dominie—all tie vocational identity to styles and powers of speech. Traditional Scots tales of social mobility, sources of the Andrew Wylie myth, often are tales of verbal power and agility. Talk for the exiled Scot became a haven of provincial reminiscence, and a good night-long blether remains the Scottish ritual of reunion. In Galt's lifetime such powers were often associated with the matriarchal figures Lord Cockburn called "Scotch old ladies." "My father," Galt recalls,

> was one of the best, as he was one of the handsomest men, but he was of an easy nature . . . My mother was however a very singular person; possessing a masculine strength of character, with great

natural humour, and a keen perception of the ridiculous in others. —In her prime, as I would call it, she indulged in queer metaphorical expressions, exceedingly forcible and original. In latter life this grew so much into a habit, that her talk to strangers must have seemed often fantastical. The rich ore of common sense, however, which pervaded her observations was always remarkable.[14]

This may be some clue to Galt's defensive feelings about the major character of *The Last of the Lairds*, the chief instance of what he calls "that kind of caricature which is at once laughable and true," Mrs. Soorocks.

So fertile and verbose is she that no manageable quotation can fairly represent her. Yet what the narrator calls her "disheveled and raveled" speech is an essential stylistic element in Galt's idea of the provincial. It is breathless in extension and parenthetical fecundity, explosively dramatic in its cascade of exclamations and imperatives and insistent questions, reckless in mispronunciation, riotously colorful in figures of homely trivia mingled with biblical allusion and proverb, self-assertive, self-satisfied, and withal good-humored and humane. But the sort of character found in Mrs. Soorocks had been celebrated earlier in Galt's most notable dramatic figure, the phenomenal Leddy Grippy of *The Entail* (1823).

The connoisseur of Galt, coming by way of the parish chronicles, may encounter Galt's most admired novel in the spirit of S. R. Crockett, for whom the subtitle *The Lairds of Grippy* is descriptive of the book.[15] For him, the story is a family chronicle, and the idea of the "entail" imposes a false unity. The false unity of the entail is not Galt's artistic error, however, but rather his protagonist's tragic flaw. The book's unity derives from the emergent meaning of the ill-fated entail, and its very persistence renders "Lairds of Grippy" a pathetically ironic label. The unity of the parish histories—*Annals, The Provost, The Last of the Lairds*—is provided by a continuity of character and community. In *The Entail* community is sacrificed to idolatry, and character is markedly discontinuous. Claude Walkinshaw, idolatrous paterfamilias, dies less than halfway through. The continuity he obsessively sought to impose is an outright, blasphemous denial of character and all it implies—freedom, autonomy, reality itself. Control passes to his noisy, seemingly simple-minded wife, his opposite, Leddy Grippy.

Claude comes to recognize his sin, better than most of his kin and some of his readers. "I sold my soul to the Evil One in my childhood," he confesses, "that I might recover the inheritance of my forebears. O the pride of that mystery!"[16] His was no simple greed for "gear"; he alone knew this. Like the rest, his mother-in-law "regarded him as one of the most sordid of men, without being aware that avarice with him was but an agent in the pursuit of that ancestral phantom which he worshipped" (76). It *is* a phantom. At first it seemed to have substance. "Laird," says he to his father-in-law, "ye ken the Walkinshaws of Kittlestonheugh are o' vera ancient blood, and but for the doited prank o' my grandfather, in sending my father on that gouk's errand to the Darien, the hills are green and the land broad that should this day hae been mine; and therefore, to put it out o' the power of posterity to play at any sic wastrie again, I mean to entail the property of the Grippy" (22). This is our one brief glimpse of the reality he dreams of and his one reference to the human realities of his inheritance.

His plight is common in Scottish fiction: it is the terrible, obsessive relation to an irrecoverable past that Stevenson thought unique to the Scot. It is the burden of elegy. The past is lost; can any gain be found in the loss? To this, Walkinshaw's is the false, blasphemous answer. He seeks to impose his will in entail on time and change, to substitute a cruel, specious legalism for a human continuity. In so doing, he denies providence and robs himself of free will in the act of seeking to perpetuate it. He is punished with infatuation; his act of entail becomes a mysterious thing with powers of its own that render his absurd. He recognizes his blasphemy at last. "O man!" exclaims the "hoary penitent" to his only friend, the old lawyer Keelevin, "ye ken little o' me. Frae the very dawn o' life I hae done nothing but big and build an idolatrous image; and when it was finished, ye saw how I laid my first-born on its burning and brazen altar. But ye never saw what I saw—the face of an angry God looking constantly from behind a cloud that darkened a' the world like the shadow of death to me; and ye canna feel what I feel now, when His dreadful right hand has smashed my idol into dust" (146-147).

In his morbid secrecy and growing isolation Claude Walkinshaw cannot function as a recorder of manners, and the manners milieu of *The Entail* has slight importance.[17] The tragic fruits of the entail are obsessive idolatry, religious despair; a story of monomanic isolation offers little room for the image of community. Such images in Galt are transmitted through open provincial consciousness; pictures of life in the parish histories are individual, eye-witnessed. Here we see only Claude. His consciousness remains, his image of reality, as remote from us as it increasingly is from those around him. Glimpses of Grippy must come coincidentally through others. It is only with the emergence of the grandson, a youth of late eighteenth-century sensibility, that we have access to a mind open to impressions, free of the secrecy and isolation of the ancestral idolatry. Otherwise, the reality of this provincial world is locked up in secret selves or darkened by the face of an angry God; idolatry results in lost reality and lost community.

Such a fictional world requires a different characterology. In the traditional worlds of *Annals* and *The Provost*, the Ayrshire of the Legatees and Andrew Wylie, character is at once original and generic. Claude, cut off from the humanity of his heritage, attempts to recreate his identity with a legal abstraction and his status with a social one. While he may see himself archetypally, he can be neither generic nor communal. His only real individuality grows from his sin; the more he loses the freedom he has tried to perpetuate, the more character he acquires. His sons inherit individuality from the same poisoned source. Charlie, romantic and feckless, has his father's inability to cope with reality. Watty, the "natural," becomes a ludicrous counterpart to his father's greed. The Snopesian George inherits the mercenary obsession with the entail. All three seem slight beside the grim moral grandeur their father acquires in his torment.

Because there is no shared reality, no community of character, Galt needs an omniscient authorial narrator to mediate between the surfaces of character and the depths of private obsession the reader must glimpse. Claude's external aspect gives no hint of "the fierce combustion of distracted thoughts which was raging within" (157). His family is "equally amazed, and incapable of comprehending the depth and mystery of a grief which . . . undoubtedly partook in some degree of religious despair" (155). From Claude's secrecy follow the surprises of secrecy in others. Watty discloses depths of sensitivity and devotion no one could have expected when his Betty Bodle dies. He transfers his devotion to their daughter and thwarts his father's good impulses as he had almost thwarted his sinful ones. Watty's idolatry is as stubborn and fantastic as his father's, and none can fathom it; hence the sharp poignancy of scenes with Claude, when the reader alone sees in the struggle of cruel infatuation with stubborn idiocy the presence of hidden kindness. Cheated at last, Watty fades into himself and out of life. The burden of secrecy remains.

Thus, a major surprise of character is provided by the widowed Leddy, the single character of the earlier chapters who had seemed open and predictable. It is on her emergence that the book's final meaning depends. "Byron said," recalls V. S. Pritchett, "that the Leddy Grippy of *The Entail* was the finest portrait of a woman in English literature since Shakespeare," but "he was thinking, I am afraid, not of literature, but of the women who had annoyed him." Others have found her a distraction from the book's tragic theme, or a mere "vehicle for displays of language."[18] But the book is about a tragic fall *and* a comic redemption. And the Leddy's triumphs of "character" are antidotes to the spread of Claude's idolatry. She seems as garrulously open as the rest are secretive; she seems utterly lacking in the private sensibility that torments them or the sinful self-seeking that drives them. She is character of a very different sort, and the others misunderstand her. For Claude she is a noisy nuisance and a threat. George thinks her a ludicrous eccentric. The lawyers think her a fool until she defeats them. She luxuriates in power (as Claude suffers in it), but hers is not sinful, for it is open and joyous, pious and humane. She acts for life, yet she acts in the face of mortality instead of trying to deny or forestall it. "To me—noo sax-and-seventy year auld—the monthly moon's but as a glaik on the wall—the spring but as a butterflee that taks the wings o' the morning—and a' the summer only as the tinkling o' a cymbal—as for hairst and winter, they're the shadows o' death; the whilk is an admonishment, that I should not be overly gair anent the world, but mak mysel and others happy, by taking the sanctified use o' what I hae—so, Geordie and Sirs, ye'll fill another glass" (279). Such is her antidote to the idolatry that curses her family.

The charge that she serves merely as a vehicle for dialectal virtuosity deserves testing. The single example below is a tirade aimed at her granddaughter, who seeks her aid in plotting an elopement.

"Eh! Megsty me! I'm sparrow-blasted!" exclaimed the Leddy, throwing herself back in the chair, and lifting both her hands and eyes in wonderment.—"But thou, Beenie Walkinshaw, is a soople fairy; and so a' the time that thy father . . . was wising and wyling to bring about a matrimony, or, as I should ca't, a matter-o'-money conjugality wi' your cousin Jamie, hae ye been linking by the dykesides, out o' sight, wi' Walky Milrookit? Weel, that beats print! Whatna novelle gied you that lesson, lassie? Hey, Sirs! auld as I am, but I would like to read it. Howsever, Beenie, as the ae oe's as sib to me as the ither, I'll be as gude as my word; and when Dirdum-whamle and your auntie, wi' your joe, are here the day, we'll just lay our heads thegither for a purpose o' marriage, and let your father play the Scotch measure or shantruse, wi' the bellows and the shank o' the besom, to some warlock wallop o' his auld papistical and paternostering ancestors, that hae been—Gude preserve us!—for ought I ken to the contrary, suppin' brimstone broth wi' the deil lang afore the time o' Adam and Eve. Methuselah himself, I verily believe, could be naething less than half a cousin to the nine hundred and ninety-ninth Walkinshaw o' Kittlestonheugh. [259]

Here is the provincial mind in which Galt delighted. The miscellaneous flow suggests her kinship to the "natural"—her son Watty—as to Mrs. Pringle of the *Legatees* and Mrs. Soorocks of the *Lairds*. Malapropism underlines her openness, for she is as full and particular as others are shrewd and secretive. Her ample stores of allusion suggest a wealth of traditional vitality and meaning from which others have been cut off, all used in the service of exuberant, unselfish self-assertion. Her role is human, familial; she scoffs extravagantly at ancestral dignities in the face of present human need. She is matter-of-fact, worldly, yet metaphoric and proverbial as well; thus she can respond to surprising realities with flexibility and wonder. In its exuberant natural piety her character is beyond tragedy; her triumph is in the traditional, provincial force that dispels the curse brought by Claude's romantic idolatry. It is no excrescence in this, Galt's most ambitious novel.

Yet, one contemporary reviewer could "wish Mr. Galt would do nothing but write imaginary autobiographies." And I agree with Ian Jack that Galt's greatness, as well as his significance at the opening of Scottish tradition in the novel, is as "the great master of this art of literary ventriloquism."[19] Necessarily overlooking, then, several later books, including the extraordinary political "memoirs," *The Member* and *The Radical*, we conclude with the most complex of Galt's imaginary autobiographies, *Ringan Gilhaize* (1823), and discover how central to Galt's view of human history and understanding is his idea of the provincial.

Ian Jack finds "a technical expertise or sophistication about *Ringan Gilhaize* which is seldom found in Scott," and the judgment would have pleased Galt, for he acknowledged that the book was provoked by *Old Mortality*. He shared with others an impulse to correct Scott's satiric distortions of Scottish presbyterianism. The Blackwoodians, touched by a new nationalism and by the evangelical revival as well, may be seen in reaction against the cosmopolitan enlightenment to which Scott belonged. In contrast with Scott, Galt deliberately exploits personality and eye-witness involvement. The narrator here is no philosophic analyst: the methods are those of memoir, not picturesque narrative history. Rather than construct a romance plot to fictionalize a historic world, Galt invents a protagonist of individual as well as generic interest and traces his role in public events. History is central; fiction is in personality of view. Ringan is not just an Ayrshire covenanter; he is *the* hypothetical covenanter who, driven by his sufferings, killed Claverhouse at Killiecrankie. In Galt's fiction (and in Hogg's and Lockhart's) the mingling of the historic and the imagined is closer than in Scott's. Galt's characteristic purpose, moreover, is to avoid caricature. In caricature, the archetypal in character is rhetorically fixed and focal. Scott's fanatics illustrate a wide diversity of fanaticisms, but they remain illustrative personifications. In *Ringan Gilhaize*, on the other hand, a character is distorted or stylized into obsession or monomania only through a psychological process, as in Hawthorne and Godwin. This is to suggest that Scott belongs with the older mode of allegorical fable and Galt with the newer romantic one of symbolic naturalism.

In another respect the historical modes of Galt and Scott seem closer. Ringan, like Provost Pawkie, strives to preserve a distinction between the "household memorial" he purports to offer and the public affairs he is unable to avoid. The close interweaving of household memoir and national history is a central Scottish motif. For Scott, the epic historian, small domesticities are caught up—given scope and dignity—by their entanglements with historic fatality. Galt's version is in the more familiar Scottish mode of diminution. Man's historic pretensions are seen in their true limits when reflected on the stage and sensibility of household and parish. Only through a provincial perspective can one see the real smallnesses of history.

The truth of Ringan is inseparable from his personal limits of vision. This narrative voice is a brilliant technical achievement. It was essential, says Galt, "that I should distinctly conceive what was a covenanter's character, in order to make him relate what such a person [his grandfather] would do with the reformers in the time of John Knox. There was here, if I may be allowed the expression, a transfusion of character."[20] The transfusion is a complicated affair of imaginative ventriloquism. The Covenanter is critically aware of his distance from his grandfather's picaresque sixteenth-century career, and his rendition of that earlier "carnal" time is a double exercise in historical imagination. But his grandfather's heroic past has become more than memory: "I am bound to say, that his own exceeding venerable appearance, and the visions of past events, which the eloquence of his traditions called up to my young fancy, worked deeper and more thoroughly into my nature, than the reasons and motives which guided and governed many of his other disciples" (I, 275-276).[21] The "transfusion of character" is part of Ringan's own identity. His apology rests on the conviction that he is his grandfather's providential reincarnation.

The struggle throughout his narrative of hereditary intention and "interest" makes of his story a sustained dramatic monologue, closely akin to *The Provost*. His mixture of local piety and prophetic force comes from the same tradition that produced Leddy Grippy. His will not be a personal complaint, yet the point of his destiny is that heredity can usurp personality. He will tell the truth about Charles and James, persecutor and usurper, with "firm and fearless pen," yet "the tale of their persecutions is ravelled with the sorrows and the sufferings of my friends and neighbours, and the darker issues of my woes" (I, 321). The recollection of his wife and children brings new horror and new resolution: "They are all gone. The flood and the flame have passed over them;—yet be still, my heart; a little while endure in silence; for I have not taken up the avenging pen of history, and dipped it in the blood of the martyrs, to record only my own particular woes and wrongs" (I, 326). But he is uniquely singled out. At last only Claverhouse and he are real. Even the "impartial historian" is possessed by "the spirit of piety which reigned in the hearts of the Covenanters," and adopts the prophetic tone: "Should aught of a fiercer feeling than belongs to the sacred sternness of truth and justice escape from my historical pen, thou wilt surely pardon the same, if there be any of the gracious ruth of Christian gentleness in thy bosom; for now I have to tell of things that have made the annals of the land as red as crimson, and filled my house with the blackness of ashes and universal death" (II, 168).

The historical pen is subject always to the local immediacy of the eyewitness. Ringan's eye catches the vivid particularity of Galt's other provincial memoirists, augmented by the visionary intensity of one possessed. His visions range from a hilarious anecdotal realism—the image of the papistical archbishop with his naked right leg slipped in Spanish leather flung over Mistress Kilspinnie's knees; the prelatical young preacher in a kirk full of "cloks and spiders": "The only sensible thing Andrew Dornock ever uttered from the pulpit was, when he first rose to speak therein, and which was caused by a spider, that just at the moment lowered itself down into his mouth: 'O Lord,' cried the curate, 'we're puzhened wi' speeders' " (II, 20)—to a prophetic fervor and a simple sublimity: "Verily it was a sight that made the heart of man dinle at once with gladness and sorrow to behold, as the day dawned on our course, in crossing the wide and lonely wilderness of Cumnock-moor, those religious brethren coming towards us, moving in silence over the heath, like the shadows of the slowly-sailing clouds of the summer sky" (II, 52).

Even at its most sublime his vision is fastened thus to a local landscape. Through many pages of flight and hiding he ranges over a named terrain, and his experience creates and recreates the contours of locality historicized by the legends of the martyrs. This intense effect of eyewitness locality, this romance of topography, really has no counterpart in Scott but looks ahead to the Scottish romancers of *Kidnapped, John Splendid,* and *John Burnet of Barns.* It is what Conrad was to call a "romance of reality," and in Galt's realizing of the provincial it provides a strongly evocative counterforce to the distancing effect of humor or obsession.

Fittingly, when Ringan comes home to find his wife and girls slaughtered by Claverhouse's soldiers, all vision fails him. His reason is lost; his time sense is gone; his home has no reality. He becomes ageless; possessed like Claude Walkinshaw by the Abraham archetype, he gives his last son, his Isaac, to the Cameronians, and lives only for his awful mission. The deed is done; the narrative ends. The madman, now sane again, leaves us with only a place name and date seven years after Killiecrankie. In this final blankness Galt is true to his dramatic conception. But, like that other of Galt's masterpieces, *The Entail,* this too may be seen as a logical extension of the art and the idea of the provincial annalist.

3

The Other
Blackwoodians

Galt's achievement becomes the more evident as one sees him in the company of his imitators and followers. His friend and first biographer, David Macbeth Moir,* dedicated his "sketches, principally of humble Scottish character," to Galt in friendship and admiration—and some would add, imitation. But *The Life of Mansie Wauch Tailor in Dalkeith* (1828) is imitative chiefly in superficial ways. This, too, is an annal of "uncos," marvelous parochial trivia, the memorializing of local "character" in anecdote. The pervasive irony is in the discrepancy between the narrator's solemn historic pretensions and his vigorously oral, compulsively thorough account of local matters and manners. The record lacks Galt's kind of theoretical center—the problem of improvement and the fading of communal individuality in historical change, for instance. There is little of Galt's interest in social history. Yet *Mansie Wauch* is a lively rendition of local personality, parochial attitude, and imperfect enlightenment.

Like Galt's fictional autobiographies, Moir's comes in response to the fad of memoir: every sort of person felt his experience to be of interest and value to the philosophic mind. Moir is parodying the fash-

*Moir, David Macbeth. Born at Musselburgh, near Edinburgh, in 1798, and died in 1851 at Dumfries. He studied medicine in Edinburgh and practiced in Musselburgh. He wrote several medical works, contributed regularly to *Blackwood's* (as "Delta") and other magazines, and became Galt's biographer. His novel *Mansie Wauch* began appearing in installments in *Blackwood's* in 1824.

ion. Mansie in his "preliminaries" relates himself to other "notable characters" who have recorded "surprising occurrences and remarkable events." A persistent mock-heroic irony, simpler than Galt's, undercuts the self-importance of the tailor; even his birth came when everyone said "that something great and mysterious would happen on that dreary night." The distinctively Scottish element is Mansie's conviction that the most trivial experiences manifest "an especial Providence"; in this he resembles Galt's autobiographers. Yet there are differences. In Galt self-deception is a problem and mystery. A character struggles to identify his role and his significance; self-justification is his governing motive, and the reader must judge. Mansie Wauch provokes no judicial activity. His petty self-importance is charming and humorous. Because Mansie places his small self at the center of the universe, we have no choice but to condescend to his narrow locality.

There is, however, a rather subtle implication. The Dalkeith tailor considers himself a philosophic autobiographer of the Enlightenment. He refers to the heathen past as "days of darkness"; he scorns superstition and your "warlock and wizard tribe." He expresses amazement at "such doings in an enlightened age and a civilized country!—in a town where we have three kirks, a grammar school, a subscription library, a ladies' benevolent society, a mechanics' institution, and a debating club!"[1] His ludicrously shallow idea of enlightenment implies how absurd it is for small and superstitious human nature to suppose itself enlightened.

The petty "uncos" he recounts are "most wonderful . . . to the eye of a philosopher." His philosophic manner leads him always to refer local experience to what he repeatedly calls "the course of nature"; it is grounded in the conviction that local realities have given him a general understanding of human nature, that Dalkeith is— as Balwhidder's Dalmailing seems to him—a true type of the world. But Balwhidder's reader weighs the possibility that he is right, and Mansie's is simply amused. "I know human nature" is Mansie's constant boast. His new apprentice arrives from the Lammermoors, and "having a general experience of human nature, I saw that I would have something to do towards bringing him into a state of rational civilization." A dreadful fire breaks out next door, and Mansie relates his heroic actions as though he were an Old Testament hero and the end of the world were at hand:

Never such a spectacle was witnessed in this world of sin and sorrow since the creation of Adam . . . The darkness of the latter days came over my spirit like a vision before the prophet Isaiah; and I could see nothing in the years to come but beggary and starvation; myself a fallen-back old man, with an out-at-the-elbows coat, a greasy hat, and a bald pow, hirpling over a staff, requeeshting an awmous—Nanse a broken-hearted beggar wife, torn down to tatters, and weeping like Rachel when she thought on better days . . . I left the hindside of my shirt in her grasp, like Joseph's garment in the nieve of Potiphar's wife, and up the stairs head-foremost among the flames . . . [191-192]

The fire is just one of the great adventures of small local life that bear out his initial claim: he who never stirred from home has witnessed as much as he who sailed the salt seas. And local catastrophes are measured by Mansie on the largest historic scale: "From the first moment I clapped eye on the caricature thing of a coat, that Tammie Bodkin had, in my absence, shaped out for Cursegowl the butcher, I foresaw, in my own mind, that a catastrophe was brewing for us; and never did soldier gird himself to fight the French, or sailor prepare for a sea-storm, with greater alacrity, than I did to cope with the bull-dog anger, and buffet back the uproarious vengeance of our heathenish customer" (260). Such adventures mingle with dire preparations for French invasion, and with discussions of other momentous historical matters in parochial perspective and idiom. That Mansie Wauch should suppose his little catastrophes to be part of the great current of human affairs reflects ironically on his parochial sense of proportion. Yet his supposition also places great events in parochial perspective and gives them human reality by fixing them in the experience of petty people. Add to this the abundant scriptural analogues, and Mansie's little world assumes an archetypal character, without ceasing to be humorously provincial and narrowly generic. This mock-heroic mode flourished in Scottish fiction from the *Noctes Ambrosianae* to the great Aberdonian novel of the Disruption, *Johnny Gibb of Gushetneuk*, half a century later.

However faulty his sense of proportion, Mansie's world does include ample evidence of the course of nature and the perversity of sinful man. The most farcical incidents show man's perversity in brutality and violence—especially those centering on Cursegowl, the butcher next door, who is a devil incarnate of grotesque violence.

When Mansie was but seven years old, he recalls, Cursegowl locked him in his booth of sheepskins and blood, a horror chamber of a farcical demonism akin to episodes elsewhere in Scots comedy from Smollett to Linklater:

> He flang me like a pair of old boots into his booth, where I landed on-my knees upon a raw bloody calf's skin . . . The floor was all covered with lappered blood, and sheep and calfskins. The calves and the sheep themselves, with their cuttit throats, and glazed een, and ghastly girning faces, were hanging about on pins, heels uppermost. Losh me! I thought on Bluebeard and his wives in the bloody chamber! And all the time it was growing darker and darker, and more dreary; and all was as quiet as death itself. It looked, by all the world, like a grave, and me buried alive within it; till the rottens came out of their holes to lick the blood, and whisked about like wee evil spirits. [29-30]

In the graveyard too the atmosphere is ghastly farce. But the most hellish grotesque is the brief glimpse of Edinburgh, the city of sin and pollution and dreadful loneliness, where Mansie spends a short time as youthful journeyman, "dreeing the awful and insignificant sense of being a lonely stranger in a foreign land." "I abode by myself, like St John in the Isle of Patmos, on spare allowance, making a sheep-head serve me for three day's kitchen . . . Everything around me seemed to smell of sin and pollution, like the garments of the Egyptians with the ten plagues" (33-35). The images and sounds of the city at night are vivid and particular, yet strongly colored by Mansie's archetypal Old Testament vision. And later Mansie understands when his apprentice feels the same desolation in Dalkeith and literally pines away for his Lammermoors.

Dalkeith as community is of the same kind as Galt's parish or burgh in its traditionary sense of idiosyncratic personality. But for all the stress on colorful individuality and extraordinary event, there is almost none of the rigid or stylized dehumanizing of character we call caricature; in this, too, Moir is following his master. Caricature, to be sure, is a relative thing, determined in large part by the norms of the narrator's vision. Mansie sees a world of marvelous yet mundane surfaces, and the extraordinary force known as "character" belongs to that world. The reader is left to make his own adjustment to it. Unlike Galt, whose narrators mediate between provincial reality and a cosmopolitan audience, Moir limits himself to a narrator unaware of his world's parochial peculiarity, and unaware of the extraordinary mixture of the archetypal and the local in his densely particularized pictures.

The problems of caricature and the adjustment of provincial perspectives are also evident in the fiction of Susan Ferrier.* She had begun writing independently years before Galt appeared in print, and in fact found Galt's fiction insufferably vulgar. The judgment may sound like genteel Edinburgh lamenting the lowness of Glasgow and the West. But vulgarity is the central problem of value and attitude in Susan Ferrier's manners fiction. Caricature and character are identified and measured on a scale of social intelligence and refinement. Perspective is managed consistently, through all three novels, by an omniscient, judicial narrator. The representation of Scottish manners is handled more in the style of Scott and the eighteenth century: provincial manners are explicitly discovered in *Marriage* and *The Inheritance* by central characters who come to rural Scotland. Even in *Destiny*, the heroine must undergo an educative process through travel and learn to balance the claims of worldly wisdom—associated with a cosmopolitan outlook—with those of local piety, traditional community, and the tranquillity of provincial withdrawal.

In the basic similarities between Galt and Ferrier we can find some important differences. Both are concerned with smallness or narrowness of mind as a central fact of provincial life. For both, in different degrees, smallness is interesting and amusing because they view it, however sympathetically, from enlightenment perspectives of breadth and tolerance, and because they associate it with Scottish local identity. For Ferrier, the application of such perspectives is apt to be satiric. Yet satire is complicated in her novels: her point of view is severely religious, and she treats satiric perspectives as spiritually dangerous. One way to test the accuracy of these distinctions between Galt and

*Ferrier, Susan Edmonstoune. Born in Edinburgh in 1782 and died there in 1854. The daughter of a friend and legal colleague of Scott, she kept house for her father and was a regular visitor in Scott's circle. Although her strict Edinburgh taste could not approve of the fiction of such Blackwoodians as Galt and Lockhart, Blackwood published her first two novels, and no doubt would have published *Destiny* had not Scott's skillful brokering brought her 1700 pounds for the novel from Cadell; hence her inclusion here among the Blackwoodians.

Ferrier is to look at the humorous older women in Ferrier's three novels. They are certainly comparable with Galt's Leddy Grippys and Mrs. Soorockses, yet differ radically in nature and function.

In *Marriage* the heroine Mary and her uncle visit two eccentric Scotswomen, one a slovenly rustic housewife and the other an ancient Edinburgh matriarch—Mrs. Gawffaw and Mrs. MacShake. Mrs. MacShake is a close counterpart to Leddy Grippy. But eccentricity here has little value in itself and almost no reference to present cultural types. Eccentricity is rather a form and manifestation of stupid worldliness—which is a fair definition of Ferrieresque vulgarity. Or, eccentricity may be the form of what the world in its blindness to truth sees as vulgarity, but which the person of true social intelligence sees as natural folly or generic simplicity.

The representative humorous old ladies in Ferrier are not the Mrs. Gawffaws and Mrs. MacShakes. Most Galtian are the three maiden aunts of Glenfern, the stark and tedious Highland estate where the heiress of *Marriage* is temporarily trapped by her runaway marriage. Like Galt's parochials, they gossip trivia, wax solemn about petty and superficial things, and write rambling letters about items of total insignificance. The narrator sums them up with characteristic severity and compassion. They are of the kind who find "occupation congenial to their nature in the little departments of life: dressing crape, reviving black silk, converting narrow hems into broad hems . . . Their walk lay amongst tapes and pickles; their sphere extended from the garret to the pantry; and often, as they sought to diverge from it, their instinct always led them to return to it, as the track in which they were destined to move."[2] For all their Highland manners, the ladies of Glenfern are here primarily to represent a kind of universal human smallness— a timeless provinciality. But the chief female humor of the novel is their local sybil, Lady MacLaughlan. The wife of a grotesque old baronet, Lady MacLaughlan is a rural bluestocking with a laboratory atop her house, with absolute intellectual self-assurance, a conviction that most other people in her world are fools (in this she is correct), and no manners whatsoever. She is a provincial termagant with no apparent compassion and yet humane wisdom. Her marvelous remedies are rural—fruits of the natural sagacity underlying the bluestocking humor—but they have no local significance. Her generic importance is strictly social and intellectual, not cultural.

The novel is about marriage, of course, and is formed around that thematic problem, more or less as an Austen or Burney novel would be formed. Marriage is a problem in social identity and maturity, and it rewards the successful completion of a social education. But Mary's social education is as distinguishable from Evelina's as from Emma Woodhouse's. Its lessons are the satiric-pastoral themes of the novel: natural goodness and stupid vulgarity are not limited to locality or class; place offers universal options of urbanity and provinciality, simplicity and luxury; a longing for one's childhood scenes is natural, and local attachments and pieties are good. Time is not, as in Galt, an ambiguous cultural improvement, but a Thackerayan mutability. In time, some become wiser—that is, less vulgarly attached to worldly things; some act impiously as though time did not touch them, like the vain ones of *Persuasion* and *Henry Esmond*.

Mary has a fine balance of sense and sensibility—or a balance of Fanny Price's piety and Elizabeth Bennett's discrimination. The second half of *Marriage* traces her successful learning of such lessons, through her entrance into fashionable society. She is sent to London to stay with her viciously fashionable mother, her coldly artificial twin sister, her uncle, and her cousin Emily. It is from Emily that her most diffi-cult lesson is learned. Emily serves as her confidante, virtually replac-ing the commentative narrator as delineator of London manners. The lesson is the one voiced by Lady MacLaughlan: there are fools every-where; one must learn to take a providential view of them. And when at last Mary must join her Aunt Grizzy of Glenfern at Bath, she has learned it: "Mary now saw, that there are situations in which a weak capacity has its uses, and that the most foolish chat may sometimes impart greater pleasure than all the wisdom of the schools, even when proceeding from a benevolent heart" (II, 246). Grizzy has other claims on her as well. "She was old, poor, and unknown—plain in her person —weak in her intellects—vulgar in her manners; but she was related to her by ties more binding than the laws of fashion or the rules of taste" (II, 247). Her deficiencies are natural and cultural; moreover, Mary views them with the eye of natural piety. Emily spells out the dis-tinction, recalling faults that "come over my fancy like some snatch of an old nursery song, which one loves to hear in defiance of taste and reason, merely because it is something that carries us back to those days which, whatever they were in reality, always look bright and sunny in retrospection . . . faults [that] are real, genuine, natural faults; and, in this age of affectation, how refreshing it is to meet with even a natural fault!" (II, 368-369).

Such views indicate a significant softening in Emily. Up to now she has been as self-indulgently satiric as Peregrine Pickle. Her satiric temperament is a problem in Mary's education, because Emily's is a valid but extreme way of responding to vulgarity and folly; it is a burdensome gift of vision. "If people *will* be affected and ridiculous, why must I live in a state of warfare with myself, on account of the feelings they rouse within me?" (II, 98). Mary's own gentler penchant for satire confirms the view, and the narrator too delights in satiric caricature.

Critics commonly speak of Ferrier as a caricaturist, without indicating how caricature is to be identified or judged. We can apply to *Marriage* D. W. Harding's astute perception of Jane Austen: the shifting limits of caricature are part of her fictional method. In the social context of *Marriage*, caricature is the representation of character too foolish or vulgar to grasp the norms of enlightened intelligence. The novel is arranged in "gradations of intellect," of taste and humanity. Dr. Redgill is a humorist-monomaniac, who cares only about eating. Lady Juliana seems incredibly selfish and naive, Lady MacLaughlan incredibly despotic and intolerant. Mrs. Douglas, the norm of enlightened piety, seems exaggeratedly compassionate and contented. But we become acclimatized to these extremes, and they are analyzed into believability by the narrator. Always, too, the narrator reminds us that the severest judgment must be tempered by a faith in providence: "Neither are the trifling and insignificant of either sex to be treated with contempt, or looked upon as useless by those whom God has gifted with higher powers" (I, 305). We should be forewarned, then, to weigh our satiric responses to caricature in Mary's London experience. The last word on the matter is Lady MacLaughlan's: fools are fools; God in his wisdom has sent them; true folly and vulgarity are to be judged by a divine wisdom and not by a worldly mind.

The humorous older woman in *The Inheritance* is unlike Lady Mac-Laughlan; and the differences call attention to basic differences between the novels, as well as suggesting the direction of Susan Ferrier's development. Miss Pratt has been compared in her bustling garrulity with Austen's Miss Bates. In some respects she may be classed with Miss Ferrier's caricatures, of which this novel is full: vulgar petty bourgeois nabobs, mothers who are nothing but mothers, aunts who represent "auntimony" and have an entire chapter devoted to them—caricatures because Ferrier focuses so emphatically on their humorously generic qualities. But Miss Pratt's role is important and individual enough to lift her above her generic level. She is a provincial busybody, always arriving everywhere for an unexpected and unwanted visit. Most enjoy her noisy pettiness if only in malice; she is a relief in dull provincial life, and everyone seeks after her and abuses her: "She was, in fact, the very heart of the shire, and gave life and energy to all the pulses of the parish. She supplied it with streams of gossip and chit-chat in others, and subject of ridicule and abuse in herself."[3] Yet, for Lord Rossville, the heroine's guardian uncle, "the provoking part of Miss Pratt was, that there was no possibility of finding fault with her. As well might Lord Rossville have attempted to admonish the brook that babbled past him, or have read lectures to the fly that buzzed around his head. For forty years Lord Rossville had been trying to break her in, but in vain" (I, 103-104). Nature cannot be overcome, and Miss Pratt's ubiquitous volubility seems a force of nature.

Because Miss Pratt is the gossipy heart of the shire and the parish, her activity and talk impart particular reality—in this she resembles Miss Bates—to a provincial world that otherwise remains somewhat abstract. Like Lady MacLaughlan's, her style has no cultural individuality—none of the triumphant stylization of a Leddy Grippy. It is characterized simply by its dashes and breathless runs, its gossipy energy. Its constant is reference to her young kinsman Anthony Whyte, who never appears and yet becomes one of the novel's most particular persons. Everything is personality to Miss Pratt, and Anthony Whyte comically attests to this fact, as well as to her essential unselfishness.

To the pompous Lord Rossville she becomes something more grotesque. Her most extraordinary arrival is in the middle of a snowstorm in a plumed hearse, commandeered from the mourners of M'Vitae the distiller. The consequence of this intrusion is even more grotesque:

Death, even in its most dignified attitude, with all its proudest trophies, would still have been an appalling spectacle to Lord Rossville; but, in its present vulgar and almost burlesque form, it was altogether insupportable. Death is indeed an awful thing, whatever aspect it assumes. The King of Terrors gives to other attributes their power of terrifying: the thunder's roar—the lightning's flash—the

billow's roar—the earthquake's shock—all derive their dread sublimity from Death. All are but the instruments of his resistless sway.
[II, 237-238]

Lord Rossville retires, unable to free himself from the train of ideas
excited by the spectacle; in the morning he is found dead. The garrulous county busybody in a comedy of provincial manners has become
a memento mori. Yet the intrusion is wholly fitting, for the comedy
has a grim, medieval piety to inform its satire of vanity and vulgarity.
Susan Ferrier is a forerunner of Muriel Spark. There is therefore no
point in lamenting the submergence of Ferrier the satirist in Ferrier the
Christian moralist: they are inseparable.

The combination is complicated further by a mixture associated
with Dickens: that is, the transformation of satiric survey into romance of inheritance. Ferrier's title, *The Inheritance*, signals a similarity to Galt's *Entail*, for here too are contrasted true and false kinds of
inheritance—worldly pomp and pride contrasted with natural and
Christian piety. The romance that develops this distinction gradually
replaces satire. The narrative becomes so preoccupied with the heroine's suffering, with the chastening of an idolatrous worldling in order
that she may come into her true inheritance, that humorous figures
such as Lord Rossville and Miss Pratt must be withdrawn. Even Uncle
Adam, having served humorously as a "Scots type well observed,"
must change from cultural humor into a moral touchstone (not unlike
Touchwood in Scott's *St. Ronan's Well*) in his unmannered simplicity.
He is also revealed as the source of the heroine's recovered ancestral
identity.

The heiress Gertrude warrants the pained attention we must give
her; and she can have no Austenite counterpart. Initially, emphasis is
placed on her naturalness as contrasted with the artificiality of her
supposed mother; and she remains essentially open, loving, and conscientious even during her temporary fall into distracted dissipation in
London. She is almost Richardsonian in distraught moral sensibility.
The lies of the great world chain her; her inheritance destroys her
natural freedom, and her pained subjection to fraud and mockery
confirms the narrator's characteristic comment, "Man is not born to
be free . . . Tis to the Christian alone that such freedom belongs" (I,
208). She must be severely chastened, lose everything, become nameless and homeless and humble, before the freedom of her true inheritance can be attained.

The ordeal suits her nature. She anticipates some of the women of George Eliot in her imaginative ardor, a trait repeatedly stressed. She lives in and by her imagination. She is capable of "agony of spirit" because "her ardent and enthusiastic nature" makes her "susceptible." Her "nature [is] lofty, and her disposition generous; but her virtue [is] impulse—her generosity profusion." Her lover Lyndsay knows her well: "I knew all the dangers that awaited one of your ardent, confiding, susceptible, but volatile nature" (II, 93, 309, 311; III, 143). The spiritual danger of this nature is idolatry, and idolatry is the growing imaginative preoccupation of Susan Ferrier.

Gertrude is duped and infatuated in her love for Colonel Delmour. Everything seems to conspire to drive her into the arms of her Lovelace: she is isolated, surrounded by mystery and vulgarity; she longs for affection and refinement, and he offers both. But he is no Lovelace, no sexual menace, and she is her own dupe. He is false, selfish, supercilious. But the key to her suffering is not in his villainy but in her idolatry. She is warned early and repeatedly. She cannot believe the warnings "because all the affections of a warm, generous, confiding heart, were lavished on this idol of her imagination, which she had decked in all the attributes of perfection" (I, 371). She is blinded. "The idol of that heart had gained an absolute ascendancy over her affections, and on it she looked—not with the steady eye of sober truth, but with the fascinated gaze of spell-bound illusion" (II, 11). Lyndsay's love is the opposite: "As his love was without idolatry, so was it free from selfishness." Delmour boasts to Gertrude of the idolatry of his love, scornfully contrasting Lyndsay's "cold-blooded, methodistical" or "puritannical" way. She sees the error: "I am afraid tis in your imagination alone I stand any chance for being deified" (III, 76). Yet in London she loves being the "idol of the day." It is only when her entire world has become unreal, her very name gone, that she can name her sin: "I had power and I misused it—I had wealth and I squandered it—I had an idol, oh! my God!—and thou wast forgot!" (III, 342).

Social satire and presbyterian piety join, then, in Gertrude's experience. The heroine who loves idolatrously and is chastened through infatuation and disinheritance is also satirically revolted by the vulgarities of petty worldliness. Indeed, worldliness and vulgarity, the objects of satire, are also idolatries; grotesque mutability and death are constant reminders of the vanity of human idols. Like Evelina, Gertrude must suffer association with her mother's kin. But she must learn the lesson of *Marriage* and Lady Emily, the lesson taught by Lady MacLaughlan. It is her true lover Edward Lyndsay who teaches her the enlightened taste and Christian piety that Susan Ferrier promulgates in her novels of manners.

"I flatter myself I am a Christian," said she; "and yet I cannot help thinking there are people in the world who are very tiresome, very impertinent, and very disagreeable; yet, I don't think it would be a very Christian act were I to tell them so." "Certainly not," answered Mr. Lyndsay, with a smile; "you may think them all those things; but if you think of them, at the same time, in the spirit of kindness and Christian benevolence, you will pity their infirmities, and you will have no inclination to hurt their feelings, by telling them of faults which you cannot mend." [I, 175]

The lesson includes a new acceptance of the humble Scottish life that surrounds her. It is fitting that her real inheritance, Uncle Adam's estate, is the one house with ancestral identity in a specific Scottish locale. It is a house bound to a legendary peasant past, associated with Adam's lost love, the peasant girl Lizzie Lundie, who turns out to have been Gertrude's grandmother. Thus, her ultimate inheritance combines the presbyterian piety her suffering has taught her with the ancestral peasant tradition in which she finds her name, her security, and her peace at last.

Destiny is Susan Ferrier's only novel of manners in the regional mode. Most commentators find it disappointingly evangelical or pietistic. In fact, the religious didacticism has not increased; rather, the satiric caricature such commentators relish in the earlier novels is virtually gone. To say that penetration of character is gone with it, however, is to overlook the changed nature and function of character in *Destiny*. We see the change if we look at the humorous older woman and also at the male figure—the idolatrous and humorous estate landlord—who replaces the grotesque Glenfern of *Marriage* and the ludicrous Lord Rossville of *The Inheritance*.

The novel opens directly on a local Highland group, the decadent chief of Glenroy, his kinsman-hanger-on Benbowie (ancestors, both, of Compton Mackenzie comedy), and his loyal kinswoman and housekeeper Mrs. Macauley. The group is Susan Ferrier's finest humorous creation, and it is also her fullest characterization of cultural locality. The closest approximation to satiric caricature is M'Dow, the Highland minister from Glasgow. M'Dow is Ferrier's Mr.

Collins, yet he is primarily a ridiculous example of the worldly Scottish minister, from a vulgar Glasgow background, whose worldliness functions like Miss Pratt's gossip. He is equally garrulous and his visits are as frequent and unexpected. His worldliness allows him to describe local manse life in exhaustive detail: he thinks only of his "augmentation," his improvements to the manse, and his food. M'Dow, however, is the only figure in the Highland section to be classed as satiric.

Glenroy himself is culturally typical in humor, totally different in kind from Lord Rossville of *The Inheritance*. Rossville combined the smallness and rigidity of mind, the pompous garrulity, of other Ferrier provincials. Milieu makes little difference in his characterization. The "petty foibles of his mind" are denoted as universals of provincial character; he is simply "a sort of petty benevolent tyrant," with a mind filled to capacity with "little thoughts, little plans, little notions, little prejudices, little whims." Glenroy, too, is provincial; but he explicitly typifies a late phase in the decadence of Highland aristocracy. His infatuated efforts to alter history make him, in idolatry and pathos, a Highland counterpart to Galt's Claude Walkinshaw. And while he remains true to type, the fluctuation of mood and the mental confusion in his development as bereaved father give him the high degree of dramatic individuality that Walkinshaw also achieves. Ferrier's preoccupation with idolatry, in short, has been made local and historical. The "destiny" of the title is more a historic problem than the "inheritance" of the earlier novel. "Idolatry" is now centered on parents and their hopes for their heirs. Glenroy's hopes center idolatrously on his son, and when his son dies, they pass over his devoted daughter (like those of Dickens's Dombey) and center with a growing desperation on his adopted heir, Reginald. Even Captain Malcolm's pious wife, longing for her "lost" son (in an Enoch Arden subplot), is susceptible, and saved only by her sober faith. Ironically, Glenroy's adoptive heir, Reginald, is himself damned as an idolater in love; and the suffering that Glenroy's daughter undergoes in loving him derives from her idolatry.

Edith's mild character should not conceal her kinship to Gertrude. And her education parallels those of the earlier heroines. At her father's death she is left disinherited to become a dependent in exile, the sad last of her line, cast among vulgar relatives in London to discover the Ferrier lesson that meanness, smallness, and idolatry can be found in the most cosmopolitan of worlds. The city bourgeoisie and her high-life relatives are equally mean. She also learns compassion for such smallness: "She felt only pity for those whose minds had been thus cramped and fettered by the bondage of their own little sphere, falsely called the great world." Likewise, her Cockney kin, the petty good-natured Ribley and his wife: "As the mind commonly finds its own level in society, it may be inferred that Mr. and Mrs. Ribley's circle of acquaintances was composed of common-place, vulgar-minded persons, like themselves, full of the paltry gossip and petty detail of the narrow sphere in which they moved."[4] Edith finds the provincial and the idolatrous everywhere. The Ribleys' nephew observes to her, "How you must despise us mercenary English . . . when you see the homage we render to mere wealth." She replies, "Is it not the universal idol, under some form or other?" "Yes," he says, "with the vulgar; even mere vulgar coin commands reverence—but you, I am sure, would be no worshipper of wealth under any form." And she answers, "Every country—nay, every heart, has perhaps its own false deity" (III, 114). Her own as well.

In identifying the spiritual ill for which Edith must suffer exile and disinheritance, the narrator uses terms almost Johnsonian: "Edith had religious feeling, but she had not religious principle; and thus, what might have been the medicine to check and mitigate the fever of her heart, had served rather as the aliment to feed and pamper its sickly sensibilities" (II, 362). She has known and forgotten that true love cannot be idolatrous—hence, in true love "there can be no illusion." Knowing that it is sinful to lavish all affections on God's creature, she claims she cannot help it. Surrounded like Gertrude with the dull, coarse vulgarity that horrifies her, she turns with relief to the graceful, refined, and inconstant Reginald, until she sees even Reginald and his high world turn to the grotesque degradation of the later chapters: her hideous mother intruding on her vain daughter's theatricals as Venus in a cart, "emblems . . . of the weak and beggarly elements of mere worldly advantages." Such worldlings are slaves of the world and time. Their destiny is perpetual slavery.

Destiny can be seen as a Scottish analogue to *Persuasion*—a romantic analogue, to be sure, and a Christian one. The vain Sir Walter has become a Highland chief, his heir is his infatuation, his daughter is as sadly neglected as poor Anne ever was. The need for time to mature judgment and affection is part of Edith's experience, too. There is no natural process of maturing; rather, Edith's is the Pauline death-rebirth cycle of Christian romance. Suitably, the true lover that was Austen's Wentworth is Ferrier's Captain Malcolm, reported dead at sea, dead to his family by choice for thirteen years (the Enoch Arden motif). Recovered from her idolatry, Edith turns unknowingly to her childhood friend Malcolm, meeting him again in the presence of the goodnatured admiral and his wife, who resemble Austen's Crofts. Her "second spring" of affection is, unlike Anne's, a religious renewal; her second love is free of the illusion of idolatry. The imagery of *Persuasion* and Ferrier's persistent religious idiom are remarkably combined in this climactic passage:

> Could it be that the lost, the lamented, had thus, as it were, started into life—that the loved companion of her childish days was now the chosen of her matured affections? And these affections, had they been lightly transferred—could affections, once so blighted as hers had been, ever again revive, and own a second spring? . . . Love had formerly been a sentiment—a false, narrow, exclusive sentiment—shared only by the object which inspired it; now it was a noble, generous, diffusive principle . . . Again she loved, but by a light which could not deceive; by that divine light which taught her not to love the mere perishing idol of life's passing hour, but the immortal soul, with whose soul her own might joy to claim kindred throughout eternity. [III, 346-347]

Time is fulfilled only through time transcended. But the escape from the provinciality of time, worldly "destiny," is also the return to childhood's local affections. Time is everything and nothing to the vulgar worldlings. The historic time of Glenroy is real, but past. Time is redeemed—in history and locality—in the true love of Edith and Ronald and the renewal of the Highland estate.

Edith's faith, rooted in childhood, has been with her throughout, in the shape of the novel's humorous older woman, Mrs. Macauley. Mrs. Macauley, unlike her antecedents Lady MacLaughlan and Miss Pratt, is a local type, a Highland widow devoted to her chief, who speaks in a soft Highland accent, reflects a distinctively simple and provincial outlook, yet in her simplicity represents Christian piety and a providential view of time. She travels to London with Edith and preserves her charity, good humor, and fidelity in exile. She speaks for providence in modest defiance of her chief, and is called a fool and a

dangerous predestinarian. And true to her Gaelic tradition, she has
the book's final word, suitably on man's blindness, God's providence,
and the destiny allotted to time and place:

> Oh, should not that make us humble and trustful, when it is shown
> to us poor, blind craaters, that it is not in man that walketh to direct
> his steps? And to see how beautifully it is appointed to us as to the
> naatral creation, to have our tribulations and our consolations, if
> we would but look to the hand that sends them! for, as the old Hie-
> land distich says, (but as you do not understand Gaelic, I must give
> it to you in English,)
>
> > There is neither knoll nor rising,
> > Nor yellow (green) grassy hillock,
> > That will not for a space of time be joyous,
> > And for a while be sad and tearful. [III, 398-399]

Through Mrs. Macauley's loyalty, there is an affirmation of local
affection not found in Susan Ferrier's earlier novels. The final return
of Edith and her devoted retainer to the Highlands is not just Gertrude's generalized return to local piety and pastoral tranquillity. The
return in time and place is specific, and at the same time romantic. It is
notable that as Scottish fiction becomes, like Susan Ferrier's novels,
increasingly focused on and evocative of particular time and place, it
also moves away from novel to romance.

The romantic discovery of time and place is more prominent in the
four novels of John Gibson Lockhart,* than in either Galt or Ferrier.
Lockhart had a more varied critical sense of the possibilities of fiction
than either, however, and his novels are four different experiments in
mode and method. *Valerius* and *Matthew Wald* are first-person narra-

---

Lockhart, John Gibson. Born at Cambusnethan, Lanarkshire, in 1794, and died
at Abbotsford, near Melrose, in 1854. The son of a minister, he studied at Glasgow
University, won a "First" in Classics at Oxford, and settled in Edinburgh to read
and practice law. He joined Wilson, Hogg, and others to make early *Blackwood's*
a scandalous success in attacking the Edinburgh Whig establishment. Blackwood
published his first book, a translation of F. Schlegel's *Lectures on the History of
Literature*, and his second, a critical-epistolary survey of contemporary Edinburgh, *Peter's Letters to his Kinsfolk* (1819). His four completed novels appeared
in the four years following his marriage to Scott's daughter Sophia and preceding
their move to London, where Lockhart began his quarter-century as editor of the
influential *Quarterly Review*. He is best remembered for his *Life of Scott* (7 vols.,
1837-38; 10 vols., 1839), but he also wrote fine short biographies of Burns and
Napoleon.

tives—one a historical romance, the other a bitter Godwinian pica-resque. *Adam Blair* and *Reginald Dalton* are omniscient third-person narratives, the first a restrained and compassionate brief narrative of tragic passion, the other a colorfully digressive, humorous romance of university life and mysterious inheritance. Lockhart, throughout his experiments, shares Galt's historical interest in provincial manners, as well as his concern for the "metaphysical anatomy" of his characters. But with Susan Ferrier he shares something more basic: the mixture of satiric vigor with a severe but compassionate piety, and a strong sympathy for presbyterian character and tradition. His peculiar artis-tic excellence as a novelist is a skillfully manipulated mobility of per-spective and variety of tone. David Craig, for whom *Adam Blair* remains among the most significant of novels in the Scottish religious tradition, suggests that for Lockhart Galt's "vein of fiction-as-social-history must have seemed nearly worked out."[5] The evidence con-firms this view. Lockhart's many theoretical statements about the novel stress repeatedly that while the novelist has access as social his-torian to endless treasures, he must never forget his primary formal obligations as an artist. And Lockhart succeeded remarkably in prac-ticing as he preached.

All four of his novels are rich surveys of local manners, or more than that, of the spirit or ethos of a milieu. *Valerius* recounts a young Roman-Briton's voyage of inheritance to the Rome of Trajan, and the Romans in the book are genre figures in the network of social and do-mestic relations of decadent Rome. *Reginald Dalton* owed its long popularity on the railway bookstalls to the gusty and colorful set-pieces of squierarchy and vicarage, of fashionable London, of the or-gies and idylls of undergraduate Oxford. *Matthew Wald* is Scottish picaresque, its proud and angry young hero an heir to Roderick Ran-dom but also to Godwin's monomaniacal Mandeville. Disinherited because of his father's honor and his own proud ferocity, Wald moves from one professional and social sphere to another, in a skillfully de-signed panorama of eighteenth-century Scottish manners. Even in *Adam Blair*, most economically focused of the four, a manners con-ception is basic. Scenes of life and death in manse and mansion, of the presbytery in session, even of passion and penance in a gaunt Loch Fine tower—all are manners pieces of the same breadth, color, and economy as the great panoramic summaries in Lockhart's biographies. Characters are representative of "the habitudes and feelings of the religious and virtuous peasantry of the west of Scotland, half a century ago." The narrator insists that the essential truth of his story is a test of Scotland's national memory. As one reviewer, Henry Mackenzie, noted, the tragic remorse of the minister after his fall can be understood only with reference to the role of Scottish clerical morality in parochial culture.[6] Yet in Lockhart's novels an interest in manners is subordinated to fictional form and meaning.

Valerius is the romance of a provincial in ancient Rome, implicated by accident with persecuted Christians, lover of a noble Christian, a convert, and finally a fugitive. An episodic plot keeps the sensitive, humane protagonist-observer almost constantly in motion; the facts of Roman place become the concrete impressions of personal experience. Unlike Scott, whose descriptions are set-pieces in the late eighteenth-century picturesque mode, Lockhart and his protagonist luxuriate in vivid local images that are suggestive of postromantic travel literature. The sensations of the stranger lost outside the Colliseum, the eyewitness impression of the passionate mob, particular faces in spiritual stress—all are nightmarishly vivid. Valerius mounts the Palatine and

> now, on one side, were all the pillars and arches of the Forum stretched out below us, as in a picture; and, on the other, lay the stately sweep of the great Circus, topped with its obelisk; while right before, from above trees and temples, rose the grey cliffs of the Capitoline, with all their crown of domes and proud pinnacles glittering in the glow of the noontide. Imagine to yourself the space between, all radiant with the arms and banners of those moving cohorts, and confess that my enthusiasm might have been pardoned, even had I been an old man, and less a stranger to spectacles of Roman magnificence.[7]

And mere spectacles they always are, hinting at fear, corruption, and restless unhappiness beneath. Anti-Gibbonian as he is, Lockhart has derived his ironic view of imperial spectacle from Gibbon's ambiguous sketch of Antonine enlightenment and prosperity. But Valerius's observations are always formed by the same contrast between melancholy superstition in the most "enlightened" and a tranquillity of countenance that suggests the mysterious transcendence of the Christian. Valerius's motive in summoning up images of his romantic voyage is part of his Christian character and experience, and essential as well to Lockhart's satiric intention.

In Lockhart's time, every remote locale of culture and history had its romantic novelist. But Lockhart's exotic localism is controlled by a satiric perspective like that found in Galt and Ferrier. Valerius's is the discovery of metropolitan manners by a dazzled provincial, who finds a restless and idolatrous vulgarity under a cosmopolitan surface. He is overcome at first by "the most refined and exalted people, whose hands have ever been invested with the dominion of the world" (I, 14). He looks with condescension back upon "the ill-cemented and motley fabric of an insulated colony" in Britain. In Rome he encounters vain metropolitans mocking the pretensions of nouveau provincials and boasting of "the air of the Capital." But the truth of the air of the Capital is blood-thirsty folly and melancholy superstition. Roman philosophers are philosophers only in name. The supposed "enlightened" and "metropolitan" are alike narrow and irrational; real enlightenment is found in what metropolitan perspectives find provincial. Lockhart's satiric intention is identical with Ferrier's: to show that the enlightened piety of Christianity is the opposite of provinciality.

One technical criticism remains to be answered. Those who compare the novel with its nineteenth-century descendants, culminating in *Marius the Epicurean*, complain that Valerius's conversion is never made explicit. In fact, it is one of Lockhart's unique skills as a novelist that he can trace highly idiosyncratic subjective experience purely by implication—that he can objectify psychological process through a vivid impressionism. It is an accomplishment comparable with Galt's autobiographers, who not only give themselves away, but present us with historical and local worlds which are themselves expressions of character and experience. Valerius's remembered impressions of Rome are formed into the implicit drama of his conversion. Every locale, incident, and character functions in this drama, not just as an external type, but also as a subjective symbol. The same is true of Adam Blair's adulterous passion and Matthew Wald's monomania.

The lively melodrama *Reginald Dalton* has its own similarities to the romance of *Valerius*. Reginald is the son of a north English vicar. His story is set at home, at Oxford, in fashionable London, and on Queen Street in Edinburgh. Here lives one of the only two Scots among the book's principal characters, Macdonald, the Writer to the Signet. The other is the old Catholic priest, Father Keith, an exile from Scotland who, after years in Germany, has returned to Oxford. The two Scots are old friends, both implicated in the mystery of the orphaned heroine Ellen Hesketh's true identity and inheritance. Lockhart characteristically chooses not to exploit the manners potential of meetings between a worldly Edinburgh lawyer and an old Jacobite priest.

The chief manners interest of the novel centers on undergraduate life at Oxford: a street fight between town and gown, college dinners, parties in "rooms," provincial ladies' teas, rowing on the river—all done in the romance mode of *Valerius* but with a distinctive tone, and all in Lockhart's favorite manner of rapid impressionistic panorama. So skillful is the economy that at climactic points Lockhart can introduce a localized manners vignette without digressive effect. Reginald in desolation is leaving Oxford after his duel with Chisney.

> In passing the door, Reginald could not avoid throwing one glance into the apartment of the Canon. The purple old man was dozing with his feet on the fender, a huge night-cap on his head, and an enormous black cat asleep on his lap. The wife, daughter, niece, or cousin, a pimpled paragon, was sitting on the opposite side of the fire, nodding over a volume of Hannah More, and a rummer of hot brandy and water—a pack of dirty cards lay half way between her and the Canon, and one of the tall unsnuffed candles was distilling a slow heavy stream of liquid tallow upon the oaken boards of a folio volume of Chrysostom. They glided rapidly past, and were in a moment in the Canon's garden, among tall sighing poplars, and a wilderness of wet sheets, smocks, and surplices.[8]

All of this evokes "the GENIUS LOCI," "that noble and ancient City of Muses," and once more, as in *Valerius*, through the passionate sensibility of a youth "born and reared in a wild sequestered province," sadly disillusioned with the reckless vulgarity he discovers in the great world, and ultimately enlightened as to the transcendent values of his own "provinciality." The pattern as well as the satiric perspective is reminiscent of Susan Ferrier. The difference is that Lockhart's narrative voices are so various and versatile that he can severely satirize worldly vulgarities and yet at the same time delineate with lively dramatic sympathy passionate scenes of juvenile abandon: drinking, fighting, hunting. Anticipating *Matthew Wald*, he seems able even to identify with feelings of violent, even brutal hatred. Yet, all of this is framed in and consistently controlled by a severe piety, a penetrating sense of the worldliness in the most admirable or gentle characters: Reginald's father the vicar is capable of romantic self-delusion and self-interest; Father Keith can momentarily be a snob and slightly drunk.

Lockhart delighted in a Scottish mixture of severe piety and boisterous animal spirits. His delight in the mixture gave him his dominant
voice in the antics of early *Blackwood's*; and the narrator he evolved
for *Reginald Dalton*, in his omniscience, his urbanity, and his extraordinary tonal range, is an identifiably Blackwoodian voice. He is
garrulous and good-humored in his comments; some of them become
colloquial essays that generalize action and character. His flexible
omniscience allows character to achieve the ironic complexity we associate with such later English Victorians as Eliot and Trollope. Such
mobility of viewpoint makes the book a remarkable conflation of brilliant surface and psychological intricacy. The conflation, like the tonal
mixture of boisterous gusto and severe piety, belongs in the Ambros-
ian atmosphere of early *Blackwood's*, anticipates the biographer of
Burns who valued equally the rantin dog and the Saturday night cot-
tar, and in general suggests how a novel can be distinctively Scottish
with little Scottish subject matter.

The novel belongs to the Blackwood group in its serious romance
plot as well. Reginald pauperizes his father and ultimately is forced to
leave the university forever, in shame but in honor and in love with
Father Keith's ward, the mysterious and disinherited orphan Ellen
Hesketh. The inheritance romance recalls Galt's *Entail* and Ferrier's
The Inheritance, each with its idolatrous pursuit of perpetual landed
power and with the pains of losing one's worldly inheritance in the interests of a higher one. Reginald, having ruined his father, delights to
surrender his bride's newfound legacy to filial piety; and Reginald and
Ellen come together under a triple religious sanction: one the child of a
methodistical baronet, the other of an Anglican vicar, and both
adopted and counseled by the old Scottish priest. The third volume
centers on three idolatrous fathers: one seeking his son's worldly
glory; another denying his true daughter's inheritance and then being
betrayed by his false daughter's artifice; and Reginald's father, still
caught in romantic idolatries of worldly inheritance. The dark places
of the human heart are in all; and all, in their struggles of conscience,
discover the blindness of human pride and the emptiness of worldly
idols. In Lockhart, as in Ferrier, the satiric and the severely pious are
closely linked.

Dalton, a young man of feeling, finds Gothic exultation in destructive emotional conflict: "There was trouble, darkness, miserable darkness within; but there was burning ire too—indignation, and

contempt, and steady scorn, and the hot thirst of blood; all these, strangely blended with the tender yearnings of a young and living love, and yet all shrouded and enveloped, more strangely still, in a profound feeling of weariness of life" (II, 328). Wald, the manic disinherited picaro of Lockhart's fourth novel, is a more extreme form of the same collection of moods. He describes himself as he leaves the home that has rejected him: "I could never describe the feelings with which I took my parting look of it from the bridge. The pride, the scorn, the burning scorn, that boiled above,—the cold, curdling anguish below,—the bruised, trampled heart."[9] His early description of the step-uncle who has beaten him illustrates the close connection of satiric acuteness, wrathful vanity, and self-disgust:

> I had heard, I know not from whom, when Mather first came to the parish, that his father was a barber. Conceive how often this recurred to me now—conceive how I grinded my teeth, as I lay counting hour after hour through the night, upon the sweet idea that I was trodden under foot by the spawn of a village shaver—that he had whipped me—that I had borne the marks of him on my back! . . . His fine large white teeth seemed to me as if they belonged to some overgrown unclean beast—some great monstrous rat . . . What exquisite vulgarity did I not see in his broad flat nails, bitten to the quick! [37]

Wald's "intense perceptions" of exquisite vulgarity are our access to his world, as though a Smollettesque Heathcliff were to tell his own story. His choleric impressionism allows many vivid sketches, some grotesquely humorous, some poignantly lovely, momentary glimpses of transcendence, of pastoral peace. His intense perceptions are animated by a deeply divided self that he himself has fractured: "I sat down again, half naked as I was, in my chair, and spurned the slipper from my foot against the mirror. It hit the line of the old crack; and the spot where it lighted became the centre of a thousand straggling radii, that made it impossible I should be henceforth offended otherwise than with sorely broken fractions of my sweet form" (69). And all from an "inexpiable stain," a secret sin of meanness he cannot forgive himself.

His father, a Hanoverian with a doomed Jacobite brother, inherits the forfeited estate, but wills it honorably to his brother's daughter, whom Matthew loves. Matthew's disinheritance is just and magnanimous. Yet Matthew allows himself to become a pawn of High Street law and fights to disinherit the true heiress, his love. He loses, but never forgives himself for his mean sin. We depend on the impulsive, anguished character engendered by such sin for our vision of his picaresque world. It is a grim and grotesque world in which character is almost always mysterious, surprising, the repository of secret pain and corruption. Meikle the kindly old minister tells the story of his son's tragedy and illegitimate child. Mammy Baird, ancient retainer in the aristocratic West Highland house where Matthew serves as tutor, tells of another orphan bastard and her mother's suicide. Matthew, when a Glasgow medical student, lives with a fanatical Cameronian cobbler and witnesses the horror of the fanatic's murder of his friend and his triumphant self-righteousness, a justified sinner, even through execution. Wald's own grotesque vision is thus confirmed. The phrases of a caustic Calvinist pessimism, heard first in *Valerius,* are repeated here: "For, oh, sir! the heart of man is a dark thing to look into." Added is a tragic compassion that echoes *King Lear*: "We weep when we come into the world, and every day shows why. Let us be merciful judges of others, and, ere we taunt the cripple, see well that ourselves be whole" (155). Yet this world's chief quality is moral surprise—the noblest man's capacity for meanness, the villain's capacity for moments of magnanimity. Wald himself, at his most judicious and humane as country doctor, testifies to this:

> I have seen the pompous stoic frightened out of his toothache by the mere sight of my forceps; and perceived, that it is possible to make an edifying appearance in church on Sunday, with one's wife and family "all a rowe", and yet to be *dans son interieur* not a little of the tyrant . . . But I have seen many more agreeable matters than these. I have seen the rough cynic of the world sitting up three nights on end at a bedside;—I have seen the gay, fine lady performing offices from which a menial would have shrunk;—I have seen heirs shed genuine tears. [224-225]

His narrative is addressed to a young friend and heir; it is seen only after Wald's death. Following his complete breakdown after killing his rival, Wald had at last recovered his sanity and become a kindly old man, yet darkly melancholy underneath—"in reality the secret slave of despondency." The heir wonders how much of the story is true and in what way its truth is to be taken. And we are left with that final gesture of Blackwoodian mystification, turned here to the service of Lockhart's perennial theme of character as dark mystery, to be judged only in humility and compassion, to be understood cautiously with an abiding sense of how complex and surprising it may be.

Lockhart's best novel is his third, *Adam Blair*. Lockhart's purpose in
Adam Blair is a fusion of cultural description and moral persuasion;
its truth is historical and normative. Like other Blackwoodians, he
seeks to correct false cosmopolitan views of Scotland's "primitive
peasantry" by showing the peasant's natural intelligence and traditional piety. With Ferrier's satire he shares the representation of enlightened sceptics chastened and in some measure restored to traditional local pieties. The urbane narrator's view of parochial piety is
expressed in what would seem condescension were it not for the tone
of quiet respect and tragic compassion. A distinction between characters of urbanity and characters of a regional typicality is suggested in
the scenes where some speak Scots and some do not. The parochial
grand old lady, Mrs. Semple, uses it: "I weel ken that nae love can
ever be like a first love; but oh! mem, it's folks' duty to struggle with
the evils of our condition; and Mr. Blair is not in the same kind of situation that he would have been in, had he been left at the head of a large
family, wi' everything astir round about him. He has naething but yon
puir bit lassie, little Sarah, and I'm sure she has as meikle reason as he
has to wish for such a change."[10] But her language is indistinguishable
from the speech of the humble elder John Maxwell, or for that matter
of the nameless old beggar who accosts Blair and Mrs. Campbell in
their garden chair. Scots is not used for intrinsic evocative value (as
Galt and Moir use it), or for social or regional differentiation (as in Ferrier and Hogg). It is used to suggest a general character of traditional
simplicities and pieties, and it is saved for characters who have them.
Strahan, the local lad of sharp parts who has become an Edinburgh
lawyer, uses no Scottish idioms at all.

Speech style has another dramatic function in the novel as well. The
letter in which Charlotte Campbell announces her visit to Adam, the
widower of her late friend, subtly suggests the dangerous self-indulgence of her sympathy:

Having been for near four weeks in Scotland, you may think it very
strange that I have not taken an earlier opportunity of saying, *what
I hope, indeed, I need scarcely say*, that I have heard with feelings of
the *sincerest* sorrow, of the *great* blow with which it has pleased
God to visit you, (I may add myself,) and of expressing, at the same
time, my hope . . . Since we saw each other last, *many, many* things
have happened which could little have been expected by either of
us; and I believe I may add, that in that time I have had *my own full
share* of the sorrows of this *world*. [40-41]

Her sentimental self-indulgence finds a subtle echo in his own, and the echo leads to Blair's sexual surrender. Her corrupt, worldly sympathy is carefully distinguished from the restrained and delicate compassion of his presbyterian parish. Indeed, the parish's quiet and profound awareness makes it seem almost speechless. There is little dialogue. In *Adam Blair*, Lockhart seems to be opposing Galt's provincial community of traditional talkers to his own of quiet, respectful concern.

Like most of the people of the novel, the narrator has a solemn and modest respect for the privacy of individual character. He has Lockhart's view, as we have seen it in *Matthew Wald*, of the sacred mystery of each human spirit, the difficulty of knowing or judging another. Often one character senses that another wishes to be alone and leaves him or remains at a quiet distance. The novel's silence is remarkably expressive. Characteristic is the incident of the humbled Blair walking to the elder's house. The narrator begins with typical caution:

> I know not whether, when he passed his threshold, he had made up his mind as to the direction in which he would go; but so it was, that he wandered over the fields until he had come very near the place where John Maxwell lived.
>
> In those days it was the custom of many of our godly peasants, and among the rest it was the custom of John Maxwell, to pray aloud, out of doors . . . it did not then enter into the mind of any body to connect its observance with any notions of pharisaical display.
>
> When Mr. Blair, therefore, had come within a few paces of the old beechen hedge at the foot of this man's garden, it was not with surprise that he heard his voice among the shade . . . he drew back to some distance that he might not be, by accident, an intruder upon the secret of that privacy. [232-233]

Perhaps it is this pervasive silence that accounts for the disturbing force of the novel's one harsh noise. Blair, being carried by the singing Gaelic boatmen up Loch Fine to Charlotte Campbell's lonely tower, goes with no anticipation of evil. On the shore, watching his approach and delighting in Blair's weakness and imminent fall, the vulgar and demonic solicitor Strahan laughs loudly and then repeats his laugh "more loudly than before." It is the demonic laugh of the one undeniably evil figure in the book. Otherwise, the crucial moments of reflection and decision, in an action filled with lonely spiritual agonies, are left implicit and quiet. The narrator is enacting his own reverential distance from spiritual stress and privacy.

Some readers feel unprepared for Blair's overwhelming adulterous passion. There is no explicit psychologizing; the passion's slow and inexorable growth is dramatized, in the way Lockhart the critic had so admired in Goethe's *Wilhelm Meister*.[11] It is done by implication, at a respectful distance. The narrator warns us that no one can know for what secret spiritual sins the bereaved minister has been punished. He provides hints of the minister's passionately solitary sensibility, his proneness to emotional self-indulgence. There is pride in Adam's stoical dignity; he never betrays his feelings to his community. He recklessly ignores the interests of others at times of stress; he flees to the woods, while others worry but respect his privacy. Charlotte's passionate nature matches his own, as does her indiscretion. Two scenes bring them into highly emotional and ill-clad proximity—once in the churchyard, where Charlotte is musing on what a great lover he must have been, and once by the water, where Charlotte has rescued both father and daughter from drowning. The community is fully aware of the dangers of their situation—the bereaved, lonely husband and a house-guest with a shady past. We cannot miss the direction of the relationship, though Adam seems blind to it. We join the community in profound sympathy, but we share the narrator's characteristic acuteness and severity in detecting spiritual weakness.

This distanced yet penetrating sense of the minister's noble weakness makes Adam Blair seem a completely individualized character. Yet his individuality is generic. He is his peasant grandfather's descendant and his father's son, a parish minister of the Scottish southwest; he has a communal identity inseparable from milieu, role, and ancestry. The narrator repeatedly reminds us of those determinants of character. The truth of the story is itself offered as testimony to the valuable reality of such a recent past: in such a place to such a man a tragedy and its triumphant outcome could have occurred. The tale is generalized in reflections about the workings of nature. There is a pervasive hint of archetypal allusion in Adam's name, his fall, his deceptive Eden, his stormy night of sin and the horrors of remorse that follow. Yet even this universality is tied to cultural particularity: the shape of the tale illustrates the spiritual workings of a particular way of life.

The evocation of local setting is restrained and subordinate. There is none of the panoramic impressionism of *Valerius* and *Reginald Dalton*. The parish churchyard, for example, belongs to the cultural and moral consciousness of the characters. It stands as witness to Blair's ancestral and communal significance. The initial temptation, too, is set there, in the subtle scene where Charlotte, newly arrived, wanders out in her nightgown to mourn self-indulgently on her friend's new grave. Adam, seeing the white figure, has a superstitious moment of thinking the figure his wife; then quietly joins her, inadvertently placing a protective hand on her bare shoulder. Likewise, the scene on Loch Fine is depicted with restrained sublimity, but functions, too, as an expression of Blair's recklessly sympathetic mood, his dangerous intensity and solitary nature. Finally, the peasant's hut to which Adam returns following his fall is a type of local ancestral shrine where he must seek purification. Rustic provinciality simply conceals the spiritual nobility and delicacy of the peasant. Lockhart is consciously a Wordsworthian pastoralist. Yet his moral compassion and severity are expressive of the specific milieu whose ethos he celebrates.

But like the narrator of *Reginald Dalton*, this narrator is capable of a sophisticated instinct for the signs of grace in fallen worldlings. Lockhart, like Ferrier and Galt (and, much later, Robin Jenkins and Muriel Spark), may be seen as a distinctively presbyterian satirist of worldliness. He treats Charlotte Campbell and her husband with urbane restraint, seeing their worldliness, yet allowing them their moments of grace. The realization of such characters is the major difference between *Adam Blair* and its oft-noted analogue, *The Scarlet Letter*. Charlotte is as complex a female character as can be found in nineteenth-century British fiction. She is such a mixture of self-indulgent weakness and self-sacrificial strength that the seeker of analogues must recall Lockhart's love of the Jacobeans, summon up the Duchess of Malfi, and place her with Manon and the Charlotte of *Young Werther*. Her buoyant will to survive anticipates Becky Sharp, but manifests a sexuality Becky lacks. She is decorous but too warm. She can feel shame, yet glory in the thought of Blair as a lover; mourn on his wife's grave, and sing a bawdy ballad at her window; love his daughter and his parishioners, reprimand Blair justly for his selfish remorse, save him from suicide, nurse him and die so doing. Her husband begins as cultural caricature and ends as a diffident agent of grace. He is "one of that numerous division of the human species which may be shortly and accurately described as answering to the name of Captain Campbell." He is bandy-legged; "his nose had been blown up a good deal by snuff and brandy, or both; his eyes were keen grey; his hair, eye-brows, and whiskers, bristly red; his bob-major dressed à *merveille;* and his Dutch uniform as fine as fivepence" (51). Upon hearing of his wife's adultery and death, however, his shame and sorrow overcome his anger, and this "hot," "violent," "vain," "rude" man feels and acts "in a style of which a great many more polished characters might have been altogether incapable under similar circumstances" (205). His brief, quiet confrontation with the convalescent Blair is the greatest scene in Lockhart's fiction. The vain, vulgar worldling forgives and protects the remorseful minister from exposure. His compassion is genuine, his delicacy remarkable. He transcends his cultural typicality, as Highland mercenary and Lowland minister meet in sorrow on the shore of a Highland loch.

John Wilson,* the most prolific of Blackwoodians, is not impressive as a novelist, but his unimportance in the origins of the Scottish novel is not simply a problem of art. It can be argued that he preferred the short sketch—the nineteenth-century prose idyll, with blank verse counterparts in Wordsworth and Tennyson—to the novel. Wilson's fiction began with *Lights and Shadows of Scottish Life*—"Scottish sentimentality of the most objectionable kind," says Ian Jack, in "stories supposed to describe the simple realities in the life of the Scottish peasantry"[12]—and Professor Wilson as "Christopher North" later flourished as "editor" of Lowland idylls. These idylls anticipate the development of a major Scottish Victorian form, generally ignored now: the parochial idyll and its curious kin, the domesticated *kunstmärchen*, "scenes," "legends," and "sketches" of regional life and tradition, raised to significant art by George MacDonald, transposed into provincial history by Dean Ramsay, Hugh Miller, and William Alexander, and carried at last into the Kailyard of Barrie, Crockett, and Watson (Ian Maclaren).

Wilson's novels are two: *Margaret Lyndsay* and *The Foresters.* Wil-

*Wilson, John. Born in Paisley, Renfrewshire, in 1785, and died in Edinburgh in 1854. He attended Glasgow and Oxford, where he won the Newdigate Prize for Poetry. His major poems were *The Isle of Palms* (1812) and *The City of the Plague* (1816). One of Blackwood's chief contributors, he compiled most of the Blackwoodian dialogues, the *Noctes Ambrosianae*, and later became identified with their editorial persona Christopher North. He became Professor of Moral Philosophy (largely through political influence) at Edinburgh University in 1820, and held the chair until 1851. In addition to his two novels, his fiction includes *Lights and Shadows of Scottish Life* (collected from *Blackwood's* in 1822).

son's mode combines ornate sentimentality and presbyterian severity in a pastoral setting. The Lyndsay family lives in a Braid Hills village just outside Edinburgh in surroundings of peace and natural beauty.

> Little sensible, perhaps, were the simple dwellers in Braehead of the pleasures which such scenes inspire; for they were the children of labour and poverty; yet Nature wastes not her power in vain, and no doubt it mingles unconsciously with the happiness of every human heart. The rising and setting sun, as its light burnishes the cottage window, does more than merely awaken to toil, or give a welcome summons to rest; and in a country like Scotland, where thoughtful intelligence has long been the character of lowly life, it is not to be supposed that even the poorest and most ignorant are ever wholly indifferent to the wonderful works of God.
>
> In this hamlet lived the family of Walter Lyndsay, the narrative of whose fortunes may perhaps not be unaffecting to those who feel a deep interest in every exhibition, however humble, of the joys and sorrows, the strength and the weakness, of the human heart.[13]

Like Lockhart, Wilson derives his ideas of pastoral simplicity and tragedy from his understanding of Wordsworth. Wilson's characters seem occasionally to have stepped out of *The Excursion*, free of Wordsworth's kind of transcendentalism, and much given to "feminine" intensities of affection, to the pieties of home and parish, and to deathbed repentances worthy of Dickens. The narrator invariably views his humble subjects with a mixture of solemn respect and generalizing condescension—"the simple dwellers," "the children of labour and poverty." His social perspective is generically Scottish, and in humble and intelligent respectability he professes to find "the native character of the race." But his intention is to show in such character the "human heart."

Minor characters are recognizable originals of Scottish parochial manners. Walter Lyndsay's mother is seen sitting palsied by the fire, reading her Bible or stories of Scottish martyrs. The Lyndsays' rough, coarse neighbor John Walker, a poor carter, reasserts Scott's Mucklebackit theme: among the poor there can be no luxury of grief, but the roughest Scots poor are capable of delicate compassion. Lucy Forester's awkward, silent suitor is the young parish scholar doomed to die young. Lucy's friend Mary Morrison has a stern Calvinist father, who has "taught, and truly taught" his daughter "that the human heart is desperately wicked." Yet the narrator, sharing Abraham Morrison's severity, is unwilling to judge: "In that dark and disturbed tumult of many passions, He who formed the heart may have seen what was hidden from human eye, for He alone judges aright, in His omniscience, the secrets that wring the souls of the children of men" (499-500). Margaret Lyndsay's father represents a moment in Scottish cultural history—an Edinburgh printer, a free-thinker infected with "deistical opinions," who becomes involved with the revolutionary Friends of the People, pollutes his Braehead cottage with a copy of Paine's *Age of Reason*, spends time in prison, goes off to live with another man's wife, and of course lives and dies a guilty, remorseful, infatuated man. Such is but one of the "trials" of Margaret Lyndsay.

The truth Wilson propounds is the same embraced by Lockhart and Ferrier. Man without the light of faith is a blind, infatuated worldling. But a gloomy and fanatical Calvinism, such as that held by the "severe and gloomy preacher" that casts Margaret's blind sister into deep melancholy, is as mistaken as complacent worldliness. Thoughtful intelligence ennobles the Scottish lowly, but feverish intellectuality without the peace and assurance of faith is worse than ignorance. Wilson's ideal is the intelligent, pious peasant, Michael Forester, who, blinded by lightning, becomes a patriarchal Job figure. His theme is Michael Forester's rejoinder to the condescending, class-conscious father of Lucy's suitor: "Do you think, Mr. Ellis, that in poor men's huts the best natural affections do not reside in as great force and purity as in the dwellings of the rich or noble?" (507). Wilson's dream of cultural conciliation and fulfillment is projected in the final marriage of Lucy Forester. She marries the son of a Westmoreland vicar, who takes her home to the Lakes, with the comfortable proviso that the families will visit annually back and forth.

Margaret Lyndsay's destiny is more varied and catastrophic. Having suffered in Braehead through her father's disbelief and desertion, she moves with her family into urban poverty under the shadow of Castle Rock and becomes a little schoolmistress among the poor, until successive misfortunes leave her totally alone. She moves to live with a charitable wealthy friend, whose brother is rash enough to fall in love with her. Finding no home in Edinburgh, she sets out for the west to find a hitherto unknown great-uncle in the pastoral place of her birth—and here she finds a home and a substantial inheritance. She is then deceived in marriage; her love must be chastened, her husband must return to suffer and die, and it is finally hinted that her home will not long be in this world. For Margaret, successive and innumerable trials lead to an earthly paradise, an innocent pastoral home, which is only the final stage on the way to a loftier inheritance. Her destiny and her representativeness are summed up thus:

> The orphan girl, brought in poverty and destitution from that miserable lane, was now in all things a gentlewoman, and worthy to sit in any parlour or saloon in the land. There may be something in birth; but hers had not been mean, either by the father or the mother's side. The Lyndsays, although now a faded, almost an extinguished family, had been highly respectable for many generations; and the Craigs had long been dwellers on the same soil, and in poverty and hardship had lived decently in their farmhouses, not poor either in intelligence or virtue. Margaret Lyndsay, therefore, though lowly, was respectably born; and in her appeared what, with due culture, was the native character of the race. [287]

Lucy Forester is a character of a different kind. Seemingly an echo of Wordsworth's Lucy Gray, she is not just a part of innocent nature but a part of locality. Her destiny too begins with disinheritance; her father (reminiscent of Wordsworth's Michael) is charged with his brother's criminal debts and must sell his home on the Esk and move as tenant to a Clydesdale farm. She too becomes the valued friend of an aristocratic lady: the noble needs the peasant girl, and their relationship is generalized into a cultural type. Their affection knows no inequality of condition: "It was so with Emma Cranstoun and Lucy Forester. Here, it might be said, met together the genii of the hall and the hut; and who could pronounce which spirit was most beautiful—the lady with her dark hair braided across her pensive forehead, and a few pearls among the lace veil that shaped her head-dress into that which charms in old pictures of our Mary Queen—or the shepherdess with her golden tresses yet as rich in ringlets as when Isaac Mayne compared it to a star twinkling in the brow of the hill" (535). Lucy's affections are confined to her idyllic Clydesdale parish. "And was Bracken Braes forgotten? The green broomy hills and treeless banks of Heriot Water—that one wooded linn, the Howlet's Nest, and he whom her heart had so often beat within her inmost bosom to meet there—Edward Ellis! No, no—all Lucy's affections were true to the place of her birth" (467). But her affections must be chastened and shifted, and the spirit of the Scottish hut finds a new love and a home elsewhere, in a greener vale.

Margaret Lyndsay's fortunes are remote from such mawkish idyllicism. Still, like the great character Chris Guthrie in Gibbon's *A Scots*

Quair, she is Scotland in archetype, the suffering daughter and wandering orphan, undergoing successive exiles in search of some true Scottish home. Her sojourn in a city slum, like her visit to her dying father in the slums of Glasgow, is an unexpectedly vivid image of the plight of rustic Scotland forced into slum streets. The city is a grim work place, a place of noise and plague; for city dwellers, memories of "the green pastoral hills of Tweeddale, or the misty glens of Badenoch" lead to another realm, set apart for "gathering May-dew on a green hill-side" or "dancing in a fairy ring at sunrise." Though in dark city streets, the innocent is tightly bound to some dear green place, some remembered idyll. But in this severely pious book, such a place has an ambiguous quality—of childhood innocence, but also of pagan indulgence. We are assured that "the love of nature lies more or less in every human heart"; but we are warned, as Margaret is warned, "What is love to the creature, without fear of the Creator?" The most idyllic local affections may prove idolatrous, vain. And Margaret at last finds her arcadian earthly inheritance painful and brief.

With such patterns and place-archetypes in Wilson, we are clearly in the borderland between novel and romance. We are also on the verge of Scottish Victorianism. For some, this means that there is nought ahead but several generations of Kailyard sentimentalists. But the novel of Victorian Scotland deserves a more careful and discriminating look.

The Scottish
Victorians:
In and Out
of the Kailyard

4

Victorian
Modes
and Models

The dominant mode of Victorian fiction in Scotland was pastoral idyll, influenced—as was its English counterpart—by Wordsworthian Romanticism. It was a fiction parochial in setting, elegiac in time sense, traditional in communality, and studiedly regional in manner and idiom.

Some critics cannot tolerate what they consider a cynical avoidance of the contemporary horrors of urban industrialism, with the result that Scottish Victorianism is lumped in a single midden and seen through the distortive lens of a long-lived anti-Kailyardism. Where was the great and outraged Scottish novelist of the thirties and forties, the terrible decades following "Reform"? One answer is, he was alive and dyspeptically well in London, under the name of Carlyle, brooding noisily on Poor Laws, Corn Laws, ballot boxes, and other Morrison's Pills, and preaching the Scottish lesson that a nation's culture can be diagnosed only in terms of its myths, creeds, and heroes. Where were the Scottish Dickens, Thackeray, Trollope, or Brontës? A preindustrial Gothic London produced Dickens. A unique mixture of Anglo-Indian disinheritance, Bohemian Paris, the Silver Fork of Bulwerism, and the Irishism of *Fraser's* produced Thackeray. A fine philistine Anglican humanism, fired by dreams of English Parliament and the English hunt, made Trollope. A gothicized Northumbria, no more English than Scottish, brought forth the Brontës.

What of George Eliot? How "English" and how naturalistic is this first literary genius of freethought and dissent? Is the exotic London of *Daniel Deronda* more current, more realistic, than the pastoral midlands of *Adam Bede* and *The Mill on the Floss?* Is the radicalism of *Felix Holt*, from the perspective of a new, urban proletarianism, satisfactory? Is Middlemarch in 1832 the best setting for confrontation with the new horrors of a laissez-faire economy? Perhaps George Eliot had been diverted by a non-English inspiration. For the author of Waverley was a name whispered reverentially in her household, and a persistent fondness for Lockhart is not surprising in one whose preoccupation with scenes of clerical life, with the persistence of narrow manners and provincialisms, with the prefigurative imagination (in *Daniel Deronda* she calls it "second sight") and the spiritual heroisms of the Dissenters, might be labeled "Blackwoodian" in spirit as well as in genesis.

The case of George Eliot ought to remind us that elegiac pastoralism in nineteenth-century fiction is not a judgment but a classification. It reminds us as well that the masterpiece of English Victorian fiction—Eliot's "study of provincial life"—appeared the same year (1871) as the masterpiece of Scottish Victorian fiction, William Alexander's *Johnny Gibb of Gushetneuk*. The kinships as well as the cultural and formal differences are revealing.

Middlemarch was set around 1832, and its moral cruxes are in large part societal. William Alexander's* "glimpses of the parish politics" of Pyketillim were set around 1843, and their cruxes are theological and political, a general cultural difference that should not surprise us. In the very year of Carlyle's *Past and Present*, Scotland suffered the cataclysmic Great Disruption of the national church, the most momentous event, says the historian Ferguson, of nineteenth-century Scotland. If the Disruption was not a cause of cultural distinctness, it surely is a complex symptom. At issue was the reaffirmation or recovery of those institutions in which Scotland traditionally based its selfhood. Thus, Scottish Victorian fiction was to be simultaneously religious and cultural, its impetus theological liberation rather than social enfranchise-

---

*Alexander, William. Born in 1826, and died in 1894. Educated at a parish school in Aberdeenshire, he worked as farm boy and ploughman until, in his early twenties, he lost a leg. As a result of the accident he turned to journalism, and eventually became editor of the *Aberdeen Free Press*. He also wrote *Sketches of Life among My Ain Folk* (1875) and *Twenty-five Years: A Personal Retrospect* (1878).

ment. And the symbolic locales of Scottish fiction remain centered on the manse, the minister, his ally or rival the schoolmaster, and his patron (or enemy) the local laird. It may well be that this preoccupation was a regrettable fact for nineteenth-century Scottish civilization; at any rate, it is a fact of major importance for the persistence of that national propensity often discounted as Kailyardism.

Johnny Gibb poses definitive questions of intention and value for Scottish fiction—questions of scope, mode, form, truthfulness, and language. I begin with it here as an approach to two of the most indefatigable of Scottish Victorian novelists, Margaret Oliphant and George MacDonald, thence to their ambiguously descended "Kailyard" heirs, and climactically to those formative early Scottish modernists, the anti-Kailyarders.

The popular literature of Victorian Scotland after the Blackwoodian *Noctes* was the sketches and anecdotal reminiscences of Dean Ramsay, Hugh Miller, and Dr. John Brown. Out of the same impulse come the sketches of Pyketillim Parish, seen retrospectively in the throes of Disruption with all its attendant crises of political tyranny, tenant displacement, and communal dissention. J. H. Millar long ago set the precedent of contrasting *Johnny Gibb*'s praiseworthy realism with the Kailyard,[1] and most recently Douglas Gifford offers the same praise. Sketching the descent from *Andrew Wylie* of "that anecdotal and episodic sentimental exploitation and distortion of Scottish Life and Character for a bigger British Audience," Gifford then cites the admirable exception: "Only when it is realized how strong a hold this distorted and debased image of Scottish rural life had on British, let alone Scottish, audiences, can the peculiar integrity and honesty of view of William Alexander's *Johnny Gibb of Gushetneuk* (1871) be appreciated."[2] J. M. Reid and Kurt Wittig, on the other hand, see in it a fatal narrowing, which they associate with its ecclesiastical focus. The limiting occasion of the book, says Reid, like the occasion of Miller's *My Schools and Schoolmasters*, is the Disruption. "No later event produced such effects. Except for Thomas Carlyle, who belongs to British rather than to Scottish literature, Scots writers seemed unable to react to the world around them after 1843." And Wittig sees in this "honest and realistic series of sketches" the repeating of Galt "on a narrower scale."[3]

But Wittig finds a redeeming advance in linguistic seriousness: it "is more seriously Scots than Galt's, and we feel that Alexander needs the

Scots words to render exactly what he means." David Craig differs on this, and lumps *Johnny Gibb* with *Mansie Wauch* as fiction in which Scots became "the subject of specialised rendering. These novels are written to exhibit 'good Scots' for its own sake, aside from serious life-interests of which speech would be only one aspect." On this muddied issue Gifford is wisely guarded and helpfully focused. He sees the question of linguistic integrity as a formal and a rhetorical one, and cites the central stylistic problem of the novel, "retaining the moral position of Victorian Scotland, curious in its gulf between standard English comment and magnificent Aberdeenshire dialect."[4]

The distance between narrator and character is one of the book's formative features. The narrator assumes a learned loftiness that might be taken for condescension but is something subtler. *Johnny Gibb* is pastoral; it contrasts a stabler, simpler rural past with the pretensions of a great and remotely cosmopolitan world, and the narrator insists repeatedly "that the habits of Pyketillim are to me of perennial interest, whether the date be a quarter or half a century ago, or more."[5] Part of the impulse is affectionately antiquarian; but part of it derives from the ironic pastoralism of Scott. Johnny Gibb is, after all, something of an aging male Jeannie Deans, forced out of his quiet unheroic life—but not out of his shrewd, pious, and brave traditional character—into the rigors of ideological heroism by the incursions of the historic world: "He was just Johnny Gibb of Gushetneuk, as he had been for the last thirty and odd years; an inconsiderable person, speaking and acting as the impulse moved him, in accordance with what he believed at the time to be right" (152); "It was not Johnny Gibb's intention to be a Disruption leader, yet he had become so *de facto*" (163). He is, we say now, the innocent radicalized. His real opponents are less the shadows of great usurpers than the betrayals of petty communal corrupters—the vain, miserly, ambitious Mrs. Birse, and her rival time-server the factor Dawvid Hadden, a pair reminiscent in their sly alliances and combats of Trollope's Mrs. Proudie and Mr. Slope.

The analogies with Trollope and Scott are just, for Alexander shares their strain of mock-heroic. Petty human affairs touched by cataclysms in the great world reflect their pettiness on that greatness. The simple, small world is seen in analogue to the no less petty great one; the sense of ironic relation is sustained by the narrator's cosmopolitan presence. In mock-heroic of this sort, the urbane narrator is a necessary ironic component, turning often against the affectations of the urbane reader:

> And here, good reader, I bethought me of giving utterance to a few moral reflections on the degraded character of our farm-servant class; and how blameworthy they are for being such immoral and unmannerly boors. But somehow my line of vision came always to be obstructed by a full-figure image of Mrs. Birse of Clinkstyle, who, you will perceive, is a very particular and intimate acquaintance of mine. Mrs. Birse *would* come into the forefront, and her husband, Peter, was vaguely discernible in the background. So I gave up the attempt. You may make it on your own account; but I doubt whether you will be able to search thoroughly into the causes of this social evil without being also troubled with the image of Mrs. Birse of Clinkstyle. [52]

Alexander differs from his counterparts in mock-heroic in his very sparing use of the narrator for narration. The novel is more scenic or dramatic than Trollope, Thackeray, or even Dickens. Episodes not fully rendered in dialogue are recounted at secondhand in vivid oral narrative by magnificent local gossips such as Meg Raffan the henwife and Hairry Muggart, whose account of the crisis at Culsalmon Kirk is at once a set-piece of folk narration and a masterpiece of contemporary historical imagination. Here the vernacular is no excrescence but inseparable from narrative mode and imagination, and all three dramatize the traditional community upon which these menacing events are now having their impact.

This, as it must be, is a communal style. Idiosyncrasy of speech in Dickens characterizes by individualizing; his people, says V. S. Pritchett, "are solitaries . . . They soliloquize . . . They do not talk to one another; they talk to themselves."[6] Idiosyncrasy of speech in *Johnny Gibb* unites a traditional community, articulating traditional norms and powers of resistance. Gossip in Barsetshire, where it is equally important, defines a provincial community in terms of the uncertainties of knowledge—such is Trollope's theme. Gossip in Pyketillim affirms the community in stubborn continuity of manners. The novel in its dialogic mode is far more societal than psychological. Johnny Gibb's own crisis, as he braves alien powers and risks the loss of his home, is never shown in an inwardly isolating moral awareness. His fortunes evolve in episodic alternation with those of his neighbors. His crisis identifies him with his community at its traditional best, and he is recognized for it. His character draws its individual strength from communal values and not from self-consciousness.

When we consider comparable English Victorians in this light, the differences are radically cultural. The Scot once-removed J. S. Mill prophesied, in the very Anglo-French essay *On Liberty* of 1859, that the question of human well-being had become the survival of individuality against coercive social pressures. Such prophecy is clearly applicable to the solitaries of Dickens and Eliot, the ambivalent Bohemians of Thackeray, the Brontës' Gothic defiers. That it had little relevance for *Johnny Gibb*, where the crisis is a survival of communal integrity, is a momentous cultural fact, not a sign of artistic deficiency. Other generic differences are no less cultural. The voice of the Victorian sage, secular replacement for prophet and priest, can be heard in the narrators of Dickens, Thackeray, and Eliot alike.[7] English Victorian narrative reflects a radical separation of prophecy and religious morality from the institutional church. The same prophetic energy in Scotland—George MacDonald is the notable exception—went into ecclesiastical disruption and reinstitution. Identifying the form of English Victorian fiction, Hillis Miller notes its thematic focus on struggles of self and society.[8] Liberation in Scottish Victorian fiction looked not forward to humanistic individualism so much as backward to the renewal of reform covenants. Individuality turned not to romantic selfhood but to traditional models of communal integrity, to the reawakening of older, less egocentric norms of heroism. If in *Johnny Gibb* this implies a narrowing of Galt's scale, it also implies a deepening. The perspective is backward, but such a perspective is inevitable in a fiction focused on crises of cultural inheritance, on the problem of redeeming one's heritage from usurpation and discontinuity. As an old matriarch tells the heroine in Mrs. Oliphant's *Merkland*, "Child, there are bairns in this generation that would fain inherit the rights and possessions of their fathers, without the ills and the wrongs."[9] Such is the theological and cultural concern of Margaret Oliphant and George MacDonald, in their novels of inheritance.

5

Mid-Victorians

J ohnny Gibb may be Victorian Scotland's most impressive single novel, but its most talented and tireless novelist had already appeared. An earlier attempt to build a fiction around the Great Disruption was the first novel of Margaret Oliphant,* written when she was only twenty, published in 1849 when she had long since moved from Lasswade and Glasgow to Liverpool, and successful enough to justify three editions and launch a long career. "When I read it over some years after," reminisced Mrs. Oliphant, "I felt nothing but foolishness and shame at its foolish little polemics and opinions. I suppose there must have been some breath of youth and sincerity in it which touched people, and there had been no Scotch stories for a long time. Lord Jeffrey, then an old man and very near his end,

---

*Oliphant, Margaret. Born near Musselburgh in 1828 and died in 1897 at Windsor, England, where she had settled to be near her sons at Eton. She began writing before she was twenty-one with Margaret Maitland, and thereafter, especially when she became a widow with several children and adopted her brother's children as well, lived a life of what the Dictionary of National Biography calls "slavery to the pen." Her nearly one hundred separate publications include over fifty novels, literary histories, biographies of Italian saints, artists, and writers, and the first two volumes of a history of the Blackwood firm (Annals of a Publishing House, 1897), for which she had long written fiction and criticism. Mrs. Oliphant's family was associated with the Free Church movement, and she herself became an Irvingite (see her biographies of Thomas Chalmers, 1893, and Edward Irving, 1862). Her Autobiography was published in 1899.

sent me a letter of sweet praise, which filled my mother with rapture and myself with an abashed gratitude."[1] Jeffrey's letter identifies the "long time" lapse, but its judgment, I think, is by no means merely sentimental: "Nothing half so true or so touching (in the delineation of Scottish character) has appeared since Galt published his 'Annals of the Parish'—and this is purer and deeper than Galt, and even more absolutely and simply true."[2]

Mrs. Oliphant's connection with an older Blackwoodian was commemorated shortly thereafter. On their trip to Edinburgh in 1851 she and her mother "renewed acquaintance with Dr. Moir of Musselburgh, an old friend of hers, who had, I believe, attended to me when, as a very small child, I fell into the fire, or rather against the bars of the grate." Such pleasing multiple connections can be misleading, however, and no less so when we recall that this "heir" to Galt and Moir was influential enough by the early sixties to help bring about the publication of George MacDonald's first successful fiction, *David Elginbrod* (1863).

Her career as Scottish novelist was mostly limited to the 1850s, when *Margaret Maitland* was followed shortly by *Merkland*, *Katie Stewart*, *Adam Graeme of Mossgray*, *Harry Muir*, and *The Laird of Norlaw*. J. H. Millar, who admired her considerably (as did Henry James), thinks *Katie Stewart*, "considered as a work of art, is probably her supreme effort."[3] *Merkland* is an exciting, strongly colored romance in the manner of *Guy Mannering*—and it is characteristic of Mrs. Oliphant to have made romance of a presbyterian drama of inheritance with a sober, quiet heroine. *The Laird of Norlaw* is also inheritance romance, but once more the execution is restrained and artful, and the theme anticipates Neil Munro in its *illusions perdus*, as well as its preference for homely, hard-working people over romantic dreamers. We will consider only *Margaret Maitland*, and then notice what changed and what did not change after 1861, the turning point in her career, when she achieved her greatest popularity as chronicler of Carlingford, in novels at first attributed to George Eliot, that other female Blackwoodian associated with "scenes of clerical life."

Those who would remember Mrs. Oliphant as author of *Salem Chapel* and *The Perpetual Curate* might also remember George MacDonald for *Wilfred Cumbermede* and *Annals of a Quiet Neighbourhood*, and this would be less than fair to either. Others may find most interesting a further similarity to MacDonald in the final phase of her popularity, the ghost stories and visionary tales called "Stories of the Seen and Unseen," where her recent biographers, the Colbys, say her best writing is found.[4] Both areas seem remote from Scotland. Apparently the market that awaited *Margaret Maitland* did not last; or perhaps these two modes—the chronicle of provincial manners and the quasimystical fable, both shared by MacDonald in a strange combination as Victorian as it is Scottish—led away from Scotland.

For all this, *Some Passages in the Life of Mrs. Margaret Maitland* (the full title recalls Lockhart's *Adam Blair*) remains a remarkable first novel, in ways even Jeffrey did not recognize. Margaret is a pious, sensible, kindly gentlewoman, living a solitary but involved parochial life, recalling a time of youthful "tribulations" when she had given up a suitor too licentious for her "precisian" tastes. She is called upon to raise and educate a young heiress. After years of mutual devotion, the girl is ordered back to a life of haughty social pretense by her aunt and her father, who try to trick her out of her inheritance. Her guardian, it turns out, is Margaret's long-rejected suitor (now chastened). Margaret's concern centers on two rough careers of young love: that of Grace the heiress and Margaret's ministerial nephew, and that of Margaret's niece and her old suitor's flighty son. Grace's relatives are balked; young Lilliesleaf is chastened under Margaret's tutelage. Both couples are happily wed, and at the end Margaret is having numerous "communings together" with her old suitor.

It is fitting that the climax should coincide historically and dramatically with a climax in the "history of the Kirk's trials . . . an old story in our country of Scotland."[5] She insists it is neither seemly nor needful "to meddle with the deep things of the Kirk in a simple history like this," but she has hinted throughout at deep and solemn things not to be spoken of directly. Her reticence is one of her most winning features, an effective check on a piety that might otherwise be self-righteous or shrill and thereby justify what the world recklessly says of it. The quiet assurance and chaste good humor of her piety in the face of the world are grounded in the Kirk and its tradition. We feel a quiet desperation in Margaret as she forces herself to defy the world, knowing as she does the flighty worldliness that has "made me a lone woman, desolate in the summer of my days" (218). Her defiance is testimony to the tradition that has made her; it is also witness to the silent anguish of one who, for all her protestations of contentment, is no happier in solitude than Austen's Anne Eliot. Her heroism is never arrogant or priggish. She has not yielded; she has risked all; and somehow she wins. When her story reaches its climax at the time when "my brother, the minister, and Claud, my nephew, and many of their brethren—as is known to the world—left their temporal providing at the appointed time, and came out with the pure and free Kirk into the wilderness" (300), we feel that this history has already been domesticated in Margaret's character and destiny. In a strictly dramatic, nonallegorical way, she is the Kirk, and her total engagement with the world has been a domestic parable of the Kirk's struggle.

Alongside the book's religious dimension, its societal aspect seems slight. There is no place in Margaret's sensibility for a Thackerayan relish of Vanity Fair, or a Trollopian tolerance of worldly casuistry, or even a zestful perception of vulgarities as by a youthful Austen or Burney. Manners here are codes of behavior by which the pious have traditionally engaged the world and defended themselves. Society functions chiefly as Margaret's rival in the struggle for the soul of the young laird. The laird is reminiscent of Austen's Henry Crawford. Ironically, his most Austenite feature is a passion Margaret awakens, a passion for "improving," for recklessly tearing down a dirty old village on his estate and building his people a new one. His shifting career as improver occasions visits to Margaret, placing her unwillingly in the role of the laird's tutor and suggesting a symbolic relation of cultural interest—a pious spinsterly kirk uneasily responsible for the social experiments of an enlightened but giddy young landlord. The suggestion is handled cautiously. What might become a simplistic conservative satire—at the expense of leveling philanthropists—retains the moderate view of progress we associate with Galt and the *Annals*.

Finally, Margaret's staunch, prudent progressivism is evident in her sense of the literary undertaking of her memoirs. Sober and pious, she is not repressively sabbatarian. A lover of children and folk song, she reads Grace the history of Scotland, and even concedes that novels are not "so ill at an odd time, when folk need a rest to their minds": " 'Whisht, bairns,' said I, 'there are worse things than novels in this ill world' " (209). When Elphinstone brings her a sickly young poet for protection, she admires him for it, and is duly disgusted when the "ladies from the castle" invade her refuge to coerce the poor wretch into supplying them with verses for their historical tableaux:

Truly I marvel that folk are not afeerd of tempting the Giver to take away from them the life that they put to such fuil uses. I read a book no long since, where the story was little but a string of such like things. Grown up folk making themselves like the figures in pictures, and playing at guesses, as bairns will do by the fire on a winter night, which filled me with wonder within myself, that poorer and wiser folk should see such unseemly guisarding and no lift up a voice, nor put forth a hand to restrain it. [180]

Yet she finds much to revere in the wisdom of bairns by the fire.

The passage well exemplifies her style. It puts no ironic distance—as in Galt's *Annals* or *The Provost*—between the enlightened reader and a writer of naive garrulousness or pawky self-righteousness. Her habits and prejudices are part of her cultural identity; her perspective is limited without being ironic. Her narrative includes linguistic extremes. Letters are in English; there is dialogue in broad dialectal Scots, associated by the mild noblesse oblige of the Christian gentlewoman with the lower classes, or with the humorously insincere stick-it minister who captures Margaret's brother's pulpit at the time of the Disruption. Evidently Margaret, for all her Scots bias and Scots rhythm and idiom, sees Scots of that dialectal kind as a cultural indignity, another instance of men acting like bairns. Nonetheless, the book closes with ceremonies of cultural reintegration. Margaret Maitland's two young ladies are wed to a purified kirk and to a humane cottage industrialism.

It was a major misfortune for Scottish Victorian fiction that Mrs. Oliphant's father emigrated to England when his daughter had only a juvenile idea of Scotland. The reader of the Carlingford chronicles may be struck by what this tireless, perceptive woman might have done with petit bourgeois Glasgow had she not grown up in Liverpool, or with Edinburgh had she not known it simply as a literary visitor to the world of *Blackwood's*. But her admirer Henry James (in *Notes on Novelists*)[6] finds persistent "scottish" things even after the shift of locale, and *Salem Chapel* offers a fascinating study of cultural translation in popular fictional form.

The Carlingford books include what her biographers call three "principal religious stories," whose unifying theme or problem is "vocation for the priesthood."[7] In *The Rector*, the awkward, shy minister comes from fifteen years as Fellow of All Souls, an Arabin type; but unlike Trollope's clergyman he is principally concerned with his own unfitness, is defeated by his conscience, and returns dissatisfied to academic life. In *The Perpetual Curate* there is the young High Church curate Frank Wentworth; in *Salem Chapel*, Arthur Vincent, young gentleman-scholar from "Homerton." But, while the setting is English, the issue of vocation echoes the Scottish situation of the principled minister in a Voluntary Church.

Mrs. Oliphant had been writing a life of Edward Irving, removed by the presbytery from his Annandale kirk, and she was shortly to become an admirer of George MacDonald, who had similar troubles. She felt a strong sympathy with the Free Kirk movement and admired Thomas Chalmers. Yet she saw a real dilemma: the Free Kirk minister, a man of strong principle, leaves the established church in an act of profound conscience. He then becomes subject to his own congregation, especially his elders (or deacons). His freedom is lost, his principles are compromised, his vocation before God is conditional on the will of his "flock." Here is the issue as Arthur Vincent sees it: How can the man of God obey his worldly flock? How can the flock choose and govern their own shepherd, who must somehow follow God, his vocation, and the social demands of his church? There is no such problem in Trollope or Eliot. It is a problem Mrs. Oliphant discovered in the Scottish Kirk and translated into English dissent.

She explains as much in her autobiography: "I knew nothing about chapels, but took the sentiment and a few details from our old church in Liverpool, which was Free Church of Scotland, and where there were a few grocers and other such good folk whose ways with the minister were wonderful to behold." The sentence that follows is marvelously ambiguous: "The saving grace of their Scotchness being withdrawn, they became still more wonderful as Dissenting deacons, and the truth of the picture was applauded to all the echoes."[8] How much and whither is the irony of "saving grace" and "wonderful"? The mercenary elder or deacon with his Scotchness would have been relished as a wonderful monster by George Douglas Brown and his neo-Calvinist kin. But for Mrs. Oliphant, what is essential is his devotion to his minister, and he is reminiscent of the elder of Lockhart's *Adam Blair*, heroic for all his simplicity or vulgarity. His Scotchness gone, Tozer the butterman of *Salem Chapel* may still be the best character in the chronicles; but his uncomfortable, vulgar devotion lacks cultural dimension.

The problem of Vincent is similar. He is passionately intellectual and idealistic, and the combination causes a social diffidence and arrogance that make it impossible for him to adjust to the demands of his congregation. Such a burning and visionary intellectuality has been seen as a traditional danger of the Scottish minister's education, but how it comes out of Homerton is less clear.

Of course the whole moral issue in the novel is blurred. Ernest A. Baker identified the blur: what looks like a "case of conscience"—to Vincent "and possibly to his creator"—is actually a case of temperament.[9] Vincent is bad-tempered throughout. He finds the green grocers and buttermen and their tea-meeting chapel vulgarity stupid and mean; and in the early pages Mrs. Oliphant manages beautifully to show it for what it is and still convey an ironic view of the temperamental young cleric. She remains ironic as he is enchanted by Lady Western, the lovely, perfumed, banal young widow behind her garden wall. Then, say the Colbys, "her interesting young hero becomes enmeshed in a cruelly melodramatic plot almost totally obscuring the important issues of the book"[10]—and such has been the dominant complaint since the book appeared in 1863.

The patron of the Kailyard, W. Robertson Nicoll, explained it thus: "There is evidence to show that when it was written Mrs. Oliphant was deeply impressed by the work of Wilkie Collins, who was then at his very best. Under his influence, she brought in the sensational element, and plunged into the region of mysteries and horrors. Thus the book seems to make two separate stories connected in an extremely forced and artificial manner."[11] The beautiful dowager, the mysterious needlewoman, the profligate seducer—all, insists Nicoll, "were totally incongruous with the admirable portion which relates to Salem Chapel and its organization." But the incongruity is at the center of the minister's suffering, and his love for Lady Western is inseparable from the horror world of her half brother. Nicoll also overlooks the fact that this odd mixture of parochial "manners" with Gothic diabolism is, as we have seen, in an older *Blackwood's* tradition and has Scottish fictional antecedents. In Mrs. Oliphant's own view, the vogue of "sensation novels" was due to the age: "We begin to feel the need of a new supply of shocks and wonders."[12] This need is crucial to her minister's experience. He is forced to begin a "coorse" of sermons on miracles when at the height of his troubles with a runaway suicidal sister. He learns—as his flock learns—that if he simply speaks to them from his heart of the darkness, loneliness, and wondrousness of life,

LIBRARY
OKALOOSA - WALTON JUNIOR COLLEGE

he will be irresistible. His entanglement with the diabolic and the ecstatic brings him spiritually and morally alive, gives him the features
of the romantic sage speaking out of the depths of his own torment.
He is akin to Hawthorne's ministers—and Mrs. Oliphant, in her
article, traces the "sensation novels" to America and Hawthorne. He is
Carlylean too, discovering the wondrous darkness surrounding
human life, and in it both ecstasy and diabolism.

Through the discovery his ministry is transformed and he ceases to
belong to the narrow manners life of earlier chapters. But his chronicler remains divided in focus. "What, then, were the poor dialectics of
Church and State controversy, or the fluctuations of an uncertain
young mind feeling itself superior to its work, to such a spectacle of
passionate life, full of evil and of noble qualities—of guilt and suffering more intense than anything philosophy dreams of?"[13] What indeed? Where is the irony, and where the narrator? From here on we
are to believe that the young minister lives a life of transcendent moral
intensity, lifted out of the mean world of Salem Chapel. Yet, with the
emergence of his mother and of Tozer as devoted deacon, with the
suffering of his sister and Mrs. Hilyard, we can only feel him to be a
selfish fool. The tension is in the narrator. The restrained moral realist
of *Margaret Maitland* is at odds with the romantic transcendentalist of
The Beleaguerd City; the novel of manners jostles strangely against
Gothic fantasy. It is a mixture not unlike the one we find in Mrs. Oliphant's protegé George MacDonald.*

Margaret Oliphant is remembered as the chronicler of Carlingford,
as visionary of the "Seen and the Unseen," as master of the Black-

---

*MacDonald, George. Born in Huntly, Aberdeenshire, in 1824, and died at Ash-
stead, England, in 1905. He attended King's College, Aberdeen, and was ordained
as a Congregational minister, but resigned after a controversy with his congregation over his independent doctrine, and managed to support himself and his family
as a writer. He remained active as a lay preacher, influenced numerous liberal and
spiritualist Victorian nonconformists, was a friend of the Carlyles, Browning, and
Ruskin, and was led through his friendship with F. D. Maurice to the Church of
England. MacDonald's over fifty separate works include poems, the *Unspoken
Sermons* (1867-1869) so influential on C. S. Lewis, the Scottish novels mentioned
here, English novels such as *Annals of a Quiet Neighbourhood* (1867) and *Wilfred
Cumbermede* (1872), and of course the tales and phantasies for which he is chiefly
remembered—such as *Phantastes* (1858), *At the Back of the North Wind* (1871),
the Princess tales, *The Golden Key*, and *Lilith* (1895).

woodian ghost story. The first of her theosophical stories appeared in book form in 1880. In it, like MacDonald, she moved easily into a fantasy world that is without locality yet intensely localized. Like his, her concern with states of transcendence and transformation, with "final things," seems remote from her painstaking concern with little manners and materialities of parochial life. She shares with him the prophetic aim of reawakening a sense of the noumenal in a time of skeptical naturalism. With him, she equates the rigors of salvation with the coldness of death, and yet conceives of an all-embracing love as the basis of divine motivation. The difference is that while the reader of Mrs. Oliphant's Scottish novels may not anticipate the fantasist, the reader of MacDonald's novels can never forget the creator of *Phantastes*, of little Diamond and the Princess tales, of *The Golden Key* and *Lilith* (his masterpieces). The novelist appeared first in *David Elginbrod* (1863); and characteristically its writer-hero finds "it is hard to write a novel when one is living in the midst of a romance."[14] In *Alec Forbes of Howglen*, too, the narrator must draw back: "But I forget that I am telling a story, and not writing a fairy tale" (70). By the 1870s, the time of MacDonald's boy-heroes Malcolm and Gibbie, the novelistic world has edged far into the borderland of fantasy. *The Marquis of Lossie* reveals "a world of faery; anything might happen in it . . . Malcolm felt as if the world with its loveliness and splendour were sinking behind him, and the cool entrancing sweetness of the eternal dreamland of the soul, where the dreams are more real than any sights of the world, were opening wide before his entering feet . . . a kind of borderland betwixt waking and sleeping, knowing and dreaming" (176, 179). It is the same borderland that provides a kingdom of faery for his fantasies.

For all their rich regional particularity, MacDonald's "novels" are actually theological romances, where the fantastic and the normal, the ideal and the real, are separated only by semivisible and shifting boundaries. Their characters are best described in his defense of Robert Falconer: "Those who are in the habit of regarding the real and the ideal as essentially and therefore irreconcilably opposed, will remark that I cannot have drawn the representation of Falconer faithfully" (396). Their subject, both romantic and theological, is the mystery of inheritance. As elsewhere in Victorian romance, the orphan and the disinherited are seeking their true fathers; but in Mac-

Donald the search for the hidden father is the way of crisis and conversion that reveals the fatherhood of an immanent, hidden God. The innocence of the child—or more accurately, the childlike—preserved in older natures such as David Elginbrod embodies an ideal of fidelity to one's childhood simplicities, social, natural, intellectual, and linguistic (that is, northeast Scots). But the providential role of the incarnate childlike must be played in time in that place of deprivation, darkness, sin, and yet love, the city; and MacDonald's redeemers—Falconer, Gibbie, Malcolm, and David—are missionaries there. The role is perilous, but the loving Father is always nearby. Evil and suffering are necessary but unreal, hence uninteresting. Villainy lacks character, "for all wickedness tends to destroy individuality." This precept from *Alec Forbes* is an essential principle, both of MacDonald's theological morality and of his narrative characterology.

Those with the most character in his novels appear evil initially; they are the stern natures, fruits of a vigorous peasant tradition but victims of a corrupt pseudo-Calvinism, who must be overthrown by the divine vengeance of love. Such problematic characters give MacDonald's fiction its moral interest but also its modal ambiguity; they must play roles at once in a theological romance and in a drama of cultural process. They are spiritual archetypes and at the same time cultural-historical representatives, a mixture we see often in Scottish fiction. Moreover, in such a mixture the narrator must play both chronicler and prophet. His historical intentions are strongly homiletic, and he is vulnerable to the charge leveled at Malcolm in *The Marquis of Lossie:* " 'You are like all the rest of the Scotch I ever knew,' said Lady Clementina: 'the Scotch are always preaching! I believe it is in their blood. You are a nation of parsons' " (174). " 'That is the right question, and logically put, my lady, rejoined Malcolm, who, from his early training, could not help sometimes putting on the schoolmaster" (184).

His romances envision the transformation of stern natures by the providential agents of divine love and the assimilation of all hells on earth into a design for universal redemption. Such a vision is sure to offend at least two kinds of readers: neo-Calvinists, for whom it is theologically "soft," sentimentally liberal; and radical humanists, for whom it is socioeconomically conservative, neofeudal, even reactionary. And since the dominant anti-Kailyarders of modern literary Scotland belong at once to both groups, MacDonald's "novels" of theological romance have little current appeal. There is truth, then, in the interesting suggestion of William Power that

> George MacDonald is perhaps the link between Galt and the Kail-yarders. *David Elginbrod, Sir Gibbie, The Marquis of Lossie* mark the change that had been wrought since Galt's day by evangelicalism and the preaching of "heretics" like Edward Irving and Macleod Campbell. The gradual departure from the old-Jewish conception of God as a jealous, revengeful, and quite arbitrary Deity had softened manners and deepened sympathy, but the controversy introduced preoccupations that were not good for creative literature. That is one reason why George MacDonald, with a far finer mind and personality than Galt, is not in the same street with him as an artist.[15]

Now, MacDonald was obviously an artist as different in kind from the Kailyarders as from Galt. And it is not safe to prescribe what preoccupations are "not good for creative literature." But the theological liberalism underlying MacDonald's books will later become the focus for hatred of the "Kailyard."

David Elginbrod introduces themes and images that will become prominent in later, better novels. It rests, for example, on a vision of pastoral nature that is traced to Wordsworth but seems inspired more by Carlyle and German Romanticism. It celebrates and appeals to the childlike, though here the childlike is found in an old peasant whose wisdom is higher innocence. David serves as a spiritual archetype, but also as a cultural representative—the simple, learned Scots peasant— and as a literary type as well: "One evening, while reading *The Heart of Midlothian*, the thought struck [Hugh]—what a character David would have been for Sir Walter" (19). But the essential David is spirit. His influence is spiritual, even ghostly, for he functions in the book's Gothic parts as the benign ghost, whose spectral counterpart, the false mesmerist and magician Funkelstein, underlines by negative contrast the truth of David's influence. Though David is culturally representative, his example transcends cultural identity. Paradoxically, the book attacks "Scotch metaphysics" while celebrating the true metaphysical in David, distinguishes the truth of Calvin from a corrupt, sabbatarian Calvinism, and defends the cultural beauty of the Scots language against those in whom it is ugly or vulgar. For MacDonald the restoration of Scotland to its cultural truth demands a freeing of its theology and its culture from false idols. And the central figure in this process is one of MacDonald's stern natures.

The stern nature in *Robert Falconer* (1868), natural successor to *Elginbrod*, is Robert's grandmother, and she too is drawn with characteristic ambivalence—presented with cultural sympathy to an English audience and with theological disapproval to a Scottish one. "Few English readers will like Mrs. Falconer; but her grandchild considered her one of the noblest women ever God made; and I, from his account, am of the same mind" (212). At the same time, "there was no escaping her. She was the all-seeing eye personified—the eye of the God of the theologians of his country, always searching out the evil, and refusing to acknowledge the good" (152). Her religion, "while it developed the power of a darkened conscience, overlaid and half-smothered all the lovelier impulses of her grand nature" (146). Her false religion condemns Robert's father and cuts Robert off from his natural inheritance. Robert moves through village and pastoral boyhood to an educational interlude in Aberdeen and finally to London, where his search for his father leads to a career as saintly, secular missionary of the streets.

His final wisdom is rooted still in "what lay at the root of his character, at the root of all he did, felt, and became . . . childlike simplicity and purity of nature." But, in this insistently typological book, his childhood is merely the type of a higher one. For a time his kite and his grandfather's violin are "full globated" symbols of a wondrous and deep glory; but his stern grandmother burns the violin, and the kite must be cut loose—and with it his childhood, a "feeble and necessarily vanishing type" of a "deeper and holier childhood." He loses his ideal lady to a more poetic soul, and must enter upon the "desert" of Teufelsdröckhian wanderings, where he is subject once more to the despair of his grandmother's theology. But the romance of his inheritance drives him to seek his lost father in London, where her false vision must give way to a new sense of humanity, and he learns to judge human nature "from no standpoint of his own, but in every individual case to take a new position whence the nature and history of the man should appear in true relation to the yet uncompleted result" (339). And now the quest for his own inheritance transcends all merely cultural identity: "His whole countenance bore self-evident witness of being a true face and no mask, a revelation of his individual being, and not a mere inheritance from a fine breed of fathers and mothers" (272-273).

The paradox is central to MacDonald's transcendental nationalism, and after him to the transcelticism of the fin de siecle Highland novel and of twentieth-century Highland novelists such as Neil Gunn and the Compton Mackenzie of *The Four Winds of Love*. It envisions a tearing away of the false, of the cultural overlay, a winnowing to the true and essential in language and "manners." The truth thus restored is a type of an emergent higher truth. To have his full force as a cultural exemplar, Robert, like Elginbrod, must die in his local self and be translated in spirit (Robert dies en route to India) to far-off places. His cultural inheritance is celebrated—"for the latter had ancestors—that is, he came of people with a mental and spiritual history" (124)—but only in the course of movement toward its transcendence. His local language survives the prudent impulse to learn English; but the rugged tongue of his cultural childhood is reinstated only to be transcended in death. The same must be true for his Scottish manners: "The ancient clan-feeling is good in this, that it opens a channel whose very existence is a justification for the flow of simply human feelings along all possible levels of social position. And I would there were more of it. Only something better is coming instead of it—a recognition of the infinite brotherhood in Christ" (399). A restored and purified Scottish culture is merely a type of a higher reality.

It is impossible to undertake here a full survey of MacDonald's eleven "Scottish" novels. But the broad, general strokes I have just drawn can be tested specifically against two of the novels. Consider the two that stand up best as narratives: *Alec Forbes of Howglen* (1865) and *Sir Gibbie* (1879).

Coming between *Elginbrod* and *Falconer*, *Alec Forbes* is a more sustained effort at narrative realism than either. Coming a decade after all three, *Sir Gibbie* is a fuller adaptation of novelistic elements to romance and fantasy. Yet they have much in common, and both illustrate the unity and modal tension characteristic of MacDonald's novels. The transvaluation of Scottish culture through exile and death to a transcendent realm, which we have seen in *Elginbrod* and *Falconer*, is not evident in them, for both end triumphantly with the young laird reinstated in his local inheritance. The reinstatement can take place only after both have survived the trials of great but false expectations, Alec Forbes by error and redemption and Gibbie by providential suffering and active faith.

The differences between the heroes are symbolized in differences of attitude toward language. In *Alec Forbes*, the novel of manners, vernacular Aberdonian is given, characteristically, to the good characters; and a rejection of Scots—as with Alec's mother, Kate the false heroine, and Beauchamp the Byronic villain—is associated with social and cultural falseness. But Alec is effectively bilingual; his mother slips into Scots and is teased for it:

> For had not she, the immaculate, the reprover, fallen herself into the slough of the vernacular? The fact is, it is easier to speak the truth in a *patois*, for it lies nearer to the simple realities than a more conventional speech.
>
> I do not however allow that the Scotch is a *patois* in the ordinary sense of the word. For had not Scotland a living literature, and that a high one, when England could produce none, or next to none—I mean in the fifteenth century? But old age, and the introduction of a more polished form of utterance, have given to the Scotch all the other advantages of a *patois*, in addition to its own directness and simplicity. [43]

Alec is educated accordingly in conciliation and accommodation. The accommodation is reflected in his chief teachers and mentors, Thomas Crann the pious stonemason and Cosmo Cupples, polymath, ex-alcoholic, and sceptical university librarian. Crann and Cupples learn to be good friends at last.

Gibbie, on the other hand, cannot speak at all. There is a physiological reason, but we never learn what it is. Speechless Gibbie, with his smile, his eyes, his strange singing, wins out over men of words. The heroine Jenny, redeemed from her father's false values (social and theological), returns to her love of nature and speaks broad Scots to Gibbie; but their betrothal scene is carried on in sign language. The book consistently mocks affected English speakers, such as the pharisaical minister Sclater and Jenny's father the false laird. Donal the sensitive poet speaks Scots. But Scots is justified as a child-speech, a special poetic medium: "To a poet especially it is an inestimable advantage to be able to employ such a language for his purposes. Not only was it the speech of his childhood, when he saw everything with fresh, true eyes, but it is itself a child-speech; and the child way of saying must always be nearer the child way of seeing, which is the poetic way" (133).

As the contrast suggests, Alec Forbes is a hero of experience, learning and growing through influence and error, enlightenment and penance. Gibbie is a hero insulated against experience, living his providential destiny, testing and restoring faith in others. He is the incarnate childlike, while Alec is never quite a child. Yet the lesson Alec must learn is the same Gibbie symbolically enacts, and it leads both heroes to the same inheritance.

For Alec, the lesson centers on the familiar romance pattern of false heroine and true. The false heroine is his romantic, deluded, antivernacular cousin Kate, with whom he falls in love at Aberdeen. The true is little orphan Annie Anderson, who idolizes him as her protector at rural school, worships him quietly, and wins him in the end when false Kate, finally deserted by the Byronic Highland cad Beauchamp, goes mad and drowns herself. The book is organized according to Alec's and Annie's parallel fortunes. Alec is natural goodness untried, a "great handsome good natured ordinary-gifted wretch," courageous, just, but a somewhat thoughtless schoolboy, capable of cruelty and violence—an unusually plausible protagonist for Victorian romance. Annie the orphan plays the sacramental role of the childlike, elsewhere given by MacDonald to a boy. While Alec struggles chiefly with romantic folly and the temporary youthful sins of drunkenness "and worse," Annie is caught in a war of sects and faiths, susceptible to the influence of natures stern and false. She is devoted to the established minister Cowie—who is spiritually a mere child to her—and yet drawn half in fear to more severe missionaries. It is Annie who has the awakening religious sensibility and providential influence, and Annie whose inheritance, so crucial a symbol for MacDonald's theological romance, is the more problematic. Alec is a dynamic and "realistic" protagonist, but Annie is the symbolic or philosophical center.

They are touched by the same forces. Alec's inheritance, through his mother's debt, is vaguely threatened by the same falseness that imperils Annie's. When her father dies, her kinsman the mean shopkeeper Robert Bruce takes her to live in his shop and garret to control her little inheritance. He is a petty miser-hypocrite who moves from church to church to improve his business and is finally expelled for stealing Annie's five-pound note from the old Bible left her by the minister. MacDonald makes a caustic cultural joke of his name: is this "Robert Bruce" what has become of heroic Scotland? But MacDonald is no novelist of manners; social issues and values are important only as they are types of theological and spiritual ones. Robert Bruce is of little interest; his creator finds trivial wickedness uninteresting, just as he does in the case of the stereotyped fraud Beauchamp.

More interesting, because closer to the center of MacDonald's imagination, are the stronger, sterner natures, the traditional types of peasant elder, schoolmaster, and scholar: Crann the stonemason, Malison the brutal schoolmaster, and Cupples. All must be saved from their own excesses by the divine vengeance of love, the influence of Annie, the perseverance of poor crippled Truffey. In Malison's tyranny over children is personified "the God of a corrupt Calvinism," but he is defended by MacDonald as the type and victim of this cultural disease. In Crann the same doctrinal harshness is at war with more loving religious impulses. Cupples is saved from a lonely and alcoholic academicism by his suffering devotion to Alec, which leads him back to the exhilaration and sobriety of nature. All are saved, and their salvations matter more than Alec's redemption from the foolish romantic excesses of his young manhood. And at the center of the marvelous, often visionary world where their struggles and salvations occur is the divinely childlike Annie.

Sir Gibbie is a male version of that ideal, and more. He is almost a force of nature and a fabulous one. To come into the inheritance lost to him by his degenerate forebears, he must go back to the archaic vitalities of nature—the mountain, the river, shepherds and beasts—but also to his foster parents, old peasants once the glory of Scotland, where he can learn a simple, pretheological Bible Christianity. He becomes a legend. He plays fabulous roles as local sprites; the natural springs of his true inheritance are inseparable from the springs of faith and wonder. Both bring him into conflict with the false Thomas Galbraith, usurper of his inheritance, who personifies the two cardinal temptations to Scottish disinheritance as MacDonald sees them: anglicization and atheism, both representing the denial of local tradition and belief.

There is a further stage to Gibbie's inheritance, and it carries him back to the city where he began. MacDonald's city seems akin to Dickens's—preindustrial, crowded, labyrinthine, a place of fear, sin, and violence. But unlike Dickens's innocents—Oliver, David, Esther, and Pip—Gibbie is perfectly at home there, an innocent protector of those who wander in hunger or drunkenness in its streets. He has no consciousness of humanity's fall. But when his father's death sets him loose and when the Negro Sammbo is murdered before his eyes, his faith in humanity fails, and he follows his drunken father's "vague urging up Daurside" to his natural inheritance. The same river, in spate, causes his return to the city, but this time as the recognized heir, a mute but resistant Pip with expectations, in the hands of Sclater the pharisee. A corrupt church now plays his foster parent and tries in vain to make him a "gentleman," but he returns to play the missionary of the city streets, a literal Christian, and ultimately uses his money to restore the Auld Hoose of Galbraith as a settlement house. Here he lives winters to care for his outcasts and strays, and summers he spends up Daurside as the kindly laird-baronet, married to the old laird's daughter. It is a curious and interesting variant on the Waverley pattern of cultural redemption.

It is also a mythic revision of *Robert Falconer*, a movement back toward the visionary or fantastic, where MacDonald is at his best and most unique. Cultural types are transposed into archetypes of theological romance, and thus the local realism of the nineteenth-century idyll is present only to be transcended. Yet in its most archetypal patterns this romance of MacDonald's has an extraordinary analogue in one of the rare city novels of nineteenth-century Scotland, *St. Mungo's City* by Sarah Tytler.

The historian E. A. Baker refers to this lady as "such natives as Henrietta Keddie (1827-1914), who wrote under the name of 'Sarah Tytler,' author of *St. Mungo's City* (1885) and *Logie Town* (1887), [and who] cultivated the 'Kailyard' before it became classic ground, and in fact went on doing so when the nickname had gone out of fashion."[16] The British Library Catalogue lists more than seventy-five novels and tales by this prodigious woman, not counting biographies, histories, and sketches for young ladies. By her own account (in *Three Generations*), two early novels failed, and she wrote without publishing until she took the classic route of Scottish novelists: "I spent a holiday in Selkirkshire, and happened to climb the hill of Pirn along with one of my sisters. On what is equivalent to classic ground in Scotland, it occurred to me that I might try to amplify and put new life into some of the traditions with which the country-side abounded."[17]

The success that followed, through magazines such as *Fraser's*, *Cornhill*, and *Good Words*, took her from Fife into the urbane Free Church world of Victorian Edinburgh (well drawn in her memoirs), thence "for the better furthering of my literary career" to London in 1870, and after ten years to Oxford and a world of Victorian woman authors living off literary magazines. But she remained a daughter of Victorian Fife. Her father was a Cupar clerk who became owner of coal pits on the south coast, and her brother was a civil engineer of some eminence in the laying of Scottish railroads. She was evidently in touch with an age of commerce and industry, as with a world of remarkable men such as Chalmers, Guthrie, Tulloch, and Norman Macleod. She knew George MacDonald. But ultimately, when she placed her own world of Fife on the classic ground of countryside tradition, the result was the provincial *Logie Town*, a better novel, in my view, than *St. Mungo's City*.

It is not surprising that those who happen upon Sarah Tytler at all are more impressed by the city novel. In *Barrie and the Kailyard School*, remarking on how the Clyde Valley was industrialized "almost overnight into a Black Country," George Blake recalls his long search for some trace in novels of what was happening. "Only two have rewarded a patient endeavour. One is a completely forgotten but remarkably solid novel called *St. Mungo's City* by Sarah Tytler, with some excellent detail about Glasgow's textile industry in the early 19th century, and one splendid chapter about a cruise on the Firth of Clyde in a popular steamboat."[18] Actually there are two climactic cruises up the water, and taken together they reveal much about the book.

In the first, the radical son of merchant prince Tam Drysdale (of Glasgow, Drysdale Haugh Dye Works, and Drysdale Hall, Lanark) becomes disgusted with his father's capitalist materialism and joins "the people" on a steamboat holiday up the Clyde. He finds himself strangely out of place; popular orgy is not to his taste, and he is thoroughly chastened. "He's no easy," his mother had said, "about the rich and the poor"; and his father had answered, "We're not here to mend the whole economy of things" (I, 114-115). But on the boat young Tam meets a half-mad Highlander with a chest full of papers containing a marriage settlement that may ruin the Drysdales. Later, when old Tam has bought the papers and struggled with the prospect of disinheritance, he rents a yacht and takes his two daughters on an autumn sail up Loch Fyne into scenes of sublimity and solitude, tells them local stories of his boyhood, and there, "alane in the presence of one's maker," where "this taste of the world as God made it" proves the frivolity of worldly wealth, Tam asks his family to go back to their poor beginnings and start afresh. It is extraordinary, this climactic chapter of "a charmed sail," a sabbatarian pastoral journey away from urban materialism to a natural oracular place, suggestively similar to Gibbie's trip up Daurside, and suggestive, too, of how little this romance of religious and worldly inheritance really has to do with the urban grimness of industrial Clydeside.

St. Mungo's City is an evangelical sentimentalizing—I do not use the word pejoratively—of Galt's *Entail.* But Auld Tam derives less from the Laird of Grippy than from Bailie Jarvie. For in him, the mercantile entrepreneur and self-made man with poetry, simplicity, and humanity underneath is celebrated and vindicated. Having proved himself charitable and free of idolatry, he wins his inheritance back. Meanwhile our glimpses of contemporary lower-class Glasgow are limited to the bewildered impressions of Rorie the half-mad North Uist man. We anticipate more. The second volume opens with the outbreak of typhoid in Glasgow, and Tam himself becomes the most active and daring of charitable workers in infected slum dwellings. A Carlylean theme is here: the separation of the rich from the poor stultifies the rich and brutalizes the poor. But we see little of the dwellings. Instead we see Tam's moral struggle, the rural highlife of the Drysdales and their neighbors, and by contrast—and in the one truly superb element of the book—the poignant and ludicrous gentility of Tam's starving old kinswomen the Miss MacKinnons, living a lie like Caleb Balderstone's in their old house in St. Mungo's Square.

They have dreamed for ages of their inheritance from Fenton of Strathdivie. Their trip to claim it is a masterpiece of bitter pathos.

> The three ladies had a look of blinking owls, as the Miss MacKinnons stood on the platform, keeping guard over their trunk, while they interfered with the traffic, got in the way of the porters and other passengers, and were more than once heartily anathematized. Even Miss Janet made mistakes, dropped tickets, miscounted her money, and entered into hopeless altercations, trotting backward and forward as fast as her stiffened limbs would let her . . . When the group were seated in a third-class carriage—for they were not yet in possession of the reversion of Jean MacKinnon's tocher—various rough jests and not too civil remarks were made by the bystanders on "the party out of the ark that had ta'en the road, forget-

ting that they had left Noehey behind them" . . . It was afternoon when the Miss MacKinnons were set down, sorely wearied, at the roadside station which was nearest to Strathdivie . . . Brickfields with their clay hillocks and smoking kilns, rows on rows of half-dried bricks, and piles of broken and crumbling-down bricks, like ungainly masses of sordid ruins, were the most flourishing form of industry. Strathdivie was in sight, a discoloured, tall and narrow last-century house, reminding the gazer of a gaunt face foul with weeping, half hidden in a neglected fir-wood . . . This was the paradise the Miss MacKinnons had sighed for. But the sight of it did not daunt them—at least Miss Janet—more than a second.

"It is an auld-fashioned pairt, without ony nonsense," said that indomitable woman; "and auld-fashioned farmin' aye paid. I dare say these brickfields have been Archie Fenton's—they say there's no such flourishin' trade now as the buildin' trade, and that there is grand profit tot out o' drain-tiles. I wouldna wonder though he has doobled his capital, and that there is plenty of stouchrie [stowed away goods] in the auld hoose." [II, 279-284]

They discover that the legacy has shrunk to two hundred pounds and belongs to the youngest sister. Out of respect to equity and seniority they burn the will, and go to jail. The terrible and ludicrous poverty and hunger of this "the cream of old Glasgow" provides the only realistic picture of city life in the novel.

The old ladies have lost touch with the strange new world about them and have kept their own spare community by withdrawal. This theme is what Sarah Tytler portrays best, and it is more central in a setting of parochial closeness and decay in *Logie Town*. The life of a Fife burgh is seen here with wholeness and urbane compassion, with a finely balanced sense of its values and deficiencies. The story is set back between Waterloo and the Reform Bill in "a small 'landward town' of robust local colouring and individual character, before the days of the penny post, railways, and universal intercommunication."[19] It is a story of straitened circumstances and narrow views: "The natives of Logie thought there was not such another town on the face of the earth, and rather resented an inhabitant's leaving it on any pretense whatever. If people could not be content with Logie, what town would satisfy them? If they could not find all they desired in Logie, they were ill to please indeed" (251). Characters are treated with neither condescension nor sentimentality. The style of witty discrimination is almost Augustan. The schoolmistress, for example, "regarded the school as the center of the universe, with the rest of the world revolving around it, but that was merely a flaw of mental vision, not a moral error. She was as dull as ditch-water under her turban and spectacle, her pedantry and pomposity; but this, again, was more her misfortune than her fault" (260). The town is to be warmly enjoyed from this critical distance. It is, for the rather sophisticated heroine, a comfortable human world where she has identity and security; and after her father dies, when her stepmother flits back to Ayr and the Miss Murdies must let her go, she is temporarily lost. Her story makes for a far more novelistic realism than the moral romance of Tam Drysdale, where the bewilderments of identity and discontinuity in the babel and flux of the city seemed to demand romance as a mode of expression. Only in the distanced but intimate traditional community was the novel possible.

6

The Liberals
in the
Kailyard

A s we turn from this brief glance at a hugely prolific novelist, Sarah Tytler, to the so-called Kailyard with which she has been facilely identified, we should bear in mind what Ortega y Gasset said of the classical novel. It is "provincial life"; its "author must see to it that the reader is cut off from his real horizon and imprisoned in a small, hermetically sealed universe . . . He must make a 'villager' of him and interest him in the inhabitants of this realm . . . To turn each reader into a temporal 'provincial' is the great secret of the novelist."[1] We should hear, too, from a critic who has understood Scottish Victorian fiction in more philosophical terms than the cliches of anti-Kailyard critics—William Power: "Though Scotland had been severely industrialized, though the number of miners, artisans, and textile workers was possibly greater than that of all agricultural workers, and though Glasgow was one of the largest of British cities, it was still assumed, for literary purposes, that the majority of Scots people lived in rustic villages . . . The Scots people were vigorous industrialists and slum-builders, but they never reconciled themselves spiritually to their own urban creations, which, indeed, were more fitting subjects for commissions and blue-books than for novels . . . The fact of the matter is that social conditions in industrial Scotland at that time were somewhat beyond the scope of realism. It was better to help to keep alive the native faith and virtues and idyllic memories of the people than to remind them of the scorching fires of Moloch through which they were passing. Not until these fires had been largely quenched was Scots literature able to face *la vraie vérité* of Scots life."[2]

How is a foreign observer to understand this intense and endless conflict of the Scottish imagination, the warfare of Kailyard and anti-Kailyard? An almost physical sense of outrage is as evident among Scots critics now as when J. H. Millar overflowed with scorn at the turn of the century: "The circulating libraries became charged to overflowing with a crowd of ministers, precentors, and beadles, whose dry and 'pithy' wit had plainly been recruited at the fountain-head of Dean Ramsay; while the land was plangent with the sobs of grown men, vainly endeavouring to stifle their emotion by an elaborate affectation of 'peching' and 'hoasting.' "[3] Avoid the Kailyard School at all costs, advised Sydney Goodsir Smith in his Kirkcaldy lectures of 1947. Power offers a more positive comment: the three chief Kailyarders were all "first-rate literary craftsmen," he allows; "The real trouble was in the public to whom these writers mainly appealed . . . a convention was somehow established." It was that "a Scots novelist dealing with Scots life should not portray anything that was sensual, base, coarse, cruel, cynical, profane, or even passionate. The treatment . . . must be essentially respectable, the kind of thing one could discuss with one's maiden aunt, one's minister, or one's adolescent daughter; and it must not cast grave aspersions upon the character of the Scots people."[4]

There are several issues here: respectability (bowdlerizing), moral realism, and national pride. The last is most strange, since so many anti-Kailyard critics find the Kailyard degrading to Scotland. The first belongs to Victorianism in general and to the anxious moral earnestness of an international evangelical ethos. The second is of most interest, for it identifies moral reality with a certain intense representation of evil and implies that such evil is absent from the fiction of Crockett, Maclaren, and Barrie.

Kailyard fiction is chiefly Victorian pastoral, sometimes neopagan (Crockett), sometimes elegiac (Maclaren), and sometimes ironic (Barrie). The anti-Kailyard revulsion, however, is much less a matter of literary mode than of theological vision. Anti-Kailyarders are offended by sentimental images of man's goodness because they find man grotesquely fallen. They find more salvific force in the evil grandeur of a Calvinist megalomania than in glimpses of kindliness behind the dour facades of Thrums and Drumtochty. When George Douglas Brown claimed his *House with the Green Shutters* was "more complimentary to Scotland," I take it he meant that it is truer doctrine to have a powerful vision of evil than a poignant vision of redemptive innocence. Perhaps he envisioned the program Hugh MacDiarmid finds in the words of J. D. Scott: "to realize the demoniac quality of the national character, to unfasten the bonds of religion, respectability, sentimentality, and success which hold it down, to find out what the Scot really is"[5]—to discover, that is, that the Scot "really is" demoniac. This anti-Kailyard furor is manifestly theological; the Kailyard was sown in an alien theological liberalism.

Few recent social historians of Scotland mention Thomas Erskine of Linlathen, whom Ian Maclaren calls "our Scottish Maurice" and George MacDonald's son calls "that loving support to all who dared preach universal redemption."[6] The exception, William Ferguson, describes as "one of the most significant and least understood of the revolutionary changes wrought in nineteenth-century Scotland" the collapse of "bare old Calvinism under sentence of death," under the onslaught of Erskine's "appealing but unreasoned universalism . . . Erskine inspired a new and more spiritual outlook in some of his younger contemporaries, including the wayward genius Edward Irving who charmed the great of London but not the presbytery of Annan which in 1833 deposed him from the ministry . . . Much healthier was Erskine's influence on another young minister of the Church of Scotland, John MacLeod [sic] Campbell. In 1830 he was deposed because of suspect views on the atonement."[7] Greville MacDonald likens Macleod Campbell to Alexander John Scott, who had been found guilty of heresy and deprived of his license to preach "for refusing assent to the doctrine that only the Elect are redeemed by Christ."[8]

The heresy struggles were with a resurgent Calvinism linked to the Disruption. The struggle had its intellectual-academic side. In *The Democratic Intellect* George Elder Davie sketches the new Edinburgh orthodoxy of the heirs of moderatism, Hamilton and his disciples, in educational and religious thought. They opposed the Mill-Maurice kind of Germano-Coleridgianism, associated with "the mysticism of men like the celebrated Erskine of Linlathen." This early importation was blocked in presbytery and academic senate, but a new German threat rose in the 1850s and 60s: "This mystical optimism associated with the Romantics, alien as it was to the majority, now at last in the 'fifties' and 'sixties' began to make headway among those who, for one reason or another, were in revolt against the educational and spiritual tradition. Hitherto, this anti-Calvinist element had . . . remained very much in the background." Then the young men—Shairp for instance —"devotees of Romantic monism" and Romantic poets, who had gone as Snell Exhibitioners to Balliol and had learned to despise the Common Sense philosophy "as prosaic and thin in comparison with Germano-Coleridgianism," came home to exert their influence. Their affinities, suggests Davie, "would be probably with the mysticism of Erskine of Linlathen, and of his disciple Macleod Campbell of Rowe, rather than the two great rival factions of the Moderate Calvinists and the Evangelical Calvinists who had combined to expel Macleod Campbell from the Church of Scotland."[9]

The strange provenance of the Kailyard may be imagined in the visit of George MacDonald to Erskine at Linlathen in 1865, when Carlyle and John Brown were also guests. The Kailyard may be seen germinating in the ferment of heresy trials, its ideological heritage the line of Erskine-MacDonald-Maclaren. The "I" of *Beside the Bonnie Brier Bush* becomes the boisterous Free Kirk minister of *Kate Carnegie,* whose anti-Calvinism is modeled on his creator's liberalism and who must undergo a heresy trial. Barrie's Little Minister has his auld licht nurture exploded, falls in love with an aristocratic gypsy of Chartist sympathies, and is torn between loyalty to his orthodox parishioners and his own new liberalism.

But first, what of poor heterodox Samuel Rutherford Crockett,* whose *Lilac Sunbonnet,* says Ernest Baker, is "probably the most unconscionable display of sentimentalism, simple and unabashed, in the work of all the school," and, says George Blake, "is hard for any reasonably literate adult of the mid-twentieth century to read . . . without nausea."[10] This adult succeeded. The book is extreme only in what its title suggests: drenched in sun, flowers, and the imagery of

---

*Crockett, Samuel Rutherford. Born at Balmaghie, Kirkcudbrightshire, in 1860, and died at Avignon, France, in 1914. The son of a farmer, he attended Edinburgh University on a bursary and worked as a journalist while studying at New College for the Free Church ministry. He was ordained and held a parish in Midlothian, but the enthusiastic reception of *The Raiders* and *The Lilac Sunbonnet* (both 1894) led him to leave the ministry and live by writing. Between 1895 and 1914 he published over forty books, chiefly novels.

Eden, it is a virtual fertility rite, localized in an agricultural Galloway. The localizing recalls the Eliot of *Adam Bede* and *The Mill on the Floss*, and early Hardy. The Pictish gypsy Jess Kissock speaks a broad Galloway Scots, and for the narrator, "Jess's good Scots was infinitely better and more vigorous than the English of the lady's maid."[11] The heroine Winsome talks a simple, forthright English—"Listen, Ralph, I want you to understand this"—because she spent her early days in England. Her grandmother teases her for it, just as the narrator quizzes Ralph for his tendentious English. The Scots varies dramatically, and the stress on regional distinctiveness is emphatic.

The picturing of physical personality is equally strong. Critics who cite merely the excessive curls of Winsome are unfair, for the girls of the story are physically very present indeed, and the first shock of bare limbs trampling blankets carries through the entire book. Innocence is frank and unabashed. Winsome is as ready for a midnight tryst in the fields as Jess Kessock is to substitute herself; and the kiss of Ralph, the mistaken lover, is genuine and lengthy. The narrator, far from damning Jess, lets her marry the heir and prosper, exuberant Eustacia Vye though she be. Winsome is associated repeatedly with "Mother Eve," the place is a sinless garden, and her "full kiss of first surrender" has few analogues in Victorian fiction, though it oddly anticipates the sinless sexuality in Alan Sharp's two novels of the 1960s. Crockett's critics call his perspective "breezy" because it amounts to an indiscriminate vitalistic naturalism, with God on the side of youth and love. *The Lilac Sunbonnet* is a deliberate idyll of a sort Barrie and Maclaren could not imagine; Crockett's lovers are young adults whose innocence is inseparable from their fleshliness.

But with the others Crockett shares the inevitable elegiac strain of the Kailyard. The book sets the world's false loves in the perspective of "an older love which was fresh and tender, sweet and true," and the Edenic allusion dominates.

> It is at once instruction for the young, and for the older folk, a cast back into the days that were. . . . Perfect love had done its work. All frayed and secondhand loves may well be made ashamed by the fearlessness of these two walking to their farewell trysting-place. . . . Overhead there was nothing nearer than the blue lift, and even that had withdrawn itself infinitely far away, as though the angels themselves did not wish to spy on a later Eden. It was that midsummer glory of love-time, when grey Galloway covers up its flecked granite and becomes a true Purple land. [424-425]

The Miltonic memory of brave partners is unmistakable, and here at parting they face "the great interior sadness, mixed of great fear and great hunger," in the midst of Crockett's four elements: "There are no finer glories on the earth than red heather and blue loch, except only love and youth" (426). But the elegiac is superficial, and in this fact is Crockett's sentimentality. He starts out with a neopagan vision of youth and love, suggests strong passions in combat (murderousness in the idiot Jock, Jess's sexual war for Ralph), opposes it all to the foolish rigidities of an old kirk—and there is no evil whatsoever. This later Eden is without the fall or the serpent, and sadness and parting are momentary. It is all real, ripe, yet intensely idyllic, a dream of sinlessness; what starts out as Eliot or Hardy drops the darker possibilities of both. The consequences of a terrible Scottish yearning for old Eden have become the concern of recent novelists such as Jenkins and Sharp; in Crockett the yearning itself blots out darker areas of the moral world.

Similar are other Crockett novels such as *The Stickit Minister* and *Cleg Kelly, Arab of the City*. At first they impress us with an unsentimental gusto in the realistic depiction of milieu; we then see the values of romance and idyll take over. There is a superficial kinship to MacDonald's city novels. Cleg Kelly's beginnings are brutal enough. Like Huck Finn, he has a drunken father; he is rough, shrewd, and boisterous. If he is an angel in disguise, the disguise is real. The city, Edinburgh, and its Victorian Pleasance are too. They surround Cleg's mother:

> The wind swirled about the old many-gabled closes of Edinburgh. It roared over the broken fortress line of the Salisbury Crags. The streets were deserted. The serried ash-buckets were driven this way and that by the gale. Random cats scudded from doorstep to cellar, dipped, and disappeared . . . So through the turmoil of the storm she came back, and ran up the evil-smelling dark stairs, where the banister was broken, and only the wind-blown fleer of the gas-lamp outside, flickering through the glassless windows of the stairway, lighted her upwards. She had once been a milkmaid, but she had forgotten how the cowslips smelled.[12]

They are palpably real for the wealthy bourgeois Sunday School teacher as she visits a Pleasance shop

> one clammy evening, when the streets were covered with a greasy slime, and the pavements reflected the gloomy sky. In the grey lamp-sprinkled twilight she reached the paper-shop. There were

sheafs of papers and journals hung up on the cheeks of the door. Coarsely coloured valentines hung in the window, chiefly rude portraitures of enormously fat women with drying-pans, and of red-nosed policemen with batons to correspond . . . There was a heavy smell of moist tobacco all about. The floor of the little shop was strewn with newspapers, apparently of ancient date, certainly of ancient dirt. These rustled and moved of themselves in a curious way, as though they had untimely come alive. As indeed they had done, for the stir was caused by the cockroaches arranging their domestic affairs underneath. [46-47]

This is urban realism for any taste, and what follows—scenes of drunken violence—is *Oliver Twist* without Dickensian sentimentality. But what begins this way ends as grotesque Gothic idyll—General Theophilus Ruff in his emblematic coffin, Tim Kelly and Sal Kavannah dead on the strong room floor. And in the middle are the adventures of the ebullient Cleg commanding his gang, caring for the Kavannah children, traveling the world of Southwest Scots railroads, and inheriting a fortune of loose sovereigns in corned beef cans. At last Cleg and Vara can live in a house by the sea and be market gardeners, but build a new club house for the less fortunate in the South Back of the Canongate. It is an interesting variant on *Sir Gibbie*, in Crockett's terms a city "idyll," where, somehow, all adventures are innocent and gay.

Those who find Crockett morally or theologically false will object differently to Ian Maclaren.* For in the idylls of Drumtochty the aura and mood of old mortality are all-pervasive; here, the only final meaning and security are in the harvest of death.

The cynical Alexander Woolcott found the final section of Maclaren's *Beside the Bonnie Brier Bush* ("A Doctor of the Old School") "that gentle and touching masterpiece . . . more moving than anything I ever read." Prefacing a 1929 American edition of the *Doctor* he recalled its source as "that best-seller of the Middle Nineties": "Not

---

Maclaren, Ian. Pen name of John Watson, who was born in 1850 in Manningtree, England, and died in Mount Pleasant, Iowa, in 1907, while on an American lecture tour. Educated in Perth and Stirling and at Edinburgh University, Watson was a Free Church minister in Perthshire and Edinburgh, then moved to the Presbyterian Church at Sefton Park, Liverpool, where he won fame as a preacher (Matthew Arnold praised him highly), and helped found Liverpool University. W. R. Nicoll, editor of *The British Weekly*, urged him to try fiction, and the three works discussed here brought international fame and wealth to Ian Maclaren. Sermons and theological works were published under Watson's own name.

quite so often as 'Trilby', I suppose, but a little oftener than 'David Harum', one saw it in the hand of every Gibson Girl, and found it, in its gray-green cover, left in every hammock and deck-chair from Kansas City to Port Said."[13] Now, in the twenties, he supposed it unread. George Blake, a more hostile witness, thought its success a mystery of the bizarre nineties, a time of great prosperity, self-satisfaction, and imperialism before Freud, Adler, and Jung, when the works of Marx "were still known to only a few cranks."[14] "It needs no fine work with elaborate critical apparatus to demonstrate that the Rev. John Watson, D.D. [prosperous minister of Sefton Park Church, Liverpool, and, less forgiveable still, quick seller of a quarter million copies in the U.K. and a half million in the U.S.], was the least gifted with real literary qualities of the Kailyard triumvirate . . . It would be a waste of time to analyse *Beside the Bonnie Brier Bush* and its successors in the same genre." Watson was a talented raconteur, but a cynic. His sketches "are no more than anecdotes, aurally conceived"; he has no plot.

We have seen before the importance for the Scottish novelist of "anecdotes, aurally conceived." Moreover, it is irrelevant to charge the author of Victorian prose idyll with having no plot; the idyll, in fact, provided an escape from the flamboyant plot demands of conventional Victorian romance and melodrama. The idyll has formal unity of other kinds.

Maclaren uses the term "idyll" and sets his dominant mood in the titular sketch of the *Brier Bush:* "It was a low-roofed room, with a box-bed and some pieces of furniture, fit only for a labouring man. But the choice treasures of Greece and Rome lay on the table, and on a shelf beside the bed College prizes and medals, while everywhere were the roses he loved. His peasant mother stood beside the body of her scholar son, whose hopes and thoughts she had shared, and through the window came the bleating of distant sheep. It was the idyl of Scottish University life."[15] The idyll's attendant image is the brier bush at the house end, "where George was to sit on the summer afternoons before he died." He sits there pale and dying, when, through the window, we overhear his mother answering the charge that she has provoked the Almighty by idolizing her bairn. The angry answer comes in the voice of Maclaren's liberalism: "Did ye say the Almighty? I'm thinkin' that's ower grand a name for your God, Kirsty. What wud ye think o' a faither that brocht hame some bonnie thing frae the fair for ane o' his bairns, and when the puir bairn was pleased wi' it, tore it oot o' his hand and flung it into the fire? Eh, woman, he wud be a meeserable, cankered, jealous body" (23). The idyllic focus is that of Scott's *Old Mortality* with *its* lamented young scholar, and the whole book has the same pathetic resonance. Its center is not kailyard but kirkyard; many sentences begin, and many sketches are prefaced, with "the kirkyard heard" or "the kirkyard was told." The kirkyard doubles as center of parish history and locus of an engulfing mortality. In their temporal perspectives the idylls are all elegiac. The same characters come and go, though we hear of the deaths of them all. The lad of the first comes home to die; many characters are the last of their lines; Carmichael's first sermon commemorates his dead mother. Maclaren's best known sketches, "A Doctor of the Old School" and "Rabbi Saunderson," culminate in deaths. The most humorous have elegiac elements and are post mortem in perspective.

The persistent theme is reconciliation, secret charity, the conversion of hard legalistic Calvinism into kindly helpfulness. Consider "The Transformation of Lachlan Campbell," whose heart "was wisened in the breist o' him wi' pride an' diveenity," but who is softened and made childlike by trouble. The session meets for presacrament examinations. Lachlan asks forgiveness, Burnbrae prays, and Carmichael the minister has this characteristic vision: "The six elders—three small farmers, a tailor, a stonemason, and a shepherd—were standing beneath the lamp, and the light fell like a halo on their bent heads. That poor little vestry had disappeared, and this present world was forgotten" (122). And it has all been elegiacally framed from the start: "I still hear Drumsheugh pronouncing the final judgment of the glen on Lachlan as we parted at his grave ten years later" (116).

The last idyll of *Auld Lang Syne*, "Oor Lang Hame," is subtle in its finality. Charlie, ne'er-do-well exile who has prospered in America, returns to desolation, visits his mother's ruined cottage, and stands long in the kirkyard. Drumsheugh, loyal last survivor, is there visiting graves. Drumsheugh takes Charlie home, where Saunders has just finished harvesting. " 'Ye thocht, Drumsheugh, we would never get that late puckle in,' " says he, " 'but here it is, safe and sound.' " " 'Ye're right, Saunders, and a bonnie stack it maks'; and then Charlie Grant went in with Drumsheugh to the warmth and the kindly light, while the darkness fell upon the empty harvest field, from which the last sheaf had been safely garnered."[16] So the book ends. Charlie will not stay, and left alone, Drumsheugh will die soon. The field is empty, the harvest safe at last. One comes home only to die; this place, living in the image of Drumsheugh's warmth and kindliness and safety, is already dead. Each idyll goes back to pick up some earlier strand of life and carry on the harvest, but each strand reiterates and reaffirms the all-embracing fact of death.

The kirkyard also functions as setting of the most definitive of Drumtochty's social acts, talk: debate centered on the sermon; communal gossip whereby persons and incidents are fixed as legend in local memory. Trials of strength and orthodoxy are carried on in full view of the kirkyard. Incidents are given dramatically. "Achievements" in diplomacy, investigation, and criticism, are reported here: "It was the birthright of every native of the parish to be a critic, and certain were allowed to be experts in special departments—Lachlan Campbell in doctrine, and Jamie Soutar in logic—but as an all-round practitioner Mrs. Macfadyen had a solitary reputation. It rested on a long series of unreversed judgments, with felicitous strokes of description that passed into the literary capital of the Glen."[17] These are wits "sharpened by the Shorter Catechism" and by the life-long study of sermonizing. These are people, too, united in a sense of national and local tradition upholding freedom of conscience. Burnbrae's situation is that of Alexander's Johnny Gibb. When his lease renewal is conditional on his deserting the Free Kirk, his deep-rootedness becomes a pastoral standard: the townsman's "houses are but inns, which he uses and forgets; he has no roots, and is a vagrant on the face of the earth." The community acts; the ministers defy the factor; the true landlord returns to save the day; the community replenishes Burnbrae's farm. The encompassing theme is no condescending one: "We respected one another's souls in the Glen, and understood the agony of serious speech." For these stern shy natures, debate is therapeutic, but silent love is redemptive.

The brief sketch of "Posty" and his heroic death in *Auld Lang Syne* offers a good example of style and texture in Maclaren's idylls. Posty is a notorious drinker. His exploits are generalized from the point of view of local legend and belief; the urbane narrative compression tends to understress the hardness and danger of rural life: "It was also believed that he had only been late twice, when the Scourie burn carried away the bridge, and Posty had to go four miles up stream to find a crossing place, and the day when he struck his head against a stone, negotiating a drift, and lay insensible for three hours." At this point the narrator's own vividness and wit are evident: "At five o'clock to a minute Posty appeared every morning in the village shop, which had accumulated during the night a blended fragrance of tea and sugar, and candles and Macdougall's sheep dip, and where Mrs. Robb, our post-mistress, received Posty in a negligent undress sanctioned by official business and a spotless widowhood."[18] Then comes dialogue in broad dialect. The narrator thus brings into juxtaposition a few vivid details of local domesticity, with an elegantly urbane view of communal sanctions, and then the color of local dialectal gossip. Is the effect what Blake describes: "a fairly unpleasant impression of a collection of rustic oddities being exposed to the laughter of foreigners"? I think not. The distance is mainly linguistic; the narrator belongs to the community, after all, in loyalty and sympathy. And the glen, as it hears these things, relishes them with its own kind of critical sophistication and stern love. These people are intelligent and self-aware; they read Carlyle and other contemporaries. They seek the correct theological interpretation of each event, and in the case of Posty, Jamie for one is pleased with Carmichael's argument that Posty surely is saved for his heroism: "When the great heresy trial began at Muirtown, Jamie prophesied Carmichael's triumphant acquittal, declaring him a theologian of the first order" (213).

The trial is yet to come in *Kate Carnegie*, Maclaren's *novel* of Drumtochty, where the narrator of the idylls is still a young, brash hero. The people of the idylls are present as chorus; Margaret Howe, the bereft mother, serves still as the true parish counselor on love and death. They are all rediscovered by General Carnegie, who retires from India with his lively daughter to their ancestral lodge, vestige of a Jacobite family. Even as we begin, the narrator tells us how brief is the return, for the race of Carnegies "has now neither name nor house in Scotland, save in the vault in Drumtochty Kirk. It is a question whether one is wise to revisit any place where he has often been in happier times and see it desolate. For me, at least, it was a mistake, and the melancholy is still upon me."[19] But the center is still the manse, and the social world is dominated still by the Disruption. The liberal young Free Kirk Carmichael has his elder counselors in the worldly but admirable Dr. Davidson, who had *not* gone out in the Disruption, and in his spiritual father "Rabbi" Saunderson, learned,

absent-minded, and fanatically Calvinist, a deeply moving figure. The
mood is elegiac and the problem is Carmichael's—in love and faith.

Can the daughter of decadent Jacobitism and ruined lodge marry
the liberal minister and join lodge to manse? Only in exile. Only by a
deathbed, and after the reckless youth's sin of inhumanity toward a
stern past has been cleansed. Carmichael is scornful of an older Calvinism even as he is scornful of Jacobite nostalgia, and the novel links
those who had "come out" with Chalmers to those who had "gone
out" in an earlier heroism. His scorn reflects his author's liberalism.
His first careless sermon—against Queen Mary as Jezebel—sends Kate
stomping angrily from the church. His climactic one, the Sacrament
sermon, causes the devoted old Saunderson, after a long night of
spiritual wrestling, to bring charges before the presbytery. The trial
comes to nought, and the Rabbi walks home to his final illness.

Carmichael's own "journey of expiation" follows the "road the
Rabbi walked with the hand of death upon him after that lamentable
Presbytery, and he marked the hills where the old man must have
stood and fought for breath." He thinks of Saunderson and the dead
"doctor of the old school" together, "who had each loved the highest
he knew and served his generation according to the will of God, till he
found himself again with the Drumtochty doctor on his heroic journeys, with the Rabbi in his long vigils. It was a singular means of grace
to have known two such men in the flesh, when he was still young and
impressionable" (349-350). It is the "means of grace" offered by
George Eliot's sacramental natures, and the narrator's comment movingly echoes Eliot, as well as her idol Scott. Compassion is required if
there is to be reconciliation of heroic past with enlightened present:

> When two tides meet there is ever a cruel commotion, and ships are
> apt to be dashed on the rocks, and Carmichael's mind was in a
> "jabble" that day. The new culture, with its wider views of God
> and man, was fighting with the robust Calvinism in which every
> Scot is saturated, and the result was neither peace nor charity.
> Personally the lad was kindly and good-natured, intellectually he
> had become arrogant, intolerant, acrid, flinging out at old-fash-
> ioned views, giving quite unnecessary challenges, arguing with
> imaginary antagonists. It has ever seemed to me, although I sup-
> pose that history is against me, that if it be laid on any one to advo-
> cate a new view that will startle people, he ought of all men to be
> conciliatory and persuasive; but Carmichael was, at least in this
> time of fermentation, very exasperating and pugnacious, and so he

drove the Rabbi to the only hard action of his life, wherein the old man suffered most, and which may be said to have led to his death. [270]

With such a theme, then, *Kate Carnegie* is perhaps the most maturely integrated of all Kailyard novels. Its world has no recognizable connection with the stereotyped Drumtochty of anti-Kailyard criticism.

T. W. H. Crosland says Thrums and Drumtochty are "little bits of Heaven dropped on to the map of Scotland."[20] J. M. Barrie's* Thrums seems almost as remote from paradise as Maclaren's Drumtochty. But then the antiromantic ironies of Barrie are so strange and unstable that it is hard to fix on a single Thrums for definition. All sense of place in Barrie is deflected by multiple subjectivities of vision. Nonetheless, an illuminating road to Thrums is by way of Peter Pan's Never Never Land and its strange adventurers.

Because he dared to write *Margaret Ogilvy*, Barrie has had the misfortune to be framed by interpreters in an upsetting mother fixation. But the treatment accorded his fantasy mothers is puzzling. For Peter Pan, a mother is a girl who tells stories and does the spring cleaning; he is too selfish to know when one replaces another. But the narrator's own elusiveness leaves us unsure what to make of the offhand news that "Mrs. Darling was now dead and forgotten," or the contraposed final assurance that each new generation's daughter will be Peter's mother "so long as children are gay and innocent and heartless." The option to gay, innocent heartlessness is the fate of the boys, who discover "what goats they had been not to remain on the island," and then grow up to be "done for" as clerks, engine-drivers, judges in wigs, and bearded men with no stories to tell. Only Wendy emerges with humanity—with divided loyalties, with genuine sadness. Yet life on the fantastic island for Wendy is so often drudgery or mistreatment that she envies spinsters.

Wendy alone grasps reality, and her assignment is a sad one. She

Barrie, James Matthew. Born at Kirriemuir, Angus, in 1860, and died in London in 1937. He attended Edinburgh University, worked as a journalist, and first became known as a Scottish novelist, with books such as *Auld Licht Idylls* and *The Little Minister*. *Margaret Ogilvy* (1896) is the biography of his mother. With the turn of the century Barrie turned to the London theater and achieved tremendous success with plays such as *Quality Street* (1902), *What Every Woman Knows* (1908), and *Dear Brutus* (1917). He was the close friend of Meredith, Hardy, and Shaw. He was elected Chancellor of Edinburgh University in 1930.

must tell reality as a fable to the terrified boys, who must learn "the difference between an island of make-believe and the same island come true." Peter is despotic enough to refuse the distinction, even as he refuses at last to allow a light that shows Wendy aging. Wendy is distressed to hear that his feelings for her are "those of a devoted son," but Tinker Bell, the vengeful, snobbish fairy, sums it up best when she calls him a silly ass. He is the tyrannical artist as child—egocentric, boastful, and heartless. He forgets years of spring-cleaning. He even refuses identity; Wendy must keep on telling him who he is. During their final duel, Hook, the more human antagonist, says, "Pan, who and what art thou?" " 'I'm youth, I'm joy,' Peter answered at a venture, 'I'm a little bird that has broken out of the egg.' " Comments the narrator, "This, of course, was nonsense; but it was proof to the unhappy Hook that Peter did not know in the least who or what he was, which is the very pinnacle of good form."[21]

Hook is impressive in his own right—final Byronic degeneration of the Jacobite outlaw, melancholy ape of Stuart attire, devilish gentleman and raconteur, and (the Freudian would add) dark father gaily dismembered by a boy. He has become a moving figure. When Peter imitates his voice and calls him a mere codfish, "He felt his ego slipping from him. 'Don't desert me, bully,' he whispered hoarsely to it. In his dark nature there was a touch of the feminine, as in all the greatest pirates, and it sometimes gave him intuitions." When Peter's cockiness drives him to destruction, the narrator bids farewell to "James Hook, thou not wholly unheroic figure" (111). Peter becomes more interesting when, in other books, he is naturalized and complicated into the strange figure of Sentimental Tommy.

One of the complexities of Sentimental Tommy is that he is a Peter Pan who plays at being Captain Hook. His is a bitterly ironic portrait of the artist as a young man, and the narrator who mocks him repeatedly as "this poor devil" admits to being his slave and sly defender. In *Sentimental Tommy* he is the fantasizing urchin of the London streets, imagining a Thrums that never was. Returned to the grimness of real Thrums, he cultivates a despotic and cold-blooded imagination: the "most conspicuous of his traits was the faculty of stepping into other people's shoes and remaining there until he became someone else; his individuality consisted in having none."[22] But his talent is purely sentimental, and tragically he comes to know it. As he comes dazedly out of his roles, Corp cries admiringly, "Oh you deevil! oh, you queer little deevil!" (235). When he reads *Waverley*, he invents a whole Jacobite myth for the children to play at in a den—trysting place for local adulterers—with himself as Charlie. Consummate role-playing leads to a bursary competition, but his boyhood ends in failure and exile. In the novel of his doomed young manhood, *Tommy and Grizel*, he is akin not just to Neil Munro's Gilian and G. D. Brown's young Gourlay, but to Conrad's Lord Jim as well. The devil of his sentimentality possesses him. He knows the truth in what Pym says: "Love! You are incapable of it. There is not a drop of sentiment in your frozen carcass . . . Young man, I fear you are doomed."[23] The tragedy, for the helplessly loyal narrator, is that Tommy could not remain an innocent heartless boy:

> Oh, who by striving could make himself a boy again as Tommy could! I tell you he was always irresistible then. What is genius? It is the power to be a boy again at will. When I think of him flinging off the years and whistling childhood back, not to himself only, but to all who heard, distributing it among them gaily, imperiously calling on them to dance, dance, for they are boys and girls again until they stop—when to recall him in those wild moods is to myself to grasp for a moment at the dear dead days that were so much the best, I cannot wonder that Grizel loved him. [II, 10]

> Have I been too cunning, or have you seen through me all the time? Have you discovered that I was really pitying the boy who was so fond of boyhood that he could not with years become a man, telling nothing about him that was not true, but doing it with unnecessary scorn in the hope that I might goad you into crying: "Come, come, you are too hard on him!" [II, 283-284]

This is a hysterical sort of Marlowe, trapping us into secret sharers of his weakness for the despotic Tommy. But it is Grizel who lives on to win our real affection, to make a myth of Tommy the perfect lover, to make a faith out of the lie that he was. The pathos of Thrums ends in the heart of darkness.

Grizel, like Wendy, can only be herself, and in so being she can cope with the weird and ironic disenchantment that is really Thrums. The fancied "home of heroes and the arts" turns out to be the place where Tommy's mother is buried in a cold, dark hole, and where poor Grizel cares for her drunken maniac of a mother, the "painted lady," who trysts with respectable local gentlemen in the den where Tommy plays his Jacobite fancies, and wretchedly dies there. Thrums drives people to secret sinfulness. Hardy conceived of nothing earthier than the local fair and carnival called the Muckley, which at night becomes a place of rough sexuality.

> With the darkness, too, crept into the Muckley certain devils in the colour of the night who spoke thickly and rolled braw lads in the mire, and egged on friends to fight and cast lewd thoughts into the minds of women . . . Grand, patient, long-suffering fellows those men were, up at five, summer and winter, foddering their horses, maybe hours before there would be food for themselves, miserably paid, housed like cattle, and when the rheumatism seized them, liable to be flung aside like a broken graip. As hard was the life of the women: coarse food, chaff beds, damp clothes . . . Is it to be wondered that these lads who could be faithful unto death drank suddenly on their one free day, that these girls, starved of opportunities for womanliness, of which they could make as much as the finest lady, sometimes woke after a Muckley to wish they might wake no more?[24]

Thrums, like Peter Pan's island, is sad for children because it can not be the place of their fancy, and because in its grim falseness it leaves them with nothing better than sentimental illusion: "Each was trying to deceive the other for the other's sake, and one of them was never good at deception. They saw through each other, yet kept up the chilly game, because they could think of nothing better, and perhaps the game was worth playing, for love invented it" (157). This is ironic pastoral indeed, grounded in a vision of loving innocence that is all the bitterer for its remoteness from the reality that is Thrums. Robin Jenkins has made better, subtler Scottish fiction of the same pastoral irony.

In *The Little Minister* Thrums is called the town without pity. This is perhaps the least defensible of Barrie's major books, but it returns us to the ecclesiastical-political center of Kailyard fiction, and to the strange mixture of regional history and pastoral romance that characterizes it. The book is pathetic romantic melodrama, centering on the plight of two improbable lovers: the young auld licht minister and the foundling aristocrat who goes about her benevolences in gypsy guise. The colorful central role is hers, but the central problem is his, for it is he whose traditional nurture is exploded and whose vocation is menaced. Babbie comes to warn the town that troops are coming to punish the Chartist weavers, and she tricks Gavin Dishart into helping and hiding her. She and Gavin are seen meeting in the woods by Rob Dow, devoted drunk, and his son warns Babbie to go away or she will ruin the minister. Humane and independent, she has been brought up by the Earl of Rintoul to marry him in his old age; in flight from him, she now faces the dilemma of how to save herself without destroying Gavin's communal vocation. Gavin, at the same time, must resolve the conflict between his loyalty to his severe community, his severe vocation, and his new love of, and respect for, Babbie.

There is also the dilemma of the narrator, old Ogilvy the dominie, long devoted but long since lost to Gavin's mother. Whether and when should he reveal that he is Gavin's father? The intricate romance of sailors supposed drowned, returning, vanishing again, has left poor Margaret with two living husbands. These several dilemmas move toward crisis. But then in the wild twenty-four hours of August 4th the rains come, floods break up the world, and all issues are drowned in adventure and melodrama. The political issue of Chartism is peripheral after all; Gavin's plight as orthodoxy in love is short-circuited; Thrums matters little except as a familiar setting with auld licht proclivities.

Thrums is much more evident in *Auld Licht Idylls*. Told by the same narrator, these are humorous, usually bleak, rather simpleminded sketches of a small-town life that differs from that of Brown's Barbie, in *The House with the Green Shutters*, only because of a stress on humor rather than irony. In *A Window on Thrums*, Thrums differs again; for this is the record of a single family, and the town is seen only through an old woman's window. The life of the house focuses on the family members, who are simply noble without being sentimentalized. Their life is grim, hard, lonely, undemonstrative. The son in London stops writing. Father and daughter die. Mother is left alone in her final weeks, and after she dies son Jamie comes home, finds strangers, and goes away again. It is, as elegiac pastoral, close to "Michael" and "The Ruined Cottage." Where is the rose-covered distortion we are led to expect in the Kailyard? *A Window on Thrums* is parochial because it must be; it is selective as all art is selective. It is sentimental only insofar as a quiet, somewhat grim domestic heroism might be named sentimental—only insofar as a resignation grounded in a sense of the pathos of human goodness might be considered sentimental from a theologically opposed point of view.

7

The
Anti-Kailyard
as
Theological Furor

I f Thrums and Drumtochty are "little bits of Heaven," then, continues T. W. H. Crosland, G. D. Brown's Barbie "is not of heavenly origin in the least."[1] Indeed not: it is hell. Maurice Lindsay is right: "Kailyardism must satisfy some continuing Scottish need."[2] But anti-Kailyardism does too: they are poles, in fact, of the same field. What Richard Chase found to be true of the American romantic imagination is true as well of the Scottish moral imagination: it is theological, but hardly tragic, hardly Christian; rather, it is deeply polarized, Manichean and melodramatic. There may be historical reasons for this late Victorian fury of neoorthodoxy. Calvinism—what Ferguson calls "that bogeyman of the avant garde from David Hume's day to our own"—receives increasingly close attention from historians these days as a cultural energy. Rosalind Mitchison sums up the positive impact: "Calvinism was a fighting faith . . . As with Marxism, men could act freely and strongly in its cause because they felt that it was inevitable that they should." V. S. Pritchett suggests the negative side: "Extreme puritanism gives purpose, drama and intensity to private life . . . Puritanism burns up the air and leaves a vacuum for its descendents."[3] Fionn Mac Colla devotes a book, *At the Sign of the Clenched Fist*, to the dreadful correlation in the Scottish historical consciousness of the principle of Voluntarism, the primacy of will, and the idea of radical evil. In Kailyard fiction, the denial of evil itself was allied with an elegiac paralysis of will. In light of such an alliance, we may begin to understand the contrary ferocity of anti-Kailyardism, so vital an impulse of modern Scottish culture.

The three most promising of early modern Scottish novels promulgate a common anti-Kailyard lesson: an enlightened liberalism cannot cope with the Manichean warfare carried on behind man's facade of civility. Robert Louis Stevenson's* Archie Weir has to learn it in circumstances of primitive violence. There is scarcely anyone left to learn it in Brown's *House with the Green Shutters*, but the theological lesson is there. The would-be destroyers of the soulless evil of Hay's *Gillespie* learn it through disaster and blood bath.

Interpretation of *Weir of Hermiston* normally dissolves, of course, into speculation as to how Stevenson might have completed his book. He still worked feverishly at it the morning he died, December 3, 1894. The Kailyard was in bloom back home; ironically, Stevenson had discussed his novel in correspondence with Barrie. Withal, there is little evidence of an anti-Kailyard motivation, and part of the reason lies in the curious condition Stevenson shares with Brown and Hay: all three identify with an acute moral sensibility embodied in the febrile son of a weakly humanitarian mother. All three identify, in hatred and pity, with a vision of radical evil that is both horrible and mysterious.

Stevenson's title suggests his dual stress on both father and son, on the identification of personality with ancestral place, and hence on the old problem of divided inheritance. Archie learns tenderness from his weak mother, and judges his brutal father uncharitably. Then, in newfound sympathy and modesty, he returns to an ancestral place and learns of primitive violence and justice from Kirstie's nephews, the four black brothers. Here, we surmise, he is to end by murdering the seducer of Kirstie's niece, be tried in his father's courtroom, be freed by the brothers, and escape to America with the girl.[4] A humanitarian tenderness proves no way to live; he must be his father's son.

From the "Introductory," the question seems to be how young Weir should be assimilated into the legendary history of his countryside. Should his destiny reaffirm a continuity of fateful tragedy, or should he break the chain and make his own world and name as his father, a stranger with unknown ancestors, has done? Is a dark archaic fate inseparable from his achievement of manhood, or is it a part of his

Stevenson, Robert Louis. See footnote, p. 154.

destiny that he must repudiate and leave behind? For Robert Kiely, Archie's journey is backward in time to a primitive source where he acquires a natural self and learns from Kirstie "an attitude toward the past which is the reverse of his former escapist fantasies."[5] Thus he goes to "one of the most primitive areas of Scotland" and to a place unsophisticated in its human motivations by the "rationalizations and hypocrisies of civilized society." But the least *civil* person is old Weir in his Edinburgh courtroom and house, and the rural brothers are normally very civilized. And if young Weir is coming here to escape from a Puritan ethic imposed by his mother, why does he go to her ancestral home, by the Covenanter's tomb, with its associations of Old Mortality?

Eigner holds that the book is "Stevenson's most complicated and most serious study of the problem of man's dual nature," that the split is between savagery and civility, such as Archie cannot put together in his father, and that "Stevenson had no solution to the problem of duality which he could bring himself to impose on his fiction." His "melodramatic and Manichean" imagination "does not settle ultimate questions; it leaves them open."[6] Thus, argues Eigner, it is fitting that the book was left unfinished; unsure of his resolution, Stevenson was likely to end in melodrama. In fact, all three novels, seeking to arouse a sense of tragic doom in a Manichean vision of evil, are susceptible to the charge of melodrama.

In imagining the brute nobility of the stern father, Stevenson, like his young hero, never fully escapes the sensibility of the weak mother and thus is caught in the same trap as Archie. Archie's overwhelming sense of a tragic past comes from his mother's sensibility. His mother comes to his mind as Christina perches by him on the tomb and they think together "of their common ancestors now dead, of their rude wars composed, their weapons buried with them, and of these strange changelings, their descendants, who lingered a little in their places, and would soon be gone also, and perhaps sung of by others at the gloaming hour."[7] Out of context this is haunting elegy; in context, however, it seems the problematic heritage of his mother's weak will. In the fragment's last lines, Archie sees "for the first time the ambiguous face of the woman as she is"; one suspects that he has been deluded up to now by elegiac sentimentality, that present harsh reality is not to be understood through a gloomy sense of archaic tragedy. Yet, with something close to the ambivalence of Barrie with his Sentimental Tommy or Neil Munro with his Gilian the Dreamer, Stevenson the narrator has vicariously eluded the demands of reality. In the first interview (the sixth chapter) he seems unequivocally identified with the innocent victims: "Fate played his game artfully with this poor pair of children. The generations were prepared, the pangs were made ready, before the curtain rose on the dark drama." One easily imagines what old Adam Weir would say of such childish fancies. He would see Archie's mother coming out in Archie's creator. In the thin line between melodramatic diabolism and elegiac idyll, one senses the close if strained kinship of Kailyard and anti-Kailyard. It is something to keep in mind, turning to Brown's *House with the Green Shutters* and Hay's *Gillespie.*

Crockett's forced gusto, Maclaren's overwhelming melancholy, and Barrie's elfin cynicism have become George Douglas Brown's* anger; and the anger has an instability that Brown's superb rhetoric does not control. Iain Crichton Smith and others have suggested that it was Brown's artistic error to let his animus pervade the book;[8] this is an error if it is distracting or confusing—and it probably is. Brown speaks to a foreign audience as a distanced, knowledgeable interpreter of Scots; his premise is that one who understands a thing cannot sneer at it, yet he sneers constantly. For all his pretense of analytic distance he is deeply implicated in the culture he portrays. His theme, Kurt Wittig finds, is in Mrs. Gourlay's Bible reading: charity is the gospel that Barbie needs.[9] But Brown as narrator shows none. His anti-Kailyardism proscribes all show of gentler virtues. He writes with the wrathful justice of an Old Testament Jehovah, with a classical Greek model, and with a naturalistic ethic. And for all that, his is one of the greatest of Scottish novels.

Many of the charges Iain Crichton Smith has recently made can be leveled against naturalistic tragedy in general, a curious post-Darwinian Victorian literary mode with an inherent instability. George Eliot and several younger contemporaries were steeped in an archaic Hel-

---

Brown, George Douglas. Born in 1869, at Ochiltree, Ayrshire, and died in London in 1902. He attended Glasgow University and went as Snell Exhibitioner to Balliol, Oxford. A Greek scholar, he lived as a free-lance writer in London, after 1895, publishing articles and short stories. Recognition and royalties came with his only published book, *The House with the Green Shutters*, in 1901. He was at work on a novel of Cromwell's time and a study of Hamlet when he died suddenly.

lenism and sought a tragic view of life to replace a providential Christianity they found no longer plausible. But they tried to adapt a tragedic decorum to the mode of critical naturalism, and the result was a cluster of interesting confusions.

Recall Butler's *Way of All Flesh*. Which does Butler hate more, the strength of old George Pontifex or the weakness of Theobald and his son Ernest? The same kind of question is provoked by Hardy, and by Brown. There is no answer, for both strength and weakness are natural facts, and the strength of strength and the weakness of weakness are viewed with inexorable unconcern by Nature and her mimic narrators as she favors the one and discards the other. But most late Victorian naturalists are driven by an ethical passion and cannot accept a naturalistic ethic. As they imagine the ruthless strong man conquering his world, they cannot help but fear him and invoke a moral law for his downfall, even though they don't "believe" in it. Gourlay's flaw, we are told, is hubris. But hubris is an error in Greek theology, and Brown's animus has nothing to do with man's struggle with gods.

The chief object of hate in *The House with the Green Shutters* is stupidity and weakness. Gourlay is stupid but strong; his son is weak and almost as dumb. For this reason his vivid imagination becomes a curse rather than a source of power. The narrator tells us repeatedly that weaklings are most dangerous, vindictive, and malignant. In his vision of human malignancy the contrast seems to be between a grand, stupid, and strong malevolence, and a weak, cowardly malevolence—and somehow strong evil is preferable to weak. In the logic of Gourlay's downfall, the weak are a means of destroying the strong; only by imitating the strong are the weak ennobled, as when mother and daughter kill themselves: "Willing her death, she seemed to borrow its greatness and become one with the law that punished her. Arrogating the Almighty's function to expedite her doom, she was the equal of the Most High" (568). The one unqualified villain is the most cowardly and mean of the "bodies" of Barbie, Deacon Allardyce. He is called "an artist in spite." He uses a feigned sympathy, "a favourite weapon of human beasts anxious to wound. The Deacon longed to try it on Gourlay. But his courage failed him. It was the only time he was ever worsted in malignity" (536). The entire book is a contest in malignity and spite.

Only the baker believes "folk should be kind to folk"; the baker is "the only kind heart in Barbie" (514-515). But he also believes Gourlay to be the only gentleman: "Brute, if you like, but aristocrat frae scalp to heel. If he had brains, and a dacent wife, and a bigger field, oh, man . . . Auld Gourla could conquer the world, if he swalled his neck till't" (515). And it almost seems he is right. But we cannot imagine Gourlay under such circumstances, for his circumstances—summed up in Barbie—are his fate. He comes from peasant stock; he does not have the brains; he married for money and helped turn his wife into a slut. And what is a "bigger field" in a world made up of Barbie? Edinburgh? Edinburgh is seen as frightful, alien, and equally bad. The only good world present is that of nature, and nature is a pastoral dream from which man in his petty malignity is cut off.

This, then, is the controlling theological vision of the book, and it is familiar to the reader of Scottish fiction from Smollett to Robin Jenkins and Alan Sharp. The book's opening paragraph contrasts the frowsy, sluttish chambermaid and her slovenly postures with the water she throws out, which becomes a smooth round arch glistening in the morning's perfect stillness. The book's last sentence shows the "dark" and "terrible" house "beneath the radiant arch of the dawn." When Gourlay is forced to mingle with the malicious "bodies" on the brake to Skeighan, the theme is sounded: "The brake swung on through merry cornfields where reapers were at work, past happy brooks flashing to the sun, through the solemn hush of ancient and mysterious woods, beneath the great white-moving clouds and blue spaces of the sky. And amid the suave enveloping greatness of the world, the human pismires stung each other and were cruel, and full of hate and malice and a petty rage" (479). This is the book's vision: a profound revulsion at man as an alien in nature, appearing first in mock-heroic satire and finally in horror at diabolical inhumanity. It is more Gothic even than Hogg's in *The Justified Sinner*. There is little reason to see as social criticism what is clearly a theological revulsion.[10] Young Gourlay sees it: "The contrast between his own lump of a body, drink-dazed, dull-throbbing, and the warm bright day, came in on him with a sudden sinking of the heart, a sense of degradation and personal abasement. He realized, however obscurely, that he was an eyesore in nature, a blotch on the surface of the world, an offence to the sweet breathing heavens. And that bright silence was so strange and still. He could have screamed to escape it" (556). He finally does escape—from the horror of his own vision.

Why must the intensity of that vision be a curse? Because the vision itself is devastating, or because he is stupid and weak? The vision is bad enough, but the book expends much energy of hate on his stupidity and weakness, when they are simply the brute given of his fallen nature. The only valid response is the baker's, when told by Drucken Wabster's wife that he was throwing tumblers at his mother: "Puir body! puir body!" Why detest the equally helpless "bodies" of Barbie? "It was not the least of the evils caused by Gourlay's black pride that it perverted a dozen characters. The 'bodies' of Barbie may have been decent enough men in their own way, but against him their malevolence was monstrous" (416). Gourlay's is the chief diabolical presence. It is evident in "the score of wild devilries he began to practise on his son. Wrath fed and checked, in one, brings the hell on which man is built to the surface" (543). The hell on which man is built. Supremely possessed by a devil of malignity, Gourlay is transformed, beyond himself in his art of spite and cruelty.

Barbie is a grotesquely hellish vision, a view of human degradation, alienation, and malignity. It is hardly the vision of a naturalist, and not the vision one normally associates with the neo-Hellenic tragic image of man's dignity. The same strange mixtures characterize John MacDougall Hay's* *Gillespie.*

In his 1963 introduction, Robert Kemp sounds the anti-Kailyard keynote: "Not there were to be found the milky pages of *The Lilac Sun-Bonnet* or *Beside the Bonnie Brier Bush.* Instead, there was all manner of original sin and disastrous behavior. In a decent Scottish town people swore, drank, cheated and broke every other commandment with dour determination."[11] Quite so, but this is not the book's major concern. Hay felt that "the growing spirit of materialism in Scotland needed a *Gillespie*" (xiii). His attack on materialism and its

*Hay, John MacDougall. Born in 1881 at Tarbert, Argyllshire, and died in 1919 at Elderslie, Renfrewshire. After a brilliant undergraduate career in Arts at Glasgow University, he worked as a free-lance journalist and served as schoolmaster at Stornoway (Lewis) and Ullapool. Following a severe illness, he turned to the ministry, and in 1909 became minister of Elderslie (though he always wanted a Highland parish). He kept up his free-lance writing, however, and *Gillespie*, his astonishing first novel, would no doubt have brought even greater transatlantic recognition had it not appeared on the eve of World War I. His second novel, *Barnacles*, appeared in 1916, and late in the war he published *Their Dead Sons*, a volume of poems.

weak sister humanitarianism is mounted from a neo-Calvinist prophetic perspective. The book prophesies the divine vengeance that will
be frightfully visited on the person and the house of the soulless
capitalist—for that is what Gillespie is. And here one of the themes of
The House with the Green Shutters is noticeably reversed. Brown
shows the petty bodies helping to cause the downfall of the idolator.
Hay's governing theme is "Vengeance is mine, saith the Lord," and
Gillespie's victims and enemies must learn this. Those who set fire to
Gillespie's fishing fleet must discover that their vengeance simply
allows Gillespie to sell them new boats. Of those who seek vengeance
by bringing a headless corpse to Gillespie's warehouse, one drowns
and the other goes mad. Gillespie is so brilliant and unscrupulous in
his entrepreneurial tricks that he exploits each new resistance.

The end is part of the same warning. It demonstrates the magnitude
of divine vengeance and makes the end of Brown's *The House with the
Green Shutters* austerely tame by contrast. Indeed, all events in *Gillespie* are drawn with a terrific extravagance, and a verbosity alien to the
fine economy of *The House*. The final confrontation in *Gillespie* is between mother and son; the son is spiritually destroyed by the vision of
his mother's degradation. The final horrors—the son with his throat
cut, the guilty mother with her head smashed, and Gillespie, his foot
pierced with a fragment of the same murderous mutchkin, dying in
slow agony of lockjaw—are more than enough to prove that a terrible
law has worked itself out, that a terrible God has taken vengeance.
There is none of the pastoral awe that closes *The House* in a radiance
of remote natural innocence. Nature for Hay is violent, erratic, in
collusion with the amoral natural force of Gillespie.

What is that force and whence does it come? Gillespie springs virtually from nowhere, is drawn as a man without psyche, grows up
suddenly, ages abruptly. If he is, as his mother hints, the demonic
product of a divided lineage, why is there no internal instability in
him? Brown offers explicit cultural explanations for his characters.
After the opening, Hay scarcely suggests such dimensions. The small
west Highland port setting is massively particularized, but Gillespie's
capitalistic war with divine justice has little to do with social setting.
The end is rhetorically confused. Son confronts mother with, "Do you
believe in the judgment of God, in Hell?" and she responds, "Gillespie
Strang is hell" (423). Yet, says the narrator, "his fate deserves some
pity . . . He had been great in his activities, and in another sphere

would have played a large part . . . [A] giant, perishing in a mean hovel, is a more pitiable sight than that of the same man dying upon the stage of the world . . . Whoever has sympathy will recognise that he had a certain earnestness and vision" (437). This simply is not so. There is no hint that the little town constrains him. There is no hint that he is a giant, except in restless greed. There is little hint of earnestness and vision. Yet the narrator must make this appeal, since vengeance is God's and man can only pity.

It appears that in the face of an evil force such as Gillespie, we must feel charity and leave justice for God. Man is God's blindest creature because he thinks he can change things, conquer heredity, take vengeance. Earthly wisdom is "impoverished and futile" when "confronted with the satire of existence" (26). Gillespie is a neo-Calvinist test of the town's theology, an awful affront to its liberal sentiments. Mrs. Galbraith, for example, is "a woman who, by nature, found in every one something to appreciate; some gift, aptitude, or virtue. Gillespie had trailed humanity in the mire. Living so much on Thomas a Kempis, she could not conceive that a predatory beast inhabited a human frame . . . She was puzzled at the triumph of evil, at the suffering of the righteous" (74). Topsail Janet, the poor widow who becomes Gillespie's household slave, is also naive: "She believed in the compassion of God, in the kindliness of man" (113).

In short, as we consider *Gillespie* at the end of Scottish Victorianism, we recognize not so much a new modernist realism as a spectacular, and confused, mixture of a sort we have seen before: a mixture of elaborate local realism—of severe cultural criticism—with Gothic theological romance. It is the ferociously neo-Calvinist other side of George MacDonald. And together with its companion anti-Kailyard denunciations, it suggests that modern Scottish fiction, seeking a mode for the realistic portrayal of modern Scottish life, was still to have great difficulty escaping the persistent invitations of romance.

The
Persistence
of
Romance

8

Romance
after the
Enlightenment

At the opening of *The Dancing Floor* (1926), John Buchan's intriguing persona Sir Edward Leithen offers his own notion of romance as "something in life which happens with an exquisite aptness and a splendid finality, as if Fate had suddenly turned artist—something which catches the breath because it is so wholly right." In his essay on Sir Walter Scott, Buchan gives a somewhat different definition: "The kernel of romance is contrast, beauty and valour flowering in unlikely places, the heavenly rubbing shoulders with the earthly. The true romantic is not the Byronic hero; he is the British soldier whose idea of a *beau geste* is to dribble a football into the enemy's trenches."[1] Romance as an exceptional interlude in the reality of mundane life is an idea we have known since the Enlightenment. The novel began in parodic repudiation of romance, and the parodic strain is strong in Scott's novels as in other quixotic fiction of the late eighteenth century. But during the Romantic period—or what I call the counter-Enlightenment—novelists who found the norms of realism too restrictive began to reintroduce the motifs and expectancies of romance as a counterparody to challenge the aesthetic and even the metaphysical adequacy of the novel. The challenge has continued; the post-Enlightenment novel has evolved in a mixture of modes—realism and romance, and sometimes what Donald Fanger calls "romantic realism."[2]

Theory of fiction in our own time includes numerous redefinitions of romance and its relative modes, fantasy and myth.[3] The genre critic concedes that the novel's action is basically a reworking of romance patterns, and that older layers survive. The psychoanalytic critic holds that all literature is a transforming of primitive wishes and fears into meaningful form, that all fictional art has its "core of fantasy." The structuralist believes that mythologies are necessary instruments of cultural survival, and the mythic critic directs our attention to the very nature of fiction-making, suggesting that "the highest use of fiction is as a way of knowing and replenishing the consciousness of the mythic." And in the English-speaking world most of these critical schools have been influenced by the romance theory of Northrop Frye.

Frye's discriminations are useful for our purposes. He defines romance under three distinct heads: as mode, mythos, and genre.[4] As mode, romance relates the adventures of a hero superior in power to other mortals. As myth, romance traces the perilous quest through struggle to ritual death and triumphant reinstatement. As genre, romance represents personality not as a social mask but as an archetype in a setting of allegorical intensity. There is, for instance, a romance pattern shared by Scott and Stevenson. The hero is a bystander representative of the reader's normal reality. He is kidnapped into significant peril in a strange world dominated by romantic adventurers—in Scott, a world of quixotic activism, in Stevenson, a world of exhilarating sensation. But in genre, Scott and Stevenson are quite different; Stevenson saw Scott as a fuller realist, himself as an antirealist. Buchan differs from both in mode. His heroes are urbane escapists fleeing the ennui of the normal and assuming the roles of adventurers. In Neil Munro, on the other hand, the normal itself has faded with the marvelous into bitter melancholy, the romance mythos into tragic irony. Yet in all four, hero and adventurer come into close, affectionate, but finally unreal kinship. The final unreality of this kinship casts a strange light on the ostensible resolutions of Scottish romance.

Paul Zweig's recent book, *The Adventurer*, focuses on these two archetypal figures, the hero and the adventurer, and provides us with useful and applicable distinctions. The hero is the protector of the community's values; he possesses courage, loyalty, resourcefulness, and above all selflessness. The adventurer, on the other hand, "undermines the expected order."[5] He possesses the hero's qualities of skill, resourcefulness, and courage; but he is the opposite of selfless. He lives by action, sheer energy, in encounters with peril, outside of the spaces of normal civility. The adventurer's career demands that he "abandon himself to adventure—*ad venio*, 'whatever comes'—to be permanently available, his mind emptied of sequence like a Zen master's, at one with the heartbeat of the world, profoundly passive."[6] He is an escape artist, and vicariously through him we experience escape from the prison-world of convention and communality. The romance of adventure has timeless and universal human appeal.

Such indulgent redefinitions of romance are not likely to find much favor with modern Scottish critics. For them, it is understandably repellent to find Scotland, even in the 1970s, still dominant on the shelves of popular romance as a land of gothic cliche. For this notoriety, Scotland has paid and continues to pay too high a price. A colorful recent example of their protest is found in Tom Nairn's essay, "The Three Dreams of Scottish Nationalism," a diagnosis of Scotland's peculiar romantic intensity and of "the great significance of the country as a locale of the European romantic fancy."[7] Nairn sees Scotland as a country cheated and haunted by its past, yet preserving that past "as a dislocated and poignant inner reality" for a people "unable to forge valid correlates of their different experience." Behind Scotland's wary countenance he finds a dream-pathology of three parts: first, the abstract, millennial dream of the Reformation; second, a nationalistic romantic consciousness that could attach itself to no viable nationhood and thus became a possessing demon; third, contemporary nationalism. For Nairn, Scottish history is the story of a land "where ideal has never, even for an instant, coincided with fact." The persistence of romance becomes, then, a tragicomic necessity. And yet Scottish culture has for ages been fascinated with history and fiercely loyal to fact. So the romance that persists is likely to be a strange amalgam of history and escape from history, of passion for fact and addiction to dream that mocks that passion. It can be expected to underlay its intense adventures into national history with irony and even despair.

The critical question is not whether romance persists, but rather, in Richard Chase's words, "to what purpose have these amiable tricks of romance been used? To falsify reality and the human heart or to bring us round to a new, significant and perhaps startling relation to them?"[8] Chase's concern, of course, is with the necessary role of romance in the American novel. For American novelists, romance

145

seemed the best means for introducing into the novel "the narrow pro-
fundity of New England Puritanism, the skeptical, rationalistic spirit
of the Enlightenment, and the imaginative freedom of Transcendentalism."[9] Since all three elements have close counterparts in Scottish history (only recall the Calvinists, Hume, and Carlyle), it would seem
easy to translate Chase's hypothesis to a Scottish context and find a
rationale for romance more constructive than Nairn's. But Chase
could hardly accept such a translation. He denies the classification of
serious romance to the tradition of Scott and Stevenson because he associates them merely with the romanticizing of the past. The relation
of romance to history must be our chief concern here.

In Scottish fiction the prose romance and the historical novel came
into being together, and Scottish romance since then has carried the
ironic burden of the national past. "The Scots are pretty good at history," mused Neil Gunn, "which, perhaps, is why most of them mistrust it. For it is full of facts, most of them ugly."[10] What does one do
when one's history seems at once to harbor a rich, hereditary identity
and a memory of tragic futilities and mean betrayals? We can expect
ambiguities of mode and rhetoric. We can expect a fascination with
historic realities and at the same time a wish to be free of these realities, to transform them into legend. The Scottish romancer comes to
resemble the traditional storyteller, for whom the line between history and legend exists only to be blurred. The romancer does precisely
what the reader of novel and history is conditioned to resist: he mingles fact and fantasy, the givens of history with the projections of
imagination. It will not do to reassure the reader that all history is fiction, for he still knows that Prestonpans happened and that Waverley's participation in it did not, and that somewhere in between,
Prince Charles Edward may really have been as he seemed to Waverley, or that, if Prince Charles Edward and Fergus MacIver and Edward
Waverley are all "equally real," they are real in three quite different
ways, whereas Scott projects all three ways imaginatively as a single
reality.

The novelist in Scotland is closer than novelists in other cultures to
the storyteller and to the storyteller's relation to his audience. The
folkteller establishes history as a property of the collective imagination to which it pertains—the family, locality, class, or nation. Tradition is a shared property of teller and audience, recreated by the teller;
if the recreation is successful, the communal property may be altered

or enriched. The auditors, presumably aware already of the tradition, help from the start to sustain the storyteller's fiction, while in turn his fiction must sustain their support by meeting their demands for credence and form. John Buchan was optimistic about the novelist's ability to keep alive and draw on his kinship with the story teller.[11] We may come to share his optimism. Or we may come instead to agree with Walter Benjamin, for whom the "storyteller" and the novelist are basically at odds.[12] For Benjamin, the discontinuities of story and novel are what matter. The story offers information and practical counsel, not motive and explanation. It stresses incident, pacing, situation, and not character, ethos, psychology. The novel arises from and appeals to the solitary individual; the story is communal and traditional in origin, and its desired impact is communal absorption or impersonal enchantment. Benjamin's distinctions are similar to Stevenson's early "remonstrances" in defense of romance. If we come to sympathize with both, then we will see the persistence of romance in early modern Scotland as a resistance on behalf of a vigorous storytelling tradition to the English Victorian establishment of the social-psychological novel.

Alexander Welsh notes a crucial structural paradox in most of the Waverley novels. Edward Waverley awakens to find that his life has so far been romance, but that its real history is now to begin. The romance is not over, however, for the history is to be equally imaginary.[13] In fact, the romance has been an adventure in history; the real history is a retreat from historic experience. The mingling of romance and history in Scott defies simple categories. Robert Kiely wisely hedges on recent critical attempts to reject Scott's "romantic" label. "The point," he says, "is that there are two distinct tendencies in most of his novels and that one of them, despite efforts to change Scott's image, is romantic."[14] The tendencies are there; they are not always distinct.

The representative Waverley protagonist is a hero who is and is not an adventurer. He is not superior to other men and is not capable (in Frye's terms) of "prodigies of courage and endurance." Circumstance and instinct cause him for a time to move around in a world where history is infused with legend and folktale. Here, temporarily, the prudent, civil hero acquires the aspect of the adventurer, vicariously at least, through his encounters with historic figures. These figures are the adventurers.

For Scott they are figures of historic charisma and dangerous fatality—possessed, fey, often doomed, yet having the power to enchant
even doubtful devotees from across cultural and ideological barriers.
They are the characters of romance and at the same time they embody
the forces of history, yet they have no ultimate place in the "real history" of the hero. The ironic Scott—the one now called a realist—sees
them as unstable, reckless, quixotic; the romantic Scott, the storyteller, surrounds them in narrative with an aura of fatal pathos. Their
interest as the magnetic centers of adventure depends on the fatal influence they wield. They include Prince Charles in *Waverley*; Queen
Mary in *The Abbot*; King Richard in *Ivanhoe* and *The Talisman*; Bur-
gundy in *Quentin Durward* and *Anne of Geierstein* (and perhaps King
Louis as well); Cromwell in *Woodstock*; Charles II in *Woodstock* and
Peveril; Rob Roy; Burley and Claverhouse in *Old Mortality*; Count
Robert; Leicester in *Kenilworth*; Redgauntlet, and the very eccentric
adventurer James VI and I in *Nigel*.

The adventures of the heroes center on their relation to these powerful adventurers; their temporary roles of allegiance or discipleship
make them unique instruments of that power. However passive, they
are strangely susceptible to perilous entanglement with such figures
and powers; and this susceptibility becomes an essential part of their
own mysteries of identity and inheritance.

Their power is dual and paradoxical. They must be able to
surrender themselves, in the words of *Waverley*, to the full romance
of their situations. But at crucial points they must be heroes, able to
withhold that surrender and act as independent, morally responsible
agents. Until such a point, Waverley must play out his bewildering,
"strange, horrible, and unnatural dream." Darsie Latimer must follow
his dreamlike quest into the country of his adventurer-uncle to solve
the mystery of his own life, which is "like the subterranean river in the
Peak of Derby . . . I am here, and this much I know; but where I have
sprung from, or whither my course of life is like to tend, who shall tell
me?"[15] Henry Morton's ordeal is no less romantic: neglected, impoverished in fortune and spirit, he must play out his destined entanglement with fanatical adventurers, undergo exile and even supposed
death, and ultimately brave Burley in his infernal cave to win his true
station and freedom. In *Mannering*, the "harassed wanderer" is the
pawn and protégé of Mannering's temporarily hostile power; from
this fact arise "the strangeness of his destiny and the mysteries which

appeared to thicken around him, while he seemed alike to be persecuted and protected by secret enemies and friends."[16] The disinherited
Ivanhoe wonders, "It seems as if I were destined to bring ruin on
whomsoever hath shown kindness to me," yet he must remain faithful
to his fanatical father and his reckless king.[17] Durward, also disinherited, fulfills his own quest for home and stability by being true to the
Machiavellian king whose destiny is somehow "under the same con-
stellation" with "this unfriended youth." Similarly, Nigel's fortunes
are linked to those of the eccentric James, and his protest might be
voiced by all Waverley heroes: he has become "a mere victim," a
"thing never acting but perpetually acted upon," as "passive and helpless as a boat that drifts without oar or rudder"; and yet at last "he
must now be sufficient to himself or be utterly lost."[18] For Ravenswood there is no escape from the mysteriously fated role as adventurer that thwarts his every effort to play the prudent, civil hero.
Earnscliff, upon coming home, finds himself in the perilous world of
Waverley, Morton, and Ravenswood and must put on the same perilous, fictive role. Roland Graeme protests the same tyranny of circumstance that robs him of "free-will and human reason" and at the same
time gives him a unique role of romantic importance: "A land of enchantment have I been led into, and spells have been cast around me—
every one has met me in disguise—every one has spoken to me in par-
ables—I have been like one who walks in a weary and bewildering
dream."[19]

To what end? To history and historic inheritance, and the civil and
domestic responsibilities of the hero. Disinheritance is the given. The
disinherited hero must suffer an adventure of moral complicity with
his own divided past and become adventurer enough to play effective
mediator in his threatening present if he is to redeem his inheritance.
His problem is cultural and moral. His adventure is to discover and
then escape from the disorders and decadences of history and the menace of divisive fanaticisms in his own historic situation. This he must
do through realizing an independent but conciliatory loyalty to his
past and to what is most humane and salvageable in that past.

Waverley redeems and relocates his dishonored Waverley Honour.
Frank Osbaldistone must shed his arrogance and save his father, and
he does so through the exemplary piety and humane prudence of Nicol
Jarvie, that model of cultural conciliation. In *Mannering*, the Bertrams
have been disinherited by an erratic inhumanity, and Bertram can be

reinstated only through the loyal support of a gypsy and a sheepfarmer, representatives of fading traditions. In *The Antiquary*, two ancient houses are at a point of crisis, and only through the uncovering of the past's truth can reckless fatality be reversed, one lost heir legitimized to marry the other, and both houses saved. Henry Morton, trapped into loyalties that threaten to reenact in him his father's career, must play out the adventure of his complicity, yet transcend it by his humanity if he is to be the redeemer of Tillietudlem. *The Pirate* and *The Surgeon's Daughter* center on rival heirs; the preference for adventure, for a foolish romanticism over a prudent humanity, temporarily threatens cultural integrity and continuity. *The Fortunes of Nigel* commence with an inheritance mortgaged to the hilt, and the very unromantic Nigel must enter a world of moral peril to confront the only source of hereditary authority who can reinstate it. Young Peveril sees in the unlit beacon of Martindale Castle the end of his race, and he must save his naive father in a world of political madness if he is to relight it. Markham Everard in *Woodstock* must win his own place by restoring Sir Henry to Woodstock and King Charles to his true kingly self. The soldiers of fortune Quentin Durward and Hereweard the Saxon, both culturally disinherited, must employ old virtues in new and compromising allegiances, and thus win renewed inheritance. For some of the disinherited—Ravenswood, Tyrrel in *St. Ronan's Well*, the Children of the Mist in *Montrose*, the MacGregors—no renewed inheritance is possible. But these are the tragic exceptions.

In general, Scott's romance expresses an optimistic Unionist ideology—a message of conciliation and restoration. His successors are more tragic and ironic, more escapist, or all three.

In the later nineteenth century, two traditions in Scottish romance can be distinguished by comparing James Grant's* *The Scottish Cavalier* (1850) and S. R. Crockett's *The Raiders* (1893). The first is

---

*Grant, James. Born in 1822 in Edinburgh, and died in 1887 (in London?). Of an old Jacobite family, related to Sir Walter Scott, Grant resigned his army commission to work for an Edinburgh architect. Moving to London, he became secretary of the National Association for the Vindication of Scottish Rights. He published some fifty novels (see, in addition to the book mentioned here, *Adventures of an Aide-de-Camp*, 1848, *Bothwell*, 1854, and *The Yellow Frigate*, 1855) and a number of biographies and histories.

clearly in the earlier Scott manner (perhaps with an obligation to Bulwer); the other is evidently Stevensonian. Grant's novel is set—massively, documentarily set—in 1688, Scott's kind of epoch, the final stages of the "killing times" when a cruel cavalierism was pitted against remnants of covenanting fanaticism. Yet the descriptive fullness of place and circumstance belongs to the Victorian manner of Thackeray and Eliot. The omniscient historical narrator is in control of the narrative and offers it to a Victorian reader as illustrative of a specific past. The hero is a Waverley variant, the orphan whose identity is doubtful, the cinderella cavalier of presbyterian heritage, whose chivalry permits the presbyterian Napier ladies to escape and who then is saved himself by Clavers. The interest is predominantly pathetic and antiquarian, rather than thematic: there is far more history and historic milieu, and yet less historical interpretation, than in Scott. And this is just one of the differences that suggest why the Scott manner in historical romance could not survive in an age of historical positivism.

The hero Walter Fenton lacks the reflective, divided consciousness of the bewildered, disoriented Scott hero. Yet the rendition of contemporary Edinburgh is densely particular; we are given a detailed model of late seventeenth-century Edinburgh—the dark crowded closes and wynds off the High Street, the Cowgate, the North Loch, St. Cuthbert's, and the Water of Leith with Drumsheugh perched over it. Every city structure has its windows and prospects; each new locale occasions a new genre piece of manners; the abundant nocturnal movements in time of intrigue and crisis permit a rich imaginative rendition of the city. This is not so much the romance of adventure as the romance of picturesque panorama. The hero's impressions are not there to provide access; we sense ourselves at a distance from this hideous, packed, and dangerous place, while the people alive in it are themselves moving against backgrounds ancient and threatening.

There is missing, also, an essential romance perspective that we associate with Scott and, differently, with Stevenson: a sense of contrast between the normal or mundane—"real history"—and the dangerous allurements of the adventurous. Such a sense appears only in the uncertain nostalgia of older characters for past persons and events. Otherwise, this is merely history romanticized, with few ordeals of allegiance or deeply felt cultural dilemmas. Yet—and this is another difference—the narrator is consistently elegiac and committed to a

historic cause. The scenes of exile at St. Germain are moving; the end
is wholly tragic. The final sympathy for the cavalier and the bitter
hatred of a Scotland disloyal to her kings are unmistakable. *The Scottish Cavalier* is an unflinchingly Jacobite novel, the kind one would
expect from a founder of romantic mid-Victorian nationalism.[20] Such
a radical shift of ideology from Scott's was bound to alter the Scott
manner considerably; and yet it is the Scott manner still.

For Grant, history is a tragic betrayal, a dead end. For Crockett,
history is the threat of mundane reality, of growing up. *The Raiders* is
done in first-person sensuous impressionism with a Stevensonian lilting quasi-Scots—a "style" in the late-Victorian sense. History has
given way to adventure, to local legend, the fabulous and the humorous mixed. There is full sensuous stress on the adventure of place; in
Crockett we recognize that Stevenson's poetry of circumstance is primarily a poetry of space rather than time. *The Raiders* might be a *Kidnapped* or *Treasure Island*, a *John Burnet of Barns* or *John Macnab*,
with its map design, its game of hunting over closely identified terrain,
its adventures of flight, pursuit, sanctuary, and hiding. The essential
authentication comes when the hero-narrator assures the reader that
he may verify the story's truth by going to the place, and that his purpose is to correct local memory from its wild legends: "It is necessary
that ere the memory quite die out, some one of us who saw these
things should write them down."[21]

The Raiders is suitably impressionistic then; Scott's local antiquarian intention has found a fitting style. The sensuous immediacy depends often on an effect crucial to Scottish romance: the perspectivist
contrast Daiches and Wittig find so pervasive from Dunbar to Stevenson, the cozy interior against the cold blast, the sense of domesticity as
shelter: "It is hard to make any who did not see it, believe in what we
saw that night. Indeed, in this warm and heartsome winter room, with
the storm without, and the wife in bed crying at me to put by the
writing and let her get to sleep, it is well-nigh impossible to believe
that any of these things came to pass within the space of a few years.
Yet so it was. I who write it down was there" (121). There has been no
doubt of it. The style repeatedly evokes the immediacy of the adventurer as observer: "I get down by the water's edge, for I am pushing on
all the time, I hear my feet crash on the shingles" (119).

Yet the very intensity is surreal, for this awareness is what is elegized. *The Raiders* is a romance of *past* exhilaration and strangeness, a strangeness that is not historic but subjective. Its "time past" is a world that is preadult, predomestic, prelegal: "It was with me the time of wild oat sowing when the blood ran warm. Also there were the graceless, unhallowed days after the Great Killing, when the saints of God had disappeared from the hills of Galloway and Carrick, and when the fastnesses of the utmost hills were held by a set of wild cairds"(21). It was a time of mischief and mythic loyalties; the mood of fun in *The Raiders* ebulliently emasculates the blood, violence, fear, and suffering. The hero can as yet afford to be "pure" adventurer; he is a boy-man teamed up with other boys on a fabulous free island menaced by pirates. We are as close to *Peter Pan* as to *Kidnapped*, and we glimpse their kinship. In a way Crockett follows the pattern of *Rob Roy*, allying his hero with a legendary, virtuous outlaw (John Faa), who has been cut off from his band and yet serves still as agent of natural justice in the countryside. In a way he follows the *Kidnapped* motif in the relations between them: young Patrick Heron loyal to the outlawed gypsy king, fighting and hiding with him. We might call *The Raiders* a Stevensonian romance of adventure, and then judge that subgenre accordingly.

And this would not be fair. For by the time Crockett was imitating his idea of the early Stevenson, Stevenson himself had changed.

9

Stevenson, Munro, and Buchan

T he change in Stevenson* can be misunderstood if we attend too rigorously to the apologetics of romance that Stevenson offered in critical essays published before *Kidnapped*. The essays do suggest, however, where he thought he began. The 1874 essay "Victor Hugo's Romances" sounds the keynotes. Fundamental is its distinction between drama and narrative romance, and fundamental to this distinction is the idea that narrative surrenders the immediacy and "vividness" of drama in return for a "power over the subject," a "texture" of continuity, a "complicated and refined" unity of impression and effect. These are possible to a method where "nothing is reproduced to our senses directly," but everything has "been put through the crucible of another man's mind." The history of modern romance is seen as an advance from Fielding, who wrote in the spirit of drama, whose characters were set in "unnatural isolation" and

---

Stevenson, Robert Louis. Born in Edinburgh in 1850 and died in Samoa in 1894. Stevenson attended Edinburgh University, then studied law and "passed advocate" in 1875. Ill health led to frequent travels, first to the Continent, then to America (1879), and to writings such as *Travels with a Donkey* (1879). Essays, sketches, and short stories were contributed to *Cornhill* and other magazines and collected in *Virginibus Puerisque* (1881) and *Familiar Studies of Men and Books* (1882). His poetry for children appeared in *A Child's Garden of Verses* (1885) and for adults in *Underwoods* (1887). *Treasure Island* (1883) made him famous. *The Master of Ballantrae* (1889) was written during his months at Lake Saranac, New York. In 1890 he settled in Samoa.

moved by "a few simple personal elements," to Scott, Hugo, and Hawthorne, who achieved the impressionistic unity of narrative and whose characters are reduced to fit into "the constitution of things," qualified by "subtle influences," subordinated to "the action and reaction of natural forces."[1] The phrases show that Stevenson saw modern romance as a sophisticated and subtle genre.

The "Gossip on Romance" (1882) and its sequel, "A Humble Remonstrance" (1884), develop and modify the position. Stevenson's best-known critical paragraph is in the first. Here he associates drama with conduct, activity, moral will, and hence "character" in the ethical sense; whereas romance is associated with "brute incident," the pleasures of passive surrender to circumstance and surroundings, the amoral and practical.[2] In the "Remonstrance" he acknowledges the novel of character, but speaks as advocate for the novel of adventure as more fixed in the "charm of circumstance," the secret of "the art of narrative." Such true art pretends to no illusions of reality, but seeks "to obey the ideal laws of the day-dream." It differs from life by virtue of being "neat, finite, self-contained, rational, flowing and emasculate." It is to be judged not "by its exactitude," but as "a simplification of some side or point of life, to stand or fall by its significant simplicity."[3]

Yet, paradoxically, this "rational" and "emasculate" art "appeals to certain almost sensual and quite illogical tendencies in man." Paradoxically, while the artist's method is "to half-shut his eyes against the dazzle and confusion of reality," the effect for the reader is to "plunge into the tale in our own person and bathe in fresh experience." Escape from reality is an access to the immediacy of experience. It "woos us out of our reserve." It does so by eluding the ethical and cognitive barrier of "particular" character in preference for the "abstract," the puppet-like character through whom we can enter circumstance and incident directly. For Stevenson, circumstance is a place to be entered; the poetry of circumstance is the romance of place. There must be "a fitness in events and places." Places speak of events; stories express the meaning of places, adventures justify places, narrative can "make a country famous with a legend." The aesthetic end to which the "charm of circumstance" and "brute incident" are the means is really immersion in the atmospheric impression of a place. And however much Stevenson emphasizes "fit and striking incident," his emphasis is stronger still on the subjective "quality" or "fitness" imparted in "the emphasis and the suppressions with which the human actor tells of them." Character must not intervene between reader and "fresh experience," but the unity and power of narrative impression demand a personal impressionist center as narrator.[4]

So much for the paradoxical theoretical background to the early romances. There is no reason to think it did not alter later. There is no reason to suppose that such theory must produce mere "boy's daydreams." What may appear as a theoretical commitment to simplicity is like Stevenson's thematic concern with "the unsophisticated": both are elusive ideals.

In *Treasure Island*, as in later more "adult" books, he presents a seemingly unsophisticated hero who becomes implicated in a curiously mixed, dangerous fidelity to an amoral adventurer. Daiches rightly finds here the "highly sensitive moral pattern" through which Stevenson explores the "desperate ambiguity of man as a moral animal."[5] Some readers find no serious morality, no psychology, only boy's game-playing in *Treasure Island*.[6] But game-playing can be fraught with moral implications; evil in romance need not be presented psychologically. There is a psychology in *Treasure Island*, not so much of evil as of infatuation with evil. This psychology is at the center of Stevenson's image of the unsophisticated and its perilous adventure.

Adventure in *Treasure Island* includes atmosphere and suspense, and the only true suspense is not the whereabouts of the treasure—this is no problem—but the problem of knowing Long John Silver. From our point of view, Silver is no heroic villain or angel-devil; he is a comic adventurer. For Jim, however, he is a moral enigma, and Jim becomes puzzled by him and responsible for him, his destroyer and savior. At first, Jim cannot believe him evil: "I would have gone bail for the innocence of Long John Silver".[7] He has feared him as an amoral force of nature: "On stormy nights, when the wind shook the four corners of the house, and the surf reared along the cove and up the cliffs, I would see him in a thousand forms, and with a thousand diabolical expressions." Jim is repeatedly at hand to see Silver's cruelty or violence; he is maneuvered into being in the enemy camp to watch Silver's struggle to keep power:

Heaven knows I had matter enough for thought . . . in the remarkable game that I saw Silver now engaged upon—keeping the mutineers together with one hand, and grasping, with the other, after every means, possible and impossible, to make his peace and save his miserable life. He himself slept peacefully, and snored aloud; yet my heart was sore for him, wicked as he was, to think on the dark perils that environed, and the shameful gibbet that awaited him. [148]

Yet Silver the adventurer will survive, for survival is what he represents—the code of the adventurer, courage, shrewdness, endurance. Maimed but resilient, he is the amoral force outside of the snug inn, the life of adventure beyond the dull world. Jim may come to feel "a horror of his cruelty, duplicity, and power" (63). But Silver is already a "personage" haunting Jim's dreams; and when at last Jim says, "That formidable seafaring man with one leg has at last gone clean out of my life"(173), we doubt it. Jim has learned to act with the adventurer's own brave duplicity and shrewdness—indeed, there has been all along something of the adventurer in Jim. Silver recognizes the kinship. Jim is fanciful and ingenious; it is Jim who overhears, goes ashore, finds Gunn, saves the ship. His conscience troubles him, but he revels in his courage; he is playing a boy's game, but in so doing he is proving the power of the unsophisticated. If this is a boy's day-dream, it is the stuff that dreams of adult adventure are often made of.

If Silver is the central enigma, Jim is the protagonist, the hero, and to confuse the two is to partake of the error of Jim's own fascination. The lasting sadness at the end of this book, and of *Kidnapped* (1886) as well, is the realization that the hero cannot be the amoral adventurer of his fancy and affection.

The bond between David Balfour and Alan Breck is very different in many ways, but it ends the same way: the hereditary hero has much to learn from the adventurer, and may even acquire a strange longing for him, but at last the adventurer must recede into ineffectual exile. The bond puzzles them both and saves both their lives. On one level, it reflects their cultural representativeness: one the pious, aggressive Lowland Whig, the other the proud, whimsical Highland Jacobite. On another level, such considerations—paramount in Scott—matter little beside the fact that one of them must assume the role of hereditary hero while the other has no choice but to remain a homeless adventurer. Yet their mutual respect and affection, their wits and endurance, bring them safely in flight through the wilderness, past hostile troops and clans, to the ambivalent resolution where the hero recovers his bourgeois inheritance in Queensferry and the adventurer prepares to escape to France.

Historic reality is essential and yet peripheral. The perils of their adventures derive from a historic assassination, and they encounter historic figures. Yet their adventures are remote from history. Topography is the pervasive reality. Their adventures are mapped in detail; they are never lost. But it is the physical impression of place and movement that matters. Stevenson wrote Colvin (in May 1892), "With all my romance, I am a realist and a prosaist, and a most fanatical lover of plain physical sensations plainly and expressly rendered," and in that spirit, he recalls, he rendered "D. Balfour's fatigue in the heather."[8] The passages of physical anguish and exhaustion are unforgettable: "birstling" like "scones upon a girdle" under the summer sun in a saucer of rocks; crawling in stooped posture endless miles; "the aching and faintness of my body, the labouring of my heart, the soreness of my hands, and the smarting of my throat and eyes in the continual smoke of dust and ashes";[9] reliving horrid images amid the rain and mud, with teeth chattering and a painful stitch in the side. Such sensations give intense and immediate reality to place and motion; there is no place for moral reflection. In this sense the adventure might seem "emasculate," the protagonists might seem to be without psyches.

But the psychic forces are there in David's strange, erratic moods. The mood word of insistent recurrence is "horror." It is David's "horror of despair," what he calls "groundless horror and distress of mind," a nightmarish "general, black, abiding horror," that is persistent. He feels it even when he is physically safe: a horror of solitude, a horror at wickedness and violence, "a darkness of despair and a sort of anger against all the world."[10] A sickening unto death, it still produces a kind of existential courage. It is no clear correlate of the sheer physical intensity of David's circumstances, but rather a mystery of his piety of character. It is the undercurrent to his endurance and to his deep attachment to Alan, the shape of his uncertain longing for Alan's unsophisticatedness. For Alan labors under no such moods; his states are best suggested by the "kind of dancing madness" David first sees in his eyes, the weird mixture of ecstasy, vanity, and love Alan feels at the height of violence, the fanatical simplicity with which Alan would die for "morals" that seem to David "all tail-first."

And here is the key to the romance. The boy of the daydream is

David; yet David is the hero, bearing a heavy weight of moral tradition, the heir who must suffer and endure to reclaim the inheritance given away by a quixotic father to the mean, destructive evil of David's uncle. His ordeal is the wilderness of savage physical sensations, and Alan's role is virtually that of savage guide. Alan becomes an amoral force for survival, and his seemingly amoral simplicity fascinates and angers David. Thus, while David has the adventures, Alan is the adventurer; and because David is caught up in the adventurer's adventures, he must compromise his own civil code and take on the amoral wildness of the adventurer to come into his own conventional inheritance. It is Alan who, at last, plays the trickster at Ebenezer's door, just as it was David who, on the amoral ship *Covenant*, saved the adventurer's life. In a situation of such moral and cultural confusion, each needs the other.

This is not to say they are psychic "doubles."[11] Their bond is sadly circumstantial. At the end there is a terrible sadness, a sense of the impossible—and here is a basic ideological difference between Scott and Stevenson, and perhaps an underlying cause of the horror. David and Alan can be brothers only in circumstance; there is no place for Alan in David's inheritance—he must remain the fugitive and exile to the end. One of the book's finest touches is its equivocal ending: the unexplained "cold gnawing in [David's] inside like a remorse for something wrong" as "the hand of Providence" brings him to the door of the bank. The strange intensities that haunt the hero throughout are never formulated as adult ethical issues; they are nonetheless pervasive. When they are explicitly confronted through the bitter dilemmas of Prestongrange in that more "adult" book *Catriona*, the result is far weaker as art. Henry James said that Stevenson "is an artist accomplished even to sophistication, whose constant theme is the unsophisticated."[12] Perhaps the older Stevenson was too pressured by sophisticated friends, for he let the "unsophisticated" dwindle from an intense and disturbing consciousness into a theme.

Stevenson criticism now divides between two attractive options: the view of Stevenson the arrested boy daydreamer who erratically grew up, and the view of Stevenson the Gothic moral psychologist who found his mature patterns and motifs early and persisted in them. Critics of the former persuasion assign books of the *Black Arrow* sort to immaturity and "tushery," while critics of the latter persuasion are tempted to find Dick Shelton to be a nineteenth-century Hamlet, caught in a "double" duplicity with Dickon Crookback (Shakespeare's Gloucester), incapable of action in a world where justice and honor are nowhere, evil is everywhere, and survival demands a constant swithering of loyalties.[13] It is significant for an understanding of Stevenson that he produced in *The Black Arrow* (1888) a light-toned, rapid-paced boy's pot-boiler—one he grew to despise himself—that is so mixed as to invite both kinds of critical extravagance.

Stevenson's biographer, J. C. Furnas, the book's most judicious critic, recognizes that "the thing is by no means altogether hackery," and that the "troubled and troubling moralist insinuates himself."[14] The insinuation is curiously oblique; it is as if Stevenson set out to prove that he could emasculate and render as pure adventure a world of bloody violence, frightful errors, and reckless ambiguity, and gradually discovered, through the growing reflectiveness of his boy-hero, that the dark and confused morality of his romance could not be eluded after all. Thus, while *The Black Arrow* cannot justify close examination, it at least suggests why the theorist of the "Gossip" and the "Remonstrance" discovered that his darkly ironic matter simply would not fit the manner of pure adventure, and turned to the less "pure" art of *The Master of Ballantrae* and *Weir of Hermiston*.

One can see the process in *Catriona* (1893),* the return of the kidnapped heir after *The Master*. The narrative picks up the moment when *Kidnapped* left off, yet Balfour has become quite sophisticated; unpolished still, but bravely ethical in a world where simplicity and innocence are duped and endangered, and where a desperate realpolitik not only forestalls David's efforts to see justice done, but is more or less understood and half accepted by him. Thwarted as he is, David has become a more active hero, and in this sense he is less romantic than the willingly passive romance hero. The more romantic problem is not David's but Catriona's. David recognizes her problem as an extraordinary and dangerous innocence, which in a corrupt and compromised world isolates her and immobilizes David. Her innocence provides a strange, alienated idealism at the center of this argumentative and ironic book.

Ironic it is—bitterly ironic in its view of political history, and ironic in mode. Physical adventure is minimal; the perils in *Catriona* are daunting moral compromises: "Peril of slavery, peril of shipwreck,

*Published in the United States as *David Balfour*.

peril of sword and shot, I had stood all these without discredit; but the peril there was in the sharp voice and the fat face of Simon, properly Lord Lovat, daunted me wholly."[15] The peril is worsened when David discovers willing compromise even in himself. Of physical sensation there is little. Henry James complained that the book subjected his seeing imagination to "an almost painful underfeeding," but it is picturesque enough, set mostly in and about Edinburgh. The senses of touch, taste, and smell are the ones starved, and fittingly so, since the adventures are mostly intellectual and moral. The book is deeply divided between the exuberant, juvenile intensity of its romantic love interest, and the dour, argumentative quality of its cynical political morality. To read the book properly in its odd mixture, one should recognize that the political interest dominates the first two-thirds, while the love interest is central only in the final one-third. David ends in total disgust with politics, and he ends the love story whimsically with a coy reference to the "funny business" of man's life and the laughter of the angels as they look on.

Catriona is far from the most interesting feature of David's adventures. The book's most powerful and persuasive figure is the Lord Advocate Grant of Prestongrange. Prestongrange replaces Alan in the book as a counterforce to David's brave and pious civility. Alan provided the fascination of a faithful but amoral natural force; Prestongrange is the opposite extreme, the over-civilized Machiavellian protector-father: "I think shame," says David, "to write of this man that loaded me with so many goodnesses. He was kind to me as any father, yet I ever thought him as false as a cracked bell" (176). Prestongrange is character of the kind excluded from Stevenson's earlier adventure novels. His influence places David far more in the bewildering role of the Scott protagonist than in the earlier role of adventurer-hero. His vigorous, and surprisingly equal, debates with David remind us of the Grand Inquisitor, and he is equally unanswerable. He anticipates the father-judge of *Weir of Hermiston*, and David survives to moderate his reckless idealism with a grudging respect for the tough pragmatism of the older man. In a world under such controls, the romance of winning Catriona must seem insulated and domestic.

Before turning back to *The Master*, we can glimpse the final state of Stevensonian adventure in the fragmentary *St. Ives*.[16] Stevenson dictated it in alternation with *Weir* in his final months, and it reveals how uninterested he had finally become in what he had done so brilliantly in *Kidnapped*. It is all escape, hide and seek, episodic encounter and peril, with a romantic French adventurer—a Napoleonic soldier-aristocrat imprisoned in Regency Britain—at its center. "It is," wrote Stevenson to Colvin (June 18, 1894), "a mere tissue of adventures; the central figure not very well or very sharply drawn; no philosophy, no destiny, to it; some of the happenings very good in themselves, I believe, but none of them *bildende*, none of them constructive, except in so far perhaps as they make up a kind of sham picture of the time, all in italics and all out of drawing." The vignettes of Regency Edinburgh are colorful but superficial.

It is symptomatic that the serious romance note is sounded only when St. Ives warns his new man-servant Rowley of the perils of accompanying him north again to Edinburgh: "I am in peril, homeless, hunted. I count scarce anyone in England who is not my enemy. From this hour I drop my name, my title; I become nameless; my name is proscribed. My liberty, my life, hang by a hair. The destiny which you will accept, if you go forth with me, is to be tracked by spies, to hide yourself under a false name, to follow the desperate pretences and perhaps share the fate of a murderer with a price upon his head" (207). But Rowley has been bred to a "secret cultus for all soldiers and criminals," and delights "to live by stratagems, disguises, and false names, in an atmosphere of midnight and mystery, so thick you could cut it with a knife" (208). In fact, St. Ives is too careless and Gallic (or "daft") an adventurer to manage such an atmosphere. Their adventures are more comic picaresque than romantic; the gruesome alternates with the slapstick and pathetic. A violent mixture of moods is characteristic of Stevenson; but here he had the formula of romantic adventure fully in mind and no serious interest in carrying it out. The ironic undercutting of romance is epitomized when St. Ives returns to his beloved's window in Swanston Cottage and a betrothal is proposed and accepted under the downpour of a faulty gutter. The very different impulse of *Weir* now held sway. *The Master of Ballantrae* (1889) had already altered Stevenson's notion of romance and, ironically, brought it closer to Scott's.

The Master is Stevenson's most interesting and easily misunderstood adventurer. He can be seen as the idolatrous old servant Mackellar sees him: a beautiful, accomplished devil. "Hell may have noble flames. I have known him a score of years, and always hated, and always admired, and always slavishly feared him."[17] Stevenson seems to have been haunted by the ideas of election and damnation, and he did say that the Master had all he knew about the devil. The Master is foolishly loved by the duped Alison; and the working of a false vision of his evil in his brother Henry's mind helps to make Henry, as Walter Allen claims, "one of the most absorbing psychological studies of degradation in our fiction."[18] But the Master of Ballantrae is no epic figure, no lost barbaric giant, no demonic hero, no Heathcliff or Ahab (he has been called all these things). To grant his evil such stature is to commit the idolatry that deludes Mackellar, degrades poor Henry, infatuates Alison, and destroys the House of Durrisdeer. He is a hollow adventurer, "a footpad that kills an old granny," a seeker after dirty money, a vulgar confidence man whose power is derived from scandal and blackmail. As Daiches says, he is Long John Silver "given psychological reality and subtlety."[19] Through him Stevenson is diagnosing the idolatry of devil-worship as a form of cultural suicide. "It is certain," Stevenson wrote in an essay, "we all think too much of sin . . . To make our idea of morality center on forbidden acts is to defile the imagination and to introduce into our judgments of our fellowmen a secret element of gusto."[20] *The Master of Ballantrae* may recall Scott's *Redgauntlet* and *Bride of Lammermoor*, but its closer kinship is with the Blackwoodians, their ironic diabolism, and their preoccupation with cultural idolatry.

The psychology of evil, as in *Kidnapped*, centers not in the adventurer, but in what happens to the pious, civilized hero when he becomes infatuated with the adventurer. Henry goes wrong, says Eigner, when he accepts James as the projection of his own evil; he cannot live with his vision of evil and makes Dr. Jekyll's mistake. "Henry is particularly dangerous, for, like Victor Frankenstein and the other justified sinners, he has set out piously on a holy war to destroy his devil."[21] His vision has become an idolatry. Eigner is right. If Henry as hero is weak and foolish, his weakness is part of his significance; a surprisingly common device in Scottish romance is to present as tragic hero one who is ironically helpless. He is helpless because the House of Durrisdeer cannot be saved. It is corrupted by vanity and idolatry and hopelessly divided as a result of its historic errors. Scottish romance often sets a tale of domestic betrayal and decay against a background of historic betrayal and futility. That is where it begins, with the absurd and dangerous futility of Prince Charles and the '45. History is not the villain; the house is doomed by its own folly. Furnas's summary makes this clear: "A father and two sons allow political and dynastic considerations to align them in positions false to all three. Exploiting this falseness with exquisite skill and malice, the elder and stronger brother destroys all three. There is no pseudo-Greek tinkering with Destiny. The original decision is responsibly made, bitterly italicized at the time by the younger: 'If we were playing a manly part, there might be sense in such talk. But what are we doing? Cheating at cards!' "[22] The rest is all a matter of reputation, a mere idea. The Master has the last word: he and Mackellar have a "common strain"; they "both live for an idea." Both are false, and between them poor Henry tries to live for his love, is degraded into the same idolatry, and is destroyed. This is ironic romance indeed, yet it is Stevenson's most mature romance.

A "pure hard crystal, my boy," wrote Henry James, "a work of ineffable and exquisite art." André Gide had trouble finishing it: "Odd book in which everything is excellent, but heterogeneous to such a degree that it seems the sample card of everything in which Stevenson excels."[23] Some have seen the book as broken-backed, at conflict with itself. Stevenson himself saw a conflict between the "fantastic elements" and the "genuine human problem." Perhaps he did shy away from his own tragic imagination. Or perhaps there is no consistent tragic mode or consistent realism in *The Master*, and what Stevenson could not face was the degree to which a blasting irony pervades the tragic. Whatever the explanation the "swithering of modes" is one more evidence of what Stevenson himself had recognized and Zabel called the conflict of "the realist and the fabulist" in his talent. It is the same odd heterogeneity—realism and fantasy, tragedy and irony —that pervades Scottish romance.

It is even more prominent, and I would say more conscious, in the romancer whose inspiration seems to have been the Stevenson of *The Master*, Neil Munro.* One critic treats Munro as a Stevenson of the Celtic Twilight and another sniffs at him as the Scott tradition going

*Munro, Neil. Born in 1864 in Inveraray, Argyllshire, Munro came from a line of farmers and shepherds attached to the Clan Campbell, and never lost his nostalgia for the southwest Highlands. After several years as a law clerk, he became a journalist in 1881 and worked for Glasgow newspapers until shortly before his death in Helensburgh, Dunbartonshire, in 1930. He began writing short stories early, including the humorous Para Handy tales and those collected in *The Lost* bad,[24] yet his finest work, *The New Road*, is a work of sustained art Stevenson could not manage and is perhaps the finest Scottish historical romance between Scott and Naomi Mitchison's *The Bull Calves*. Neil Munro is remembered in Scottish fiction as the author of humorous Para Handy tales. "His heart and genius," writes George Blake, who knew him, "were in the writing of romances, and yet his instinct and his talent were for journalism." He was never, insists Blake, the "solemn romanticist"; yet "Neil Munro lurked shy and sensitive behind the protective barrier of laughter and chaff set up by his *alter ego*."[25] Munro would not admit his romantic attachment to his native countryside of Inveraray, but chose instead to mock the romantic spirit. He saw in the fin de siècle Gaelic imagination a softness of blight and rot. The result is devastatingly ironic romance.

For example, *Doom Castle*, a novel whose title suggests stereotypes of mood and motif that belie its sophistication, is over-rich in romance qualities. There is the Gothic of the mysterious, demoniac castle, the erotic of the mysterious lady and her secret lover, the pastoral of beloved home countryside, the historic pathos of the ruined family, its "secrecy and decay" in sustained contrast to the prosperous orderliness of Argyle's castle. The hero, Count Victor of Montaiglon, seeks romance as an escape from the tawdriness of France and the dullness of civility, and his mission is a romantic adventure: to find and punish the spy who betrayed and caused the death of a lady Count Victor had loved. But the romance he finds is largely in his mind; he is a quixotic hero involved in various ludicrous situations and misapprehensions.

Romance and antiromance are in close, uneasy juxtaposition. From the outset Victor's expectations are played against a background of illusion. He comes at once into "a country of marvels and dreads," a country of dirty bandits and mean danger. He comes expecting chivalry and sees instead a squat, grotesque ruin on an island. At certain times and moods the castle appears to have something archaic and sinister about it, but its mysterious baron's mystery turns after all on the fact that he plays at masquerade in his garret with outlawed dress and arms and keeps his daughter locked in an upper chamber to prevent her affair with a gallant he does not like.

Pibroch (1896). He then turned to historical romance, and later and less effectively to more contemporary novels such as *The Daft Days* (1907) and *Fancy Farm* (1910). The best of these is *Gilian the Dreamer* (1899).

The gallant is the counterprotagonist, Simon McTaggart, Argyle's chamberlain and factor, whom one suspects early to be the spy Victor seeks. McTaggart is no simple villain, no adventurer in the mode of the Master of Ballantrae. For he is presented repeatedly as wearing "some odd air of mystery and romance," as being a "creature of romance and curious destiny," as sensing sadly the thwarted nobility of his life. At the end, with a searing fatalism "he saw himself plainly for what he was in truth—a pricked bladder; his career come to an ignoble conclusion, the single honest scheme he had ever set his heart on brought to nought."[26] He has been, like Munro's John Splendid, involved in the commerce and legalism of a modern dispensation. He is pursued lustfully by a groveling attorney's wife, Kate Petullo, a small-town Argyllshire Emma Bovary. But the Baron of Doom's daughter, trysting with the same gallant, does not seem too different from Kate Petullo.

In a world, then, of complex grotesquerie, we see various thwarted or disillusioned romantic personalities yearning pathetically for a lost nobility. We find Jacobites worshipping a lost homeland while Victor knows from St. Germains what a tawdry business Jacobitism in exile is. We hear Victor laugh at the ambiguous reality of his plight and regret his quixotic mission. We see hints that behind the facade of law and order lurk a pathetic romanticism and a possibility of archaic violence. Yet there is romance here, in thwarted potentialities of nobility, idealism, and passion. It is the modern world of Munro's *Gilian the Dreamer* set back in time.

An odd romanticism of character is even more central in *John Splendid* (1898). Munro calls it a "winter tale," and the history behind the romance is the devastation of the Lorn homeland by Montrose. Melancholy has replaced bitterness; the elegiac keynote is that "the essence of all human melancholy is in the sentiment of farewells."[27] Some elude it by remaining rootless. But the sense of farewell or imminent exile can come in the midst of life's merriment, and with it the sudden chilling notion of "life's brevity." The sense of romance for the narrator is an abrupt musing in the midst of adventure on the mysterious sadness of life. What is distinctive about experience in the book is, in fact, the abrupt juxtaposition of intense and immediate perceptions with tranquil, melancholy retrospects, which make the most vivid perceptions somewhat grotesque. On one page it will be: "Sitting cosy in taverns with friends long after, listening to men singing in the cheery way of taverns . . . I could weep and laugh in turns minding of yon winter's day" (84), and on the next: Splendid, "his eyes flashing wild upon the scene, the gristle of his red neck throbbing." The strange vividness of a present image suddenly recedes into a long remembered past and takes on a quality both elegiac and ironic, with no counterpart in Scott or Stevenson. For example, Elrigmore the melancholy, pacific narrator-hero and John Splendid the adventurer are helping defend a hill fortress near Inveraray. An enemy scout has been shot down at the edge of the wood. The narrator watches the man below as he "writhed to his end with a red-hot coal among his last morning's viands." From this empathic close-up of pain the next paragraph shifts in perspective: "Long after, it would come back to me, the oddity of that spectacle in the hollow—a man in a red fealdeag, with his hide-covered buckler grotesquely flailing the grass, he, in the Gaelic custom, making a great moan about his end, and a pair of bickering rooks cawing away heartily as if it was no more than a sheep in the throes of braxy" (99). The remembered vividness withdrawn to a temporal distance suddenly looks oddly unreal; and so the adventures seem to Elrigmore, all unreal, child's play, or, summed up in that word central to Munro, "daft."

Elrigmore is more a melancholy philosopher than fortune's warrior. He speaks from a safe old age; even in the midst of adventure, lost on Rannoch Moor, a fugitive after the sacking of Inneraora, he seems distant and views his adventures as a mere dalliance with fate; even then he seems to speak from a more stable, domestic world. Thus, his friendship with the adventurer Splendid is fatefully strange. Their bond is reminiscent of the devotion of Waverley to Fergus MacIver or of David to Alan Breck. But Splendid is complex, a figure of a cultural fatality, diversely motivated, a man of practical instinct, a natural leader, a devious play-actor whose sincerity shows in distress or danger, an adventurer with no real place in a dawning civility, no business being Argile's manager of mines. He is Argile's cousin and is fiercely loyal, yet is finally driven to break with his chief by Argile's cowardice. Argile's character is a mystery to Splendid, as Splendid's is to Elrigmore, and the book's chief interest is fathoming the odd and mysterious in character. In this respect, Munro is much closer to Scott than to Stevenson. But in romantic mood he is unlike either. Romance is child's play, but also dance-of-death, grotesque fin de siècle elegy.

The mood persists in *The New Road* (1914). It is a romance of bit-

ter, progressive disillusionment with the naive hero's "glamoured notion of the North."[28] The pattern is like that of *Kidnapped;* the deluded heir must be gotten rid of. He has his older version of Alan
Breck in a wily agent of Argyll's named Ninian Macgregor Campbell.
But the disillusionment is that of *Catriona.* This hero too has a wise
pragmatist for teacher in Duncan Forbes of Culloden. Forbes is the
one who tells him what General Wade's New Road means: "The
hearts of all of us are sometimes in the wilds. It's not so very long since
we left them. But the end of all that sort of thing's at hand . . . Ye saw
the Road? That Road's the end of us! The Romans didna manage it;
Edward didna manage it; but there it is at last, through to our vitals,
and it's up wi' the ell-wand, down the sword!" (215-216). The New
Road is history, haunted for the hero by the ghosts of broken men.
History is hateful. Yet it is paradoxical, too. For the New Road is the
way back into the discovery of the past; and the New Road "will some
day be the Old Road, too, with ghosts on it and memories." All
changes; the note of elegiac futility in *Splendid* is repeated. Yet little
changes. To uncover the past is to discover there the same mean rack-
eteering that curses the present. What Aeneas the hero comes to suspect is "that, after all, the heroes of the ceilidh tales—the chiefs and
caterans—were, like enough, but men of wind as this one seemed"
(89). The opportunists of the present are the old savages thinly ve-
neered. Duncanson, for example: he hasn't even his own name; he has
stolen his estate, is cheating his master Argyll, and rules the Highlands
as Argyll's agent to serve his own racket.

> The notion came to Aeneas as he stood looking at him, he had never
> rightly seen the man before, but always in a mask or a veneer, made
> up of clothes and studied manners; this creature, stripped of all that
> gave to him the semblance of a person schooled and prudent, stood
> stark-nakedly revealed a savage, club or dagger only wanting to
> give murder to his passion. Under eaves as coarse as heather were
> his eyes recessed and glinting like an adder's. [42].

It is only by finding the savage once more in one's self that one can
deal with such men. This is the course that Ninian Campbell urges.

Such is the "great adventure" of Aeneas's life. It ends only when the
poor tutor has discovered that he has been robbed of his heritage.
Drimdorran is rightly his. His father was not killed in Glen Shiel fighting for the Jacobites, or drowned in Loch Duig shortly afterwards, but
murdered and buried in the dovecot fireplace at home by Duncanson,

an imposter. The family legend of Jacobite heroism is a mere cover-up. Aeneas's reward is his liberation from false romance and his discovery of the mean savagery that persists along the road of history. Historical romance has gone as far as possible in the ruthless deromanticizing of history. The veneer of civility is periodically stripped off; the savagery lasts—the savagery and the long sad memory.

John Buchan the Borderer,* with his "very thin crust of civilization," is not far off. Essential to the evocative beauty of Munro's romance is the bitter melancholy, the elegiac fatalism, which Stevenson largely excluded. With John Buchan—allegedly master of the Tory adventure tale—the picture changes again. His more than twenty novels depend largely on traditional and repeated patterns, and we can be fair to them in general without stressing minor differences. But there is one major difference that Buchan himself took seriously. And while the adventures overlap, Buchan's pilgrimage of modern adventure divides along three distinct paths with three very different protagonists: the South African Scots soldier of fortune Richard Hannay (*Thirty-Nine Steps, Greenmantle, Three Hostages*); the retired Glasgow provisioner and romantic descendant of Nicol Jarvie, Dickson MacCunn (*Huntingtower, Castle Gay, The House of Four Winds*); and the prosperous Scots London lawyer and M.P. Edward Leithen (*The Power House, John Macnab, Mountain Meadow*). All are seekers of "romance" in different ways. Hannay the skillful, powerful engineer is ordered into action for his commando talents; MacCunn uses his retirement to pursue a "goddess" of romance; Leithen seeks wild adventure to relieve the tedium of professional urbanity. The adventures of Hannay, MacCunn, and Leithen will have more meaning if we

Buchan, John. The son of a Free Church minister, Buchan was born in Perth in 1875, but spent his youthful holidays in the Borders. He was educated at Glasgow University and at Oxford, was admitted to the Bar in London, and began his career of public service in 1901 in South Africa. Upon his return, he was a partner in the publishing firm of Thomas Nelson. During World War I he was a war correspondent and became director of information for the government. He served as a Conservative M.P. from 1927 to 1935, when, as 1st Baron Tweedsmuir, he went to Canada as governor general. In addition to thirty works of fiction, he wrote biographies of Scott, Montrose, Ralegh, and Cromwell, and a four-volume history of the 1914-1918 war, as well as a history of the Church of Scotland, of which he was an elder for thirty years and lord high commissioner in 1933-34. Buchan died in 1940 in Montreal.

see them in perspective after the early *John Burnet of Barns*, the fascinating "boy's adventure" of *Prester John*, and the book Buchan thought his finest, *Witch Wood*.

Having spoken in *Pilgrim's Way* of his stories of modern adventure, Buchan recalls that "besides these forthright tales of adventure I was busy with a very different kind of romance. The desire to recover the sense of continuity . . . prompted my first serious piece of fiction."[29] There followed several carefully wrought books in "this kind of romance," and of these he thought *Witch Wood* the best. Yet *Witch Wood* is atypical; it differs even from other "serious" romances such as *The Free Fishers*, a "bustling yarn" in historical disguise. It comes out of his profound, presbyterian, and scholarly sympathy for Montrose. It is noticeably omitted as evidence from Gertrude Himmelfarb's fine sketch of the Scotch Calvinist Tory,[30] perhaps because it is a denunciation (in the manner of Lockhart's *Wald* and Hogg's *Sinner*) of perverted popular Calvinisms and is as liberal a plea for tolerant humanity as anything Scott produced.

"Being equally sensitive to the spells of time and of space," Buchan recalls, "to a tract of years and a tract of landscape, I tried to discover the historical moment which best interpreted the *ethos* of a particular countryside, and to devise the appropriate legend. Just as certain old houses, like the inns at Burford and Queensferry, cried out to Robert Louis Stevenson to tell their tales, so I felt the clamour of certain scenes for an interpreter." *Witch Wood* took the scene of "the Tweedside parish of my youth" and found its ethos in a time "when the rigours of the new Calvinism were contending with the ancient secret rites of Diana."[31] *John Burnet of Barns*, written when Buchan was still in his teens, came from the same intimate locality but chose for its moment the next generation. The search for continuity is equally strong, but the differences are striking. *John Burnet* was written in the nineties when "Stevenson filled the bill completely"; Stevenson was a companion, young in heart, who also thrilled to "the lights and glooms of Scottish history; the mixed heritage we drew from Covenanter and Cavalier; that strange compost of contradictions, the Scottish character; the bleakness and beauty of the Scottish landscape." Stevenson was "a preacher at heart, as every young Scotsman is."[32] *Witch Wood* was published thirty years later by the mature adventurer-politician who was far along in his researches into Montrose and at the beginning of his life of Scott. The self-conscious Scottish romancer now had a choice of models.

John Burnet is full of Stevenson. The countryside is upper Tweed; Hannay will retrace it in *Thirty-Nine Steps* without knowing the names:

> I feared to come to Dawyck too early, so I forded Tweed below the island, and took the road up the farther bank by Lyne and Stobe . . . The haze was lifting off the great Manor Water hills; the Red Syke, the scene of last night's escapade, looked very distant in the morning light; and far beyond all Dollar Law and the high hills about Manorhead were flushed with sunlight on their broad foreheads. A great gladness rose in me when I looked at the hills, for they were the hills of my own country; I knew every glen and corrie, every water and little burn.[33]

And scarcely one is missed. The setting is so densely topographical as to seem surreal—mazelike, vivid, detailed like a relief map or game board.

The game is, as in *Thirty-Nine Steps* and other tales, hide-and-seek, played in earnest with John's dangerous rival-cousin, over a girl both love. Yet the game is caught up in the historic situation, the persecution of Covenanters; cousin Gilbert is a hunter, until James II flees, William becomes king, and the hunter becomes hunted. John is a fugitive more by accident, but he is linked in fortune with the fugitive groups who share his countryside, Covenanters and gypsies. The Covenanters he meets make claims in his father's name (as Burley does with Henry Morton); yet, while he sees their suffering, he never becomes one of them. His encounters do lead to one confirmation; he meets Covenanters of reasonable mind and lofty purpose, "and thus I have ever found it, that the better sort of the Covenanters were the very cream of Scots gentlefolk, and that 'twas only in the *canaille* that the gloomy passion of fanatics was to be found."[34]

Buchan remained a defender of the Kirk against its fanatical perversions. From boyhood he had had a vision of earth that combined fairy tale and Norse myth with "the old Calvinistic discipline," and "that discipline can have had none of the harshness against which so many have revolted, for it did not dim the beauty and interest of the earth." For him the traditions were joined in his "constant companion" among boyhood books, *Pilgrim's Progress*, with "its picture of life as a pilgrimage over hill and dale, where surprising adventures lurked by the wayside, a hard road with now and then long views to cheer the traveller and a great brightness at the end of it." It is suggestive of local-archetypal reality in a Buchan setting that "John Bunyan claimed our woods as his own," and that the young university student of philosophy "came to identify abstractions with special localities . . . Sin, a horrid substance like black salt, was intimately connected with a certain thicket of brambles and spotted toadstools . . . [and later] the processes of the Hegelian dialectic were associated with a homely Galloway heath, and the Socratic arguments with the upper Thames between Godstow and Eyndham."[35] It says much, too, of the portrayer of Kirk and Covenant that Buchan saw Montrose as the hero of a betrayed Covenant, saw the full austere passion of Covenanting conviction, and could share the dream of the first reformers.[36]

But these complex sympathies belong to the later novel. The gypsies matter more in *John Burnet.* John is mistaken for a Covenanter. Impersonation—a central impulse of Buchan adventure—is essential; he becomes a gypsy, puts on gypsy disguise, and then: "The romance of the thing took me captive; it was as well that a man should play all the parts he could in this world" (341). When the battle of the gypsies begins, he tries to shed his role and cannot. And though the violence is fatal to almost no one, he has been obliged to discover in himself a capacity for primitive violence. He has discovered, too, that his fate binds him to romantic outlaws and other adventurers. In the wild, haughty gypsy leader's face he sees "such shrewd kindliness that I found it in my heart to like him." He is bound to the hunter-hunted game with his cousin as if "some impelling fate" were "driving me forward to meet this man, who had crossed me so often" (368). We recall the brothers of Ballantrae when, "as I looked on him I hated him deeply and fiercely, and yet I admired him more than I could bear to think, and gloried that he was of our family" (415). John is saved from being Gilbert's killer and returns to his familiar, pastoral place. Flight and violence recede into "remembered romance," and "the shadow of the past seemed to slip from me like an old garment" (429). But the adventure has been a complex pilgrimage all the same. He has mingled with and survived elemental forces, discovered mixed allegiances, and confirmed his kinship with the primitive continuities of his local world.

We can see Buchan's obvious Stevensonian inspiration, and see how easily the Buchan pattern translates overseas, in his boy's adventure,

Prester John.[37] This is *Kidnapped* again, with a difference. It is once more an adventure in topography. The romance centers chiefly on two things: the locale, a terrain over which we accompany the hero, with intense physical effort, again and again, covering extraordinary distances by night, or blindfold, or in a half hallucinatory state; and the fabulous black adventurer who is the enigmatic aim of the pilgrimage. John Laputa has been compared with John Silver and Alan Breck, but he is more in the mold of Scott's Burley. He is the civilized native leader returning to impersonate an archaic hero, something better and higher than "civilization." David Crawfurd is drawn not just in moral fascination, but in genuine hero-worship—drawn out of himself to fulfill a destiny of protecting Laputa. Yet he is fated to be the little prosaic youth who is the great man's undoing.

From the first view of Laputa on Kirkcaple Shore, he feels a spell cast, feels "somehow shut in with this unknown being in a strange union." From the beginning he determines to get to "the heart of the matter"—the phrase is often repeated—and the heart is in dark Africa, in a legendary cave of treasure, in the extraordinary heart of a great man. In the unforgettable climax we again recall Scott's Burley: "It was burned on my mind that Laputa was alive," says David, "nay, was waiting for me, and that it was God's will that we should meet in the cave" (232). In the cave he finds Laputa dying, sees him jump over the edge into the torrent, and then escapes by climbing the crags. He has found the place with the secret. It has been a lonely pilgrimage. "I alone knew of the devilry in his heart, and I could not but believe that some day or other there might be virtue in that knowledge" (31). He is pleased to realize that he is alone in the secret; yet he is frequently aware, too, of being "hemmed in by barbarism, and cut off in a ghoulish land from the succour of my own kind' (78). We are reminded of the young minister of *Witch Wood*, compelled to go alone in his knowledge of devilry.

In *Witch Wood* we are back in the local world of *John Burnet*. Once more the pilgrimage is a quest for continuity with a barbaric past. The barbarism, however, is linked not to the personality of a charismatic adventurer, but rather to the conflict caused by religious repression. The conflict originated imaginatively in Buchan's vision of the familiar place. One evening, looking at "that decorous landscape, prim, determinate, without a hint of mystery," he "saw it with other eyes," and thereafter "the colliery headgear on the horizon, the trivial moorish hill-tops, the dam-bred-pattern fields, could never tame wholly for me that land's romance, and on this evening I seemed to be gazing at a thing antique and wolfish" (12). The "antique and wolfish" lurks in paradise. The ancient forest surrounding the village is a place of paradisal innocence and a place of pagan abomination. Here the hero, young minister David Sempill, meets his beloved Katrine, and here the dour, respectable citizens hold their witch sabbaths on Beltane and Lammas. David fights in vain to cleanse the diabolism, but the town defeats him, his presbytery excommunicates him, his charities are misrepresented, and his humanity to a wounded officer of Montrose is used against him. Katrine dies and he disappears. Local legend has him carried off by the devil or the queen of faerie; the novel shows him departing for continental exile. Woodilee settles back into its sickly divided life.

His erratic supporter drunken Rieverslaw offers a diagnosis David's orthodoxy cannot accept: "What do your Presbyteries and Assemblies or your godly ministers ken o' the things that are done in the mirk? . . . They set up what they ca' their discipline and they lowse the terrors o' Hell on sma' fauts like an aith, or profane talk on the Sabbath, or giein' the kirk the go-by, and they hale to the cutty-stool ilka lass that's ower kind to her jo. And what's the upshot? They drive folk to their auld ways and turn them intil hypocrites as well as sinners" (143). One timid, sickly minister, who tries to speak out on David's behalf, has his doubts, and they become David's. His is the statement of Buchan's own creed: "At times I'm tempted to think that our way and the Kirk's way is not God's way, for we're apt to treat the natural man as altogether corrupt . . . If there's original sin, there's likewise original innocence . . . If you ban this innocent joy it will curdle and sour, and the end will be sin. If young life may not caper on a Spring morn to the glory of God, it will dance in the mirk wood to the Devil's piping" (154). If David can regard the coven of Woodilee with "curious pity and friendliness" as "misguided innocence," then he can work for its redemption. He does come to realize that "men might frequent Melanudrigill for hideous purposes, but the place itself was innocent" (227). But his charity is erratic, and his vision of evil is intense; there is a capacity for fanaticism in him, and he is divided between spiritual militancy and indiscriminate charity. His Manichean vision of the wood persists and defeats him. He succeeds only in destruction; he confronts his enemy Ephraim Caird—pious elder, king-devil, justified sinner—and, almost rejoicing, drives him to madness.

The evil figure of Buchan's modern adventure tales is an adaptation of this vision of sublime fanaticism, of the master impersonator whose power-lust and unshakeable self-righteousness are hidden behind a facade of urbanity. In modern despotisms Buchan saw this archetypal figure collectivized into a vague international conspiracy. There is imaginative plausibility in the kinship, and historical plausibility in his linkage of heroic Covenanter and socialist revolutionary. But the analogy is pursued without the cultural particularity of *Witch Wood*. And it simply serves the stereotypical needs of his "bustling" adventure tales, providing the fascinating bogeymen against whose conspiratorial machinations his modern adventurer-heroes carry on their game-like missions.

The formula is recognizably inspired by Scottish romance; yet, says Buchan, it came to him by way of the first master of international thrillers. E. Phillips Oppenheim had transformed the wide historic world of Scott's romance into sinister, explosive modern Europe; the Buchan protagonist is charged extra-legally with saving it. The lesson imparted by Heritage to Jarvie's descendant Dickson MacCunn in *Huntingtower* is an echo of Waverley's message: "It sounds ridiculous, I know, in Britain in the twentieth century, but I learned in the war that civilization anywhere is a very thin crust."[38] The strategy is to play in exhilarating earnest at a game, to meet the wilderness as a lover on its own terms (the wilderness in fact replaces woman in these tales), and to find in atavistic adventure the vitality and shrewdness to guard civilization beneath the crust.

From *Thirty-Nine Steps* on, the enemy is a "power house," a "big subterranean movement going on, engineered by very dangerous people," "away behind all the Governments and the armies."[39] But there are other antagonists as well: natural forces, time and space, and the aim of the game is to reach a far-off place of destined climax at the right moment. Buchan recalls, "I was especially fascinated by the notion of hurried journeys. In the great romances of literature they provide some of the chief dramatic moments, and since the theme is common to Homer and the penny reciter it must appeal to a very ancient instinct in human nature. We live our lives under the twin categories of time and space, and when the two come into conflict we get a great moment. Whether failure or success is the result, life is sharpened, intensified, idealised."[40] The great speedster Sir Turnour Wyse (in *Free Fishers*) is miraculous by virtue of his skill as coach-driver, and the miraculous Sandy Arbuthnot crosses Europe to Turkey (in *Greenmantle*) far ahead of the rest because he commands mysterious disguises and routes. The Gorbals Die-Hards of *Hunting-tower* and other MacCunn expeditions flourish by the tactical brilliance of their maneuvers over extensive, difficult terrain, and are never even lost in the dark. Even in modern Gothic London of *Three Hostages*, the victory goes to those who master the territory, and the intricately charted shooting preserve of *John Macnab* poses the same challenges. Every Buchan adventure has an implied frontispiece of map and game-plan.

Triumph over time and space is the power of the boy, and the hero-adventurer must recover that power to survive. His antagonist possesses the power already, for his fanaticism is a perverted form of the power of youth and innocence. Hence, the boy and the fanatic have a curious kinship. Yet the antagonist, opposing youthful power, also plays the role of age and death, of denial and mockery; and thus the combat has vitalistic roots deeper than those of conventional morality. This is why the moral and cultural stereotypes that give Buchan's adversaries their surface of melodrama and reactionary cliché matter little, and why the combat at its deepest level is against death or spiritual torpor. But when the antagonisms transcend stereotype and preserve something of a theological complexity, the fanatics retain a moral fascination. In *Prester John* it is the child's fascination with the dreaded but beloved pirate or revolutionary. In *Three Hostages* it rests uneasily on a Bulweresque image of occult hypnotic power. In *Greenmantle* it becomes the exotic, ambiguous attachment of adventurer and fatal amazon, Sandy and Hilda von Einem. The adversary is the one who sets the game going, and it must be played on his (or her) terms. This demands a hero who, while basically a "normal" person of conventional decencies, can come close to the power figure through the agility and shrewdness of the child and the skill and conviction of the master impersonator.

The quintessential Buchan adventurer is Sandy Arbuthnot. Near death (in *Mountain Meadow*), Leithen recalls him as "the central star, radiating heat and light, a wandering star who for long seasons disappeared from the firmament." Buchan biographers suggest he was a distillation and blend of Montrose and Lawrence of Arabia. Whatever his derivation, Sandy more than any other embodies Buchan's guiding idea of the Scots adventurer, and perhaps he reaches his zenith in *Greenmantle:* "We call ourselves insular, but the truth is that we are the only race on earth that can produce men capable of getting inside the skin of remote peoples . . . Sandy was the wandering Scot carried to the pitch of genius. In old days he would have led a crusade or discovered a new road to the Indies. To-day he merely roamed as the spirit moved him, till the war swept him up and dumped him down in my battalion."[41] So says Hannay, and as we follow Hannay in his slow, perilous journey across wartime Germany, down the Danube, to the Middle East and the battle of Erzerum, Sandy travels swiftly, alone, in his legendary underground way, and is already in Constantinople in powerful disguise to protect the others. He is leader of the maniacal Companions of the Rosy Hours, "the most eldritch apparition you can conceive. A tall man dressed in skins, with barelegs and sandalshod feet . . . He capered like a wild animal" (154-155). He reveals himself at last, and in a "spasm of incredulity, a vast relief," Hannay greets him: "Sandy, you're an incarnate devil." Not quite, but he plays the role brilliantly.

They are all playing roles. "I've been playing a part for the past month," says Hannay, "and it wears my nerves to tatters" (182). They must do so to contend with the fanatical Hilda von Einem, leader of the German plot to stir the Turks into religious war against the British and Russians. Hannay pales at the menacing sexual challenge in her stare. But Sandy she loves, and to Sandy she offers a mate's share of her Napoleonic destiny. Sandy must replace the dead prophet Greenmantle, and "Sandy was a man of genius—more than anybody I ever struck—but he had the defects of such high-strung, fanciful souls . . . he might go stark crazy. The woman, who roused in me and Blenkiron only hatred, could catch his imagination and stir in him—for the moment only—an unwilling response" (265). When Sandy returns from her, he seems drugged and raves of having lived a few days in hell, calls her she-devil: "evil—evil—evil." It is Sandy to whom, on the edge of defeat, she appeals in vain, and Sandy sadly buries her when she is killed. At the end, as the Allies ride triumphant into Erzerum, Sandy *is* Greenmantle: "He was like the point of the steel spear soon to be driven home . . . He was bare-headed, and rode like one possessed, and against the snow I caught the dark sheen of emerald" (320).

Buchan's romance of impersonation approaches operatic tragedy in *Greenmantle*. In *John Macnab* it approaches comic myth.[42] Three eminent Tories—Leithen, late attorney general; Lamancha, colonial secretary; Palliser-Yeates, a powerful banker—suffer from ennui. As Lamancha says, in a familiar Buchan figure, "The light has gone out of the landscape. Nothing has any savour" (18). Renovation comes with the book's basic premise: "Most men at heart are poachers" (23). The mythical John Macnab is created; challenges are sent to sporting land-lords of Wester Ross: during such a time period John Macnab will poach a stag or salmon, delivering it up, and paying a handsome prize, win or lose. The book is the carrying out of the challenge. John Macnab mostly wins, is rounded up voluntarily; dinner ensues at a landlord's house, and all is harmony. But the landlord is baffled; had he known who they were, he would have invited them to hunt and fish. Cries Lamancha, "You are missing the point. Don't you see that your way would have taken all the gloss off the adventure and made it a game?" (282).

The line is a subtle, elusive one, and it runs through Buchan's ro-mances: it was all merely a game, yet it kept the gloss of adventure. Lamancha despairs: "We've been making godless fools of ourselves. We thought we had got outside of civilization and were really taking chances. But we weren't." Silly, romantic Lady Claybody's consola-tion is trivial yet truthful: "You have had the fun of thinking you were in real danger, and after all it is what one thinks that matters. I am so glad you are all cured of being bored" (283-284). The reader, of course, has had the same therapy at a further remove of vicariousness. The book's unique interest is in its enactment of the game aesthetic of romance.

The "gloss of adventure" is real. The adventure variously illustrates — in its absurdities, coincidences, entrapments— "the unplumbed pre-posterousness of life." In Leithen, "a philosopher, with an acute sense of the ironies of life," it arouses not just the atavistic zeal of "the large streak of bandit in his composition," but "helpless mirth" as well (192, 243). The situations demand all the skills of impersonation and the tactical subtlety of the *Greenmantle* team. They demand a keenly charted grasp of the terrain of three wilderness estates; the book has its frontal map for guiding image, and the narrator and reader must remain in painfully direct contact with the poachers in their campaign of hunt and diversion, hide-and-seek, strain and exhaustion, and never become seriously lost. The possibility of danger, physical and social, must remain dire, even as the reassurance of the game-like must be always present. As one tenant puts it, "I'd like to think it *could* happen. The permanent possibility of it would supple the minds of your legislators. It would do this old country a power of good if now and then a Cabinet Minister took to brawling and went to jail" (131). The old life is going and all that remains is property, no justification at all. The romantic heroine offers a radical creed: "Nobody in the world today has a right to anything which he can't justify . . . I mean that people should realise that whatever they've got they hold under a perpetual challenge, and they are bound to meet that challenge" (155-156). Her suitor forgets his political speech at a rally, and what comes out is "the apologue of John Macnab": "John Macnab, he said, was abroad in the world today, like a catfish among a shoal of herrings. He has his defects, no doubt, but he was badly wanted, for he was at bottom a sportsman and his challenge had to be met." "He ca's himself a Tory," says one wild-eyed auditor. "By God, it's the red flag that he'll be wavin' soon" (180-181). The spirit of John Macnab thus serves Gertrude Himmelfarb well in her case for Buchan's Scottish Toryism: it "was radical rather than romantic, and he respected enterprise as he respected labor." It came from Disraeli by way of Morris, and perhaps it began in Ned Leithen's endless reading of Walter Scott.[43]

The theme of the book, says Gertrude Himmelfarb, "is not only the natural and rightful authority exercised by some men by virtue of their breeding, experience, and character, but also the natural and rightful impulse to rebel against that authority." The theme is continuity, too; Macnab is whimsically identified as Harald Blacktooth, Viking ancestor to the heroine, the link that assures rebirth. Finally, the theme is that more apprehensive side of Buchan's ideology: humane decency and civility are precious and fragile; the adventurers "Macnab" are its guardians, playing the game by its rules and roles, playing it humanely, and returning, then, to the life of the civil hero.

The final test of the spirit of John Macnab—and of Sandy Arbuthnot— comes in the wilds of Canada, in *Mountain Meadow*;[44] the American title misleadingly focuses on the pastoral spot Leithen picks for burial, while the British title, *Sick-Heart River*, properly marks the place of testing and the spiritual nature of the test. Leithen knows he is dying, and he goes seeking a place, a way, and a time to die. Buchan's landscape of the Canadian North is beyond history, archetypal, a "queer thing" that demands an ultimate discipline of spirit. It provides a dark night of the soul—for Leithen, for the fugitive he seeks, for his Scottish-Indian guides, for the poor Hare Indians to whom Leithen, playing the medical missionary, sacrifices his life. It is a suitable apocalyptic setting for the final revelation of Buchan's romantic Calvinism. A missionary priest calls it a place "where man is nothing and God is all"; Leithen is now "alone with God. In these bleak immensities the world of man had fallen away to an infinite distance . . . He was an atom in infinite space, the humblest of slaves waiting on the command of an august master" (88, 151). The Calvinism has its coordinate social imperative, however: "It was the brotherhood of all men, white and red and brown, who have to fight the savagery of the North" (218). But it is no facile "brotherhood." Leithen "had always been in his own way a religious man. Brought up under the Calvinist shadow, he had accepted a simple evangel which, as he grew older, had mellowed and broadened. At Oxford he had rationalised it in his philosophical studies, but he had never troubled to make it a self-sufficing, logical creed. Certain facts were the buttresses of his faith, and the chief of them was the omnipotence and omnipresence of God. He had always detested the glib little humanism of most of his contemporaries" (149).

The Buchan romantic pilgrimage is seen at last in its essence. Leithen must die; the race against time and space must end. Faced by the limits, "there was a plain task before him, to fight with Death. God for His own purpose had unloosed it in the world, ravening over places which had once been rich in innocent life" (250). The antagonist—beneath the nay-saying fanaticisms, the "incarnate devils" of history—is a spiritual torpor that is death, the sick heart. The missionary priest sees it as "the fear of the North or, perhaps more accurately, as fear of life. In the North, man, to live, has to fight every hour against hostile forces; if his spirit fails and his effort slackens, he perishes" (269). God had left a suitable battlefield here, a borderland with its paradise and inferno, a "watch-tower as well as a sanctuary . . . a frontier between the desert and the sown." For Leithen it evokes "the spell which had captured him here in his distant youth. It was the borderline between the prosaic world, where things went by rule and rote and were fitted to the human scale, and the world as God first made it out of chaos, which had no care for humanity" (54-55). It is the place of archaic romance. Life is summed up in its peaks of loneliness, and heroic adventure passes into a legend of martyrdom.

10

Mitchison

and

Later Romancers

Romance, like Scottish nationalism, makes for strange ideological kinships. Leithen's death in the Canadian wilderness can be placed beside a similar vision of a death in Bechuanaland, the personal vision of Naomi Mitchison.* With confidence in cultural assimilation and practical technology, this extraordinary heir to the Haldanes went to Africa in the early 1960s and became mother to the Bakgatla tribe and its chief Linchwe II. Her memoir appeared as *Return to the Fairy Hill* (1966), and this romantic title of a pragmatic record says much about her. The book is to be a practical study of "the mechanics of a completely non-racial relationship," a "study of commitment," a commitment perilously complete. "I think probably I shall, sooner or later, be killed; I hope at least that I shall die a useful death. But if I die here in Mochudi I want to be buried in the great

---

*Mitchison, Naomi (*Haldane*). Born in Edinburgh in 1897, educated at Oxford, Lady Mitchison lives at Campbeltown, Argyllshire. Daughter of the physiologist J. S. Haldane, sister of the biologist J. B. S. Haldane, she married G. R. Mitchison, an influential Labour M. P., and herself ran for Labour M. P. for the Scottish universities, as well as serving on the Highland and Islands Advisory Council and other public commissions. She became tribal adviser to the Bakgatla of Botswana in 1963. She has written sixteen novels, six collections of short stories (beginning with *When the Bough Breaks*, 1924), and three dozen other books, many of them biographies and fantasies for young readers. Alexander Scott finds that in Scottish subjects she is at her best in fairy tales such as *The Big House* (1950) and *Five Men and a Swan* (1958).

Kraal where Chief Molefi was buried, and let the cattle trample out all marks of where my body lies. And I do not want any religious service, nor yet to have my body put into any coffin, but into the skin of some beast; I would like best for it to be a lion skin."[1] Yet she remains a practical, romantic Scots citizen of the world, "singing 'Scots wha ha'e' to myself, thinking always of Africa." Talking to the black porter in a white African railway station "was like talking to a Glasgow porter about poaching salmon"; the Highland situation is relevant to Africa. Her sense of modern Scotland sent her to look in Africa for what had been lost elsewhere in the West: "the open secret that we all know and which binds all life together. The sense of continuity between past and present. The stream of life which makes the individual both more and less important, which takes away fear" (83).

She realizes the romantic dishonesties of her own culture pattern, where, she says, "every kind of love is tangled up with romantic attitudes, the stuff of Northern poetry, the blind bairn god" (208). As a novelist she has stressed "imaginative sympathy towards the characters and their historical situations . . . feeling with their muscles, reacting to their hormonies [sic]" (69). Now she wonders whether her tribal role is simply a creation of her fiction, whether "me-and-the-tribe was in some way a recap of my own books. Had Linchwe anything to do with Meromic or Beric (blondes both of them)? Was he Tarrik or Kleomenes? Above all, I didn't want him to be Kleomenes" (73). Are her personal mythologies imposing roles? "Even if now I was only the Winter Queen, I was with my Corn King—but no, he was the Rain King. Without rain no corn. But the Fairy Hill was Marob, my place imagined over half a century, now real" (52). The romantic irrationalist, however, is not fully at ease. The creator of the barbarian Tarrik and archaic Scythian Marob had begun her lifelong quest in less romantic precincts: "All my life I have looked for the just society since as a child I sat on the back of the dining-room sofa reading Plato's *Republic*. I had felt that without justice there could be no real civilization. I had turned my mind on Athens, not only the historical Athens but 'all that we mean by Athens,' and on other parts of the ancient world" (86). The complex results appear in many books.

The Bull Calves (1947) is the most interesting of Scottish romances after Buchan. It is carefully historical, and at the same time a transformation of history into myth. It is romantic, yet the romance is set in a closely drawn picture of domestic manners. At its center is a pair of imaginary lovers, psychologically real yet archetypal, and culturally generic. And Mitchison's voluminous notes about the book's creation constitute an essential critical text of the novel in Scotland. The notes connect this domestic romance of Scottish history with the fictions of ancient life, Mediterranean and Gaulish, for which Naomi Mitchison is generally remembered. Her work is as unified as it is fixed in Scottish tradition.

The three most extensive and available of Naomi Mitchison's fictions are all occasional works. *The Corn King and the Spring Queen* (1930) expresses a deep interest not just in Spartan history, but also in *The Golden Bough* and other sources in Mediterranean ritual and myth. It interweaves historic figures and events of Greece with imaginative archetypes of archaic Scythia. *The Conquered* (1923) calls for a familiarity with ancient Gaul, but the occasion is the political struggle of modern Ireland. The chapter epigraphs are from contemporary and traditional Irish poetry. *Blood of the Martyrs* (1939) is equally occasional. The dedication acknowledges a great number of collaborators, members of worldwide socialist resistance to tyrannies old and new, comrades in "the Kingdom which we all want in our hearts"— the kingdom furthered by the primitive Christian martyrs who make up the book's chief characters. In mode and style it is less romantic, more consistently naturalistic and deliberately colloquial, and more explicitly propagandistic—a free interpretation of proletarian Christianity in the time of Nero.

The Conquered could easily be read without reference to modern Irish analogues.[2] Its style is terse, vivid; its narrative mode is annalistic and spare. There is little suggestion of complex motive or consciousness. The governing theme is unmistakable: we know of ancient Gaul through Caesar, but what of the experience of the conquered? Do they not belong with those conquered by tyrants throughout history? The familiar device of the culturally divided hero in an ordeal of mixed allegiances provides the only complexity. Meromic, son of Kormiac the Wolf, is well treated by his Roman master Titus: "Can't you see, Lerrys? There's half of me aching to get off, to be fighting on my own side, the side I ought to be on; and there's the other half—oh God, Lerrys, I'd give my life for him, I would truly; he's all I've got, he's wife and child and home and everything. I don't care what he does to me—not really. There's nothing I can be sure of except friendship" (199). The brief triumph of the youthful Vercingetorix, embodiment of a nationalist ideal, intensifies his dilemma, and after Vercingetorix's defeat and capture by Caesar, Meromic flees from his master. "I have to go. I have been faithful up to now. Have I paid you for what you did for me? There is another debt to pay; whatever else I may be I am a Gaul, so *he* was my General. I should have gone before . . . I think that Gaul is conquered for ever and Rome is the conqueror; but still I must go" (242). He is found later by Titus, his right hand chopped off by the Romans, and is taken to live in peace outside Rome. But the reports of the treatment of Gaulish leaders in Rome awaken again his sense of what he is. With murder in his heart, he takes his knife down. The wolves howl nearby as he asks to be taken back to Gaul. There are only wolf tracks left, as if Meromic has become his father the wolf and fled north—but to what? There is no answer.

It is in keeping with the narrator's muted voice. The book's events are related concisely without interpretive sophistication. Little comment is offered, little attempt is made at psychological interpretation. In the forward to *The Corn King*, written just after *The Conquered*, Naomi Mitchison gives her theory of character in historiography: "It is very doubtful whether, at a distance of more than two thousand years, one can ever get near to the minds, or even to the detail of the actions, of the people one is writing about, although they are in a way nearer to one than one's living friends . . . it is all a game of hide-and-seek in the dark and if, in the game, one touches a hand or face, it is all chance."[3] In *The Conquered*, character is drawn with little generalization, philosophical or archetypal. The historic world of Caesar is presented, but not emphatically enough to complicate the book's world of action and pathos. The primary sensations and passions—loyalty, friendship, a hatred of slavery and a love of freedom—predominate. The actions are those of Stevensonian romance—exile, flight, return, hiding, all the adventures of topography but without the physical and imaginative exhilaration. Language also serves to minimize any quality of romance. Naomi Mitchison had thought much about the problem of historical language in romance; later, in notes to *The Bull Calves*, she records her decision to translate ancient language "into current English," while trying always "to keep an edge of my thought parallel with the original language, so as to try and get as near as might be to ancient ways of thought, with the deep influence that phrasing and words must have on ways of thinking."[4] Thus, while the world of the novel must seem remote, the kinds of distance, reson-ance, and intensity associated with romance are carefully excluded. If *The Conquered* seems in any way romantic, it is merely by virtue of its setting and its radical simplicity of motive and feeling.

Subject matter makes *Blood of the Martyrs* even less romantic and more historical, and in its intention and point of view, more didactic. The book offers an interpretation of primitive Christianity in Rome and finds in it a parable for Europe in 1939. There is little historical atmosphere. Neronian Rome becomes familiar and particular, but only through the casual use of place names and directional signals. Part One accumulates numerous small personal histories of a group of Roman slaves. The group is of Crispus's household, under the man-agement of Beric, a British prince. These brief chronicles provide the book's only romantic narrative. The emphasis instead is on the natural simplicity of early Christianity, on the experience of slavery, on the freedom offered by the new faith, whose essence is love, respect for the person, and equality among the conquered. Imperial Rome is a dehumanizing power, economic and military, and against this are set the selfless love and nonviolence of the Christian community. The faith of the slaves is simple and undogmatic; the hero refuses to be baptized by Paul. It is a natural faith; when the central figures are slain by beasts in the arena, no attention is given to the question of immortality. The slaves insist that their faith is not magic, but simply freedom and love. It is a proletarian faith, and the forming of the com-munity is a representative proletarian movement. It is a faith of per-sonal commitment, set against contemporary epicureanism, stoicism, and Egyptian mysticism.

Mitchison, like Lockhart, chooses for her hero a British aristocrat, Beric, who is caught in the corruption and power of Rome through his affair with Crispus's cruel, sensuous daughter. In his newfound sym-pathy for the Christians, he resorts to murder, and they suffer for his violence. His final temptation is to save himself from public execution. But he announces himself a Christian and is baptized in prison, acting ultimately out of loyalty to his lowly friends and a sense of his own sinful violence. He is no Marius; he is not the Scott hero caught up in the ordeal of cultural conflict. He is the *homme moyen sensuel* who errs into violent activism and at last discovers through personal com-mitment that Christianity is a creed of love, freedom, and humanity.

Blood of the Martyrs is in no definitive sense romance, unless prophetic history must be so classified. It is simple historical reconstruction governed by universal humanistic norms and rendered in a style of restrained modern colloquialism. But Mitchison's two most impressive fictions are more ambitious in conception than *The Conquered* and *Blood of the Martyrs*, and their complexity demanded the archetypal figures and patterns of romance.

The Corn King and the Spring Queen consists of more than six hundred pages arranged in eight unequal parts and an epilogue. Setting in place and culture is dual, and the layers of dualities that give structure and theme in the book are sometimes as enigmatic as they are momentous. The book fluctuates between mythic and historic phases of human time; and while it suggests that the birth of history is irreversible, it also suggests that the mythic will outlast or replace the historic, that the prehistoric will be reborn as the posthistoric. The dual settings are Spartan Hellas and Scythian Marob—one real, the other imagined— an old, unstable Hellenism counterpointed with an older agrarian primitivism. Under the guidance of its god-king Tarrik, the barbaric culture of Marob is seeking a road across to the future. The moment has come for a new consciousness, both historic and personal, and with it the moment for two archaic leaders to become self-conscious, moral individuals, to struggle for the first time with the mystery and the necessity of their godhead. The Spring Queen Erif Der says to the Corn King Tarrik, "Has it never happened in the past? Surely other men and women have found that they could not always be gods!" And his answer is a keynote: "They have never thought about it before, so it has never happened. We two are different from any Corn King and Spring Queen that Marob has ever had" (278). Continuity and identity are lost; Tarrik and Erif Der must save themselves spiritually as individual human beings, acquire a new consciousness, and in so doing become once more the gods of their people.

Their separate quests for enlightenment and renewal begin under the doubtful influences of decadent Hellas. Both are led to Greece, and finally to Alexandrian Egypt, where they try to share sympathetically in the moment that has come there—a moment in history. These are the new times of social justice brought by the revolution of Kleomenes, a brief and ambiguous glory that ends in defeat, exile, and, for Kleomenes, violent death. Yet somehow, through the sacrificial death of the Spartan king in history, Tarrik and Erif Der find a personal wholeness, a healing, a sense of transcendent purpose, and can return to Marob and to the future. They have discovered a right way for leaders to serve their people in time.

In what ways is it meaningful to associate this book with the persistent traditions of Scottish romance? To begin with, there is the sense of place, romantic yet intensely local. Tiny, remote Marob opens on a huge historic world; Tarrik must carry his idea to all the world, yet return to be king of his own place. Kleomenes' Alexandrian ambition to conquer the world is a betrayal of his revolution, for, as in *Blood of the Martyrs*, the true kingdom is a universal brotherhood of the small, the parochial, against cosmopolitan imperialism. Marob remains at the center of Mitchison's sense of her book. Place can be known intimately only by the exile, the fugitive, the conquered. Place is the locus of legend.

Second, there is the book's curious sense of time and history. History is the field of human consciousness, yet history is a record of betrayal and defeat, and finally history is less real than myth. The book conveys an elegiac sense of lost powers and integrities that can be recovered only by stepping back to an archetypal self at some moment of explosive historic transition. One seeks in the past for a lost identity of culture and of self to project into a utopian or millennial future; radical toryism becomes utopian socialism, and Mitchison's kinship with Buchan and Scott becomes clearer. Historic transition is the confrontation of cultural polarities followed by a synthesis of the old power with the new humanity. Characters are paired in cultural counterpoint, protagonists are divided into complementary options, lovers progress toward union in a struggle for mutual fulfillment. Lesser characters are tempters who prevent or falsify integrity and yet provoke the protagonists to new stages of consciousness. This dialectic is presented as history, but it is too absolute to be historical and must therefore be expressed in romance.

Third, there is the protagonist's ethical dilemma of how to survive revolutionary transition, how to live by the new code or ideology and yet be loyal to traditional humane obligations. Here is the god-man problem, the problem of fanaticism and idolatry central to Scottish romance. Scottish romance persists in an ambivalent fascination with the demigod, the charismatic sacrificial leader—Mary, Prince Charles, Montrose, Dundee—and yet repudiates its own idolatry in a severe critical impulse to humanize, to demythologize. A major theme of *The Corn King* is the superceding of archaic god-worship by new, sacrificial gods of humanity, as if the birth of true history were a ritual iconoclasm: "About kings dying. About sacrificing kings. Taking a living man and mixing him with pain and death—yes, mixing him—like a cook—and making a god. I have made a god that way. A new form of god" (702). The sacrificial king or god-man must embody an idea, but if he is so wedded to it as to forget his humanity, then his divinity is diminished. Tarrik and Erif Der constantly struggle to find new ways to reunite their humanity and their godhead, and this struggle is a movement of consciousness toward the incarnation of Christ. Yet both in their sinfulness need purification as humans before they can reassume godhead.

Similarly paradoxical is the romancer's conception of the preenlightened or preternatural. The narrator speaks with a high degree of conceptualized sophistication to an enlightened reader about naive or "superstitious" people, yet the narrative derides "enlightened" points of view in characters who condescend to the "superstitious." Such is the role of Hellas vis à vis the "barbaric," analogous for Mitchison to the role of the cosmopolitan English relative to the Scot, or of the Lowlander to the Highlander. It is noteworthy in Mitchison that her philosophical homes are Greek—Athens, Sparta, the Republic of Plato—while her imaginative homes are Marob, the fairy hill, archaic Gaul. The two can have no real coalescence in history. Tarrik cannot be friend to Kleomenes; there is nothing for Tarrik in Sparta. Yet through Erif Der, the queen-woman, there is something for Marob. Kleomenes of Sparta must die in history if Marob is to be whole again beyond history: here is the central mystery of the book. And it is through Erif Der's ritual participation in that death—becoming its Isis, its protective serpent—that Tarrik can be healed and Marob can again be complete in its natural life. Death has entered the seasons, and this is not to be understood philosophically but to be confronted ritualistically. Yet the narrator remains highly philosophical; a marked philosophical distance vies with intense individual sympathy for character. It is this duality that makes the book a philosophic romance.

Finally, the problem of history in *The Corn King* is complicated by the problem of what is real. One of its resolutions is historic: to reground the divine in the human, the ritualistic in the collective. Another is to conclude that history is unreal. Kleomenes' son Nikomedes says to Metrotime that to be man is now the ultimate necessity: "One

189

can't get behind knowledge, behind the real thing." It is the definitive historical perspective. She answers, "Yes, one can, and must" (596). Beyond historic reality is what the book calls the *kataleptike phantasia*, the possessing vision.

After the abstractions of *The Corn King and the Spring Queen*, it is relaxing to come home to *The Bull Calves* (1947). Surprisingly, this book comes closer to the historical romance of Scott than any other later Scottish fiction I have read. Not least reminiscent are the one hundred twenty-five crowded pages of notes appended to four hundred uncrowded pages of narrative. And the notes have the same paradoxical effect as Scott's: they stress the author's close dependence on sources in social and domestic history, and the liberties she has taken to make a fiction. "It is a queer business altogether, this family continuity, in time and place. And it can be used well and ill. If used well, one may perhaps be justified in trimming it into a kind of mythology" (412). What is the kind of mythology?

The Bull Calves is a story of middle-aged love and affection, of Kirsty Haldane, sister to the Haldanes of Gleneagles, and William MacIntosh of Berlum, son of a Jacobite martyr of the '15. The lovers represent a union of Episcopal Highlands and Kirkish Lowlands, in Perthshire, the middle of Scotland. "What is the knotting," asks Naomi Mitchison, "in this net of events between Highlands and Lowlands that has us caught, why should the fresh knot come now, timeously to its place, and myself in the centre of it?" (412). This is to be a unionist myth, but the partners in union no longer include England.

The families are real; the lovers are imaginary, invented to accompany "only names in two family trees. They died young. I have given them the lives they might have had" (407). Kirstie, once married to a fanatical minister, had been charged with witchcraft and with causing her husband's death. William has been a thief and adulterer in North America and is believed to have once become a savage Indian and to have deserted his Indian wife. They bring different barbarous pasts into a peaceful union, to live together lovingly without full disclosures. The book, set soon after their marriage, centers on mutual confessions. Its climax is William's realization that he must not enlighten Kirstie about the horrors of his past. Thus, the problem of truth versus discretion is a central condition of the relationship, and storytelling is an essential part of the domestic continuity to which they belong. So much of the book is taken up with accounts of their separate pasts that

Kirstie and William act chiefly as traditional storytellers. Each progressively reveals parts of extreme and adventurous histories. Their revelations are interrupted by arriving guests and by their own impulses of kindly prudence. Suspense in this quiet book is provided by repeated threats of exposure or dissension. The alternating accounts of romantic past and comic present weave together in calm domesticity to achieve the classic counterpoint of Scottish romance: past adventures, betrayals, and extremisms resurfacing to threaten the humane prudence of an enlightened present.

The domestic crisis of Kirstie and William is part of a family myth. It poses the problem of whether the family can hold together in the face of past divisiveness. The book makes the point that it must, and in this respect it offers a paradigm for modern Scotland. The union, as in Scott, demands humor, tact, prudence, and a concerted opposition to threats of division. Divisiveness is embodied in Highland cousin MacIntosh of Kyllachy, who has been a betrayer in the past and who now threatens to betray Berlum and to reveal the presence in the attic of a Jacobite fugitive, Robert Strange. The threat is comic as *Redgauntlet* is comic. Strange, whose presence is insignificant and accidental, does not matter; the Haldanes have not been involved with the '45. But two members of the party have slipped Strange into the attic and now the problem is how to keep the secret from Mungo Haldane, magistrate and head of the house, and, once he has heard of it and decided to remain silent, what to do when Duncan Forbes of Culloden arrives for an overnight stay. By the time Culloden finds out, Strange has escaped, and Culloden chooses to do nothing. Kyllachy leaves in defeat, the "kindly house" ends in harmony and love, and the romance of history and ideology closes in comic resolution.

The counterpoint of comic domesticity and romantic past is further elaborated by the introduction of a modern romance dimension. Halfway through writing *The Bull Calves*, Mitchison read Jung's *The Integration of Personality* and found in it a confirming apparatus for the eighteenth-century version of "integration" or soul-saving she had conceived for Kirstie and William. She conceives of both Kirstie and William as descending into "dark waters" of past irrationality to achieve integration. Of course, "they need to put the thing as it might have appeared to them in words and ideas of their own time, with the additional help of Gaelic phrasing. But, because the archetypes of the unconscious are no less of the eighteenth century than of the twentieth— or any other fully human century—so some of the images will be the same" (514). Hearing Jung speak of "the general impoverishment of symbolism," she sees her book as helping to provide "mythologies which will be potent and protecting for our own era . . . not merely as protection for the individual, but also as social glue" (515-516). And so, in *The Bull Calves*, an archetypal process of individual and social therapy is interwoven with historical and comic romance. Character and event have their meaning on what allegorical critics would call three levels—historic particularity, cultural and ideological generality, and psychic archetype. An unusual achievement of this book is that all three are meaningfully integrated, and with this achievement Naomi Mitchison joins her great contemporaries in modern Scottish fiction, Lewis Grassic Gibbon and Neil Gunn.

In the years since *The Bull Calves* was published, there have been few signs in station bookracks or druggists' paperback shelves that Scotland has lost its unique position as the stereotypical land of popular romance. Perhaps only a social anthropologist could hope to interpret the current hunger for the Gothic, but it persists; and clearly romance, an embarrassment to the aesthetic solemnities of early modernism, has become a highly salable commodity to the frankly fabulous tastes of postmodernism. But the garish covers often hide thoroughly researched fictionalized histories and biographies. They are almost all by women, most of them non-Scots—though it is. noteworthy that *noms de plume* include "Jean Plaidy." And when D. K. Broster published her effective and exciting redaction of *Waverley*, *The Flight of the Heron*, she dedicated it as an Englishwoman's act of penance to the Scots poet Violet Jacob in homage.

It is too easy to pass off the phenomenon as merely exploitative or fraudulent; in fact, the talents are formidable and prolific and deserve far more than the glance accorded them here. In the 1960s, Jane Lane focused a number of sensitive, economical novels on the familiar tragic events of Scottish history: *Fortress in the Forth* on early Jacobitism, *Farewell to the White Cockade*—surprisingly good—on the latter days of the last Stuarts, *Queen of the Castle* on the last months of Mary Stuart, *A Wind through the Heather* on the Sutherland Clearances. Jane Oliver's novels—such as *Alexander the Glorious*, *The Lion is Come*, and *The Lion and the Rose*—are informed, if conventional, fictionalized biographies of Scottish monarchs, including of course the endlessly romanticized Mary. In two books—*The Captive Queen of Scots* and *The Royal Road to Fotheringay*—Jean Plaidy has offered a less conventional, ultimately psychoanalytic version of Mary. The single serious male contender in the field at present is Nigel Tranter,* whose long list is now capped by a large-scale trilogy on Robert Bruce, *The Steps to the Empty Throne, The Path of the Hero King,* and *The Price of the King's Peace.*[5]

Here, the manner of fictionalized biography continues fundamentally unchanged. The fitting of a conventional narrative formality to moments of consciousness and the inept sexual episodes merely call attention to the obsolescence of the mode. Interpretive historical biography would be more persuasive and original, while true romance would be more daring and imaginatively evocative, and the resurgence of both in recent years has left fictionalized biography, whatever contemporary touches are added, somewhat old-fashioned. Tranter's psychology is muted and simple; the torments of Bruce's conscience over the Comyn murder are alluded to occasionally for "moral" interest. Bruce is not presented as a complex, historical personality, but as "the hero king," with unusual emphasis on his partly Celtic ancestry and with thematic focus on his efforts to unite a divided nation against a common enemy. Battles and campaigns are laid out in orderly, clear fashion, but little attempt is made to include social history. The overall effect says something about the present state of the genre. While such books appeal to conservative romantic tastes, they have almost excluded romance elements and qualities and adhered to traditional realisms. And while they are more a branch of popular historiography than of imaginative fiction, they appear more and more an evasion of historical understanding.

A striking exception, Dorothy Dunnett,† promises something more

---

Tranter, Nigel. Born Nigel Tredgold in 1909 in Glasgow, Tranter studied at Heriot's College, Edinburgh. A full-time writer and television broadcaster, he has published over forty novels in addition to the Robert Bruce trilogy (see also the Master of Gray trilogy). He has written juvenile action stories and (under the name Nye Tredgold) Western adventures, and has published a three-volume study of the fortified house in Scottish architecture. He lives in Aberlady, East Lothian.

†*Dunnett, Dorothy.* Born in Dunfermline, Fife, in 1923, Dunnett is married to the former editor of *The Scotsman* and lives in Edinburgh. A professional portrait painter, she has exhibited at the Royal Scottish Academy. She has also written a series of mystery novels (the Johnson Johnson books), such as *Murder in the Round* (1970) and *Murder in Focus* (1973).

artistically exciting. She has published a romance cycle on the huge scale of Compton Mackenzie's *The Four Winds of Love,* in a style of equally ornate brilliance, and with a comparable hero of superhuman versatility. Six long volumes, appearing over fourteen years, trace the fabulous sixteenth-century mercenary career of the Byronic Francis Crawford of Lymond and Sevigny, betrayed and outlawed borderer, soldier of fortune, and protector par excellence of the child queen Mary Stuart (a minor figure in the cycle). He travels from Scotland and England to France, to Malta and Turkey, to the Russia of Ivan the Terrible (whose armies he commands), to the perilous London of Mary Tudor, France again, and finally—his strangely incestuous identity revealed, his legitimacy proved, his body and soul healed— home to Scotland. It is too soon to assess this intricate and ornate opus, but I will offer a general comment on its possible significance for present and future Scottish romance.

To begin with, it is ironic that romance itself in Scottish fiction has been the slowest of fictional modes to be liberated from realism. Scottish romance began in Scott with a decidedly antiromantic motive, an ironic aim of demythologizing the romantic past. In Dunnett's saga of Lymond the process is reversed—as, in other ways, Stevenson and Mitchison sought to reverse it. Reviewers' allusions to Dumas, Sabatini, and Ouida suggest the degree to which Dunnett has reinstated romance in all its exotic extravagance. The world of the cycle is densely historical. But the entire narrative design is governed by the ploys and artifices of chess, as the titles make clear: *The Game of Kings* (1961), *Queens' Play* (1964), *The Disorderly Knights* (1966), *Pawn in Frankincense* (1969), *The Ringed Castle* (1971), and *Checkmate* (1975).[6] Amid colorful violence and melodramatic power struggles, the game aesthetic prevails; the maneuvers of sixteenth-century Europe and the Middle East are surveyed in summary as on a chessboard; and the hero, Lymond, is one "whose game with life was a strange and rootless affair played with the intellect" (*PF* 126). At all costs the child queen is to be saved, and Lymond's most intimate alliances must be mere pawns in the game. On one occasion the structural metaphor becomes horribly literal: in the sultan's seraglio at Stamboul Lymond must play a living chess game in which captured pieces are killed, and one of them may be his own illegitimate son.

The flamboyant style conforms with versatility to the game-like design, adding a witty, aesthetic dimension to the most improbable of adventures—bizarre, bloody, farcical, grotesque, operatic. It is a style that accommodates breathtaking speed and heavily exotic texture and delights in everything from byzantine ritual to rooftop pursuit.

The sea slapped and hissed up and down the low freeboard, and on deck sprays of fire bloomed from gunplace to gunplace, sizzling in the burnt-orange haze. The sun had gone down, and although it was afternoon still, falling chiffons of light brown and russet concealed the light from the sky and enclosed the three ships and the glittering, indigo water in a strange saffron dusk. [*PF*, 44]

Fragile terror filled the black air, with the buffeting of wings and the confused music of flutes. The air held all the life of the garden: the scent of blood and of jasmine, the stench of candlegrease and of singed and burned taffeta. From the ground below there was no sound after Vishnevetsky, thrusting his shoulder among the green leaves, had stifled the flames, and taking fresh grip on his knife stood waiting, somewhere, as his eyes widened in the dark. A siskin, crying, touched Lymond's cheek and beat wildly off, its heart pulsing. [*RC*, 200]

They sprang from niche to balcony and swung between pillars. They arrived at ground level and freed a mastiff and unshackled the door of a pig sty: at first floor, and found looms and a great role of silk which streamed and bounded, calendating all their assailants; at second and third and fourth floors, and found sacks of flour to upset, or a bucket of slops or a wallsconce to send flying downwards, first from her hands and then from his, watched by the winged lions and griphons on the ceiling bosses, the angels guarding the windows; the fanged faces grinning from corbels or spewing open-throated from gutters above them. [*CM*, 86]

Narrative motifs, like styles, are extravagant, formulaic. It is difficult to recall a single romantic or mythic topos that is not included: the hero's mysterious birth and lineage; his love-hate struggles with his civil, prudent brother; his odyssey in quest of his bastard son, twin to the son of his archenemy, the fanatical fallen angel of the Maltese Knights known as Gabriel; the incredible coincidences and ambivalences of his look-alike bastard half-sister; his miraculous victories, betrayals, survivals. His brilliant career as mercenary general involves him with all the great sixteenth-century powers—"Lymond's life was lived on this level: the level on which the future of whole communities could be steered or reshaped, improved or jeopardized by a handful of people" (*RC*, 112)—and all, at one time or another, seek to exploit, possess, betray or destroy him. "But everyone," says his half-sister, "either abominates Francis Crawford or longs to possess him" (*CM*, 66), and most do both. A libertine yet curiously chaste, he is dominated by powerful, jealous women: Margaret Douglas, Countess of Lennox; Mary of Guise; his French fortune-teller and benefactress, the mysterious Dame de Doubtance; the magnificent Turkish courtesan "Güzel," who rescues him from opium addiction and primes him to rule Russia; the fanatical Irish patriot Oonagh O'Dwyer, who bears his child and is immolated by his diabolical enemy; his ultimate mate Philippa Somerville, brave, earthy, virginal Northumberland girl; and always his noble mother, whose favorite he has always been, and who calls on him frequently and largely in vain to recognize his proper Scottish destiny and come home.

> And in Scotland, what was there? A divided leadership. The French Dowager fighting the Earl of Arran for the Governorship during Queen Mary's childhood and wittingly or not, with every French coin she borrowed, ensuring Scotland's future as a province of France. And since England dared not have another France over her border, England was ready to seduce any Scottish noble, from Arran downwards, who did not care for the Queen Dowager, or France, or the old Catholicism. A divided nation; a divided God; a land of ancient, self-seeking families who broke and mended alliances daily as suited their convenience, and for whom the concept of nationhood was sterile frivolity . . . what could weld them in time, and turn them from their self-seeking and their pitiable, perpetual feuds? [*DK*, 216]

The romantic answer appears to be Lymond. And all factions appear bent on betraying him or keeping him unjustly exiled, just as all have sought to buy his extraordinary powers and have made him the desperate cynic he is. He is superb in will, wit, intelligence, and passion. He is commando leader, detective, scholar, musician, lover, actor, and indefatigable rhetorician. "I wish to God," says Philippa's father, "that you'd talk—just once—in prose like other people" (*GK*, 362); and the reader may well agree, for as Lymond concedes, "Nothing arouses suspicion quicker than genuine, all-round proficiency" (*GK*, 383). He is seen as "a brilliant young man going to waste" (*DK*, 240), a cold-blooded voluptuary of "scathing theatricality" (*PF*, 80); he is suspected of betraying his country, killing his sister, sacrificing his child. He himself is haunted by a sense of terrible crimes and betrayals, of a doom that destroys all who love him, and a sense that in every camp is one plotting to betray him. The epithet "Byronic" is inevitable. Yet above all he is a man of action, a Juanesque confidence man who almost conquers the world but comes home at last, fitted to be Scottish hero-king but denied by destiny and a corrupt world his proper role, and rewarded at last with legitimacy and pastoral true love.

With Lymond the persistence of Scottish romance achieves a new fictive apotheosis. Its effect on the novel proper cannot yet be conjectured. Yet, as we turn now to the novelists of twentieth-century Scotland, it becomes clear that the Juanism so prominent in Lymond's myth had already had significant impact in more modest precincts.

The Novel
and
National Myth
in
Modern Scotland

11

Contemporary Scotland
in
Fact and Myth

The ecological fact of mid-twentieth-century Scotland is whimsically captured by Michael Grieve in a spaceship image:

Narrow and ugly, slum-cluttered, Scotland's industrial belt stretches tight across the 24 miles from the estuary of the Clyde to the Firth of Forth. On the east coast, the belt expands to include Dundee—yet it is on this strip of development that one measures the size and importance of the Lowlands—and gauges the present strength of Scotland. Black from the toil of yesterday and today—with the islands of bright, cardboard-like factories on special estates—this industry-studded belt secures the flapping underpants of Scotland's south [the "borders" of legend and romance], and pins the spectacular but moth-eaten blouse of the Highlands.[1]

But for its violent contrasts—of postindustrial blight and pastoral loveliness, of megalopolis and wilderness—it seems hardly a landscape for romance and myth. Yet, while the romancer continues to refurbish old myths, the novelist shares newer ones with the social and political critic.

"The dominant myths of contemporary Scotland," writes H. J. Hanham, "are the continuity and distinctiveness of Scottish culture, the unique character of Scottish democracy, and the capacity of the Scots to run their own affairs better than they are at present run from Whitehall."[2] To these one might add two other dominant myths. First, however tongue-in-cheek, the most sophisticated of Scottish analysts are willing still to speak of "the Scot" as a national type; second, their discussions inevitably focus on the wholeness of Scotland. These myths, like the others, cannot but complicate the difficult situation of the modern Scottish novelist. It is hard for him to elude the many-sided question of national identity, and the generality of the question must seem a disconcerting intervention between the local reality and the universal issue that have come to be the novelist's twin poles.

Of late, the debates of Scottish identity and destiny have passed from literary hands to those of political economists, and this fact in itself suggests major changes. The Scottish novel began in times when the gradual disappearance of Scottish institutions and manners seemed to the ideologues of Unionist progress a foregone conclusion. Nationalism was relegated to the dreams of romance, and a fatalistic cultural nostalgia prevailed. The Scotland of fiction came to be seen, whether in love, hate, or an anguished mixture, at a distance as if with the eyes of exile, while the real Victorian nation moved into its North British heyday of imperial prosperity and farflung colonial enterprise. Political nationalism was never dead, but flickering, until the Home Rule agitations of the later nineteenth century. The trauma of World War I, the collapse of heavy industry, and the prolonged economic decline changed the "North British" atmosphere irreversibly: as Eric Linklater says, "A victorious peace brought few rewards other than unemployment and disillusion, and voices, more numerous than before, began to cry angrily for self-government."[3]

The Scottish Home Rule Association, born in the Gladstonian 1880s, uneasily raised amid Irish controversy, fostered by founders of the Independent Labour Party such as Keir Hardie, convened the Scottish National Convention in 1926 and gave way in 1928 to the new National Party of Scotland. It merged with the newer and more conservative Scottish Party in 1934 to form the Scottish National Party, which is alive and well forty years later, in spite of a history as turbulent and divisive in its way as the history of the nineteenth-century Scottish church. It has survived its own social and ideological divisions. It has survived the early and erratic role of its literati. "In the early 1960s," writes James Kellas, "a change came over the movement. Respectable, sober-minded businessmen and teachers started to join, and the fratricidal activities died down."[4] The 1960s saw the SNP achieve a new magnitude of support. When I lived in Scotland in the midfifties, political nationalism was seen with a mixture of condescension and comic alarm as a reckless tartan nuisance. When I returned a decade later the change was palpable, and the statistics of party growth prove it: from a membership of 2,000 and 20 individual branches in 1962 to a membership of 100,000 and over 500 branches in 1968, with the total SNP vote in general elections climbing from 7,000 in 1951 to 12,000 in 1955, 22,000 in 1959, 64,000 in 1964, 130,000 in 1966, 308,000 in 1970, and 733,000 in 1974. But where does the phenomenal growth lead? Even within the SNP ranks, the federal model has more support than full separation. In the Scottish Covenant drive launched in 1949 by John MacCormick and his allies, a majority of Scottish adults signed a demand for self-government within the United Kingdom framework; and Gallup polls still put popular approval of separatism at low percentages.

Argument over the degree and form of Scottish self-government has been one major part of the "Scottish Debate" in recent years.[6] The nuances of the debate illustrate painful contradictions that still characterize Scottish national consciousness. Secretary William Ross was not so peculiar when on the one hand he opposed further devolution and on the other he admonished Westminster not to interfere with Scottish institutions. Political and economic schizophrenia is widespread. Especially painful is the issue of whether nationalism itself is a dangerously reactionary tendency or, in its postwar manifestations, a legitimate libertarian movement, a resistance to the imperialism of the superpowers. Is the SNP merely an antilabor bourgeois movement, a focus for negative protest, a simplistic panacea? Should Scottish identity be sacrificed to an allegedly international drive for social progress, or can Scotland contribute more forcefully to that drive if it first institutionalizes its own sense of national unity?

Climactically, there is the issue of confidence. For centuries Scots have demonstrated their extraordinary resourcefulness, skill, and administrative talent on a worldwide scale. Now there are doubts as to whether Scotland has left the human resources and expertise to undertake self-government. Eric Linklater wondered what sort of legislators will be found to carry on Home Rule.[7] A Labour intellectual told Douglas Young that in practice a Scots Parliament might be no better than a Glasgow Town Council. Some Scottish members of Parliament conclude that they are unable to run their own country.[8]

A national mythology, centered on distinctive institutions, has kept alive these institutions and at the same time preserved nagging doubts about their viability. Church, education, law, and mercantile enterprise, conservative by nature, have survived through determination to preserve their traditional character, with the result that they have been reluctant to change. Take the law, for instance. James Kellas summarizes: "Legal rights in Scotland are based on the principles of a weak crown (that is, Executive), a strong Church, a strong feudal oligarchy, and a predominantly liberal criminal and civil code."[9] If we note the strong features, we can understand the view that a conservative legal elite stands in the way of much legal reform. Similar is the role of the church. Religious institutions have been paramount in preserving a semblance of unity in Scotland; the popular, national character of the Kirk has kept it alive, and there is agreement that religion continues to play an influential role in Scottish society. There is a disputacious presbyterian energy even among anti-Calvinists, and many of us have heard of the angry Scot who insisted that he was a Presbyterian atheist. But Calvinism remains, as William Ferguson calls it, "that bogeyman of the avant garde from David Hume's day to our own"[10]; one of the chief energies of literary nationalism is the obsessive debunking of the church. Finally, the long-lived myth of Scottish democratic education is now challenged. Having achieved its own Education Department, Scottish education discovers self-doubts. Traditional strengths are seen as obstacles to progress: a generalist arts tradition obstructs specialist training; an "argumentative" or "deductive" mode of learning is found uncreative or abstract. In Scottish popular myth the sadistic dominie gives way to the feckless academic sentimentalist. The two stereotypes combine wondrously in that extraordinary character Miss Jean Brodie.[11]

Behind the lack of confidence lie the desolate statistics of emigration. The net loss by emigration from 1861 to 1951 was 1,585,000 people, forty-three percent of the natural increase. Emigration during the 1960s averaged 35,300 annually, an increase of 10,000 over the average of the previous decade.[12] The tendency has long been there. Some celebrate the Scots as born wanderers and Scotland as a land of escapes and emigrations. Alastair Reid's secret hero in a Border boyhood was "a vague uncle, who turned up only twice in my life, but who had lived in the Cococ Islands, and filled my ears with such towering stories in the course of one small walk that my fantasy and my present life were divided for ever after."[13] I asked Neil Gunn once why he left Dunbeath when he was twelve, and the answer was to the effect that "it was just the thing to do." But the tendency, long established, became a cause: the example was magnetic, and growing numbers of Scots abroad provided the means by which more could make their way. And while the exodus pattern is age-old, romantic, and self-nourishing, its economic motive and its cumulative impact on confidence at home are undeniable. The emigré grows large at a mythic distance, while the remnant that stays home, feeling inferior and defensive, makes compensatory myths and laments the drain of the able and ambitious. This, at least, is the image that haunts the modern literary consciousness.

How did the mighty fall? It is a sop for Calvinist morality. In the days of farflung imperial opportunity, emigration was an adventure for wealth and status. The economic shift seemed so sudden and drastic as to invite superstitious awe and tragic saga. Scotland had led the world in heavy industrialization. First came the romance of Scottish Victorian fame, technological and entrepreneurial; then the romance ended and Scotland paid the price. Heavy industry and agriculture declined, and unemployment reached almost thirty percent in the early 1930s. World War II brought an artificial recovery, but the problem of chronic unemployment remained, part of a vicious circle of emigration, low wages, and poor housing. New industries have begun, but much advance has been held back by inadequate retraining programs. The 1960s brought the beginnings of regional planning, but such efforts seemed doomed by Britain's overall economic plight. The problem, commentators agree, has not been natural but human. Analysts of different persuasions agree with Malcolm Slesser, chemical engineer at Strathclyde: "I can see that Scotland has every national asset necessary for her to become a modern prosperous state . . . yet its most talented sons and daughters are obliged to leave their homeland year by year to seek elsewhere the opportunities they cannot find at home. Why? Because Scotland is like a ship without a rudder."[14]

Growing numbers point to other small nations that control their own affairs. The emergence of modern Scotland into a world of Cold War politics and massive bureaucratic powers has awakened her kinship with other small nations likewise dominated or menaced. Her role in colonial administration and missionary enterprise has now brought her home again. Her internationalism makes of her small-nation consciousness a sense of union with defeated cultures and an awareness of new models and alliances. Decentralism has become a strong trend. The economic policies of the SNP are compared to those of Norway, Switzerland, and Israel. Housing policies are measured by those of Sweden; linguistic preservation is contrasted with that of the Faroese. In a world struggling to survive, suggests J. M. Reid, Scotland may have a unique place: "In an international society nations will still be needed—nations conscious of their individuality and free to develop their own qualities, but conscious also that the life of mankind must be preserved by their agreement. Scotland, whose identity has survived so many trials and changes, is perhaps peculiarly suited to take her part in such a future."[1]

In a paradoxical new small-nation internationalism, Scotland's nagging sense of provinciality takes on a new meaning. Cosmopolitanism has generated giant neocolonial bureaucracies trapped in paranoid arms races. Cultural and ethnic pluralism, no longer merely picturesque, becomes a recipe for civilization's survival. It becomes the wisdom of humility and moral realism to recognize that man's is a "village mind," that allegiances are most real when local. For Scots, parochial allegiances remain strong. The "wee burgh" remains the most comprehensible environment for many, and even in the large cities what Clifford Hanley calls "the *Gemütlichkeit* of close society" is a deeply planted factor.[16] The fears of depersonalizing urbanization, the horror of new urban renewal housing projects, have been keynotes of modern Scottish fiction from George Blake's *Mince Collop Close* to Iain Crichton Smith's *My Last Duchess* and Elspeth Davie's *Creating a Scene*.

The point is not that Scotland is unusual in its "village" mentality. Urban ethnographers may well discover otherwise. The point is that Scottish observers have long stressed it primarily with dismay or condescension, but recently with a perceptibly positive shift of tone. In a world where local attachment and cultural pluralism seem essential to human survival, the phenomenon need no longer be a cause of dismay or denigration in Scotland. The Scottish example evinces a capacity to remain vigorously identified with a small and homogeneous community and at the same time to flourish as a citizen of the world. We will see this salutary paradox slowly growing as a theme in the course of the twentieth-century novel.

12

Novelists
of the
Modern Renaissance

W hat is now a call for economic renaissance began as a celebration of literary renaissance half a century ago. "In
1928 there was much cause for discontent," recalls Linklater; and with the founding of national convention and party came
the revival of letters. There were numerous men and women of genius
and energy at the time: MacDiarmid and Muir in poetry; Gibbon,
Gunn, Mackenzie, Linklater, Naomi Mitchison, Blake in fiction; Bridie in drama; and older figures of romance, such as Cunninghame
Graham, Buchan, and Spence. The extraordinary influence of Mac-
Diarmid makes it too easy to see in the Renaissance only a preoccupation with poetry. And while generously praising a few novels, Mac-
Diarmid has often expressed the view that the novel is an inherently
inferior form, with the result that the novelist has had to face the
scepticism or hostility of the Scots Renaissance establishment. In the
early 1930s, Edwin Muir saw the lack of vitality in the novel as an
index of disbelief in Scottish society. In 1935, Linklater endorsed this
unhappy diagnosis and saw the novelists' choices as sorely limited:
"They may avoid Scottish themes; or deal with them in a parochial
spirit that belittles what is already small enough; or confine themselves to some remote parcel of geography, to some distant fragment
of life, and find in that solitary corner a significance that is clearly
lacking in the whole."[1] Even so, the novel offered a means of representing the Scottish situation on a scale and in a mode available to no

other form. Around 1930, as Willa Muir confirms in her recent memoir, the novel was clearly in "the air." Even she and Edwin tried it.

Willa Muir's* first novel, *Imagined Corners* (1931), "had enough material in it," she recalls, "for two novels, which I was too amateurish to realize at the time."[2] The book is a *Middlemarch* of a modern northeast Scottish coastal burgh torn by sexual and religious conflicts, with its Miss Brooke struggling temporarily in a provincial web. The Eliot model is evident in the book, though the polarities are distinctively Scottish, and the represented burgh recalls G. D. Brown and anticipates Gibbon's *Cloud Howe*. Replacing Eliot's structural metaphor of the web is the image of a crystal dropped in a solution, suggesting the reactions and precipitations of a taut, traditional, seemingly segmented community when a new element is introduced.

The new element is widowed Madame Mütze, long-ago renegade from the burgh, fugitive sister of the propertied Shand family. Her return precipitates the middle of the action; her departure closes the novel. She has saved one derelict of Calderwick, the deserted wife she takes with her, and has discovered her moral limits in learning she is powerless to save more. She has returned after twenty years, a scornful exile, to see if Scotland has any integrity, ideological or cultural. She rediscovers her home, her self, her limits, and stays long enough to lose her contempt for Calderwick and to find beneath the mill town's gossipy, mean, and dull exterior a severe honesty and a genuine if limited charity:

> An undercurrent of kindly sentiment that runs strong and full beneath many Scots characters, a sort of family feeling for mankind

*Muir, Edwin and Willa. Edwin was born in 1887 in Deerness, Orkney; Willa (Wilhelmina Anderson), in 1890 in Montrose, Angus, of Shetland parents. Edwin's farm family migrated when he was in his teens to Glasgow, where both parents soon died. Ill and neurotic, Edwin worked as an office clerk. Willa attended St. Andrews on a bursary, and was a lecturer on psychology at a London training college when they met in 1918; by this time, Edwin had read his way from evangelical Christianity through socialism to Nietzsche and was writing "propagandist poetry." They were married in 1919; their marriage of forty years is movingly detailed by Willa in *Belonging* (1968). He worked as a London journalist, and when his income as a successful free-lance critic permitted, they moved to Prague, and thereafter lived in Germany, Italy, and Austria, where their careers as translators began. Their translations comprise forty-three volumes; best known are novels by Kafka and Broch. During World War II Edwin went to work for the British which is expressed by the saying: "We're all John Tamson's bairns" . . . It is a vaguely egalitarian sentiment, and it enables the Scot to handle all sorts of people as if they were his blood relations. Consequently in Scotland there is a social order of rigid severity, for if people did not hold each other off who knows what might happen? The so-called individualism of the Scots is merely an attempt on the part of every Scot to keep every other Scot from exercising the privileges of a brother . . . The whole of Calderwick is bound together by invisible links of sympathy . . . It is not everyone who can live without embarrassment in a Scots community.[3]

Nonetheless, the culture is deeply polarized. Elizabeth, one of the Shands' exploited women, remembers "only the two extremes of her vision." The extremes are religious and sexual, and the dual polarities are analogous. William the minister is inattentive and impractical because he has believed only in the peace of God and a sinless world, whereas his brother Ned, his polar self, has seen nothing but evil and hence has gone mad. William must discover that God's anger is as real as his love, that on this side of eternity are both heaven and hell. But the only result of his discovery is hell-fire preaching; he finds no balance, no integrated self—and, symbolically, he drowns at the end. Polarized likewise are visions of body and spirit. The Shands have divided between a horror of the body and a wild sexuality. Hector Shand is raised in an unbalanced world, "between the two poles," in a family whose men are a legend of unbridled sexuality and whose repressed women are trapped in a myth of wifehood. Through a series of fugitive affairs and disgraces, he, too, must learn that only in balance and integrity can body and mind become a self, but that even the achievement of a self does not lift one above this provincial world or one's own caprice. Such is the lesson that Madame Mütze learns from her rediscovery of Scotland.

Council, which sent them, following 1945, back to Prague and then Rome. Back in Scotland, Edwin headed Newbattle Abbey College from 1950 to 1955. He was Norton Professor of Poetry at Harvard in 1955-56, and then they retired to Cambridge, England, where he died in 1959. His poetry achieved late recognition, and is now widely admired: see *The Voyage* (1946) and *The Labyrinth* (1949). Willa and Edwin both wrote volumes for the "Voice of Scotland" series begun by J. Leslie Mitchell—she, *Mrs. Grundy in Scotland*, and he, *Scott and Scotland*. He has been called Scotland's first truly philosophical modern critic—see *The Structure of the Novel* (1928) and *Essays in Literature and Society* (1949). His *Autobiography* (1954) is a masterpiece of modern life writing. Willa has also published *Living with Ballads*.

The book includes many counterpointed variants on its theme. Its method is that of *Middlemarch*, with a structure of alternating centers of consciousness and parallel domestic plots; each tangles increasingly with the rest yet maintains its separateness. Culturally particular and psychologically general, the book has its additional burden of representativeness. Divided Calderwick is the Scotland of the Muirs. Character types abundantly localize Calderwick as a Scottish burgh: the minister, the sceptical doctor, the disgraced and lunatic student, the wives risen from farm and rural school, the Shand heritage—one brother the red Highland Viking, the other dark, sensitive, lecherous. The book opens in witty "kailyard" conjecture as to how northern twilights "may have first sharpened the discrimination of the natives to that acuteness for which they are renowned." But the heroine's quest for Scottish community and ideology becomes chiefly the means to her compassionate discovery of the universal plight of human narrowness, especially for women, and of the limits and flaws of human love. The book points ahead to Robin Jenkins, whose novels it resembles far more than it does the novels of Willa Muir's husband.

Willa explains Edwin's unsuccesses in the novel thus:

> Edwin had apparently decided that prose novels had better not come out of the "queer part" of himself which produced his poems, and that he could distance his personal emotions sufficiently by setting his scene in the sixteenth century, as in *The Three Brothers*. The result was not quite convincing nor was there enough romantic glamour in it to draw public interest. Undaunted, Edwin then wrote *Poor Tom* as a purely contemporary study of life in Glasgow, again using his own family experiences, but again in this book, which contained much that was finely imagined and moving, he failed to attract a public.[4]

At the time, Edwin thought *The Three Brothers* (1931) "the best thing I've done up to now." The most impressive parts, P. H. Butter feels, portray the inner world of the young protagonist.[5] This is so, for the novel *does* come from the same Muir that produced the poems, and it is not a conventional historical novel. It is a theological novel of personal crises, after the manner of J. H. Shorthouse or Pater's *Marius*, in which the hero's maturing centers painfully on a collision of faiths and allegiances dramatized at an historic moment, that of Beaton and the young Knox. David Blackadder awakens to the horrifying polarities of Scottish life, and the options of faith are the ways available for trying to live with them. The motif of the brothers recalls novels such as Scott's *Monastery* and Mérimée's *Chronicle of the Reign of Charles IX*, in which ideological differences split up families and domestic situations become the emblems of historic conflict. David's mother remains Catholic; his father, after years of exile in Europe, is a Rabelaisian humanist. The three sons all become Calvinists at college in St. Andrews, and their various struggles with Calvinism are the chief matter of the novel.

Their conflicts are personal. David is withdrawn, pacific, timid; Archie is outgoing, rough, adaptive; the oldest, Sandy, is an outcast because he was born just two months after his parents' wedding and has grown up warped by rejection, obsessed with guilty sexuality. The wee error of his father and mother, he says, has ruined his life, and his big lustful wife Alison is his horrifying vision of adult sexuality as sadistic and punitive. He sees her, too, as a Calvinist's Satan or one marked by the devil to be his scourge. In a single figure are joined his guilty dread of sexuality and the horrified infatuation of his Calvinism.

The book's burden is Muir's characteristic war with Calvinism, which is fought with fearful admiration and is somehow won by being lost. "Calvinism," says Sandy, "makes all the other creeds look like bairn's play, it takes all into account that you can take into account, and there's a kind of satisfaction in that, too." But here is no resting place for David. Moreover, the anabaptism of his swashbuckling young friend Cranstoun leads only to sexual rivalry and violence. The humanist alternative—his father's secret black books and neopagan sexuality—remains distant and ineffectual as his father, home from exile, ages into a dull peasant. All that transcends Calvinism is the red worm that stretches its head up from his mother's grave, "up and up as if in blind unending prayer—wreathing its long length out of the mould in the sunshine, and it was like an inarticulate sign, a dumb announcement."[6]

David's grim Scotland is unacceptable as a place, narrow and brutal. The Falsyth of his pastoral boyhood is best; the Edinburgh where Sandy lives and dies is a place of noise, stench, violence, and sexual menace. Return to the farm offers only dull stagnation. David's Scottishness is disintegrated throughout. In a world where Scots is spoken, his long, impressionistic reflections and dreams are in English, recalling the strange bifurcation of communication and thought, of experience and feeling, which Muir found symptomatic of the emptiness at the center of Scottish culture. For David as for Muir, Scotland offered only painful psychic polarities and cultural options either frightening or stagnant.

Poor Tom (1932), set in modern Glasgow, is a very different novel, yet the Scotland depicted there is essentially the same. David Blackadder was overwhelmed with the stench and sinfulness of the city, and a profound regret courses through poor Tom at having come to this awful place. Tom is a pathetic victim of the city and of his inability to adapt to its peculiar falsenesses, religious and sexual. The stringent Calvinism of burghal orthodoxy has turned to a sickly Baptist respectability, a naiveté of Scout marches and sentimental insincere socialism; the ambivalent but tough Calvinism of the Blackadders is now condemning a soft, urban middle-class "puritanism." The gusty, real sexuality that young men of the northern islands had found by climbing through windows to their sweethearts' beds has given way to middle-class appearances and a vague pregenital sexuality that stops with genteel kissing and looks back in guilt at childhood games. Poor Tom takes to drink and brooding by the fire. One night he falls off a tram, and the neglected head wound produces a tumor, recurrent and increasing fits or strokes, and eventually death. Much of the later book is the family's waiting for Tom's death. His illness comes to symbolize the wounded and doomed emptiness that sits at the center of their lives, and it finally destroys the facility of their adaptation to this strange place—the "atmosphere disinfected by the future" in which they live. Yet they make little effort to understand and deal with what that emptiness means.

Tom's brother Mansie, his rival and opposite, becomes the exception and Tom's sympathetic custodian. Tom's fate becomes something of a corrective to Mansie's facile adaptation to the city's falsenesses. Its pseudosexuality is fine with Mansie; he joins the Christianity of nicely scrubbed Baptists, the hollow talk of the socialists, the Clarion Scouts in their May Day march, the club dances and whist drives. Though Mansie comes to embody Muir's detestation of Glasgow's cultural void, he is nevertheless a sensitive, Muir-like center for the novel. His walks through the slum streets are rendered fully and impressionistically; he copes emotionally with the horror and dirt by distancing it with naive eroticism and juvenile socialism. Yet he struggles self-consciously to serve and to understand Tom's fate, as he blames himself—or what he has come to represent—for that fate.

What Muir is doing becomes clear. As modern Glasgow is realized through the evasive but adaptive sensibility of Mansie, the protective sentimentalities—social and political—by which it survives are condemned. The condemnation is conveyed with the sympathy but severity of one for whom Calvinism with its harsher vision of the fallen human city still "makes all the other creeds look like bairn's play." The book, like *The Three Brothers*, is a struggle for an adequate, theologically valid way of envisioning the cultural emptiness of modern Scotland. Yet it remains a carefully focused tragic story of a few lives, deliberately limited in its social and historical scope, modestly true to its own narrative limits.

The aspirations of the Muirs' contemporaries in narrative fiction were far more ambitious and abstract. The novel was "in the air" of Scotland in the early thirties because, for a number of novelists, it invited the creation of national epic or myth. In seeking to make so much of the novel, they sometimes neglected its limits or diffused its powers. Modern critics would not place together the Glasgow and Garvel fictions of George Blake, the *Four Winds* tetralogy of Compton Mackenzie, and the *Scots Quair* of Leslie Mitchell. Yet all are part of a single epic impulse or phase of the Scottish novel of the 1930s.

George Blake* is remembered chiefly as the author of a major novel that failed, *The Shipbuilders* (1935). Eric Linklater thought it failed because Blake, whatever his talent for epic panorama, did not believe in his principal characters and consequently sentimentalized them out of plausibility.[7] Blake himself, judicious in his appraisal of the novel in modern Scotland, was more just in identifying his own limits. In a late fifties British Broadcasting Corporation retrospect, he "pleads guilty to an insufficient knowledge of working-class life and to the adoption of a middle-class attitude to the theme of industrial conflict and despair." He grants modest approbation to his own fictional retirement to Garvel, its genteelly decadent mercantile bourgeoisie, its perilously

*Blake, George. Born at Greenock, Renfrewshire, in 1893, and died in Glasgow in 1961. He studied law, but after service in World War I, where he was wounded at Gallipoli, he turned to journalism. He wrote for the Glasgow *Evening News*, moved to London to edit *John o' London's Weekly*, spent some years as director of a publishing firm, then became a full-time writer. In addition to some two dozen novels, he wrote criticism (*Barrie and the Kailyard School*, 1951), travel (*The Heart of Scotland*, 1934), and the partly autobiographical chronicle of his favorite subject, the Clyde, in *Down to the Sea* (1937).

haunting Firth of Clyde background, its West End domestic problem-dramas of enfeebled dynasts and their nobly stoic widows and daughters. And he cites "above all, his respect for the architectonic verities of the novel," for "the architecture of a long novel": "here is a sort of norm, like that of a Scottish Arnold Bennett."[8] The estimate is perceptive, fair, and courageous. But it concedes too much when it singles out just *The Westering Sun* (1946) as a full display of Blake's qualities.

The several Garvel novels that followed *The Westering Sun*—*The Paying Guest* (1949), *The Voyage Home* (1952), *The Peacock Palace* (1958), and others—continue the use of a milieu and a mode established earlier. But the question of how the author of *Mince Collop Close* (1923) developed into the author of *The Westering Sun* is of interest for an understanding of the early modern Scottish novel. And *The Shipbuilders*, while best known, is by no means the only remarkable work in the process of this development.

The first two of the seven novels to be discussed here[9] predate the ambitious, "epic" program of the early thirties, which Blake shared with Compton Mackenzie and Leslie Mitchell. *Mince Collop Close* is the lively chronicle of a Glasgow slum Moll Flanders named Bella McFadyen. *The Path of Glory*, five years later, is a devastating short novel about a misty-minded Benbecula tinker amid the grotesque horrors of trench warfare. The tinker is dimwitted kin to Munro's Gilian the Dreamer and Barrie's Sentimental Tommy, wandering lost in the trenches of Gallipoli. *Mince Collop Close* recalls Crockett's *Cleg Kelly* and looks forward to Jenkins' *The Changeling*.

Bella, having survived the efforts of a middle-class philanthropist to remove her from her gang-ridden, filthy home, grows up "firmly determined and well equipped to work out her destiny according to her own ideas." They are ideas of survival and power, and she becomes Queen of the Fan-Tans, dealing ruthlessly with rivals, playing an unsentimental Robin Hood, with a hunger for adventure and reward, a "fierce passion for efficiency," and a hatred of tyranny. The picture is vivid and unforced, the style terse and jocular, the character of Bella free of the typological weight that later Blake protagonists must carry. The narrative is episodic—no ambitious architectonics in sight. Bella grows up, discovers softer longings as a woman, and stows away with her Danny on a steamer for "the promising shores of the New World." It seems that only a triumphant child—or a dim-witted tinker—can survive amid the horrors of modern Glasgow or Gallipoli. These early

214

Blake protagonists elude the problems of adult consciousness, insulating us by their brutal innocence from the graphically real modern worlds we see them in. The characterological challenge of *The Shipbuilders* was still to come.

It was similar to the challenge faced simultaneously by Mackenzie and Mitchell. The epic novel of modern Scotland was to project a new ideology of national survival and at the same time demythologize a past that had become a force of romantic betrayal. Each demanded a protagonist with strong roots in a national past who could still present an admirable, viable identity in the face of a hostile, depersonalized modern world. Mackenzie with John Ogilvie went unblushingly the way of archetypal romance, and Mitchell's Chris has the qualities of myth in a real world mythically transfigured. Blake went the way of the naturalist-realist, and the result in Danny Shields the shipbuilder is a figure with many weaknesses, yet with a lonely nobility. But Danny's characterization is insistently generic, and hence his nobility is considerably softened, his reality is compromised, and the combination results in what some would call "sentimentality."

The parallel structure of *The Shipbuilders* follows the destinies of two men through the Depression months, when the Glasgow shipyards were closing, and through their personal crises as husbands and fathers. The wealthy manager Leslie Pagan of Pagan's Yard is last heir to a shipbuilding tradition. His loyal servant Danny Shields the riveter is the traditional artisan, protected temporarily by his boss, kept on as gardener and handyman, then out of work. The book contrasts the elegant waste and defeatism of Pagan's life with the poverty and gradual degradation of a Partick tenement, until at last Pagan has resigned himself to his wife's southern ways and become an English country gentleman and Danny has survived the temporary degradation of drunkenness, fights, and fifteen days in jail, lost his nagging wife, and settled happily into middle-aged adultery at the country-smelling little house of an old friend's kindly widow. Pagan and Danny are essentially good, but helpless, and weak; both seem pathetically alone in the collapsing world they try in vain to share. And while this is the world of the commerce of shipbuilding, Danny is scarcely ever seen at work because the work is gone, and Leslie, gradually resigned to closing his father's yard, sees the industry only as a past glory or a dream to pass on to his son.

The problem is that while both characters are presented as cultural types, what they typify is no longer real or effectual; in fact, the typicality of each seems a noble illusion in the mind of the other. Yet the illusion seems half-shared by the narrator. Both are trapped in a system that is rotten and unjust, doomed by economic necessity. Yet for them the tragedy is beyond economics, and they try to live with the illusion that each is large enough, representatively real enough, to provide the corrective. The hope is clearly futile. But is its futility primarily economic or moral? Both men are weak, but does it matter? The narrator never quite settles the implications of their human weaknesses, never quite denies the illusion by which they attempt to live, never achieves the analytical distance from which its futility might be judged and accepted.

Moreover, the architectonics dictate using the two men as central consciousnesses. The complexity of their economic situation is clearly beyond the understanding of both. But there is no clear sense of alternative, no controlled dramatic irony. So while their conceptions of their plight are pathetic, partial, even illusory, somehow we are left with them. Danny has only "some dim sense of the economic crime that had been committed" and Leslie does not have a great deal more, yet the narrator's own view is obscured by his sympathies and we are forced to wonder: does he not share Danny's dim sense or Leslie's pained confusion? It is symptomatic that the narrator's intense involvement focuses with love and pity on Danny and his boss and turns in hatred on Danny's nouveau-riche sister-in-law and her con-man gambler husband Jim. They are pasteboard vulgarians. Yet they, too, are products of this ugly, queer new environment; in fact, they are mastering it, they are more sharply aware of the social truth than Danny and Leslie, aware in a way the narrator, in his love for central figures he knows to be weak and deluded anachronisms, cannot tolerate. The naturalist in Blake admits that Jim too, has degenerated, from a decent dairy foreman to a clever investor "with his queer, ambiguous interests in bookmaking, the films, boxing, and, indeed, all those activities that, catering for an uneasy generation, shelter and sustain in affluence so many latter-day pimps." The naturalist sees Danny's brutalized son Peter, who becomes involved in a gang knifing of a bookie's runner at a dance hall in Govan, as another awful product; yet Peter wins no sympathy from Danny or the narrator. While Blake the naturalist must include Lizzie, Jim, and Peter, Blake the romantic cannot separate them from Danny's own simple, traditional moral vision.

The narrator is similarly divided in the presence of the tragic pageant of the once-glorious Clyde. We hear of the great tradition when Leslie Pagan drives his sickly son down the river and discovers, in the history he tells his child, "the splendour of the story his family had lived for generations." Yet now: "It was written. The supreme glory had departed." Was the glory ever real, except as a story told to a child? Was the truth a tale of brief, brutal capitalist warfare leading to exploitation and collapse? The glory is revisited, and each time the chastisement is repeated; Leslie's son catches little other than a bad chill and near pneumonia from the futile escapade with his romantic father. It is a deflationary effect repeated with devastating control in Jenkins' *Changeling*. Lurking behind Blake the romantic elegist is an uncertain Calvinist, and this vivid panorama verges on idolatrous fraud.

Blake would mature as a novelist only when he could face artistically the ambivalence at the heart of his vision of the Clyde, with the suspicion that the romance might be real only for a child. It is meaningful that he turned from the uncertain success of *The Shipbuilders* to *David and Joanna* (1936). Before settling into his ultimate locale, he returned to the Glasgow of Bella McFadyen, or, at least, of juvenile adventure, rebellion, and escape.

David and Joanna offers Blake's link between the strange ironies of Barrie's Peter and Wendy and the more caustic ones of Robin Jenkins' characters. The rebellious young lovers are in yearning flight from Glasgow's vulgar commercialism and mean repression. David is in love not just with Joanna but with his new bicycle and his dreams of edenic innocence and free love up Lochlomondside. He is an orphan raised by the awful presbyterian Aunt Ashie and the absurd fake invalid Uncle Daniel. From Blake's genre pictures of a dull, sabbatarian Glasgow home, the young lovers flee to the pastoral Scotland of their ancestors. The narrator shares their yearning for escape from the dingy repressive city to green and sinless places. But their idyll is invaded by the respectable, by the holiday hordes, by gross city kinfolk who, like the grotesques of Jenkins' *Changeling*, break with infernal humor into the earthly paradise of the glen. The villains, however, are not just external. The idyll is illusory. If freedom and defiance are only youthful adventure, based on a faith that sinless summer can go on forever, they are not real. And finally the bicycle is broken, the tent site is washed out by the rains, Joanna is pregnant and must be trapped into a wedding her bohemianism deplores, and David settles down as bartender in Brodie's pub.

Blake sees a terrible pathos in the plight of "these children of an industrial civilization" and of "the doctrines of John Calvin," but he sees a terrible irony, too, in the way their illusions betray them. David is a grand self-deceiver, a weakling, and Joanna, though stronger, is betrayed by his divided, immature defiance. He is trapped not just by Glasgow but by his own "romantic tendencies" and his sentimental attachment to the sabbatarian world of Aunt Ashie. The key to David's weakness is the book's subtlest character, one of Blake's finest creations, Aunt Ashie's pleasant mercantile lodger Mr. Balharrie. With his seeming sympathy, his bent toward the feudal and the antiquarian, his aging boyish passion for maps and place names, his comic obsessions, Balharrie is the believable, unwitting devil whose kindly respectability traps David into docility, and leaves pregnant, defiant Joanna with nothing but dreams of their next escape.

The book's jarring ironies are controlled and strangely moving. And they prepare one for the burghal world of Garvel in the book that follows, *Late Harvest* (1938). This is not yet the Garvel of Victorian shipbuilding romance and elegy, but the industrial town of the depressed twenties and thirties, the Garvel of *Green Shutters* tradition, repressive kirk, mean respectability, awful shopkeepers, and sniggering about sex—the Garvel of Webster Urie, Session Clerk of Martyrs U. F. Kirk, his orphaned niece Livvy (the novel's strong heroine), and the two weak or unstable males who represent her narrow alternatives for escape.

This book achieves the large-scale architectonics of which Blake modestly boasts. It is organized in eight long chapters, each with episodic subchapters that keep many complementary centers of consciousness operative and keep numerous facets of theme and situation before us. The unpleasant central fact of Garvel is shown through various eyes as a single problem. The three lives of the love triangle are deliberately alternated and interwoven, each in its way a rebellion against Garvel. Livvy is the strong and stable one, an orphaned woman struggling with her choice between Roddie, heir of the aristocratic but daft Drummonds, and Duncan Troup, the kindly and liberal but dull, weak, and sentimental new minister. Poor Troup is an extraordinary character, deserving, courageous, yet compromised; and his plight is the plight of the kirk in Garvel. A lonely bachelor, he fails at last in his wooing as in his ministry. Livvy chooses Roddie because she must finally choose the dream of freedom, of escape, yet he is a "daft Drummond," evasive, feckless—a problem to love, a boy:

> He would never cease to delight her, never cease to astonish her. Handsome—but that was little enough. It was his fun, his boldness, his wildness, his unexpectedness, and always his tenderness. There was, she knew, a lot of plain common sense and serious goodwill behind what Garvel disapprovingly called his daftness. But so difficult to find him serious! He would wriggle like an eel from between the clutching fingers of any grave problem. With herself he had to sublimate emotion in a parody of gallantry. She knew that, for some deep and mysterious reason, he feared emotion and sentiment. Perhaps because he was afraid of being betrayed by them? Perhaps because his childhood had been lonely and his temperament made him conspicuous in the safely ordered world of Garvel? A sort of Changeling?[10]

The changeling theme is central, as again in *The Constant Star*. For the free spirit, no adjustment, no reality is possible, and escape is the only choice. It is pathetic that the mature, strong Livvy must choose the eccentric, immature "older way" of the Drummonds; but for Blake it is preferable to West Garvel, and for Blake, the East Garvel of the working classes scarcely exists.

Garvel will become the deliberately restricted arena of the later novels—these the limited alternatives—this the endless plight of woman, the moderating realist, forced to choose among history's male alternatives of feckless or corrupt weakness. But in *Late Harvest* the central figures carry no such archetypal burden, and Blake's craftly realism flourishes at a safe remove from history and romance. Not so in the first full historical romance that exploits Garvel, *The Constant Star* (1945). Here, the symbolic weight, the large-scale architectonics, the stress on history as spectacle and on character as eternal polar conflict bury the realist. The book spans sixty years and three generations of Garvel's shipbuilding Oliphants, from the arrival in 1807 of the two nephew heirs, through the coming of steam and iron, to Crimea, Civil War, and Suez. Ship types symbolize historic epochs and cultural phases and options, and characters can do little more.

The nephews come inevitably from Ayrshire parish (Mark the ruthless capitalist power lord) and Highland manse (Julius the designer, the dreamer). Julius loves and marries the remote, half-French cousin Barbara Rait, whose unillusioned strength and wisdom are unmatched in the world of male eccentricities and failures. It is Barbara who sees all history as a struggle against "the Mark Oliphants of this world," a "war which never ends"; it is her brother Bob Rait, cynical ship's captain, who serves as the book's enduring raisonneur. But too much of the book is seen through the eyes of Julius: "It would have been fine, he thought, to stand on the escarpment before the Mount and from there, pensive and aloof, watch history pass in a moving picture under his eyes"—or to see "the small interior as if it had been a scene on the stage of a theatre." Julius's flaw is his aestheticism, and it is disastrous in the eternal war against the Mark Oliphants; but in *The Constant Star* it is not clear that Blake offers any more viable antagonist, or indeed has resolved his own attitudes toward the historic necessity of the Mark Oliphants.

Mark, on the other hand, must fail because he confuses grace with worth, has no eye "for the value of a tradition rooted in the soil," "has no sense of time or history." But what valid tradition is available? And is not the book's "sense of time and history" limited and diffused among Barbara's patrician view of endless war, her brother's cynical sense of decadence and dotage, and the futile elegance of Julius, unaware of evil? The star is not "constant," yet the symbolic spectacle is all the book finally offers.

And so, with a nice old-fashioned formality, the dignity of the Eighteenth prevailing into the Nineteenth Century under the spars of a tall ship, the two generations passed into family council.

There was silence in the little room for a space, and again Walter was visited by the subtle sense of a large significance in the small gathering. He suddenly saw his own father [Julius] as an aging, indecisive man, bewildered by portents and tempted to retire into the gracious ease of the past, while the other dark man of equal age pushed his way out of an insufficient environment towards power, greater and greater power, that most alluring houri of all the ambitions. His literary fancy saw the eighteenth and nineteenth centuries in opposition, the philosophical part of his brain thought to behold a special staging of the eternal conflict between Thinker and Doer. In his young and romantic imagination the afternoon sunlight in the parlour seemed charged with a sadness intolerably sweet.[11]

The problem of the book is here: a vision of eternal conflict in history undercuts itself as mere "literary fancy," and is suffused at last with only a sweet sadness. The "sort of sequel" that is *The Westering Sun* (1946) begins, as its title suggests, in the same insistent and bewildering mode, but then settles into a novel that justifies Blake's claims of "vast improvement in technique and understanding on its predecessor, *The Constant Star.*"

In *The Westering Sun*, Blake the panoramic social historian lingers. Early we hear of the last Julius Oliphant—"A whole complex of economic processes and social assumptions coalesced in the person of this beautiful boy, lying unbefriended on the shores of a Scottish sea-loch" —and our prospect of the character groans under the abstract thematic weight. We are not surprised to be told that individuals and family groups at Garvel pier—if seen by that Hardyesque busybody, "a disinterested observer of the scene"—are "each in his, her or its way thoroughly representative of the middle-classes of industrial Scotland"; or that the hats men wore "formed a perfectly representative picture gallery of the period"; or that sending the Oliphant children away to boarding school "was a new thing altogether in the evolution of industrial society . . . a wheeling movement in the progress of the wealthy by inheritance from the pioneer traders of Victoria's period"; or that in 1910 "the fortunes of the Oliphants passed their peak and went into slow corruption with the bulky person of Edward the Seventh."[12] But the social historical mode served its time, and in this novel it recedes. The successive patterns of generational typology fade out. To the fore at last is a single, sensible woman struggling for her deserved independence.

The book gradually settles into the life story of this last of the Garvel Oliphants. The foolish Julius dies in 1918, when Bell, his daughter, is almost thirty; and her own death on a mobile canteen mission in a Glasgow air raid during World War II closes the novel. At her father's death she determines to flee the prison of her brothers' trivial bachelordom; she takes her half-sisters, leaves Garvel, moves into a Glasgow flat, and gradually prospers as the busy entrepreneur of a chain of city tearooms, cheerfully exploiting the nouveau riche wives of a middle class she despises. Her inspiration is Betty Bell, Highland ex-schoolteacher, who sums up the book's stalwart matriarchal perspective: "It's a queer thing, Bell, but women like you and me are needed now and again. We're odd fish, goodness knows, but we seem to pop up just when our men-folk have lost heart."[13] The strong woman who survives the ideological warfare, the foolish and violent ups and downs, of male-dominated history: it is a central conception shared with Blake's contemporaries in Scottish fiction, Gibbon, Neil Gunn, and James Barke.

Distanced by her plainness and lack of interest from the sterile comedy about her, Bell serves effectively as a critical central consciousness. Free of romantic vision and illusion alike, her sense of history is informed; but it is a "feeling for the endless flow of human living, that queer process which the more it changed, the more it was the same thing" (220). Her sense of her own integrity and her will to survive are stronger. She may recall her life as a tapestry and see in the decline of the Oliphants "almost the beauty of an aesthetic pattern" (208), but hers is not the aesthetic or philosophical view. Romantic and Calvinistic extremes alike repel her; she looks with a humorously sensible compassion at herself and the world around her: "It's awful never to be able to be tragic, always to be seeing both sides of things, as if everything were really ridiculous" (227).

Her Glasgow years take her through epidemics, strikes, riots, and finally war, but she is always the figure of practical charity. Denied marriage and children by her father's snobbery and then her lover's death in World War I, she is the courageous survivor, free of self-pity, always the realist at the center of the novel's realistic mode, a believable and congenial point of view for Blake. She echoes the survival talents of Bella McFadyen, with a maturity Bella never won. Finding her, Blake found the necessary center of technique and understanding that could make *The Westering Sun* the satisfactory long novel he had been trying to create.

When Compton Mackenzie* began publishing *The Four Winds of Love* in 1937, he had already enjoyed a quarter-century of recognition as one of the younger English novelists praised by Henry James and as a fabulous cloak and dagger figure of World War I. *Sinister Street*

*Mackenzie, (Sir Edward Montague) Compton. Born in 1883 in West Hartlepool, England, and died in Edinburgh in 1972. Educated at Oxford, he headed the British Aegean intelligence service in World War I, receiving the O.B.E. and the Legion d'Honneur. He was one of the founders of the Scottish National Party in 1928, and was Rector of Glasgow University from 1931 to 1934. He lived on Barra in the Hebrides for several years, but settled at last in Edinburgh. In addition to the

(1914), a romance of Oxford and of London's underworld in which Michael Fane's Oxonian chivalry confronts Sylvia Scarlett's Petronian neo-Calvinism, seemed to some a book of genius. Frank Swinnerton thought Mackenzie "one of the few writers able to dramatize the Cockney scene" but inclined, when inspiration lagged, "to relapse into romance, Cornishness, and a rather *fin de siècle* emotionalism."[14] There is much in the early novels that anticipates the Juanesque extravaganza of *The Four Winds of Love*. *The Four Winds* is so huge and complex a work as to permit only sketchy consideration, which is perhaps why it seldom receives even that. Eric Linklater said once that he thought only three or four people had ever read the entire book, and that he was glad to be one of them.

The book was published from 1937 to 1945 (owing to wartime delays) in four parts, six volumes, approximately three thousand pages, and perhaps a million words.[15] The action opens in 1900 when Juan Pendarves Ogilvie is a schoolboy and closes on the eye of World War II when Ogilvie, aged fifty-four, marries for the second time and settles into a long-awaited Hellenic stasis on an island of the Cyclades. *The East Wind* traces his early loves, travels, friendships, and loyalties, and climactically his escape from that abomination, the English public school. Early loves and friendships introduce the politico-erotic romance scheme to be hugely elaborated in ensuing volumes. *The South Wind*—the most romantic and adventurous—covers 1912 to 1917 and centers in the Mediterranean. The successful young playwright Ogilvie, fresh from transatlantic successes and idylls in France and Italy with his new mistress, becomes a swashbuckling secret service officer in the Aegean, survives Salonica, and makes himself a Byronic vicegerent in the Grecian isles until tragic love and dysentery send him into prolonged convalescence in his Sarracen tower on the Neapolitan coast.

The third part (*The West Wind of Love* and *West to North*) covers the five years following the end of World War I, to the time when Mussolini is forming his cabinet and Ogilvie is purchasing his Hebridean island preparatory to his move to Scotland. "West" suggests

---

ten "Octaves" of his *Life and Times* (1963-1971), Mackenzie published almost a hundred books, including forty-seven novels (counting the *Four Winds* volumes separately), plays, biographies, juvenile books, and several volumes on cats (he was president of the Siamese Cat Club 1928-1972).

America, Ireland, Cornwall. The American South gives John a wife; Athene replaces his lost Hellenic maiden Zoe but has the same name as his Cornish mother. West is now also the bitter tragedy of Ireland. One of John's closest school friends has become a fanatical Irish patriot and is finally a martyred victim of the Free Staters. Ogilvie has been preoccupied from boyhood with the plight of small nations, Poland, Greece, Cornwall, Brittany, Ireland—and finally Scotland. The fourth and last wind calls him, in the echo of a swan of Tuonella more Celtic than Scandinavian, more Iberian than either, and finally Atlantean, to the far northwest of Scotland.

The North Wind (in two volumes) begins after an eight-year lapse. Ogilvie is already established as a Scottish Nationalist leader with numerous responsibilities and abundant ready cash. His wife dies, and he retires to play Prospero and Sir Austin Feverel to an only daughter in his island kingdom. He counsels and subsidizes a young Nationalist group suitably called the Airts in an abortive Stone of Destiny ploy. His long-awaited conversion to Rome has occurred without detriment to his Goethean ideal of world culture. He travels widely and sentimentally to earlier places trying somehow to collect his world into a single Catholic-communist-Celtiberian federation. There are sentimental, politically frightening visits to the France of his former mistress, the England of his earliest loves, the Neapolitan Cirano now under Fascist podesta; a disillusioning return to the Ireland of the early thirties; trips to Poland, Asia Minor, and other vantage points from which to glimpse the growing Hitlerian menace that has ended the promise of youthful Italian Fascism. *The North Wind* grows more menacing, a Lutheran Nordicism of which Hitler seems the ultimate avatar. Further Scottish separatism must be postponed. Ogilvie rediscovers a lost love in the Greek Euphrosyne, "symbol of the true heart of Hellas," and the novel ends in the Cyclades with double weddings, celebrations of Greek Independence Day, and talk about a necessary Mediterranean stasis in temporary shelter from the raging north wind.

The book is a vast excursionary romance with a cultural prophet-artist-pedagogue for hero, a solemn, densely historical modern Don Juan legend; but its three thousand pages are also filled with ideological discussion and declamation. The reader who cannot tolerate a hero of superhuman talents in love, politics, talk, and travel should steer clear of Ogilvie. The reader intolerant of symbol, pattern, and exposition in ideological romance-anatomy will not get far. The romance patterns are intricately overdesigned. The incremental symbolism of place should be obvious from the above summary. Julius Stern exclaims to John of his Cycladean villa, "Grace of God! If this house were large enough to hold the world!" (*NW*, II 304). The Hebridean castle Tigh nan Ron, with John's dream of a meeting there of all his anti-English friends to plot a postcapitalist West, is temporarily closed, but remains typical of his longing for a place which is world-home for him and center of renewed civilization for a sick world. The novel's title comes from his guiding metaphoric fancy for the structure and meaning of his life: "A fancy I had to divide my life into the four winds" (*SW*, 351). Every place has its influence according to the then prevailing wind. His Neapolitan tower is a temporary symbol of the centricity his fancy dictates: "That room at the top would make a splendid library—a room he had always wanted, with windows opening to the four winds" (*SW*, 206). It is a defense post, too, a vantage point of warning. Ogilvie dreams of standing in for the master personification of his life, the Polish trumpeter in the four-sided tower room over St. Mary's in Cracow.

The crucial episode is the climax of the first part. One morning in Cracow Ogilvie forsakes the marketplace for mass in St. Mary's. He no longer feels a stranger, feels a momentary transcendence, is "absorbed into seven hundred years of prayer," knows a "moment of burning acquiescence," responds with love to the reality of every stone. Coming out of the church, he hears the trumpeter sounding the hour from his tower room where, for seven hundred years since a Tartar arrow pierced the trumpeter's throat, the trumpeter has ended on the same wavering note his admonitory blast: to the east defiance against the Tartar; to the south defiance of the Turk; to the west against Mohamet; to the north against Luther and "any new German assault upon the spirit of man." Ogilvie is receiving a gift of transcendent life and love at the center of Christian Europe. With the widowed mother of his friends Julius and Paul he visits a Polish salt mine; Miriam sits by John beside an underground pool, a sybil in the underworld where the boy has come to find his destiny, and confesses her months of suppressed love. Back at the hotel they spend one night together, and on leaving her room at dawn he hears the trumpeter again and sees his life in design: "Eastward it sounded. Southward it sounded now. Westward it would sound, and northward. And always with that broken wavering note at the end. He listened, the cool breath of dawn upon his face. For nearly seven hundred years by night and by day, hour after hour, that tune defied time. Its strength was in the feeble wavering note at the end. Its triumph was its failure." [*EW*, 409].

The four winds suggest four seasons, a seasonal pattern in man's knowledge of love. Like the chaste but magnetic Juan that he is, John is loved by women of all ages and nationalities, and falling in love with a woman is falling in love with a new nationality, a "new airt," a new cultural possibility. There is Miriam Stern first and last (the lost mother, the moral guardian, Madame de Warens or Rachel Esmond), whose son is John's best friend and whose grandson will marry John's daughter (making John his own ancestor: ultimate dream of the world-maker). The young John is then jilted by the daughter of old Jacobite legitimist Fenwick and by Rose Medlicott, symbol of the England of his youth. These loves of the early, chill east wind must come to nought. The south wind brings two loves, both symbolizing a Byronic Hellas. The little "maid of Athens," Zoe, is drowned; he is seasick with sorrow. The American Athene really symbolizes the West of America and Cornwall; John is her first and last love, yet the reality of their love is lost between the formal complexity of her symbolic position and the unexamined psychological complexity of her loveless earlier marriage. Her death marks the end of a phase. His return to Euphrosyne marks another. A subtle study of "the four winds of love" is artistically compromised if a sequence of adoring women must serve as symbols of political and cultural phases. Nor is the love-study helped by the fact that in his most intimate erotic situations John tirelessly expounds his ethno-metaphysical ideas.

No brief quotation can do justice to John's verbosity and wit. People of all sexes and ideologies are astounded by his priestly catholicity of understanding. One puts it tenderly: "You understand almost too much" (*WN*, 119); as friends and lovers are regaled by indefatigable exposition, the reader recalls Shaw's Jack Tanner. From early manhood Ogilvie lectures, berates, admonishes friend and foe alike. He is a devastating critic of English imperialism and a flamboyant theorist of Celtiberian superiority. His lasting preoccupation is with the survival of small nations, the inevitable decay of imperialisms, Ireland as the timeless source of Christian renewal, the poisonous individualist capitalism spawned by Lutheran Germany. Music is the one dominant passion of which he is no master, but with his musical Jewish friends he can indulge another favorite speculation, the history of the persecution of the Jews. He lectures Irish ministers on Ireland, Poles on Poland, priests on Catholicism, Greeks on Greece, Scots on Scotland, and his father on English law. Some lecture back. Many of the conversations are witty, penetrating, exciting. Narrative is held in abeyance while dialogue becomes an end in itself. But the basic rhetorical problem lies with the characterization of this prodigiously wise, lovable, loquacious hero.

The book is the modern historical experience of one sensitive, influential observer. But the observer becomes as important as the world he struggles to recreate, and the novel is ultimately about Ogilvie. Ogilvie must be more than a mouthpiece or authorial surrogate. He must have a problematic life of his own, engage and provoke the reader as he attracts and infuriates his lovers and kin. Ogilvie would be a fascinating central character for a novel about such a character in such a world; but Mackenzie seems still to be following the rules he set himself for dealing with Michael Fane in *Sinister Street*: to limit his own ken to his character's consciousness and not to psychologize about him. We are left to wonder. Obsessed with the need for a transcendent center in time and place, Ogilvie seeks to create out of his far-ranging and disordered experience a world of his own, tutored, governed, financed by himself. Is he the mad utopist or is he the founder of a new world religion? His complacency as world reformer and at the same time opportunist stage farceur, his histrionic proteanism, the fertility of his egocentric fantasy, all are manifest to those in the novel who know him best. "You were always the same," says Emil Stern,

> always looking back into the irremediable past to find a remedy for the present and a panacea for the future. You're Gothic, John, you're Gothic. Your mind sprawls. You feel, you don't think. You aspire: you cannot plan. You're living in a lumber room. I become impatient with you now that you're closing in on forty. When you were seventeen you could carry off your romantic individualism. I had my own romantic dreams about you. I used to feel like Rebecca the Jewess with Ivanhoe. At that age your Jacobitism and Chopinism and Byronism added to your charm, but now at thirty-seven you're going to a fancy-dress ball in an unsuitable costume [*WN*, 42].

Emil, of course, is unreliable. But Miriam his mother is wiser and more trustworthy, and she suggests early that Ogilvie dramatizes all

227

of his experiences and enters them merely as a dramatist: "But John, you are so Protean. You are too easily capable of being transformed by your surroundings. Not in a chamelion way by taking the colour of them. That wouldn't so much matter. But you are transformed more deeply. You actually become what you are doing at any given moment. That is an incalculably useful quality for a dramatist, but I dread what an active participation in this war might make you become, even temporarily" (*SW*, 237).

John's creator appears free of such apprehensions. There is no hint that we are to take John's fertility of role as Shandean comedy or as the ironic romance of a Teufelsdröckh or a Tanner. Seldom is there any hint of critical distance on the narrator's part; seldom are the dilemmas John's destiny imposes actually examined. The shape of that symbolic destiny matters more to Mackenzie; occasional long stream-of-consciousness reverie recapitulates the design as if it had all been a fine musical harmony. And because John must play so many roles in that design—observer, prophet, pedagogue, lover, savior—the problem of his role-playing character remains unformulated. Crucial decisions are made; conversions take place; ideologies undergo significant modification; but the formative, semiconscious torments that must have led to them are only hinted at, and Ogilvie is seldom ruffled, indecisive, or inarticulate. The result is a character who in his inner life is almost wholly sentimental or intuitive and in his public roles is tirelessly dialectical; the fusion between them is slight.

There are ample suggestions, in *The Four Winds* and elsewhere, that this was deliberate. Mackenzie deplored the methods of the psychological novelist: thank Heaven, reflects Ogilvie, that while Meredith and Conrad are dead, we always have Jane Austen. It would be pointless to wish Mackenzie's novel were something its author rejects. But in its verbose evasions and disintegrities it is symptomatic, not least in the company of Blake and Mitchell. Its emotion remains intensely romantic, while its intelligence is abundantly forensic. John's friendly critics are right: his affinities are with the Byronic tradition of Juan, transcendent picaro, romantic *eiron*, discovering in his succession of roles only the reality of his countless loves and defiant fancy. Byron's Juan seems to have been the Aberdonian ancestor of much modern Scottish fiction; but the lineage, ornately politicized in *The Four Winds of Love*, is more fruitful in the fiction of Eric Linklater.

First, however, a different and third possibility for nationalist myth had been tried with momentous impact by the Scottish exile James Leslie Mitchell, who called himself Lewis Grassic Gibbon.* Many would say that the novel in Scotland was born again with the great trilogy *A Scots Quair* (1932-1934). How new was the new beginning? How did the pastoral realism of *Sunset Song* or the caustic antiburghal historicism of *Cloud Howe* emerge from the Georgian romance and fantasy of the anglicized Leslie Mitchell? "What is a Scottish author like you doing in Welwyn?" Compton Mackenzie wrote. And George Blake urged, "You really must think of coming up here."[16] Mitchell's English novels are hard to find, but their disappearance is not surprising.

The connected stories in *Cairo Dawns* (or *The Calends of Cairo*, 1931)[17] are tales of melancholy exile, filled with fantasy and exotic symbolism, of place evoking in a Near Eastern setting the pre-Raphaelitism of the Celtic Twilight, with a late romantic nature mysticism, and with a belief in racial memories, a kind of archetypal reincarnation whereby modern individuals dissolve into eternal types. A modern girl can become identified with the girl of an Attic vase, and a young adventurer is the golden Cro-Magnard hunter reincarnate. The priestly fanatic is a timeless destroyer, "little jingo" nationalisms echo the hatred of the Neanderthalers, and the prophet of a prehistoric humanism sees in the return of the archaic to modern Cairo the promise of a creedless God. The celebrant of "the adventure-soul in man" mocks the self-delusions of the self-proclaimed "realist"—"though where was ever yet realist who dipped pen into the inks of reality?"[18] and the visionary symbolist sees with an ornate Pateresque impres-

---

*Mitchell, James Leslie (*Lewis Grassic Gibbon*). Born in 1901 in Auchterless, Aberdeenshire, Mitchell spent his boyhood in the agricultural Mearns of Kincardineshire between Aberdeen and Dundee; he died suddenly following emergency surgery in 1935, in Welwyn Garden City, England. After two years as a journalist and several in the army and the R.A.F., serving mainly in the Middle East, he settled to writing and archaeological study in the south of England. His first book, *Hanno, or the Future of Exploration* (1928), was an "essay in prophecy." He was encouraged in the short story by H. G. Wells and Leonard Huxley, and most of his stories were published in *Cornhill*. He collaborated with Hugh MacDiarmid on *Scottish Scene* (1934) and organized the "Voice of Scotland" series, to which MacDiarmid, Gunn, Linklater, Mackenzie, and the Muirs all contributed volumes at his invitation. His nonfiction includes a biography of the explorer Mungo Park (1934) and *The Conquest of the Maya* (1934).

sionism the spirit of a civilization in a street or a face. Contemporary domestic tragedy wears an aura of legend.

With the same Egyptian setting and narrator, *The Lost Trumpet* (1932) is the search of two humorous archaeologists for the lost trumpet of Jericho, a talisman with the power to break down all the walls that make of civilization a maze of alienation. Doctor Adrian serves here as the exponent of Mitchell's archaeological "Diffusionism," his theory of a golden age of man, the sane and happy hunter, "no gods, no magics, no mystic hates or hopes; no patriotisms, no clothes, no communists . . . no savages and no pacifists, no taboos, no culture and no cruelty . . . before in Upper Egypt they tamed the first growths of corn," and civilization followed with all its brutalizing inhibitions and fanaticisms.[19] The trumpet is found. It is blown once in silence by a blind harlot-goddess, and she and the trumpet are turned to death and dust by lightning. But the talismanic impact is felt by all, and the homesick exile narrator and his beloved ex-princess leave Egypt for the dreams and perils of their (now Red) Russian homeland.

The fantasist prophet of prelapsarian man is more at ease in the unabashedly fabulous science fiction of *Three Go Back* (1932),[20] an "adventure in pre-history." The three—a popular, promiscuous woman novelist, a young militant pacifist physician, and a munitions millionaire—survive a mid-Atlantic earthquake when their dirigible is thrown back twenty-five thousand years through a space-time spiral and crashes on Atlantis on the eve of the fourth ice age. They are saved by a tribe of cheerful, kindly Cro-Magnard hunters, who speak a kind of proto-Basque. The munitions maker dies converted. The woman follows custom and takes a Cro-Magnard lover for the dark winter days. And when the dark days prove to be the beginning of glacial disasters for Atlantis, the doctor, torn by his Diffusionist faith between saving the Cro-Magnards for their Fall into history and preventing history by letting them perish with Atlantis, opts for the thwarted promise of their survival and leads them to safety through glacial winter and the malevolent hordes of attacking Neanderthalers. The couple, now lovers, "die" and reawaken in the modern Azores. The woman now recognizes in the modern doctor her Cro-Magnard lover reincarnate, even as before she had seen in her archaic golden lover the archetype of her young twentieth-century love, torn and dying on the barbed wire of World War I. Knowing that man was once unfallen, the two live in the hope that the golden humanity still alive in them may yet outlive and triumph over civilization with all its cruelties and cannibalisms, "the eager, starved, mind-crippled creatures of the diseased lust of men," the eons of the bestial Neanderthalers.

Much of *A Scots Quair* is already visible. Young war-torn Ewan is here, as are the long, tormented prophecies of Robert Colquohoun the consumptive minister. Anticipated are the creedless visions of the eternal Chris, the merging of the novelistic character into archetype ("race-type, race-memory, blood of his blood"), the overwhelming nostalgia for a golden paradisal anarchy, the terrible Calvinist view of history born in a Fall, and the sense of life as a thwarted adventure. What cannot be here, of course, is the passion for the land, the croft, the traditional community. For Mitchell the Diffusionist saw in agriculture the beginnings of the horrible errors of history. And Gibbon the elegist of the agricultural Mearns never quite subdued the Diffusionist view, the yearning for a life that needs no local attachments, no inhibiting family pieties. Thus, the nostalgia of the *Quair* is not so much excessive as ambiguous, a yearning far beyond Blawearie to a prehistoric dream. The grim but lyric realism of the *Quair* is actually the surface that veils an archetypal romance of poignant archaic perseverence. The shifting identity of Chris is actually grounded not in national myth so much as in a prophetic humanist vision of world history.

This vision commands Mitchell's finest non-Scottish novel, *Spartacus* (1933),[21] the story of the slave revolt in Italy in 73 B.C. and of its legendary leader. Comparisons with Flaubert's *Salammbo* were inevitable: *Salammbo* had been a favorite of Mitchell's, and his subject and vivid impersonality are reminiscent of Flaubert's. Yet for Flaubert the flight to ancient Carthage was consciously escapist and amoral, while for Mitchell the desperate, doomed revolt of many oppressed peoples against "the Masters" (as the Romans are always called) was an occasion for pained sympathy with the tortured and conquered of all time.

The artistic shift and advance from the speculative fantasist of Egypt and Atlantis to the narrator of *Spartacus* is as remarkable as the emergence of Lewis Grassic Gibbon, and the two changes may well have been interdependent. It is arguable that *Sunset Song* gave Mitchell the impressionistic realism and lyric fluency he needed for *Spartacus*, while *Spartacus* provided the pastoral Gibbon of *Sunset Song* with a necessary transition into the historic world of *Cloud*

Howe. The narrative style of *Spartacus* is close to the hypnotic fluency of linear narration in *Sunset Song*, but without its dialectal pungency and central female consciousness.

> Now ten years passed on the great White Islands and the secret sailings from their windy coasts. Thoritos levied tribute across many routes, and his riches grew, and Kleon became his first captain. Yet he had no love of ships, though the sea he loved, sight and sound and smell of it in the long, anethystine noons, when his bed was set on a westward terrace and the world of the Islands grew still. Crouched at his feet one of Thoritos' women would sing and brush the flies from his face, and bring him cool wine to drink when he woke from his daytime dreams. And Kleon would drink and doze again, though he slept but little, lying still instead, companioned with thought. [17]

Kleon, later a castrated Roman slave, becomes the chief lieutenant and philosophical mentor of Spartacus; and his bitter sadness over lost manhood, combined with a fierce Platonic utopianism, provides the book with its strange, problematic, yet highly suggestive central consciousness.

The book moves in two directions. As the revolt builds through successive triumphs toward its fated collapse, the character of Spartacus grows at once into an awesome legend and a hardened political master whose role puzzles and pains him. The hardening is Kleon's doing. The slaves wish only for freedom and homeland—all are sad exiles driven by "hate built on memories dreadful and unforgivable, memories of long treks in the slave-gangs from their native lands, memories of the naked sale, with painted feet, from the steps of windy ergastula, memories of cruelties cold-hearted and bloody, of women raped or fed to fish to amuse the Masters from their lethargy, of children sold as they came from the womb, of the breeding-kens of the north, where the slaves were mated like cattle, with the Masters standing by" (97). Kleon, obsessed with his "republic," strives to turn their hate into a ruthless revolutionary force and to mold the simple giant leader into his vision of a king for a Platonic Republic in Italy. He competes for the soul of Spartacus with the woman Elpinice, and when she and her child are butchered by the legionaries, it appears that Kleon has won. Spartacus makes a heroic effort to discipline his anarchic forces into a cohesive body on the model of the Roman legion; and he approximates in himself the cold, passionless statesman of Kleon's bitter vision. But still he is haunted by cruelty, and increasingly he is conscious of becoming one with "all the slave host, bound in a mystic kinship of blood," one with "the hungered dispossessed of all time": "None of his marchings and plannings had been his alone, but an essence of the dim wills in the minds of the multitude, in the Negro slave who had starved and shivered up the Rhegine dyke, the Thracian shepherd who limped with a bloody heel, the Bithynian porter who disputed with the Thracian land-serf the name for victory and defeatlessness. He was but a voice for the many, the Voice of the voiceless" (264). The various slave leaders stand for and dispute many ancient creeds; Spartacus alone stands for a compassionate universal humanity, resembling in his plight and growth of consciousness the figure of Chris in the *Quair*. Kleon is eventually not so much repudiated as transcended; and it is Kleon who, in his final agony on the cross, has the vision of Spartacus as one with the humanist savior who would die on the cross a century later. This struggle and this resolution parallel the central conflict of *Cloud Howe*. A new prophetic-historic perspective entered the *Quair* at this point, as did a further elaboration of the consciousness and significance of Chris Guthrie.

The elaboration of the central character in the *Quair* is inevitable, given the complexity of Gibbon's scheme. The book was conceived as a trilogy; yet, as its three parts appeared, they had been separated by time, change, and much intervening work. There was also the burden of knowing that, once *Sunset Song* had met with acclaim on both sides of the Atlantic, critics and friendly readers would be wondering if *Cloud Howe*, and then *Grey Granite*, could confirm the promise and fit their notion of a suitable sequel. Inevitably attention would focus on the element of change—the distinct, culturally representative locales, from agricultural Mearns of the dying croft culture, to the narrow, often corrupt, vitalities of the small burgh of Segget, to the amorphous industrial city of Duncairn—and on the element of permanence in change, Chris Guthrie the educated croft girl who "becomes" in her successive marriages Chris Tavendale-Colquhoun-Ogilvie. Perhaps the growing critical reservations were inevitable.[22] But whatever the problems or flaws of *Cloud Howe* and *Grey Granite*, they are essential to the total meaning.

It has become fashionable to interpret the *Quair* in terms of "levels" of meaning and to judge it as allegory. For J. T. Low it has three levels, the personal, the social, and the symbolic; for Kurt Wittig its three levels are the personal, the social, and the mythic.[23] But they are less levels than alternating, sometimes conflicting, sometimes coalescing modes of experience and understanding. And their evolution and interplay constitute a problem for both Chris and her narrator, sometimes distinguishable, sometimes not.

For Wittig the personal level is the story of Chris's development as a daughter, woman, wife, and mother, and of the inherent conflicts of her individual character. In *Sunset Song*, standing with her long retrospects up by the Standing Stones, Chris is already a complex, solitary figure, set apart by her intellectuality (she has been away to academy and college). As a result, "two Chrisses there were that fought for her heart and tormented her. You hated the land the coarse speak of the folk and learning was brave and fine one day and the next you'd waken with the peewits crying across the hills, deep and deep, crying in the heart of you and the smell of the earth in your face, almost you'd cry for that, the beauty of it and the sweetness of the Scottish land and skies . . . And the next minute that passed from you, you were English, back to English words so sharp and clean and true" (37). Later there are the demands of a "third and last Chris," the woman hungering for lovers and love. But the initial conflict between the two Chrisses is obviously social and historical. And there is the ambiguous suggestion that the "third and last Chris" supercedes or resolves the conflict of the first two. If so, then on the personal level the social level becomes meaningless. Ultimately, Chris is integrated and alone.

The social level, for Wittig, is the succession of locales and social groups: the death of the crofting community; the historical corruption and disintegration of small-town society in the burgh; the city in revolutionary ferment. But Chris's relations to all three are problematic and growingly tenuous. The first is dead or dying even as she becomes aware of it; the second concerns her only through the doomed humanitarian efforts of her minister-husband; the third belongs to her estranged son, never to her, and she leaves it to return to the land of the first. Wittig sees the three levels as unified and meaningful only on the third level, where "the personal and the social history are part of a larger, mythological cycle, where nothing endures but the land, the seasons, and the links with archaic ancestors." And so it is, says Wittig, that Chris becomes "more and more, 'Chris Caledonia,' Scotland herself."

Does this mean that Chris becomes Scotland through her successive marriages, but must be herself and return alone to the land that alone endures? Or that Chris fulfills her identity with Scotland by thus being herself at last? I would argue that Chris's personal resolution is actually a coalescence of the personal and the mythical in repudiation of the social and historical. The doomed marriages that involve Chris in several social worlds of Scotland are phases she must go through in order to reach her lonely personal wholeness at the end. In a larger sense they are simply distractions, for Chris is personally whole from the climax of *Sunset Song*. The real conflict from then on is between Chris herself and her temporary social and ideological Scottish associations. Is she ever in reality "Chris Caledonia," or is that simply an abstraction from the mind of the tormented Robert Colquohoun? Clearly she is more than that, just as the myth of the novel is more than a nationalist myth. Its nationality is subordinate to the wholeness of human history, the perspectives and voices of all the oppressed and conquered. History is an unceasing struggle between the true feminine with its courageous, naked self, independent of ideological "clouds," and the successive male creeds and fanaticisms that come and go, deluding, dividing, corrupting. What Chris stands for comes clear only in her final conflict with her son, and in his words: "There will always be you and I, I think, Mother . . . the fight in the end between FREEDOM and GOD" (*GG*, 143). Thus, her struggle is finally individual and theological—or, if you will, antitheological, which is the same thing.

Returning to *Sunset Song*, then, we are surprised to realize the degree to which it is a novel of community, and to discover that for a time Chris is not so much a character of special significance or depth as a center of awareness. The life she observes begins in Gibbon's commemorative regionalism: the record of passing communal customs in the crofting Mearns. Regionalism was bound to be dangerous: on the one hand was the risk of an elegiac sentimentality; on the other was the risk that honesty would arouse hostility. As the *Kirriemuir Press* said in attacking the book, "It's an ill bird that fyles its ain nest."[24] And there is evidence that Gibbon felt the tension in the thoughts he gives to Kinraddie's new minister: "He was to say it was the Scots countryside itself, fathered between a kailyard and a bonny brier bush in the lee of a house with green shutters . . . And then, when the porter had picked him up and was dusting him, the Reverend Gibbon broke down and sobbed on the porter's shoulder what a bloody place was

Kinraddie! And how'd the porter like to live 'tween a brier bush and a rotten kailyard in the lee of a house with green shutters? (*SS*, 31, 73). But kailyard and green shutters are not otherwise included.

Chris's awareness centers primarily on the hard rhythms of nature and the fury of sexual longing they awaken, gossiped over by a narrow, conventional society. For woman, the life is dominated by the fear of childbearing, the exhaustion and pain, the hatred of man who forces it upon her. In this setting Chris grows to womanhood, surviving the torment and suicide of her mother, the elopement of her brother, her stern father's hard despotism, and after his death Kinraddie's disapproval of her marriage to the "coarse" Highland "tink" Ewan Tavendale. Ewan goes off to war, returns brutalized to maul her on his final leave, and is shot as a deserter on the western front. Word is brought back to Chris of how, on the battlefield, he had suddenly waked up to Blawearie as his only land, his only reality, and had set out to go back and tell Chris he had not been himself on that last leave. A madness has taken the men of Kinraddie—even Long Rob of the Mill, the resister, the rebel—away to a foreign war. These people have no land but Kinraddie, and no reality but the land; there is no nation for them—this is the gist of the lesson Chris learns:

> And then the queer thought came to her there in the drooked fields, that nothing endured at all, nothing but the land she passed across, tossed and turned and perpetually changed below the hands of the crofter folk since the oldest of them had set the Standing Stones by the loch of Blawearie and climbed there on their holy days and saw their terraced crops ride brave in the wind and sun. Sea and sky and the folk who wrote and fought and were learned, teaching and saying and praying, they lasted but a breath, a mist of fog in the hills, but the land was forever, it moved and changed below you, not at a bleak remove it held you and hurted you. [97]

Here, too, is the remarkable language and voicing of *Sunset Song*. It was, Neil Gunn wrote, as if the land itself had been given a voice, or as if Chris was the voice of the land—even as Spartacus had become the voice of the voiceless. One reviewer complained, "He never seems to have heard of any stops except commas." But the incessant, all-encompassing fluency was deliberate and functional; even question marks for dialogue would have destroyed the sought-for unity of voice. Munro justifies it well: "Leslie Mitchell had a precise if largely instinctive sense of his art. His aim was to keep a single unity of expression in which narrative, description, thought, and dialogue were one—each a part of the 'folk-mind.' The prose had to be continuous; inverted commas would have made a sharp break instead of merely a change of inflection. There must be no end and no beginning—the voices coming and going—the flow endless, always incomplete, yet always exciting in its variations."[25] It is this remarkable unity of multiple voices and moods that makes the analytic discriminations of allegorical level seem so false to the novel. This unity also makes the emergence of the voice of the new minister at the end of *Sunset Song* problematical, as he seeks to lift the action onto a plane of historical allegory. The last of old Scotland; the last peasant Scots; "Chris Caledonia," the nation-woman—it sounds ironically pretentious, as if the unity were gone and now in the face of loss it were necessary to endow the lost with "significance."

And yet the intrusion of a new style, a new conceptualization, is symptomatic of the elegiac shift from *Sunset Song* to *Cloud Howe*, to a world where the lonely integrity of Chris seeks temporarily to accommodate itself to "clouds," to the creeds and ideologies of a revolutionary minister. Narrative mode must change in *Cloud Howe*. We have left the grim but enduring unity of the land for the town, for a disjointed human situation of a thousand persons, and the vital principle is not the seasonal life of the agricultural community but the traditional social life of the burgh with all its "characters," humors, gossips. The story of Segget can never be Chris's experience as *Sunset Song* was her experience. It is rendered as before in her successive tragic retrospects; each phase of her experience—and the collective historic experience hers particularizes—is "finished," realized in elegiac memory, inevitable in its pervasive and sometimes bitter nostalgia. But the problem is whether and how Chris can actually fit in here as wife of a progressive minister; an analogous problem is that the narrator has a livelier and more catholic sense of life in Segget than Chris can have, and her consciousness is no longer the integrative center it was in *Sunset Song*.

Segget is the small-town life of Scotland that Robert Colquohoun cannot save. Chris knows somehow that he cannot—hers is a tragic view free of historic ideology and available to no one else. For her, ideological clashes can mean little more than passing clouds, and yet she must take her place and ally herself to the Cronins, the Spinners with their red flag. From Robert she hears that man was once a simple hunter in a golden age, that history is a fall from that innocence. Yet she cannot escape the view that all creeds are clouds, pillars of cloud followed briefly by doomed men, and in her large sceptical view she is set apart from and above all current ideologies. This is dramatized at the climax of "Stratus" when, pregnant, she pursues Robert at the time of the May socialist strike, goes into premature labor, and loses her baby—as if sterilized by ideological conflict. At the end of the book the country verges on economic collapse, and there is general misery. Robert and Chris hear of an evicted family whose child's thumb was chewed off by rats. The shock brings Robert back from his Christly visionary pietism, and, dying as he is from gas damage in the war, he preaches one final angry sermon about the death of Christian man in the West and dies in the pulpit, blood streaming over the Bible. But not Chris. She has sought in vain to share Robert's creeds, but she has remained closer to the narrator's ironic vision. And she sees with a deep prophetic pity, unavailable to men with their flitting activist creeds, what has made them all in Segget "the pitiful gossiping clowns that they were, an obscene humour engrafted on their fears, the kindly souls of them twisted awry" (CH, 81). She foresees a new ice age coming. But up at the Kaimes at the end she blesses the people of Segget.

The crofter girl intellectual, widow of one who saw in her a nation, has become a historical prophet, almost a female Christ of timeless humanity. In terms of characterization there is no satisfactory portrayal of the growth in Chris of such a consciousness. She is too limited to encompass the life she sees, yet she has somehow become elevated and distanced enough to comprehend and atone for it. But while *Cloud Howe* is flawed in characterology, its adaptation of style is remarkably functional. The single style, at once incantatory and palpably colloquial, still slips easily between persons—third for distance and externality, second for a single or collective involved consciousness:

> They saw not a soul as they passed the Mains, then they swung out into the road that led south; and so as they went Chris turned and looked back at Kinraddie, that last time there in the sun, the moors that smoothed to the upland parks Chae Strachan had ploughed in the days gone by, and Knapp with no woods to shelter it now, Upperhill set high in a shimmer of heat, Cuddiestoun, Netherhill—last of them all, high and still in the hill-clear weather, Blawearie up on its ancient brae, silent and left and ended for you; and suddenly, daft, you couldn't see a thing. (CH, 25-26)

The style easily becomes the pharisaical voice of the burgh: "And that was just daft, if Ake spoke true—that Mr. Colquohoun could mean it of folk, real coarse of him to speak that way of decent people that had done him no harm. It just showed you the kind of tink that he was, him and his Labour and socialism all" (*CH*, 97). It serves the other collective voice of the burgh, the proletarian weaver, the "tink." At times it is neutral, the omniscient narrator's voice, a burghal Tiresias. And often it is the inner voice of Chris herself, her consciousness, limited and dynamic, subtly distinguished from the narrator's. It is a style still integrative and functional.

It cannot remain so in the urban, strange world of *Grey Granite*. The let-down of this third part of the trilogy can be accounted for variously, but it is important to distinguish between a disappointment over technical faults or deficiencies and a sense of the lessening of intensity and of the narrowing of concern; for this sense is an inevitable part of the trilogy's meaning and form.

William Montgomerie wisely noted that *Grey Granite* has no prelude or postlude because the city for Gibbon—as Munro summarizes it—"is a city without a history, without development, without depth, without background."[26] The main characters have come too late and too limitedly to the city to have any broad sense of it, to hear or become its voice. They have fled from one kind of history and only partially come into another: the Marxist history of class struggle that Chris's son Ewan and his new friends wish to become part of and learn they cannot escape. This is history with no local character, and for that reason one with little imaginative reality for Gibbon: "A hell of a thing to be History, Ewan!" Ewan's world of the foundry, the strikes, the socialist meetings, and the stone quarry is sparsely represented. His betrayal, false arrest, and beating are graphically and angrily drawn, it is true; but the world of the keelies and the boardinghouse are never integrated into, never become representative of, city life. We do not even sense that the city is cut off from reality, as Segget in its pathetically fallen state is cut off from its own bloody and absurd heritage. Duncairn's fragmentariness is seen in the little broken vignettes with which the narrative is punctuated. Duncairn contains fragments of moral vision but is not one itself; Segget is. The coherent moral universe of the Scottish novelist in Gibbon—whether in derision or blessing—is the small burgh. Cloud Howe is the howe of this world in all its smallness and fallen meanness.

The real conflict that gives a center to *Grey Granite* merely uses Duncairn as a backdrop. It is the conflict between mother and son. Throughout the short novel the two lives develop separately with little significant parallel or counterpoint. Ewan is lost in the city; Chris is more insulated than ever before. She helps Ma Cleghorn run the boardinghouse—and abruptly Ma Cleghorn dies. Ake Ogilvie from Segget turns up, moves in, offers her capital and marriage—and then abruptly good Ake decides they should not have married and goes off to Saskatchewan, leaving her with the capital but no will to remain in the city. She and Ewan have decided quietly to lead their separate lives, and Chris moves back alone to the childhood croft, to dissolution and death in nature.

Yet the conflict between mother and son, as Ewan defines it, is momentous. He has turned from a flinty archaeological passion to an equally flinty communist fanaticism. He says he has found "a creed as clear and sharp as a knife." But Chris characteristically responds, "The world's sought faith for thousands of years and found only death or unease in them. Yours is just another dark cloud to me—or a great rock you're trying to push up a hill." His reply is: "There will always be you and I, I think, Mother. It's the old fight that maybe will never have a finish, whatever the names we give to it—the fight in the end between FREEDOM and GOD" (*GG*, 143). Is this definition of the conflict any more reliable than the abstract and cloudy formulations of that earlier intervening male intellectual, the minister Robert? Are these efforts at finding a significance for Chris merely falsifications, in nationality and theology, of her true meaning?

That meaning is inseparable from her womanhood, and the males in her life fail to comprehend it. It is most fully articulated in *Cloud Howe* when Chris herself counsels pregnant Cis Brown. Her tale is all tales, and they are all about how women replenish life while men sail their cloud-ships. Woman is eternal, precivilized, prehistoric; man is the civilizer, the betrayer, the fanatical creed-seeker. Woman alone is able to live without believing in anything but the permanence of change, the reality of the land, her naked self. *Grey Granite* confirms this meaning in Chris's growing alienation from her son, and in her final withdrawal from social life altogether. But it adds little, and in the process Chris dwindles, and the great voicing of the trilogy's language, inseparable in its integrity from her stature, dwindles too into an uncertain style.

Perhaps, then, all of these ambitious experiments toward a modern national epic in novel form had to falter under the conceptual burden of their own large ambitions. But all—those of Blake and Mackenzie, as well as Gibbon—were impressively symptomatic of a grand design. And *A Scots Quair*, whatever the uncertainties of its over-all design, has left an enduring model and stimulus, not least in its brilliant adaptations of language.

In different ways, two ambitious works of Scottish fiction beg comparison with the *Quair*. James Barke's* *The Land of the Leal* (1939) is comparable in scope and design, while Sydney Goodsir Smith's *Carotid Cornucopius* (1947, 1964) is comparable in linguistic brilliance and versatility of mode.

Barke's *The Land of the Leal*, misremembered for a doctrinaire socialism, is as moving and believable for its characters as any novel produced by modern Scotland. Its intention is fairly put by Barke in his prefatory note: "If honesty compels us to face the major political and economic issues of our generation then we confront an obligation which we must discharge, not as politicians or economists (far less as propagandists of a political party), but as artists, conscious of our tradition, grateful for our heritage."[27] It is the story of a late-Victorian working-class marriage of a half-century. True to his tradition, Barke presents the wife, Jean Ramsay, daughter of a pious and violent old Galloway farmer, as strong, aggressive, and practical. Her husband David is weaker, a poet-musician, an idealist-dreamer, easily overwhelmed by the repeated shocks and inequities of their itinerant working lives. At least in the novelistic sense, Jean and David are far more believable in their individual complexities than the romantic and mythic characters of Mackenzie and Mitchell, and at the same time more genuinely representative than the dynastic antagonists of Blake.

The book is a big one in every respect, spanning almost a century of

---

*Barke, James. *Chambers Biographical Dictionary* reports that Barke was born in 1905 in Kincardine-on-Forth, but he refers to a "Border birthplace" in his autobiography, *The Green Hills Far Away* (1940). At any rate, his parents were migrant farm workers from Galloway, and his boyhood was spent at Tulliallan on the borders of Fife, Clackmannan, and Kinross. He started as an engineer, but turned to writing. His other novels include *The World His Pillow* (1933), *The Wild Mac-Raes* (1934), and *Major Operation* (1936). He is best known for the cycle of five novels about Robert Burns, *Immortal Memory*, published from 1946 to 1954. He was a lifelong student and editor of Burns. He died in 1958.

Scottish time, from the middle-Victorian years of Jean's and David's childhood to Jean's fading widowhood in 1938. It carries the couple from job to job as dairy workers in a great geographical arc from their "bonnie Galloway" to their "Border ballad," on to the "West Neuk of Fife," and finally to Glasgow in its period of shipyard depression. The chronology of the book is effectively muted, and as they are forced to move and discover with each new exhausting job a new part of Scotland, each region is skillfully defined as a new phase in Scottish social and economic history: Galloway is the grim world of old farming; the Borders are dominated by enlightened, snobbish post-Scott North British landlordism; the Fife estate is owned by a Highland gentleman and his aristocratic foreign wife; the final move buries them in modern industrial Glasgow. As they move, they romanticize bonnie Galloway in memory, but when finally they return for a visit, David learns the desolate historic lesson that informs the book: "There was no way back to that life: there was no way forward. He had come back to find that the past was dead or dying and that the future was more uncertain than ever it had been" (518). Their children, meanwhile, have grown up, some have emigrated or died, and those who survive look at their parents with a mixture of compassion, bitterness, and awe.

The book in its deep sadness is nevertheless full of humor and conflict. The episodic structure matter-of-factly illustrates social history. Yet even the countless place-names of Galloway are sounded off with an elegiac passion beyond simple realism and equally remote from doctrinaire ideology (109-110). One is reminded of *A Scots Quair*, not least in the way the heroine becomes symbolic in the eyes of the hero while remaining in her own solitary strength and reality far more effectual than the introspective male whose prophetic vision "gives" her symbolic significance. David is "a dreamer and something of a metaphysician," and Jean becomes a pragmatic tyrant; yet it is she who resists and copes with their transient and terrifying world. They are both "pawns in the development of economic cause and political effect," we are told, but neither has the time to brood on it, and the narrator is restrained in his own reflection. He is too busy portraying the widespread realities of his mise-en-scène, too busy with a huge number of subordinate characters, and too busy with a rich but softened discrimination of Scottish regional speech. Jean, her Galloway dialect complicated by "ten years in the Borders and thirteen in Blackadder," narrates buying a chicken from a Partick shopkeeper:

"How would this one suit?" says he, raking down an auld leghorn that had been past laying—"six shillings." It's a hen I want, says I, no' the invoice o' one. His birss got up right away. "That's a lovely young pullet, madame," says he. It was a pullet about the same time as you were a cockerel—look at the legs o' it and the comb—or the plucking for that. "You're a country-woman?" Heth, I'm that. "Come through to the back shop—I see there's no good trying to deceive you, mistress. Now, would any of these suit you?" And he pointed to a wheen he had in a wire-netted box. That's something like it, says I. Just thraw the neck o' that Buff Orpington there. (613)

But, while the "Scottish dialects are of great variety and beauty," Barke disclaims any attempt to "record them phonetically" as of "no import to the reader."

Linguistic realism is equally remote from the purpose of Sydney Goodsir Smith's* Urquhartian extravaganza, *Carotid Cornucopius*, a recasting of Rabelais's mock-epic in cascades of bawdy Scots puns among the more bibulous locales of contemporary Edinburgh. Smith, like Hugh MacDiarmid in his celebrations of the book, prefers to "get rid of realism altogether." And this is a familiar impulse of much mid-twentieth-century fiction. But if part of Smith's intention was to save the novel from realism, it was hardly consistent to deplore Lewis Grassic Gibbon's "poeticized rhapsodizings" and insist (in his 1947 Kirkcaldy lectures, the year of *Carotid's* first publication) that poetry and prose are distinct arts and cannot mix. It is strange, too, that MacDiarmid, having rejected "realism," should argue for the unique genius of *Carotid* among Scottish novels on the mimetic premise that its "complex word-play" is real Scottish discourse raised to a level of genius.[28] To rid the novel of "realism" and at the same time find the "conventional novel" doomed by the unreality of its language is hardly consistent. In fact, the endlessly ingenious language of *Carotid* is as

---

Smith, Sydney Goodsir. Born in 1915 in Wellington, New Zealand, and died in Edinburgh in 1975. He moved to Scotland when his father became professor of forensic medicine at Edinburgh; Smith studied history at Oxford and medicine at Edinburgh, then turned to verse in "Lallans." "The Burns *de nos jours*," MacDiarmid called him; Kurt Wittig calls him "after Grieve himself, the most important living poet who writes in Scots." Among his many collections of poetry, beginning with *Skail Wind* (1941), his elegies, *Under the Eildon Tree* (1948), are perhaps the greatest. His plays include *The Wallace* (produced at the 1960 Edinburgh Festival) and *The Stick-up* (1969). He was a painter and an art critic. He edited Gavin Douglas, Burns, and a collection of essays on Robert Fergusson. His *Short Introduction to Scottish Literature* appeared in 1951. No account of the novel can even hint at his singular greatness among modern Scottish writers.

artificial in its way as Gibbon's, and is closer to the language of Smith's splendid poetry than to prose.

But language cannot settle the issue of whether *Carotid*, by any stretch of definition, can suitably be considered a novel—if, that is, a novel must be a prose narrative. Only in later "fitts" (parts) does the book become predominantly narrative. In the first of eight published fitts, Carotid the hero, "Caird of the Cannon Gait and Voyeur of the Outlook Touer," is seen at home. His name is explained; his library is described; the catalogue of his drinking vessels fills a page, and another goes to the drinking places they have come from. His lineage and cronies are introduced in long mock-epic catalogues, and with his cronies he sits drinking in "the Chimera Upscrewa in the Ootluik Touer that stanes on the Kisselkill jist ayant the tap of the Looanmerkit in Alt Raikie in the Cuntie of Dedlothian, frae whicshsh he could phew (the auld voyeur) the haiell shitty and enfirons."

In the second fitt, two of his special friends are introduced with resumes of their Fumbly Trees: the "least Drouk of Hardbile" (with pages of the Drouk's associations) and his estranged wife Colickie Meg, paramour of Carotid, native of the Cowgate, and now (by marriage settlement) mistress of the Ben Nevis Bar on "Damnubile Strait" by the Water of Leith, given her as a "kinna duinafashal lollimoney or uninfinishall valeminnie." In Carotid's embraces she conceives "a bairn doustrained to be ane of the goatest hairyos aver broacht furth in Sotland," one who is to be "a vurry Panthergrowle o' a bab."

The love triangle is set aside so that the third fitt can introduce Rorie, but the Auktor or "Auk" now finds (in increasingly Shandian fashion) that he has lost his characters, and the Caird turns up in jail by "the Huge Gurk or Cathetertroll of Sanct Jowl's at its Aist Ond juist besod the intrunts til the Polis Affhats of the Oddanbeerie Cantsapuleerie in Parlyvooment Squeer."

The fourth fitt, still in Shandian fashion, is a prologue; the fifth is the birth of Rorie, after the Rabelaisian model, with pages cataloguing equipment for the great lying-in. In the sixth Rorie is off to the wars, and his destined bride is born. In the seventh he returns, falls in love, attends school; the games he and Biddie play—mostly sexual puns—are catalogued for two and a half pages. In the eighth there is a great birthday feast for Rorie and Biddie, with long debates over the menu, and the book closes for the nonce.

Such a summary is largely irrelevant to the book's brilliance as a linguistic virtuoso piece, but it does identify the Rabelaisian mock-epic motifs through which Smith transforms contemporary Edinburgh into a bawdy goliardic saga. Whether such a medium could be adapted to the minimum norms of presentational realism and narrative logic still expected in the novel remains to be answered. One novelist of modern Scotland has sought that answer, and Smith recognized the kinship.

The Rabelaisian talent of Eric Linklater won Smith's approval. In his Kirkcaldy Lectures of 1947, Smith placed Linklater's *Juan in America* in the tradition of goliardic folk tales, associated its satire with Dunbar and its wit with Byron, and found it almost the equivalent in prose—albeit English prose—of MacDiarmid's *A Drunk Man Looks at the Thistle*. This last claim should surely be reserved for *Carotid Cornucopius*. But if no modern novel can quite justify such associations, the problem is not so much language as mode. The barrier is the realism that Smith and MacDiarmid had sought to throw out, and through his long career as a novelist Linklater struggled with this problem himself.

13

Novelists
of
Survival

Shortly after the untimely death of Lewis Grassic Gibbon, Eric
Linklater* saluted him as "the only Scots writer of his generation to dare suppose that playing football with the cosmos was
his chosen mission." It was a time when "social life in Scotland" had
"no peculiar and individual significance" and was "derivative and provincial," and Scottish writers reacted in a way "likely to be evasive, or
lacking in conviction, or minutely selective."[1] Yet the same year Linklater published in *The Lion and the Unicorn* a defense of the humane
utility of small nations against modern bureaucratic imperialism. It is
characteristic of him to have juxtaposed an adventurous manifesto
and a hard-headed admonition of limitation.

Introducing his collected stories in 1968, Linklater wrote, "Critics, I
am told, prefer an author who . . . will mark his territory and stay
within it . . . I rarely write the same thing twice."[2] There may be a real
clue here, for Linklater had extraordinary insight into literary
decorum and his own relation to literary history. In his autobiog-

*Linklater, Eric. An Orkneyman by lineage and lifelong devotion, Linklater was
born in Penarth, Wales, in 1899; he died in 1974 in Aberdeen. He attended the
Grammar School at Aberdeen and studied medicine at Aberdeen University before
switching to English literature. He worked as a journalist in India, spent a year as
Commonwealth fellow in the United States, and turned professional writer. His
"third essay in autobiography," *Fanfare for a Tin Hat* (1970; the first two are *The
Man on My Back* and *A Year of Space*), recalls his miraculous survival in the
trenches of 1918 France and his lifelong fascination with men at war, out of which

raphy *Fanfare for A Tin Hat*, he identifies "the moment when I forfeited all claim to be recognized as a serious novelist" with the time (in 1931) when he declined the urgings of Jonathan Cape and Edward Garnett to follow up *Juan in America* with sequels, and sat down instead to write the ninth-century Orcadian saga of Thorlief Coalbiter and his sons, *The Men of Ness*.[3] In making such a switch—and he did it repeatedly—he gave up the way of the giants ("a true novelist is one who imposes his own character, his own way of thought and fashion of writing, on every page that leaves his table") for a "more humble and realistic way." In the belief that in literature, expression ultimately counts for more than content, he chose to vary his subjects widely as occasion and inspiration suggested and to allow "my subjects to determine the style and temper in which I have written of them." Linklater was a markedly occasional artist, trained in professional journalism. Yet among British novelists he was as well-read as Scott, whom he resembled in various ways: in his Scottish Toryism, his Episcopalianism, and the ease with which critics underrate his prodigious talent and confuse his creativity with potboiling or frivolity.

But while he may have denied it and critics may have missed it, the definitive quality is there in his twenty-three novels in thirty-eight years. The high points are the third (*Juan in America*, 1931) and the eleventh (*Private Angelo*, 1946), and these two ironic heroes—the Byronic-Aberdonian cosmopolitan aristocrat and the Italian peasant —have much in common, and are akin to the rest, not least in the romantic and ironic phenomenon of their will to survive.

White-Maa's Saga (1929), recalls Linklater, "had some of the virtues of green things," "most of the faults of inexperience," and "relied, like many first novels, on an autobiographical substratum which had to be raised, falsified, and decorated to make a good story."[4] It is a romance of *bildung* whose hero, Peter Flett, struggles in vain to pass his medical exams at "Inverdoon," spends his summers in Orkney, courts a crofter's daughter, engages in desperately witty and extended talks

---

came an official history of the 1940s campaign in Italy and several military pamphlets. He biographized several Scottish monarchs, and his volumes of history include *The Survival of Scotland* (1968). His pride in and interpretation of Norse tradition are best seen in *The Ultimate Viking* (1955), and the title of his Aberdonian rectorial address, "The Art of Adventure," sums up his creed. He also wrote several plays, "conversations," short stories, and fantasies for children.

with his student friends, eats, drinks, fishes, and fights like the "etio-lated Viking" he is, kills the despicable Orcadian villain, and finally agrees to sail to Vancouver with his Orcadian sweetheart.

For all the wit and exuberant evocation of local custom, it is a moody story of "the swift sadness of the beauty of youth" and "Grey-beard Time wearing a cap and bells, and carrying a pig's bladder in-stead of a scythe." Peter and his friends are already old; they are filled with the war they have survived as "a lively memory" (it is 1921-22)—"most of the men who filled the Scots universities had seen death in stranger disguises than the frigid decency of the mortuary, and life painted more vividly than immaturity can paint it." One of Peter's girl friends says, "We're not really young, are we? We only have a kind of hard, make-believe youth that's lasting longer than the real thing would." But the make-believe youth is taken seriously for the most part. The "raised, falsified" bouts of passion and wit and preening self-doubt mingle strangely with the vivid realism of Orkney's traditional life. The gypsy primitivism is falsified by idyllic sentimentality and complicated by Rabelaisian gusto. The germs and talents of later books are here but without the formal control, the fine decorum of mixed modes, or the characteristic episodes of fantastic farce.

Linklater spent the months following the completion of *White-Maa's Saga* partly in research for a thesis on Jacobean comedy and partly in writing a second novel which was "an exercise from which I hoped to learn something of the strategy and tactics necessary, as I be-lieved, for the construction of a novel."[5] *Poet's Pub* (1929) is a comedy of southern English manners, a "fantastic idyl," located in a fashion-able rural inn managed by a young Scottish poet whose zest for art in food, drink, and adventure is more robust than his talent for poetry. He has thought of writing "a Gargantuan epic of food, of inventing a young Gargantua who should eat his way through France and Eastern Europe to Russia . . . A gastronomic Tamburlaine." A mock spy-thriller plot intervenes: an American confidence man steals secret plans for converting coal to petrol; Nelly Bly, a gossip columnist, steals Keith's manuscript poem; the bartender believes his blue cock-tail recipe has also been stolen; and the whole company drives wildly north to Scotland in a cavalcade of flight, chase, picaresque encounter, and coincidental victory. Much of the Linklater mixture is here: the Peacockian metier of elegance and wit; the Gargantuan mock-epic of gustatory orgy; the farcical, fantastic adventure; the artist-hero de-

signing an art of life; the remotely-hinted-at real world of suffering
and struggle. The tragic element has still to be assimilated. A suitable
protagonist has not yet been conceived. A way of using the mixture to
interpret the anxious contemporary world has still to be tried.

Linklater's genius for literary tradition and decorum led him to send
an exiled descendant of Aberdonian Byron's Don Juan (Juan Motley)
on a picaresque epic-farce foray across Prohibition America. Linklater
claims that *Juan in America* (1931) is a historical novel, a vision of
some "vestigial or stubborn remnant" of innocence beneath fabulous
wealth, "remedial crime and sentimental well-being".[6] What suited
him so perfectly was the discovery of a giant reality ripe for satire,
yet patently fantastic and romantic. "Fantasy lived here. Satyrs
walked in the woods and millionaires built with the large and unstudied imagination of Haroun-al-Raschid. America was the last home of
romance and anything could happen there" (65). "America," Juan
drunkenly tells a distinguished audience in Washington during
Hoover (Bloomer)'s inaugural, "is really a quaint old-fashioned land.
Personally I like it. But that does not blind me to the fact that it is the
last abode of romance and other medieval phenomena" (285). The
hero, generated out of an ironic saga of dynastic identity and suspect
legitimacy (a Scottish mock-romance motif), in boyhood is a child
satyr or gypsy Christ come to destroy respectability and humbug
"with a keen perception of the grotesque and ridiculous." He falls
temporarily into the seductions of romance—" I mean a certain kind of
silliness on a large and pleasant scale; I mean a denial of tasteless common sense for the sake of pungent nonsense" (99)—and carries this
propensity into a wild travelogue. He survives Manhattan's sudden
violence, failure as a college football player, bootleg boating on the
Canadian border, gang warfare in Red-eye Rod Gehenna's Chicago,
the crushing passion of Olympia the amazonian operacrobat, the jealousy of a Negro rival in South Carolina swamps, the perilous idyll
with his Haidee, Red-eye Rod's daughter, on an edenic Carolina island, parachute escape from his California-bound plane into the midst
of an Oklahoma lynching party, and finally the complex unrealities of
Hollywood, whence he escapes to join the beautiful Kuo Kuo in Dr.
Salvator's mystical Arroyo Beach nudist colony. He sees himself
sometimes boisterously, sometimes sadly, as a gypsy exile; he is
moved by "something between fear and antic laughter." In his wildly
drunken ecstasy, in the company of bootleggers, he has bawdy priapic

visions of the many-wombed brotherhood of man, a "polychromatic but monogene world."

The cascading virtuosity of Linklater's grotesque is seen in the gangland murder Juan attends in a New York speakeasy:

> The first bullet, rising high, had missed Wenny altogether and smashed the aquarium tank above his head. It hit, indeed, the globular gaping fish that had so long and stupidly stared into the smoky room. Wenny disappeared under the deluge of water and broken glass and the unexpected draught of fishes, and the bullet-struck fish, its silver skin laced with its golden blood, lay on the floor unseen. Its shining plump companions flopped and wriggled beside it, drowning in the hot air of the speakeasy, trampled on by the panic-feet of the men they had seen so often and so uncomprehendingly. Their fishy eyes stiffened into dead jelly, and their silver mail was broken on the floor where the customers had thrown the butts of their cigarettes. So, killed astonishingly by a gangster, one by one the silver fishes died, far from the cold native silence of their sea, and the jungle softness of waving weed, and the white labyrinthine shelter of coral reefs. And by-and-by a policeman spoke their epitaph in blasphemy as he trod on one, and slipped, and fell bluntly to the wet floor. [88-89]

George Blake writes that "this was not characteristically Scottish writing." Neither, to be sure, was Byron's *Don Juan*—and yet the peculiarly Scottish quality T. S. Eliot sensed at work in the first descends to its heir. "We may wonder," says Blake, "what such comic pieces as *Poet's Pub, Ripeness Is All,* and *Private Angelo* have to do with Scotland." Hugh MacDiarmid had found an answer when he placed the best of Eric Linklater in the company of Stevenson, Brown, Hay, Gibbon, and Sydney Goodsir Smith's *Carotid Cornucopius*; Smith, when he recalled goliardic Scots folktales, the satire of Dunbar, Byron's *Don Juan,* and MacDiarmid's *Drunk Man.*[7]

After *Juan,* Linklater went home literarily (and, not long after, domestically) to "pillage the Icelandic sagas" of *The Men of Ness* (1932)—his unique contribution to a brief flourish of archaic recreation in the novel (Gibbon, Gunn, Mitchison, and others)—and to chasten the stylistic exuberance of *Juan* into "a stark simplicity that banished all Latinisms from its sentences and relied almost entirely on a vocabulary that could, with some latitude, be called Anglo-Saxon." He had read the Orkney Saga as a boy.

Now Orkney was the southernmost home of that pagan heroism which had changed the shape and temper of all northern Europe, and in its heroism—destructive though it had been of much that was valuable—I was beginning to discern a principle that had little reference to the common motive of profit . . . a superior motive that showed itself in a code of behaviour dominated, not primarily by a prospect of material gain, but by wish or determination idealistically conceived . . . to complete an action in accordance with a pattern that was artistically satisfying.[8]

This historical thesis was to be worked out later in *The Ultimate Viking* (1955): the Vikings were unwitting "artists in conduct"; "they were unabashed by social obligation, undeterred by moral prohibition, and they could be quite contemptuous of economic advantage and the safety of their own skins. But they saw clearly a difference between right and wrong, and the difference was aesthetic"; "within the conventions of a brutal heroism would be disclosed the formative spirit of an artist."[9] It is akin to that quintessential Linklater manifesto, the 1945 Aberdonian rectorial address, "The Art of Adventure."

There is no critical language for the novel applicable to the terse matter-of-factness of *The Men of Ness*. One finds no thematic weight, no mythologizing, as in Gunn's *Sun Circle* or Mitchison's *The Corn King and the Spring Queen*: saga is the norm; unstudied brutality, proverbial admonition, and stark humor alternate. Ninth-century Viking history is broadly sketched without anachronistic interpretation; motives are limited to fame, property, security, and, most of all, atonement.

> Skallagrim said, "I will let you go free on this condition: when evening comes you will ride straightway to Ivar and tell him that Skallagrim Thorlief's son, Ragnar Hairybreeks' son, and Kol Cock-crow his brother, are come out of Orkney seeking him in the matter of that atonement which he did not pay for Bui of Ness, whom he killed, and also in consideration of certain wrongs he did to Signy my mother, Thorlief's wife and Bui's. Tell him that we shall wait here till he comes, for we have travelled far and do not mean to go bootless home.[10]

The saga comes to focus on the travels of Skallagrim and Kol, and the long chronicle of their stormy voyage in the North Sea is done with a magnificent simplicity equal to anything Linklater has written. Finally, both brothers must die, and only a lone survivor, their peasant neighbor Gauk of Calfskin, goes home to tell the tale. Gauk is not a hero but a little man content to hide in his little place. Gauk the little peasant, who survives at the end of the story, supplies something of a final comment on the heroic aesthetic of the men of Ness—a comment that will later be embodied in Linklater's most memorable hero, not a Viking bent on the art of adventure but an Italian peasant committed to the art of survival. For Linklater is no connoisseur of violence; while courage and beauty may be found in the horrors and absurdities of war, it is on the archaic will to survive that his notions of heroism ultimately focus.

This new focus produced in *Magnus Merriman* (1934) Linklater's first large-scale novel of modern Scotland. Magnus is White-Maa grown older, home from India and America, successful first-novelist, and Orcadian survivor of the Great War. He is a Juanesque victim of his own seductions, an epic drinker, and the first of Linklater's heroes to be conceived as a victim of a destiny that is both tragedy and farce: a fool, a brilliantly argumentative reactionary, an artist, and ulti- mately a peasant trapped into workaday Orkney domesticity by a beautiful, shrewd, and despotic farmer's daughter. His love for the very soil of Scotland is romantic enough, and the book characteristi- cally and repeatedly deflates it. Yet it survives his ludicrous incursion into nationalist politics, and focuses at last on Linklater's view of the validity of small nations—that man at his most cosmopolitan remains a creature of local attachments, that "the human mind is essentially a village mind." "Life was the flowering of a single land, and love of country was no virtue but stark necessity. Patriotism and the waving of flags was an empty pride, but love of one's own country, of the little acres of one's birth, was the navel-string to life . . . life could not be whole save in its own place."[11] The long middle of the book carries Magnus through a thinly fictionalized satire of Edinburgh and the nationalist movement of the early thirties. The follies and crimes of his campaign and his manager are sketched in broad caricature. Some political and literary figures are caricatural portraits in a roman à clef, mingling with plausibly mimetic characters such as Magnus and his numerous paramours and with more typical manners figures. Satiric realism fuses with various kinds of fantasy—farcical, erotic, and even gothic—as when a mildly erotic episode in Edinburgh is bracketed by a reminiscence of frightening witchcraft, or when the manners comedy of Edinburgh respectability gives way to the mock-epic of interna- tional Rugby, or when Miss Beauly naively devastates the urbane Tarascon Restaurant by emptying Meiklejohn's snuffbox into the mouth of a nearby saxophone, producing a storm-ravaged orgy of

sneezing. Such great setpieces of grotesque hilarity, erupting cata-
strophically in the midst of elegant manners milieux, will become one
of Linklater's trademarks.

One of the most splendid examples occurs early in *Ripeness Is All*
(1935). Lady Caroline Purefoy, wife of the Vicar of Lammiter, tireless
patron of humane causes, gives a large garden party to benefit the
Brackenshire Association for Improved Slaughterhouses and to demonstrate old and new ways of killing pigs. The demonstration pigs
break loose in the lovely vicarage garden; the quality of the long, grotesque episode can only be suggested:

> The porker kicked its feet out of the rope and galloped headlong for
> the pergola. It was a fearsome sight. Its black body was convulsive
> with rage and speed, its hugh ears flapped, and as it galloped it dia-
> bolically screamed . . . The scene of confusion in the garden was
> now almost indescribable. Most of the guests were women, and
> many of them were old . . . Brandishing their umbrellas like clubs, or
> stabbing with them as though they were assegais, they drove a reso-
> lute way to safety . . . The second pig had taken refuge among the
> rhododendrons, and though it could not be seen its progress might
> be marked by the shaking of the bushes and the occasional destruc-
> tion of syringas and the remaining azaleas . . . In the meantime, the
> first pig, after a spirited pursuit round the garden by Miss Ram-
> boise and several other athletic young women, was busily destroy-
> ing the rose-garden. In such evident fury as to daunt even Miss
> Ramboise, it attacked a magnificent Golden Gleam, whose yellow
> petals fluttered in the air and fell like dapples of sunlight on its black
> satanic hide. Half a dozen ruined Duchesses of Athol lay behind it,
> their bloom an orange carpet for the soil, and the dark red blossom
> of l'Etoile de Holland lay like blood in the wasted snow of Madame
> Butterfly. The raging pig uprooted a fine Shot Silk; pink petals were
> mingled with the red, the creamy white, the yellow, and the gold,
> and the gross black brute, its swart ears flapping, trampled the
> lovely wreckage underfoot. Rain fell thick and steady now, and the
> least percipient was sensible of something awful in this sinister spec-
> tacle of wrath beneath a hostile sky.[12]

The pigs take refuge and are captured in the lily pond. Lady Caroline
is soaked, takes cold, then pleurisy, then pneumonia, and in a few
days is dead, leaving the poor vicar with six children. The hilarity of
delicate patrician elegance devastated by gross beastliness leads to
domestic tragedy. Yet this farcical novel celebrates life, fertility, ripeness. The episode is fitting: in an effete postwar pastorality, the gross
will to survive tramples less fruitful orders into muddy chaos. A fan-

tastic vitality crashes among the manners—it is a familiar motif of Scottish fable. And the ominous real world of 1935 is kept at an idyllic distance.

The book's occasion, Linklater remembers, was "exuberant delight" at the birth of his own first child. Shortly, the new father left his Orkney retreat, "returned to the clamorous world from which I pretended to have escaped," and sailed for China to develop a background for Juan Motley's only return appearance, in *Juan in China* (1937).[13] War is the main strand of Linklater's autobiography; he sees it as tragic folly emblematic of the absurd resilience of human destiny. His books so far had celebrated the delight of having survived a past war and the Primavera of renewed human vigor. The problem now was to adapt fantastic farce to the portents of renewed war. Sending Juan with his tireless wit and his amoral love of the adventurous, the free, the grotesque and heteroclite, to China's corrupt warlords and incipient Japanese invasion was a brave experiment.

The situation is appalling: internal corruption in the face of disaster, an early *Catch-22*. Juan's paramour Kuo Kuo seeks to recover a document of great price, which ultimately proves worthless, while Red-eye Rod Gehenna's former henchman Colonel Rocco and an obese Englishman arrange the sale of General Wu Tu Fu's Japanese-made tanks. The tanks in battle are discovered to have an armor plate of wood covered with tin. But they were paid for with bundles of phony money; and the battle that the tanks have lost Juan wins by throwing up the money to be blown over the Japanese lines, followed by hordes of avaricious Chinese.

The hilarious confusion on the battlefield is a variant on the devastated garden party or the murdered fish in the speakeasy, yet here humor wins an odd victory. "At first a very proper sympathy and decent feeling kept Juan from laughing. But laughter was like an acid that soon dissolved such soft metal, and presently his sobriety vanished, and from all over his body, as it seemed, there started small tides and currents of mirth that gathered and grew stronger" (356). The problem that pervades the book is the problem of laughter and of Juan's determined lack of seriousness. He is left overnight for safety in a Buddhist monastery and finds himself alone in a maze of idols. One is "a glaucous deity whose face was twisted in wild and diabolical laughter . . . Laughter that tore the very fabric of life. A god more evident than the others—despite his lineaments of the devil—for only a god could see such comedy in the world and have the courage to laugh at it . . . a god, but clothed in sackcloth and rags, heaven's outcast, perhaps, because he had mocked the foundations of heaven in the same breath . . . Or a god, it might be, who was God's jester" (138). From this "dreadful apotheosis of humour" Juan hastily retreats, coming next upon a "Chinese Gargantua" who amazes him with the realization that the Chinese have "no sense of sin" but instead a "gross and unpardonable innocence . . . capable of the most appalling misconduct." The stage is set for tragedy; the recurrent effect is of tragedy falling into farce.

When Juan is wounded, gives up the adventure, and goes home, the moments of triumphant laughter are underlain by a "stupid feeling of desolation," and it seems clear that the Juanism so marvelously suited to medieval Prohibition America has proved unfitted to a new tragic-farcical situation. The critics, Linklater recalls, found the book guilty of "heartless ill-taste." Juan was dead, and his true successor only emerged with Private Angelo nine years later. Meanwhile, the problem intensified and the experience multiplied with *The Impregnable Women* (1938) and *Judas* (1939).

But first came a brief picaresque tale, *The Sailor's Holiday* (1937).[14] The germ may be seen in *Juan in China*: "All men are sailors," says the narrator; "We men of action are incurably loquacious," says Juan. Henry Tippus, an impecunious English sailor home on holiday, is as loquacious and fertile a romantic liar as Arthur Gander of *Ripeness Is All*, and his adventures make a modern fabliau. Bawdy errors and providential accidents alternate with his fertile and nonsensical inventions, with gobs of speculative anecdote and dialogue. The effect is of Peacock shot with bawdy and farce: the blowing up of the demonstration model Little Beauty Washing Machine, overcharged with soap, in the market square of rural Whippleford; the lowering of the heroine, locked up with suspected appendicitis by her faith-healer father, out of her window in her bed. Indestructible, romantic Henry finds and loses again his own plain beloved and survives to complete his circle and to go back to sea, in his common blood the mingled blood of "princes and potentates" and in his name the echo of his mythic ancestor. The first of the sea-going Tippuses, his great-aunt Hannah had told him, sailed strange seas in the ship Argos; and "the story that Henry was telling, whether he knew it or not was a rude version of the voyage to Colchis and the Golden Fleece" (177). The survival of the archaic sailor, in his veins the illegitimate blood of kings, traveling in a world of bawdy adventure and poignant romance—here is the essential Linklater myth in an unpretentious gem of a book. It looks to *Private Angelo* and beyond to *Position at Noon*. Set entirely in England, it has the markings of Scottish folk fabliau.

The claims of serious comic art pulled Linklater back to more ambitious adaptations of legend. *The Impregnable Women* (1938), one of his least successful books, was "a novel inspired by angry revulsion against the prospect of war's renewal."[15] It supposes the renewal of European war sometime in the 1940s. The war begins with air raids, but an oil embargo sends the armies back into the grisly trench warfare of 1914-1918—and this, Linklater says accurately, he described "with sufficient realism . . . in a high, resounding style."

But trench realism gives over to mythopoeia, Dionysiac ritual, and farce. Linklater's own judgment is characteristically judicious. "I should have opposed to war a down-to-earth, bawdy ridicule. I should have let bawdy nature be the conqueror, and peace the reward of those that preferred four bare legs in bed to the profitless cavorting of honour and probity and such-like tattered concepts. But I was too serious for that. I looked at war with realistic eyes, and tried to defeat it by a farcical extension of war. And there was my mistake. I should have purged myself of emotion, pushed realism out the window, and relied on rough and dirty mockery." This is a central statement of the classic rationality of Linklater's most fantastical art. The mixture of fantasy and grotesque farce with serious and plausible adult characters is quite typical. It is a difficult mixture to manage. At his best—as in *Juan in America*, *Position at Noon*, and *A Man over Forty*, Linklater succeeds. But the next two books represent more cautious and monochromatic economies.

Judas (1939) is a book of stunning economy and tact. Linklater associates it in retrospect with *Men of Ness* as another example of how he let his topic determine his style "almost as a sculptor lets his material—marble or wood or clay—dictate the manner of his work . . . I told the story in modern terms, as if the betrayal of Jesus were a contemporary tragedy, and I was aware that no attempt to heighten or decorate it could be tolerated."[16] It was a betrayal he chose to recreate in response to a contemporary tragedy—the failure of Britain and France to come to Czechoslovakia's aid and block Hitler's truculence. The events of Holy Week are retold indirectly, so as to permit intense concentration on Judas and his hysterical and neurotic point of view. Most biblical events are bypassed and hinted at in retrospective gossip, rumor, shocked memory. The presence of Jesus is really the presence of a problem, moral and political: What is he for? Judas complains bitterly that Jesus has changed from the man of peace to the man of war, rebellion, defiance. And this problem is paralleled by and reflected on Judas's uncertainty: Why is he a pacifist? The book draws Judas with extraordinary complexity in a few pages. He seems overwhelmingly sincere in his pity for the poor and the crippled, and yet is crippled himself by his neurotic need for money, security, and peace.

Uncle Phanuel's judgment of Judas is the author's: "He hadn't enough appetite for life. To enjoy life you must take it as it is . . . The world isn't all it should be, but if you have a good appetite you don't mind the sour bits and a bad smell here and there." Yet it was this fastidiousness, this idealism, that drew him to Jesus. And the self-named realists are self-deluding, self-defeating, in their efforts to deal with the Romans. The book carefully avoids simple answers. It also avoids mere dialogue or parable. Dramatic reality and ideology are carefully balanced, which is crucial in a book that translates an ancient event into such a contemporary idiom. What detail there is stands out in vivid economy. "Jerusalem was like a city desolated by plague. The sun glared on empty streets, on windows unshuttered and shops where the shutters hung half-open. A country-man's staff lay on the roadway, and there a torn cloak. A dead man was huddled on a doorstep beside a pool of blood. Two or three figures hurried furtively round a corner, and a lost child was crying in the street. As if it saw ghosts, or the moon hiding behind the sun, a dog howled at the staring sky" (183). The suggestion of eclipse through the dog's eyes is typical, as is the image of Tamar in despair, leaving Judas after the crucifixion: "She went down the road like a rook with a broken wing" (196). Linklater's stylistic versatility and tact are extraordinary.

After the long hiatus of World War II came *Private Angelo* (1946), out of Linklater's war experience in Italy. Following the fall of Rome he drove across Umbria to the Adriatic: "I had already given much of my heart to Italy, and now—though the local wine was bad—I renewed my dedication." The conception of his wry, wondering Candidean peasant hero—"no anti-hero, but a true one"—came a decade earlier, from observing and hearing about the peasants on the Villino

Medici estate, particularly about one man who managed to survive and come home from war owing to his fortunate lack of the *dono di coraggio*.[17] Angelo has "the most useful of all accomplishments, which is to survive!" A deserter from the Italian army, he is dragooned into the German army, prevents his deportation by volunteering for the Italian front lines, deserts again and becomes attached to a commando group of the British Eighth Army, arrives in Rome for the liberation, is enlisted in one of the new Italian regiments, loses a hand, and is discharged home to rule benignly over a menage of wife, mistress, sisters-in-law, and several polychromatic or international children, the waifs of foreign soldiers and increasing numbers of his own. Parallel to Angelo's fortunes run the fortunes of his patron, landlord, and evidently his natural father, the Count of Piccologrande, a refined, amoral patrician blackmailed into poverty by the despised Germans.

Angelo's happy penchant for flight keeps him out of major military events, and the book sedulously avoids narration of the Italian campaign—although Linklater was War Office historian of the campaign. It is a deliberate control, for Angelo is ideally suited to play naive ironic observer and might have been used primarily as a medium for ironic history. But Linklater has other designs:

> The subject of my novel was not only war and its capacity for destruction, but Italy and its genius for survival. War in Italy has a character all its own; it was tragical, as war inevitably is, but also ludicrous because its waste and folly were underlined, emphasized and thrown into toppling-high relief by the accumulated riches and beauty that Italy had created . . . War was hateful—anyone could see and say that—but war in Italy was also irrelevant because the forces of civilization, and the benignities of art, were clearly so much stronger, more informative and more permanent. War, in Italy, was a drunken, destructive and impertinent clown; to deal justly and truthfully with it one had to keep one's temper cool, one's judgment clear, and write a comedy.[18]

The effort is a triumph of tone. But the mode of drunken clownishness is absent, for the perspective of the book is either the count's poignant Panglossian urbanity, or Angelo's tongue-in-cheek Candidean irony. Amid the bloodshed and destruction their elegant dialogues go on, and the potentialities for grotesque farce are wisely muted. "Realism," Linklater recalls, he carefully avoided, but not in the interests of fantastic farce. The ironic lucidity of Angelo's sad bemusement is a little miracle of rational order:

"Would you say that this village has been liberated?" asked Angelo.

"Oh, properly liberated," said the soldier. "There isn't a roof left in it."

"It makes me sad to look at such destruction," said Angelo. "I am Italian, you see." [82]

"Do I, in any way, resemble Cassino?" he asked Simon, as soon as he was allowed to visit him.

"There is no apparent similarity," Simon answered.

"Then why was I bombed?"

"We all make mistakes from time to time."

"We do not all carry bombs. To make a private mistake in your own house is one thing, but to make a public mistake with a bomb of two hundred and fifty kilograms is different altogether."

"Year by year," said Simon philosophically, "science puts more power into our hands."

"So that we may throw bombs at the wrong people?"

"Science, like love," said Simon, "is blind."

"I prefer love," said Angelo. "It makes less noise." [90]

Angelo marvels at life, at survival, at the miracle of his own body; the count complements him with his own sad resignation to absurd misfortune:

All the days of his life joined themselves together to make a Chinese scroll of the most rich and delectable entertainment . . . He saw himself swollen with the toothache and badgered by the ear-ache . . . Sleep-walking at seven, a clap at college, the piles at forty—he had fallen from his horse in the pincio, he had choked on a fishbone when dining with the Colonnas, he had gone to the races with his buttons undone . . . And yet, though they were ten times as many, life would still be good. (100)

He is the indestructible patrician, the passionate individualist who speaks for Linklater's conservative antipathy to "Great Powers, great causes, great events—and how dull they are!" and sings Linklater's paeon to the survival of man the phoenix in his smallness.

This, one of the finest of Linklater's novels, seems remote from Scottish inspiration. Yet his typical fusion of Voltaire and Byron is here, together with his own persistent self-image as the urbane peasant in league with the resilient patrician, and with his conservative nationalist feeling for the survival of traditional community and value, of small nations and simple people, against the forces that liberate peoples and nations by enslaving or destroying them. *Private Angelo* is one of the best demonstrations of how a vision nurtured in Scottish tradition can interpret events and motives on a worldwide scale.

From 1949 to 1956, Linklater published six novels of extraordinary variety and uneven success. The very versatility is a problem. He was evidently trying for more serious tones, perhaps in response to a critical denigration of comedy and farce. Though confessedly out of sympathy with realism he seems to have been uncertain as to what fantastic or romantic modes were best suited to his interests. He experimented with placing contemporary dilemmas against long historical backgrounds, primarily Scottish; how to integrate them was not always clear. Running through all six novels is an urgent dislike of inhuman rationalism, political giantism, and vulgar bureaucracy.

A Spell for Old Bones (1949) is a Cold War fable set in Galloway and Garrick at the time of the Roman invasions.[19] Its hero is a poet, Albyn, whose preference for love over war and whose prudent behavior in battle are reminiscent of Angelo. The fable is without fantasy except for the giants and for the superb climactic scene of resurrection, when the scattered bones of the armies killed in the war between two giants come to life again after the giants have destroyed each other.

Giants are an unnatural joke. "Anything that grows too big is a joke! Whatever swells, or sprouts, or assumes too much is ludicrous. For children, and the poor, and little things we're sorry; little things are pathetic. But at giants, and rich men bloated by their wealth, and things that have grown big beyond proportion, we want to laugh, and we're right to laugh" (84). Two Linklater themes are apparent. First, a sense of proportion and natural propriety is the most adequate ground for social judgment; the artist, governed by aesthetic standards, is the wisest political moralist. Second, the destructive forces of the world are best treated by laughter. Underlying these themes is Linklater's epicureanism: the end of life is happiness, the real danger in giants lies in their neurotic unhappiness, an unhappy man is more dangerous than a criminal. Furbister and McGammon—presumably the United States and the Soviet Union—hate each other because they are unhappy, and are unhappy because of an infantile hatred of their parents. Furbister is an erratically benign big baby, and McGammon is a giant caricature of despotic socialism. They war against each other out of hatred and fear, and the little people caught between them are destroyed temporarily. Albyn is buried alive under the dead giants, but he returns from his living grave, and the resurrection scene follows; the bones seek out their comrades in gleeful dance and become living men again.

Another experiment followed in *Mr. Byculla* (1950). Here the macabre replaces the fabulous, but the murderous perils of neurotic unhappiness persist. The agent of evil is a reincarnation of Indian Thuggee in unhappy, rootless London, and the hypothesis is that the Thugs did their ritual murders out of sympathy for their miserable victims. It is a picture of amoral weakness and self-pity begging for destruction at the hands of a compassionate fanaticism—a suspenseful variant on the Linklater grotesque, a variant he did not repeat except in his strange, dreamlike final novel, *A Terrible Freedom*. The Scottish element is muted yet significant: Byculla's murderous fanaticism comes in part from his McKillop blood.

Laxdale Hall (1951) is a boisterous return to Scotland. It is set in Compton Mackenzie country: the transient civilities of the shooting lodge, the colorful and erratic Highland villagers, the intermeshed plots of battling the commercial poachers from the city and battling the related invasions of bureaucrats. The framing plot, remarkably fitting, is the outdoor production of a Euripidean play, called *Bacchanals* in the novel. The play is the climax, and the play's meaning, variously interpreted by the characters, is the thematic center. The novel is farce, while the play is tragedy—the definitive Linklater mixture. The plotting is wonderfully improbable; the characters, circumstantial in history and trait, act according to comic stereotype. The Glasgow poachers flee just as the poached stag has been hidden in the local hearse, where the guilty gamekeeper will leave the visiting bureaucrat in drunken sleep to be found *in flagrante delictu* by the constables coming with their summonses for the rebellious locals, who refuse to pay their road tax.

The bureaucrat Pettigrew is as grand a caricature as his false leg. He shares with Macaulay, the fanatical minister, the role of Euripides' foolish King Pentheus, "excessive and inopportune rationalist" who had "stopped the sap and robbed the joy of life." The Euripidean theme that "you can't ignore nature, without nature having its revenge" is reenacted in Linklateresque pastoral.[20] The modern women of Thebes—the Highland women—take their Dionysiac revenge. Pettigrew urges them to give up Laxdale as obsolete and become resident workers on his faraway industrial estate. He grossly violates their sabbath, and they dismember this foolish Pentheus by following him to his naked swim in the millpond, pelting him with clods, and capturing his artificial leg. The scene is farcical but grotesque. The bureaucrat retreats hurriedly, and leaves the Laxdalers to their small triumphs and their remote, nonutilitarian place.

The book is a witty mixture of romantic adventure, farcical incident, and crotchety debate. The lengthy arguments of Matheson and Pettigrew over the Highland economy are serious, but leavened by the debates of two of the general's guests: the fugitive Shetland novelist Swanson (romantic veteran of two wars, in the first of which he lost most of his chin) and the Greek professor Crantit, from "an ancient" Scottish university. Swanson bespeaks Linklater's playful anticontemporary tastes, while Crantit blames the world's ills on the spread of the German work ethic to Russia and the United States. Crantit is a snob and an aesthete: "I'm a roaring snob . . . Every good man is. The lifeforce itself may only be sublime snobbery" (261); "you, as a writer," he instructs Swanson, "cannot afford to waste your respectability on life. Keep it for your muscular sentences and comely paragraphs" (263). The truest morality is style. Yet, for all his sense, Crantit is deflated by the earthy wife of Pettigrew. And the same vulgar, lecherous, but good-hearted lady tells Swanson the novelist off: "Oh, don't talk like an intellectual! I read one of your books once, it was full of words, but if you got past them there was plenty of fun and games in it" (121). It is Linklater's marvelously apt deflation of his own book.

Crantit and Swanson are next transposed into more poignant figures in a Gothic melodrama called *The House of Gair* (1953).[21] Crantit has become Hazelton Crome, elegant Yellow Book anachronism living in archaic Sutherland. Swanson the maimed writer has become Stephen Coryat, struggling with his novel of the Clearances in a lonely cottage by Dornoch Firth. A storm and an empty petrol tank bring Coryat to Crome's "House of Gair." Both men are morally ill: Crome is a literary blackmailer; Coryat's mutilated life is symbolized in a crushed foot and an unfaithful wife. In their long dialogues on art and life is a fascinating assortment of views. Coryat the novelist-hero is a virtual anti-Linklater, and Crome speaks for the author. "My art—such as it is," says Coryat, "is an expression of myself," to which Crome replies, "Oh dear me, what a dreadful thing to say!" (45).

Crome instructs his maimed young secret sharer in the supremacy of comedy as a mode of confronting evil: "If only you had realized that Sodom and Gomorrah lie within the Tropic of Comedy; and to describe their geography and sociology you need perfect confidence and a great deal of gross humour" (44). Crome insists that "style is the hard bone of writing," and provides a prideful epigraph for Linklater's future *Fanfare:* "I'm a writer of the old breed from Pliny the Elder to Dickens, who saw marvels in the world and wrote to express what they saw, not to transcribe the rumblings of a queasy conscience. The writer wasn't born to cut a figure in the world, he was born to work; to make a legend, to mold human figures out of dust and sweat, and breathe life into them! And to match a hundredth part of the variety of life, he should go to work in a hundred different styles and fashions!" (80). *The House of Gair*, which opens with the promise of a "richly comical acquaintanceship" by a speaker who feels "the need of comedy; or, at any rate, of the sanity that inspires it," settles into a suspenseful macabre and ends with extortion, murder, and suicide. Linklater seems to be reaching for Coryat's seriousness: a tragic Highland theme, contemporary in setting, suggestive of the radical options of art, and related analogically to the Highland tragedy of the Clearances. Through his complicity in Crome's survival, Coryat is working out his own maimed past. It is a past both personal and cultural, for Coryat is descendant of a maimed Highland civilization and of two Kildarroch ministers who "must have been agents in the crime" of the Clearances. It is an ambitious conception, whose links and parallels are suggestive. But the historical implications are mostly subordinate to aesthetic issues and to the extravagant plotting of melodrama. The serious modern novel of personal complicity in a Highland past of cultural betrayal is more nearly accomplished in *The Dark of Summer* (1956).

There intervened *The Faithful Ally* (1954), a tale of genial urbanity and perilous adventure in a mythical sultanate. The picture of civility triumphing over savagery is a variant on the strange image of Crome in Sutherland and is another Linklateresque image of survival. The maculate, resilient hero is also familiar. The playboy sultan has a boil on his bottom, an endless supply of champagne in his luggage, a scandalous Rumanian widow—allegedly communist—for a new mistress, an ideological antagonist in solemn British colonial bureaucrat Morland, and a dangerous problem in his highlands where a religious messiah leads the credulous natives in brief and abortive rebellion.

One of the sultan's sayings provides an epigraph to *The Dark of*

Summer, Linklater's single venture into serious romance. "Irony," says the sultan, "or the recognition of it, is one of the major graces of a decent life. Without irony history would be quite intolerable."[22] The story intertwines personal and cultural past. Both are maimed, and the war-wounded protagonist must, through his own suffering, atone for his brother's cowardly death and for his own complicity in the suicide of "a man called Mungo Wishart." Wishart is "a landed proprietor in Shetland, whose mind, to a singular degree, had been shaped, or misshaped, by a family tradition of long unhappiness: a history that started from sedition, murder, and dark uncertainties, and was continued through purposeless and wasteful litigation to no better end than the deformity of a man's reason and a new project of sedition."[23] The start was a usurpation of property occasioned by the Jacobite uprising, a thwarted marriage, a disinherited heir, and a long family feud; the "new project" was the embittered Mungo's secret dealings with Quisling early in World War II. The structure recovers past within past, reminiscence and family memoir; the style is filled with metaphors of the darkness of time and the curse of memory. The protagonist Chisholm tells his own story, warns that he is no writer, and the result is a stammering, awkward, but painfully expressive style, another triumph of Linklater's decorous versatility.

Chisholm is on a counterintelligence assignment for the War Office in the Faroes. His naval escort Lieutenant Silver believes in aesthetic congruousness as the governing force in human acts: "Moral standards have usually been odious . . . The only agreeable standards are the standards of propriety, of fitness" (80). It is Silver who proposes the "blatantly theatrical scheme" of confronting Wishart with the dead Quisling agent, which leads to Wishart's suicide. As in *The House of Gair*, the maimed modern hero becomes involved with a decadent aestheticism and must in compassion act out that involvement, thereby healing himself and his own wounded past. The dark secrets of the past must be dug up—just as Chisholm and his wife, Wishart's daughter, dig up the old Jacobite Dandy Pitcairn when making their new beach road. Complicity with the ironic betrayals of that unearthed past demands a kind of sacrificial maiming—a bad leg, a lost arm, a lost hand (for Angelo)—as the price of exorcism and survival. But then the sheer wonder of survival—the exhilaration that echoes through Linklater's life and work—prevails over bitterness in the renewal of life. "To have survived," says Chisholm, "so much is, I think, something of an achievement, and I admit a persistent sense of wonder about the why and the how of survival" (6). A wound, it is suggested, may be indispensable to that survival. Memory is a wound—at least for the "sort of romantic Puritan" that Chisholm is. It is a sombre, absorbing book. What is missing from its irony is some of the wonder, and while it includes a "grotesque adventure in the Faroes," one misses the extravagant blend of farce and wit with which Linklater ordinarily faces the tragic ironies of history.

In the last chapter of his history, "Mungo Wishart spoke with a curious malice of his father and grandfather" and here, as so often in Linklater, one glimpses the germ of the novel to follow. *Position at Noon* (1958) is, for me, Linklater at his best. Linklater has recorded his "deep" disappointment at "the indifference which attended its publication," since "in conception, as well as in execution, it is the wittiest novel I have written, and wit is a quality that I value and expect to be valued."[24] The word "wit" may suffice, so long as it can include a richly informed sense of historic irony, a repertoire of historical styles, an agility in stylistic modulation and counterpoint to embrace the most heterogeneous narrative modes. For in *Position at Noon*, Linklater's despondent, slothful martinet of a bankrupt modern hero takes for his model God's own fiction: "The vast, tragico-romantico-comico-bawdy novel that God began to write before there was paper to write on, and still is writing when all the forests of the world are being felled to make paper for the novelettes that so many of His faithful apes are writing" (228).

The speaker is a failed antique dealer in a provincial English town, trapped in a dull marriage, with a sluttish mistress at the town hotel, an indestructible devotion to good taste, an exuberant will to survive, a conviction that his misfortunes are owing to his father's folly, and finally a determination to flee to a new life as major domo to a Texas millionaire. The ironic theme echoes at the climax of each chapter in the backward march of dynastic time: "The dice were loaded against me from the start . . . my old booby of a father" (77). The story is of the guilts and follies of the fathers. It moves generation by generation back over two and a half British centuries and eight generations of Vanbrughs, always in disgrace or decline from the days of "The Founder," a bastard found in a coach outside the theater after a play by Vanbrugh. The mixture is often what a chapter title calls it: "Tragedy and Farce."

The narrator's father was a pathetic and bemused survivor of World War I. His father Tom was disgraced in an act of romantic chivalry and lost his commission in imperial India. His father Eustace went through every ideological eccentricity of the mid-Victorians, achieving scandalous notoriety as a Darwinian fanatic who sought experimentally to prove the persistence of a vestigial tale in the female of the species. His father, in Reform days, served in brave dumbness against Napoleon, and became the foolish follower of Regency sportsmen before his wits faded. His father literally stumbled over the bodies of Annette Vallon and William Wordsworth in revolutionary Blois, returned to become Coleridge's "Person from Porlock," suffered from fainting fits, and lived to be Wordsworth's most determined and least welcome guest at Grasmere. His father, reported dead at Bunker Hill, after years of humiliation as a captive manservant to American trappers, returned to spend years preparing the first volume of his *Collapse and Doom of Rome*, only to learn that one Edward Gibbon had anticipated him by a decade. His father—the foundling Moses Van Brugh—made his way to a nabob's fortune through his skill as a footman; and now the eighth in line will begin it all again as a butler in Texas. Each heir is a fumbler—"the only measure he can tread is the *faux pas*" can be said of them all. And yet through all the farce and misfortune runs the thread that is picked up by the speaker in the concluding chapter—a superb paragraph that could serve as an epigraph for all of Linklater's books:

And now—now—do you see the change of temper in me? In the dark hour of my despair, reeling in the vertigo of an oceanic hangover, I could find no straw to cling to—God had vanished, God was not—but God returned when I began to think of my father, and beyond him of my life's long provenance. Belief came back as I rehearsed the troubled tale of my ancestry, because—though patched like a cottage quilt with farce, futility, and gross ineptitude—it was a tale so stiff and stubborn with intent to live, to propagate and persist. A patchwork quilt of folly and fatuity and a brutal appetite for life: of temperance and intemperance, neither much better than the other: of faith and despair, neither enduring: of love like sunshot, pricking showers in April (there must have been that), and the withered herbage of parched and barren years: of great meals, oysters and turtle soup, partridges and venison and ruby dripping sirloins, with beer in the barrel and cellars full of wine—and shrivelled lips dribbling their gruel: of health and sickness, labour pains, and death-beds as reluctant as a never-opened pelvis to let out the soul:

of little piddling desires, trumpery little men and their cackling little women, and the drum-thumping, purple-canopied history they composed. (228-229)

The conception of *The Merry Muse* (1959) is as witty as that of *Position at Noon*, but its execution is uncertain. The discovery of Burns's handwritten bawdy in a defunct schoolmaster's copy of *The Merry Muses of Caledonia*, lost then in Edinburgh and passed surreptitiously around the sedate city with Dionysiac effect, is promising and characteristic. It is, however, subordinated to the leisurely exposition of the central figure, Max Arbuthnot, prosperous Edinburgh solicitor and bon vivant sexagenarian Don Juan. The book aspires often to great farcical-grotesque scenes: the ill-fated tugboat trip on a rough rainy day to disperse old Charlie's ashes at open sea; the catastrophic drunken hearse, which tangles with a regiment of troops marching to Leith. The urn of ashes is opened too soon, and the wet guests are covered with bits of old Charlie. The devastated hearse tosses out the coffin, and a soldier finds the bawdy book and carries it off to the Far East, where it has the same Dionysiac effect. The festive transformation of Edinburgh sits strangely with Max's complex aggressiveness. When Max's daughter and Max's mistress have their rough and tumble in Max's office, the battle lacks humor because both of the women are mean, selfish sensualists. There is too much plot about recovering the lost manuscript and too little about its wide-ranging effect; Max's long hard search for a Landseer to buy seems inconsequential, and the departure of Max's military son-in-law to quell rebellion in the New Brabant of *The Faithful Ally* belongs elsewhere. The book has all the makings of a grand Linklater comedy, but it fails in integration and proportion.

And a new problem arises. How well will bawdy epic farce serve as a response to old age and death? In *Roll of Honour* (1961), Linklater seems reluctant to find out, and instead creates yet another style, with a chronicle rhythm similar to that of *Position at Noon*, but with a quiet, sequestered serenity as frame for Andrew Birnie's long reminiscence of the war dead, an old retired schoolmaster's memorial to sorrow and waste. Andrew Birnie lives alone, resigned to his housekeeper's hen-pecking, contented in the perfect ritualizing of his simple weeks of walk and golf and cinema. The obituary of his old schoolmaster sends him to memorial volumes of the boys of their school who had died in the century's wars. The effect is surprisingly varied, as

Andrew Birnie's long roll covers many years and continents, all re-called in the small town gossipy milieu of Inverdoon by this survivor: "He had survived his reverses. They had not defeated him. And the ability to survive, and the fact of survival, clearly enhanced the inter-est of his life."[25] Then comes the other survivor, Simon Kyle, a novel-ist no longer popular, with artistic principles akin to Linklater's, with a draggy limp from World War I. It is a brief and extraordinary inter-vention in Birnie's peaceful elegy. Kyle is angry, and he speaks with Linklater's voice: "There's nothing plain and simple and orderly. You come up against tragedy and go to a box-room to look for your top-hat to dress up for the funeral; but some damned conjurer has been there before you, and there's a nest of white rabbits in your hat-box. — Or you meet nobility—not often, but sometimes, and you may be reluctant to recognise it; but you make the effort, you acknowledge a moral superiority—and the next thing you see is farcical intervention that's undoing its buttons" (171).

Kyle is there only long enough to introduce Birnie to the pleasures of rebellious whisky drinking. As he turns back to one final reminis-cence, Birnie takes a bottle of Glenlivet with him, accidentally pulls over a bookcase of Victorian masters, sings of the goodness of life in those older witnesses, and goes to sleep contentedly amid the ruins of his civilization.

Husband of Delilah (1962) is an odd diversion from the main line of the last novels, masques of old age, addresses to death. While it is narrated with Linklater's facility and economy, it is misconceived. First, he sees Samson as a folk hero like Robin Hood and Till Eulen-spiegel but dignified by his relationship to God. He is "a combination of the indomitable outlaw and the jester"—or the "God-intoxicated mountebank."[26] But even Samson speaks of his life and his strength in utterly rationalistic terms, and the narrative avoids all supernatural suggestion even as it recreates the major events. Second, Samson is a mixture of "village saint" and "village toper," with a "village philos-ophy"—yet in dialogue he is as urbane as a Don Juan. Linklater says he "tried to refurnish the core of reality in a heroic myth" (viii), but this means naturalizing and domesticating, and the "heroic myth" be-comes a superficial element of fable. Third, Linklater's "excuse for re-telling the story . . . in modern terms" lacks artistic validity: the Phili-stines are "a mercantile people . . . a modern and modernising power in conflict with a conservative and pastoral habit of life" (vii), the "lost cause" Samson represents. The bureaucratic Philistines speak for history, and Samson speaks for God—but he actually speaks for a way of life, a consciously backward pastoral culture, which is not persuasively represented. Linklater has little imaginative sympathy for the power of the fanatic. Finally, while Delilah is richly, realistically drawn as an awesome prostitute and astute business tycoon, and while her love for Samson and his surrender are the focus of the middle of the novel, her role is irrelevant to the ideological "excuse." Moreover, the title suggests a mock-heroic tone, and yet the book is very short on mockery or any other comic mode. Samson says, "There's only the thickness of onion-skin between disaster and a joke." There is very little joking in this book.

A Man over Forty (1963) is my favorite Linklater novel. It triumphantly combines elements in a way that one has learned to expect when Linklater is at his best. It belongs with other late masques of age. Though Balintore is far short of being elderly, his full, extravagant life is behind him, and he must flee from it to save his sanity. Balintore is a return to *Juan in America* and to the pastoral urbanity of *Merriman*. As in *Laxdale Hall*, contemporary farce is played against archaic Greek legend and tragedy, and the tragic is so mingled with the farcical as to leave them in uneasy and yet effective solution. What is different is the new concern with a survival that is not physical or aesthetic but moral and religious. It is remarkable that a novel which operates hilariously on the levels of farce can move into a realm of mystery and religious illumination in its final chapters among the Greek isles. But even this mixture is reminiscent of the Byronism of *Juan in America*.

The "man over forty," though he does not know it, is in flight from and to his uncertain Scottish self. He is a God-obsessed romantic rogue, a London television "character," who collapses before the cameras when his past is probed, and flees before Furies. His flight ends with self-recognition in a Greek monastery. He has been forced to uncover his ancestral sin: out of love for his dead adoptive father he killed his cruel adoptive mother by filling her insulin bottles with water. Peace comes with the recognition of his Scottishness: the Calvinist conscience and God-obsession of an Edinburgh boyhood are not to be evaded, even though their provinciality is transcended in the isles of Greece.

Balintore is an aging schoolboy, a fool, a Don Juan, a would-be

Alan Breck: one can hardly share the surprise of the young lady who says to him, "I didn't know you were Scotch."²⁷ He is a middle-aged Orestes, in quest after thwarted quest for a paradise where he can hide. For all his well-traveled cosmopolitanism, he is a village philosopher. He is conscious of the mixture of tragedy and farce in his history; he had once produced a "monologue on the uneasy relationship between tragedy and farce." Shivering after an icy midnight pursuit of a lady that ends at Central Park Zoo, Balintore announces, "I've been involved in tragedy, and I've behaved like a clown: that's the pattern of the story"—and it is indeed. The mystery of Balintore's Scottish identity has a special complexity. His old Scottish boyhood friend, Peter Ricci, is an Italian now living in Australia. Balintore is a foundling; his Scottish identity may be merely adoptive. He is intrigued by the richness of ancestral identity available to his far-descended secretary Palladis; but Palladis was sterilized by mumps in boyhood and talks in a "pleasing mezzo-soprano," and his descent seems on occasion to have depended on burly footmen and lovely Jamaican Negresses. Like Alan Sharp's Scottish foundling Moseby and Muriel Spark's Sandy Stranger, Balintore yearns for "genetic identity." Palladis's reaction to the yearning poses a dilemma: which is worse, he asks, total anonymity or descent from a known regicide and a reformed whore? Balintore's Scottish preference is for ancestral guilt and folly; he has learned that anonymity is not innocence.

The conscience-stricken Scottish child buried in Balintore has driven him from Eden to illusive Eden—Jamaica, Ireland, Greece. In Jamaica he is caught by a man convinced that Balintore has stolen and used his dead brother's novel manuscript. In New York, in wild pursuit of a new "secretary," he runs into his second wife, new mistress and model to Inga Pomador, Mexican "action artist"—and we are back in the flamboyant satiric world of *Juan in America:*

> Already he had done more than any other of the action painters to expose the faded insufficiencies of orthodox art, and the shallowness of mind that had characterised the so-called masters from Cimabue to Chagall. He had bicycled over furlongs of wet paint, and thrown small furry animals into pools of crimson lake and Chinese white. He had flung vegetable refuse at ochre screens, and pushed wheel-barrows across canvases splashed with Prussian blue to spill upon them loads of mica and dried blood. With boxing-gloves soaked in cadmium red he had punched the incontestable image of his vigour on to shivered panels smeared with Naples yel-

low; and dabbed a tight-stretched pair of *pantalon de toile* with the varnished entrails of bats, young pike, and hamsters. (101)

The new secretary proves loquacious, and Balintore flees to Palladis in County Mayo. Here the precarious Eden is a fine Georgian manor house. A slightly mad geologist mines for gold in adjacent fields. During a manorial dinner the nearby miners get drunk, set double charges, and almost blow up the house, shattering one of two great Waterford glass chandeliers and with it another of Balintore's hopes of edenic refuge. The pilgrimage resumes. "All good travellers are pilgrims at heart," says Palladis. "Pilgrims or fugitives," groans Balintore. The aging Juan, "a deeply religious man," finds (like his Aberdonian ancestor, Byron) his identity at last in a Scottish guilt.

Psychological disintegration is more advanced in *A Terrible Freedom* (1966), whose protagonist-narrator is as old as the century, a wealthy and retired manufacturer of window blinds, a long-time cultivator of his extraordinary dream life. He decides: "I would record in future all such dreams as survived the little death of waking up, and seemed under critical appraisal to be worth recording; and as a framework for them I would write, but very briefly, the mundane or daily part of my autobiography."[28] The incessant echo throughout all the novels, the trauma of having survived World War I, when Gaffikin was buried alive like the poet of *Old Bones* for two days, sounds more clamorously than before. Linklater's fifty-year fanfare for a tin hat— for the miracle of having returned from death on the battlefield— sounds here in a melancholy key. "I was a lonely man when the war was over," says Gaffikin, "and so remained for most of my life" (158). As his son notes in a postscript, "He speaks of the desolating effect, on his mind and body, of the war in which most of his contemporaries and all of his friends were killed, and it is perfectly clear that he never recovered from the psychological wounds of that war. His retreat from life, his *fugue*, was the direct consequence of what he had suffered" (222).

Linklater said in 1967 that the novel had been received with indifference. The dream sequences early in the book are sometimes farcical, sometimes dystopian, always irrational. Evan's conscious life is the story of the survivor who succeeds in the world, flees from the prison of his success, enjoys a furtive romance, and is otherwise alone. The book is an attempt to experiment with the dream-life and to treat satirically the obsession with death that Linklater sees as the stock-in-trade of a tradition in fiction that has lost its way. As always he manages a strange style with assurance and polish. But what it offers of his fantastic vigor for serving life "by crystallising its dilemmas and excusing its defeats in a mood of civilized acceptance"—or in a mood of bawdy hilarity and Dionysiac fury—is not clear. Linklater's has always been a fiction of survival, and the weird and serene death impulse of *A Terrible Freedom* is either a personal emotion out of tune with his art or a new aesthetic adventure whose form is uncertain.

Eric Linklater and Robin Jenkins* are novelists of survival. A fiction of survival centers on the antihero, a chastened quixote, and on the perilous folly of harboring romantic attitudes in a fallen world. Like other Scottish fantasists, Linklater and Jenkins are haunted by images of innocence, and both find the betrayal of innocence to be an inevitable sin. The innocent eye perceives divinity in a ludicrously fallen world, and the effect is grotesque. The grotesque serves both novelists well in their visions of the city: an absurd vitality erupts through Edinburgh gentility; a humanity that must be loved survives in a Glasgow slum. But the novelists differ, too. For Jenkins, ripeness is not all; not even the *dono di coraggio* is enough. The problem of survival for him is moral.

The Scottish situation as Jenkins portrays it is desperately polarized between natural beauty and human ugliness; he dwells on the illusory temptation of pastoral retreat in the face of urban degradation. He pictures faith corrupted into football worship and into the loveless fanaticisms of orthodoxy. His imagination centers on two figures: the innocent child and the quixotic guardian. His innocents are most moving when they are both naive and corruptible; his guardians, when in their love of innocence they learn to know its limits and acquire humility.

Ten of the sixteen novels are set in Scotland.[29] Three are set in the Near East—Afghanistan, "Nurania," India. Two are in Southeast Asia, "Kalimantan," a sultanate between Singapore and Hong Kong. One is set in Catalonian Spain. The Scottish settings alternate between

---

*Jenkins, Robin. Born in 1912 at Cambuslang, Lanarkshire, he attended Glasgow University and has taught at Dunoon Grammar School. He has held several teaching appointments abroad, in Kabul (1957-1959), Barcelona (1959-1961), and Sabah (1963-1968).

Glasgow or the Lanarkshire industrial towns and the south western Highlands of hunting estates and reforestation projects.

Jenkins's purpose leads him into large-scale books with many characters and complex plots resting on numerous evolving relationships. It is hard to judge whether this challenge of scope and complexity stirs Jenkins to his best, or whether a limited, intense focus serves him better. Three of the largest books—*The Thistle and the Grail, Guests of War,* and *A Love of Innocence*—are among his best. But so are four of the most sharply focused: *The Cone-Gatherers, The Changeling,* and more recently *A Very Scotch Affair* and *The Holy Tree.* In the larger books a comprehensive moral interest requires a complex structure of thematic parallel and variation. In the smaller ones it requires characters of extreme symbolic weight—archetypal figures rendered psychologically in polarized settings.

So Gaily Sings the Lark (1950) sends a sensitive young Lanarkshire miner to the Highland forestry service in flight from the cold, gray inevitability of the mining town, in search of a place to be rooted and content like the trees. The narrative is a simple episodic sequence of local places, events, character types variously illustrative of natural and religious attitudes. Rivalries in love, trials of faith, thwarted yearnings for nature, anger over the loss of a pure way of life, how to survive without it, how to love in the face of vulgarity and unchastity —these shape the hero's struggle. The love of Kirstie the croft girl, a character of robust natural strength and compassion, leads him to a truer sense of what he is and what life he has found. Alexander Reid is unhappy with the happy ending, since "Kirstie is nature and nature (as Jenkins sees it) tends to go bad—the good is always a miracle."[30] But in this first novel the miracle lasts.

In *Happy for the Child* (1953), the protagonist is the weak, broodingly oversensitive boy attending academy on a bursary; his bond with a proud, austere charwoman mother is at the center of his struggle. Both characters are endowed, somewhat improbably, with subtle moral awareness, the boy with a cunningly intricate understanding. No innocent, he pursues his innocence as a romantic myth, knows ecstasies of destructiveness, hungers to confront an angry God. The plot parallel to this austere melodrama, radically different in tone, anticipates the later novels. It follows another boy, dunce and delinquent Sam Gourlay, his "small, sleekit, idle" unemployed socialist miner father, his "huge cruel desperate" bawdy slattern of a mother,

273

his kind sister with her idyllic vision of saving him and her guilty sexual fears of God's wrath. The domestic wars of the Gourlays set a satiric frame for the Byronic boy-hero's torments. Here in germ are the school figures of *Guests of War*, the grim, often bawdy domestic ethos of *The Changeling* and *A Very Scotch Affair*, and what will become the pervasive problem of innocence betrayed and betraying in its struggle to survive.

Jenkins moved to a larger, livelier canvas in *The Thistle and the Grail* (1954), and conceived the angry, ostracized Andrew Rutherford, town industrialist and president of Drumsagart Thistle football club in its year of triumph. The town is seen in all the orgiastic humor of its football fanaticism. The president, good man and local magnate, is pulled down by malicious rumor and mean, toadying detractors, the tragic pattern of Brown's *House with the Green Shutters*. Rutherford is forced to choose between a hopeless loneliness and a capitulation to his shrewish wife and to his own despair at the spectacle of self-tormenting Scottish meanness where only football replaces the "faith and purpose" of a Covenanting heritage. Will he give up Drumsagart in its quest for the football grail? In all its ugliness and fraud it shows signs of vitality and courage. Will he capitulate to his brother-in-law and flee to a corrupted sanctuary of suburban nature? He has already done so, he believes, and surely there by the lovely Firth "there could be some kind of salvation."

In *The Cone-Gatherers* (1955), Jenkins returns to the lovely, ambivalent world of *The Lark*, where, in time of war on a patrician estate, the superficially humanitarian Lady Runcie-Campbell gives patriotic permission for two simple forestry workers to gather the cones of her majestic trees for seeds of reforestation. The simple-minded hunchback brother Calum is the object of the insane hatred of Duror the gamekeeper, who sees in Calum a "personification" of his own "stunted, misshapen, obscene, and hideous" life with a love-hungry, obese invalid wife. Duror's plots to drive out the brothers are slow to ripen. But when the embittered older brother refuses to help rescue the lady's son from a tree-top, Duror has his excuse for violence. He shoots Calum in his tree and then kills himself. The horrified, chastened lady kneels beneath Calum's macabre crucifixion and finds "pity, and purified hope, and joy" in "the blood and the spilt cones." A weird, sacramental sacrifice engineered by a pathological perfectionist somehow brings hope of social justice grounded in sad humility.

Ritualistic intensity recedes, and the humorous large scale returns, in *Guests of War* (1956), which introduces what will become a recurrent motif: the risks to innocence of haphazard pastoral adoption. Once more the clichés of rural kindness and urban inhumanity are set forth for qualification. The expectation in 1939 that "Gowburgh" will be bombed provokes a mass exodus of children and mothers to remote Langrigg on the Borders, a comic epic of uprooting and adoptive transplanting. The central figures are a romantic, rebellious young schoolmaster and an energetic slum mother. Both are effective guardians. But she, whose rural childhood and yearnings for escape make her see herself as a betrayer of her Gowburgh home, undergoes struggles of conscience. Her son Sammy, her "substitute for those meadows and hills," is killed accidentally; once more the innocent is sacrificed to chasten the self-indulgent idyllicism of the supposed guardian. An aging Chris Guthrie, she drags the weariness of her fifty years part way up nearby Brack Fell in a final act of rededication and vows to return to the city.

In *The Missionaries* (1957), a book confused in mode and tone, we are back in *The Thistle*'s world of decayed faith. A Glasgow sheriff, two clerks, and six constables go as "missionaries of Authority" and representatives of an "era of decayed faith" to evict a small community of fanatical "sectarians" who live illegally on a holy Hebridean island owned by a wealthy cosmopolitan and his attractive, shallow daughter. The eviction is opposed by the sheriff's nephew, a university debater with the quixotic self-image of a modern Jason pursuing the fleece of his soul. The missionaries are touched in various miraculous ways—healing, illumination, paralysis, death—by this holy place. "Jason," having made a solemn commitment to the threatened community, discovers with wonder that they are in fact "small-minded, crafty, grasping, lecherous bigots" prepared to blackmail and seduce him. He sheds his illusions, acknowledges the humanity he must share with them—"so swift a re-orientation was nothing short of miraculous" (the miracle muddles the art)—and returns chastened to the worldly comforts of his island Medea and her wealthy father.

The Changeling (1958) translates the figure of the quixotic liberal in his later years back into the rebellious and facile schoolmaster of *Guests of War*. Charlie Forbes is a flabbier quixote, a naive Peter Pan; and the innocent victim, Tom Curdie, adopted by the Forbeses to share their Firth of Clyde holiday, wears only a mask of ghetto stoicism. The superficial kindness and erratic resentments of the family shatter the mask. They come to see Tom as a changeling, a demonic invader of family love, and he becomes one, wondering at the strange divided thing he has become, yearning to belong, unable to escape the old, ugly attachments. Charlie Forbes feels helplessly betrayed by this strange innocent—"Was not adult life a series of such ambushes from the past?"—and shrinks as his godliness is thwarted. Tom's final despair comes with the arrival of his Glasgow kin bent on blackmail; and sought by the police, unwilling to return to the city, he hangs himself, leaving the bourgeois Forbeses to survive in the exposed limits of their humanity.

For all its stunning effectiveness, *The Changeling* reveals problems that Jenkins solved only intermittently in later books. The severe, compassionate moral realist is unevenly served by the grotesque fantasist. The tragic naturalist depends too easily on psychic polarity and sacramental catastrophe. The artist of psychological intensity is betrayed by an excess of complex characters, with the result that some characters seem overburdened with tormenting moral awareness. If some admirers were disturbed by the next book, *Love Is a Fervent Fire* (1959), it may be because these problems surface there with a vengeance.

The world of *The Lark* and *The Cone-Gatherers* has shrunken into a Highland version of G. D. Brown's Barbie, seething with destructive gossip, neurotic lechery, and hysterical sorrow over lost innocence. The town amply confirms the moral vision of Jock the barman (the book's only sensible, compassionate figure): "The truth was he felt, with his heart as tender as scaled teeth, that every human being, from murderer to saint, was at the mercy of passions, desires, and appetites that crept out of the dark forests of the mind like ravenous wolves . . . Christ pity us all" (86). The new forestry officer, a cynical, drunken war hero, desperately seeks atonement for his part in the recent war. He somehow thinks to find it in loving a decayed aristocrat with a bastard daughter and a moronic brother.

The lady plots to yield to the officer, then reverts to hatred and plans his murder. His forgiveness is a burden she is not sure she can bear, and his sense of atonement may well arouse in the reader the response she feels: "She felt then like screaming to him what right had he to believe his heart was cleansed, that atonement had been made?" (223) But abruptly they set out together in the slow cultivation of love and forgiveness. One reader has called *Love Is a Fervent Fire* "that strange anguished novel";[31] certainly for Jenkins it is a revealing, central one.

It was fitting that he escape temporarily from the fiery anti-Kailyard of his Scotland. Escape came with the first group of "expatriate" novels. In *Some Kind of Grace* (1960) the enigmatic central figures, lost and found in the wilds of Afghanistan, are fanatical Scots, however, and the novel is a variant of *Love Is a Fervent Fire:* a sighting of signs of grace amid perverted love and misery. The perverter here is a fiercely ascetic Christianity in a missionary couple, she pregnant, he unable to believe he broke his vow of chastity to beget the child, she fostering the myth that she was violated by drugged natives. The momentum of the book comes from the quest of the diplomat McLeod, who hates their religion, yearns for his own vision of natural innocence, and discovers grace and nobility in the wretched villagers.

Dust on the Paw (1961) retains the Near Eastern setting, but returns to the world of baffled schoolmasters and endangered innocents. The Asian protagonist, schoolmaster Wahab, is at once a betrayed innocent and an opportunistic politician. We are shown the risks and tests of adoption: the plight of half-caste children in a prejudiced world of superficial liberals. Schoolmaster Charlie Forbes reappears as the disintegrating Moffatt, married to a lovely Chinese wife but afraid to have mixed children. In a setting of international tension, cultural revolution, and domestic power politics, Wahab imports, deflowers, and marries a plain, lame, brave Scottish spinster, and the unfolding of their joint courage counterpoints the betrayals, humiliations, and ultimate hopefulness and fruitfulness of the Moffatts. It is a large, handsomely formed book, and remains Jenkins's most ambitious achievement.

In *The Tiger of Gold* (1962) his inspiration seems to have run temporarily dry. The result is a modernizing of Scott's *Surgeon's Daughter.* Sheila McNair, Scott and Scotland never out of her mind, travels in India, finds it no tiger of gold but filth, disease, and suffering, almost marries a maharajah's heir, plays off her "romance" against her kirkly background, loses her maharajah, learns antiromantic humility, gives up dreams of her "dark" lover, and returns to Edinburgh University.

There was a need for Jenkins, too, to go home, and *A Love of Innocence* (1963) is a welcome return to Scottish settings, a mature, postwar sequel to *Guests of War* in a Hebridean setting. The offspring of lust and violence in a Glasgow children's home are brought for adoption, with all its risks and tensions, by the island's barren women. Point of view is mobile and well-dramatized; melodramatic polarities and explicit atmospheric symbolism are gone from this reflective study of the mature need for love and the dangers of guarding innocence. The central lovers are a fortyish Glasgow social worker, who returns at last like Bell McShelvie to the commitments of her muddled city, and the fiftyish island bigamist, who is one of Jenkins's most interesting characters—cynical raisonneur, but compassionate moralist. The narrative traces their affair to its end, and traces several of the trial adoptions to their hopeful conclusions. In the muted background is the imminent death of the island locale, but the possibilities of human love, not the warnings of cultural prophecy, are what matter.

Off again, then, in *The Sardana Dancers* (1964), this time to Catalonia, where a "graceful" international set of expatriates, as frivolous as they are morally sophisticated, wonder whether to join the sardana dance of life, and if so, how—by politics, art, or love. Love wins, in a survey of elegant manners seemingly uncongenial for Jenkins. Perhaps he is too much his own angry, antiphilistine Glaswegian artist Lynedoch, who despises Scotland, yet knows "it is in your blood, and in the remotest crannies of your brain; you cannot get rid of it." The common cultural plight of Scot and Catalonian is made explicit. But Scotland and art are nagging thematic problems left hanging.

Spain returns in an effective though subordinate role after a four-year lapse and after another remarkable homecoming in *A Very Scotch Affair* (1968). This is the short, restrained, and probing story of Mungo Niven, Glasgow insurance supervisor, his gross and dying wife, his opportunistic son, his stoic daughter, his small boy, and his brittle intellectual mistress, who twits him with his out-of-date Scottish conscience, takes him from his pathetic wife, and dumps him after a seven week affair in Barcelona. The news of his wife's death reaches Spain by a wire slipped under the hotel room door while he is in bed with a Rubenesque whore, uneasily cleansing his conscience in ample flesh. He goes home for the funeral. Mungo's pretentious return to a neighborhood where his wife's friends are likely to murder him is as fine an episode as Jenkins has written. Mungo must decide whether to patch up with his kids. In a whimsical, moving finale he bids them goodbye and settles back in his cab "to think of Italy or some other beautiful place of banishment." Relatively free of explicit themes, the book derives its economical force from the character of Mungo. Raised in a ghetto by a charwoman, erratically afflicted with "Scotch conscience," intellectually ambitious and vain, feebly lecherous, a shallow humanitarian, Mungo assimilates many Jenkins motives into a credible antihero, a changeling who survives.

His heir in *The Holy Tree* (1969), a low caste Southeast Asian Tom Curdie, fails to survive. Michael Eking is caught in a postcolonial social web and betrayed by a lust for education and sex as the keys to status and escape from his primitive village life; he is an innocent already corrupted by naive self-love and a hypocritical world. The ironic title alludes to the tree near his college hostel, which Michael identifies as his, and which recalls Katherine Anne Porter's *Flowering Judas*. Michael sees in the tree a Christian God bleeding for him, and yet Michael is the book's Judas. He wins entry to college by betraying the hiding place of his people's nationalist leader. Under his tree Michael, guilty but still bewildered, is assassinated by the son of the man he has betrayed.

The Expatriates (1971), set mostly in Michael's Malaysia, returns to the Forbeses and the Moffats. Expatriate Ronald McDonald, rich Glasgow businessman, tells his self-righteous bride he is determined to retrieve his half-caste bastard daughter. After a flight to Kalimantan, an unpleasant few days of feuding with old colonial friends and fornicating with old mistresses, he brings his former housekeeper to surrender her little girl. The family departs for Scotland, and the quiet, bereft native mother kills herself. Another innocent is sacrificed, and another tormented family, their thin humanity measured, their love exposed in its imperfections, feels chastened and glimpses a hope of forgiveness and grace.

As this survey suggests, Jenkins's novels show a remarkable continuity of motif and theme, a cluster of situations and problems alternatingly worked and reworked, without marked shifts in mode or method. His feelings for Scotland fluctuate widely between anger—for what his artist in *Sardana Dancers* calls "the cold, murk, and inspissated philistinism" that "tormented him too into vision"—and a marveling compassion for the sheer will to survive in those ground down by a life of Glasgow poverty. Bell McShelvie's life in *Guests of War* is the tale in a nutshell:

It had been a tale of crudeness, ignorance, paganism, violence, hardship, selfishness, and greed; unfolded in hovels in the country and grimy tenements in the city; without the alleviation of what was called culture; purposeless, unless eating, sleeping, working, and reproducing were purposes; and unredeemed even by any sense of suffering, of crucifixion, of being kept out in the wilderness with paradise shut off by a wall as high as a mountain, over which nevertheless the tormenting fragrances were wafted. [242]

Jenkins's concern with the degradation of modern Scotland is not that of the socioeconomic naturalist, but rather that of the theological moralist, with ways of living in the face of that degradation, and in the face of another undeniable given: a love of innocence. Innocence is always the lovely menace, the source of renewal and hope, but also the temptation to forget how far one is from Eden, how limited is one's humanity, how flawed one's love.

Lovely, ambiguous nature can provide "a morning that seemed to beguile the mind with recollections of a time of innocence before evil and unhappiness were born" (*Cone-Gatherers*, 41), or a place which seems to the deluded romantic a "kingdom, where regret, humiliation, mercenariness, and failure, did not exist" (*Changeling*, 69). The reminder comes often in the figure of the child; Jenkins, like the schoolmistress in *Love Is a Fervent Fire*, is never without the faculty "of being able to see in any man or woman the child betrayed and corrupted" (30). Even an old pauper in *The Thistle and the Grail* feeds such a faculty: "Tinto, bound for the Calvinist hell, despite his dirt, disease, and randiness, could give one a glimpse whiles of that carefree, far-off, mythological life under blue skies and green trees" (121). The protagonist Rutherford glimpses it in his shrewish wife Hannah: "Obscurely he realized there must be deep in her a green sunny meadow shut off by thick stunted trees and rocky deserts" (32). For one of the foster parents of *A Love of Innocence*, thinking of the cast-offs of lust and murder brought to her peaceful island from a city orphanage, it seemed "miraculous that out of so much human misery and sordid violence two such delightful little boys should have emerged, not only innocent in themselves, but inspiring innocence in everyone who met them" (144). Why is it, then, asks the cone-gatherer Neil, "that the innocent have always to be sacrificed?" (167). Why, as the town councillor's wife in *Guests of War* comes to see, should there be in her husband, "as in all humanity . . . a dark hell where she and his children suffered for his sins"? (152). Often, Jenkins implies, it is because the guardians of innocence have not yet discovered the risks and imperfections of their love and the narrow limits of their humanity. It seems an innocent must die to impart the lesson.

Jenkins's protagonists often find themselves in the trap discovered by Moffatt in *Dust on the Paw*: "He found himself tormented by his love as by an enemy who knew him profoundly" (67), or by Margaret Mathieson in *Love of Innocence*: "The need for love had revealed to her imperfections that only love granted could cure" (122). Angus, her Lothario, speaks for all of the novels: "The truth was, of course, that everybody fundamentally could love only himself; selfless love was beyond the capabilities of human beings; when it appeared to exist it was really self-love in some pathetically ineffectual disguise" (202). One such disguise leads quixotic Charlie Forbes of *The Changeling* into a terrible failure. He and his wife at last "both knew in their hearts, she in her way and he in his, that love had failed amongst them, and for the rest of their lives they, and their children, must live in the shadow of that failure" (154). Yet, says Old Gourlay in *Happy for the Child*, "you can't scunner love. It's unperishable" (185). Love may be grotesque or perverted by a lust for perfection. But "love had to be accepted, in all its shapes; to sift and censor it, and leave out all that was neither respectable nor aesthetic, was to destroy it as an adventure"— so learns Andrew in *The Missionaries* (227). "Love by its nature is bound to be a little grotesque, but it need not be destructive." "Cherish love," comes the imperative, "especially if it's maimed or ashamed or comic" (*Sardana*, 13, 265), and the novels specialize in such versions of love. The result is a melancholy vision of "the vaster universal sorrow of humanity thwarted in its love by its own limitations" (*Guests of War*, 220). The central revelation is always the same: "Maybe it's a miracle that love is able to exist here. But it does" (*Scotch Affair*, 106).

The discovery of one's love as a coward or betrayer, the sensing of one's distance from Eden, brings with it the chance for "that maturest of virtues," humility (*Fervent Fire*, 19). Charlie Forbes can no longer return in enchantment, a romantic Crusoe, to his glorious holiday heritage on the Firth of Clyde. He has learned that "his heart was of ordinary size, composition, and quality; only if he acted accordingly would he find peace; that it would be the peace of mediocrity could not be helped" (*Changeling*, 186). The romantic heroine of *The Tiger of Gold* must give up her visions of her maharajah and go home, "resolved to cultivate a little humility" (157). Bell McShelvie won't allow herself false hopes: "There was, then, Mrs. McShelvie knew, to be no complete redemption, no cleansing and healing of the wound. A little humility had been learned, and might as soon as tomorrow be forgotten" (*Guests*, 219). The West Highland minister of *Gaily Sings the Lark* advises: "We are none of us bare-footed world-renouncing saints, remember. We are entitled to put up a fence round our own little bit of existence. If we can we make excursions of unselfishness through the gate, but we must always return and close the gate behind us. Close the gate, Grant" (173).

Love without humility, Jenkins suggests, is cruelly perfectionist; and in the face of its pretensions, betrayal is inevitable. Mungo Niven, deserter of his slatternly wife, realizes too late that "if she had since degenerated, so had he; and he was not so sure now that she had contributed more to his degeneration than he had to hers. He had perhaps blamed and punished her for inadequacies neither of them could help" (*Scotch Affair*, 142). Rutherford of *The Thistle and the Grail* realizes, "he had no right to judge any human being, weigh that being's worth as if it was easily measurable, reject any hope of information, and smugly accept the incurable mediocrity" (123). Lynedoch, the artist of *Sardana Dancers*, finds the want of humility a national trait: "I took a scunner because we're a small country that has never had the humility to admit its smallness, or even to recognize it. We stand on our own midden and try to blow our heads off crowing. Who hears? Who notices? Not even the English. In the past it was a miserably small contribution we made to the world's art. Now we make none, and never will. How can we? We've neither faith nor interest" (217). Moral humility demands cultural humility. The two go hand in hand, like Paula and Wahab of *Dust on the Paw*.

Humility is "the maturest of virtues," but without a love of innocence it turns into amoral quietism or despairing renunciation of the "world's falseness and triviality" (*Expatriates*, 149). The challenges and commitments are not to be shunned because "we're not fit to face them." Such are the words of one of many deniers, and the deniers are always inferior in humanity to fools such as Charlie Forbes.

The deniers give up human community and long instead for the conscienceless grace of nature, a kind of innocence not to be recovered. In *Some Kind of Grace*, McLeod knows it for a moment: "Trembling, he sat and gazed at the house. His hand still hung down, as if maimed.

Out of some green vines that covered part of the wall a bird flew, with a crest and a soft, cooing call. He watched it alight on a tree. For a moment he seemed to escape into life, where morality did not exist" (212). Calum the hunchback is more at home with trees than with humanity; but then so is the pathological gamekeeper Duror. A large elm stands outside Duror's house: "Here was a work of nature, living in the way ordained, resisting the buffets of tempests and repairing with its own silent strength the damage suffered: at all times simple, adequate, pre-eminently in its own proper place. It had become a habit with him, leaving the house in the morning, returning to it at night, to touch the tree . . . Now the bond was broken" (28-29). Because he can show no compassion for his invalid wife, nature has no grace to offer him, and Calum, the image of natural innocence, becomes an obsession of destructive hatred. It is not the image that is at fault. David Sutherland is fascinated by trees—"their fixity, their patient growth in their ordained places":

> Surely it should be easier in these surroundings to regain the sanity the world had lost, for the most important thing was first of all to feel at home on the earth, to be able to meet even a caterpillar crawling across the road and feel with it the kinship of living creatures. In the city it could be done . . . But here, under so generous a width of sky, it was a less tormented kinship: the caterpillar making for its green food on the other side of the road could be watched with a freer less desperate love. [*Gaily Sings the Lark*, 263]

But in their rootlessness, their vulnerability, people need more love than trees, not less.

To love people is to love a radical mixture of betrayal and corruption, innocence and evil. It is the lesson Margaret Mathieson learns from bigamist Angus. It is the lesson Charlie Forbes cannot quite learn as he leads the children up Canada Hill to enjoy the magnificent view:

> On this green hill that boy with the chubby knees had been Balboa once. Today he was an unsuccessful dominie, still fat, still clutching nothing, but still surely with a trace of that wonder left . . . The grass around the cairn was littered with gluttonous sun eaters, lying on their backs, with their mouths open. Young lovers lay entwined in public lust . . . He led the way through the little pine wood. The path was overgrown with bramble bushes so that he had to thrust recklessly past in places. Hanging to one bush, like an obscene fruit, was an object, the most disenchanting on earth: a contraceptive. It was too high for him to kick it out of sight, and there was no time to search for a stick . . . As he stared at [the children], seeking signs of

their having seen that dismal symbol here in the midst of nature's prodigality, he saw bobbing among the bushes another similar symbol, the red-blue-green-white cap of the half-wit pursuing them. He could not help connecting the one symbol with the other. [*Changeling*, 166-168]

This is one of those moments of disorientation that justify the term "grotesque" and link Jenkins with a Scottish tradition from Smollett to Muriel Spark. The grotesque in art, we recall, images a subversion of the natural order, in the monstrous, the sinister, and the absurd, and thus expresses a sense of estrangement. "The alienation of familiar forms ... creates that mysterious and terrifying connection between the fantastic and the real world which is so essential for the grotesque." The grotesque feeds on violent contrast with the sublime its opposite. In it all ingredients are distorted, and different realms are fused. In art, the grotesque represents a sudden breaking down of categorical proprieties in nature and feeling: the animate and the inanimate; the human and the bestial; the real and the fantastic; the tragic and the farcical; horror and humor. It offers a demonic vision of the world; some would say it is an attempt to control the demonic.[32]

We find in Jenkins several states of life that call for the term grotesque. There are the innocents who by some mystery are monstrous—the diseased rabbit in *The Changeling*, Tom, Calum the hunchback, Michael Eking, or Laura Johnstone, the limping heroine of *Dust on the Paw*. There are the physically battered or gross figures of middle age in whom, almost hidden, the innocent child still lingers. There are the degenerate, aging women feigning a naive sexuality in their longing for love. There is poisoned love breaking out of repression into perverse violence. All these states are tests of love and compassion, trials in humility; to those who cannot pass the tests but cling fanatically to a vision of edenic innocence and loveliness, they seem grotesque. So must the hunchback seem to Duror; so, momentarily, must the half-wit Sheila, naked by the Sanctuary Stone, seem to Andrew; so Donald Kemp must see his pregnant wife (in *Some Kind of Grace*), and Constance Kilgour see the encroaching trees in *Love Is a Fervent Fire*, and Charlie see the Curdies when they arrive to beg and blackmail at his paradise by the Clyde. For Charlie, who has already come to see Tom as a changeling, who has begun to "give way to the feeling that he was in the grip of inimical nonhuman forces, whose instrument was indeed

Tom Curdie" (60, 113), these figures indeed seem like "malevolent folk of the other world," grotesque fairies who evoke a preternatural horror as well as a worldly humor. But the horror need be no more than natural pity and revulsion and amusement at what modern Glasgow makes of human beings, or what human beings make of themselves and one another. There are no clear hints from Jenkins that we need to believe in a hell or a heaven outside of the human psyche and human society.

Yet the hints, however unclear, must be recognized. For Jenkins is nothing if not a religious moralist, and some of his most potent images and key terms are theological in suggestion. There is the negative side, the bitter attack on puritanical morality and Calvinist theology, from the frightening self-righteousness of Charlie Forbes's mother-in-law, to that of spinster-virgin Margaret Ormiston in *The Expatriates;* from the "lecherous bigots" of *The Missionaries* to the holy hypocrites who feel no charity for Mungo in *A Very Scotch Affair,* reaching a peak of intensity in the ascetic fanaticism of the missionaries in *Some Kind of Grace.*

But that title is subtly elucidated. It is not just the sarcastic reference of the searcher McLeod to the way these ascetics must have made love: "There could be little doubt that before it she would have gasped out some kind of grace and after it a thanksgiving" (188). To Jenkins, all kinds of grace, like all kinds of love, must be cherished. McLeod, whether he knows it or not, is searching for some kind of grace, the kind to be found in the filthy, suffering Afghan poor, or in the call of a bird, or in Kemp's remembered vision of Eden on a Wester Ross mountain top. The trick is in learning to recognize signs of grace. In *Love Is a Fervent Fire,* the conservator glimpses it in Carstares' wit: "Such self-condemnation, fairly seasoned with wit, was, he thought, a sign of grace" (11). Andrew Doig learns more generous thoughts in *The Missionaries:* "They did not take into consideration the eccentricity of grace, which in human beings could assume strange shapes. God sometimes chose to honour those whom their fellow mortals would never have thought of honouring" (212). At tea with his sluttish, dying wife, Mungo Niven says, "I suppose it's too late for grace," and she replies, "It should never be too late for that, Mungo" (*Scotch Affair,* 29). Bell McShelvie reflects on the miracle that people somehow "by their very separate existence on the earth were granted this virtue of diminishing the accumulated evil that was in the world. Some called it, she knew, the grace of God" (*Guests*, 283). She is no church-goer and presumably would not think to call it that.

It appears not to matter what Jenkins would call it. It remains for him a central miracle, and perhaps faith in such miracles is the faith whose loss he laments. But Andrew Rutherford, remembering his Covenanting heritage while en route over the moors to Carnick, finds football a poor substitute for faith: "Scotland was a country where faith lay rotted like neglected roses, and the secret of resurrection was lost. We are a dreich, miserable, back-biting, self-tormenting, haunted, self-pitying crew, he thought. This sunshine is as bright as any on earth, these moors are splendid: why are not the brightness and splen-dour in our lives" (*Thistle and Grail*, 166). What faith, what love, could redeem such a crew? For Andrew, "If human love failed, was there not God's love to revive and strengthen it?" Another good man—Uncle Dave of *A Very Scotch Affair*—"sought always to find good in people, not because he was a Christian, for he never went to church, but because it was simply a seeking he had been born with" (86).

Is grace, then, an accident of birth? Or faith an accident of national culture? Jenkins is too much a natural moralist to offer answers to such questions. But his narrative preoccupations and his explicit, moralistic stances as narrator repeatedly raise them. The same themes —the fascination and the perils of innocence, the many grotesque shapes of love, the terrible imperatives of humility, the eccentricities of grace—are investigated anew in each novel; in a few basic plots, with each novel growing from a germ in an earlier novel, or returning with a new view or emphasis.

14

Kennaway,
Spark,
and After

After Linklater and Jenkins, the task of identifying the Scottish novel becomes as difficult as the talents are abundant. Made cautiously, however, the attempt proves a valuable key to interpretation. The two most widely praised "Scottish" novelists of the 1960s, James Kennaway* and Muriel Spark, appear to represent a new phase of London literary expatriation. Familiar Scottish locale, plot, and theme virtually fade away. Yet the essential exile from Edinburgh that Muriel Spark identified as a key to her life is a suggestive idea with which to read her fiction. And the strange ambivalence of a haunting Scottish memory is inescapable in at least four of Kennaway's seven novels. More controversial will be my judgment that each novelist achieved his or her finest work in the most explicitly Scottish of novels—Spark in *The Prime of Miss Jean Brodie* (1961) and Kennaway the same year in *Household Ghosts*. Each novel personifies a destructive spirit in a betrayer, exiled from a Scottish vitality that it must love and hate, admire and destroy. David Dow of *Household Ghosts*, schoolmaster's son, sterile technologist, explains:

"For many years, usually when drunkish, I have bored my friends with the suggestion that the Scots, of all people, are misunderstood.

*Kennaway, James. Born in Scotland in 1928 and killed in an accident near London in 1968. Educated at Oxford, he served as an officer in the Cameron Highlanders. He worked as an editor for Longmans Green from 1951 to 1957, then be-

A glance at their history or literature (and especially if you count Byron as a Scot, which after dinner, at least, is permissible) reveals what lies underneath the slow accent, the respectability and the solid flesh. Under the cake lies Bonny Dundee."[1]

The passage is unique in Kennaway's novels, yet applicable to all.

His books appeared with deliberate speed. *Tunes of Glory* (1956) is a relatively simple book, a Hardyesque tragedy of a coarse, anachronistic, yet heroic military Scot. *Household Ghosts* (1961), remarkably wide and complex for its modest size, concerns a decadent squirearchal Scottish family on a dairy farm up the Tay from Dundee. *The Mind Benders* (1963), a strained psychological thriller of the instinctual life fighting to survive the ravages of modern technology, is set in scientific Oxford. The scientist-hero Longman is American; his wife Oonagh, who fights for his passional soul against a world of intellectual violence, is vaguely Gaelic-Norse in an Orcadian way. In *The Bells of Shoreditch* (1963) the theme is the same, and the marital triangle recalls *Household Ghosts:* the young London couple tied to city banking and finance; the wife Stella Vass from Glasgow's Kelvingrove struggling for life, battling her Scottish socialist background; the lover a brilliant, ruthless banker; the husband a coward who learns to fight back. *Some Gorgeous Accident* (1967) has no "Scottish" element at all. Instead, the Juanesque hero is an Irishman à la Donleavy. James Link of Belfast is a photographer, the lover of Susan Steinberg, an American magazine writer, and the rival-friend of (ancestral Scot) Dr. Richard Fiddes, who keeps a London surgical clinic. The mode is fantastic in motley like Link himself; the triangle is here as before, and its dialectic becomes more explicit. Next, *The Cost of Living like This* (1969), published after Kennaway's early death, is about a dying young Oxford economist, his blonde wife, and his life-seeking affair with a black-haired cockney secretary. The struggle and the dying are transported to Glasgow, to scenes of student violence, and to a flamboyantly Scottish setting. This penultimate novel, with its death-obsessed Scottish return, shows, according to Alexander Scott (an admirer of *Some Gorgeous Accident*), a "lack of contact with the contemporary Scottish environment"—a not unusual lapse in the imaginative returns of expatriate writers.[2]

---

came a full-time writer. He wrote several screenplays (including those for *Tunes of Glory* and *The Mind Benders*); his play *Country Dance* was performed at the Edinburgh Festival of 1967. His last novel was *Silence* (1972).

No catalogue of "Scottish" elements adds up to meaningful Scottish structure or theme in the novels. Rather, the point is that Kennaway worked toward the expression of a coherent vision, one that is articulated through the sexual triangles of the novels and the struggles for vitality, honesty, and love that they express. The struggles involve polarities that are national and cultural, and the idea of Scotland is indispensable to the articulation.

The idea is scarcely operative in the spectacular, straightforward novel *Tunes of Glory*.[3] Ex-piper Jock Sinclair, aging war hero of much gusto and little subtlety, for some years acting colonel of a Highland battalion, is replaced in command by a tense man who is his intellectual antithesis. There is a short, unequal struggle between them, in which Jock is disgraced and Barrow the rival, actually a historian of the battalion and a worshiper of Jock's heroism, is forced to preside over Jock's downfall. The burden is too much, and in a sudden reversal Barrow commits suicide and Jock is in command again. The long final section is one agonizing scene in which Jock orders Barrow's funeral procession and breaks down completely. Every element in the narrative is there to reflect on Jock, and it all builds him up into a noble, yet dumb, doomed man. The actress Mary Titterington, Jock's mistress, worships him unashamedly: "Oh, Jock, you're always talking about your soldiers, and your Battalion, but it's you that doesn't see the half of your men . . . you're a child, Jock . . . You expect too much of them. You expect them all to be the same as yourself, and you're twice the man of any of them." He protests that "it isn't true any more," but she persists: "Jock, man, you're a bloody king" (158-160). And as long as we are absorbed in the tragic process, it is true.

The "tunes of glory" seem gloriously real in memory; the man was a demigod, and in his fading glory the brutality, coarseness, and vanity are all but forgotten. It is the casting off of the terrible burden of command that we see. He is "the anonymous commander in the long coat moving through the night, alone. He is the guard" (95). He is the Sauchiehall Street piper who drinks and shouts too much, and also the figure with a brave, classless vitality who appears in later Kennaway novels, in more "mannered" contexts. His story is simple and awesome—no questions are asked, no moral insights learned. It is a fine scenario for the film it became, with great scenes, the "obligatory ones" (David Dow of *Household Ghosts* calls them) that do not quite happen in the later novels. It is a novel of heroic catastrophe, and the later ones are about very unheroic survival, about the limits one must learn to accept and the lies one must tell. In a way, it was a spectacular dead end for Kennaway; its admirers could hardly have guessed what was to come. There is significance in the lapse of five years between *Tunes of Glory* and *Household Ghosts* (1961).

Consider the hauntings, for example. Jock is, we are told, perhaps the "most superstitious of men." He lives in a wintry northern landscape, haunted by echoes. It is the Scotland of Victorian elegy, of Celtic Twilight; and in the grim northern twilight the lonely dull giant towers, worshipped and feared by lesser beings—one recalls Brown's *Green Shutters.* "All cities are lonely at night, but the old Scottish ones are lonelier than all. The ghosts wander through the narrow wynds and every human is a stranger surrounded, followed, and still alone. The ghosts always unnerved Jock" (31). The "household ghosts" belong to an equally Scottish landscape but have a different reality. David Dow, the schoolmaster's son, offers the definition in one of his letters of expiation: "You know I always used to tell you that everybody and especially those mixed-up characters, the children of the angelic, are six people at once? Haunted perhaps, by a lot of ghosts of their fathers who have committed no sins except sins of omission, all saying 'Go on, take everything, we never did!' I don't really think the haunted idea bears examination" (114-115). But it does, and finally in his terrible destructiveness, David learns: "We look into the dark and there's always someone there. We look into the dark and see the faces of those we have already destroyed, by our own ignorance of ourselves; our immaturity. We look into the dark, sweet cousin, and no wonder we are afraid" (187). This is a very different sort of Gothic from *Tunes of Glory.*

It will no longer do to be a destructive child. The vain immaturity of Jock is now the egomaniacal solitude of David: he is the one who is afraid; Mary survives and lives. The world of Jock has become the odd world of Mary's father, the colonel disgraced in some mysterious officer's club gambling scandal and retired to his lonely dairy farm, where his children grow up weaving their own myths, making their private language. David, destructive Calvinist become Oxford-London scientist, determines to shatter the myths, force Mary and Pink into mature reality; but it is he that turns out to be the child and the self-deceiver.

He accuses her of having no morals. To her brother Pink she herself wonders: "Old flesh . . . I sometimes wonder if we've any bones. Moral bones" (90). But schools and "a touch of poor Macdonald," the old nanny from Lerwick, have left their mark of the old "Moo-morality." "We've got an awful lot of Moo tucked away" (110), says Pink; and "God's moosh is just like Macdonald's, big, gloomy, hurt, disapproving and so irritatingly patient" (83). David expresses the enlightened view: "It's better to start with life and find out about right and wrong than to be burdened with so many hoodoos that you spend all your time in revolt, and miss out on love and life altogether" (182). But it is David who misses out, whereas old Macdonald transmits the love and truth of the past to Mary.

Mary and Pink, with their private language and their domestic myths, are not so untrue after all. They have talked "in a private and complicated language . . . since their night-nursery days" (10), a "curious code, a language drawn from anecdote and limerick; from family jokes and nursery rhyme; from a lifetime spent together; from a myth they had had to weave for themselves" (16). They are like the pathetic brother and sister of Scott's *St. Ronan's Well*, and their language is skillfully defensive; yet it develops an "accuracy of the ear" which immediately distinguishes truth and falsehood. David Dow, self-appointed truth-sayer, on the other hand, is a scientist of "communication engineering," of "complicated signal and response systems," who deals with Mary's "lies" as he experiments surgically with cats. In fact, David is the liar, and hers are "sinless lies" made to cope with the strange past of her household. Her childish lies, he lies, make her afraid of life, incapable of love; but it is he who is afraid and incapable.

The tragedy is hers. Her father is disgraced, her husband Stephen is impotent, and her lover David is destructive. Yet her tragedy is mixed with farce, and in the farce is bitter hope. She ultimately wins the war against the ghosts to save her imagination from the threats of David's cold-blooded positivism. The figure of the woman as myth-maker, as tragic but triumphant life-giver against the sterile ideological passions of man, becomes an essential motif in Kennaway's novels, as it is in many other novelists of Scotland.

It is the motif of *The Mind Benders*, in which the slightly fey Oonagh must save her husband from his destructive experiments. It is the same in *The Bells of Shoreditch*, whose heroine Stella Vass is the only lively, lovable person in the book. Her Glasgow background is tied to what is lovable in her: "In those eyes, there was a whole, smoky city, with wynds and cobbles and men on strike and dark churches set on bright green grass." She dreams in London of the Scottish bourgeois life she must not have: "All the Maggies and Grizels in Glasgow and Aberdeen, married happily to big husbands on good salaries, giggling in coffee shops, in big department stores, gossiping about age, about hats, about eccentric acquaintances, always with good humour. She envied them now" (98-99). She has what her husband calls a "Kelvingrove hangover," and this leads her away from reality into political postures, into "the Jimmy Maxton—the old I.L.P.—in me and for some reason the only thing I can think of doing is blame you and all your works. And I see myself sitting astride you singing the Red Flag. And I'm sure that's dead psychosomatic. God knows what of. Of something—maybe life in Kelvingrove with the I.L.P. yelling at one end of the park and the couples in the bushes at the other" (29). By the book's fierce ending, the Scottish dreams are gone.

Andrew her husband, fired by Sarson after an abortive rebellion, is now on his own in finance. Stella's affair with Sarson has been broken off, but Sarson visits her to offer help. When Andrew comes home and learns of Sarson's visit and where he had come from, the news is a clue to an investment, and Andrew immediately phones instructions to friends in the city. Here is the novel's end:

> At last he replaced the receiver, to find Stella silent, at the other end of the hall. She stood in the shadows, her feet apart, white-faced, staring at him as if she would be insulted no more. He had kept her waiting like that for almost ten minutes, but he had no intention of apologising. He too stood still, his hands behind him on the sill where the telephone stood. For a long, long time, they remained like this, fixed and hostile, like brother and sister hoarse and naked in the back street; which is to say reduced to that blazing attachment where passion starts.
>
>
>
> When will you pay me?
> Say the Bells of Old Bailey.
> When I grow rich,
> Say the Bells of Shoreditch. [211-212]
>
>

There is some grim triumph of honesty and self-assertion here. She will now find a strength in her formerly weak, timid husband that she has had to find previously in Sarson. Like Mary of *Ghosts*, she is the strong romantic figure afflicted with weak or destructive males, and in hostility she finds strength. It seems the only way for her, with her Jimmy Maxton ideals, to come to terms with life in her amoral exile.

She has prostituted herself. Now the only way to face a world of Sarsons is to become as fierce and cold as they.

Susan Steinberg of *Some Gorgeous Accident* (1967) must learn a similar lesson. Mandy-Margaret, the tart whose abortion loses Fiddes his practice, has sounded the title keynote when she collapses in court, crying for her child: "It was as if she were now quoting some lines that obsessed her and that she didn't quite understand. 'I want some new.' (Not 'something new,' not 'some news.') 'I want some new. Some happening. I want some fucking crucifixion. Some gorgeous accident!' " (219). But when Susie is hit by a lorry in the snow, she lashes out at Link: no, she was not trying to destroy herself. "Don't make me into somebody else now. I'm not to do with destruction, I swear. I don't want your gorgeous accident. I just lost my glasses in the snow" (250-251).

Fiddes has failed her in his egoism, and she refuses to stay hooked to Link, for that is sterility and cowardice. Yet Link, homeless and seemingly damned himself, speaks most clearly for Kennaway as artist (as David Dow has spoken for him as moralist in *Ghosts*). He sees no pattern in his career as photographer and reflects on Dylan Thomas's early death. To Fiddes, the sentimental egoist of Scots ancestry, he defines his stance:

> I've got to keep going. Except in blank moments like this, therefore, when I'm victim to the Fiddes in my soul, I see I've only got one thing to do. To live. Keep living. Then I see we're all doing the same thing. You and the grey ones are scowling at the empty sky. I'm buzzing and buzzing about, ignoring its emptiness. The same game. Just a question of styles. Your tension lies between the fear of pain and pain itself. Mine in the wild pursuit of pain for pain's sake. [76]

To the lawyer Clarke he is the novelist speaking:

> For those of us not knit into the Right-side, the motive-game, the love game, the whole business of analysing who's up to what and why—well, Clarky, believe it or not, that's our life. We may be overplaying it. That makes us on the sick side. That's why we're all so afraid of Virginia Woolf. Meaning she's the greatest, quite the greatest at our game, but she fell the other side, the crazy side. [163]

And Link wants to stay sane. But through the analysis of the motive game, the love game, comes a perception of what is life-giving, loving, true, and what is destructive, egoistic, false.

These are books of vitalistic life and death struggle. Julian's death in *The Cost of Living like This* (1969) is a fitting finale. It is the time when he seeks life with a passion that has been denied him, presumably by his Oxford training, his English pessimism, his wife's treatment. She (Christabel) describes his moral philosophy to the improbable Glaswegian Mozart Anderson, in Glasgow, where, as Anderson says, all is philosophy. From his Anglican parish parents, Julian derived faith and discipline and joy; yet he lost the faith and joy and kept only the discipline, the "discipline of impossibility," a joyless pessimism. He sees death as merely a fatal illness. Christabel has tried, wrongly she thinks, to make him less serious. But somehow with Sally the cockney secretary he finds a passionate reality that his wife's frivolity has denied him.

For a few moments with Sally he feels a miracle; the pain is gone, and there is no death. The miracle is set by Loch Earn, and after it he returns to a Glasgow hospital to die; Scotland is the place of miracles and final things and eccentric moral philosophers. Julian has sought in Scotland a place of passionate gaiety and rootedness, a place of romance, which his English wife cannot understand. Mozart Anderson has the last futile words or thoughts: "Only on his way north did he think of all the things he should have said to her; how she was doing for her children what she had done for Julian, how she was turning her eyes from the blazing truth that passions such as Julian's have always deeper roots? How we can't go on and on, like this?" (199). Kennaway could not go on like this, and before the book was published he was dead, a restless, extraordinary talent in and out of the Scottish novel gone.

The problem of Muriel Spark's* relation to the novel in Scotland is more subtle. Her thirteen novels to date are sparse in identifiably Scottish elements.[4] While possible, it is hardly fair to force a reading of the other novels into the mold of the Edinburgh *Miss Brodie*. The

---

Spark, Muriel. Born in 1918 in Edinburgh, half-Jew, half-English, Muriel Spark attended Gillespie's School for Girls (evident prototype for the school of Miss Brodie). During World War II she worked in intelligence for the British Foreign Office. She edited *The Poetry Review* in London (1947-1949), and, turning to fiction, won the *Observer* short story prize in 1951. Other early work included literary biographies or editions of Wordsworth, Mary Shelley, Emily Brontë, J. H. Newman, and John Masefield. Her conversion to Roman Catholicism in 1954 just preceded and in some ways occasioned her appearance as a novelist with *The Comforters* (1957). Her most recent novel is *The Takeover* (1976). She now lives in Rome.

others are set explicitly elsewhere. *The Comforters* (1957), *Memento Mori* (1959), *The Ballad of Peckham Rye* (1960), *The Bachelors* (1960), and *The Girls of Slender Means* (1963) are novels in and of contemporary London; *The Abbess of Crewe* (1974) concerns an English abbey. *Robinson* (1958) is on an Atlantic island; *The Mandelbaum Gate* (1965) is in and about Israel and Jordan; *The Public Image* (1968), Rome; *Not to Disturb* (1971), Geneva; *The Hothouse by the East River* (1973), New York; and *The Driver's Seat* (1970), some south European holiday metropolis as unlocated as the island of *Robinson*. Does it matter? That depends on the nature of place in Muriel Spark's fiction: they may be all one place, or all idiosyncratic place-atmospheres, or no real place at all because all fantastic, all of the mind. The universal and the particular are strangely real and unreal in the irony—sometimes romantic, sometimes Augustinian—of Spark's vision of earthly cities. Can the most eminent living novelist nurtured by Scotland be recognized, then, in her eminence, in her eccentricity, as a Scottish novelist? Behind that question is the question that haunts this book. Can the question of national identity in art be answered honestly, usefully, and not merely in the dogmatic mode of territorial aggrandizement?

Most of her critics are preoccupied with other things. Is she serious or an elegant trifler? Gothic or Catholic or both? A catalogue of "Scottish" elements is offered by Derek Stanford: her taste for the Old Testament with its archetypal figures and gestures, for the "classic economy" and "laconic" violence and "mordant irony" of the Border Ballads; her "straight way of dealing with facts," an "ethic of emancipated spinsterhood," learned "from Miss Brodie's Scotland"; her alien response to a "lush and cozy" England and its romanticism; and, climactically, her deep ambivalence over Scottish Calvinism, the Edinburgh birthright of which Miss Brodie's Sandy Stranger felt deprived, the "something definite to reject" that her search for identity demanded.[5]

This last, one suspects, led Stanford to think "that much of Muriel Spark's fiction is a kind of imaginative denial of her roots," that "truth, for Muriel Spark, implies rejection." It is this, perhaps, that created in Jean Brodie Spark's most formidable character so far, and in Jean Brodie's betrayal by the disciple Sandy her fiction's most complex moral action. One insightful critic says of it: "Surely the conflict which gives the book its special character, so enigmatic, so wryly amusing and yet profound, is that of Mrs. Spark's own life. The excitement infused into all her best fiction, that duality which I attempted to define at the outset, derives from some formidable positive charge of Edinburgh Calvinism against its opposite, the negative of mystical Catholicism."[6] This is a difficult, fascinating thesis to test. It recalls the Manichean warfare between Kailyard and anti-Kailyard, a battle of orthodoxies one does not expect to see outside of Scottish fiction.

She has spoken for herself about her past, in a 1962 essay in the *New Statesman*.[7] She remembers, on awaiting her father's death in Edinburgh, an "outpouring of love for the place of my birth" inseparable from her own "exiled sensation": "Edinburgh is the place that I, a constitutional exile, am essentially exiled from. I spent the first 18 years of my life, during the 1920's and 1930's there. It was Edinburgh that bred within me the conditions of exiledom; and what have I been doing since then but moving from exile into exile? It has ceased to be a fate, it has become a calling." Essential exile as a fate and a calling is common in the Scottish tradition. But there is more. She recalls Edinburgh as the place where she was first understood as an artist. "The puritanical strain of the Edinburgh ethos" was "not necessarily a bad thing. In the south of England the puritanical virtues tend to be regarded as quaint eccentricities." Spiritual joy comes with difficulty to "the puritanically-nurtured soul." She had no faith in politics, because she had breathed "the informed air of the place, its haughty and remote anarchism." Most of all, she recalls the pivotal word of her Edinburgh experience—"Nevertheless." "I believe myself," she says, "to be fairly indoctrinated by the habit of thought which calls for this word . . . I find that much of my literary composition is based on the nevertheless idea. I act upon it. It was on the nevertheless principle that I turned Catholic."

The claim suggests an extraordinary unity of habit, and of this habit Edinburgh remains a dramatic emblem: "The Castle Rock is something, rising up as it does from pre-history between the formal grace of the New Town and the noble network of the Old. To have a great primitive black crag rising up in the middle of populated streets of commerce, stately squares and winding closes, is like the statement of an unmitigated fact preceded by 'nevertheless.' " The "nevertheless" principle—"this word of final justification"—this black primitive crag of inevitable intervention, rising amid civility and elegance and material order, and recalled as a condition of essential exiledom: such is the Edinburgh genesis of Muriel Spark's fiction. But what, specifically, in her novels, does it mean?

One finds a strange relation between place and the exiled protagonist who cannot and will not belong there. Her heroines are strangers. Even the stately Abbess of Crewe chants of her homesickness. The very nature of place is mysterious—real and yet fantastic, local and yet transcendent. Robinson's island seems allegorical to some. The protagonist-narrator January imagined it a displaced memory of her life after death, saw its contours and persons in an archetypal way; and as it sank finally, it rose in her thoughts transformed into "a locality of childhood, both dangerous and lyrical" (176), an "apocryphal island" whose remembrance makes all things possible. Caroline Rose, lying in her hospital ward in *The Comforters*, supposes her Typing Ghost author "has not recorded any lively details" because "the author doesn't know how to describe a hospital ward" (175). But the diabolist Baron Willi supposes her "embroiled in a psychic allegory"; Spark's diabolists all deny the materiality of the world. The geriatric London of *Memento Mori* is undeniably material, with all the awkward, ludicrous conditions materiality places on the very old. In *The Ballad*, Peckham Rye is a vivid reality of manners and ethos—and Dougal Douglas, itinerant angel-devil, never eludes its reality, except by his con-man wits. For a time, his diabolism exercises itself in the zany choreographing of commercial Peckham; he feeds off its solemn triviality but is finally driven out, exorcised. What he leaves behind, however, is a hint of transfiguration that makes this material place at once beautiful and remote: "Humphrey drove off with Dixie [the book ends] . . . it was a sunny day for November, and, as he drove swiftly past the Rye, he saw the children playing there and the women coming home from work with their shopping-bags, the Rye for an instant looking like a cloud of green and gold, the people seeming to ride upon it, as you might say there was another world than this" (376).

The vision that at once transfigures place and challenges its reality is frightening, socially because it deprives the seer of a mundane reality to belong to, and theologically because it opens the way to demonisms that lead to damnation. The yearning of Sandy for "some quality of life peculiar to Edinburgh" is hinted at in the "dark and terrible" emblems of St. Giles and the Tolbooth. The quotidian London of *The Bachelors* is pervaded by forgery and fraudulent spiritualisms. Ronald

Bridges, the epileptic graphologist who is and is not a priest, walks round the houses counting the bachelors and sometimes surrendering to his devilish vision that they are all "fruitless souls, crumbling tinder . . . demons of the air." Likewise, the postwar poverty-stricken London of *The Girls of Slender Means.* Their doomed May of Teck Club, a solid, amply particularized establishment, is turned by a delayed bomb into an infernal place where an "action of savagery"—the rescue of a Schiaparelli dress—provides a "vision of evil" sufficient to send the forger Nicholas Farringdon to conversion and a martyr's death. Only the gossip columnist, Jane Knight, remains to search out the mystery of Nicholas's martyrdom and to recall that other victim, Joanna, whose selflessness and sense of hell had made Jane feel "suddenly miserable, as one who has been cast out of Eden before realising that it had in fact been Eden" (143).

Spark's most ambitious evocation of place comes in *The Mandelbaum Gate.* The place is Israel and Jordan, its dividedness focused on that gate between the two Jerusalems. Its reality is accessible only to the pilgrim (Barbara Vaughan) and to those who, out of their own dividedness and homelessness, manage glimpses of a unity that is divine. The reality can be seen only by those in disguise, those who are spies. An English priest sneaks a sermon into the mass for his flock of pilgrims at the Holy Sepulchre, and its text is from St. Paul: "We have an everlasting city, but not here." It affirms what the book affirms: these streets and shrines are real; the archaeology is real though it deals in mere probabilities of faith; true prayers can be said at false shrines; pilgrimage to a real place, though it produces after much effort only a "small moment, here and there," does permit "a meeting . . . materialized." And such materializations have the effect of transfiguring mundane lives. "Well," says Barbara, "either religious faith penetrates everything in life or it doesn't. There are some experiences that seem to make nonsense of all separations of sacred from profane—they seem childish. Either the whole of life is unified under God or everything falls apart. Sex is child's play in the argument" (344)— sex, that is, and all the other "problems" humanity finds to help it evade the only real problem of division.

Jerusalem, as the pilgrim discovers it, is a real unity, the ultimate home that is here and not here. The Manichean "nevertheless" principle may well have prevailed in the earlier novels, but in *Mandelbaum Gate* the essential exile seems to have found a true pilgrimage and with it a hard-won spiritual joy. The novels that follow might be expected to differ radically from those that preceded. Certainly time and place have altered, as if the perspective of eternity had been won. *The Driver's Seat*, *Not to Disturb*, and *The Hothouse by the East River* are narrated in present tense. The artist and the theologian advance together in Spark, and the butler Lister in *Not to Disturb*, himself a consummate artist, says: "What's done is about to be done and the future has come to pass"; "let us not strain after vulgar chronology."[8] The protagonists—acting in the illusion of being "in the driver's seat"—"have placed themselves, unfortunately, within the realm of predestination" (45). Their elegant choreographies of self-destruction articulate just that "predestination" that had fascinated and repelled the earlier Caroline, Sandy, and Ronald. In *The Hothouse*, the anarchic "nevertheless" principle is left to the anxieties and deflections of the poor muddled husband; for his wife, smiling serenely at the Nothing that casts a strange light on her from the East River, all things are possible with God because predestination has already finished with them. In New York of the 1970s she knows they have been dead since a V-2 hit their train in London in 1944.

Place can hardly be what it was before. Lise, the methodically romantic suicidal heroine of *Driver's Seat*, comes from a northern city where she has worked for sixteen years in an accountant's office and lived in an austerely functional, prize-winning flat, "as clean-lined and as clean to return to after her work as if it were uninhabited. The swaying tall pines among the litter of cones on the forest floor have been subdued into silence and into obedient bulks" (12). She flies on vacation to a southern city, bent on finding the "type" to carry out her murder. In *Not to Disturb* the Baron and Baroness Klopstock and their male secretary act out their predestined murder-suicide in the locked library of their villa, while the servants complete their plans for inheritance, press exploitation, and Hollywood movie rights in the servants' hall. Neither place is particularized significantly. New York, in *The Hothouse*, is more particular, yet highly conceptualized; it is a version of purgatory:

Home of the vivisectors of the mind, and of the mentally vivisected still to be reassembled, of those who live intact, habitually wondering about their states of sanity, and home of those whose minds have been dead, bearing the scars of resurrection. [9]

The mental clinic . . . where we analyze and dope the savageries of existence . . . the sedative chamber where you don't think at all and you can act as crazily as you like and talk your head off all day, all night. [78]

It is the place of countless "problems" where a preternatural sign, such as the wife Elsa's unnatural second shadow, can be seen by others only as her problem "externalized," though she serenely assures them the problem is theirs.

Here, too, is a fitting admonition to critics who have made of the Spark mode a "Gothic" psychological romance, a surrealist black humor. Hoyt's phrase "Jane Austen of the surrealists" is suggestive but it needs modification: "Jane Austen; nevertheless, the grotesque."[9] The spirits are undeniable. Yet they have such desperate impact on human self-sufficiency, and the puritanic sense of sexual degradation and social idolatry is so pervasive, that the Catholic sounds more Augustinian-Calvinist than might feel comfortable in modern Rome. And here is where the real tension is found: not between secular and supernatural ideologies (she despises ideologies, she says), but between two Christian orthodoxies. Muriel Spark was led to Rome by Newman, after all, and the agonizing conflict of faith in Sandy Stranger is between a Presbyterianism denied her and an equally austere Catholicism that brings no easy spiritual joy.

Spark's conversion, she said, "gave me something to work on as a satirist. The Catholic belief is a norm from which one can depart."[10] But what is this norm in her fiction? There are few if any Catholics among her characters who can be seen as "normative"; most are uneasy converts such as Caroline, January, and Sandy, or moral blackmailers such as Mrs. Hogg. Rather, the norm operates chiefly through the mode, and because the mode is at once so familiar and so foreign to contemporary tastes and assumptions, the norm seems as elusive as the reality. But the world is real; in it, by divine presence or intervention, all things are possible. When divine messages are neglected, the effect is a loss of reality, or that inverse side of sacramentalism, the anarchic flowering of individuality. To Spark, normalizing Catholicism means a spiritual discipline that assures the reality of the self and of the external world—what Malkoff calls "strict controls based outside the individual."[11] "One who has never observed a strict ordering of the heart," warns the Abbess of Crewe, "can never exercise freedom" (30). Can the Catholic realist be a fantasist in the modern absurdist vein, a fantasist who blurs the distinctions between the real and the nonreal? There is nothing blurred in Spark's supernaturalism; in her satire those who do the blurring are the purveyors of a fraudulent spiritual order and freedom. Her true believers are diabolically tempted. Caroline cannot be sure that her Voices are not from some infernal source. The would-be priest, epileptic Ronald in *Bachelors*, is suspected of having "a diabolical side" to his nature. Only by repeating to himself the passage from Philippians—"all that is gracious in the telling"—and applying it "to the company of demons which had been passing through his thoughts," can he force "upon their characters what attributes of vulnerable grace he could bring to mind" (113).

The fullest delineation of Catholic perspective is in Barbara of *Mandelbaum Gate*, and that novel is largely free of both satire and fantasy. Half Jewish and half English-gentry, a Catholic convert, Barbara's "habits of mind" at the start of her pilgrimage are "inadequate to cope with the whole of her experience." Now suddenly she is homeless in a place as divided and filled with exiles as her life. From Mount Tabor the Place of Transfiguration she recalls her divided life, and tirelessly returns to the question of identity:

> Barbara thought, "Who am I?" She felt she had known who she was till this moment: She said, "I am who I am" . . . She decided, therefore, essentially "I am who I am" was indeed the final definition for her. But the thesis-exponent in Barbara would not leave it at that . . . By the long habit of her life, and by temperament, she held as a vital principle that the human mind was bound in duty to continuous acts of definition. Mystery was acceptable to her, but only under the aspect of a crown of thorns. She found no rest in mysterious truths like "I am who I am." [26-27]

By the end of her pilgrimage she has found such rest. Categorical public "identities" jostling menacingly, generating disguises and forged documents of identification, become meaningless. Her answer not only sticks, but becomes the answer to *why* as well as *who:* why a half-Jew Catholic convert? why a pilgrim? "Questions were things that sufficed in their still beauty, answering themselves. What am I doing here on a pilgrimage, after so much involvement? Because I am what I am" (337). To get here, she has had to depend on others similarly homeless or divided. Depending on fellow exiles, she drops out of official existence, assumes disguises, and is elated by a surrender of control and an evasion of the incessant questions. Loss of identity comes with exile, and "she sagged with relief. It felt marvelous to be homeless" (190). Freedom for Barbara is freedom from worldly inheritances and homes, freedom from problem-centered questions and public, ethnic disguises, and freedom from the moral tyrants who impose them—the divisive forces, the agents of predestination. Such freedom, once materialized in acts of presence, transfigures one's life, though appearances may not change much.

The dark or grotesque side of Barbara is Jean Brodie, but their kinship can easily be missed by those who read through secular romantic assumptions. Jean Brodie is one of the spiritual tyrants, whose egoistic romanticism is the link between an obsessive Calvinist doctrine of the Elect, of Justification, and the fascism of Mussolini and Franco, whom Miss Brodie in her prime adulates. Generically she is the Scottish spinster *entre deux guerres*, "indifferent to criticism as a crag" (the Castle Rock of "nevertheless"), the eccentric of Scottish tradition, the character obsessed with character who "thinks she is Providence, thought Sandy, she thinks she is the God of Calvin, she sees the beginning and the end" (176). She is close kin to the justified sinners; her formidable piety is tragicomic madness. She could find normalizing discipline only, thinks Sandy, in the Catholic Church; but she acknowledges only a self-discipline, claims freedom from all conventional restraints, plays God with her girls, and thus dooms herself and them to predestination. She is a fusion of the haughty anarchism and the moral tyranny that are the dark grandeur of the Edinburgh Muriel Spark must "betray" in repeated acts of exile. The Abbess of Crewe is not unlike her.

There is a key here to Spark's other eccentrics and tyrannical blackmailers. Her critics invariably begin from the presumption of grotesque eccentricity. The gargoyles are gimmicky but effective, stylized parody figures. Their exaggerated individuality is taken by some to be Spark's polemic against collectivity.[12] Yet their individuality should not be misread, for hers is no stance of romantic individualism. Romantic personality is essentially a fraud, a heresy of self-assertion; it is, as Stanford says, "merely a mask, a *persona*, disguising an essential emptiness within. And because the inner ego is unreal, the self is asserted all the more by the speaker. The *persona* becomes a character-ideal, and the pursuit and worship of this false self obscures from the man all knowledge of his true nature and its actual failings. It also precludes him from attendance upon, and submission to, God,

302

who is the only valid ideal for those who accept the Christian hypothesis."[13]

The characters of a Spark novel are a gallery, an obsessive plenitude, representative of a cultural situation. Their behaviors defy their collectivity by various forms of absurd self-assertion, romantic, anarchic, antinomian. The theologian must see these self-assertions as diabolical forgeries of true individuality, which is found only through the self-surrender of the orthodox Christian. Yet the artist cannot help but show a creative sympathy for—a humorous nostalgia for—her illusorily free "characters." She sees the cult of character-worship as an anarchy generated by the romantic egoism that grew from Calvinism. Her style of ironic cliché and mock-heroic disproportion undercuts that anarchy, while at the same time mocking the superficial conventions and disciplines that oppose or seek to contain it. Her false individualists are grotesquely unreal and at the same time diabolically alive: the extreme nominalist and the Catholic realist are at war. Diabolism, the shadow side of religious conviction, may seem a joke or a fraud, yet the secular Calvinist—as in Nick Farringdon—knows that "a sense of Hell" and "a vision of evil" may effectively initiate salvation, that the religious visionary may well feel demon-possessed, that "the Christian economy seems . . . so ordered that original sin is necessary to salvation." Spark's Christian economy, in short, is a grotesque, demon-ridden one, where an ambiguous battle goes on between fraudulent romanticism bent on self-assertion, self-destruction, and a tyrannical moral collectivity that imposes discipline by blackmail.

Blackmail is the activity of the fraudulent spiritual disciplinarian, the wielder of an order that only apparently deals with the antinomian anarchy of human ego, the false priest who intervenes in no real way in the terrible progress of predestination. And for Muriel Spark, heritor of a Calvinist distrust of fictions as spiritual forgeries, the role of the moral blackmailer is precariously close to the role of the artist. Both play at godly powers; both impart a creaturely reality and freedom that are unreal; both consort with demons and spirits, and are ultimately as unfree as the creatures they manipulate. The Abbess of Crewe's electronic blackmail is turned ultimately upon herself. "In life," notes the novelist Charmian in *Memento Mori*, "everything is different. Everything is in the Providence of God" (163).

Mrs. Georgina Hogg in *The Comforters*, formerly "a kind of nursery-governess," "suffers from chronic righteousness, exerts a sort of moral blackmail," a "fanatical moral intrusiveness, so near to an utterly primitive mania" (29, 159). Caroline the heroine controls her by thinking her "not a real-life character . . . only a gargoyle" (152). Caroline's author assures us that this gargoyle climbed to "her mousy room at Chiswick" and "simply disappeared" because she had "no private life whatsoever" (170). But the real danger is what Mrs. Hogg could become in Caroline's mind—"She began to reflect that Mrs. Hogg could easily become an obsession, the demon of that carnal hypocrisy which struck her mind whenever she came across a gathering of Catholics or Jews engaged in their morbid communal pleasures" (44). To make her an unreal gargoyle, says the author, is to lapse "into that Catholic habit of belittling what was secretly feared" (194)—a traditional Scottish linguistic habit, too. "I don't say there isn't great evil in it," says Caroline of the Black Mass. "I only say it's a lot of tomfoolery." "I wouldn't dismiss it so lightly as that," protests her lover Ernest. "It depends," says Caroline, "on how you regard evil" (98).

Allegorical critics find the characters of *Robinson* "real" chiefly as psychic forces in the heroine's mind. The island where she is planewrecked offers two opposing moral tyrants for her to struggle with, and it is hard to say which is more fraudulent: the misanthropic owner Robinson, ex-priest who is "constitutionally afraid of any material manifestation of Grace" (100) and who forges his own murder merely to avoid company, or Tom Wells, the literal blackmailer, editor of *Your Future* magazine, traveling salesman of "religious" charms. It is Wells whom she thinks a murderer. But Robinson is a subtler threat, as Jean Brodie, to Sandy, is the most dangerous of tyrants; it seems no accident that the brother-in-law Jan thinks of as resembling Robinson is named Ian Brodie. To Robinson's kind of austere anarchy Jan can speak easily enough: "I chucked the antinomian pose when I was twenty. There's no such thing as a private morality" (163). But earlier, she had seen him "as an austere sea-bound hero, a noble heretic who, to follow his mystical destiny, had hidden himself away from the world with only a child-disciple for company . . . he took on the heroic character of a pagan pre-Christian victim of expiation" (132). When his fraud is exposed, his myth must be deflated. The island, shortly after their rescue, suitably vanishes; and Robinson, for Jan, remains in nostalgia—like Jean Brodie—"a locality of childhood, both dangerous and lyrical," an austere anarchy in a never-nevertheless-land.

The moral blackmailers in *Memento Mori* are two—Mrs. Petti-grew, the housekeeper who makes her fortune out of capturing lega-cies from her ancient charges, and Dr. Alec Warner, aged sociologist, who studies old age without quite believing that other people exist, without learning that the reality of death makes them real. Their hu-morous vividness in the novel derives, to be sure, from the various absurd ways they respond to the phoned memento mori, going about their pettinesses heedless of the disciplines known to the book's two truly free—hence real—individuals, Jean Taylor the retired house-keeper, and Henry Morton the police detective. Other intensities are vivid but unreal, hence a cosmos of grotesques; other disciplines are absurd, though they make for lively social comedy.

Muriel Spark describes her creative process as a matter of obsession with a subject that peoples the world, a "narrow little small world . . . full of whatever I'm studying."[14] The "role" played by Edinburgh "Arts" man Dougal Douglas in the little world of industrial Peckham is essential to Spark's art. He is hired by a manufacturer to "bring vision into the lives of the workers" through "motion studies" that will "speed up our output." The motion studies of class life in Peckham amount to a devilish choreography of the romantic clichés of young Peckham life, in the midst of which Dougal assumes many guises, dis-rupts marriages, and provokes one manager to murder his girlfriend.

> "I have the powers of exorcism," Dougal said, "that's all."
> "What's that?"
> "The ability to drive devils out of people."
> "I thought you said you were a devil yourself."
> "The two states are not incompatible." [330-331]

His fraudulence is obvious; the legend he creates and exploits is unde-niably real. To the vulgar little rituals of Peckham class-consciousness he brings an atavistic violence. Having caused disruption and para-noia, he is driven out, but the hint of a "vision" of another world per-sists with his legend, his "ballad."

Patrick Seton, the medium, forger, and police informer of *The Bachelors*, is a less ambiguous devil. The ambiguity here is in his exor-cist, Ronald Bridges, epileptic, would-have-been priest, and expert graphologist in the detection of forgeries. Seton has embezzled his middle-aged mistress's funds, dreams of his diabetic young mistress's murder, but remains the charismatic medium of "The Wider Infinity" and its secret "Interior Spiral." The materiality of tawdry London is particularized in the various "characteristic" but drearily similar lives of countless bachelors. The point of constructing a novel jointly on the timorous sterility of bachelordom as a social class and on the rituals and rivalries of an absurd spiritualism becomes clear. "There are only two religions," insists Ronald, "the spiritualist and the Catholic" (175). Yet when his friend singles out the common problem—"You've got to affirm the oneness of reality in some form or another" (87)—Ronald tries to deny it. His epilepsy gives him no choice, leaving him the helpless victim of his vision: "For Ronald was suddenly obsessed by the party, and by the figures who had moved under Isabel's chandelier, and who, in Ronald's present mind, seemed to gesticulate like automatic animals; they had made sociable noises which struck him as hysterical. Isabel's party had begun to jump off the stage, so that he was no longer simply the witness of a comfortable satire, but was suddenly surrounded by a company of ridiculous demons" (11). The similarity to the disquieting post-Calvinist vision of Carlyle and his Teufelsdröckh is noticeable. For Ronald there is no recourse but to chant his charm from Phillippians and seek friendly absolution from "the maker of heaven and earth, vigilant manipulator of the falling sickness" (116), a theological pun affirming Ronald's belief that original sin is necessary to the Christian economy. The others go instead to the false priest Seton, whose childhood was haunted by J. M. Barrie, and who can justify murder of his pregnant girlfriend because he "denies" the reality of the flesh.

The destinies of the Brodie girls are plotted by their own false priest. They are to be triumphantly idiosyncratic individualists, each "famous" for some accidental, one of the Elect above good and evil and loyal only to Miss Brodie. They are taught to scorn "the team spirit," yet they are as despotically collective a team, all "in unified compliance to the destiny of Miss Brodie, as if God had willed them to birth for that purpose" (46). When Teddy Lloyd paints them they all look like Miss Brodie, for that is where her individualism really leads, and this is the "near-blackmailing insolence of . . . knowledge" (150) that leads Sandy to betray her. To understand her is to recognize in her anarchy, her spiritual fascism, one who prides herself on descent from that infamous Deacon Brodie who prospered in commercial and civic respectability, kept mistresses, and died on the gibbet cheerfully for his night burglaries. Denied or protected by "enlightened people" from her Calvinist birthright, Sandy can sense the direct connection "in the

curiously defiant way in which the people she knew broke the Sabbath, and she smelt them in the excesses of Miss Brodie in her prime"
(159). Among the squares and streets of civility and elegance rises the
primitive crag of "nevertheless."

The crème de la crème of *The Girls of Slender Means* are linked by a
superficial individualism and a genteel poverty. Their shared sacrament is a Schiaparelli taffeta evening dress. The exile from this cosy
nonsociety, Nicholas Farringdon, begins as a fraudulent anarchist and
poet with false visions of the collective. Jane Wright, forever at her
"brain work" of forgery and commercial blackmail, later to become
gossip columnist, feeds Nicholas information that fits his ideal of the
place: "It was a community held together by the graceful attributes of
a common poverty" (106). Nevertheless—the community and its disciplines are tested by catastrophe. The bomb in the garden explodes,
and the great primitive crag of savagery that looms up is a vision of
evil sufficient to send Nicholas to a martyr's death.

The communities of Jews, Palestinians, and Jordanians in *Mandelbaum Gate* are equally specious. Barbara seeks an identity more real
than the ethnic and religious disguises of her milieu. Freddy's friend
Abdul, and Abdul's sister Suzi, transcend their disguises differently.
They share a "pact of personal anarchism." But Suzi is capable of finding liberation in love, and of coping with the book's moral tyrants and
blackmailers, all having only the common reality of blackmail.
Freddy's freedom is harder won from his mother, "a peculiar type of
tyrant-liar whose lies could only with difficulty be denounced because
of her long-sustained tyranny, and whose tyranny could hardly now
be overthrown because of her long-condoned lies" (66). Only through
betrayal can she be stopped; Freddy betrays her by destroying letters
that might prevent her murder, and like Sandy he must carry the burden of his betrayal through life.

The blackmailers of *The Public Image* are double. Screen tiger-wo-
man Annabel Christopher's weak husband stages a suicide to trap her
in the fraud of her obsessive "public image." Billie O'Brien attempts to
blackmail her by demanding money for the false letters the husband
has left. Annabel struggles to prevent the shattering of her image by a
predatory press. She finds her only reality in her baby; and in this
hold on a reality beyond public image, she finds the determination to
defy the blackmailer in court.

Lise of *The Driver's Seat*, compelled toward her own death, we know almost nothing of. Her taut, brief story is an exercise in the mysterious externality of the new novel: "You know nothing whatsoever about me," she says to her pursuer; "I'm only a tourist, a teacher from Iowa, New Jersey . . . I'm a widow . . . and an intellectual. I come from a family of intellectuals. My late husband was an intellectual. We had no children. He was killed in a motor accident. He was a bad driver, anyway" (83). She leaves a trail of deliberate self-concealment. She seems without home, without nationality. "Our home is in Nova Scotia," says her elderly fellow tourist, Mrs. Fiedke, "where is yours?" "Nowhere special," she answers; "It's written on the passport"—the passport she carefully buries behind a taxi seat (57). At the climax, " 'Kill me,' she says, and repeats it in four languages" (117). On the surface—and what more is there?—she is a stereotyped spinster tourist, hungrily seeking her "type" of man. She decks herself in bright colors and carries as her banner of invitation a green and white paperback with author's name in "blue lightning streaks," and "in the middle of the cover . . . a brown boy and girl wearing only garlands of sunflowers" (21). She finds a reluctant sex maniac, gives him the bright bonds to tie with and the carved knife to stab with. The only intervention comes from fellow passenger Bill, on his way to open a macrobiotic restaurant for the Yin-Yang Young of Naples. He presses upon her his diet, his regimen of one orgasm a day, the spilling of his rice seeds in the backseat of a taxi. He is clearly not her "type." He is a comic grotesque; she is a doomed romantic. No one could blackmail Lise.

In *Not to Disturb*, the servants make up an international chorus of domestic blackmailers, under the tight order of Lister the butler. The inevitable catastrophe is reminiscent of Lise's. The Baroness Klopstock "hasn't been playing the game." She went, we are told, "to a finishing school in Lausanne and learnt to eat an orange with a little knife and fork without ever touching the orange" (72). "Why did she suddenly start to go natural," lose her shape, fall for the secretary Victor, and do "a Lady Chatterley" on her pornophiliac husband? Romantic defiance of her sterile predestined life is, as we know from Jean Brodie, a logical outcome of that life. She begs to be blackmailed, murdered; that is what her romanticism amounts to. The blackmailers have her on tape; "the machine emits two long, dramatic sighs followed by a woman's voice—'I climbed Mount Atlas alone every year on May Day and sacrificed a garland of bay leaves to Apollo. At last, one year he descended from his fiery chariot' " (53-54). Lady Chatterley's anarchy is as obscene as her husband's pornography. The only fruitfulness in this nightmare is the kicking five-month pregnancy of Heloise the youngest maid, raped by the Baron's idiot brother. To insure their inheritance, the servants engineer a marriage. Lister always knows "what is right" and orders the chaos of the house, not unlike the Abbess of Crewe with her electronic "bugs," in the interests of blackmail. Samuel and McGuire, recording technician and candid photographer, members of the Baron's blackmail team, are on hand to help stage the entire predestined catastrophe. Lister's opening epigraph from Webster's *Duchess of Malfi* seems fitting.

The Hothouse by the East River opens with a different Jacobean epigraph: "If it were only true that all's well that ends well, if only it were true." The "end" is well in a purgatorial sense, though the setting is emphatically infernal: "hothouse" is a pun on the artificiality and the hellishness of New York life. The book is a ghost story, a scene of feverish civility crossed and transfigured by a preternatural shadow. It keeps the present tense of Spark's late novellas, but returns to the dominant time shift of *Jean Brodie*, *Girls of Slender Means*, and *Mandelbaum Gate*. But here it is the present that becomes unreal: "Now is never, never. Only then exists. Where shall I turn next," moans the poor husband. The answer comes in the appearance of a long-dead German World War II double agent who had been the wife's lover in England in 1944. The answer is, as before, death, death as a fait accompli that must at long last be accepted.

"Character" is back; one of the living dead is an extravagant caricature Princess Xavier, founder of a London employment agency specializing in foreign exiles, now the incredibly fat owner of a silkworm farm on Long Island. "She is in the habit of keeping the eggs of her silkworms warm between and under her folds of breasts; she also takes new-born lambs to her huge ancestral bed, laying them at her feet early in the cold springtime, and she does many such things" (34). But in the winter time in the hothouse, grotesque things happen: "Under the protective folds of her breasts the Princess, this very morning, has concealed for warmth and fear of the frost a precious new consignment of mulberry leaves bearing numerous eggs of silkworms. These have hatched in the heat. The worms themselves now celebrate life by wriggling upon Princess Xavier's breast and causing Garven to scream" (46). Garven is the wife Elsa's psychoanalyst, her false spiritual director. Of her, he understands nothing; she says, "I came to

Carthage," but he misses the Augustinian reference. She sits and gazes at a "Nothing" over the East River with whom she shares a strange, often wacky slapstick humor and from whom comes a preternatural light that casts her strange second shadow. New York is the place of countless "problems" invented to cover up the real one. Yet Elsa is serene, self-contained, enigmatic, almost "eastern." She appears to know they are long dead; she awaits her husband's enlightenment.

Their effete son Pierre produces an off-Broadway version of *Peter Pan*—"a very obscene play," says Pierre—and "everyone who's acting in it is over sixty." It is done with money Pierre extorts from his father. "It's blackmail, of course," Paul says. "Everything's blackmail" (67). On the opening night Elsa, armed with overripe tomatoes, awaits the appearance of Never-Never Land—"now is never, never. Only then exists"—"The scene is the traditional Never-Never Land, the island of Lost Boys. Garven breathes heavily with psychological excitement as Lost Boys of advanced age prance in fugitive capers with the provocative pirates, then hover over the crone, Wendy. Enter, Peter Pan. At this point Elsa stands up and starts throwing squelchy tomatoes one after the other at the actors" (96). This climax of grisly farce, bringing back dead comrades from 1944, precipitates Paul the husband's realization that she is dead, he is dead, their children were never born. Their comrades follow them about by car in one last evening on the town, and it is Paul who says, "Come Elsa, we can go back with them. They've been very patient, really." "She turns to the car, he following her, watching as she moves how she trails her faithful and lithe cloud of unknowing across the pavement" (146). She is a divine innocent; she has ready access to spiritual joy; she is free of blackmail. Her presence, casting rotten tomatoes at an obscene and geriatric Peter Pan, an unreal Manhattan, all adds up to a remarkable cosmic joke. The "nevertheless" persists; the essential exile has become metaphysical. This world has no reality at all, no sacramental force. The waiting is purgatorial, and who but Muriel Spark would fashion her purgatorio in farce around a geriatric version of *Peter Pan*?

The 1960s and early 1970s have seen the emergence of a number of versatile talents in the novel of Scotland. Even a glance suggests a new vitality and seriousness, a consciousness of precedent, an ability to renew Scottish situations and motifs without shutting out the international scene, a degree of liberation from the self-consciousness of past artists with overly ambitious nationalistic aims and themes. Most of the new careers are young, and early novels are subject to experimental confusion and excess. But if such easy allowances are made, the picture is promising.

The first two novels of Alan Sharp's* trilogy may well be obsessive in their concern with exile and sexual guilt, but their talent is prodigious. *A Green Tree in Gedde* (1965) is a flight from and to Scotland.[15] Of its four main characters, two are Greenock Scots and three are sexually obsessed. One stays home in Scotland in onanistic broodings, one in a grim North Manchester flat in the same condition; two take to the road into the illusive possibilities of freedom and license promised by London, Paris, and the Black Forest. In this remarkable odyssey, sexuality becomes a key to regional identity. One of the four (Gibbon) finds happiness—the one most firmly possessed of a Scottish identity, most tranquilly reconciled to his regionality, his past.

The fevers of all four are haunted by a vision of Eden in the remembered career of Gibbon's uncle, ancestral prophet whose preachings supply the book's titular vision, idyllic wanderer who preached in the wilds of Wigtownshire and fathered bastards in the same fields. The legend of his pilgrimage to a religious and sexual paradise mocks the empty, haunted fever of modern sex. Moseby's affair, for instance, "was, in this new sense, Glaswegian; it had this incarcerated, airless aura to it, this unease that lay upon the city dweller . . . Was it that yearning for the garden genesis, old green Eden, wherever and whatever it had been?" (249). For Moseby, the realization reveals "what being West Coast Scottish meant, with its preoccupation with guilt and sex and sin and its image of man as a monster" (87), and "Hide, Mr. Hyde," he screams at himself, finding himself—a foundling with dual identity and none—in the Scottish myth (255). "What people don't realize about us," explains his Glasgow tutor, "is that we are existentialists, classically so, and that the twin pillars of our existentialism are religion and sexuality . . . Existential mystics. Passionately

---

Sharp, Alan. Born in 1934 in Alyth, Scotland, adopted by a shipyard worker, he attended Greenock High School. After working in the Clyde shipyards, he taught English in Germany and worked as construction laborer and dishwasher before settling in London to work as a television and radio playwright. *A Green Tree in Gedde* won the Scottish Arts Council Award in 1967.

concerned with the world as our domain, yet obsessed with the dream of transcendence . . . Only all our avenues of transcendence have been Calvinist" (329, 362). For poor Moseby the very prison of Greenock, of regional self, offers an insistent metaphor of transcendence: "Had not the town urged this on him without respite, like some great metaphor of the mind, the world beyond the province of the self, the true idea of transcendence" (368).

The Cuffees, English brother and sister, yearn negatively for transcendence. For them there is no home, but only a stale, fraudulent domesticity that drives its offspring to onanism and incest. For Harry Gibbon, Greenock carpenter, on the other hand, there is a rich, ancestral identity and an almost sexless tranquillity. He follows his prophetic great uncle's advice—"if you don't go, you can't come back" (263)—and takes flight from Scotland in order to return: "I have to go back. Don't you ever feel, well, lost because you don't want to go home. I mean, that's how you know where you are, isn't it, because you know where you come from" (340-341). But Gibbon learns that regional place itself may point to transcendence: " 'You will not find it down on any map,' he said to himself, then aloud, 'True places never are' " (342).

In *The Wind Shifts*, the pace slows, and the several pairings change, but the quest for identity continues, and the obsession with exile and home is if anything stronger.[16] Cuffee the incestuous Byronic romantic seeks new metaphors for the central reality of evil and for a "sense of location that makes the problem of identity seem an irrelevance" (271). He finds both—and a violent end—in Germany. His sister, judging Gibbon an inadequate lover, takes up with Moseby—now a London exile—but finds his world "almost completely obsessive, shut in behind walls of guilt and distorted Christian imagery, soured through with his bitter self-abusive wit and sweetened by the soft centre of his nostalgia for Greenock and Victorian stability" (233). An Edenic nostalgia, and a longing for a home that never was, are strong. "All problems," says Cuffee, "are problems of geography" (205). And his sister Ruth seeks always "the true address of home" (174). The yearning is for a transcendence beyond history, beyond guilt, beyond identity, and they are all the same. Only Harry the naif, with his "yearning that everyone should love everyone else" (207), seems free.

The "objective correlative" that Eliot missed in *Hamlet* seems miss-

ing here, and the same diagnosis might apply to William McIlvanney's* *Remedy Is None* (1966),[17] in which the echo of *Hamlet* is explicit. Charlie Grant is called home from Glasgow University to the small
town near Kilmarnock where his father is dying and his girl thinks she
is pregnant. The sole concern of his life becomes his obsession with the
meaning of his father's death and its connection with his mother's desertion and her life with another man—wealthy, sophisticated:

> Did his father's suffering have no meaning? It could have no mean-
> ing if everything else was to continue exactly as it had done. Was it
> simply to be accepted with the reflection that this was the way
> things were? . . . Was there nothing more dynamic than this to con-
> nect these two images that haunted Charlie's imagination: the image
> of one man peeled of flesh and illusions, a skeleton of bitter hope-
> lessness, lying in a lonely room; and the image of two people some-
> where in another room living in quiet content? For he knew that for
> anything to matter these two images must be made to meet, must
> fuse to one. [51]

Nothing else does matter. His girl, not pregnant after all, is treated
like Ophelia; his two university friends—jolly Scots Rosencrantz and
Guildenstern—have little effect. The mother and her new husband
come to visit and help; there is a fight, and Charlie kills the husband.
The terrible irony follows: Charlie asks only the justice of having it
understood why he did it, but instead he is offered only impersonal,
procedural justice, which seeks not to explain but to explain away.
Now the guilt is his, for "Charlie had played at being God," had denied to all others what he claimed had been denied his father. And
now that the guilt is his, his own injustice permits him sympathy and
love for others. His guilt is "not familial or parochial but universal"
(241).

Yet it is parochial too. The images of family life, the local factory
dialect, the scenes of party and football game and town park, even the
Scots spoken by Charlie and his university friends—the lawyer insists he speak English since, after all, he has been to the university:

McIlvanney, William. The son of a miner, McIlvanney was born in Kilmarnock, Ayrshire, in 1936. He attended Glasgow University and became a schoolmaster in Irvine. He won the Faber Memorial Prize in 1966 for *Remedy Is None*
and the Scottish Arts Council Award in 1968 for *A Gift from Nessus* and in 1975
for *Docherty*. His autobiographical essay, "Growing Up in the West," appeared in
Memoirs of a Modern Scotland, ed. Karl Miller (1969).

the universal tragic pattern is fleshed out in local style and experience. A major problem is that the narrative manner is highly analytic and completely English; the figurative psychography of complex and extreme inner states overripens at times, and the authenticity of a simple young rustic's nightmare is occasionally lost in the over-analysis of the university novelist. The dialectal Scots is remote from the narrator. As a result, it is hard to say whether Charlie's inability to act meaningfully is part of the universality of his problem or part of his cultural simplicity and his youth.

A Gift from Nessus (1968) is a finer book—indeed, an extraordinary one.[18] It is Kennaway's *Bells of Shoreditch* translated into a contemporary Glaswegian world, a severely compassionate view of the moral illusions and penances of a modern marriage, quite in the manner of Jenkins, yet with a style and a narrative economy subtler and more versatile, a moral vision less insistent. A Jenkins theme and a Jenkins title echo centrally: "All they could do was surrender to each other, go on again and again making that ultimate act of mutual submission, in the hope that from the recurrent ashes of their passion would come some kind of benediction, some kind of grace in the coolness of whose shadow they could meet. If they couldn't irrigate the desert, at least they could lay the dust" (57). The "grace" comes to Eddie Cameron, "Hamlet of the suburbs," and his coolly self-protective wife, as in Jenkins, only through sacrificial destruction of an innocent. Eddie's mistress, deserted by Eddie and separated from her family by a fiercely righteous Scottish father, drowns herself in desperation—pitiable Ophelia of the bathtub. Eddie, successful area salesman and now in line for management, acts at last decisively, leaves the modern Glasgow business labyrinth, openly attends the girl's funeral, confronts her hostile brother in a fine moment of mutual compassion, terrorizes his wife into acceptance, and sets about being true to himself. Milieu and motive are fixed throughout in modern, urban Scotland, and yet the consciousness of being Scottish neither defines the problem nor offers a solution. "Glasgow happened by the way. The feeling he commonly had on entering Glasgow after a day's driving was that of surrendering his own motivations to those of the city . . . But today his purposefulness protected him. The frenetic urgency of the city was no more than a background noise, something from which he was separate" (183).

James Allan Ford's* *A Judge of Men* (1968) follows McIlvanney and Jenkins as the study of a modern marriage in disintegration, yet its Edinburgh setting is as crucial as its problems are nonparochial.[19] Lord Falkland of the High Court of Justiciary is a "hanging judge" in the most contemporary terms: "All of a sudden, he's set himself up as a judge of our morals" (12), and his court when dealing with sex cases has been named the Bullring. His wife, a former actress, is anonymous sponsor of the "Salamander Prize" of five hundred pounds for a modern Scottish play; the play chosen by the committee is in gross defiance of Falkland's puritanical tastes. The winning playwright David Wilde and his friends engage in a campaign of anonymous threatening letters against Falkland. The prize is withdrawn, a copy of the play destroyed; Wilde comes for the surviving copy to Lady Falkland, and refuses when she offers him the five hundred pounds.

Neither antagonist, Wilde or Falkland, is content with the position in which he finds himself. Wilde is more conscientious than his mod friends, and Falkland has no desire to be the hero of the remnant of "grim Scottish paternalism." "In an age of satire and fantasy, even the most balanced of views could be interpreted as narrow-minded. At a time when the modish totem was a wild horse, it was bound to be up-hill work reminding people of the general advantages of harness" (51). Such are Falkland's thoughts in his loneliness, against even the pleadings of his judicial friends and colleagues. At the climax of his troubles and his misunderstanding with his wife, Falkland suffers a stroke and dies. Wilde is determined to take back nothing, just as Falkland took back nothing, and he would oppose Falkland again as the symbol of the medieval power of law in Scotland. Yet one senses they have become worthy enemies, each more honest and courageous than his allies and fans. The war over the moral well-being of contemporary Edinburgh is presented with fairness and balance, though the effort to do justice to Falkland's side may be harder and the temptation to satirize the obvious quirks of artistic permissive youth easier.

*Ford, James Allan. Born in Auchtermuchty, Fife, Ford attended Edinburgh University and has held numerous executive posts in the Scottish Civil Service. From 1966 to 1969 he was registrar general for Scotland; in 1969 he became director of establishments in the Scottish Office. *A Judge of Men*, his fourth novel, was preceded by *The Brave White Flag* (1961), *Season of Escape* (1963), and *A Statue for a Public Place* (1965).

In talent, versatility, and artistic assurance, Gordon Williams* impresses me most. *The Last Day of Lincoln Charles* (1965), a moving account of parochial Lancashire and a maltreated black American soldier's homicidal outburst, gave little suggestion of Williams' extraordinary command of contemporary Scottish material or of his tragicomic virtuosity and scope. But to take only two other Williams novels, *From Scenes like These* (1968) often recalls and even adapts stylistically the manner of Gibbon's *Quair*, and *Walk Don't Walk* (1972) echoes and often equals, in a later milieu and idiom, Linklater's *Juan in America*.[20]

In *From Scenes like These* local experience—farm labor, dancing, football—is rendered in vivid detail, without any distance of viewpoint, in a colloquial English that includes and assimilates Scots dialectal words and rhythms, often in the second-person used by Gibbon but without the pastoral lushness or nostalgia. A harsh realism is set forcefully against the title's idyllic recollection of Burns. But the bleakness and coarseness are not distorted—the texture is too closely and even sympathetically woven for that. The setting Kilcaddie is an industrial sprawl gradually gobbling up the remaining farms, but the housing scheme, grim center of several recent Scottish novels, has its own "real scheme edge" in speech and life. The tragedy is that Dunky, the protagonist with real promise as a writer, clearly lacks the will to escape and turns instead to football and whisky.

Walk Don't Walk is subtitled *A Scots Burgh Boy's Dream of America*. The boy is now London Scots novelist Cameron, newly successful, brought to America by publisher Tannenbaum on a promotional tour for his new novel. Williams' dedication is to Nelson Algren, whom Cameron and evidently Williams think "America's only living novelist worth a fart." The hero-narrator alternates between "I" and "he" throughout a wildly comic narrative in which the United States is toured from a honky tonk dreamland to Westchester to cousins in rural east Texas to a brief, final sexual success in Hollywood with a fast-aging, slow-witted gossip columnist. The rendering of numerous American regional dialects is brilliant, if exaggerated. Cameron falls in totally with the huckstering principle of his hosts, plays the insane

---

*Williams, Gordon M. The son of a policeman, Williams was born in Paisley, in 1934. He lives and writes in London. He won the Scottish Arts Council Award for *From Scenes Like These*. His other novels include *The Last Day of Lincoln Charles* (1965) and *The Siege of Trencher's Farm* (1969).

games symbolized in the pedestrian lights WALK DON'T WALK, is usually drunk and lecherous, and makes a great, witty hit on television talk shows. His growing obsession is to "get laid" and specifically, for all his comic erotic fantasies of starlets, to conquer his touring guide, the frigid, aggressive Sally Weber, who babies him but never surrenders. He finally grows pathetic and gives up to hurry back to tolerant London wife and babies.

Cameron's Scottish background is always there as a sort of compulsive joke as he tries in vain to play the wild young author, haunted by memories of Behan and Dylan Thomas. "The whole of Glasgow is America daft." The rapid present tense panorama, recalling Juanesque impressions of a weird land of zany make-believe, presents a hilarious, surreal travelogue remote from the vigorous, ugly realism of *From Scenes like These.*

After the fantastic humor and bawdy of *Walk Don't Walk*, the comic novels of Clifford Hanley* seem a return to more provincial Scottish music hall traditions. But while their origins may be there, the achievement transcends the origins. *The Hot Month* (1967)[21] is a story of a wild and "wicked" Highland holiday; Alexander Scott finds it much more laughable than the whole Ben Nevis series of Compton Mackenzie. The resemblance is meaningful, for Hanley is exploiting the same small range of improbable local Highland stereotypes, and Lilian Beckwith is not far off. The Glasgow pater familias, successful artist Nat Boag, is blessed with a television talkshow impersonative wit that, alas, never deserts him; his family is equally compulsive in its humor. His novelist sister is a foolish amazon in search of a Highland Peyton Place—and not far wrong: the unloved sassenach landlord has a moronic fop of a son who creates numerous farcical possibilities by seeking to seduce numerous females of the Boag family. The locals, mechanics, constables, lady-butchers, and the rest, are exuberantly eccentric and amoral. Dionysus rules; puritans and snobs are discom-

*Hanley, Clifford. Born in 1922 and educated in Glasgow, Hanley has been journalist and columnist for Glasgow newspapers, and a television critic, director, and social commentator. He is vice-president of Scottish P.E.N. and a member of the Scottish Arts Council. He is the author of several musical plays and, as "Henry Calvin," of mystery novels such as *The Chosen Instrument* (1969). The two novels mentioned here were preceded by *Love from Everybody* (1959), *The Taste of Too Much* (1960), and *Nothing but the Best* (1964). *Dancing in the Streets* (1958) is his Glasgow autobiography, and *A Skinful of Scotch* (1965) is his irreverent contribution to the long Scottish travel bookshelf.

fited predictably. The Boags' in-laws, hidebound and henpecked, re-treat. Summer romance, sex, whisky abound—and yet it all seems playful and innocent enough, such is the idyllic juvenility of West Highland towns such as Ochie when drawn in broad colors for sum-mer farce. There is the inevitable poaching by Nat and his local cronies, and the dynamiting of salmon, and the drunken funeral when heirs fight to strip old Maggie's house of its furnishings; the climax is the young master's twenty-first birthday celebration with fireworks, the same night as the grand concert in the village hall. No one has any feelings to be taken seriously beyond the affection of Nat and his family for each other. It is well-made popular farce.

On the surface, *The Red-Haired Bitch* is manifestly by the same author as *The Hot Month*. But now he has a real year-round world to expose—the world of contemporary Glasgow theater—and a number of plausible and strained domestic relationships are involved. A com-mercial "angel" tries losing money in the theater by producing a musical comedy based on Mary Stuart's life. Such a burlesque occa-sion appears improbable to serve for another total farce, but surpris-ingly, the theatrical professionalism of Hanley and his chief characters takes over, and the new music hall rendition of the old story suddenly makes serious claims. The actress playing Mary, a nightclub singer and a Glasgow mobster's moll, involves the group in a near murder, and an old music hall comedian turns John Knox "from an elegant voice of doom to a coarse, passionate politician with a policy of ideal-ism and a cunning sexy twinkle" (217). The cynical author of the script has seen nothing happen "in this dump since William Wallace, and he was a romantic with the death wish. Tartan and comic songs and slag-heaps and Presbyterian yahoos" (43). This, it seems, is how he saw it. Maybe the music hall has the truth about the Scottish past after all. And the present in theatrical Glasgow, down to Johnny MacGill's brutal, sentimental drunken father, is given with a grim veracity ut-terly lacking in *The Hot Month*.

The two novels suggest that Hanley can do two very different modes of comedy—a highly artificial and stereotyped farce when he works with reality, and something far more significant and moving when he works through his own metier of the theater.

With Williams' *Walk Don't Walk* and Hanley's *The Red-Haired Bitch*, the artist novel has evidently come into its own in Scotland, and with it questions about the connections between art and reality, fiction and fact, and which is which. In two of the most polished of recent Scottish novels, the artist is also a teacher: Elspeth Davie's* *Creating a Scene* (1971) and Iain Crichton Smith's† *My Last Duchess* (1971)—particularly suitable examples with which to finish this chapter.[22]

The question of *Creating a Scene* is whether the artist's creativity can make of modern urban Scotland a scene with a human reality, a scene where human life can be real. The old city school setting—Canongate, the Crags, Castle Rock—is an archaic reality peculiarly immutable, yet spectacular. The new housing scheme that now blocks out the sea is, by contrast, strikingly unreal. The grotesque and unreal spectacle of the new giant "scheme" of Scottish urban planning has a force of horror for the social imagination that haunts the current Scottish novel. Why? It is far from unique. Yet it is, as a dehumanizing menace, unusual by contrast with the traditional image of the "close," or the full connotative range of Scots *gemutlichkeit* with its relish of closeness, human density, human collectivity, and the diminutive as a gesture of affection and accommodation.

And characteristically, the students who are hired to humanize the scene by turning a derelict swimming pool into a "meeting place" turn their wall murals into a scene of paradise, which enrages a local teddy boy into his own reactive creativity of destruction.

The novel centers on the contrapuntal development of two student artists, with the emergence of their middle-aged teacher, Foley, as a minor but integrated theme. For Joe the chief artist, the question is whether art can or should be subjected to any restraints, moral or metaphysical. For Nicola, his female counterpart, the question is whether art can ever approximate human involvement in human reality; posing for him, she discovers her own identity in the ageless Eve forever subservient to the male ego. For Foley, the question is one of schoolmastering: how much freedom should he give his students? how responsible is he? And for all, it is a question of how to be aware —of how to see creatively—without merely seeing, without turning reality into pigment.

Davie, Elspeth. She was born and is living in Edinburgh, where she attended university and art college and where her husband teaches philosophy at the university. *Creating a Scene* is her second novel; the first was *Providings*. Her fine short stories have been collected in *The Spark and Other Stories* (1968).

†*Smith, Iain Crichton.* See below, page 327.

The handling of visual space and color in the novel is itself worthy of attention. In a remarkably subtle and delicate way, and on a small scale, this slight novel has the resonance of an open parable, and as an art work it is perhaps second to none among recent Scottish novels.

As in *Creating a Scene*, teacher and artist are uneasily conjoined in Smith's *My Last Duchess*. The distanced perspective that sees only spectacle makes the artist or the teacher unreal; the teacher who liberates, the artist who sees beyond his own paradise to the creativity in another's chaos, bring hope.

When diffident, withdrawn Mark Simmons and his young artist wife Lorna visit the little church in one of Scotland's loveliest Lowland towns, two teddy boys from "the city" knock over her easel and ruin her painting with bootprints. Mark's only response is to give in and take her to see a little ancient church and its effigy of the local saint, who protected white deer. A little old man offers his company, and it turns out he is the minister's father, and a retired headmaster. "Christ, another of them, thought Mark, you can't go anywhere without running across them. Even in the Garden of Eden Satan would turn out to be an academic" (124). The image is revealing, for the schoolmaster in his ambiguous, powerful role appears repeatedly in recent Scottish fiction; and so does the terrible preoccupation with Eden and its destruction.

Mark is a paralyzed modern Scottish intellectual, with his "dour Calvinist conscience," his *New Statesman* mentality, his loss of both his young wife and his faith in literature, in words, in a world where communication for some is still a pathetic fitful effort and for others is wordless violence. His Scottish milieu is sparely hinted at. He teaches at a training college in a "nice" town seven miles from Glasgow; he journeys back in a vague search for lost self to "the northern city," "a city made of silver [that yields] nothing to his digging" (52). Faced with the "great slabs of multi-storey flats" and "an open precariousness" replacing a remembered density, he imagines "the ancient closes with their blue gas lighting," "the warm closeness of people" (106, 111). Numbed by the grinning destructiveness of vandals and by the garrulousness of an old antiquarian, he senses for a moment "the presence of an ancient holiness" in a little legendary church.

Yet as the Browning title suggests, his desolate unreality is of his own making. The bleak, quiet story is of his own sterility, and the question is whether that story connects itself in any significant way with the locale of a changing Scotland in the "Wilson era." The seminal equation that comes upon him in the violent climax—the episode on a train when he goes to "see" the new city violence his friend Hunter has been studying, the episode where he sits by and sees two cool teds take off a "colored" salesman to a lavatory to knife him—is that the terrible aloneness, the utter barrenness of affection, the moral unreality of the new city savage are in fact identical with his own unreality. At the end he is left to survive with intellectual honesty, but he has learned that coarser values—the small town family, the young baker's domestic Christmas in Aberdeen—are closer to what makes survival possible.

This is, of course, nowhere near Iain Crichton Smith's beginnings as poet and novelist. In some respects he belongs, with Neil Gunn, Fionn Mac Colla, Jane Duncan, George Mackay Brown, and others, to a different Scottish tradition.

The Novel
of the
Highlands

15

The Tragedy
of the
Clearances

Any cultural comment on Celtic Scotland begins with the fact of centuries of exploitation and its effects. By the later eighteenth century, an isolated remnant of Christian Europe's oldest continuous civilization, long denied its cultural identity, had become parochial, just as long ago it had lost the very name of "Scots" to the Anglo-Saxon Lowlands. An ancient Christianity had been mostly suppressed by a severe Calvinist hegemony; an environment had been repeatedly abused in the name of progress; a rich language had been displaced by oral dialects; an often reckless discontent had been exploited by anachronistic royal dynasties; a marginal agrarian economy with many regional problems had been administered by indifferent foreign politicians; a proud, complex people had been stereotyped as servile, lazy, devious, but fecklessly romantic savages. The very survival of such a civilization would remain doubtful even if its unique problems were to be imaginatively grasped. The emergence in such a situation of a modern literary form such as the novel was certain to be a rather special phenomenon.

The region as setting had already been flamboyantly appropriated by romancers. The Highlands of prose romance had been personified, sometimes with tragic splendor, more often with melodramatic extravagance, in the outlaw chiefs and fanatical clansmen of Scott, in the boyish Jacobite adventurers of Stevenson, and, most interestingly, in Neil Munro's conflation of Stevenson's adventurers with Ferrier's decadent Highland lairds. Moreover, the Highlands and Islands did not—could not—develop anything comparable to the socioeconomic urban world that had served elsewhere as a precondition to the rise of the novel. The transition from patriarchal militarism, foraging, and cattle-raising to a world of absentee landlordism, sporting preserves, coastal fishing villages, and marginal farming obviously would provide no suitable subject for a Defoe, Richardson, Austen, or Eliot. The classic novelist's preoccupation with self and society arose out of a collision between a new psychological and economic individualism on the one hand and a new commercial bourgeois morality on the other. But in a nonurban, preindustrial, and (from the bourgeois perspective) classless society, self and society was not a crux of moral identity. Rather, the crux was self and land, or self and archaic community, or self and suppressive theocracy. Finally, Gaelic Scotland remained rich in archaic and sophisticated oral narrative traditions, remote from the norms of the novelist yet central to the community the Highland novelist would necessarily represent, and so centered on vignettes of local character and incident, heroic or humorous, as to make the long developmental patterns of the novel less congenial than those of the short story.

For the romancer, the essential Highland tragedy or tragicomedy had been Culloden, the ultimate quixotry of lost causes, the awful "end of an auld sang," the coup de grace of a system already anachronistic. By contrast, it may be argued that the novel could take hold only when the writer acquainted with the ordinary realities of Highland experience substituted for the epic absurdity of Culloden the more comprehensive and domestic tragedy of the Highland Clearances, going on largely ignored even as Sir Walter was creating his Jacobite anachronisms. While utilitarian economists applauded and opportunistic ministers connived, the agents of chiefs-turned-landlords depopulated glens of poor subtenant crofters, in the name of progress, of economic efficiency, even of humanity. Some were forced to emigrate; others were driven into the harsh circumstances of coastal villages, and the ancestral lands of the evicted were profitably rented to Lowland speculators in sheep ranching. Less angry historians, whatever their views of the economic rationale, would have to agree with Ian Grimble on the methods and effects: "The coming of the sheep involved the expulsion of a minority ethnic group from the country they had inhabited since time immemorial, without the slightest consultation, and frequently with little warning . . . The full devastating effect of the coming of the sheep has now materialised in one of the most mutilated regions of Europe."[1]

It was a bitter human tragedy arousing widespread compassion. The bitterness survives; the compassion, say some, was the first bond to link Highlands and Lowlands in a common nationality. The humanitarian pretensions of landlords who still appealed to loyalties once due them as partiarchs; the rationalizations of "progressive" economists; the ethnic animosity of Lowland factors (land agents); the cowardly opportunism or hypocrisy of ministers who admonished their docile flocks to bow to eviction and exile as a divine judgment; and the abject or bewildered defeatism of a people cowed by centuries of subtle genocide: history shows little to equal it. "But the tragedy," says Eric Linklater, "is indisputable, unrelieved, and irreparable; and because there is no profit in crying over spilt milk, irony is the way to deal with it."[2]

Patrick Sellar emptied and burned Strathnaver in 1814, when many men were away fighting for their "chief" against Napoleon, but the Clearances extended from the 1760s to the 1830s and 1840s. Then as the nineteenth century wore on and the sheepish prosperity proved short-lived, there came the final insult of committing ancestral glens to the protected wilderness of grouse moore and deer forest (3.5 million acres by 1912), purchased by English and foreign sportsmen, often themselves titillated with the misty popular mythology of a post-Waverley age of kilted and Balmoralized Hanoverians. The Highlands remain today largely the desert of the Clearances. In the face of such a grim parade of economic realities, the question becomes whether the novelist can either use such a story or leave it alone, or whether, using it, he can transcend or universalize its manifold local bitternesses. We begin, then, by glancing at three modern novels of the Clearances. Iain Crichton Smith's* *Consider the Lilies* (1968; in America, *The Alien Light,* 1969) is the first, not quite successful, novel of a fine modern poet in both Gaelic and English. The earliest of the

Smith, Iain Crichton. Born on Lewis, in the Outer Hebrides, in 1928. He attended Aberdeen University, and since 1955 he has taught English at Oban High School. He is chiefly known for his poetry in both Gaelic and English, such as *Deer on the High Hills* (1960), *Thistles and Roses* (1961), and *Biobuill Is Sanasan Reice* (1965). His Gaelic plays have been produced in Glasgow, and he has published short stories in English and Gaelic. His four novels are *My Last Duchess* (1971), *The Last Summer* (1969), *Consider the Lilies* and *Goodbye, Mr. Dixon* (1974).

three is an early novel of one of Scotland's greatest novelists, Neil Gunn: *Butcher's Broom* (1934). *And The Cock Crew* (1945) is the second novel of the author who called himself Fionn Mac Colla. So tempting is it for the Highland novelist to see the Clearances as the story of his people in modern history that he must be hard pressed to realize comprehensiveness in time, place, and culture and still manage the novelist's focus on individual lives and relationships. Only Neil Gunn has tried the panoramic novel of community, but in fact none of the three has found it suitable to follow the traditional way of the historical novelist, perhaps because history itself, a foreign enemy, seems an irrelevant or inadequate mode of comprehension.

Smith insists he has not written a historical novel.[3] He is not, he says, "competent to do an historical study of the period," but has done, rather, "a fictional study of one person, an old woman who is being evicted." It is, he repeats, "only the story of an old woman confronted by eviction. A way of life may emerge indirectly but it is not explicitly documented." The historicity of his subject is not so easily muted; the mind of the old woman is not easily abstracted from the way of life her story comes to represent; and besides, Smith has made the woman a unique center of concern for a group of characters whose place in history is unforgettable. Patrick Sellar the factor, John Loch (historically James Loch), Donald Macleod the stone mason who wrote influential indictments of the Sutherland actions—all are shown earnestly vying for the old woman's loyalty and acquiescence. How, then, can the reader make himself "forget" Smith's multiple anachronisms? The woman is old; her husband is long dead in the Peninsular campaign; yet the Strathnaver actions of Sellar took place in 1814 and his trial was the year of Waterloo, when the historic Macleod was still an unmarried youth. If none of this matters, then Smith might have avoided the distractions of anachronism by not having historic antagonists argue the issues of the Clearances in the old woman's little croft house and in her bewildered presence.

But there it is. Inevitably one tries to understand history and old Mrs. Scott's personal tragedy together, and this means seeing her story as somehow in metaphoric relation to the movement of "history." The facts of her life, given us in alternating flashbacks of reverie, are few and grim. Her crofter father died; her senile mother, in a religious mania, was hers to care for. At twenty-nine, she was alone at last. A younger neighbor married her for the house, gave her a son, and fled. Her husband almost forgotten, she brought up her only child, quarreled with him about his girl friend, and lost him when he too left her to emigrate to Canada. Now she is old, alone, bullied by Patrick Sellar the factor, facing eviction, and refused help in her resistance by friend, elder, and minister alike. The book's turning point comes when she goes in vain for help to the minister, faints when looking into the river, wakes in bed at the Macleods, and from then on is drawn to the freethinker Macleod and away from her church. Macleod invites her to join their household, but she refuses. She will stand alone. She has triumphed, somehow, against church, against the hellish repressiveness of her own past, against what Sellar represents. Macleod "knew that his hatred was not simply for those who were bent on destroying the Highlands, not simply for the Patrick Sellars, but for the Patrick Sellars in the Highlanders, those interior Patrick Sellars with the faces of old Highlanders who evicted emotions and burnt down love" (139).

For she has told Macleod her story, and he, suddenly kneeling at her feet like the son she has lost, sees her story as the essential human reality of the issue he has intellectualized in writing his pamphlets— the history "that had always been and might always be, like a sea rising and falling for ever . . . this waste, this terrible waste" (138). And this very achievement of story is, in Highland community and Highland novel, of thematic moment. She tries next day to tell Macleod's children a story, and since she has no stories any more— such is the cultural impoverishment of the "terrible waste"—she tries fitfully to make a fairy tale of her own truth. Macleod tells her she is doing well. As the chronicler of the tragedy, he stands, in a sense, for the force of storytelling against the church's suppression of local tradition. She stands at last, against threat and bribery, in defense of Macleod, against the church and factor alike; thus, she triumphs over the fearful waste, the emotional evictions, of her own past, and somehow the particulars of eviction no longer matter much at the end.

This is to impose on the book a schematic burden of meaning it perhaps will not bear. But the potential suggests at least that the old woman is inseparable from an interpretation of her cultural situation. And it suggests as well the implicit kinship of *Consider the Lilies* with the essential life-and-death struggles that give thematic scope to two very different novels of the Sutherland Clearances.

Fionn Mac Colla's* *And the Cock Crew* goes to an opposite extreme.[4] From Smith's deliberate dramatic restriction it moves to cosmic conflicts of perspective. The central character possesses extraordinary spiritual power and insight, is capable of violent convulsions of vision. He is a conscientious minister who, just as Peter three times betrayed Christ before the cock crew, three times betrays his people as they await his leadership in resisting eviction. "Maighstir" Zachary's essential conflicts are two: one with the factor, the "Black Foreigner" Byars (an obvious pun on Sellar), who fears and hates and vows to root out Gaelic humanity from the Sutherland estates; the other with the old traditional bard, Fearchar the poet, who had led the community until twenty years before, when the zealous young Zachary came to force him and his "paganism" out of the community.

Zachary appears first as an effective and defiant leader. But abruptly, seeing his own sinfulness reflected in the secret "sin" of a pregnant girl, he is morally paralyzed and sees sin everywhere, even in his own vision of his community and the natural wholeness and harmony of its life:

> To destroy it seemed an outrage and a violation, the triumph of chaos over order . . . He could not contemplate that more crudely pastoral life of the sheep men without a deep sense of the incomplete, of frustration . . . On every count it represented a regression, a reversal of the natural line of vital growth. But above all it was dissatisfying to him because it was a life without roots, not growing out of the soil but taking from it an illicit sustenance as it were by stealth, not needing any particular place, fixed nowhere, and therefore without vital relation to any single countryside, permanently incapable of taking root and forming with, and within, its surroundings a unity and a whole. (26).

Such is the aesthetic way of the poet he had rooted out of himself in youth. Now the triumphant theological vision whispers to him with the voice of Judas that the imminent destruction of that wholeness is

---

*Mac Colla, Fionn. Born a MacDonald in Montrose, Angus, Mac Colla, like MacDiarmid, adopted an emphatically Celtic name and heritage. After working as a schoolmaster in the northwest Highlands, he spent several years teaching in Palestine; he returned to Scotland in 1929 at the time of depression and resurgent nationalism. From 1940 he was headmaster of various schools in the Highlands. He retired to Edinburgh, where he died in 1975. His psycho-historical study of the errors of post-Reformation Scotland, *At the Sign of the Clenched Fist*, appeared in 1967; his autobiography, *Too Long in This Condition* (*Ro fhada mar so a tha Mi*), in 1975.

God's judgment. His betrayals follow: "From that one Uncertainty his judgment was all unseated, and his mind reeled before the possibilities involved in the simplest and most natural act; for spirit is not Size and in the smallest act could be a whole universe of sin" (75). He fails to resist as Byars burns the heather. He wrongly advises the crofters who come for his counsel as to future sowing. On the verge of the evictions he opens his Sabbath sermon with the text from Deuteronomy 8 prophesying forty years of wandering in the wilderness, and then collapses speechless and sobbing in his pulpit as his people leave in despair.

Prior to this final betrayal, literally in the dark night of the soul (set vividly in the hellish flickering of the smithy), he has gone groping to his defeated rival the old poet, seeking forgiveness but still unable to see his error. Their dialogue is the long center of this short book (78-104), and as Fearchar argues the necessity of leadership and Zachary counters with his own theological rationalization of inaction, the book's scope as a parable of visionary conflict becomes evident. Zachary now "sees" impending events as if they have already happened, can understand events "only as produced in the tensions between the Divine and human wills; and not otherwise was he able to understand the world. Hence he was unable to think historically, for that is as it were horizontally; incapable from the very nature of his mind of recognising the validity of a view which might seek to explain events as the product of factors working out in a process that must be called historical"(95). Fearchar tries in vain to tell him that the Clearances are simply the latest part of a seven-hundred-year-old campaign of England the enemy to destroy Gaelic Scotland, that the genocide can never succeed unless the way of life fails to resist. Centrally, then, the book opposes two absolute visions. It is an irony that the powerfully evoked theological vision is artistically dominant over the pagan, poetic vision in whose favor it is rejected. But perhaps the two are equally theological, for in Fearchar's theodicy England is the eternal enemy and "history" an almost timeless dimension.

Centered on the same events, Neil Gunn's* *Butcher's Broom* is profoundly different from both, in scope, focus, and mode.[5] The definer of genres might consider it the only historical novel of the three, and history is part of its central issue. The essential conflict here is not be-

*Gunn, Neil M. See below, page 348.

tween humanism and Calvinism, or between poetry and theology, but between mythic and historic views of personality and community, and it is a conflict that will persist in the dialectic of Gunn's novels. The title identifies a bitter irony in the clan badge of the Sutherland, the sign of a matriarchal protectorate turned into an emblem of brutal rejection. The enemy is neither genocidal England nor a love-evicting creed: Gunn could never satisfy himself with the epic chauvinism of one, and he is too compassionate a critic of presbyterian severity to rest with the other. The enemy is the "improving" spirit.

Gunn finds essential in the historic situation the fact that when the "improvers" came to clear Sutherland glens, they found the young men away, conscripted for their chief's service in a foreign war. The women, as from time immemorial, were left with helpless old men and children to defend their land and their homes. This fact is framed in Gunn's matriarchal view of archaic community. What man in his callous rationalism calls "history" is really a legendary continuity of "innumerable women whose suffering and endurance were like little black knots holding the web of history together" (321). Suitably, the novel is focused on a matriarchal counterpart to the Bitch Countess, and the delicate central relationship is between her—Dark Mairi—and the deserted and unwed mother, Elie, whom Mairi takes to live with her and her grandson. Their domestic grouping, elemental, outside of man's narrow vision of legitimacy, is the novel's central reality and the point of view from which the community is progressively understood.

> The firelight enriched the skin on their faces and glistened in their eyes. Davie's soiled legs glowed brown beneath his bony knees on which the plate rested. Elie's legs had a reddish tinge in their tan and her ankles were strong and yet delicate. Her broad stained feet had short smooth toes. Davie's face was smudged as by sleep. The fire-tongues played with the gloom around them, and the smoke curled upwards toward the opening in the black roof. In the centre of this gloom was the fire, and sitting round it, their knees drawn together, their heads stooped, were the old woman, like fate, the young woman, like love, and the small boy with the swallow of life in his hand.(31)

Dark Mairi is the tragic center, but by her nature she cannot serve as a central consciousness like Smith's Mrs. Scott or Mac Colla's Zachary. And this is one of the novel's problems. She is the epitome of the traditional wisdom and practicality menaced by history in the guise of the scientific arrogance of the "improvers." That arrogance must be fully drawn, and for this reason Gunn's novel must be much larger in narrative scope than Smith's vignette or Mac Colla's parable-dialogue. Mairi and Elie must be seen moving in a complex community, where Mairi stands for a wise continuity with the past, an earthy tolerance beyond "moral" barriers. The "improvers" are destroyers, and she is in direct opposition: her role in the community is as its healer. Born by the sea, she is first seen carrying its specifics and simples back for the medicine of her people in the glen. Her life and power are rooted in the local earth, and both are magical, amoral, and utterly practical. She is no dreamy "primitive" of the Celtic revivalist: "Where all is magic, only the utterly practical person like Mairi can use it, troubled neither by the self-consciousness of the sceptic nor the idealism of the poet" (319). Exiled at last with her people back to the sea, she wanders dazed to the glen and is destroyed with ritual brutality by the dogs of the shepherd who has displaced her people. The book's end is her death march: "The father and son set out with the body of Dark Mairi for the distant shore." Yet her own death is presumably to affect the reader as the tragic legends she tells help to heal other innumerable and nameless women wounded by male history. Thus, "by some still more profound alchemy, the very tragedy which ended Mairi's story gave to the possibility of tragedy in Elie's story the last strength of all" (284).

The idiom is enough to suggest that the novel's meaning is far beyond the conscious understanding of Mairi or Elie or their community. There is an interpretive narrator whose own vision must comprehend both the "logic" of Mairi's practical vision and the other "logics" by which men cut off from her archaic wisdom rationalize its destruction. Their pretensions to an illusory historical pattern called Progress must be seen analytically for what they really are. The narrator sees what is continuous with and yet beyond the archaic vision of a Mairi: modern "history" is no progressive succession of events after all, but primordial motives enacted in temporary new guises. The factor's murderous hatred is to be explained not in Smith's psychological terms or Mac Colla's theological and political ones, but in terms of the myth of life itself: for "when any man opposes the fundamental principle of life in another, he must, by the irksome consciousness or subconsciousness of what he is doing, become antagonistic and violent, and will hunt about in the other's life for what he can despise and hate" (268). Violence always begins as spiritual violence directed against the vital principle in another's life. The narrator must encompass and somehow transcend both the archaic vision of a Dark Mairi and the "historical" understanding of the improvers. His purpose could not be served through the mind of Smith's simple, lonely old woman, or through the absolutist intelligences of Zachary and Fearchar. The risks had to be taken.

If there is excess here, it is in the rhetorical overemphasis of tragedy. Tragedy is called the ultimate vision, the "last strength of all," but tragedy is powerful enough in the brute facts plainly perceived and stated by the old people of the community. Gunn's own vision is ultimately comic; he could never be easy with a view of "humanity's final logic" as tragedy.

However impressive, all three novels of the Clearances are not quite at ease with their subject. But here is the Highland novelist in what is perhaps his essential subject. What fictive power or meaning is to be derived without damaging falsification? The subject is the continued destruction of an archaic, impoverished community. If it is to be depicted by the unrelenting naturalist, the effect can be only a sense of unmitigated futility and despair. If it is envisioned as it was or could be, the effect may seem romantic or utopian. If it is to be thoroughly localized for an uninformed world, the burden of exposition is enough to threaten imaginative vitality. If not, the result may be pastoral parable or allegory, the communal reality lost in abstraction. If the narrator adopts the storytelling modes of the traditional community itself, how then is he to make a meaningful story for a novel oriented cosmopolitan audience? If he adopts the perspectives and patterns of the modern novelist, how will he adapt them without condescension or sentimentality to the very different rhythms of a remote, archaic community? His chief logistical problem will be how to manipulate the necessary "distance" without overwhelming the reality of the world. The tension will be between local realism for its own sake and parable in which local reality is lost in transcendent theme or intention, in tragic archetype or comic stereotype. And if character tends to be both local and archetypal, he must offer a cultural explanation for this fact.

With some of these problems and possibilities in mind, we should turn back to some facts of historical development. The cliché has it that until World War I and perhaps beyond, the novel of the Highlands was lost in the mists of Victorian pseudo-Celticism. The cliché lumps together the sunsets of William Black and the perpetual glooms of Fiona Macleod. Let us briefly unlump them and try to see this alleged pseudo-Celticism for what it was and what it meant for the novel.

16

Late Victorian
Celticisms

lmost no one has a good word for William Black.* He is remembered if at all for his Hebridean sunsets. Even the generous Ernest A. Baker labels him a businessman who supplied
fin de siècle circulating libraries with salable formulas.[1] Grouping him
with the "milk and water" school of late Victorian domestic novelists,
Hugh Walpole quotes the incident wherein Macleod of Dare presents a
London actress with a large Highland salmon, and comments: "That
gigantic salmon that has passed through the hands of the landlady and
Cousin Janet and 'should be cooked at once' is the hero of most of
William Black's novels."[2] George Blake credits him with being merely
clever. "By exploiting the romantic-sentimental aspects of his native
country he became a popular favourite and, out of his American royalties, could afford to drive up and down the front at Brighton in a
horse-carriage of his own."[3] The combined allegations ought to be
enough to save Black from any critical resurrection, and I do not in-
tend one. Nevertheless, the Highland novel begins with Black, and the
interpreter has something to learn from his formulas.

Consider a small but representative group of novels, probably in-

---

*Black, William. Born in Glasgow in 1841 and died in Brighton, England, in
1898. He began as an art student but turned to writing and moved to London,
where he worked as a journalist. He served as war correspondent during the
Franco-Prussian War of 1866 and was assistant editor of the Daily News for several
years; his success as a novelist led him to resign in 1874.

cluding his best: *A Daughter of Heth* (1871); *A Princess of Thule* (1873); *Macleod of Dare* (1878); *In Far Lochaber* (1888); and *Donald Ross of Heimra* (1891). Baker sees the Black formula as intended "to contrast the garishness of society and fashion with Highland simplicities, usually by marrying a hothouse flower from the English metropolis to a brave and dignified young chieftain . . . or transplanting an unspoiled girl from a Highland home to fast life in London . . . Obviously, all this was mainly according to Blackmore's recipe".[4] It is accurate enough to emphasize the combination in Black of the marriage of cultural strangers with the plight of the exile and the contrast of fashionable society and rural simplicity. In *Daughter of Heth* a French-Scottish orphan comes to live with her uncle, an Ayrshire minister. In *Princess of Thule* a London painter wins the daughter of a Lewis laird and carries her off into grief and misunderstanding in London and Brighton. The hero of *MacLeod of Dare*, last son of an ancient Mull family, becomes infatuated with a London actress, and, when she refuses both him and his Hebridean solitude, kidnaps her in the Thames and carries her off to an accidental watery grave in the Sound of Iona. *In Far Lochaber* varies the formula slightly. The daughter of a Free Kirk minister in late Victorian Lanarkshire, on a merry scenic visit to Highland relatives at Fort William, falls in love with and eventually marries the Roman Catholic son of a Highland laird. Donald Ross of Heimra, a bright and constructive variant of Macleod, joins forces with and marries the English heiress who has inherited his ancestral estates in Wester Ross and is determined to redeem their economic and human potential.

Obviously, such formulas call for patterns of excursion and description, as numerous major characters undergo the adventures and cultural ordeals of tourism. And this fact, combined with the wondrously erratic character of Highland weather and the ambiguities of Highland light and color, warrants scene paintings, rightly called Turneresque by Black's biographer and understandably praised by Ruskin, their master. Indeed, art itself plays a prominent role in some of the novels, and the painterly fullness with which local settings are rendered has various thematic functions. But scenic sublimity and picturesqueness do not sentimentalize Black's contrasting locales. If London and Brighton are masque-like, and towns in Lanark and Ayr are hellishly gloomy, Highland locales are differentiated and presented in their harshest aspects—remoteness, loneliness, bleakness, spareness of life. The presentation is in no way the stereotyped melancholy mist and grandeur we are supposed to associate with Celtic revivalism.

The social philosophy of the books is late Victorian too. While recognizing the moral nobility of traditional presbyterian character, Black is liberal and catholic in his attitudes. His lovers are chaste but lively, reserved but affectionate; his good parents are kindly and compassionate. His protagonists know or discover the gospel of work, and the Victorian noblesse oblige of the gentleman social reformer inspires his lairds and chieftains when they take their social roles seriously. Traditional community is worth saving; Highland land leagues and crofters commissions are real responses to real grievances, but the only effective remedies are to be sought under the kindly but firm aegis of the Tory reformer who as chief respects his people and earns the renewal of traditional loyalties.

These are the serious themes of this "popular romancer." But popular romance is replete too with archetypal figures, however peripheral and thin, and Black is no exception. Certain figures and motifs recur in the five novels: the exile, the disinherited, the maiden deserted, the intermarriage doomed by a foolish romanticism or a mean fanaticism. Macleod chooses for his wife one with only a false, romantic idea of what he is. Lavender the young English artist thinks he is marrying a princess of Thule, and his devotion lasts only as long as his foolish fancy. The most genuinely pathetic of the maidens is the daughter of Heth. Her choice of husbands is narrowed to a noble "Rochester," secretly married, and her young cousin "the Whaup," the wild but feeble bird, the boy-man of Scottish romantic tradition. The one happy romance of the group is the least plausible in plot and most matter-of-fact in theme, that of Donald Ross. Here the heroine is not just a romantic heiress, but a strong and practical New Woman, who perseveres until the disinherited young chief is thoroughly demythologized and domesticated, joins forces with her, and marries her. The ideology of this progress to union and land reform is interesting. But the improbable germ of the romance—the heiress, left a Highland estate as a toy by her uncle, proves efficient land manager and radical matriarch—simply strengthens my suspicion that Black's genuine fictive impulses were tragic. His best books are those of inexorable tragedy, and he had to defend himself against public protest at unhappy endings. *In Far Lochaber* avoids such an ending only by employing a surrogate for the heroine: her sister dies in her stead, after she has miraculously escaped the fate of a Lucy Ashton.

Such figures are related to romance archetypes; the problem of such relation is part of their experience. The titles—*Daughter of Heth, Princess of Thule*—suggest mythic identities for the heroines, but their experiences elucidate and reject such identities. Mary Stanley (in *Donald Ross*) is teased as a Godiva, yet she succeeds in the role. Macleod's Gertrude is Fionaghal, the fair stranger, but the actress quickly tires of the role and in so doing forces a fatal role on Macleod. Alison Blair (*In Far Lochaber*) tries hard to play the stern descendant of Covenanters, but her nearly fatal exiles from Lochaber teach her a truer heritage and, as the title suggests, a truer antecedent in Princess Deirdre. What in Gunn's novels becomes an atavistic self-discovery— finding one's true self in enacting one's archaic forebear—is a formative experience of Black's protagonists. But the romance of archaic identity is menaced by false romanticisms. Reality itself in Black's Highlands is romantic, set in a weather and a light of visionary ambiguity where the line between sublimity and deception is shifting. For Black the substitution of a false romanticism for reality is always destructive.

Such complexities make *Macleod of Dare* one of the most interesting of Scottish novels between John Galt and George Douglas Brown. The young hero undergoes a subtle metamorphosis. At the outset he is careless and cheerful, and he fits easily into London society: "How could anyone associate with this bright-faced young man the fierce traditions of hate and malice and revenge, that makes the seas and islands of the north still more terrible in their loneliness? . . . He was playing with a silver fork and half a dozen strawberries."[5] Here he thrives on the gift of the traditional storyteller. Forgetting himself as he tells his legends, he captivates the histrionic Gertrude, who associates him with them. He supposes naively that the reality behind the actress is easy to find outside the theater, and she is equally naive about finding the real Macleod. It is her father who, as the earnest apologist for art, sees the realities of self and role that they miss. He insists that art requires a full surrender of self, but his daughter is too selfish to make it. Macleod, on the other hand, gives himself so wholly to the traditional role that he has no self left.

He remains the superstitious Highlander; his protestations of the distance of the past become more and more ominously ironic. The return to Castle Dare shows a reality in Macleod that Gertrude is not likely to understand—the firm but friendly master—while he in turn begins transforming her into the legendary figure of Fionaghal the Fair Stranger, "the fair poetess from strange lands." Yet he cannot summon up any satisfactory vision of her; she is a phantom, she appears in a hundred shapes. Meanwhile, she is turning him into the "fair Glenogie" of her ballad. Two cultural strangers who think they are in love are victims of the tyranny of legend, and the readjustment to reality comes too late. In the kindly, brave, and practical Macleod she finally sees only barbarism, and Macleod kidnaps his Fionaghal, convinced that eventually she will play her part. There is certainly more in Black at his best than mere formulas of exotic cultural confrontation and metamorphosis.

Fiona Macleod (pen name of William Sharp)* is different from William Black, just as Yeats or AE is from Ruskin. He is not a romantic transcendentalist, but a legendary moralist, and this crucial term of his—"legendary morality"—derives from his understanding of the late Victorian Celtic Revival, in which he played an influential role. To treat his Celticism as merely an aspect of later Victorian romanticism (hence of no real significance for the student of Scottish fiction) would be to beg important questions—for example, to what extent late Victorian romanticism is itself a product of the Celtic revival codified in the 1860s by Matthew Arnold.[6] Sharp owed his entry into London literary circles largely to his friend Rossetti, and he became Rossetti's biographer and Pater's disciple.[7] This was years before *Pharais* introduced the mysterious feminine alter ego Fiona Macleod. By the time of

---

*Macleod, Fiona (William Sharp). Fiona was the feminine Celtic soul Sharp came to believe lived within him and authored most of his later works. Sharp was born in Paisley, Renfrewshire, in 1855, and died near Taormina, Sicily, in 1905. A Highland nurse filled his imagination with Gaelic folklore, and as a boy he sailed the lochs and firths of the western Highlands. Leaving the University of Glasgow and brief work in a law office, he settled in London, and during the late seventies and eighties he was a member of the Rossetti circle (he published a biography of D. G. Rossetti in 1882). The eighties were a decade of literary hackwork and editorships, but his second trip to Italy, in 1890, marked the big break in his life, and he returned to an enthusiastic study of Belgian impressionism and the Celtic revival then in full swing in Edinburgh. His association with Yeats and Ireland dates from the late eighties. The mysterious Fiona Macleod appeared first in *Pharais* (1894).

Fiona's appearance, Sharp was already heir to the Irish Renaissance of Yeats and AE.

A Yeatsian idea of Celticism appears in *For the Beauty of an Idea* and *Anima Celtica:*[8] the Celticism of the Highlands and Islands is the bequest of a civilization doomed and mostly gone, but as idea it is a power incarnate in the spiritual history of man; a Celtic fiction contributes a fiction of idea to an ongoing spiritual evolution, by reawakening ancestral memories, primordial states and modes of expression. Hence, Fiona Macleod seeks to recreate the legendary, to rediscover a pre-Christian or "pagan" mythopoeic impulse in marking the historic end of the Gael's distinct destiny. This is a step beyond Arnold in the direction of Yeats.

In his 1897 essay "The Celtic Element in Literature," Yeats redefines Arnold's touchstones of the Celtic.[9] Arnold, he says, did not understand "that our 'natural magic' is but the ancient religion of the world, the ancient worship of Nature and that troubled ecstasy before her, that certainty of all beautiful places being haunted, which it brought into men's minds." Substitute, then, for Arnold's "Celt" the "ancient hunters and fishers and . . . the ecstatic dancers among hills and woods." Modern Celticism becomes, for Yeats, an escape from "mere chronicle of circumstance, or passionless fantasies, and passionless meditations" through the flooding in of "the passions and beliefs of ancient times." The function of a Celtic movement is to open a "new fountain of legends"; "none can measure of how great importance it may be to coming times, for every new fountain of legends is a new intoxication for the imagination of the world," a new power for reacting against the rationalism of the eighteenth century and the materialism of the nineteenth.

In the essay "Celtic," Fiona quotes Yeats's sentences with approval as giving the "inward sense and significance of the 'Celtic Movement,' " yet goes a step further.[10] He speaks for a Celticism that is to give its spirituality to a potential greater "English" race to which , he believes, all British Celts actually belong. He writes against the irreconcilables, writes from a growing distrust of "pseudo-nationalism," from no great belief in " 'movements' and still less in 'renascences.' " He warns against the passion that the idea of Celtic nationality has awakened in Ireland, insists "there is no racial road to beauty, nor to any excellence," and becomes vehement against the new Celtophiles: "When I hear that 'only a Celt' could have written this or that passage of emotion or description, I am become impatient of these parrot-cries, for I remember that if all Celtic literature were to disappear, the world would not be so impoverished as by the loss of English literature, or French literature, or that of Rome or of Greece." These are surprising words coming from the most extravagant of Scottish Celtophiles. And it is noteworthy that such warnings against a narrow racialism come at the beginnings of a modern fiction for Gaelic Scotland.

Fiona shows earlier affinities as well. The prose poems called *Sospiri di Roma* recall the ornate dream-fugue impressionism of DeQuincey. And Fiona's most provocative defense of the Celticism of his fiction comes in the dedication of *The Sin-Eater* volume to "George Meredith in gratitude and homage: and because he is prince of Celtdom."[11] Fiona's Gael, he insists here, is not a "rounded and complete portrait of the Celt." He gives only "the life of the Gael in what is, to me, in accord with my own observation and experience, its most poignant characteristics." To those who "complain of the Celtic gloom that dusks the life of the men and women I have tried to draw," he argues that his doom and gloom heroes are true Celtic types, and that the gloom "to many Gaels if not to all, is so distinctive in the remote life of a doomed and passing race." Then follows shortly the most revealing statement of all:

> A doomed and passing race. Yes, but not wholly so. The Celt has at last reached his horizon. There is no shore beyond. He knows it. This has been the burden of his song since Malvina led the blind Oisin to his grave by the sea. 'Even the Children of Light must go down into darkness.' But this apparition of a passing race is no more than the fulfillment of a glorious resurrection before our very eyes. For the genius of the Celtic race stands out now with averted torch, and the light of it is a glory before the eyes, and the flame of it is blown into the hearts of the mightier conquering people. The Celt falls, but his spirit [the feminine—the *anima* Fiona] rises in the heart and the brain of the Anglo-Celtic peoples, with whom are the destinies of the generations to come.[12]

It is the Arnold keynote of a triumphant defeatism, and a fit symbol for a fin de siècle world: "The sense of an abiding spiritual Presence, of a waning, a perishing World, and of the mystery and incommunicable destiny of Man." Such is the spiritual Celticism of "this book of interpretations." But it can be bestowed only if its own tragic and mythic possibilities are recovered from those that have sought to destroy them: "In Celtic Scotland, a passionate regret, a despairing love and longing, narrows yearly before a bastard utilitarianism which is almost as great a curse to our despoiled land as Calvinistic theology has been and is."[13]

Fiona Macleod's intentions, then, are to remythologize a doomed Celticism into a spiritual bequest; to provide a fitting myth of life lived in the face of ceaseless change and mysterious destiny; to do this through interpretation as opposed to documentation of life; to renew a sense of life against the twin villainies of Calvinism and utilitarianism. Scholars of Celtic literature will find gross falsification in such a program. But John Kelleher's wise justification of literary Ireland's turn from the activism of Young Ireland to the Celticism of the fin de siècle may well apply. After many defeats and betrayals, he suggests, the hoary and stale assurances of a poetry of patriotic activism had little to offer. "A more subtle rationale than this was needed to hearten a nation that was now used to defeating itself. Poetry in Ireland would have to accept the atmosphere of defeat as its first ingredient; and out of defeat and melancholy it must somehow make the ultimate victory not only credible but expected."[14]

For the Tauchnitz collection *Wind and Wave* (1902), Fiona selected representative tales divided "broadly into tales of 'The World That Was,' and 'The World That Is.' " The distinction is revealing: "The colour and background of the one series are of a day that is past, and past not for us only, but for the forgetting race itself: while the colour and background of the other, if interchangeable, is not of a past but only of a passing world."[15] In either it would be pointless to expect from a Paterian impressionist a documentary naturalism. And behind Pater is Arnold's scorn for the claims of the "timely."

"The Dan-nan-Ron" illustrates the "World That Is." The heroine's tragedy turns on the archaic rivalry of her cousins and her suitor. They are descended, legend says, from the Sliochd nan Ron (People of the Seal). The cousins use the legend for their own selfish purposes, while the girl mocks such foolish, impossible tales of "the far-back forebears." One cousin is killed by the suitor; another, a flutist of hypnotic power, mysteriously survives. The young wife dies in childbirth; the husband, cursed and pursued by the wraithlike flutist, goes mad and swims to his death among a pack of seals. The story is based on a Hebridean superstition found also, Yeats reported, in the West of Ireland. Narrative description is vivid and terse; the violence is detailed in the simple basic colors of Morris's Pre-Raphaelite manner.

343

There is neither languor nor "spirituality" here. Character is simply and elementally motivated: the husband is good, the wife is strong, determined, loyal, the brothers are selfish.

This, then, is "The World That Is," and the other tales are similar. In them, modern Highland character is conceived in terms of the interplay of elemental motive and legendary force, with periodic outbreaks of atavistic madness. Problems of communication and identity are linked to attitudes toward story and storytelling, to "that strange, obscure, secretive instinct which is also so characteristically Celtic, and often even prevents Gaels of far apart isles, or of different clans, from communicating to each other stories or legends of a peculiarly intimate kind."[16] The seal-man motif signifies an atavistic force against the gray asceticism of conquering Christianity. The seals are enchanted pagans from the north, antisabbatarians with a penchant for Sunday frolicks on the shore. "The Sea-Madness" tells of "a man who keeps a little store in a village by one of the Lochs of Argyll . . . [he is] about fifty, is insignificant, commonplace, in his interests parochial, and on Sundays painful to see in his sleek respectability."[17] Periodically he "is suddenly become what he was, or what some ancestor was, in unremembered days," and he disappears, goes to the shore, strips himself and sits on the rocks, or throws handfuls of water into the air while screaming strange Gaelic words.

The Sin-Eater, the longer legendary tale not included in *Wind and Wave*, shows Macleod the potential novelist at his most economical. The setting on the wild Ross of Mull, the man Neil Ross walking alone from the west on his way back to Iona, the old woman who offers hospitality—all are done in a spare folk realism. Neil has come to curse an old man Adam Blair (a name from Lowland Covenanting history) who convinced Neil's father to break his troth to Neil's mother. Blair, cursed by all, has just died. The old woman recommends the destitute Neil as the sin-eater, the one who, in a ceremony all profess to find idle and obsolete, eats bread and drinks water from the corpse's chest and thus takes on his sins. Neil does the job for two half-crowns, just so that later he may throw off the sins and cause them to pursue the old man's soul in eternity. The narrator offers no critical view of such superstitions, but reports without comment the stages of Neil's ensuing madness. Neil tries in vain to throw the sins off into the sea, becomes fascinated and horrified by the sea, and dies strapped, drowning, to crossed spars. Having used the ritual as a means for personal revenge, he dies mad in an archetypal suicide.

The locality of this bare and impressive novella is essential yet muted, reminding us of what Fiona says at the opening of "The Winged Destiny": "In tragic drama it is authenticity of emotion and not authenticity of episode that matters. It is of lesser moment whether the theme be imaginary, or historically of this country or that, or of this age or of another age."[18] Had the story been expanded into a novel, the particulars of life on Mull and Iona would inevitably have been elaborated, and "facts and descriptions" have nothing to do with "spiritual history." "I have nothing to say of Iona's acreage, or fisheries, or pastures: nothing of how the islanders live. These things are the accidental. There is small difference in simple life anywhere."[19] This is why Fiona's novel-length narratives are so few.

Pharais (1894) is called "a romance of the isles," but its affinities are rather with the prose poem of DeQuincey. It purports to be "a story of alien life," but story is subordinate to vision. It is another tale of the working out of a hereditary curse of madness, filled with traditional Gaelic prayers and incantations and with experiences of The Sight. It is set in the same world as Black's novels—the same steamer *Clansman* calls at the islands, and a professor of medicine must be consulted in Glasgow—and yet the image of island life is of a continuity from time immemorial. A young couple, about to have their first child, learns that the husband has the madness of his fathers and seeks to die. He finally succeeds: such is the plot. Actions are ceremonial; emotions are simple, elemental passions—love, superstitious fear, devotion. Also pervasive is a neopagan Pre-Raphaelite ecstasy at the beauty of the body, the surreal violence of nature, the cold serenity of death, and the nearness of paradise (the title). There is no clear line between the human and the nonhuman, the subjective and objective, and we are in a world of symbolic romantic parable, or what Fiona came to call "legendary morality."

The Mountain Lovers (1895) is longer and better.[20] In scope and mimetic complexity it comes closer to "novel." Sorcha and Alan are the children of old enemies—and old lovers. Sorcha's father, blind old Torcall, loved and then rejected Anabal, Alan's mother, who in anger married another. In lustful fury, Torcall seduced Anabal. Later, Torcall and Anabal feuded and banned the marriage of their children,

Sorcha and Alan. Not caring, Sorcha and Alan live together in woods and caves, in a bliss of natural paganism and innocent sexuality. Their idyll is in extraordinary contrast with the major plot, the tragedy of Anabal and the doom of old Torcall. There is stylistic contrast as well: the children's love is given a vaguely mystical description, while the events of the tragedy are etched in horrible detail.

The events unfold gradually with forceful suspense. The effect depends on the use of innocent and devoted bystanders. Oona passes for Torcall's foster child, and Neil, who receives shelter and food from him, thinks of him vaguely as God or king. Their awarenesses provide narrative perspective, and the tragic meaning rests on their archetypal nature. Oona is like Pearl of Hawthorne's *Scarlet Letter*, a nature sprite, loving, innocent, yet mischievous and free. Neil is equally but differently "natural." He is an ugly misshapen elf-man, alleged to be a changeling, a child of a demon woman and a solitary shepherd. He is said to have no soul and spends much time in lamentation seeking one. Beside these four characters—the vengeful, mad old lovers, and their strange, natural watchers—the lovers themselves are thin and unimportant. Their love means little to the main story, until the birth of the child, Joy, and the serene death of Sorcha. Alan dedicates the child to the Lord, and it is suggested that he and the child and Oona will go away to some visionary far isles where Joy's ministry is to occur. This exile becomes meaningful in the historical context provided by the narrator:

> The tragic end of Anabal Gilchrist, the doom that had fulfilled itself for Torcall Cameron: what was either but a piece with the passing of the ancient language, though none wished it to go; with the exile of the sons, though they would fain live and die where their fathers wooed their mothers; with the coming of strangers, and strange ways, and a new bewildering death-cold spirit, that had no respect for the green graves, and jeered at ancient things and the wisdom of old—strangers whom none had sought, none wished, and whose coming meant the going of even the few hillfolk who prospered in the *machar*, the fertile meadows and pastures along the mountain bases? *It was to be: it would be.* [380]

The child represents a break with the local past, with the old bitterness of anger, jealousy, and sorrow. The locale is poisoned by an ancient sin; providence will wreak its punishment through natural instruments, Oona and the dwarf. Together they represent a grotesque but innocent natural order. Sorcha cannot survive because she is the child of a marriage conceived without love; but Alan can survive—and with him Oona the half-sister to help foster the child Joy.

The term "legendary morality" is fitting. The figures are localized by name and language, by ceremony and superstition. They move in a world of local legend; yet they are elemental, too, archetypal creatures of ecstasy, of natural freedom, love, gloom, and anger. The combination of legendary and archetypal characterizes Macleod's fiction, and its intention is to contribute in a dual way to Celtic renaissance: to awaken the mythic consciousness of Europe by creating new symbols, and to create a Celticism of the spirit, archetypal, unlocalized, as part of a future Anglo-Celticism. The double purpose demands exclusion. The Celticism of legendary morality or spiritual history must be abstracted from cultural particularity. The realities of Highland life are no longer relevant; naturalistic environment has no place. Given such a program, Fiona Macleod could hardly find the form of the novel congenial.

17

Neil Gunn

F or Neil Gunn,* local reality and transcendent meaning had to
be related in a different way. Gunn's short stories contain half-
serious jokes hinting at a loyalty to Fiona Macleod. But there is
a basic difference between them. Gunn's is finally a genius for humor;
his ultimate vision is of a wise humor triumphant over the harshest
realities of modern Highland experience. He is no mere regionalist, but
the realities must be faithfully perceived, for they are the source of the
humor, the wisdom, and the triumph.[1]

The development of his vision can be traced by several paths. First
came *The Grey Coast* (1926) and last, *The Other Landscape* (1954);
the titles suggest his continuing concern with Highland locality. But
the perception of place is no more central in Gunn than the perception
of time, revealed often through the innocent eye of youth. His three

---

*Gunn, Neil M. Born in 1891, in Dunbeath, Caithness, and died in 1973 in Inver-
ness. The son of a Caithness fishing captain, he entered the civil service in his
teens, and thereafter served for thirty years, most of that time as excise inspector
of distilleries in the Highlands and Islands (see his *Whisky and Scotland*, 1935,
contributed to Gibbon's "Voice of Scotland" series). He resigned in 1937, encouraged by the reception of his sixth novel, *Highland River* (awarded the Black
Memorial Prize), to become a full-time writer. He began as a short story writer: see
the collections *Hidden Doors* (1929) and *The White Hour* (1950). He published
several short plays and wrote many articles (uncollected) for Glasgow newspapers.
His meditative nature essays are collected in *Highland Pack* (1949); his autobiographical books are *Off in a Boat* (1938) and *The Atom of Delight* (1956).

novels of Highland boyhood are *Morning Tide* (1930), *Highland River* (1937), and *Young Art and Old Hector* (1942); the boy ages in *The Serpent* (1943) and *The Drinking Well* (1946). A less personal dimension of time has been seen already in *Butcher's Broom* (1934), and Gunn's sense of history can be further articulated through *Sun Circle* (1933) and *The Silver Darlings* (1941). In a sense, these are all "early Gunn." With the mythic antiutopia, *The Green Isle of the Great Deep* (1944), Gunn's themes were expanded and displaced into urgencies of the mid-twentieth-century world. They are anticipated in *Wild Geese Overhead* (1939), a first novel of physical and intellectual violence in a modern urban setting. Later variants of this fiction of violence appear in *The Shadow* (1948) and *Bloodhunt* (1952), and in two novels using popular suspense motifs, *The Key of the Chest* (1945) and *The Lost Chart* (1949). But Gunn's ultimate form emerged in *The Silver Bough* (1948), *The Well at the World's End* (1951), and *The Other Landscape* (1954). It is the aging modern intellectual's quest for his own renewal, and it takes him into primordial place and atavistic time. Enigmas bewilder him onto what Gunn, growingly influenced by Eastern thought, would call "The Way"; humor nudges him onto an "other landscape."

The immediate landscape predominates in *The Grey Coast, The Lost Glen* (1932), and *Second Sight* (1940). Here the contemporary Highlands are perceived as a place of severe economic depression and depopulation, of the social decay and bitterness attendant on the disappearance of old life-giving rhythms. *The Lost Glen* sums up best:

> The land was too old. Scarred and silent, it was settling down into decay. The burden of its story had become too great to carry . . . It was not that the spirit was dead but that it had passed. There was no longer any meaning in living there . . . He hid his mind in what had been friendly and fresh and full of labour and leisure and happiness; the old music, the games, the fierce passions, the fights, the stir, the excitement, the loneliness, the grey mists, the sun, the sea; life centred on itself, young life fierce or glowing or dreamy, but life, with belief in its time and place. [58, 60]

This is the lost reality of Highland place. All three novels focus on intricate character groupings, individualized in roles at once culturally representative and archetypal. Each relationship is in a state of silent spiritual conflict; each is a power struggle for selfhood and mastery. The three climaxes are plotted on murders, accidental deaths, or triumphant self-destructions; the violences evolve from sexual threat, socioeconomic conflict, and ideological warfare—the three are closely interrelated in Gunn's novels.

The conflicts take several forms. In *The Grey Coast* there are four characters: Maggie, niece and housekeeper on the croft of her uncle "ould Jeems," is loved quietly and hopelessly by young and desperately poor fisherman Ivor Cormack, and lusted after by Donald Tait of Tullach Farm, a despotic small landowner. Tullach maintains his power by helping keep up Jeems's poor croft, not knowing that Jeems, sly old sailor, has hidden gold. The plot is the quiet, tense development of these relationships against the domestic rhythms of a hard croft life. The book's technical triumph is the rendition of Maggie's consciousness. But the focus of meaning is Jeems: his sly playing with Tullach, his oblique pimping for his unwilling niece, his defiant poaching on Tullach's land, his decision to side with youth against middle-aged avarice by willing his gold to Maggie and robbing Tullach of his power. The conflict between Jeems and Tullach is a subtle Highland contest of words and wits, and it suits its locale on the gray coast of Caithness. This is the place where sea and land meet in a "fierce mating." Place and its conflict are eternal. All four characters come at last to see themselves as primordial figures of legend; yet they remain fully psychologized figures on a naturalistic landscape, young lovers and their aged collaborator fighting for a little life against the nay-saying Tullachs.

Such struggles of person and place culminate in moments of vision at once atavistic and portentous. The landscape reacts with the growth of inward vision to produce them. The mind "of its own inscrutable volition pursues hidden ways of dream and thought," far beneath the gray surface of daily croft life. "And of all places, such a grey strip of crofting coast, flanked seaward by great cliffs, cliffs 'flawed' as in a half-sardonic humour of their Creator to permit of the fishing creek, was surely of this duality of the mind, whereby the colourless, normal life becomes at once a record of the stolidly obvious and of the dream-like unknown" (14). Here is the genesis of that "other landscape" on which, throughout Gunn's fiction, essential roles and actions are played out.

The Lost Glen is less successful. In shifting his dramatic center from the simple croft girl Maggie to the young Highlander returning disgraced from his university, Gunn loses the naturalistic intensity of the first novel. But the device was necessary. To explore the survival of

Highland civilization from a sophisticated modern point of view he used the returned native or the educated stranger. *The Lost Glen* uses the alienated native (as *The Serpent* and *The Drinking Well* are to use him); *Second Sight* (like the late novels) uses the sympathetic stranger. But the conflict recalls *The Grey Coast:* a fusion of sexual, social and ideological struggle. The destructive menace is Colonel Hicks, retired Indian soldier, hunting and living where he can luxuriate in power on a small income and "expose" the lazy deviousness of the locals. His compassionate, romantic niece sees in him what we shall recognize as Gunn's essential vision of evil: a shadow "coming between one and the sweet freedom of life . . . tinging things, taunting them, in spite of one-self. It was bigger than that; in some way it transcended the personal altogether; as if it were not merely her uncle's mind, but an altogether bigger mind, the mind of a world . . . a sort of human motley in the sunlight; grotesque. Yet though one might use words like these, one wasn't defining the violence itself; for it was no more than a shadow on thought at best, an insidious destruction of humour, a corrosive taint" (257). The final response to such a shadow will be that of archaic comedy, but only bitter, destructive irony seems available to the young gillie Ewen.

Disgraced as a student, responsible for his father's drowning, fading into "this bloody menial service" of the gillie Ewen has replaced his earlier spiritual ardor with "terrible and blasting irony." He is the hero as tragic young "Gael," yet his humor and ironic honesty almost save him for us. When he is drunk he sees "that the Colonel and himself were chance figures in a drama that affected the very earth under his feet. Being chance figures, they did not matter—were indeed figures of melodrama. But none the less did the earth await the outcome of their secret strife, as if they stood for an ultimate conquest or defeat" (110). Their strife reaches a violent outcome when the arrogant, hysterical colonel gives way to his lust and tries to rape the crofter's daughter Ewen loves. Ewen procrastinates, brooding like Hamlet—"his spirit as the spirit of his people" (337-338). He resolves not to murder, but ac-cident leads to a confrontation; and having throttled the colonel and tumbled him over a cliff, he sets forth to his own death at the scene of his father's drowning. This is tragedy marred by melodrama.

What, then, does the "loss" of the title mean? The "lost glen," a pibroch by Ewen's friend, commemorates the myth of a glen "innocent of the human being," and for Ewen it recalls the lost locus of innocence which "the leaders of humanity had all searched back for." Is not the loss, then, the "lost glen" of Ewen's people? The book's integrity hinges on the question of the relation of these losses to two kinds of innocence: one glen known always in vision, the other in time and place on this old land now given over to "the degradation of poverty in a world where money was the supreme power."

In *Second Sight* (1940), the local setting remains the same, but the terms of the struggle have been redefined. The browbeaten gillie is the victim of a vacationing hunter whose arrogance is intellectual, whose destructiveness is a will to "analyze" and invalidate all such archaic modes of experience as "second sight." The hunter's spiritual adversary Harry, with whom he competes for the killing of a legendary deer, is acquiring his own form of second sight, "as if the scales had come off your eyes." As one antagonist self-destructively loses himself, the other finds himself in a renewal of vision and finds love. The coming of vision and love is a freeing of the true self—Gunn would later call it the second self—from all the menacing forces of modern intelligence. The climax for Harry is a moment of vision on the mountain top when the mist lifts; for the destroyer, it is a moment when brutal triumph turns into self-disintegration. *Second Sight* introduces the linked themes and motifs of Gunn's later fiction: the imperative of renewed vision, the translation of traditional superstition into an experience of self-transcendence. Place becomes the "other landscape" of the hunt, where the ethic and ceremony of hunter and hunted are eternal and the hunt is personal and sexual as well as social and cultural. Evil, unchanged in its original character, is incarnate in the pseudo-scientism of the self-destructive analytic intelligence. The working out of evil is traced superficially on the level of popular mystery. The urbane protagonist is in need of a restorative withdrawal into the archaism of boyhood or "primitive" vision.

The achievement of a plausible character for the boy-visionary himself is difficult. But the three early novels of boyhood remain for many readers Gunn's most admirable: *Morning Tide* (1930), *Highland River* (1937), and *Young Art and Old Hector* (1942). Hugh, Kenn, and Art are as different as the books they dominate. But all are shy, loyal, fiercely proud, defiant in their instinct for freedom and self-preservation, secretive, violently adventurous, and intensely aware of places and persons in their immediate surroundings. *Morning Tide* is an impressionistic account of "the boy's" proud and loving discoveries of archetypal domesticities and rivalries: red sister and dark sister, men and women ("like a group caught in a gray dawn of history, or legend, their separateness from the men fateful and eternal"), his mother the earth and his father the sea. The first of three parts is his discovery of his father, the fishing captain, climaxing with the storm and his father's triumph of seamanship. The second is his struggle with the loving repression of his mother, ending in the tragic economic necessity of his brother's departure. In the third, with his father away and his brother gone, with his sisters in sexual danger and his mother dangerously ill, he learns the power and exhilaration of his own manhood, the inevitabilities of fear and flight and death. In each he is "the boy's eyes," opening in wonder, and the boy's passions in response, concrete and archetypal, instinctively delicate: "All that had happened throughout the evening flashed through Hugh's mind, not so much in vivid images as in a vivid impressionism" (65). His essential response is not gloomy introspection, but rather the ecstasy that breaks upon moments of sheer unreflective delight. The three parts have the same ending: a joy in the triumphant courage of life consummated by the urge to be "off and away":

> Hugh ran. Tears were streaming down his face . . . red ecstasy of the dawn! [111]

> A flush of happiness bathed his heart. His head turned quick as a hawk's. He started running. [208]

> Unless he went to the woods—for an offering? His head turned. And all at once he started running, his body light and fleet, his bare legs twinkling across the fields of the dawn. [287]

The boy Kenn of *Highland River* is different. Kenn the man, mathematician, physicist, wounded and gassed veteran of World War I, is central. The boy is the locus of remembered experiences whose lasting significance the man sets out to discover. Place and time are the same as in *Morning Tide*, but different types of hero and plot make for different symbolic localities. The "morning tide" is the first timeless phase in the boy's awakening self-consciousness, in a pattern of daily time without historic dimension. Archetype and individual remain so close that the locality of place transcends itself. Kenn's Highland River is from the outset archetypal. The book's topic is the problem of the relation between specific boy and specific river. This relation has become the ground of the man's entire experience, indestructible "through his boyhood approaches," and carried over "to every other environment in life."

Individuality begins in a relation between person and place that evolves so as to generate self-transcendence in both: the place reveals an "other landscape," the person discovers a "second self," and the two fuse in transcendent vision. No mystical vagueness is tolerated; precise knowledge complements the sense of wonder, as when Kenn looks at the salmon pool and *knows* that the epic capture of the fish happened there. The search moves always toward greater and greater explicitness: "Kenn has an urge to be explicit, even to labour what is infinitely elusive, because the farther he goes towards the source of his river the more he feels there is in this very elusiveness the significance he would like to hold." This urge gives the book its form, as difficult as *Morning Tide* is simple. The reconstructive intelligence is always in control of design, choosing and interweaving the immediate perceptions of the boy with the later experiences and reflections of student, scientist, and soldier. But the reconstructive intelligence is conscious, too, of the pitfalls of its own imagination. The two worlds of person and past, person and place, boy and river, must interpenetrate without violating each other's integrity: "Kenn is sensitive to false symbolism here . . . All that has happened is that in the acuteness of his vision the inessentials have faded out. The figure may be ageless, but it is a living figure to whom in time past his erratic emotions were directed: who once, in a bitter cold, took Kenn's hands and warmed them in his hair" (55). The archetypal imagination must be austerely precise, fixed in the sensory reality of original apprehension. Yet it must seek an image of transcendent significance. As in *The Grey Coast*, the mode of vision in which place and time are transcended must be traced back to the place that produced it—for only back there is the "other landscape" to be found.

The transition from Kenn to *Young Art and Old Hector* is a shift of setting, as well as a sharp change in mode and form to gnomic comedy and dramatic episode. The river is now a far away boundary between here and "the world beyond." The narrator simply presents scenes and sensations, while the comments come from the wondrously devious and whimsically wise Old Hector. The method is as dramatic as the method of *Highland River* is meditative or the method of *Morning Tide* impressionistic. The book began as a series of periodical sketches, freeing the author from more ambitious structural ideas. The episodes center on the relationship of a boy and a neighbor, a relationship beyond the home; Art is initiated into a community, a human locale, rather than into a family or a natural setting. The transferral of wisdom from Hector to Art defines the place that has produced and preserved that wisdom. Each new stage of illumination is an immediate experience for the boy and an emblem of life for the old man; reality and myth are fused. The fitting climax comes when at long last Hector takes Art to the river.

Art has long been frustrated in his desire to visit that far-off "dark stranger of his dreams." When Hector on his own farewell journey takes him there, it is to discover that he must go home again, that he *has* his place, that in fact he is taking Hector's place: so ends the process of transferral and traditional inheritance. Here at the river the little world ends and the great one begins. The littleness and the wisdom of this world are now to be justified together. Art asks Hector whether he is sorry now, "at the end of the day," that he never left this place.

> "Well, if I had gone away, I wouldn't have been here walking with you, for one thing. And for another, I like to be here. You see, I know every corner of this land, every little burn and stream, and even the boulders in the stream. And I know the moors and every lochan on them. And I know the hills, and the passes, and the ruins, and I know of things that happened here on our land long long ago, and men who are long dead I knew, and women. I knew them all . . . It's not the size of the knowing that matters, I think," said Old Hector, "it's the kind of the knowing. If, when you know a thing, it warms your heart, then it's a friendly knowing and worth the having." [250]

The place is a small coastal crofting community "in the West"; nearby, the Clash, now forbidden land, is the real place in the history of these people, but the Clearances ended that. But time and place are remarkably free of the domestic particulars that localize *Morning Tide* and *Highland River*. What matters is wisdom, and wisdom is a gnomic, oblique, loving humor for which "nowhere" and "somewhere," "going" and "coming" are more than anything the counters of playful paradox. Art is a dramatic and enigmatic center in the process of acquiring wisdom and place, growing into the heroic boy, the force of anarchic and defiant innocence that he would become in *The Green Isle of the Great Deep*. The later book is in some respects Gunn's most important, but the earlier has something more precious; and in the simplicity of its scenic form, its understated style, and its comic vision, it is matchless among Gunn's books.

Before *The Green Isle* (1944) came *The Serpent* (1943) and not long after it *The Drinking Well* (1946), two ambitious extensions of Highland boyhood into critiques of Highland culture and economy. Tom the philosopher and Iain Cattanach are young men from Highland villages who go away, are educated into the early twentieth-century world, and return, one a disgrace and the other a philosophical rebel. Tom of *The Serpent* is the "New Man" as agnostic intellectual; Iain of *Drinking Well* is the social rebel, eventually a new breed of Highland farmer. Each engages in bitter conflict with an orthodox father; each is a youth at a certain moment in history. Yet, as both titles suggest, each must go beyond history to find the sources of life.

The Serpent begins and ends with the death of its hero, "a death so startling that deep in the mind of the countryside the old menacing images would stir and lift their dark heads" (5). The old man is off for a sunny climb up a hill near his village. His expanding retrospects are punctuated by climbs and rests—the method of Lewis Grassic Gibbon's trilogy. He is moving toward the height from which humans moving slowly at crofting tasks give "the illusion of an inner meaning or design that never changed." He is climbing back to old ways exiled by the Clearances, to a view of the past that contradicts his own radically progressive attitudes. Up on the deserted moor he rests in a state of blissful transcendence, an adder slips from the heather stalks, he feels its touch, and dies. His friend the young shepherd finds him, picks him up, "Whereupon a serpent of monstrous length issued, as it seemed, out of the left arm, out of the very hand . . . The shepherd turned and ran, and in the first few steps he lived through those years of his youth, the impressionable years of prophecy and curse, with the Serpent that would devour the atheist who had killed his own father" (256).

Two serpents have warred in Tom. He had been called back from the exhilarating scepticism of late Victorian Glasgow as a young man when his father was disabled. The conflict between them leads up to a violent confrontation when the thundering elder denounces Tom for having delivered himself to the serpent. The dying father, the "grey face, the grey beard, the blazing eyes . . . The power of the father created in the image of God. The tribal power," lifts a staff to chastise his blasphemous son, and pitches forward dead. The elder was partly right. The father-son conflict is so carefully, movingly managed as to cause a difficult division of feelings in the reader, for he sees that Tom has delivered himself to a serpent, and that it will take another to free him. Tom's sceptical modernity has become a cunning destructiveness, a serpent of intellectual negation. The serpent of wisdom is the counterforce. The tragedies that touch Tom occur on a landscape where no superficial intellectual freedom can be effectual. His intellectuality belongs to specific decades, and throughout the narrative he is associated with clocks and clock-time. Yet his association with timeless tragedies of love and domestic conflict, and with the warfare of the serpents, suggests the archaic timelessness of his real struggle.

Tom is a sceptic of the turn of the twentieth century. Iain Cattanach is the young man *entre deux guerres* debating political and economic issues on the future of the Highlands. His return from the city, like Tom's, brings on conflict with his father, carries him through an ordeal of personal redemption, and ends in the same archaic love of the land that prevails at Tom's death. *The Drinking Well* suffers from discursive overabundance and arbitrary symbolic design. Yet it has splendid panoramas unmatched in better novels: the brawl in an Edinburgh law office, the drunken visionary night walk up the Royal Mile, the vivid ordeal of Iain's shepherding over a Grampian pass in an early spring snowstorm. Visions of city and of pastoral land vie for reality. The city is history. The land of the sheep and the snow is nonhistoric, and it is by love of the land that Iain is haunted and saved. The title indicates the symbolic place where that love is renewed. The well of the "mad" old woman appears empty; yet the emptiness is only an optical illusion—the well is never really dry. Such is the love of the land. And Iain, having rationalized that love, having been exonerated from charges of cowardice and reconciled with his father, gets his girl and his experimental farm. The future of the Highlands is to be in hands such as his. The novel is the fullest text of Gunn's ideas of modern Highland history.

Sun Circle (1933) and *The Silver Darlings* (1941) are historical novels in the more usual sense. Yet both end their accounts of historic convulsion with comic affirmations of life and the delight at its center: "For there is a secret here that neither the lovely dead nor the swift gods know. It is the immortality of life, the young heart against the mother heart, and its music sets a man brooding or walking in defiance, and the memory of it can in a lonely place make him shout with defiance and laugh, for he knows the challenge of his own creation against the immortality of the jealous gods" (*Sun Circle*, 234). The title might apply to both books, as to other Gunn novels. Deriving from an archaic charm, "sun circle" denotes for Gunn the principle of personal wholeness and self-preservation. "As the Sun put a circle round the earth and all that it contained, so a man by his vision put a circle round himself. At the centre of this circle his spirit sat, and at the centre of his spirit was a serenity for ever watchful. Sometimes the watchfulness gave an edged joy in holding at bay the demons and even the vengeful lesser gods, and sometimes it merged with the Sun's light into pure timeless joy" (365-366). To be divided within, to disintegrate in spirit, is to surrender to darkness—such is the wisdom acquired by two rival leaders, Haakon the Viking and Aniel the Celt. The novel is so concerned with the moral and political education of the young leaders that it is rich in instruction and hence the novel in which a "philosophy of life" is most fully expounded. It is philosophical romance rather than novel. It was written at a time when novelists, excited by new developments in primitive anthropology, experimented with archaic psychology in pre-Christian settings. The temptation to mingle imaginative psychology with a highly conceptualized "primitivism" is evident in most, and *Sun Circle* is no exception. It is, for Gunn, too, a unique opportunity to expound a historical prophecy of the Celt. It represents the defeat of an ancient Celtic people by Norseman and Christian, and does so with the schematic character groupings and counterpoints of romance. The protagonist is a young druid who must learn his vocation as priestly artist. He must accept the spiritual destiny of his people as nonhistoric, yet as the permanent ground of all creeds and powers. History for the Celt is a legend irrelevant to Celtic destiny.

Butcher's Broom (1934), by virtue of its specific historical subject, is not so free to mythologize history. *The Silver Darlings* (1941) is quite different; it is Gunn's masterpiece of regional history and one of his finest books. He resists the temptation to make a "romance of the herring industry in the Moray Firth," in the manner of Neil Paterson's *Behold Thy Daughter* or the Clydeside romances of George Blake. The book does include enough to please such tastes: the rise of prosperous communities on the shores of the Firth, the first shocks to the new prosperity, the plague, the colorful activities of fisherman and curer, the fishing voyages round Cape Wrath. But the novel remains primarily one of more essential and personal dilemmas. Evolving human relations, while illustrative parts of the regional "epic," are free of the romance schematism in *Sun Circle* and the forcing of symbol in *Butcher's Broom*.

From Helmsdale, Catrine's young husband is carried off by a press gang. Catrine envisions him dead, and she walks north to "Dunster" (evidently Dunbeath, Gunn's birthplace, scene of *Morning Tide*, *Highland River*, and *Sun Circle*), where she lives as Kirsty Mackay's adopted daughter and heir. Here, in the byre, her son Finn is born. The young widowed mother's painful growth into her tragic role is the first narrative center. Then comes a suitor Roddie Sinclair, prosperous Dunster fishing captain; and the unfolding world of herring fishing centers on the growth of Finn, his rivalry with Roddie for his mother, his heroic exploits on Roddie's boat, his achievement of manhood. Narrative setpieces of suspense and excitement—the fight with the press gang, the stormswept trip around Cape Wrath, the drunken brawl in Stornaway, Finn's heroic climb up the precipice—abound; yet they alternate with delicate episodes in the world of mother and son. Catrine, for all her tragic role as the bereaved woman, is as pro-foundly individualized a female character as any in all Gunn's books. Roddie, the menacing but heroic fisherman, is as fine a male figure as Gunn has drawn (it is no accident that the book is dedicated to the memory of his father). Finn is brother to Hugh and Art, with the additional dimensions given by his representative role in a regional history and, paradoxically, by the vocation of traditional storyteller, which lifts his most vivid adventures out of historic time and sets them in the perspective of heroic legend.

He is no mythic or legendary Finn; his individuality is precious to him. Yet this individuality depends for its completion on his becoming legendary in his own eyes. Through legend the historic self survives and yet transcends itself, translating its matter of fact into something "eternally right, like the movement of a figure through the mesh of fate in one of Hector's old stories, or like a swan on the Irish sea in the legend by Finn-son-of-Angus" (549). To this other Finn, an old story-teller on North Uist, he first tells of his fantastic climb up the Flannan precipice. Only as Finn begins his story, as he learns "the power of the story-teller," does its meaning become clear. The old Finn's praise defines the thematic importance of storytelling (and describes Gunn's own ideal of narrative art):

You told the story well. You brought us into the far deeps of the sea and we were lost with you in the Beyond where no land is, only wind and wave and the howling of the darkness. You kept us in suspense on the cliffs, and you had some art in the way you referred to our familiars of the other world before you told of the figure of the man you felt by the little stone house. There you saw no-one and you were anxious to make this clear, smiling at your fancy. It was well enough done. It was all well done. It was done, too, with the humour that is the play of drift on the wave. And you were modest. Yet—all that is only a little—you had something more, my hero, something you will not know—until you look at it through your eyes, when they are as old as mine. (540)

By the power of the storyteller, Finn separates himself from his mother, reconciles himself to a stepfather, and becomes himself. Only the ultimate comic invasion of life itself can touch him, and in the final chapter, the salutary conquest is imminent. Finn, his manhood achieved, hears love and life coming for him, "the hunters in the primordial humour . . . closing in"; life, a humorous hunter, invades his circle. A myth of triumphant individuality prevails over a novel of regional history.

Finn belongs with Young Art, whose two stories follow his, and who also triumphs through becoming legendary. But this happens in a very different book, one that sets the direction for Gunn's later fiction as surely as *The Silver Darlings* recapitulates the earlier novels. The new challenge came, Gunn recalls, in Naomi Mitchison's reaction to *Young Art and Old Hector*: wasn't this escapism? was his art restricted to the reinterpretation of Highland values? could he cope in the forties with the growing complexity and murderousness of the modern world? The challenge was taken up in the "antiutopian" parable, *The Green Isle of the Great Deep*. Troubled by reports of totalitarian brainwashing, Gunn decided to send river-bound Art and Hector by accident to a legendary Celtic version of Huxley's *Brave New World*. The wise whimsy of earlier Art-Hector episodes is now joined with Edenic myth and totalitarian nightmare.

Tangling with a salmon in a pool, Art and Hector fall through the pool's bottom into a collective dream. Together they become utopian voyagers. The "strangeness" of discovery is essential to the voyager's ambivalent vision of paradise; Hector becomes a deeply troubled "stranger in the Perfect Place" as the horror dawns on him. He is weak and becomes a hopeless "insider," and in his capitulation to the behav-

ioral engineers, we see a paralysis of will analogous to the somatose
infantilism of *Brave New World*. In his interview with the Dostoev-
skian Questioner, Hector finds that there is little interest in his sins but
much curiosity about his happinesses. The "atomic psychologists" of
antiutopia benignly remove the anarchic factor from man's spirit. A
nonphysical violence lays the self bare in the "exciting game of teasing
the human mind into its strands, of combing the strands, and leaving
them knotless and gleaming and smooth over one's arm or the back of
a chair" (78). It is "all being done for the best," Hector concedes, in the
true antiutopian pathos.

Art reacts differently. Like Finn, his essence as young hero is to
resist with devious fury or dumb flight any threat to his intact self.
Repeatedly he escapes the authorities until his power of flight is
rumored to be a force of legendary magic. The legend of Art reaches
an absentee God, and like the Good Landlord hearing of his evil factor, like Shakespeare's "duke of dark corners," God returns to paradise and returns paradise to itself. The hunted, Art and Hector, become the hunters, the ultimate threat to the urbane managers, who
have been so intrigued by the indestructible bond between old man
and boy. "An interesting form of atavism," they call it; it is too
natural or primordial a loyalty for them ever to ferret out.

One thinks of Zamiatin's naked tribes beyond the wall, of Orwell's
"proles," of Huxley's savages—and the kinship raises a question.[2]
Huxley concluded that *Brave New World* had failed to offer reasonable alternatives. His criterion recalls the humanistic origins of utopianism. Antiutopian fiction has repudiated not just utopian visions in
particular, but utopianism itself, thus rationalizing the status quo and
denying even hypothetical existence to rational alternatives.[3] Anti-
Christ alone is an able dialectician, and the good man, whether Christ
or Billy Budd, can reply only with a stutter or a silent kiss. Has Gunn
offered only a choice between the rigid pseudo-intellectualism of the
Questioner and the sullen evasiveness of a primitive poacher? Hector
is a far wiser norm than this.

But it is the folly of the misguided utopian Questioner that is central
to true antiutopian satire. However diabolical his delusion, the utopian planner is a fool. In contemporary antiutopia only the diabolism
remains, and the planner has become the evil center of a tragic vision.
"A utopia," says Richard Gerber of *1984*, "cannot bear such tragedy.
A utopian tragedy tends to be hysterical or sentimental."[4] *The Green*

Isle avoids both. It affirms the comic direction of Gunn's fiction, returning to the comic or satiric origin of antiutopianism. The Managers, ultimately foolish rather than evil, reach their limits when God baffles his vicegerents at their own game of dialogue, not because they are dialecticians, but because they are nothing more. Divinity reconquers knowledge with wisdom and magic. It was Huxley who made a title of the *Tempest* tag, but it is Gunn's utopian fable that, like Shakespeare's play, transcends the irony of Miranda's naiveté with the divine comedy of a triumphant innocence in an anti-antiutopia both brave and new.

Here, then, are the lineaments of Gunn's mature vision, a comic view of life beyond the tragedy of history, surviving in the indestructible whimsy of wise age and fugitive youth. The issues of escapism are seriously broached here, as are the related issues of primitivism, and Gunn discriminates true escapisms and primitivisms from false ones. These are to be the themes and attitudes of his later novels. But to trace them, we need to go back a bit first.

After *Highland River* (1937), his most sophisticated treatment of Highland boyhood, Gunn turned in *Wild Geese Overhead* (1939) to a very different world and recounted a city reporter's efforts to validate his escapist impulses and intuitions amid the grimmest facts of modern urban life. The novel is quite close to its predecessor, specifically in its unifying concern with a momentary experience of transcendence. The sudden struggle with the great salmon has become the sudden lifting apprehension of "wild geese overhead." Will, the aptly named hero, seeks to assess and recapture a single moment of visionary delight, to measure that moment against urban violence and despair, to understand why modern intellectuals find such menace and betrayal in the delight of such moments, and to triumph over "those who took life's central purpose of delight and smothered it, out of fear and self-importance and egotism, and the devil's thrill of power over others" (75).

His chief antagonist is the Mephistophilian figure we have seen already in the caustic destroyer of *Second Sight* and the Managers of the Green Isle. Yet Will and his enemy are friends, drawn to each other, hunter to hunted; each is the other's shadow self. Will's simplest relationships all belong to this spiritual battle, and he is imbued with his creator's archetypal vision: "Out of humanity in the reaches of time appear figures like Christ the saviour, Nero the destroyer . . . In every little circle, in every village, town, country, walked the individual saviour, the individual destroyer" (266). He has the double vision of the "other landscape" as well. What makes everything come "rounded and alive, with depth and, above all, an extraordinary amount of light" is a stereoptical habit. He sees the city as the remembered stereopticon of his boyhood saw everything, in "an oddly double way: the actual scene itself and the same scene as part of the aerial vision of the city" (167), giving a deeper, more detached and impersonal interest. In true vision, "the ego [is] lost in the calm uprising of the second self, the deeper self, into conscious freedom" (187). Here is the earliest statement of Gunn's ultimate theme.

Such a novel can have only limited plot value. In the novels of 1937-1940 (*Highland River, Wild Geese Overhead, Second Sight*), Gunn was too preoccupied with finding his modern themes, probing escapist impulses or experiences for their archetypal truth, to attend much to values of narrative pattern. After *The Green Isle*, he found the plot conventions that would best serve these serious purposes. We can see the change in a later novel of the modern city: *The Lost Chart* (1949).

The title, like *The Key of the Chest* (1945), suggests the structural idea: the dangerous quest for a lost paradigm or "key." Leisurely, meditative elaboration of theme (as in *Wild Geese*) is replaced by a plot of suspenseful action. The urban setting is an unnamed Glasgow. The hero, a young shipping clerk, is involved with Highlanders carrying on Fifth Column activities in the Cold War. The plot turns obsessively on time: the time is a day of crisis, and the times pervade thought and feeling, suggesting that another dark age is coming. The question of escape arises with the horrible new urgency of Cold War crisis. The "lost chart," stolen from Dermot and recovered in an exciting battle in a sea-loch, is a map of sea approaches to Cladday, a remote, serene Hebridean island. Its location makes it of strategic military importance, but for Dermot it is a pocket of salvageable humanity where life may reassemble when the missiles hit the city.

Meanwhile, "behind the talk where the real meanings and animosities stalked around," the issue is more than political. The hunt becomes a hunt for a mental chart of "another landscape," the one humanity has lost, the chart that is the power of vision. Humanity must "go back" to find that chart, and the book becomes a discrimination between "the two kinds of regress," the "crawling back" of the totalitarian and the creative atavism of the artist. The painter and the traditional singer are the true imagemakers in a world seeking imaginative renewal. It is the painter who defines the test: "There cannot be a regress when you're searching for light." Indeed, he sounds the triumphant comic theme of all the later novels: "The darkness creates drama ready-made for men; but man has to create his own drama of the light" (178). To do so is to go back for the way that has been lost, and to go back is to find oneself on another landscape. Such is the "drama of the light" enacted on the "other landscape" of Gunn's post-World War II novels.

Three of the novels express the murderousness of the modern world in acts of individual murder and their impact on traditional Highland community. For Gunn, as for Marlow in *Heart of Darkness*, "the meaning of an episode was not inside like a kernel but outside, enveloping the tale which brought it out." The episode of *The Key of the Chest* (1945) is the death by strangulation of a Swedish seaman during his rescue from a sinking freighter. His rescuer, Charlie, is suspected of his murder; Charlie's brutish brother, Douglas, a shepherd, is suspected of stealing money from his chest. Like other Gunn protagonists, Charlie and Douglas live physically and morally on the outskirts of their community. They are in longstanding conflict with the minister, a spiritual despot on whom life has taken its revenge by awakening a love for his daughter both incestuous and idolatrous. Charlie is his rival; the minister sacrifices his whole position in a death hunt to drive the brothers to destruction. The lovers are rescued and the minister is chastened. The "key" is in the mysterious bond of the brothers, reflecting in turn the brotherhood of the sea, and echoing the brotherhood of Cain and Abel. Both brothers are accused of wearing the mark of Cain. The novel explores the problem of Cain's query: how *can* one be one's brother's keeper? Ironically the Cain-like Douglas supplies the answer: by instinctively knowing how to defy the destructive forces that threaten his brother. Brotherhood requires a most delicate tact, a respect for individuality. This is the "key." This is Gunn's deepening vision of the absolute spiritual contrast between traditional community and totalitarian collectivity.

The structure of the book is complicated, its image of community large, its centers of consciousness numerous. The doctor, a focal figure of humane concern in the community, serves well as a center. Intellectual yet urgently practical, he is bound to his people by instinctual ties yet drawn to sophisticated outsiders such as the energetic young hunting laird Michael Sandeman and his pedantic but kindly guest Gwynn. Gwynn's hunt for the key to modern "primitivism" in art has brought him to the traditional community and made him a Gunn spokesman. Sandeman and Gwynn engage in lengthy dialogues; the doctor retreats into silence from their aggressive curiosity and rush of words. The key of the chest is to be found not in words, but in vision and brotherhood. The novel is Gunn's most ambitious fusion of narrative and ideological complexity.

The title of *The Shadow* (1948) refers to the shadow cast upon a Highland village by the robbery and murder of an old hermit. It happens during the convalescence of a young woman who has had a nervous collapse during the London Blitz and has come to her aunt's Highland farm for peace and rest, only to have "the living figure of destruction . . . come away from the city where he had been impersonal and many-shaped, shapes flying across the sky, come at last to the country, to the quiet countryside" (26). The result is the second of the novel's three parts—"Relapse." The third part, "Recovery," is the outcome of a complex inner war—her own "drama of the light"—and of an outer war among friends and lovers, who claim her spirit on behalf of their conflicting ideas of her illness and of the world illness it embodies. Aunt Pheemie, watching her struggle, comes to this remarkable vision: "The child, wandering up through the daylight fields, trying to clean the shadow from the world . . . The thistledown, the soft eager balls, seeds on the wing—changing into the grey steady eyes, the searching eyes of the policeman. Changing, in his turn, into the youth with the tommygun on his knees and the cigarette in his mouth, while love in its naked family waited in the trench; he mowed them down as a pernicious corn" (207). Nan's lover Ranald, descendent of the Green Isle Managers, is one of Gunn's intellectual destroyers. In argument he "gets pale . . . and logical in a remorseless way." He enjoys tearing his opponent's "mind into small bits." But the point of the book—perhaps of all the later novels—is that the Ranalds must be saved, not defeated; through the recovery of the Nans, they must be made whole.

Gunn has by now become the anti-Freudian so visible in his autobiography, *The Atom of Delight* (1956). He is no Lawrentian anti-intellectualist either, though the echoes of Lawrence are important. In the relations of Nan and Ranald, the menace of spiritual disintegration is linked to illicit sexuality. The destroyers of Gunn's fiction wear an aura of sexual menace because they are dividers of spiritual wholeness. In drawing his image of wholeness, Gunn frequently uses the word "intact" and recalls the primitive fear of "touching." Wholeness demands a kind of spiritual chastity. Self-transcendence is never the surrender of self to the forces of "blood" or darkness. Wisdom is never to be gained by an abdication of reason. Nan's cry sums it up: "We have to rescue the intellect from the destroyers. They have turned it into death rays, and it should be the sun" (42). The destroyers pervert reason into the shadow of itself: "Reason's noise. One who makes too much noise will never see a fawn in a glen. But there are fawns in glens."⁵ To save reason from itself, then, is "not to disparage reason or intellect and opt wholly for the dark gods, the irrational flesh." Like Thomas Mann, Gunn moves only experimentally among the anti-intellectuals.

Seeking to recover an instinct for life, Nan is the hunted animal, fleeing from violence, but also from the disintegrative rationalism that labels her as neurotic. Her flight carries her too far, and she gives an instinctive, perilous allegiance to one she thinks the murderer, the strange young hunter in the woods, appropriately named Adam. But she derides the talk that "Nan is going all D. H. Lawrence" (42). She must work her way through the allegiance; Adam and Ranald must fight, and their fight is the clash of the instinctual man with the analytic utopian. No one wins. Adam slips into the river, but survives. Ranald goes back to Nan exhilarated by a rare surrender to instinct. No one can win this fight; Nan cannot choose Adam but must work for Ranald's redemption.

Bloodhunt (1952) as narrative is simpler than *The Key* and *The Shadow*, but carries the same symbolic meaning. A likeable young man has killed the rival who got his girl pregnant. The bloodhunter, a policeman, is the murdered man's brother. An old retired seaman, Sandy, living in peaceful isolation on the edge of the community, is destined in spite of himself to become "secret sharer" of the young murderer. Sandy carries on tragicomic intrigues to hide and feed the fugitive, resists the invasions of a "well-meaning" Widow Wadman from the next farm, and protects the pregnant girl. The hunt goes on. The hunter is brutalized; the fugitive is caught and killed. Sandy, knowing all, remains silent, bringing an end to violence, and finds new life in the girl and her baby, born in Sandy's barn. As Sandy sees them, the events are a "sacred repetition": "The manger and the hay and life's new cry; beyond it, that hunt. Of all the stories man had made only two were immortal: the story of Cain and the story of Christ" (233). Sandy chooses his own story, as it were, and enacts his own "drama of the light." In the "secret country" of Sandy's mind, a war goes on between dark and light, the tribal law of vengeance and an older law, "the warm feeling at life's real core." In his own secret country every man is hunter and hunted. Life is participation in life; Sandy finally accepts the law of love and rejects the law of Cain behind it. It is remarkable how wide a vision of human alternatives is embodied in this parable, how much is implied in the shift of Sandy's allegiance from the fugitive murderer to the girl and her bastard, while outside in ritual circles the bloodhunt draws to its own destruction. This, the next-to-last of Gunn's novels, is one of his best.

A last grouping of novels reveals a final development, a development beyond narrative itself in the direction suggested by *Highland River*, the direction of philosophical comedy and dialogue. Three novels share the impulse: *The Silver Bough* (1948), *The Well at the World's End* (1951), and *The Other Landscape* (1954). The three protagonists have much in common: all are academics, and all are in pursuit of the primitive. By vocation, all are questers in words, and all discover the nonsense of their academic categories in the deviously learned talk that is Gunn's highest humor. All three engage in humorous dialogues in caves, caves whimsically associated with archaic man's sources of magical power and with the "spirit" secretly made there. Here the talk becomes a form of magic; the mundane academic has gone underground into the world of the gods.

The Silver Bough opens the way. The bough of the plot is story, song, and child's talismanic toy; it is the price of entry to the underworld and the prize for which a foolish king traded his wife and child to the king of the sea. The "foolish king" here is a landowner who, sickened by war, has never married his "wife" and has disowned her child. The horrors of jungle warfare have turned him into a bloodhunter, and he must be rescued. This becomes the unwitting mission of the archaeologist's voyage to the underworld. *The Well at the World's End* is another novel of rescue; the academic protagonist rescues himself from the perilous doldrums of middle age. He almost dies trying to rescue a lamb trapped on a cliff. Wounded, he fights against the will to die. He seeks the help of a local "wild man" or primitive, only to learn the man is dead. Yet, mysteriously at night in a cave he is visited by the wild man's spirit and is reborn in the will to live by virtue of the kinship. This is the "something" he finds in the well at the world's end. It is not a source of cultural renewal (as in *The Drinking Well*), but a source of personal reanimation. The shift is characteristic of Gunn's later fiction. In *The Other Landscape*, too, there is little concern with cultural renewal. Vision is no longer a cultural power so much as a universal creative force both artistic and religious. The rescue of Douglas Menzies, withdrawn composer living on the cliffs, alcoholic widower, is ironically reversed as Menzies becomes the hero of the cliffs, the rescuer, and then is released to his own death, as he repeats his daring climb for some rum to give the old fisherman he has rescued. He has found his own rescue in a lonely spiritual struggle, but he has drawn on the powers of traditional community: love, brotherhood, art, humor.

The three novels emphasize humor. Yet, the background to humor is the same murderousness that provides the "modern" foreground of books already discussed. What was lost and found in *The Key of the Chest* and *The Lost Chart* was of solemn urgency; what is found and lost in *The Silver Bough* is a crock of gold, stumbled upon by the archaeologist-hero and stolen by the village idiot: "All this he had done—to be foiled by an idiot in the guise of prehistory" (139). The archaeologist's confrontation with the idiot is "damn funny." The earth about him seems filled with the humor of life: "The grasses flattened themselves, wiggled, in a green mirth that held on. The rowan tree was a more solemn riot, full of convolutions of itself and high bursts of abandon, but sticking to its own root at all the odds" (224)— a fine description, by the way, of the dialogue in these novels. The protagonist's own self-discoveries evoke laughter: "The more he penetrated, the more he discovered of himself, *the nearer he drew to the crock of gold.* That was no myth: it was simple fact. In a momentary wonder that it should be so, he laughed" (291).

The Well at the World's End is a middle-aged academic's holiday of picaresque humor, off and away from his wife and his serious thoughtful self, in search of the sources of eternal youth. It opens with an empty teapot and a visit to a well that appears empty. Nothing is seen there but something is there indeed. The professor's adventures take him into the well of man's illusions, his lingering superstitions, in quest of the "something" that is there when "nothing" is seen. The pattern is episodic. The form is a complex, ambiguous circling back to his wife and his own beginnings. At each new revelation, a humdrum

Highland world uncovers the exhilarating, ludicrous magic of rituals supposedly lost. The climax comes when, near death from his fall, Peter Munro nurses voraciously at the acrid udder of a bereaved ewe and gains nourishment for survival. This, the most extraordinary incident in Gunn's novels, hovers beautifully between the grotesque and the archetypal, with the humor of the drop that poises precariously on the old woman's nose as she pours Peter's cup of tea. We have had the near-tragic "prank" at the haunted cottage, the night of hilarity in the cave of the whisky still, the love magic of marital renewal, the wild street fight at the country-town dance, the heroics of a storm off the coast. What matters in all of it is the humor of which legend is born, and all that avails when Peter faces the gray nihilism of the visionary he-goat of modern life is laughter: "And the more he couldn't laugh, the more he knew that laughter, deep laughter from beneath the belt, was the only specific for the goat, the sole charm against its evil eye, its whole spectrum, its spectral tee-totum" (232).

The humor of *The Other Landscape* is most pronounced and difficult, because most closely tied to tragedy. Menzies' wife had died the night of a storm because he could get no help. Since then, he has been on a lonely search: "I saw this search by Menzies as more than a search for Annabel, though it was primarily that. I saw it as a sort of warfare into these regions which (to call on the image) the Wrecker inhabits. There could be only one end to that search, that warfare: tragedy" (164). But the end is beyond tragedy.

It transcends tragedy through the powers of legend and humor. The feature that for George Eliot makes ordinary human destinies tragic—recurrence—for Gunn lifts them beyond tragedy. An old Gaelic air can tell of a recurrent human tragedy "so winnowed by the generations that it could be sung, hummed, as a lullaby to a child. I know of no essentialising process more profound than this" (54). Tradition winnows the rhythms of life, eliminating the temporary "as the crofter's winnower eliminated the chaff. What was left was cleansed of the personal in the sense that all great art is impersonal and thereby achieves the ultimate expression of the personal."

Destruction is part of godhead, but there is more to it, and the more is humor. "There is a grey humour in the eyes of God when he is not the Wrecker. The morning of the earth has pointed ears" (117-118). Face the tragedy, and there is always *something more*—and to sense this something more, says the academic narrator, is a humorous revelation: "Presently I found myself sitting again like a fool in the twilight. I could not help laughing under my breath at my astonishment, and when I realized I was laughing I had a look around . . . It was laughable and delicious; like imps of the night dancing in a ring. Nothing was quite real. There was *something more*" (152). Always at the height of his debaucheries of talk with Menzies, "there was a smile in his eyes and the outer corner of his left eyelid quivered very slightly in a critical, understanding humour . . . the humour was there" (303). The negative side of the humor is in the old major, the despotic retired attaché who stays in the hotel, goading his gillie, doubting the locals, seeing in Menzies only a man drinking himself to death. He is the nihilistic destroyer of Gunn's earliest novels, reborn in humor. He believes in hell only. The limits of his belief are humorously exploded when his hell comes to pass, his embassy candles set his room afire, and amid the comic inferno stand the tormented gillie and his equally tipsy friends, drenching the major and his hell with the hose. The major is chastened, and following the death of Menzies he does not return again to the little hotel.

The issue between Menzies and the major has nothing to do with crises of Highland culture. The problem of evil is no longer psychological and cultural, but metaphysical. Gunn's novels have shifted to a new level of concern, from magic and science to religion and art. Menzies and the major hold opposed conceptions of godhead; the "wrecker" is a part of divinity, not humanity; there can be no absentee Jehovah to set things right, as in *The Green Isle*. The questing narrator's search for the "primitive" is lost in Menzies' search for the ultimate mystery. For these reasons, *The Other Landscape* remains a startling new departure for a final novel, its author's least "Highland" book.

All stories, says Gunn, are one story. The one story is found in myth and legend, and it is a story of timeless conflict between affirmative and negative visions of life, between delight and those who would destroy it. This is not a theory of history, yet Gunn found it throughout history and in its terms Gunn understood the modern world. The forces of modern violence are expressions of an egoistic nihilism that is archetypal in human experience, and its triumphant antagonist is an equally archaic impulse of delight and personal wholeness. The fact that such a conflict is repeatedly played out on the stage of the modern Highlands is, in a sense, accidental; yet it is profoundly fitting, too, because for Gunn the Highlands was a place of unique access to the archaic. Hence, his novels are scrupulously observant of local reality. And, as we have noted in *Highland River*, it was essential to Gunn's code as author that local and historical reality not be lost or compromised into mere metaphor. Not all are convinced by his version of that reality but his commitment to it was strong and abiding.

How then could Fionn Mac-Colla* claim that *The Albannach*, published in 1932 after Gunn's first novels, was "the first novel to treat life in the Gaidhealtachd in a realistic manner"?[6] Is this merely a distinction between Gaelic Scotland and Caithness? Is it an attack on the validity of Gunn's realism, or does it signal some difference of intention? Has Mac Colla "come to grips with the realities of the situation of the Gael in his day"?

The reality that preoccupies Mac Colla in *The Albannach* is a repressive religious morality. At the time of his death some of Mac Colla's keenest admirers regretted that his lifelong battle with Calvin and Knox had distorted his art and his idea of historical Scotland.[7] But we have seen already in *And the Cock Crew* that his anti-Calvinism can engender an aesthetically powerful theological vision. *The Albannach* has the same complexity.

Murdo Anderson grows up in Wester Ross, the son of a narrow Free Kirk elder. Murdo's determination to escape is focused on the twin demons of religious morality and an Anglophilic notion of respectability. His means of escape is familiar: he goes off to Glasgow University, where he flourishes until news comes of his father's death. He is trapped into settling down to his father's croft and shop, surrenders to the gross allurements of the leering minister's lecherous daughter, becomes sullen, alcoholic, and eventually suicidal. On the brink of self-destruction, he is saved by an awakening of compassion; he is reconciled with his pathetic wife, joins his community, finds meaning and contentment in the seasonal rhythms of his hard pastoral life, becomes the local piper and poet, and leads the rebellion in music and dance against puritanical repression. The summary suggests little of the mixed inner struggle of Murdo, which is actually the book's subject. In his 1971 foreword, Mac Colla notes that "the point of view . . . is from inside the hero's perception throughout: we are supposed

*Mac Colla, Fionn. See above, page 330.

to apprehend the state of his consciousness at any moment by seeing things as he was seeing them" (vii). But he also insists that Murdo is "the protagonist of my own attitude . . . which I had not then, of course, completely worked out intellectually" (iv), and that the book must be understood in terms of its "allegoric intention." Not surprisingly, Murdo cannot be fully realized as an independent character when he must be at once a central dramatic consciousness and an allegorical protagonist.

Edwin Muir admired the novel's gallery of portraits as of "almost startling lifelikeness," but the portraits are uniformly grotesque, like the millions of Glaswegians Murdo sees in hallucination, "deformed, malformed, idiot-faced, loose at the mouth, with pendant ears" (195), or the "lower animals" he sees "moving about the world only partially metamorphosed into human beings" (116). A pious old sermon-lover predictably shows "one big yellow tooth . . . in his mouth as it hung open and a long slaver ran down his beard" (38). The minister John MacIver is exposed "at his meat. A trickle of grease at the end of his mouth showed in the lamplight. The fat throat, collarless, rose white out of the neck of his shirt, and the round belly bulged unsuspectedly big through the unbuttoned waistcoat" (232). The point is that Murdo "had never been able to stand this beastlike in man" (250), and that physical deformity is what Murdo must learn to love if he is ever to "share in the condemnation of his fellows" and not be "cut off alike from their salvation and their damnation" (261). In his terrible isolation he sees an old woman with a club foot pass by: "He used to be a little revolted by that club-foot, but now it seemed to him almost a beautiful deformity" (262). He is saved from suicide by the sight of an ostracized sea gull with a broken leg; disgust and hatred at the imperfections of flesh are what Murdo must be cured of, and with compassion for the crippled bird his coldness thaws. But the compassion is not permanent, for Murdo's ultimate triumph over the godly is in the shape of a hilarious satiric song depicting John MacIver as "a leering Presbyterian faun" (327), and the final defiant dance he engineers is an archaic orgy. The "old life" has returned.

The old life is a vision of lost power, a myth of Gaeldom's golden age:

Life must have been good here in the old days. The folks were a lusty race in those old times, with a song never far from the lips and feet ever itching to be at the dancing. And the fine piping there must have been! But then the dark days came, with a new kind of religion that changed old ways, stopped the song on the lip, and let the wind out of the pipes with a squealing of drones. [33]

There had been old people in it, old men and women with a life-time's memories and the full of their heads of old songs and sgeulachd—what talk and what singing on winter evenings by the lamplight while the moon shone outside. There had been young men and lasses, and they at the courting on summer evenings in the woods of lapping water. There had been little children running about the grassy braes and knolls, shouting to each other in their play. [284]

The old life, it seems, can be recovered only in orgy; the new life is a grim cartoon of Gaelic Holy Willies. No peace between them is possible; the "godly" must wake up "to find their authority shattered and the fashion of constipation and the long face fallen into perpetual disrepute" (319). The whole edifice must be thrown down. But when Murdo supposes he has done so, the results are disquieting. In Glasgow he finds intellectual, cultural, and sexual freedom: the instrumental books are not specified; the whisky and sex are, and they lead to temporary madness, from which Murdo quickly and inexplicably recovers, feeling cleansed. It is unclear that his final orgiastic triumph is significantly different, except that it is at home.

The realities of agricultural life in modern Wester Ross are sparingly portrayed in *The Albannach*, and without them one is unpersuaded of Murdo's triumphant "affirmation." It may well be part of Mac Colla's meaning that, as Herdman says, "the origins of our troubles [are] not in impersonal economic or social forces but in the motivations of the human will." But if so, what are we to make of the claims of being first "to treat life in the Gaidhealtachd in a realistic manner"? As a drama of the redeemed will, *The Albannach* is ambiguous; but even so, it is better appreciated for the powerful novel it is when viewed in such a way than when it is measured on a scale of mere local realism.

18

Highlands
of the
Humorists

T he humor of the Highlands is to some degree humor in the
Gaelic or "Irish" tradition defined by Vivian Mercier in his
Irish Comic Tradition.[1] Especially in later books, Neil Gunn's
protagonist oscillates wonderfully between hero and child, visionary
and clown; Jeems of *The Grey Coast*, like Sandy of *Bloodhunt* and
Peter Munro of *The Well at the World's End*, is the old man who refuses to act his age. Fantasy and humor are inseparable, and what
Mercier calls a "divine prankishness" is as evident as the archaism and
conservatism he considers characteristically Irish. Humor, for Mercier
as for Gunn, is to be understood according to Huizinga's view of
primitive *Homo Ludens*, and the archaism of Irish tradition means
remaining in touch with "the play-spirit of a more primitive society,"
with a refusal to be solemn even about one's gods and myths: archaic
man "seems to believe in myth and magic with one-half of his being,
while with the other he delights in their absurdity." And when Gunn is
most solemn—as in his intricate riddling colloquys, his witty dialectics, his debaucheries of "blether"—he is most humorous.

It is in part the presence of such humor that makes Allan Campbell
McLean's *The Islander* (*The Gates of Eden*, 1962) such a fine Highland
novel, and the *Geordie* sort of thing, without it, woefully thin and
sentimental. It helps to explain, too, why Angus Macleod's contemporary mysteries and fantasies seem so well set in the Highlands,[2] and

why Compton Mackenzie's often hilarious "farces" (the word is his own) seem strangely foreign to Highland humor. It is definitive in characterizing the otherwise Proustian long novel of the Highlands' most prolific contemporary novelist, Jane Duncan.

The most popular form of narrative humor in the modern Highlands has been the episodic sketch, from the highly popular Para Handy series of the 1900s by Neil Munro to Lillian Beckwith's Hebridean grotesques of the 1960s. "It was shown in a former escapade of Para Handy's that he wasn't averse from a little sea-trout poaching. He justified this sport in Gaelic, always quoting a proverb that a switch from the forest, a bird from the hill, or a fish from the river were the natural right of every Highland gentleman."[3] The solemn casuistry, the appeal to tradition in Gaelic, the devotion to a traditional right to nature's bounty and to an ideal of gentility, the penchant of the mild, aging skipper of the Clyde Firth coal-steamer for "escapades"—all are familiar. The devotion to his ship, "the most uncertain puffer that ever kept the Old New-Year in Upper Lochfyne," is equally characteristic of his brand of daft idealism. Her owners do not appreciate the *Vital Spark*, laments Para Handy: "Oh man! she wass the beauty! She was chust sublime! She should be carryin' nothing but gentry for passengers, or nice genteel luggage for the shooting-lodges, but there they would be spoilin' her and rubbin' all the pent off her with their coals, and sand, and whunstone, and oak bark, and timber, and trash like that" (5). Equally strong is his devotion to the memory of the demigod, his sometime shipmate, swashbuckling Hurricane Jack. Para Handy romanticizes Jack's past and his own. His capacity for fanciful expansion involves him often in ludicrous self-deception. Take, for instance, "An Ocean Tragedy" (402-409), a study in what the recorder calls "the strange psychology of the liar." After bringing the *Vital Spark* upchannel from Tarbert to Cardwell Bay without lights in a storm, Para Handy leaves her temporarily and entrains at Gourock for Glasgow, only to find how bad the storm had become and himself a hero for having struggled in it. His anecdotes barely keep pace with the fanciful demands of his fellow travelers for wild tragedy, and a "consolatory bottle" helps, until he has both ship and mate sunk and can no longer tell what is true and what imaginary, so vivid and detailed has his picture of horror become. His wife orders him back to the "sunken" ship, where of course he finds ship and crew all well, and nothing lost in the storm but "a jar, and a Bucket, and your own sou'wester." "My Cheve!" he exclaims. "Things is terribly exaggerated up in Gleska."

Even when undeceived himself, Para Handy's fertile fancy seldom deserts him. Caught poaching, he is far too quick-witted and polished an actor for the authorities. The *Vital Spark*'s punt, he reports, had been stolen by thieves who then used her for poaching. So well does he carry it off that local sympathy is aroused to the tune of a two-pound-ten philanthropic collection for the purchase of a new punt. " 'I wouldna touch a penny,' protested Para Handy, 'if it wass not for my vessel's reputation; she needs a punt to give her an appearance' " (283). The mixture of the Highland gentleman's pride in appearance with the superb fraudulence and casuistry of the confidence man is characteristic. Applied with patient skill, then, to the bargaining process, it secures a dinghy for the two-pound-ten, which is swapped a fortnight later for "a punt that suited the Vital Spark much better, and thirty shillings cash" (287). The cash is used to replace his poaching net.

Such a combination of stateliness and shrewdness carries the captain through many similar episodes, helping the helpless with charity and delicacy, perpetrating solemn pranks, managing minor extortions, dreaming of Hurricane Jack's gentility, boasting of the breadth of his experience and the supremacy of his boat, a humane and devious sage in whimsical mock-romance sailing on small waters. The "tales" are attributed to Munro's alter ego "Hugh Foulis" as a holiday from serious fiction. George Blake sees through this disguise: Munro's finest characters, he notes, are always complex humorous figures of this sort.[4] Para Handy is not out of place in the romantic, ironic world of Gilian the Dreamer, Ninian Campbell, and John Splendid.

If we jump fifty years to the most recent sketches of Highland humor, we find something quite different. The anecdotes of an English schoolmarm are bound to be, and the inner Hebridean locale of "Bruach" is far from Clydeside and Loch Fyne. I do not know the provenance of Lillian Beckwith's* reminiscences of the island "Gael," but

*Beckwith, Lillian. Born in 1916 in England, Mrs. Beckwith lives on the Isle of Man. Since the great success of her first three books, discussed here, she has published six books: *Green Hand* (1967), *A Rope in Case* (1968), *About My Father's Business* (1971), *Lightly Poached* (1973), *The Spuddy* (1974), and a collection of short stories, *Beautiful Just! Scenes from Bruach* (1975).

her sketches—*The Hills Is Lonely* (1959), *The Sea for Breakfast* (1962), and *The Loud Halo* (1964)—portray a development of attitude, in a modern female Matt Bramble, toward the dirt and barbarism of her new neighbors.[5] As a convalescent visitor in the first, she is "infinitely relieved" to retain a "few shreds of dignity"; in the second she decides to settle into a place of her own; and at the end of the third she is evidently sorry to leave. She has found a simple, essentially humorous alternative to the "noisy clutter of life in England where nowadays it seems there is too much prosperity for real happiness; too much hurry for humour" (*SB*, 13). She has gradually come to accept the absurdities of the alternative, "so much so that I was only amused when I heard that Alistair Beag, a lazy man even by Bruach standards, had been taken to hospital after rupturing himself when trying to lift a load on to his wife's back" (*SB*,37). But even as she "learns" that here "time is practically non-existent and that the clocks are as much out of touch with reality as are their owners," the distance between their barbarism and her civility is no less real.

She becomes almost as honest with herself as she is critical of other writers on the Highlands:

> Whereas most writers on Highland subjects deem it their duty to depict the ceilidhs with a romantic pen—lamplight; peat fire flames playing on a cluster of honest friendly faces; rich Highland voices, joking, singing and story-telling; cups of tea and home-baked scones—I was never able to forget that the room was likely to be ill-ventilated; that the tight-packed bodies would be hot and unbathed; that the pipe-smoking old men would be spitting indiscriminately; that the boots of the company would be caked with dung and mud; that more than one of my neighbors might be belching with threatening violence, and the clothes of the others reeking of stale peat smoke and sour milk. [*HL*, 156]

The account that follows gives a balanced and amiable account of the ceilidh. But Miss Beckwith remains the lady of sensibility these amiable, happy primitives could never comprehend; and even in the third book the impression persists that she has somehow managed to "become" a crofter, and yet preserve her temporal proprieties and her natural sensibility. The latter is manifest in highly literary evocations of natural surroundings, as she wanders off to find "pleasant spots for meditation," and creates ornately mixed metaphors for the scene: "The Bruach hills and moors, hardly yet aware of the tentative prodding of spring's green fingers, offered an intricate patchwork of browns and greys. Rhuna and her companion isles, which a loitering winter had left sprinkled with snow, reposed lightly on the strangely still water, looking as fragile as meringues on a baking board, needing only a palette knife slipping under them to lift them cleanly from their calm, blue base" (*HL*, 140).

The books have three styles, leading one to suspect a consciously literary talent behind the schoolmarm Miss Peckwit: the "sensibility" style just illustrated; the "Smelfungus" style, its opposite, reflected in an obsession with dirt and smell, but productive of vivid interiors and episodes; and the style of grotesque humor, as when Johnny and Lachy carry the corpse of Ian Mor downstairs and Johnny gets the corpse's big toe caught in his mouth and remarks much on the flavor thereof. Miss Beckwith somehow finds violent farce, often almost Jacobean, in the most solemn occasions, as surely as Ian Maclaren found a brier bush among the kail. The difference between the account of old Farquhar's domesticated rats and the antics of Janet's trained ferret in Jane Duncan's *Miss Boyds* is illustrative. And following the rats comes the scene where Johnny and Lachy take a break from grave digging to play their ghoulish game of knocking out a skull's teeth, while the grave's former occupant waits in the bushes, and Miss Peckwit, ubiquitous observer, perceives in stark contrast the loveliness of the night.

Amid such scenes of prankishness and deviousness, she finds "true Hebridean politeness," "a very moderate degree of sanity," and an ability to endure discomfort. It is difficult to believe that this is not a deliberate antidote to the "writers on Highland subjects" and "books on crofting life" to which she often refers. The books bear somewhat the same relation to the sentimental farces of Compton Mackenzie that George Douglas Brown's "Barbie" had borne to the Kailyard: equally condescending, equally remote from realism if we accept as "reality" the island world of that fine Hebridean novel, McLean's *The Islander*. Fictional value cannot be based upon social realism, of course, but critical judgment must surely find a flaw in the accidental way the "Bruach" trilogy reflects ironically back on the unanalyzed self-flattery and literary pretentiousness of its narrator.

Likewise, while it would be improper to fault Compton Mackenzie's* Ben Nevis and Todday farces for being what they are, it is rele-

---

*Mackenzie, Compton. See above, page 222.

vant to recognize in them, too, a humor that is always at a distance from its own materials. "Farce" is the author's own label. Mackenzie's hero in *The Four Winds of Love*, John Ogilvie, writes farces for London and New York stages, although there is nothing in his romantic life and solemn personality to suggest farcical genius or perspective. In his earlier fiction of cockney London and effete Sorrento, Mackenzie was capable of brilliant humor and wit. When he turned north to Scotland, he came with a strong ideological and sentimental view of Gaelic Scotland, and without access to the Gaelic or Nordic archaism underlying the farcical humor of Gunn, Linklater, and Jane Duncan. Significantly, the most colorful humorous character in the Todday books is old Mrs. Odd, Midland mother of the sergeant-major who loves the islands at first sight. It is arguable, too, that the most humorous display of his two decadent Highland lairds, Mac-Donald of Ben Nevis and Cameron of Kilwhillie, occurs when he sends them far from the Highlands to imperial India in *Ben Nevis Goes East*. Here, Ben Nevis's traditional comic function is most clearly revealed, and it has little to do with his Highland background. Even in the Highlands, Mackenzie remains the Hellenist he and his hero Ogilvie have always been, and fittingly his humor or "farce" is in the sentimental mode of arcadian comedy.

The Ben Nevis group began first, alternating and interlocking with the Todday group, cheerful reading for wartime and postwar, and comic occasion for an attack on modern bureaucracy.[6] The first group includes *The Monarch of the Glen* (1941), *Hunting the Fairies* (1949), *Ben Nevis Goes East* (1954). Ben Nevis and his allies appear in the first of the Todday books, *Keep the Home Guard Turning* (1943), and are alluded to in *Whisky Galore* (1947), followed a decade later by a less "genial" farce, *Rockets Galore*.

In the manner of Trollope's Barsetshire, the books all share a county, and the county is conservative as Barsetshire is. The dominant mode of humor is the same: mock-heroic, with its ironic elevation of a small world at the expense of a large one. Mackenzie's comic Highlands are idyllic, for the most part innocent, parochial, defiant of time, resistant to invasions of Saxon efficiency, garrulous. The only "serious" descriptions of this world are those supplied in excerpts from the books of the imaginary Celticist traveloguer, Hector Hamish Mackay, whose absurdity, though patent, is curiously never repudiated. Place is evoked merely as the setting for a comedy of manners or a farce. Mackenzie's is the lucid, unambiguous world of the comic Hellenist, and noticeably absent are children and the child's transforming eye for locality, person, and natural magic. This is not to disparage the books, but simply to suggest why their humor seems unrelated to their Celtic subject.

Ben Nevis and Kilwhillie are those perennial figures the "last of the lairds." They are staunch traditionalists, devoted to a way of life that must indeed be moribund if they, in their naiveté or amiable feebleness, are its only surviving defenders. *The Monarch of the Glen* recounts a mock war between rough, arrogant, loveable Ben Nevis and the National Hikers Union, a satiric metonym for cockney democratic bureaucracy, against whose vulgar invasions Highland laird and Glaswegian Nationalist Scot ultimately join forces. The latter learns—and this may be the book's only "message"—that

> there was something to be said for Highland chieftains of long authentic lineage in possession of their land, as the Chieftain himself was now inclined to admit that there was something to be said for young men who desired the glory and grandeur of Scotland. In reaching this opinion [Ben Nevis] was much encouraged by the performance on the pipes of *Mac'ic Eachainn's March to Sheriffmuir* by Colin Campbell, the student who had been responsible for desecrating the air of Glenbogle with *The Campbells are Coming*. To sit in his own Great Hall and hear a Campbell piping that tune to a MacDonald was compensation for many historical events which had taken the wrong course. [287]

Cockney democrats are cast out by one they consider an "old fascist," but more wealthy, foreign elements are nicely assimilated, and in this facile comic realm assimilation is easy. Ben Nevis himself, after all, is married to a fine Englishwoman with money to restore Glenbogle Castle. And now, from North America, come the Roydes—fat Chester of the orange kilt and his wife Carrie, Canadian descendant of a tenant of Ben Nevis's ancestor, exiled during the Clearances. Here, with a vengeance, is a farcical exploitation of Highland tragedy. The sad memory is part of the story's setting, neutralized by humor, and explained away as pleasantly providential. Had her ancestor not been "cleared," Carrie could not come back with her rich husband to support Ben Nevis against the cockney invaders and buy a piece of Kilwhillie's ancestral lands as a forty-thousand-dollar toy.

Farcical incident mocks local tradition. Caves where Charlie and his wretched Jacobites hid become mock-heroic battle sites. Mac 'ic

Eachainn's Cradle, the legendary castle dungeon, serves as jail for hikers and Highlanders alike. No serious picture is offered of Celtic civilization, and even the language becomes a source of incidental humor, as tourists mistake serious Gaelic phrases for funny English ones and resort to *Gaelic without Tears* to end the confusion. Ben Nevis's own view of Highland life is mindless; the fanciful vision of idiotic Americans is laughed at, then romanticized in mild, amorous little ways, then somehow legitimized or assimilated. In such a setting, Ben Nevis is like Falstaff at Shrewsbury, the festive fool. He has vitality, resiliency; he harbors no grudges; he is formidable and amusing as general of his troops, enjoyable, even lovable, as long as farce shuts out satiric implication.

Shy, melancholy Kilwhillie, the Laurel to Ben Nevis's Hardy, is more complex, a poignant comic protagonist with a capacity for tenderness, a sense of place, a hunger for authentic tradition. The book focusing on Kilwhillie, *Hunting the Fairies*, is humor of a different kind. Comic romance of inheritance replaces the mock-heroic of *The Monarch of the Glen*. The conflict is between two silly American women, one a Campbell and the other an ally of MacDonalds and Camerons, rival queens of American Ossianic cultism, Mrs. Urquhart-Unwin (Yu-Yu) and her shrewd rival for presidency of the Boston Ossianic Society, Mrs. Linda Wolfingham. They come to the Highlands as rival collectors of fairy lore. Local Celts are either bewildered or flagrantly opportunistic about the quest. The battle climaxes when the fairy lady Yu-Yu has seen turns out to be the nutty Jacobite sister of the local antiquarian Aeneas Lamont. Linda Wolfingham is certain to disclose this back in Boston, and Yu-Yu needs protective blackmail. While Linda is transcribing the tales told her by a fraudulent old tinker in exchange for whisky, Yu-Yu parks her clarsach behind a fairy hill and plays mysterious music; when Linda is thoroughly fooled, Yu-Yu plays a tape of her trick at lunch. Deadlock in blackmail leads to reconcilation.

Meanwhile, poor Kilwhillie has fallen in love with Yu-Yu's daughter Deirdre, and although the magic he discovers is simply the excitement of touching her fingers on a Ouija board, it is nonetheless real. Kilwhillie, with his memories of a noble ancestor in the '45, is the end of a heroic Jacobite line, periodically selling land to keep his original estate. He sells more and more land to a London stockbroker and hunting laird, Sydney Dutton, who calls himself Glenbore. Then abruptly he meets, likes, and evidently intends to adopt Dutton's schoolboy son as his heir. This prospect of real inheritance follows upon the disappointment of Deirdre's rejection. The two plots are brought together in Yu-Yu's tactful letter to Kilwhillie: "You and I have both been hunting for fairies in a different way. Can we say that if we failed to find our fairies we have each found a dear friend?" (272). Behind the ludicrous quest, the hunt is real enough, a hunt for some kind of magic, for a power of renewal and continuity, however fragile. Follies are transformed into kindness; the fraudulent foreigner has brought something real to a decadent world. There is more value in Yu-Yu's Ossianism than in the opportunism of local parasites: such is the romantic implication of the farce.

The power of humor passes to Ben Nevis and Kilwhillie themselves, and their real comic nature becomes clear when, in *Ben Nevis Goes East*, their triumphant innocence carries them through the decadence of British India in the 1930s. It is a tawdry world of marital and political adventurers—nabobs, lady novelists, film stars, public school maharajahs, and visiting politicians. Ben Nevis has come to save his son and heir from the marital trap of an Anglo-Indian divorcee. His boyish faithfulness is a transforming power, as he and his school chum the maharajah play at being "Nosy" and "Banjo" at Harrow once more. Remote from the Highlands, the innocence of the lairds acquires comic virtue; archetypally humorous aspects of character and situation can be stressed: Ben Nevis bellowing mightily in a Himalayan rickshaw, playing Santa Claus, practising for a panther shoot, and accidentally killing a pig kept by "Banjo's" stuffy neighbor. His innocent humor makes reconciliation and even cultural assimilation possible.

The Todday books are different. They are comedies of exclusion. The green world of their islands must triumph over the pompous military bureaucrat. The polarities in these mythical Hebrides are those of festive comedy in modern dress: the autocratic precisian, the Malvolio, Captain Paul Waggett, organizer of the Todday Home Guard, who tries in vain to enlighten the childlike, inefficient islanders to the modern reality of "there's a war on"; and his antagonist, Chestertonian Falstaff, Father Macalister, boisterous, jovial leader of the local resistance. Always underlying are the traditional rivalries. Great Todday and Little Todday are inhabited still by mythical rival clans, Macruries and Macroons. Great Todday, moreover, is sternly Protestant, severely sabbatarian, while Catholic Little Todday is more primitive, traditional, alcoholic, and festive. But such divisions mean little in the face of a common foe. The foe is not England at war, but the puritanical solemnity and inhumanity of a cosmopolitanism that seeks to deny the values of simplicity, individuality, and joyous spirituality.

Keep the Home Guard Turning, the first, centers on the absurdity of trying to effect a warlike regimentation in such a place, and on the outbreak of old rivalries far more real than remote English wars, climaxing in the mock-heroic affair of the Home Guard exercise. Ben Nevis leads his own troops in a mock invasion of the islands, in which the real objective has to do with a bureaucratic foul-up over the issue of boots.

Whisky Galore is a comedy in which the incident of whisky salvage serves as a means of precipitating confrontations of manners and faiths. The plot focuses sentimentally on two marriages involving unyouthful suitors: Sergeant-major Odd is forty-five, and George Campbell the schoolteacher is thirty-five. The whisky—fifty thousand cases at full proof bound for America to "help with the war effort"—is supplied by a kindly providence to overwhelm the agents of repression: George's stern old mother and pompous Waggett. Life and love and merriment triumph, and marriage feasts are the natural conclusion.

Rockets Galore, in the same setting with the same characters, is different. As the author recognizes in his prefatory note: "*Whisky Galore* was a genial farce: *Rockets Galore* is a bitter farce. It is difficult to be genial when a way of life that seemed, with all its hardships and all its disgraceful neglect for sixty years by the Government of the day, to be a good way of life is in danger of extinction." The threat is now far more real than the Malvolio Waggett. The Toddays are to become part of the rocket range, and the population of Little Todday is to be resettled on the mainland. No providential whisky courage can defeat this new folly. Rather, it takes the skillful fraud of a sympathetic outsider, who dyes enough herring gulls pink to convince bird fanciers of the appearance of a rare new species, and to arouse British public opinion against government policy. All the heroism of Father Macalister, Mrs. Odd, and Duncan Ban, the ex-University poet, are to no avail; only the trick succeeds, with the aid of shrewd exploitation of the public media. Meanwhile, in such a farce, the "way of life" itself must be taken largely for granted; the real possibilities of defiance are short-circuited, the problem of fatalistic despair cannot be explored. Much space is taken up with speeches and editorials. Farce and ideology jostle together strangely, and we are reminded once more of John Ogilvie in *The Four Winds*, the indefatigable ideologue who wrote stage farces. The serious novel of latter-day Clearances was to come later with George Mackay Brown's *Greenvoe*.

19

Jane Duncan
and
George Mackay Brown

Mackenzie's achievement in the best of his tartan farces is to dramatize genuine crises of value in the comic stereotypes of arcadian romance. For Jane Duncan* all stereotypes are a diminution of truth, an aggravation of the problem of knowing oneself and other persons.[1] Her heroine Janet Sandison's incessant striving for identity is a delicate process of demythologizing, of discovering what one represents without sentimentality: "I see no reason why we should be turned into stags at bay and monarchs of the glen" (*Muriel*, 153). All Highland lasses do not sit "at spinning wheels crooning melodies (with English words by Kennedy-Fraser) beside peat fires" (*Rose*, 167). The dark peasant drama of the regionalist—Grassic Gibbon, or Hardy, or Mary Webb—is wrong, too. "There was not, either, any Celtic twilight or Kailyard about it. The light is clear at my home and we grow our vegetables in neat rows in the back garden." Yet the nineteen novels in the Reachfar story, studies in the pain of

---

Duncan, Jane. Born Elizabeth Jane Cameron, in 1910, near Glasgow, the daughter of a Dunbartonshire policeman and the granddaughter of crofters on the Black Isle of Easter Ross. There she spent her holidays on the farm, "The Colony," which became Reachfar, her "private country of the mind." She took a masters degree in English Literature at Glasgow University. In the 1930s she worked at secretarial jobs in London, and during World War II she served as an intelligence officer in the WAAF. Working for an engineering firm in a Lowland town following the war, she met her future husband, and in 1948 she joined him in Jamaica, where they lived until his death in 1958. She then returned to Jemimaville on the shores of

demythologizing one's lost past, are also studies in the profound need for compensatory myth.

Jane Duncan's Highlands are more personal than historical. Janet's grandmother is from the West, to be sure, and has grown up hating sheep, and she is the lawgiving center of Janet's Reachfar. But the problem of exile is independent of memories of the Clearances. The Reachfar of place and time was the small croft of Janet's grandparents on the Black Isle. In a succession of exiles—losses, disorientations, on various personal levels—Janet grows through recalling the life and law of Reachfar. Even in the childhood years of *My Friends the Miss Boyds* she had learned that the idyllic, "real" Reachfar was doomed— by the forces of history, by the "earthquakish" influences of those mysteriously separate but inescapable entanglements called "friends." From her first horror at seeing a gift doll as a "dead baby," from her first glimpse of one of the sexually frantic, old-maid Miss Boyds with the soldier in the quarry, Janet had in fact lost her Reachfar. In *My Friends the Hungry Generation*, built thoughtfully around Wordsworth's "Immortality" ode, the loss is placed even further back. History and society merely externalize the sad imperatives of personal growth. But each new loss produces a deeper personal fidelity to what Reachfar had been. It is the central paradox of elegy: the exploration of loss transforms the lost beloved into a reality of transcendent power; space and time become a new dimension in memory. Reachfar has been a unique stability, "a thing that was ever there and never changed." "It is," says *My Friend Sashie* (185), "the only place where you have ever belonged but you had to get around to it in your own tortuous and self-torturing way." Reachfar itself had taught that "one wants to believe that everything lasts forever, but it doesn't." Only the final loss permits the final, immutable possession—"It belonged to me in a fashion far deeper and truer than it would ever belong to anybody else" (*Father*, 228; *Zora*, 76; *Macleans*, 138). Reachfar evolves as a personal symbol of both change and permanence. In *The Hungry*

Cromarty Firth, and here she lived and wrote until her sudden death in October 1976. She had written seven novels while in Jamaica; Macmillan accepted three by mail, and on her return from Jamaica with the remaining four, all seven were accepted before the first was published. Since the twenty books mentioned here, she has published *My Friends the Misses Kindness* (1974) and *My Friends George and Tom* (1976). She also wrote several children's books. Her literary autobiography, *Letter from Reachfar*, appeared in 1975.

Generation, the symbol has been transferred to a new generation, Janet's niece and nephews, and this, too, means further adjustments and growth for Janet. In the lovely elegy of *My Friend the Swallow*, it has become the "remote and mysterious" world of a fugitive girl who somehow embodies the transiency at once of Janet's Reachfar childhood and of her life with Twice Alexander.

Reality is paradoxical in the Reachfar story. Like Dickens, Jane Duncan is fascinated equally by the separateness and the menacing interconnectedness of things—of events, persons, places. Autonomy is both desirable and terrifying. Interconnectedness can be the "feeling of all life having led up to this one instant of completeness in the 'here' of space and the 'now' of time" (*Zora*, 68). It can also be the invading "sense of the terrible interconnectedness of life" (*Macleans*, 136). It is bewildering to take an arbitrary first step in "beginning" a new story: "I defy anybody to say where any story that is about life had its beginning. One has to choose some arbitrary point" (*Sandy*, 2). Formerly peripheral events are explored in full foreground complexity in later novels; persons on the edges of concern, supposed stable and definite, shift into problematic centrality. "Coincidence," the accident of interconnectedness, is essential. "Fate," laments Janet, "is as good a name as any for the trouble I get into" (*Zora*, 51). "We are all links in a chain," chants Madame Zora; and "life," says Janet, "would be much simpler if it were not so interwoven" (*Monica*, 30). This is the "paradox that seems to be at the root of life and to be its main driving force" (*Annie*, 227).

The most trivial event can be a turning point. The most negative personalities have "some force, some potential for good and evil" (*Martha's Aunt*, 164). These are the ambiguous monsters called "friends." Without her friend Muriel, Janet would not have met Twice; without her despicable stepmother Jean and her friend the amoral trull Annie, she would not have had the courage to "marry" an undivorced man. Had she not met again the flamboyant, obscene Rose, she might have married Alan Stewart. Had her "friends from Cairnton" not turned up in West Indian "St. Jago," she and Twice might not have survived the separation of his illness. And had Percy, the swallow-like girl, not arrived to make Twice's and Janet's last months youthfully joyous, then Percy's sudden departure would not have precipitated Twice's death. Such a "frightening paradox in human relationships" (*Sashie*, 120) is crucial to what is impressive about the Reachfar books. And when, in *My Friend Sashie*, we encounter such a figure of pure and yet trivial evil as Anna, together with the only friend (Sashie) who remains at once good and close to Janet, we sense the paradox fading, the art changing, and the less interesting world of Jean Robertson emerging.

So strong is the "sense of contingency" in Janet that she finds the idea of free will an absurdity and the idea of human autonomy both fascinating and terrifying. Those impervious to influence and experience, those seemingly free, fascinate her. Annie Black did the impossible: "She tossed the only little bit of tradition that was in her out of the window," and showed herself pure "character," beyond innocence or evil, "rapt, flower like, in her own secret self" (*Annie*, 293, 276). Rose resembles her in amoral autonomy, and Roddie Maclean appeals in the same way: "In the sunlight, he turned to smile at me, the bold, reckless smile that comes only to those who have the world before them and no old debts to the past and no old doubts from the past trailing behind them" (*Emmie*, 218; *Macleans*, 17). Janet yearns for the kind of autonomy they reveal. Faced with the mystery of infancy in her new nephew, she confronts the paradox in its purest form: "He was utterly complete in himself and yet, at the same time, utterly dependent on us all and in the face of this paradox one could only look with wonder and not think or say." For her, identity lies in the contingencies that make freedom an absurdity; and a momentary vision of her own separateness, "of the core of aloneness in us all which can never reach out to involvement with the family, the rest of the world or the generations," brings cold panic: "To face the total separateness of the self's identity is, paradoxically, to become an autonomous cipher suspended in a meaningless void" (*Hungry Generation*, 114, 249-250). At the end, even Twice becomes for Janet "a separate identity who might be moving forward into a relationship in which I had no share," for Twice finally shares the intimacies of his own past with her, and yet he refuses to accept the separateness of Janet's own secret life in memory and art (*Swallow*, 39, 252).

Men's minds are small—and yet at the same time, "men's minds are the sum of their race inheritance and their individual experience." But inheritance and experience root them in a small place paradoxically named Reachfar. Places and persons are closely related in identity. Each place has its own quality of time and space, its own distinctive logic of events. Cairnton is "a place where nothing happened" (*Annie*,

189); St. Jago is "crowded with events . . . and situation arose out of situation, as suddenly and garishly as the passion vines grew overnight from branch to branch" (*Sandy*, 123); and time at Reachfar has a mythic, Old Testament quality and a substratum of changeless rock with which Janet often identifies herself. "The rocks of Ross-shire, I am informed, are of the Archaean schist type and . . . I am something of an Archaean schist myself" (*Martha's Aunt*, 6). Disorientation of place must be a crisis of identity, and this is the meaning of exile at the center of the Reachfar story.

Janet is not "very good at this thing of moving from one sort of country to another." She is like her father, who "belonged so deeply to Reachfar and the Highlands, you see, that he regarded the sending of people into exile as a deadly sin" (*Sashie*, 166). Adjustment is hard for one blinded to the smallnesses of life by the view from Reachfar. The unreality of St. Jago becomes personal. But the disorientation had begun long before. The "home me" was itself the product of exile, and the creative vision that now defines the "home me" originated with the instability of Reachfar, doomed by history, by human imperfection, by Jock Skinner and "Poop on the Miss Boyds!" Each new generation is hungry for its own vision, despotically transforming reality into the dream; and each new generation must learn that clinging to a shattered vision is an insult to reality. Old Madame Dulac, plantation matriarch of St. Jago, wants only "to remain the mistress of this world that she had ruled for so long, to remain unaware that it was disintegrating around her" (*Swallow*, 65). In *My Father*, Janet learns of this hunger in her own parents; and in *The Hungry Generation*, her brother's children practice the despotism on her, refusing for long to allow her to be the "Janet" of their own recreated Reachfar story.

Reachfar persons and codes must somehow be adjusted to the realities of other places. Other places function as counterparts in the various narrative patterns of the novels, and as several places play against each other, Janet's consciousness of her own identity grows in depth and definition. Perhaps the most intricate in its manipulation of place and time, *My Friends from Cairnton* shows Reachfar lost and gained; Cairnton, the hated Lowland place, is rediscovered and reassessed; and both processes lead to a sober acceptance of St. Jago as the place where life must continue. But St. Jago, like Reachfar, is a place where history is being denied. Reachfar came to its historic end in Janet's youth, and St. Jago is doing so in her middle years: "Why," she asks, "is it that I always seem to come in just at the end of every epoch?" (*Sandy*, 107). The waning of the plantation festival of "Crop-over" sends her mind back to the last Harvest Home at Poyntdale in 1918 (in *The Miss Boyds*). Places may be radically distinct, but what happens to Janet in St. Jago has happened to her everywhere. And her growth in vision as an artist remains always and everywhere the continuing heritage of Reachfar.

The heroine-narrator of the Reachfar story is becoming a Highland novelist, her art continuous with the communal tradition from which she comes. But the lessons she has learned from those variable and mysterious beings she calls friends complicate that tradition. Her storytelling springs from an inheritance of legends rich in characters. But the characters of legend are fixed, heroically or humorously unchangeable, whereas her experience has taught her that the knowledge of character is variable and relative. Her tradition carries with it the imperative of identity: "It is essential to me to know my own truth or where I stand and I would like you to recognize that truth too." Her art, on the other hand, is based on experience that makes identity uncertain. Only in her art can a traditional identity be created. Only through becoming an artist can the Reachfar child, amid the shocks of variability and impermanence, hope to recover and preserve her tradition.

Jane Duncan wrote four novels that Janet Sandison might have written, but they are surprisingly remote in many ways from Reachfar and the artist Janet became (*Swallow*, 50).[2] Janet is an elaborated mythic self-projection of Jane Duncan; Jean Robertson has no such relation to (or reality for) her supposed author Janet. Jean starts off as a wise, shrewd, tough little child of an impoverished Lowland small town. Too easily she becomes the secure and powerful custodian of genteel old ladies at "Laurelbank" in her town of Lochfoot. Too easily she inherits evil Old Pillans' tremendous wealth. Two young men narrate two of the four novels, and through their eyes and those of the old ladies Jean is unfortunately reminiscent (despite her petty thievery and illegitimate son) of Esther Summerson. Nor is this the only Dickensian quality. The plots of catastrophic climax, occasional distractions in the Reachfar novels, become dominant, and the complexity of character is sometimes lost in moral emblem. The "problem" of the Jean novels is not character, but money, a vicious materialism externalized in the various iron men of decor and statuary that cast their literal and figurative shadows, as does the dark, menacing figure of Old Pillans, Lochfoot's secondhand dealer and ravenous plutocrat. There is a logic, then, in the death of Jean's lover Colin Adair, his head pierced by the spike of a falling suit of armor at Laurelbank, and in the death of ruthless Isabel, Colin's sister, as her powerful new blue car plunges into the burn. But it is a surface logic.

Moreover, the interconnectedness of lives that is so subtle a mystery in the Reachfar story has become literalized. Mysterious illegitimacy abounds; lost sisters and half-brothers inevitably turn up. Identity is an external puzzle. Jean's pervasive influence on others is literal as well as moral, with none of the stubborn paradox of friendship that commands the Reachfar books. Their influence on her can never become strands in the texture of memory, for Jean is not a figure of memory or of consciousness, constantly reassembling her lost pasts into changing patterns of association. The social world she comes from and comes to control never can have the rocklike depth and mythic permanence of Janet's world. In the Reachfar story, the alternative worlds of Cairnton and St. Jago derive their reality by contrast with remembered Reachfar. Lochfoot is neither loved nor hated, and without these intense feelings there cannot be the power that makes of the Reachfar story a legend and an elegy.

Indeed, while Reachfar is irrevocably lost and can only be regained in mind, memory, and art, Jean acquires the power and wealth to literally reassemble the Lochfoot of her childhood. Laurelbank under her custodianship becomes a kind of Bleak House; the exiled figures of her past gradually return, until Lochfoot is regathered under her control. The Castle becomes hers, presumably to provide a camp for refugee Jewish children in the "iron" age of the 1930s. Thus, the loss and regaining of Reachfar have been literalized in a Lowland setting remote and somewhat unreal for Janet, if not (in fact) for Jane. The effect is paradoxical: Reachfar acquires the deep reality of a mythic place, whereas Lochfoot for all its external literalness becomes increasingly fictional or fantastic. These are not the novels a Reachfar child would have written.

The Reachfar child's instinct for persons is never truly lost. Janet inherited "a good touch of her old witch of a grandmother," says Monica: "It's a kind of instinct for people and events" (*Zora*, 130-131). Reachfar life was a mixed comic idyll with a precise value: the sort of living in detail that Janet feels the modern world has lost. The child brought up in lonely places, her whole world "concentrated in the persons of the few people sitting round the Sunday dinner table," came to know "every shade of expression on their faces, could interpret every glance of their eyes, could identify to hairbreadth precision the meaning of every inflection of their voices" (*Miss Boyds*, 65). Only the child has such power. Children have "a detachment, a clearness of vision that is fuddled and clouded when age and experience overtake us" (*Cairnton*, 25-26). For the adult Janet, the problem of knowing other persons is the problem of knowing what has become of the child's power. As Janet watches her niece and successor Liz in *The Hungry Generation*, she sees that even for the child the problem is complicated by a hunger for vision.

The adult's narrative power is a continuation of the child's love of mimicry and word-play, of playing a repertory of persons with Uncle George and Tom the handyman. Her fascination with words and names—the queer, the picture-making, the oddly distinctive—is tied to a primitive faith in the power of naming. "Talking about shibboleths, though, I think that shibboleth is a lovely word. I am very keen on words. Yes, I am a *person like this*: I am very keen on words. But I like words in a particular way—I like them 'for queer' as they say in parts of east Scotland, and the queer words form themselves into a picture of my mind" (*Muriel*, 28). With George and Tom, Janet's storytelling is the clowning word-magic of Gaelic archaism. George's habit of "playing the clown" was to "pronounce words in a queer way," and this "was a signal for me to play the clown too." And for the adult Janet, "Words, just as words, quite simply in themselves mean more . . . than they do to most people" (*Cairnton*, 48). Person and place fuse in the mystery of bye-naming: "Some bye-names derive from a physical peculiarity in their owners: some from a personal idiosyncracy of their owners; some from a comic incident in the lives of their owners, and many are related to the lands or other material possessions of their owners. It is as if my countryside has a genius for picking out the most uncommon and unusual feature about a person and turning it into a bye-name" (*Flora*, 3). The place names of St. Jago—New Hope, Canaan, Content, Paradise—"turn St. Jago into a fantasy world for me" (*Emmie*, 15). The fantasy is a new threat to identity, for Janet's identity is composed of the names and words associated with persons and places that influence her. In her collapse into suicidal alcoholism following Twice's death, it is her St. Jagoan nurse who says, "I am a person like this, I am a person, a person," and in "stark terror," unable to believe in her identity, Janet shudders and grips the arms of the chair (*Sashie*, 111).

And here is the central paradox of all the Reachfar novels. To be herself, Janet must assimilate in words the influences of person and place without which she feels she has no existence; she must rediscover, after each "earthquake" of disorientation, the "connections, coherences, the interrelations which are the fabric of life" (*Hungry Generation*, 13). Yet the Reachfar child in her longs for the autonomy of the person, the solitude of the Reachfar hill top. Retreating instinctively from the benumbing bombardment of "friends," she realizes that "I had pursued solitariness all my life . . . as primitive man must have pursued the food that would satisfy his hunger and keep him alive, without recognizing that he was in fact pursuing the essential means of his survival" (*Annie*, 137). It is the passion for privacy, for remaining intact in one's circle, that Neil Gunn also has repeatedly dramatized. Each new possibility of friendship is a new menace to one's privacy, one's stable self. Yet those who achieve an autonomy amid friends are egoists: Cousin Emmie, Annie, Rose, Roddie Maclean, Martha's aunt. And in them Janet fears she finds herself, "tremendously egotistical and selfish," thinking of "friends" only relative to herself, and "as part of the furniture of certain periods in my life" (*Rose*, 184). In the Reachfar paradise that is lost, the autonomy of the child safely at home, one could somehow have both: integrity as a person and identity in a system of stable relationships. Yet the Reachfar of space and time itself taught the lesson of the fall: the contingency of "friendship," the variability of character and relationship. Thereafter, only in memory and vision can one hope for a dimension that transcends the mutabilities of time and place and the mysteries of identity.

The most original novel to come recently from northern Scotland is George Mackay Brown's* *Magnus* (1973).[3] Far from the novel's

---

*Brown, George Mackay. Like Muir and Linklater, Brown is an Orkneyman. He was born in Stromness in 1921, studied at Newbattle Abbey College when Muir was Warden, and went on to receive a masters degree at Edinburgh and to do postgraduate work on the poetry of G. M. Hopkins. His books of poetry include *Loaves and Fishes* (1959), *The Year of the Whale* (1965), and *Poems New and Selected* (1971). He has received awards for his short stories, collected in *A Calendar* traditional forms, it derives its originality from local legend and ritual. As a student at Newbattle Abbey, Brown was associated with Edwin Muir, his fellow Orkneyman. But for Muir the novel provided only a temporary and restrictive alternative to poetry, whereas for Brown poetry and fiction are closely and fruitfully allied. We can see new hope for the novel as an art form in Scotland when accomplished poets such as Brown and Iain Crichton Smith become novelists. In Brown's case, there is the additional resource of achievement in the short story and dramatic pageant.

How far can the novel transcend its conventional restrictions—written prose, private experience, and social realism—in the direction of communal ritual, dramatic presentation, and a poetic orchestration of styles? *Magnus* derives from saga, saint's life, religious pageant; it is homily and ritual recitation, morality play played out on a sacramental earth beneath a cosmic sky. It celebrates the mystery of a martyrdom and, as the narrator says, "to celebrate the mystery properly the story-teller must give way to a ritual voice" (25). The ritual voice expands and alternates to include everything from a modern slang journalese to religious meditation, from a jeweled formulaic style to stark, sagalike matter-of-fact or evocative romantic symbol.

> Fell then a sudden death-dread upon the ships, and voices that urged return, and hands were held out yearningly towards the hither healthful shore . . . A death-lust on listening faces about the mast, a weaving of warped words.

> I was hoping to set a few creels the next day off the west of Rousay. I had seen the two yacht-type boats come in at the pier earlier on. It had nothing to do with me. I met a sailor off one of the yachts and we smoked a cigarette together beside my boat. He told me he was one of the Erlendson lot. I hadn't asked him. It was none of my business who he was.

> Bright foot by dark foot, they trudged northwards all morning. They said nothing. The hills stood behind them now. They went between ripe oatfields. Noon threw short shadows in front of them. Westwards the sea glutted itself in the caves of Yesnaby and Marwick; and collapsed, wave after long curling crested wave, on the beach of Skaill in white ruin; and sang further out in many distant

---

of *Love* (1968) and *A Time to Keep* (1970). *A Spell for Green Corn* (1970) is a dramatic chronicle. *An Orkney Tapestry* (1969) is a guide to the islands, where he still lives and writes.

Atlantic voices. The song of the sea could be heard everywhere in Hrossey island. [123, 134, 186]

But everywhere is the controlling idea of the sacramental reality of the mass: "It takes place both in time, wherein time's conditions obtain, and also wholly outside time; or rather, it is time's purest essence, a concentration of the unimaginably complex events of time into the ritual words and movements of a half-hour . . . The end and the beginning. All time was gathered up into that ritual half-hour, the entire history of mankind, as well the events that have not yet happened as the things recorded in chronicles and sagas" (139). The sacramental aesthetic of the mass fused with the luminous starkness of Norse saga: such is the style of *Magnus*, and in such a linguistic world, historical and domestic realism have little place.

The historical matter is the life and death of the Orkney Saint Magnus Martyr, Magnus Erlendson, twelfth-century earl, and his cousin-rival Earl Hakon Paulson. Their wars for supremacy spread ruin through the Orkneys, until finally a peace conference is arranged, and Paulson cheats and murders Magnus. Paulson begins a long and constructive solitary rule, Magnus is canonized, and the implication is that the sacrifice of Magnus provided a necessary cleansing, a miraculous healing. The implication is somewhat confused when the narrative of Magnus's murder is translated into an unnamed Nazi concentration camp and identified with the butchery of a Lutheran pastor. But the suggestion is that time and place are all one, and the conflict between the earls is the eternal conflict between the unworldly saint and the practical man of action. Historical character is barely sketched. The local reality of the harsh lives of the peasants, Mans and Hild, and the tinkers, Jock and Mary, is suggested with genuine compassion, but their dominant role as universal human chorus overrides cultural representativeness.

In *Greenvoe* (1972), Brown's first novel, locality, mystery, and ritual are, I think, more effectively fused; here, too, Brown's extraordinary talents as short story writer are impressively adapted to the more complex form.[4] In the fictional Orkney fishing village of Greenvoe on the island of Hellya, Brown portrays the wide diversity of a Scottish culture and the blighted wholeness of its history, suggesting at the same time the hidden persistence of its archaic life in ritual. It is a pattern we have seen before in Gibbon and Gunn, with the further elaboration, seen in *Magnus*, of a rich stylistic orchestration. The two books on the shelf of the young ferryman Westray suggest the range: *The Orkneyinga Saga* and *On Love Carnal and Divine: Seventeenth Century Sermons;* echoes from Brown's study of Hopkins and Dylan Thomas are also heard. Within the orchestration each character and domestic grouping carry their own cultural idioms and narrative modes.

The chief characters include three fishermen: one a figure of Old Testament piety and presbyterian cant (Samuel Whaness); one a radical atheist and local historian (the Skarf); one a lazy drunk (Bert Kerston)—all plausible and at times heroic, all free of caricature. Also included are a retired world sailor, Ben Budge, and his devoted sister; the promiscuous spinster Alice Voar and her numerous children by different fathers; the virginal schoolmarm from Edinburgh's Morningside, Margaret Inverary; the "norse god" ferryman and casanova Ivan Westray; the local dimwit Timmy Folster with his burnt-out house and his methylated spirits; the hotel proprietor and his illegal whisky; the merchant-postmaster-county-councillor and his malicious wife; the laird Colonel Fortin-Bell, his horsy niece, and his Lawrence-obsessed granddaughter; the Indian pedlar (and part-time narrator); and of course the weak but kindly, secretly alcoholic minister, Simon McKee, and his guilt-ridden Edinburgh mother. As the list suggests, there are many little plots here, and one extensive plot—the pathetic story of McKee and his mother (Scottish bourgeois tragedy of the manse). All have their own suspenses and resolutions, deaths, exiles, and reconciliations. All develop in close juxtaposition. The cumulative effect is of a parochial history with wide cultural representativeness.

Yet in a sense, all these lives are thwarted or decadent, and all are set against the two opposing forces of history and prehistory in whose timeless conflict they are caught. Bureaucratic Man has arrived secretly on the island, and the island is doomed to make way for Operation Black Star, a mysterious defense project. The bureaucrat's index cards, "brief cryptic biographies," reject the islanders as insignificant; and shortly they are followed up by the bureaucrat's bulldozers. But the bureaucrat's "history" is a temporary invasion. The hidden prehistoric life of seasonal ritual, having punctuated the book with its ceremonies in the barn at The Bu, returns at the end to the now derelict island. Having scaled the cliff and eluded the fence encircling the island, the children of the exiles hold their harvest ritual in a ruined broch—"this navel had attached many generations of Hellyamen to the nourishing earth" (277)—and bring the word of "resurrection," light and blessing to the "kingdom of winter," "however long it endures, that kingdom, a night or a season or a thousand ages" (279).

What is this resurrection that is promised? Is it purely transcendental, or is it cultural? These are the real children of Hellya, and they have returned to their real place; the fence cannot keep them out. The potent Highland myth of the Clearances has been reenacted on a Cold War stage, with the bull-dozers of the bureaucrat. The latest betrayers are gone, and with them the doomed dregs of a community, and the effect, as in *Magnus*, is of cleansing. The ruins of this latest historic betrayal are starkly displayed:

> It took three days to demolish the baronial hall, with its turrets and battlements and coat-of-arms. The Fortin-Bells, grown rich once more with compensation, stalked deer in the west. Agatha and Inga rode their horses with style across the strath. The colonel pulled great lithe leaping sklinters of bronze out of Highland rivers; the salmon fishing was good that year. In Hellya the skyline flowed on uninterrupted by the hall. Among the heather a sandstone shield crumbled slowly; one could still discern, after a winter, a faintly sculpted stylized horse and half obliterated words WE FALL TO RISE. The rain fell. The sun shone. The horse melted into the stone. A blank shard lay in the heather. [273]

The exiles have survived. In the archaic remnants of their island is the power to believe that life will return. Time will outlast history; for "time is not a conflagration; it is a slow grave sequence of grassblade, fish, apple, star, snowflake" (265).

Retrospect:
Notes for a Theory
of Scottish Fiction

"The service of philosophy, of speculative culture, toward the human spirit," says Pater, paraphrasing Novalis, "is to rouse, to startle it to a life of constant and eager observation." In some such spirit, it will be useful at the close of this essay to generalize and synthesize some of the things we have seen, and to take a few tentative steps toward theory. We have traced the development of the novel in Scotland through several historical phases. We have identified certain motifs. We have encountered a few persistent problems. What all of these say about the past is interesting; what they suggest about the present and the future may be of greater importance.

Prior to the late appearance of the novel in Scotland, two figures of importance emerged, Mackenzie and Smollett. Mackenzie observed the strangeness of the new English form to "Scottish genius," published three novels in the 1770s, and turned away to more congenial forms. The emigré Smollett followed the new English example, but moved increasingly to two seemingly contradictory modes that were to define the beginnings of the Scottish novel: Gothic fantasy and social history. The first major phase opened a generation later. The intentions of Scott, as well as those of Galt and others associated with Blackwood, were social-historical; in Scott and the same group, notably Hogg, may be found distinctive Gothic tendencies, nourished by folk legend and local tradition, infused with the patterns and motifs of romance. Historically, this first generation belonged to a late defensive phase of Unionism in Scottish political ideology, and to the beginnings of Tory nationalism.

The nationalist impulse flickered; North Britain settled into its mid-Victorian years of entrepreneurial wealth and industrial squalor, its chief cultural preoccupation being religion. The 1840s saw a new stimulus to cultural awakening in the crisis of the Kirk, and with it came the next self-conscious stirrings in the novel, led by Margaret Oliphant and George MacDonald. Regional locale expanded slightly into the burgh and city of Sara Tytler and the neofeudal Highlands of William Black. The fictive impulse of late Victorian Scotland took shape in the resurgent romance of Stevenson. Romance in the 1890s turned to fatalistic escape and antimaterialistic melancholy; in Neil Munro it turned to a strange elegiac irony. Regionalism was spiritualized in the twilit Celticism of Fiona Macleod and sentimentalized in the pathetic, ironic idylls of the Kailyard. The hellish realities of industrial urbanism seem to have been beyond the imaginative tolerances of the novelist; but the consolations of parochial reminiscence and exotic romance, while quite understandable as a therapeutic reaction, appear disturbingly ironic or funereal.

With the new century came signs of an extreme—I have interpreted it as a neo-Calvinist—anti-Kailyard reaction. With it, too, came a new phase of imperialist romance. Brown, Hay, and Buchan, depicting the blight of provincialism or evoking the romance of reality in volcanic Europe, make strange contemporaries. Following World War I, in a cycle of depression, class war, and emigration, the blighted Highlands produced a new naturalism in early Gunn and Mac Colla, while in the Lowlands the Muirs probed the same desperate question of Scotland's cultural survival. Hope came with the reawakened nationalism of the 1920s and 1930s, in what I have viewed as the nationalist epic ambition of Gibbon's trilogy, Mackenzie's cycle, Gunn's historical novels, Blake's Clyde sagas, and the radical chronicle of James Barke. Once more nationalism hesitated, fading this time into British anti-Fascism. The end of World War II saw in fiction an urgent concern for the survival of small nations—in Linklater, for instance—and of limited visions, notably in Jenkins. In the several fictional Highlands of Gunn, Mackenzie, and Duncan, the concern was for the survival of traditional vitalities against threats of remote bureaucracy, imperialist brainwashing, and other forces destructive of personal and communal integrity.

The 1960s and early 1970s, years of economic and political separatism, saw a new separation of literary activity from political activism—perhaps, as in the Ireland of Yeats and Joyce, a needed corrective. A new expatriate generation—Spark, Williams, Kennaway and Sharp—took exile, homelessness, and flight as existential metaphors, but also as inevitable betrayals of a cultural inheritance at conflict with itself. Yet among growing numbers of younger novelists working (some of them) at home, there are signs of a new freedom from cultural self-consciousness, of a new finesse. The economic crisis of contemporary Britain casts in shadow the question of what Scottish federalist independence may do for the renewal of a literary tradition long grounded in elegy and exile.

The novel of Scotland has displayed several distinctive and often paradoxical motifs, which can be summarized under three heads: history, community, and character.

Stevenson found distinctively Scottish an obsessive relation to an irrecoverable past. From its beginnings in Scott and Galt, the Scottish novel has been historic, yet history has generally been seen as a long roll of deceit, betrayal, and illusion, or an ironic saga of survival. "The Scots are pretty good at history," to repeat Neil Gunn's understatement, "which, perhaps, is why most of them mistrust it. For it is full of facts, most of them ugly." History, then, is romanticized, but romance must be historical, and even in romance the romantic who is trapped by loyalties to the past appears a fool or a fanatic. For Ferrier, MacDonald, and Fiona Macleod worldly inheritances are unreliable and must be transcended to be made real. Mitchison and Gunn, faithful to historic reality, pit history against the archaic, the prehistoric, in search of a continuity beyond history, in search of the *kataleptike phantasia*, the possessing vision. History, for Gibbon, is hell, or is at least an unreal procession of ideological clouds. For Blake, it is an illusory glory; for Jenkins and Sharp, it is a haunting pastoral myth. The lost past is an obsession for Duncan, yet it is being constantly demythologized, and out of this process, paradoxically, comes its real possession and the possessor's only autonomy.

The past, for many Scottish novelists, is inseparable from the demonic scapegoat, Calvinism. Calvinism is portrayed as a suppression of life, a betrayal of culture, but also a force of ancestral dignity and independence. The severest anti-Calvinist seems unable to escape a sense of its power, or for that matter to shake off its conviction of man's pettiness, idolatry, delusion, and distance from old Eden, the green tree in Gedde. Devil-ridden Calvinism is portrayed by Stevenson as a national idolatry; its other side is an atavistic, sometimes demonic vitalism. Buchan seems unique in his mingling of Norse myth, fairy tale, and *Pilgrim's Progress* into a "romantic Calvinism." Yet, in the sentimental Barrie and Maclaren, as in the antisentimental Lockhart and MacDonald, Calvinism is a communal piety not to be carelessly slighted. In Hay's *Gillespie*, it implies an awful cosmic justice that petty humanitarianisms cannot fathom. Muir recognizes its terrible comprehensiveness, and respects the fearful piety of his three brothers far more than the Baptist sentimentality of poor Tom. It is a "negative charge" that Muriel Spark's Sandy must have in order to reject; it is part of the theological anger that impels Gibbon's young Ewan and his step-father Colqouhoun into radical humanitarianism. It underlies the ambivalent pastoral of Jenkins, Blake, and Brown. In short, it haunts the Scottish sense of the past.

Finally, history, in its public guise, is an arbitrary, external force that invades the close communities of real life. "Real" history is local and domestic, subsisting in lore or in personal relationships that public history ignores or discredits. This is the paradoxical theme that Scott introduced into the historical novel, and it appears, too, in the perspectives of Galt's burghal annalists and Moir's Mansie. Oliphant's Margaret Maitland finds in her quiet, domestic existence the crisis of kirk and community, and Alexander's Johnny Gibb inadvertently becomes a hero of resistance on his remote parochial stage. Household memoir counterpoints national history in such novels as these, and in very different fictions as well: Stevenson's *Master of Ballantrae*, Mitchison's *Bull Calves*, Gunn's *Silver Darlings*, Gibbon's trilogy of Chris Guthrie, Linklater's *Position at Noon*, and Kennaway's *Household Ghosts*. The domesticating of history, like that of the devil, is a strategy of diminution noteworthy in Scots humor, an expression of distrust in history itself, and a sign of traditional Scottish affection for the close, small community.

A noteworthy feature of Scottish fiction is the moral primacy of community, the faith (some would say Calvinist in genesis) that community is the ground of individual worth and a condition of salvation. From Galt to Duncan, it is implied that true community nurtures genuine individuality; for Lockhart, Alexander, and Gunn, a denial of community is a threat to personal integrity. Idolatrous selfhood destroys community; false community, in Spark's *Miss Brodie, Girls of Slender Means*, and other novels, fosters only a specious individual discipline or private morality. For Mac Colla's Albannach, the only fulfillment is through reassimilation into a traditional community. For Duncan, community is the terrifying fact of interconnectedness, without which one's identity is in doubt. For George Mackay Brown, Calvinism is the historical villain that has temporarily destroyed a communal life rooted in ritual and myth; for Gunn, egoistic rationality has had the same effect.

True community, for the Scottish imagination, is small: the close mentality makes appalling the cosmopolis, the housing estate, the city. The city is unreal or remote, the fallen world of MacDonald's Gibbie, Muir's poor Tom, and the end of Gibbon's trilogy. The city is peripheral in Galt's *Entail* and Tytler's *St. Mungo's City*; for Blake it is the fancied battleground from which he retreated to the burgh of Garvel, and for Jenkins it is the infernal setting from which one longs guiltily to escape. The small burgh is the arena of Kailyard and anti-kailyard. The ironic anticosmopolitan impulse can be traced all the way from Galt to Linklater, where it emerges as a normative small-nation mentality, and to Mitchison, where it is felt as a sense of brotherhood with all the weak, vanquished communities of world history. It is a paradox of Scottish fiction that closeness to small community is access to the most far-flung world in space and time. Cultural humility is key to a universal compassion in Linklater and Jenkins. Hence the ambiguity of place in Scottish fiction: the "other landscape" of Gunn; the ontological irony of setting in writers as different as Spark and Barrie; the preternatural suggestion in Hogg, MacDonald, and Buchan that local site is a gateway to the archaic; the ritual power of place outside of history, as in Mitchison and Fiona Macleod.

On the other side of community is the equally ambiguous preoccupation with exile. The exhilaration of the fugitive, the adventurer, the imperial Don Juan mingles strangely with the strong nostalgia of the homing instinct. The homecoming is a troubled yet absorbing dream—of Andrew Wylie's triumph and Sentimental Tommy's disenchantment, of harvest and mortality. Exile, as for Sharp, Spark, and Gibbon, may be an essential condition; for the more romantic and pious, such as Ferrier and MacDonald, one's true inheritance may require losing one's earthly home. The agony of retrieving Jane Duncan's Reachfar, so often lost, is a gradual surrender of remembered place. This strange remoteness from home, this divided yearning for escape and return—"I'm off! I'm away!"—has caused the Scottish novelist's uncertainties of perspective, voice and tone. It has also posed problems of narrative mode. For the story-telling norms of traditional community are sometimes uncongenial to the novel form. Some of the most memorable, and garrulously suspect, characters in Scottish fiction are communal storytellers whose relation to the stances and styles of the novelist is problematic or uneasily ironic. Finally, the preoccupation with small but transcendent community has affected the characterology of Scottish fiction.

Certain characters cluster repeatedly. Prominent in the domestic grouping is the mother, often stronger and more practical than the father, often alone. Galt's matriarchs are more naturally humane than, for example, Scott's important male figures, who are, by contrast with the Jeanie Deanses, unprincipled, quixotic, or passive. Oliphant's Margaret Maitland is the stoic survivor of male divisiveness and immaturity. MacDonald may be the exception that proves the complex rule; he stresses the quest for the Father, but not, finally, the earthly father. Matriarchalism is strikingly evident in Blake, Gibbon, Gunn, and Barke; Jenkins's strongest figure is Bell McShelvie. Kennaway's Mary, Stella, and Susan are strong antagonists of male folly and avarice. Iain Smith remembers the Clearances through one lonely, brave old woman, as, in a different way, Barrie's Thrums is seen through the eyes of another.

Fanatic or quixotic, the father is out of touch with reality. In Gunn, an exception to this, we often see the archetypal figures of mother and son, or the boy with the older man who is not his father. A tragic discontinuity is repeatedly rendered through the conflict of father and son. The father, such as Weir, Gourlay, and Gillespie, is sometimes a figure of barbaric titanism; the son, often standing in for the novelist, is weak, febrile, over-imaginative. The pattern invites psychological as well as anthropological interpretation. In the fiction itself, it often has explicit cultural meaning. The father fails as ancestor (as in Galt's *Entail*, Linklater's *Position at Noon*) because he is foolish or fanatic; the mother, as in Gibbon and Gunn, remains close to the land, to traditional wisdom, to the community, and comes to represent a nonhistoric, nonideological continuity or survival.

The figures of community are predictably institutional. At the cen-

ters of authority are the minister, schoolmaster, and (through his for-
bidding surrogates, the factor and gamekeeper) the landlord. The
minister appears and reappears as enforcer of parish morality, often
the overburdened or divided carrier of that morality. Galt's annalist,
Lockhart's Blair, Hogg's holy hypocrite, the tormented minister of
Oliphant's *Salem Chapel*, MacDonald's philistines and missionaries,
the erring Carmichael of Drumtochty and his confused counterpart
of Thrums, the hapless exorcist of *Witch Wood*, the doomed visionary
of *Cloud Howe*, the false spiritualists of Spark, the clerical betrayers of
the Clearance story in Mac Colla, Gunn, and Smith: any such survey
reveals how troubled, even quasi-tragic, is the figure of the minister.
Likewise, the schoolmaster or schoolmistress. He or she is the uneasy
instrument of the community's militant faith in learning as the way to
status, mobility, escape to a larger world; he may be a "stickit
minister," a figure of pathos, while the failed student may return to
become community pariah. The schoolmaster is perverted often to
sadism or sentimentality, to the flabby humanity of Jenkins' Charlie
Forbes or the megalomania of Jean Brodie; often he is caught in the
dilemma of whether to foster or betray a local culture irrelevant to the
cosmopolitan world. Against these are the figures of rebellion, often
also the figures of tradition and nature: the child, the poacher, the
poet, the publican, defying boundaries of property, culture, and
fancy, affirming the self but also the truer community. The figures of
authority are often at war with themselves; they fight over the survival and integrity of communal culture; they are forces in more
archetypal conflicts. Indeed, the weight and complexity of their representativeness is a feature of characterology we have often noticed.

Central characters from Scott, Galt, and Lockhart on seem
burdened with various determinants of significance. They belong to a
traditional community that favors individuality; "character," even eccentricity, is the stuff of legendary, hence communal, survival. They
must also play generic roles in cultural history. Yet, so persistent are
the absolutes of romance or myth that they also carry or discover
archetypal roles. Galt's Balwhidder and Lockhart's Blair, while highly
individual, represent cultural types and moments in Scottish social
history, yet they also participate in timeless moral conflicts. Romance
characters in Scott, Stevenson, and Buchan play archetypes in the
formulas of romance, while also embodying historical process and
achieving (Stevenson's early dicta to the contrary notwithstanding)

individual complexity. Problematic individuals in MacDonald enact a drama of cultural conflict and a theological romance; Barrie's are figures in both regional history and pastoral idyll. In Willa Muir's Calderwick, character types localize the Scottish burgh, populate the heroine's quest for national integrity, and represent psychic polarities, sexual and religious; the same is true in Edwin's *Three Brothers*. A multiple typology sometimes overwhelms the characters of Blake. Mackenzie's *Four Winds* abound in individuals who are cultural exemplars and psychic alternatives. Multiple roles burden the characterization of Gibbon's *Quair*; Gunn's local representatives find their individualities in archaic selves; characters in Black and Munro are trapped into legendary roles; Jenkins's intricately psychologized characters carry extreme symbolic weight. Only Naomi Mitchison seems to have theorized the phenomenon, deliberately counterpointing the individual, generic, and archetypal identities that overlay or clash in single characters.

The burdens of multiple role are a part of character in Scottish fiction. They are also a central meaning in that fiction, a sometimes desperate expression of the problem of identity in a national culture doubted, polarized, multileveled. In Scott's protagonists, for instance, as in figures as different as Barrie's minister, Galt's Ringan, and Mitchison's Tarrik and Erif Der, the recognition of generic or archetypal role is a burden or obsession for individual consciousness. Gibbon's Chris, already sensing herself divided, must resist the roles imposed on her by male ideologues. Gunn's hunted flee the intellectual hunters who would seek out and stereotype the individual core of life, yet, in the process, both hunted and hunter become archetypal. In MacDonald, cultural artifice or adulteration overlays true local nature, but true nature fulfills itself only on a transcendent level. Character in Scottish fiction is a flight from the hapless generality of historic role to the archetypal identity of communal legend. But meanwhile, survival in a world of historic role requires skillful impersonation. An agility to sustain multiple roles is the traditional magic of an Andrew Wylie; and skillful impersonation is a fabulous power in Buchan's Scots adventurers. But in Hogg's *Justified Sinner*, the power of impersonation is characteristically the devil's, and it wears a comparable demonic aura in the blackmailers of Muriel Spark.

The complexity of character is symptomatic of one of the persistent problems of the Scottish novelist: the problem of scope and intentionality. In every phase of the novel's Scottish history can be seen a fidelity to local truth, to the particulars of communal place and time; at the same time an intention to represent national types and whole cultural epochs; and finally an impetus to transcendent meaning. With such scope, one sometimes finds the tendency to force implication, to make the particular mean too much on too many levels, with the coordinate effects of sentimentality and abstraction.

Moreover, the novelists' intentions may reflect conflicting assumptions. The aim of local realism assumes a historian's loyalty to the transient, the passing facts and customs of a particular milieu; the generic analyst assumes a social typology, a Scottish consciousness that endures; the archetypal fabulist assumes a reality of nature and motive that transcends local and cultural configuration. There is no theoretic reason why a fiction cannot have meaning on multiple levels, so long as the levels do not contradict each other in terms of their assumptions about what is real. They sometimes do in Scottish fiction, perhaps reflecting ontological conflict in Scottish consciousness: the nominalist historian, the social theorist, and the absolutist theologian coexist uneasily. The local antiquarian can be compromised by the nationalist historian, and both may be overwhelmed by the theological moralist, for whom history is a war of psychic polarities.

The second problem is a complexity that is sometimes at conflict within itself. What David Craig called a "swithering of modes" and others have named "antisyzygy" or "dissociation of sensibility" has consistently appeared as a modal feature of Scottish fiction. The mixtures have been numerous: grotesque humor and pastoral sentiment; broad satire and severe piety; history competing with legend and romance; romance repeatedly undercut with irony; austere realism jostling with fantasy; tragedy and farce. Are such rapidly alternating and extreme responses to experience to be explained as cultural distinctiveness or cultural dissociation? Social anthropologists and psychologists may have answers. For the literary historian, the fact is that they persist in the fiction, and the problem is whether such switherings or radical conjunctions can be successfully assimilated into narrative art. The problem, I believe, is to be solved in terms of the integrities of individual works. Fantastic and surreal, satiric and romantic, tragic and farcical responses to reality can be artfully coordinated so long as historical realism is not an obtrusive norm. One impressive solution was Galt's: to dramatize the mixture in the person of the narrator. But Linklater's long struggle to exorcize realism altogether, to make way for tragic farce or pastoral irony, may be more emblematic of the Scottish novelist. In such terms, in terms of a versatile management of artistic mode, the talents of Galt and Linklater may be the most impressive in Scottish fiction to date.

But like most Scottish novelists, neither seems quite to have solved the third problem: the problem of uncertain narrative voice. Galt's narrators appear to many uncomfortably "provincial," suspiciously ironic. Linklater, however distinctively Scottish in mode, speaks in a repertory of literary English voices. The problem of a national language is still with us. If local realities and affiliations matter, then authentic local speech matters. If local speech is seen as a test of cultural fidelity, then the faithful narrator may seem insular and the distanced narrator is hard pressed to seem anything but an accomplice of the betrayers. If, in his evident foreignness, the narrator acts defensively on behalf of local speech, the effect will seem sentimentality or exploitation to some. The solutions are various but not quite satisfactory: to avoid local subjects; to create (as Gibbon did) an artificial voice that is foreign, yet identifiable with local speech; to dramatize the problem with linguistic disunity in the narrator himself; or to pretend that local language is no longer distinctive enough to record.

All three problems reflect unsettled issues in Scottish culture. And if the issues continue to exist as significant features of Scottish culture, then a fiction that slights or conceals them cannot be culturally authentic. There is still this much truth in Edwin Muir's gloomy diagnosis of the novel in Scotland, but the truth need not lead to his despair. Honest cultural diagnosis need not perpetuate a lack of confidence.

Underlying the problems has been the assumption that cultural survival is doomed or unlikely, and that the novelist must stridently resist the inevitable, meet it with polemic, or compensate for it with elegiac urgency. If a master novelist could write with a measure of ease about the cultural survival of Scotland—could feel free of the obligation to preserve, memorialize, avoid, or transcend—then the problems might fade or prove soluble. But supposing that he sought merely to write with conviction about human experience in Scotland, in a language essentially true to his ear, what fictional precedents could he safely follow? The models of the past carry their problems with them. Yet, if he avoids them altogether, his precedents must be foreign and in some degree irrelevant. Perhaps if some Scottish precedents could be recognized as impressive (if incomplete) successes, later writers would acquire the confidence of knowing it could be done.

Has the past that we have surveyed provided instances of such proof? I believe there is evidence of more than a few. The remaining problem is that so few believe it; and, not believing it, many cannot bring themselves to look and see. The attitude toward the past in Scottish culture is still very much what Stevenson described. It comprises two extemes: one is defensive, obsessive, uncritically proprietary; the other is hostile, cynical, willfully uninformed. The first adopts traditional fiction with condescending affection; the second acknowledges its existence only as a moribund joke. The future of the novel is Scotland depends on the achievement of a more measured and balanced view. Likewise, the future of Scottish cultural identity. To find the past not all glory and romance is not to conclude that it is sham and betrayal. Blasting irony is often the neurotic other side of obsessive romanticism. A truer humility is the maturest of virtues, as Robin Jenkins has said; a wise and humorous acceptance of human smallness is a surer way to survival.

NOTES

INDEX

Notes

Introduction

1. Douglas Young, *Scotland* (London: Cassell, 1971), p. 11.

2. See I. Budge and D. W. Urwin, *Scottish Political Behaviour* (London: Longmans, 1966). On the strength of Scottish local tradition, see T. C. Smout, *A History of the Scottish People 1560-1830* (New York: Scribner's, 1969), pp. 63, 158; Laurance J. Saunders, the chapter on regional variety in *Scottish Democracy 1815-1840* (Edinburgh: Oliver and Boyd, 1950); James G. Kellas, *Modern Scotland* (London: Pall Mall, 1968), pp. 26-27, 42, and the chapter on local government.

3. Walter Benjamin, "The Storyteller," in *Illuminations*, tr. H. Zohn (New York: Harcourt Brace and World, 1968), pp. 83-89.

4. Smout, *History*, pp. 97-100; Rosalind Mitchison, *A History of Scotland* (London: Methuen, 1970), p. 115; see also Lord Ritchie-Calder on the Scottish Enlightenment in *Alistair MacLean Introduces Scotland*, ed. A. M. Dunnett (London: Deutsch, 1972), p. 170.

5. Smout, *History*, p. 99.

6. Edwin Muir, *Scott and Scotland*; David Daiches, *The Paradox of Scottish Culture* (London: Oxford University Press, 1964).

7. Muriel Spark, "What Images Return," in *Memoirs of a Modern Scotland*, ed. K. Miller (London: Faber and Faber, 1970), p. 153.

8. See chap. 1 of G. Gregory Smith, *Scottish Literature* (London: Macmillan, 1919); and Hugh MacDiarmid, *Lucky Poet* (London: Methuen, 1943), pp. 74, 82, 111.

9. Quoted in H. W. Thompson, *A Scottish Man of Feeling* (London: Oxford University Press, 1931), p. 108.

10. Daiches, p. 11.

11. Thompson, *Scottish Man of Feeling*, p. 3; David Daiches in *Scottish Poetry: A Critical Survey*, ed. J. Kinsley (London: Cassell, 1955), p. 152.

12. Daiches, *Paradox*, pp. 27-28.

13. David Craig, *Scottish Literature and the Scottish People 1680-1830* (London: Chatto and Windus, 1961), pp. 72ff.

14. Daiches, *Paradox*, p. 23.

15. Quoted in Thompson, *Scottish Man of Feeling*, p. 191.

16. Quoted in Thompson, *Scottish Man of Feeling*, p. 47.

17. Thompson, *Scottish Man of Feeling*, p. 107.

18. Ibid., pp. 108, 112.

19. *The Man of Feeling*, chap. 34.

20. Kurt Wittig, *The Scottish Tradition in Literature* (Edinburgh: Oliver and Boyd, 1958), p. 250.

21. Thompson, *Scottish Man of Feeling*, pp. 148-151.

22. Ibid., p. 193.

23. *Blackwood's Magazine*, 11 (1822), 350.

24. Quoted in Thompson, *Scottish Man of Feeling*, p. 178.

25. Ian Watt, *The Rise of the Novel* (London: Chatto and Windus, 1957); G. A. Starr, *Defoe and Spiritual Autobiography* (Princeton: Princeton University Press, 1965); Kenneth MacLean, *John Locke and English Literature of the Eighteenth Century* (New Haven: Yale University Press, 1936).

26. Gladys Bryson, *Man and Society* (Princeton: Princeton University Press, 1945); Louis Schneider, ed., *The Scottish Moralists* (Chicago: Phoenix, 1967); "The Athenian Age," in G. S. Pryde, *Scotland from 1603 to the Present Day* (London: Nelson, 1962).

27. Smout, *History*, p. 95.

28. Mitchison, *History*, p. 345.

29. W. Ferguson, *Scotland 1689 to the Present* (Edinburgh: Oliver and Boyd, 1968), p. 313.

30. N. T. Phillipson, "Nationalism and Ideology," in *Government and Nationalism in Scotland*, ed. J. N. Wolfe (Edinburgh: Edinburgh University Press, 1968), pp. 167-188; J. A. Smith, "Scott and the Idea of Scotland," in *Edinburgh University Journal*, Spring 1964.

31. Martin Price, *To the Palace of Wisdom* (Garden City, New York: Doubleday, 1965), pp. 343-389; see also Francis R. Hart, "The Experience of Character in the English Gothic Novel," in *Experience in the Novel*, ed. R. H. Pearce (New York: Columbia University Press, 1968), pp. 83-105.

1. Scottish Variations of the Gothic Novel

1. The following discussion of Smollett, Scott, and Hogg is a revised and expanded version of my essay "Limits of the Gothic: The Scottish Example," in *Studies in Eighteenth-Century Culture*, ed. H. Pagliaro (Cleveland: Case Western Reserve Press, 1973), III, 137-153.

2. Robert Spector, *Tobias George Smollett* (New York: Twayne, 1968), pp. 87-88.

3. Spector, *Smollett*, pp. 102-103.

4. Donald Bruce, *Radical Doctor Smollett* (Boston: Houghton Mifflin, 1965), pp. 42, 44-45, 52-53, 138.

5. Wittig, *Scottish Tradition*, pp. 43-44, 84-85, 249-250, 268, 334. Wittig does not associate the phenomenon with Smollett.

6. Tobias George Smollett, *The Adventures of Ferdinand Count Fathom*, ed. D. Grant (London: Oxford University Press, 1971), p. 141.

7. Tobias George Smollett, *Roderick Random*, ed. G. Saintsbury, 3 vols. (London: Gibbings, 1895), I, 88-89.

8. Wolfgang Kayser, *The Grotesque in Art and Literature*, tr. U. Weisstein (New York: McGraw-Hill, 1966), pp. 35-37, 79, 138, 184-185.

9. E. A. Poe, "The Imp of the Perverse," *Selected Tales*, ed. J. Curtis (Harmondsworth, Middlesex: Penguin, 1956), p. 358.

10. V. S. Pritchett, *The Living Novel* (London: Chatto and Windus, 1946), p. 20; M. A. Goldberg, *Smollett and the Scottish School* (Albuquerque: University of New Mexico Press, 1959), pp. 59-79.

11. Tobias George Smollett, *The Adventures of Peregrine Pickle*, ed. J. L. Clifford (London: Oxford University Press, 1964), pp. 239, 288-289.

12. Sir Walter Scott, *The Miscellaneous Works of Sir Walter Scott* (Edinburgh: Black, 1880), III, 177.

13. Modern interpretation of Scott as historical realist begins with two influential essays by David Daiches, "Scott's Achievement as a Novelist" and "Scott's *Redgauntlet*," both reprinted in *Walter Scott: Modern Judgments*, ed. D. D. Devlin (London: Macmillan, 1968), and with Georg Lukacs, *The Historical Novel*, tr. H. and S. Mitchell (London: Merlin, 1962). The tradition is carried on by Edgar Johnson in his magisterial *Sir Walter Scott*, 2 vols. (New York: Macmillan, 1970). My own *Scott's Novels: The Plotting of Historic Survival* (Charlottesville: University Press of Virginia, 1966) follows the same trend.

14. See *Scott: The Critical Heritage*, ed. J. O. Hayden (New York: Barnes and Noble, 1970), especially the essays of Carlyle and Stephen. More recently, see Alexander Welsh, *The Hero of the Waverley Novels* (New Haven: Yale University Press, 1963); Avrom Fleishman, *The English Historical Novel* (Baltimore: Johns Hopkins University Press, 1971); Robert Kiely, *The Romantic Novel in England* (Cambridge: Harvard University Press, 1972).

15. Cf. "Charles Brockden Brown and the Invention of the American Gothic," in Leslie Fiedler's *Love and Death in the American Novel*, rev. ed. (New York: Stein and Day, 1966); also, Hart, "Experience of Character," in *Experience in the Novel*, ed. R. H. Pearce, pp. 96-99.

16. Anthony Winner, *Great European Short Novels*, I (New York: Harper and Row, 1968), p. 497.

17. James Hogg, *Private Memoirs and Confessions of a Justified Sinner* (London: Cresset Press, 1947). With an introduction by André Gide.

18. Gide in introduction to Hogg, *Justified Sinner*, p. x.

19. Hart, "Experience of Character," in *Experience in the Novel*, ed.

Pearce, pp. 83-105.

20. Edwin Eigner, *Robert Louis Stevenson and Romantic Tradition* (Princeton: Princeton University Press, 1966), pp. 24-26.

21. Hogg, *Justified Sinner*, pp. 113-114.

22. Ibid., pp. 119, 178, 183.

23. Craig, *Scottish Literature*, p. 193: "The unsatisfactoriness of the novel is in its swithering from mode to mode."

24. James Hogg, *Tales and Sketches by the Ettrick Shepherd*, 6 vols. (London: Nimmo, 1878), II, 122-123.

25. Ibid., I, 110.

26. Ibid., I, 18.

27. Ibid., I, 117-118.

28. Ibid., III, 66; *Winter Evening Tales*, 2 vols. (Hartford: Andrus, 1845), I, 227, 243, 252.

29. James Hogg, *The Three Perils of Man*, ed. D. Gifford (Edinburgh: Scottish Academic Press, 1972), p. vii.

30. Ibid., pp. 253, 276.

31. Ibid., p. xix.

32. Ibid., p. xvi.

2. John Galt

1. Craig, *Scottish Literature*, p. 219.

2. Eric Linklater, *The Survival of Scotland* (Garden City, New York: Doubleday, 1968), p. 328.

3. *The Ayrshire Legatees* (with *Annals of the Parish*), in *Works of John Galt*, ed. D. S. Meldrum (Edinburgh: Blackwood, 1895), pp. 265-266.

4. Quoted from Galt's *Literary Life* in F. H. Lyell, *A Study of the Novels of John Galt* (Princeton: Princeton University Press, 1942), p. 51.

5. John Galt, *Sir Andrew Wylie of That Ilk*, new ed. (Edinburgh: Blackwood, 1854), p. 31.

6. John Galt, *Annals of the Parish*, ed. J. Kinsley (London: Oxford, 1967), p. 4.

7. Craig, *Scottish Literature*, p. 144.

8. George Kitchin, "John Galt," in *Edinburgh Essays on Scots Literature* (Edinburgh: Oliver and Boyd, 1933), p. 113; Ian Jack, *English Literature 1815-1832* (Oxford: Clarendon, 1963), pp. 229-230.

9. G. Armour Craig, "The Unpoetic Compromise," reprinted in *Discussions of the Novel*, ed. R. Sale (Boston: Heath, 1960), p. 33.

10. John Galt, *The Provost and The Last of the Lairds*, in *Works of Galt*, I, 118; the two novels are printed together in two volumes, *The Provost* in volume I.

11. Craig, *Scottish Literature*, p. 159; Douglas Gifford, introduction to *Scottish Short Stories 1800-1900* (London: Calder Boyars, 1971), p. 15.

12. See Wittig, *Scottish Tradition*, p. 249.

13. Galt, *The Provost and The Last of the Lairds*, II, 249, 252.

14. John Galt, *Autobiography*, 2 vols. (London: Cochrane and M'Crone, 1833), I, 12.

15. S. R. Crockett, introduction to *The Entail, or the Lairds of Grippy* (*Works of Galt*, ed. Meldrum), I, xiii.

16. References are to Ian A. Gordon's edition (London: Oxford, 1970); this passage is on pp. 149-150.

17. Pritchett (in *The Living Novel*, p. 41) sees the book as a "complicated satire of Glasgow manners."

18. Ibid., p. 37; Jack, *English Literature*, p. 234; Craig, *Scottish Literature*, p. 261.

19. Jack, *English Literature*, pp. 233, 231.

20. Galt, *Autobiography*, II, 161.

21. References to *Ringan Gilhaize* are to the Meldrum and Roughhead edition, 2 vols. (Edinburgh: Grant, 1936).

3. The Other Blackwoodians

1. David Macbeth Moir, *The Life of Mansie Wauch Tailor in Dalkeith* (Edinburgh: Foulis, 1911), p. 333.

2. Susan Ferrier, *Marriage*, 3rd ed., 2 vols. (Edinburgh: Blackwood, 1826), I, 304-305.

3. Susan Ferrier, *The Inheritance*, 3 vols. (Edinburgh: Blackwood, 1824), I, 102.

4. Susan Ferrier, *Destiny*, 3 vols. (Edinburgh: Cadell, 1831), III, 112.

5. John Gibson Lockhart, *Adam Blair*, ed. D. Craig (Edinburgh: Edinburgh University Press, 1963), p. xii.

6. *Blackwood's Magazine*, 11 (1822), 350.

7. John Gibson Lockhart, *Valerius; a Roman Story*, 3 vols. (Edinburgh: Blackwood, 1821), II, 51-52.

8. John Gibson Lockhart, *Reginald Dalton*, 3 vols. (Edinburgh: Blackwood, 1823), II, 334-335.

9. John Gibson Lockhart, *The History of Matthew Wald* (Edinburgh: Blackwood, 1824), p. 91.

10. Lockhart, *Adam Blair*, p. 99.

11. See *Blackwood's*, 15 (1824), 624.

12. Jack, *English Literature*, pp. 336-337.

13. Passages are quoted from *Works of Professor Wilson*, 12 vols. (Edinburgh: Blackwood, 1858); vol. XI includes the "Tales," discussed here; this passage is on p. 198.

4. Victorian Modes and Models

1. J. H. Millar, *A Literary History of Scotland* (New York: Scribner's, 1903), p. 619.

2. Gifford, *Scottish Short Stories*, p. 15.

3. J. M. Reid, *Modern Scottish Literature* (Edinburgh: Oliver and Boyd, 1945), p. 15; Wittig, *Scottish Tradition*, p. 253.

4. Craig, *Scottish Literature*, p. 268; Gifford, *Scottish Short Stories*, p. 15.

5. William Alexander, *Johnny Gibb of Gushetneuk* (Edinburgh: Douglas and Foulis, 1948), p. 197.

6. Pritchett, *The Living Novel*, p. 78.

7. John Holloway, *The Victorian Sage* (New York: Norton, 1965).

8. J. Hillis Miller, *The Form of Victorian Fiction* (Notre Dame: University of Notre Dame Press, 1968).

9. Margaret Oliphant, *Merkland; or, Self-Sacrifice* (New York: Stringer and Townsend, 1854), p. 107.

5. Mid-Victorians

1. *Autobiography and Letters of Mrs. M. O. W. Oliphant*, ed. Mrs. H. Coghill (New York: Dodd Mead, 1899), p. 22; on Moir, see pp. 28-29.

2. Quoted in Vineta Colby and Robert A. Colby, *The Equivocal Virtue: Mrs. Oliphant and the Victorian Literary Market Place* (Archon, 1966), p. 16.

3. Millar, *Literary History of Scotland*, p. 616.

4. Colby and Colby, *Equivocal Virtue*, p. 87.

5. Margaret Oliphant, *Margaret Maitland of Sunnyside* (New York: Putnam, 1856), p. 292.

6. Henry James, *Notes on Novelists, with Some Other Notes* (New York: Scribner's, 1914), pp. 452-455.

7. Colby and Colby, *Equivocal Virtue*, pp. 44-45.

8. Oliphant, quoted in *Equivocal Virtue*, p. 46.

9. Baker, *History of the English Novel*, X, 204.

10. Colby and Colby, *Equivocal Virtue*, p. 49.

11. Margaret Oliphant, *Salem Chapel*, ed. W. Robertson Nicoll (London: Dent, 1907), p. ix.

12. Oliphant, quoted in *Equivocal Virtue*, p. 50.

13. Oliphant, *Salem Chapel*, p. 99.

14. George MacDonald, *David Elginbrod* (London: Cassell, 1927), p. 341. Subsequent references are to the following: *Robert Falconer* (London: Cassell, 1927); *Alec Forbes of Howglen* (New York: Harper, 1867); *Malcolm* (London: Cassell, 1927); *Sir Gibbie* (London: Cassell, 1927); and *The Marquis of Lossie* (London: Cassell, 1927).

15. William Power, *Literature and Oatmeal* (London: Routledge, 1935), p. 123.

16. Baker, *History of the English Novel*, X, 160.

17. Sarah Tytler, *Three Generations* (London: Murray, 1911), p. 255.

18. George Blake, *Barrie and the Kailyard School* (London: Barker,

1951), pp. 8-10. *St. Mungo's City*, 3 vols. (London: Chatto and Windus, 1884).

19. Sarah Tytler, *Logie Town* (New York: Lovell, 1888), p. 1.

6. The Liberals in the Kailyard

1. José Ortega y Gasset, *The Dehumanization of Art and Other Writings* (Garden City, New York: Doubleday, 1956), p. 83.

2. Power, *Literature and Oatmeal*, pp. 163-164.

3. Millar, *Literary History of Scotland*, p. 657.

4. Power, *Literature and Oatmeal*, pp. 160-161; Millar, *Literary History of Scotland*, p. 658.

5. Quoted in MacDiarmid's foreword to Sydney Goodsir Smith, *Carotid Cornucopius* (Edinburgh: Macdonald, 1964), p. 19.

6. Maclaren (John Watson), *Kate Carnegie* (New York: Dodd Mead, 1896), p. 296; Greville MacDonald, *George MacDonald and His Wife* (New York: MacVeagh, 1924), p. 194.

7. Ferguson, *Scotland 1689 to the Present*, p. 336.

8. MacDonald, *George MacDonald and His Wife*, pp. 192-193.

9. George Elder Davie, *The Democratic Intellect* (Edinburgh: Edinburgh University Press, 1961), pp. 266-268, 326-328.

10. Baker, *History of the English Novel*, X, 183; Blake, *Barrie and the Kailyard School*, pp. 47-48.

11. S. R. Crockett, *The Raiders and The Lilac Sunbonnet* (London: Collins, 1954), p. 330.

12. S. R. Crockett, *Cleg Kelly, Arab of the City* (New York: Appleton, 1896), p. 19.

13. Ian Maclaren, *A Doctor of the Old School* (New York: Coward-McCann, 1929).

14. Blake, *Barrie and the Kailyard School*, pp. 32-39.

15. Ian Maclaren, *Beside the Bonnie Brier Bush* (New York: Dodd Mead, 1895), p. 32.

16. Ian Maclaren, *The Days of Auld Lang Syne* (New York: Dodd Mead, 1895), p. 366.

17. Maclaren, *Brier Bush*, p. 140.

18. Maclaren, *Auld Lang Syne*, p. 195.

19. Maclaren, *Kate Carnegie*, p. 71.

20. T. W. H. Crosland, *The Unspeakable Scot* (London: Grant Richards, 1902), p. 87.

21. J. M. Barrie, *Peter and Wendy* (with) *Margaret Ogilvy* (New York: Scribner's, 1913), pp. 60, 131, 188.

22. J. M. Barrie, *Sentimental Tommy* (New York: Scribner's, 1923), p. 207.

23. J. M. Barrie, *Tommy and Grizel*, 2 vols. in 1 (New York: Scribner's,

1913), I, 27.

24. Barrie, *Sentimental Tommy*, pp. 226-227.

7. The Anti-Kailyard as Theological Furor

1. Crosland, *Unspeakable Scot*, p. 87.

2. Maurice Lindsay, *By Yon Bonnie Banks* (London: Hutchinson, 1961), p. 120.

3. Mitchison, *History*, p. 115; Pritchett, *Living Novel*, p. 110.

4. This is the intention Stevenson described to his step-daughter, reported in Sidney Colvin's note to the fragmentary novel.

5. Robert Kiely, *Robert Louis Stevenson and the Fiction of Adventure* (Cambridge: Harvard University Press, 1964), p. 254.

6. Eigner, *Robert Louis Stevenson*, p. 227.

7. *Selected Writings of Robert Louis Stevenson*, ed. S. Commins (New York: Modern Library, 1947), p. 449.

8. Iain Crichton Smith's excellent essay, "The House with the Green Shutters," is in *Studies in Scottish Literature*, 7 (1969), 3-10.

9. Wittig, *Scottish Tradition*, p. 266. References to *The House with the Green Shutters* are to the recent reprinting in *Minor Classics of Nineteenth-Century Fiction*, ed. W. E. Buckler, 2 vols. (Boston: Houghton Mifflin, 1967), II, 389-571.

10. Cf. John Speirs, *The Scots Literary Tradition* (London: Chatto and Windus, 1940), pp. 161-176.

11. J. MacDougall Hay, *Gillespie* (London: Duckworth, 1963), p. xii.

8. Romance after the Enlightenment

1. Quoted in Gertrude Himmelfarb, "John Buchan: The Last Victorian," *Victorian Minds* (New York: Harper, 1970), p. 258.

2. Donald Fanger, *Dostoevsky and Romantic Realism: A Study of Dostoevsky in Relation to Balzac, Dickens, and Gogol* (Cambridge: Harvard University Press, 1965).

3. Allusions in this paragraph are to Maurice Z. Shroder, "The Novel as a Genre," in *The Novel: Modern Essays in Criticism*, ed. R. M. Davis (Englewood Cliffs: Prentice-Hall, 1969), p. 45; Norman H. Holland, *The Dynamics of Literary Response* (New York: Oxford, 1968), pp. 30-31; Warner Berthoff, "Fiction, History, Myth: Notes toward the Discrimination of Narrative Forms," in *The Interpretation of Narrative*, ed. M. W. Bloomfield (Cambridge: Harvard University Press, 1970), pp. 266, 276.

4. Northrop Frye, *Anatomy of Criticism* (Princeton: Princeton University Press, 1957), especially pp. 33, 36-37, 186-203, and 303-309.

5. Paul Zweig, *The Adventurer* (New York: Basic Books, 1974), pp. 34-35.

6. Ibid., p. 71.

7. Tom Nairn, "The Three Dreams of Scottish Nationalism," in *Memoirs of a Modern Scotland*, ed. K. Miller, pp. 35-41.

8. Richard Chase, *The American Novel and Its Tradition* (Garden City, New York: Doubleday, 1957), p. 21.

9. Ibid., pp. viii, x.

10. Neil Gunn, *Off in a Boat* (London: Faber and Faber, 1938), p. 179.

11. John Buchan, *The Novel and the Fairy Tale* (Oxford: English Association, 1931).

12. Walter Benjamin, "The Storyteller," in *Illuminations*, tr. H. Zohn (New York: Harcourt Brace and World, 1968), pp. 86-101.

13. Alexander Welsh, *The Hero of the Waverley Novels* (New Haven: Yale University Press, 1963), pp. 147-148.

14. Kiely, *Romantic Novel*, p. 140.

15. References are to the Dryburgh Edition of the Waverley Novels, 25 vols. (1892-1894); the present reference is to *Redgauntlet*, p. 74.

16. Scott, *Guy Mannering*, p. 324.

17. Scott, *Ivanhoe*, p. 263.

18. Scott, *The Fortunes of Nigel*, p. 263.

19. Scott, *The Abbot*, pp. 296-297.

20. H. J. Hanham, *Scottish Nationalism* (Cambridge: Harvard University Press, 1969), pp. 76-78.

21. Crockett, *The Raiders and the Lilac Sunbonnet*, p. 21.

9. Stevenson, Munro, and Buchan

1. Robert Louis Stevenson, *Travels and Essays* (New York: Scribner's, 1900), XIV, 19-27.

2. Ibid., XIII, 329.

3. Ibid., XIII, 348-357.

4. Ibid., XIII, 327-339.

5. David Daiches, *Robert Louis Stevenson* (Norfolk, Connecticut: New Directions, 1947), pp. 32ff.

6. Kiely, *Robert Louis Stevenson and the Fiction of Adventure*, pp. 79-80.

7. Robert Louis Stevenson, *Treasure Island*, in *Selected Writings of Stevenson*, p. 46.

8. Quoted in Eigner, *Stevenson and Romantic Tradition*, p. 96n.

9. Robert Louis Stevenson, *Kidnapped* (New York: Collier, 1962), pp. 166, 182.

10. For the phrases from *Kidnapped*, see pp. 80, 109, 115, 162, 186, 188, 192.

11. Eigner, *Stevenson and Romantic Tradition*, pp. 92-95.

12. Quoted in Kiely, *Robert Louis Stevenson and the Fiction of Adventure*, p. 19.

13. Eigner, *Stevenson and Romantic Tradition*, p. 66.

14. J. C. Furnas, *Voyage to Windward* (New York: Sloane, 1951), p. 221.

15. Robert Louis Stevenson, *David Balfour* (New York: Scribner's, 1925), p. 57.

16. Robert Louis Stevenson, *St. Ives* (New York: Scribner's, 1925)—which includes the final chapters by Quiller-Couch.

17. Robert Louis Stevenson, *The Master of Ballantrae*, in *Selected Writings of Stevenson*, p. 365.

18. Walter Allen, *The English Novel* (London: Phoenix, 1954), p. 270.

19. Daiches, *Robert Louis Stevenson*, pp. 81-82.

20. Quoted in Kiely, *Robert Louis Stevenson and the Fiction of Adventure*, p. 173.

21. Eigner, *Stevenson and Romantic Tradition*, pp. 177-187.

22. Furnas, *Voyage to Windward*, p. 272.

23. Quoted from James, et al., in Kiely, *Robert Louis Stevenson and the Fiction of Adventure*, pp. 202, 227.

24. Cf. Angus Macdonald in *Edinburgh Essays on Scots Literature*, ed. H. J. C. Grierson (Edinburgh: Oliver and Boyd, 1933), pp. 160-161; J. M. Reid, *Modern Scottish Literature*, p. 16.

25. George Blake, introduction to Munro, *The Brave Days* (Edinburgh: Porpoise, 1931), pp. 8, 10, 17-18.

26. Neil Munro, *Doom Castle* (Edinburgh: Blackwood, n.d.), pp. 166, 318.

27. Neil Munro, *John Splendid* (Edinburgh: Blackwood, 1955), p. 143.

28. Neil Munro, *The New Road* (Edinburgh: Blackwood, 1930), p. 89.

29. John Buchan, *Pilgrim's Way* (Boston: Houghton Mifflin, 1940), p. 196.

30. Gertrude Himmelfarb, "John Buchan: The Last Victorian," in *Victorian Minds*.

31. Buchan, *Pilgrim's Way*, pp. 196-197. References to *Witch Wood* are to the London: Hodder and Stoughton, 1963, edition.

32. Buchan, *Pilgrim's Way*, p. 33.

33. John Buchan, *John Burnet of Barns* (London: Nelson, 1951), p. 72.

34. Ibid., p. 252.

35. Buchan, *Pilgrim's Way*, pp. 5-7.

36. John Buchan, *The Kirk in Scotland 1560-1929* (London: Hodder and Stoughton, 1930).

37. John Buchan, *Prester John* (New York: Doran, 1926).

38. John Buchan, *Huntingtower* (New York: Doran, 1922), p. 175.

39. John Buchan, *Thirty-Nine Steps* (London: Nelson, 1960), p. 6.

40. Buchan, *Pilgrim's Way*, p. 194.

41. John Buchan, *Greenmantle* (New York: Popular Library, n.d.), pp. 27-28.

42. John Buchan, *John Macnab* (London: Hodder and Stoughton, 1967).

43. Himmelfarb, "John Buchan," in *Victorian Minds*, pp. 265-266.

44. John Buchan, *Mountain Meadow* (Boston: Houghton Mifflin, 1941).

10. Mitchison and Later Romancers

1. Naomi Mitchison, *Return to the Fairy Hill* (New York: John Day, 1966), p. 212.

2. References are to *The Conquered* (New York: Harcourt Brace, 1923), *Blood of the Martyrs* (London: Constable, 1939), and *The Corn King and the Spring Queen* (New York: Harcourt Brace, 1931).

3. Mitchison, *The Corn King*, p. 11.

4. Naomi Mitchison, *The Bull Calves* (London: Cape, 1947), p. 408.

5. Originally published 1969-1971; the latest American editions are from New York: Ballantine, 1973-74.

6. References in my text identify the novels by initials and are all to the American editions (New York: Putnam) except for *Checkmate* (London: Cassell).

11. Contemporary Scotland in Fact and Myth

1. Michael Grieve in *Whither Scotland?* ed. D. Glen (London: Gollancz, 1971), p. 39.

2. H. J. Hanham, *Scottish Nationalism* (Cambridge: Harvard University Press, 1969), p. 25.

3. In *Alistair MacLean Introduces Scotland*, ed. A.M. Dunnett (London: Deutsch, 1972), p. 113.

4. James Kellas, *Modern Scotland* (London: Pall Mall, 1968), p. 202.

5. Rosalind Mitchison in *MacLean Introduces Scotland*, ed. Dunnett, p. 104.

6. See, for example, *The Scottish Debate*, ed. N. MacCormick (London: Oxford, 1970), pp. 33, 78; also, *Whither Scotland?* pp. 51, 86, 91.

7. Eric Linklater in *MacLean Introduces Scotland*, ed. Dunnett, p. 115.

8. Young, *Scotland*, p. 153.

9. Kellas, *Modern Scotland*, p. 115; see also *MacLean Introduces Scotland*, pp. 174-176, 191-192; Young, *Scotland*, p. 58; Mitchison, *History of Scotland*, p. 416.

10. Nairn in *Memoirs of a Modern Scotland*, p. 37; Young, *Scotland*, p. 72; *Whither Scotland?* pp. 122-123; *MacLean Introduces Scotland*, pp. 197, 170, 239; Mitchison, *History*, p. 115; Smout, *History*, p. 99; Ferguson, *Scotland 1689 to the Present*, p. 209; Kellas, *Modern Scotland*, pp. 9, 51, 74.

11. Young, *Scotland*, p. 94; *Whither Scotland?* ed. Glen, p. 60; Kellas, *Modern Scotland*, p. 90. For *The Prime of Miss Jean Brodie*, see the discussion of Muriel Spark below.

12. Kellas, *Modern Scotland*, p. 21; Mitchison, *History*, pp. 399-400; *Whither Scotland?* ed. Glen, p. 26.

13. J. M. Reid, *Scotland's Progress* (London: Eyre and Spottiswoode, 1971), p. 181; *MacLean Introduces Scotland*, p. 12; *Memoirs of a Modern Scotland*, ed. Miller, pp. 118, 156.

14. Mitchison, *History*, pp. 406-410; *MacLean Introduces Scotland*, pp. 104, 95-96; Hanham, *Scottish Nationalism*, p. 206; Kellas, *Modern Scotland*, p. 204; *Whither Scotland?* pp. 44-45.

15. *Memoirs of a Modern Scotland*, ed. Miller, p. 71; *MacLean Introduces Scotland*, p. 31; Reid, *Scotland's Progress*, pp. 179, 188-189; *Future of the Highlands*, ed. Grimble and Thompson, p. 153.

16. Clifford Hanley in *MacLean Introduces Scotland*, pp. 38-47; Young, *Scotland*, p. 22; Mitchison, *History*, pp. 403-404.

12. Novelists of the Modern Renaissance

1. Eric Linklater, "The Novel in Scotland," *Fortnightly Review*, 144 (1935), 621.

2. Willa Muir, *Belonging* (London: Hogarth, 1968), p. 163.

3. Willa Muir, *Imagined Corners* (London: Martin Secker, 1931), pp. 339-340.

4. Willa Muir, *Belonging*, p. 151.

5. Peter Butter, *Edwin Muir* (Edinburgh: Oliver and Boyd, 1962), pp. 42, 44.

6. Edwin Muir, *The Three Brothers* (New York: Doubleday Doran, 1931), pp. 208, 147.

7. Linklater, "The Novel in Scotland," p. 622.

8. *Annals of Scotland 1895-1955* (British Broadcasting Corporation, 1956), p. 32.

9. *Mince Collop Close* (New York: McBride, 1924); *The Path of Glory* (New York: Harper's, 1929); *The Shipbuilders* (London: Faber and Faber, 1935); *David and Joanna* (London: Faber and Faber, 1936); *Late Harvest* (London: Collins, 1938); *The Constant Star* (London: Collins, 1945); *The Westering Sun* (London: Collins, 1946).

10. Blake, *Late Harvest*, p. 203.

11. Blake, *The Constant Star*, pp. 278, 162.

12. Blake, *The Westering Sun*, pp. 48, 63, 66, 181, 207.

13. Ibid., pp. 260-261.

14. Frank Swinnerton, *The Georgian Scene* (New York: Farrar and Rinehart, 1934), p. 299.

15. *The East Wind of Love* (1937), *The South Wind of Love* (1937), *The West Wind of Love* (1940), *West to North* (1940)—all New York: Dodd Mead. *The North Wind of Love*, bk. 1 (1944) and bk. 2 (1945), London: Chatto and Windus. References in the text identify the volumes by initials.

16. Quoted in Ian S. Munro, *Leslie Mitchell: Lewis Grassic Gibbon* (Edinburgh: Oliver and Boyd, 1966), p. 130.

17. James Leslie Mitchell, *Cairo Dawns* (Indianapolis: Bobbs-Merrill, 1931).

18. Ibid., pp. 134, 241.

19. James Leslie Mitchell, *The Lost Trumpet* (Indianapolis: Bobbs-Merrill, 1932), pp. 144, 166.

20. James Leslie Mitchell, *Three Go Back* (Indianapolis: Bobbs-Merrill, 1932).

21. References are to the recent edition of *Spartacus* by Ian S. Munro (London: Hutchinson, 1970), where the author is given as Lewis Grassic Gibbon.

22. Abundant excerpts from the criticism are given by Munro.

23. See Low's commentary to Lewis Grassic Gibbon, *Sunset Song* (London: Longmans, 1971); references to Wittig are to *The Scottish Tradition in Literature*, pp. 330-333. References by initials to the three novels of the *Quair* are to the Jarrold's edition (London, 1950), in which the novels are printed together but paginated separately.

24. Quoted in Munro, *Leslie Mitchell*, p. 76.

25. Ibid., pp. 78-80.

26. Munro, *Leslie Mitchell*, p. 176.

27. James Barke, *The Land of the Leal* (London: Collins, 1939).

28. Hugh MacDiarmid, *Sydney Goodsir Smith*, a Tribute at the Presentation of the Urquhart Award, December 14, 1962, Fales Coll. No. 19, signed. Cf. MacDiarmid's foreword to *Carotid Cornucopius* (Edinburgh: MacDonald, 1964); my excerpts are taken from this edition.

13. Novelists of Survival

1. Eric Linklater, "The Novel in Scotland," *Fortnightly Review*, 144 (1935), 621-624; *The Lion and the Unicorn* is in the Voice of Scotland series (London: Routledge, 1935).

2. Eric Linklater, *The Stories of Eric Linklater* (London: Macmillan, 1968), p. 11.

3. Eric Linklater, *Fanfare for a Tin Hat* (London: Macmillan, 1970), p. 133.

4. Linklater, *Fanfare*, pp. 103-104; quotations from Eric Linklater, *White-Maa's Saga* (Harmondsworth, Middlesex: Penguin, 1963) are from pp. 57, 51, 10, 185.

5. Linklater, *Fanfare*, p. 104; quotations from Eric Linklater, *Poet's Pub* (London: Cape, 1933), are from pp. 22, 74, 77.

6. Linklater, *Fanfare*, pp. 121-122; references in the text are to Eric Linklater, *Juan in America* (London: Cape, 1931).

7. Blake, *Annals of Scotland*, p. 28; MacDiarmid's forward to Smith's *Carotid Cornucopius*, p. 14; and see Wittig, *Scottish Tradition*, pp. 328-329.

8. Linklater, *Fanfare*, p. 132.

9. Eric Linklater, *The Ultimate Viking* (New York: Harcourt Brace, 1956), pp. 8-11.

10. Eric Linklater, *The Men of Ness* (London: Cape, 1932), p. 245.

11. Eric Linklater, *Magnus Merriman* (London: Cape, 1934), pp. 298, 352.

12. Eric Linklater, *Ripeness Is All* (New York: Farrar and Rinehart, 1935), pp. 41-44.

13. Linklater, *Fanfare*, pp. 149, 155; Eric Linklater, *Juan in China* (London: Cape, 1948).

14. Eric Linklater, *The Sailor's Holiday* (London: Cape, 1937).

15. Linklater, *Fanfare*, pp. 157-160; Eric Linklater, *The Impregnable Women* (London: Cape, 1938).

16. Linklater, *Fanfare*, p. 161; Eric Linklater, *Judas* (London: Cape, 1939).

17. Linklater, *Fanfare*, pp. 300, 146; Eric Linklater, *Private Angelo* (New York: Macmillan, 1946).

18. Linklater, *Fanfare*, p. 316.

19. Eric Linklater, *A Spell for Old Bones* (London: Cape, 1949).

20. Eric Linklater, *Laxdale Hall* (London: Cape, 1951), pp. 50-51, 53, 134.

21. Eric Linklater, *The House of Gair* (London: Cape, 1960).

22. Eric Linklater, *The Faithful Ally* (London: Cape, 1954), p. 252.

23. Eric Linklater, *The Dark of Summer* (New York: Harcourt Brace, 1957), p. 7.

24. Linklater, *Fanfare*, p. 326; Eric Linklater, *Position at Noon* (Harmondsworth, Middlesex: Penguin, 1964).

25. Eric Linklater, *Roll of Honour* (London: Rupert Hart-Davis, 1961), p. 49.

26. Eric Linklater, *Husband of Delilah* (London: Macmillan, 1962), pp. vii, 197.

27. Eric Linklater, *A Man over Forty* (London: Macmillan, 1963), p. 143. Portions of the discussion of this novel appeared in my "Region, Character, and Identity in Recent Scottish Fiction," *Virginia Quarterly Review*, 43 (1967), 597-613.

28. Eric Linklater, *A Terrible Freedom* (London: Macmillan, 1966), p. 17.

29. References in the Jenkins discussion are to the following: *So Gaily Sings the Lark* (Glasgow: MacLellan, 1950); *Happy for the Child* (London: Lehmann, 1953); *The Thistle and the Grail* (London: Macdonald, 1954); *The Cone-Gatherers* (London: Macdonald, 1955); *Guests of War* (London: Macdonald, 1956); *The Missionaries* (London: Macdonald, 1957); *The Changeling* (London: Macdonald, 1958); *Love Is a Fervent Fire* (London: Corgi, 1961); *Some Kind of Grace* (London: Macdonald, 1960); *Dust on the Paw* (London: Macdonald, 1961); *The Tiger of Gold* (London: Macdonald, 1962); *A Love of Innocence* (London: Cape, 1963); *The Sardana Dancers* (London: Cape, 1964); *A Very Scotch Affair* (London: Gollancz, 1968); *The Holy Tree* (London: Gollancz, 1969); *The Expatriates* (London: Gollancz, 1971).

30. See Reid's fine essay on Jenkins in *Scotland's Magazine*, October 1958.

31. Alistair Thompson, "Faith and Love: An Examination of Some Themes in the Novels of Robin Jenkins," *New Saltire*, 3 (Spring, 1962), 57-64.

32. Wolfgang Kayser, *The Grotesque in Art and Literature*, tr U. Weisstein (New York: McGraw-Hill, 1966), pp. 122, 154, 58, 79, 188.

14. Kennaway, Spark, and After

1. James Kennaway, *Household Ghosts* (New York: Atheneum, 1961), p. 174.

2. Alexander Scott, "Literature," in *Whither Scotland?* pp. 214-215.

3. References are to the following: James Kennaway, *Tunes of Glory* (New York: Harper, 1956); *Household Ghosts; The Mind Benders* (New York: Atheneum, 1963); *The Bells of Shoreditch* (New York: Atheneum, 1964); *Some Gorgeous Accident* (New York: Atheneum, 1967); *The Cost of Living like This* (New York: Atheneum, 1969).

4. References are to the following: *The Comforters* (1957; New York: Avon, 1965); *Robinson* (1958; New York: Avon, 1969); *Memento Mori* (1959; New York: Avon, 1973); *The Ballad of Peckham Rye* (London: Macmillan, 1960); *The Bachelors* (London: Macmillan, 1960); *The Prime of Miss Jean Brodie* (1961; Philadelphia: Lippincott, 1962); *The Girls of Slender Means* (London: Macmillan, 1963); *The Mandelbaum Gate* (New York: Knopf, 1965); *The Public Image* (London: Macmillan, 1968); *The Driver's Seat* (London: Macmillan, 1970); *Not to Disturb* (New York: Viking, 1971); *The Hothouse by the East River* (New York: Viking, 1973); *The Abbess of Crewe* (New York: Viking, 1974).

5. Stanford, *Muriel Spark* (Fontwell, Sussex: Centaur, 1963), pp. 25-26, 37-40, 45.

6. C. A. Hoyt, "Muriel Spark: The Surrealist Jane Austen," *Contemporary British Novelists*, ed. C. Shapiro (Carbondale: Southern Illinois University Press, 1965), p. 141.

7. "What Images Return," reprinted in *Memoirs of a Modern Scotland*, pp. 151-153. For a book-length consideration of Spark's novels as constructed around the "Nevertheless" principle, see Peter Kemp, *Muriel Spark* (London: Paul Elek, 1974).

8. See Spark's statement in *Partisan Review*, 30 (1963), 81: "I express it in the past tense, but in the actual process, as far as I am concerned, it happens in the present tense."

9. Hoyt, "Muriel Spark," p. 126.

10. Quoted by Frank Baldanza in "Muriel Spark and the Occult," *Wisconsin Studies in Contemporary Literature*, 6 (1965), 190.

11. Malkoff, p. 5.

12. See Carol Ohmann, "Muriel Spark's *Robinson*," *Critique*, 8 (1965-66), 82; Renata Adler, "Muriel Spark," *On Contemporary Literature*, ed. R. Kostelanetz (New York: Avon, 1954), p. 594; Malkoff, p. 11.

13. Stanford, *Muriel Spark*, p. 94.

14. *Partisan Review*, 30 (1963), 79.

15. Alan Sharp, *A Green Tree in Gedde* (New York: New American Library, 1965).

16. Alan Sharp, *The Wind Shifts* (New York: Walker, 1967).

17. William McIlvanney, *Remedy Is None* (London: Eyre and Spottiswoode, 1966).

18. William McIlvanney, *A Gift from Nessus* (London: Eyre and Spottis-woode, 1968).

19. James Allan Ford, *A Judge of Men* (London: Hodder and Stoughton, 1968).

20. Gordon Williams, *The Last Day of Lincoln Charles* (New York: Stein and Day, 1965); *From Scenes like These* (London: Secker and Warburg, 1968); *Walk Don't Walk* (London: Hodder and Stoughton, 1972).

21. Clifford Hanley, *The Hot Month* (Boston: Houghton Mifflin, 1967) and *The Red-Haired Bitch* (Boston: Houghton Mifflin, 1969).

22. Elspeth Davie, *Creating a Scene* (London: Calder and Boyars, 1971); Iain Crichton Smith, *My Last Duchess* (London: Gollancz, 1971).

15. The Tragedy of the Clearances

1. Grimble, *The Future of the Highlands*, p. 22.

2. Paton, *The Claim of Scotland*, p. 162; Linklater, introduction to Ian Grimble, *The Trial of Patrick Sellar* (London: Routledge and Kegan Paul, 1962), p. xv.

3. Iain Crichton Smith, *Consider the Lilies* (London: Gollancz, 1969).

4. Fionn Mac Colla, *And the Cock Crew* (Glasgow: MacLellan, 1945).

5. Neil M. Gunn, *Butcher's Broom* (Edinburgh: Porpoise, 1934).

16. Late Victorian Celticisms

1. Baker, *History of the English Novel*, IX, 293-294.

2. Hugh Walpole in *The Eighteen-Seventies*, ed. H. Granville-Barker (Cambridge: Cambridge University Press, 1929), pp. 39-40.

3. Blake, *Annals of Scotland 1895-1955*, p. 8.

4. Baker, *History of the English Novel*, IX, 294.

5. William Black, *Macleod of Dare* (New York: Harper, 1902), pp. 24-25.

6. See Matthew Arnold, *Lectures and Essays in Criticism*, ed. R. H. Super (Ann Arbor: University of Michigan Press, 1962); "On the Study of Celtic Literature," and note, pp. 491-492. See also John V. Kelleher, "Matthew Arnold and the Celtic Revival," in *Perspectives of Criticism*, ed. H. Levin (Cambridge: Harvard University Press, 1950), pp. 207-221.

7. See Barbara Charlesworth, *Dark Passages* (Madison: University of Wisconsin Press, 1965), p. 37; J. D. Hunt, *The Pre-Raphaelite Imagination* (Lincoln: University of Nebraska Press, 1968); Flavia Alaya, *William Sharp—"Fiona Macleod" 1855-1905* (Cambridge: Harvard University Press, 1970), esp. pp. 42-44, 48.

8. In Fiona Macleod, *The Winged Destiny: Studies in the Spiritual History of the Gael* (New York: Duffield, 1911).

9. In W. B. Yeats, *Essays and Introductions* (New York: Macmillan, 1961), pp. 176, 184, 186-187.

10. In Macleod, *The Winged Destiny*, pp. 172, 190-197.

11. Fiona Macleod, *The Sin-Eater and Other Tales* (Edinburgh: Geddes, 1896), dedication and pp. 5-8.

12. Ibid., pp. 8-9.

13. Ibid., pp. 11-13.

14. Kelleher, "Matthew Arnold and the Celtic Revival," p. 204.

15. Fiona Macleod, *Wind and Wave* (Leipzig: Tauchnitz, 1902), p. 6.

16. Ibid., p. 71.

17. Ibid., p. 131.

18. Macleod, *The Winged Destiny*, p. 367.

19. Macleod, *The Divine Adventure; Iona; Studies in Spiritual History* (New York: Duffield, 1910), pp. 94-95.

20. *Pharais* and *The Mountain Lovers* (New York: Duffield, 1909).

17. Neil Gunn

1. References to Gunn's novels are as follows: *The Grey Coast* (London: Cape, 1926); *Morning Tide* (Edinburgh: Porpoise, 1931); *The Lost Glen* (Edinburgh: Porpoise, 1932); *Sun Circle* (Edinburgh: Porpoise, 1933); *Butcher's Broom* (Edinburgh: Porpoise, 1934); *Highland River* (London: Faber and Faber, 1937); *Wild Geese Overhead* (London: Faber and Faber, 1939); *Second Sight* (London: Faber and Faber, 1940); *The Silver Darlings* (London: Faber and Faber, 1941); *Young Art and Old Hector* (London: Faber and Faber, 1942); *The Serpent* (London: Faber and Faber, 1943); *The Green Isle of the Great Deep* (London: Faber and Faber, 1944); *The Key of the Chest* (London: Faber and Faber, 1945); *The Drinking Well* (London: Faber and Faber, 1946); *The Shadow* (London: Faber and Faber, 1948); *The Silver Bough* (London: Faber and Faber, 1948); *The Lost Chart* (London: Faber and Faber, 1949); *The Well at the World's End* (London: Faber and Faber, 1951); *Bloodhunt* (London: Faber and Faber, 1952); *The Other Landscape* (London: Faber and Faber, 1954). Parts of my discussion of Gunn have appeared in the following: "The Hunter and the Circle: Neil Gunn's Fiction of Violence," *Studies in Scottish Literature*, 1 (1963), 65-82; "Region, Character, and Identity in Recent Scottish Fiction," *Virginia Quarterly Review*, 43 (1967), 597-613; "Beyond History and Tragedy: Neil Gunn's Early Fiction," *Essays on Neil M. Gunn*, ed. D. Morrison (Thurso: Caithness Books, 1971), pp. 52-67; "Comedy and Transcendence in Neil Gunn's Later Fiction," *Neil M. Gunn: The Man and the Writer*, ed. A. Scott and D. Gifford (Edinburgh: Blackwood, 1973), pp. 239-257.

2. Eugene Zamiatin, *We*, tr. G. Zilboorg; Orwell, *1984*; Huxley, *Brave New World*.

3. See Paul Goodman, *Utopian Essays and Practical Proposals*; David

Riesman, "Some Observations on Community Plans and Utopia," *Yale Law Journal*, December 1947; Margaret Mead, "Towards More Vivid Utopias," *Science*, 126 (1957).

4. Richard Gerber, *Utopian Fantasy* (London: Routledge and Kegan Paul, 1955), p. 129.

5. Neil M. Gunn, *The Atom of Delight* (London: Faber and Faber, 1956), pp. 210, 291.

6. Fionn Mac Colla, *The Albannach* (Edinburgh: Reprographia, 1971), p. i.

7. See Alan Bold and John Herdman in *Scotia Review*, August 1975, pp. 27, 31.

18. Highlands of the Humorists

1. Vivien Mercier, *The Irish Comic Tradition* (Oxford: Clarendon, 1962).

2. Angus Macleod, *The Body's Guest, The Tough and the Tender, The Eighth Seal, Blessed Above Women, The Dam.*

3. Neil Munro, *Para Handy Tales* (Edinburgh: Blackwood, 1958), p. 281.

4. George Blake, introduction to Neil Munro, *The Brave Days* (Edinburgh: Porpoise, 1931), p. 20.

5. References are to Lillian Beckwith, *The Hills Is Lonely* (London: Arrow, 1967), and to *The Sea for Breakfast* and *The Loud Halo* in the New York: Dutton editions.

6. Compton Mackenzie, *The Monarch of the Glen* (London: Chatto and Windus, 1951); *Hunting the Fairies* (London: Chatto and Windus, 1949); *Ben Nevis Goes East* (London: Chatto and Windus, 1949); *Keep the Home Guard Turning* (London: Chatto and Windus, 1943); *Whisky Galore* (London: Reprint Society, 1951); *Rockets Galore* (London: Chatto and Windus, 1957).

19. Jane Duncan and George Mackay Brown

1. What follows is a revised and updated version of my article, "Jane Duncan's Friends and the Reachfar Story," *Studies in Scottish Literature*, 6 (1969), 156-174. The "Friend" novels, published by Macmillan (and St. Martin's in the United States), appeared as follows: *My Friends the Miss Boyds* (1959), *My Friend Muriel* (1959), *My Friend Monica* (1960), *My Friend Annie* (1961), *My Friend Sandy* (1961), *My Friend Martha's Aunt* (1962), *My Friend Flora* (1962), *My Friend Madame Zora* (1963), *My Friend Rose* (1964), *My Friend Cousin Emmie* (1964), *My Friends the Mrs. Millers* (1965), *My Friends from Cairnton* (1965), *My Friend My Father* (1966), *My Friends the MacLeans* (1967), *My Friends the Hungry Generation* (1968), *My Friend the Swallow* (1970), *My Friend Sashie* (1972), *My Friends the Misses Kindness* (1974), and *My Friends George and Tom* (1976). Page references are to these editions ex-

cept in the cases of *Martha's Aunt*, *Madame Zora*, and *Cousin Emmie*, where references are to Pan editions.

2. Jean Robertson [Jane Duncan], *Jean in the Morning* (1969), *Jean at Noon* (1971), *Jean in the Twilight* (1972: Pan ed., 1974, cited), *Jean towards Another Day* (1975), London: Macmillan.

3. George Mackay Brown, *Magnus* (London: Hogarth, 1973).

4. George Mackay Brown, *Greenvoe* (New York: Harcourt Brace, 1972).

Index

Adam, Robert, 5
Adler, Alfred, 121
AE (G. W. Russell), 340
Alexander, William, 80, 88-92, 401; *Johnny Gibb of Gushetneuk*, 55, 88-92, 93, 123, 401; *Sketches of Life among My Ain Folk*, 88n.; *Twenty-five Years: A Personal Retrospect*, 88n.
Algren, Nelson, 316
Allen, Walter, 163
Arnold, Matthew, 340, 341, 342, 343
Austen, Jane, 41, 59, 60, 62, 96, 228, 300; *Emma*, 60; *Mansfield Park*, 59, 96; *Persuasion*, 59, 66-67, 95; *Pride and Prejudice*, 41, 59, 64

Baker, Ernest A., 99, 109, 117, 336, 337
Balzac, Honoré de, 44
Barke, James, 222, 241-243, 399, 403; *The Green Hills Far Away*, 241n.; *Immortal Memory*, 241n.; *The Land of the Leal*, 241-243; *Major Operation*, 241n.; *The Wild MacRaes*, 241n.; *The World His Pillow*, 241n.
Barrie, James, 80, 115, 118, 126-130, 132, 134, 214, 217, 306, 310, 401, 402, 403, 405; *Auld Licht Idylls*, 126n., 130; *Dear Brutus*, 126n.; *The Little Minister*, 117, 129-130, 404, 405; *Margaret Ogilvy*, 126 & n.; *Peter and Wendy*, 126-127, 128, 129; *Quality Street*, 126n.; *Sentimental Tommy*, 127-129, 133-134, 214, 402; *Tommy and Grizel*, 128; *What Every*

Woman Knows, 126n.; *A Window on Thrums*, 130, 403
Beckwith, Lillian, 317, 375, 376-378; *About My Father's Business*, 376n.; *Green Hand*, 376n.; *The Hills Is Lonely*, 377-378; *Lightly Poached*, 376n.; *The Loud Halo*, 377-378; *A Rope in Case*, 376n.; *The Sea for Breakfast*, 377-378; *The Spuddy*, 376n.
Behan, Brendan, 317
Benjamin, Walter, 2, 147
Bennett, Arnold, 214
Berthoff, Warner, 144
Black, Joseph, 5
Black, William, 335, 336-340, 345, 399, 405; *A Daughter of Heth*, 337, 338, 339; *Donald Ross of Heimra*, 337, 338, 339; *In Far Lochaber*, 337, 338-339; *Macleod of Dare*, 336, 337, 338, 339-340; *A Princess of Thule*, 337, 338, 339
Blackmore, Richard D., 337
Blackwood's Magazine, 8, 13, 31, 44, 50, 53, 73, 75, 76, 80, 88, 94, 97, 99, 100, 163, 398
Blair, Hugh, 5
Blake, George, 165, 207, 213-222, 228, 229, 241, 250, 336, 358, 376, 399, 400, 401, 402, 403, 405; *Annals of Scotland 1895-1955*, 213-214; *Barrie and the Kailyard School*, 110, 117, 121, 124, 213n.; *The Constant Star*, 219-221; *David and Joanna*, 217-218; *Down to the Sea*, 213n.; *The Heart*

of Scotland, 213n.; *Late Harvest,*
218-219; *Mince Collop Close,* 206,
214-215, 222; *The Path of Glory,*
214-215; *The Paying Guest,* 214; *The
Peacock Palace,* 214; *The Shipbuild-
ers,* 213, 214, 215-217; *The Voyage
Home,* 214; *The Westering Sun,* 214,
221-222
Bold, Alan, 373
Bosch, Hieronymus, 16
Bridie, James (O. H. Mavor), 207
Brontë, Charlotte, 87, 92; *Jane Eyre,* 40
Brontë, Emily, 87, 92; *Wuthering
Heights,* 74, 163
Broster, D. K.: *The Flight of the Heron,*
192
Brown, George Douglas, 98, 116, 128,
130, 131, 132, 134-137, 208, 250,
274, 276, 290, 339, 378, 399, 401;
The House with the Green Shutters,
116, 128, 130, 131, 132, 134-137,
138, 218, 235-236, 274, 276, 290, 403
Brown, George Mackay, 384, 393-397,
402; *A Calendar of Love,* 393-394n.;
Greenvoe, 384, 395-397; *Loaves and
Fishes,* 393n.; *Magnus,* 393-395, 397;
An Orkney Tapestry, 394n.; *Poems
New and Selected,* 393n.; *A Spell for
Green Corn,* 394n.; *A Time to Keep,*
394n.; *The Year of the Whale,* 393n.
Brown, Dr. John, 89, 117
Browning, Robert, 320
Bruce, Donald, 15
Bruce, Robert, 107-108, 193
Brueghel, Pieter, 16
Buchan, John, 143, 144, 147, 169-181,
182, 188, 207, 399, 401, 404, 405;
Castle Gay, 169; *The Dancing Floor,*
143; *The Free Fishers,* 170, 176;
Greenmantle, 169, 176, 177-178; *The
House of Four Winds,* 169; *Hunting-
tower,* 169, 175, 176; *John Burnet of
Barns,* 52, 152, 170-172; *John Mac-
nab,* 152, 169, 176, 178-179; *The
Kirk in Scotland,* 169n., 171-172;
*Mountain Meadow (Sick-Heart
River),* 169, 176, 179-181, 182; *The
Novel and the Fairy Tale,* 147; *Pil-
grim's Way,* 170-176 *passim; The
Power House,* 169; *Prester John,* 170,

172-173, 176; *Thirty-Nine Steps,* 169,
171, 175; *Three Hostages,* 169, 176;
Witch Wood, 170, 173-175, 404;
biographies of Cromwell, Montrose,
Ralegh, and Scott, 169n.
Bulwer-Lytton, Edward, 87, 151, 176
Bunyan, John, 171-172, 401
Burney, Fanny, 59, 96; *Evelina,* 63
Burns, Robert, 4, 5, 8, 27, 73, 267, 316;
The Merry Muses of Caledonia, 267
Bussy, Dorothy, 23
Butler, Samuel, 135
Butter, P. H., 210
Byron, George Gordon, 18, 48, 127,
143, 194, 196, 223, 226, 227, 228,
245, 249, 250, 259, 271, 274, 288,
312; *Don Juan,* 197, 223, 224, 228,
249, 250, 268, 269, 402

Calvinism, 2, 9, 44, 49-50, 51, 63-64,
75, 81-82, 102-104, 108, 115-117,
122, 125, 131, 138-139, 146, 163, 170,
171-172, 174, 180, 204, 205, 211, 212,
213, 217, 218, 222, 223, 231, 269,
277, 280, 285, 290-291, 295, 296,
297, 300, 302, 303, 306-307, 311-312,
320, 325, 329, 330-332, 343, 356-357,
371, 372, 373, 399, 400-401, 402
Campbell, John Macleod, 102, 116, 117
Cape, Jonathan, 247
Carlyle, Thomas, 10, 31, 87, 89, 100,
103, 111, 117, 124, 146, 306; *Past
and Present,* 88; *Sartor Resartus,*
104, 228, 306
Celtic twilight, 164, 229, 290, 335, 336-
347, 385
Cervantes Saavedra, Miguel de, 21
Chalmers, Thomas, 98, 110, 125
Characterology, 1, 20, 34, 35, 37, 39,
42, 47-48, 50, 56, 57, 58, 60, 64, 75,
78, 96, 102, 103, 108, 148, 154-155,
159, 167, 176, 183, 184, 185, 188,
192-193, 210, 215-216, 219, 221, 226,
228, 234, 238, 241, 242, 269-270, 276,
290, 302-303, 304, 306, 309, 317, 332-
333, 334, 338-339, 344, 346-347, 349,
350, 352, 354, 359, 372, 382, 388,
390, 396, 403-405
Charles Edward ("Bonnie Prince Charlie"), 146, 148, 163, 188, 380

Chase, Richard, 131, 145-146
Chesterton, G. K., 382
Chopin, Frederic, 227
Church and ministers, 2, 10, 64-65, 70, 78, 88-89, 92, 95-96, 98-100, 104, 107, 109, 110, 116-117, 123, 124-125, 129-130, 170, 171-172, 174, 202, 204, 235-236, 237-238, 263, 303, 330-331, 364, 371, 399, 404
City, 33, 34, 56, 71, 84, 102, 108, 110, 114, 119-120, 206, 211, 212, 213, 239-240, 244-245, 272, 280, 295, 298, 311, 314, 319, 320-321, 357, 362, 363, 399, 402
Clark, Kenneth, 2-3
Clearances, 10, 192, 262, 263, 325-334, 355, 356, 380, 384, 386, 397, 403, 404
Cockburn, Henry, 44
Colby, Robert and Vineta, 95, 97, 98, 99
Coleridge, Samuel Taylor, 116-117, 266
Collins, Wilkie, 99
Colvin, Sidney, 158, 162
Community, 9, 33-34, 45, 47, 56, 77, 91-92, 112-113, 123, 144-145, 146-147, 184, 186, 208-209, 235, 239, 259, 306-307, 330, 332-334, 364, 393, 396, 401-403
Conrad, Joseph, 52, 128, 228; *Heart of Darkness*, 364; *Lord Jim*, 128
Cornhill Magazine, 110
Counterenlightenment, 31, 44, 50, 53-54, 70-71, 143, 189, 361-362, 366
Crabbe, George, 38
Craig, David, 4, 31, 42-43, 48, 69, 90, 406
Craig, G. Armour, 40
Crockett, Samuel Rutherford, 45, 80, 115, 117-120, 134, 150-151, 152-153, 214; *Cleg Kelly, Arab of the City*, 119-120, 214; *The Lilac Sunbonnet*, 117-119, 137; *The Raiders*, 117n., 150-151, 152-153; *The Stickit Minister*, 119
Crosland, T. W. H., 126, 131

Daiches, David, 3-4, 152, 156, 163
Darwin, Charles, 266
Davie, Elspeth, 206, 319-320; *Creating a Scene*, 206, 319-320; *The Spark and Other Stories*, 319n.
Davie, George Elder, 116-117
Defoe, Daniel, 3, 326; *Moll Flanders*, 214
DeQuincey, Thomas, 342, 345
Diabolism, 22-24, 55-56, 116, 137, 138, 162, 163, 173-175, 177, 180, 297-298, 301, 303, 304, 306
Dickens, Charles, 34, 62, 81, 87, 91, 92, 108-109, 120, 263, 387, 390-391; *Bleak House*, 390-391; *Dombey and Son*, 65; *Oliver Twist*, 120
Disraeli, Benjamin, 179
Dissociation of sensibility, 2-3, 161, 164, 189, 208-209, 210-211, 228, 296-297, 406
Donleavy, J. P., 288
Dostoevsky, Fyodor, 361
Dumas, Alexandre, 194
Dunbar, William, 4, 30, 152, 245, 250
Duncan, Jane, 375, 378, 379, 385-393, 399, 400, 401, 402, 403; *Letter from Reachfar*, 386n.; *My Friend Annie*, 387, 388-389, 393; *My Friend Cousin Emmie*, 388, 392, 393; *My Friend Flora*, 392; *My Friend Madame Zora*, 386, 387, 391; *My Friend Martha's Aunt*, 387, 389, 393; *My Friend Monica*, 387; *My Friend Muriel*, 385, 387, 392; *My Friend My Father*, 386, 389; *My Friend Rose*, 385, 387, 393; *My Friend Sandy*, 387, 389-390; *My Friend Sashie*, 386, 387, 388, 389, 392-393; *My Friend the Swallow*, 387, 388, 389, 390; *My Friends from Cairnton*, 387, 389, 392; *My Friends George and Tom*, 386n.; *My Friends The Hungry Generation*, 386-387, 388, 389, 392, 393; *My Friends the Macleans*, 386, 387, 388, 393; *My Friends the Miss Boyds*, 378, 386, 389, 390, 392; *My Friends the Misses Kindness*, 386n.; as "Jean Robertson": *Jean at Noon*, 390-391; *Jean in the Morning*, 390-391; *Jean in the Twilight*, 390-391; *Jean towards Another Day*, 390-391
Dundee, John Graham of Claverhouse, Viscount, 25, 27-28, 50-52, 148, 151, 188, 288

Dunnett, Dorothy, 193-197; *Check-mate*, 193-197; *The Disorderly Knights*, 193-197; *The Game of Kings*, 193-197; *Murder in Focus*, 193n.; *Murder in the Round*, 193n.; *Pawn in Frankincense*, 193-197; *Queens' Play*, 193-197; *The Ringed Castle*, 193-197

Economics, 9-10, 114-115, 201, 202, 205-206, 326-327
Edgeworth, Maria, 31
Eigner, Edwin, 23, 133, 159, 160, 163
Elegy, 118-119, 122-123, 133, 166, 167, 168, 217, 231, 386, 387, 391, 399
Eliot, George, 44, 63, 73, 87-88, 92, 94, 98, 118, 119, 125, 134-135, 151, 326, 369; *Adam Bede*, 88, 118; *Daniel Deronda*, 88; *Felix Holt*, 88; *Middlemarch*, 88, 208, 210; *The Mill on the Floss*, 88, 118
Eliot, T. S., 2, 250, 312-313
Erskine, Thomas, of Linlathen, 116-117
Euripides, 261
Exile, 32, 65, 84, 105, 159, 162, 166, 188, 204-205, 208, 216, 232, 287, 291-292, 296, 298-299, 301-302, 310, 311, 312, 333, 346-347, 356, 386, 389, 396-397, 400, 402-403

Fanger, Donald, 143
Ferguson, Adam, 5
Ferguson, William, 2, 10, 88, 116, 131, 204
Fergusson, Robert, 4
Ferrier, Susan, 57-68, 69, 71, 72, 76, 79, 82, 325-326, 400, 402; *Destiny*, 57, 64-68; *The Inheritance*, 57, 60-64, 65, 73; *Marriage*, 57-60, 64
Fielding, Henry, 3, 18, 154; *Jonathan Wild*, 41
Flaubert, Gustave, 231; *Madame Bovary*, 166; *Salammbô*, 231
Folklore, 14, 22, 24-25, 27, 30, 96-97, 147, 153, 168, 174, 189, 245, 250, 268, 284-285, 339-340, 343, 344, 356, 358, 359-360, 367, 368-369, 381, 396-397, 398
Forbes, Duncan, of Culloden, 168, 191
Ford, James Allan, 315; *The Brave White Flag*, 315n.; *A Judge of Men*, 315; *Season of Escape*, 315n.; *A Statue for a Public Place*, 315n.
Fraser, J. G., 184
Fraser's Magazine, 87, 110
Freud, Sigmund, 121, 127, 365
Frye, Northrop, 144, 147
Furnas, J. C., 160, 163-164

Galt, John, 3, 5, 9, 25, 30, 31-52, 53-54, 56, 57, 58, 59, 69, 71, 76, 77, 79, 89, 92, 94, 96, 103, 339, 398, 400, 401, 402, 403, 404, 405, 407; *Annals of the Parish*, 36-39, 43, 44, 45, 47, 94, 96, 404; *Autobiography*, 32n.; *The Ayrshire Legatees*, 32-34, 47, 49; *The Entail*, 45-49, 52, 61, 62, 65, 73, 111, 402, 403; *The Last of the Lairds*, 33, 43-45, 49; *Lawrie Todd*, 32n.; *Literary Life*, 32n.; *The Member*, 32n., 49; *The Provost*, 33, 39-43, 45, 47, 51, 97; *The Radical*, 32n., 49; *Ringan Gilhaize*, 25-26, 49-52, 405; *Rothelan*, 32n; *Sir Andrew Wylie of That Ilk*, 34-36, 37, 44, 47, 89, 402, 405; *The Spaewife*, 32n.
Garnett, Edward, 247
Gerber, Richard, 361
Gibbon, Edward, 70, 266
Gibbon, Lewis Grassic (J. Leslie Mitchell), 83-84, 192, 207, 208, 213, 214, 215, 222, 228, 229-241, 243, 244, 246, 250, 316, 356, 385, 395, 399, 400, 401, 402, 403, 405, 407; *Cairo Dawns*, 229-230; *The Conquest of Maya*, 229n.; *Hanno, or the Future of Exploration*, 229n.; *The Lost Trumpet*, 230; *A Scots Quair*, 83-84, 213, 229, 231, 233-241, 242, 275, 316, 356, 399, 401, 405, (*Cloud Howe*, 208, 229, 232, 233, 237-239, 240, 404; *Grey Granite*, 233, 239-240, 402; *Sunset Song*, 229, 231-232, 233, 234-237); *Scottish Scene*, 229n.; *Spartacus*, 231-233, 236; biography of Mungo Park, 229n.
Gide, André, 23, 164
Gifford, Douglas, 28, 30, 42-43, 89, 90
Godwin, William, 23, 50, 69; *Mandeville*, 69

Goethe, Johann W. v., 78, 79, 224; *The Sorrows of Young Werther*, 79; *Wilhelm Meister's Apprenticeship*, 78
Goldsmith, Oliver, 6, 7, 34, 38-39; *The Vicar of Wakefield*, 38-39
Good Words, 110
Gothic novel, 10, 13-30, 73-74, 99-100, 103, 120, 136, 139, 159, 165, 192, 227, 290, 295, 297-298, 300, 398
Graham, R. B. Cunninghame, 207
Grant, James, 150-152; *Adventures of an Aide-de-Camp*, 150n.; *Bothwell*, 150n.; *The Scottish Cavalier*, 150-152; *The Yellow Frigate*, 150n.
Great Disruption (1843), 2, 10, 88-89, 93-97, 124
Grieve, Michael, 201
Grimble, Ian, 326-327
Grotesque, 15-18, 29-30, 38, 55-56, 61-62, 66, 75, 137, 165-167, 173-174, 250, 253, 262, 265, 267, 272, 276, 281, 284-285, 286, 300, 302, 303, 309, 319, 346, 369, 372, 378, 406
Gunn, Neil M., 105, 146, 192, 204, 207, 222, 236, 250, 251, 331-334, 339, 348-373, 374, 379, 393, 395, 399, 400, 401, 402, 403, 404, 405; *The Atom of Delight*, 348n., 365, 366; *Bloodhunt*, 349, 366-367, 374; *Butcher's Broom*, 328, 331-334, 349, 358, 359; *The Drinking Well*, 349, 351, 356, 357, 368; *The Green Isle of the Great Deep*, 349, 355, 356, 360-362, 363, 365, 370; *The Grey Coast*, 348, 349-350, 351, 354, 374; *Hidden Doors*, 348n.; *Highland Pack*, 348n.; *Highland River*, 348n.; 349, 352, 353-354, 355, 359, 362, 363, 367, 371; *The Key of the Chest*, 349, 363, 364-365, 366, 368; *The Lost Chart*, 349, 363-364, 368; *The Lost Glen*, 349, 350-352; *Morning Tide*, 349, 352-353, 354, 355, 359; *Off in a Boat*, 348n.; *The Other Landscape*, 348, 349, 367, 368, 369-370; *Second Sight*, 349, 351, 352, 362, 363; *The Serpent*, 349, 351, 356-357; *The Shadow*, 349, 365-366; *The Silver Bough*, 349, 367-368; *The Silver Darlings*, 349, 357, 358-360, 401; *Sun Circle*, 251, 349, 357-358, 359; *The Well at the World's End*, 349, 367-369, 374; *Whisky and Scotland*, 348n.; *The White Hour*, 348n.; *Wild Geese Overhead*, 349, 362-363; *Young Art and Old Hector*, 349, 352, 354-356, 360
Guthrie, Thomas, 110

Hamilton, William, 116-117
Hanham, H. J., 201
Hanley, Clifford, 206, 317-318; *The Chosen Instrument*, 317n.; *Dancing in the Streets*, 317n.; *The Hot Month*, 317-318; *Love from Everybody*, 317n.; *The Red-Haired Bitch*, 318; *A Skinful of Scotch*, 317n.; *The Taste of Too Much*, 317n.
Hardie, Keir, 202
Harding, D. W., 60
Hardy, Thomas, 118, 119, 128-129, 135, 221, 288, 385; *The Return of the Native*, 118
Hawthorne, Nathaniel, 50, 100, 155, 346; *The Scarlet Letter*, 79, 346
Hay, J. MacDougall, 132, 134, 137-139, 250, 399, 401; *Barnacles*, 137n.; *Gillespie*, 132, 134, 137-139, 401, 403; *Their Dead Sons*, 137n.
Heller, Joseph: *Catch-22*, 254
Henryson, Robert, 4
Herdman, John, 373
Himmelfarb, Gertrude, 170, 179
History, 5, 19, 20, 21, 22, 26, 36-39, 40, 43, 46, 50-51, 55, 65, 67, 90, 125-126, 129, 133, 145-146, 147-148, 149, 151-152, 158, 163-164, 168-169, 170, 171, 180, 183, 187, 188, 189, 190, 193, 219-222, 231, 234-235, 237, 239, 263, 264-265, 267, 269, 318, 328, 331-332, 333, 334, 341, 342-343, 345, 349, 356, 357-360, 370, 386, 389-390, 395, 396, 397, 398, 400-401, 402, 404-405, 406, 408
Hobbes, Thomas, 15
Hoffmann, E. T. A., 20, 23
Hogg, James, 14, 22-30, 50, 76, 136, 398, 402, 404, 405; "The Bridal of Polmood," 24-25; *The Brownie of Bodsbeck*, 25-28; *Domestic Manners*

and Private Life of Sir Walter Scott,
22n.; *Jacobite Relics of Scotland,*
22n.; *Memoirs and Confessions of a*
Justified Sinner, 22-24, 30, 136, 170,
404, 405; *The Queen's Wake,* 22n.;
Tales of the Wars of Montrose, 22n.;
The Three Perils of Man, 27-30;
Winter Evening Tales, 22n.
Holland, Norman, 144
Holloway, John, 92
Hopkins, Gerard Manley, 393n., 396
Hoyt, C. A., 295-296, 300
Hugo, Victor, 154, 155
Huizinga, Johan, 374
Hume, David, 5, 131, 146, 204
Humor, 16-18, 38-39, 42-43, 48-49, 52,
57, 58, 60-61, 62, 64-65, 73, 124, 244-
245, 249-250, 252-253, 254-255, 260,
262-263, 265, 267, 305, 316-318, 348,
349, 355, 367, 368-370, 374-384, 392
Hunt, Leigh, 8
Hunter, John and William, 5
Hutcheson, Francis, 5
Hutton, James, 5
Huxley, Aldous: *Brave New World,*
360-362

Idolatry, 22, 45-47, 48, 63, 65-67, 71,
73, 84, 163-164, 188, 217, 298, 300,
302, 307, 401-402
Idyll, *see* Pastoral idyll
Impersonation, 7, 24, 49, 50-51, 127-
128, 172, 173, 175, 176-178, 301-302,
405
Inheritance, 21-22, 46, 60, 62-65, 73-
74, 82-83, 84, 92, 101-102, 104-105,
107, 108-109, 111-112, 149-150, 159,
249, 255-256, 263, 264, 270, 311,
338-339, 345-346, 355, 389, 400, 402
Independent Labor Party, 202, 292
Irony, 40, 41, 53, 54, 90, 128-129, 145,
160, 162, 164, 165, 178, 194, 218,
249, 258-259, 264, 295, 379, 399,
406, 407, 408
Irving, Edward, 98, 103, 116

Jack, Ian, 40, 49, 80
Jacob, Violet, 192
Jacobitism, 21, 74, 124-125, 127, 128,
152, 157, 163-164, 166, 168-169, 190,
191, 226, 227, 264, 325, 326, 380,
381
James, Henry, 94, 97, 159, 161, 164,
222; *Notes on Novelists,* 97
Jeffrey, Francis, 93-94, 95
Jenkins, Robin, 79, 119, 129, 136, 210,
214, 217, 272-286, 399, 400, 401,
402, 403, 404, 405, 408; *The Change-*
ling, 214, 217, 273, 274, 275-276,
280, 281, 283-284, 284-285, 404; *The*
Cone-Gatherers, 273, 274, 276, 280,
283; *Dust on the Paw,* 277, 281,282,
284; *The Expatriates,* 279, 282, 285;
Guests of War, 273, 274, 275, 277,
279-280, 281, 282, 285-286, 403;
Happy for the Child, 273-274, 281;
The Holy Tree, 273, 279; *Love Is a*
Fervent Fire, 276-277, 280, 281, 284,
285; *A Love of Innocence,* 273, 277-
278, 280, 281, 283; *The Missionaries,*
275, 281, 285; *The Sardana Dancers,*
278, 279, 281, 282; *So Gaily Sings the*
Lark, 273, 274, 276, 282, 283; *Some*
Kind of Grace, 277, 282-283, 284,
285; *The Thistle and the Grail,* 273,
274, 275, 280, 282, 286; *The Tiger of*
Gold, 277, 281-282; *A Very Scotch*
Affair, 273, 274, 278-279, 281, 282,
285, 286
Johnson, Samuel, 41, 66
Joyce, James, 400
Jung, C. G., 121, 191-192

Kailyard, 80, 84, 87, 89, 103, 109, 114-
126, 131-132, 134, 137, 210, 235-236,
296, 378, 385, 399, 402
Kames, Henry Home, Lord, 5
Kayser, Wolfgang, 16, 284
Kellas, James, 202, 204
Kelleher, John V., 343
Kemp, Robert, 137
Kennaway, James, 287-294, 400, 401;
The Bells of Shoreditch, 288, 291-
293, 314, 403; *The Cost of Living like*
This, 288, 293-294; *Country Dance,*
288n.; *Household Ghosts,* 287-288,
289, 290-291, 292, 401, 403; *The*
Mind Benders, 288, 291; *Silence,* 288;
Some Gorgeous Accident, 288, 293,
403; *Tunes of Glory,* 288, 289-290

Kiely, Robert, 133, 147, 156
Kitchin, George, 40

Lane, Jane: *Farewell to the White Cock-ade*, 192; *Fortress in the Forth*, 192; *Queen of the Castle*, 192; *A Wind Through the Heather*, 192
Language, 2, 4-5, 26-28, 32-33, 34, 37, 38-39, 41-43, 45, 48-49, 61, 76, 89-91, 97, 103-104, 105, 106-107, 118, 123-124, 152, 158, 166-167, 185, 195, 211-212, 232, 236-237, 238-239, 240-241, 242-245, 251, 291, 313-314, 316, 325, 377-378, 392, 394-395, 407-408
Law, 10, 46, 48, 204, 315
Lawrence, D. H., 365-366, 396
Lewis, M. G., 16, 23
Lindsay, Maurice, 131
Linklater, Eric, 31-32, 56, 202, 203, 207, 213, 223, 228, 245, 246-272, 287, 316, 327, 379, 393n., 399, 401, 402, 403, 407; "The Art of Adventure," 246n., 251; *Collected Stories*, 246; *The Dark of Summer*, 263-265; *The Faithful Ally*, 263-264, 267; *Fanfare for a Tin Hat*, 246n., 247-265 *passim*; *The House of Gair*, 262-263, 264; *Husband of Delilah*, 268-269; *The Impregnable Women*, 255, 256; *Juan in America*, 245, 247, 249-250, 256, 269, 270, 316; *Juan in China*, 254-255; *Judas*, 255, 256-257; *Laxdale Hall*, 261-262, 269; *The Lion and the Unicorn*, 246; *Magnus Merriman*, 252-253, 269; *The Man on My Back*, 246n.; *A Man over Forty*, 256, 269-271; *The Men of Ness*, 247, 250-252, 256; *The Merry Muse*, 267; *Mr. Byculla*, 261; "The Novel in Scotland," 207, 246; *Poet's Pub*, 248-249, 250; *Position at Noon*, 256, 265-267, 401, 403; *Private Angelo*, 247, 250, 255, 256, 257-260; *Ripeness Is All*, 250, 253-254, 255; *Roll of Honour*, 267-268; *The Sailor's Holiday*, 255-256; *A Spell for Old Bones*, 260-261, 271; *The Survival of Scotland*, 247n.; *A Terrible Freedom*, 261, 271-272; *The Ultimate Viking*, 247n., 251; *White-Maa's Saga*, 247-248; *A*

Year of Space, 246n.
Local attachment, 1-2, 10-11, 33, 34, 52, 64, 67, 68, 72, 76, 83, 108, 123, 165, 171, 206, 231, 242, 252, 349, 355, 357, 386, 389, 397, 406, 407
Locke, John, 9
Lockhart, John Gibson, 8-9, 10, 30, 50, 68-80, 82, 88, 186, 401, 404; *Adam Blair*, 8, 69, 76-80, 95, 98, 404; *Lectures on the History of Literature* (trans. from F. Schlegel), 68n.; *Life of Scott*, 68n.; *Matthew Wald*, 8, 68-69, 72, 74-75, 170; *Peter's Letters to His Kinsfolk*, 68n.; *Reginald Dalton*, 69, 71-74, 78, 79; *Valerius*, 68-69, 70-71, 72, 78; biographies of Burns and Napoleon, 68n.
The Lounger, 8, 9
Low, J. T., 233

McAdam, John, 5
Mac Colla, Fionn (T. Douglas MacDonald), 131, 328, 330-331, 332, 371-373, 399, 402, 404; *The Albannach*, 371-373, 402; *And the Cock Crew*, 328, 330-331, 332, 334, 371; *At the Sign of the Clenched Fist*, 131, 330n.; *Too Long in This Condition* (*Ro fhada mar so a tha Mi*), 330n.
MacCormick, John, 203
MacDiarmid, Hugh (Christopher Murray Grieve), 116, 207, 243, 245, 250; *A Drunk Man Looks at the Thistle*, 245, 250
MacDonald, George, 80, 89, 92, 94-95, 98, 100-109, 110, 116, 117, 119, 139, 399, 400, 401, 402, 403, 404, 405; *Alec Forbes of Howglen*, 101, 102, 105-108; *Annals of a Quiet Neighbourhood*, 94, 100n.; *At the Back of the North Wind*, 100n.; *David Elginbrod*, 94, 101, 102, 103-104, 105; *The Golden Key*, 100n., 101; *Lilith*, 100n., 101; *Malcolm*, 101, 102; *The Marquis of Lossie*, 101, 102, 103; *Phantastes*, 100n., 101; *Robert Falconer*, 101, 104-105, 109; *Sir Gibbie*, 35, 103, 105-109, 120, 402; *Unspoken Sermons*, 100n.; *Wilfred Cumbermede*, 94, 100n.

MacDonald, Greville, 116
MacDonald Greville, 116
McIlvanney, William, 313-314, 315; *Docherty*, 313n; *A Gift from Nessus*, 313n., 314; "Growing Up in the West," 313n.; *Remedy Is None*, 313n., 313-314
Mackenzie, Compton, 64, 105, 207, 213, 214, 215, 222-228, 229, 241, 261, 317, 375, 378-384, 385, 399, 405; *Ben Nevis Goes East*, 379, 382; *The Four Winds of Love*, 105, 194, 213, 223-228, 379, 384, 399, 405; *Hunting the Fairies*, 379, 381-382; *Keep the Home Guard Turning*, 379, 382-383; *Life and Times*, 222n.; *The Monarch of the Glen*, 379, 380-381; *Rockets Galore*, 379, 382-384; *Sinister Street*, 222-223, 227; *Whisky Galore*, 379, 382-383
Mackenzie, Henry, 3, 5-9, 70, 398; *Julia de Roubigné*, 7-8; *The Man of Feeling*, 3, 6-7; *The Man of the World*, 7, 8; "Story of La Roche," 8
Maclaren, Ian (John Watson), 7, 80, 115, 116, 117, 118, 120-126, 134, 378, 401; *Auld Lang Syne*, 122-124; *Beside the Bonnie Brier Bush*, 117, 120-123, 137, 235-236; *Kate Carnegie*, 117, 124-126, 404
McLean, Allan Campbell: *The Islander* (*The Gates of Eden*), 374, 378
Macleod, Angus, 374
Macleod, Donald, 328-329
Macleod, Fiona (William Sharp), 335, 340-347, 348 399, 400, 402; *Anima Celtica*, 341; "Celtic," 341-342; *The Divine Adventure; Iona; Studies in Spiritual History*, 345; *For the Beauty of an Idea*, 341; *The Mountain Lovers*, 345-347; *Pharais*, 340, 345; *The Sin-Eater and Other Tales*, 342-343, 344-345; *Sospiri di Roma*, 342; *Wind and Wave*, 343-344; *The Winged Destiny: Studies in the Spiritual History of the Gael*, 341-342, 345; biography of D. G. Rossetti, 340n.
Macleod, Norman, 110
Macpherson, James, 5

Malkoff, Karl, 300
Mann, Thomas, 366
Manners, 9, 13, 36, 43, 46, 57, 59, 64-66, 69-70, 71-72, 96, 99, 100, 108, 151, 183, 235, 242, 253-254, 337, 345, 347, 379, 383
Martz, Louis, 14
Marx, Karl, 121, 131, 239
Mary Queen of Scots, 125, 148, 188, 192-193, 196
Maturin, Charles Robert, 22-23; *Melmoth the Wanderer*, 23
Maurice, F. D., 116
Maxton, James, 292
Melville, Herman: *Billy Budd*, 361; *Moby Dick*, 163
Mercier, Vivian, 374
Meredith, George, 228, 342; *The Ordeal of Richard Feverel*, 224
Mérimée, Prosper: *Chronicle of the Reign of Charles IX*, 211
Mill, John Stuart, 92, 116-117; *On Liberty*, 92
Millar, J. H., 89, 94, 115
Miller, Hugh, 80, 89; *My Schools and Schoolmasters*, 89
Miller, J. Hillis, 92
Milton, John, 119
The Mirror, 5, 8, 9
Mitchison, Naomi, 165, 182-192, 194, 207, 250, 251, 360, 400, 401, 402, 405; *The Big House*, 182n.; *Blood of the Martyrs*, 183, 184, 186-187, 188; *The Bull Calves*, 165, 183-184, 185, 190-192, 401; *The Conquered*, 183, 184-186, 187; *The Corn King and the Spring Queen*, 183, 184, 185, 187-190, 251, 405; *Five Men and a Swan*, 182n.; *Return to the Fairy Hill*, 182-183; *When the Bough Breaks*, 182n.
Mitchison, Rosalind, 9, 10, 131
Mock-heroic, 37, 41, 54, 55, 90-91, 136, 244-245, 252, 269, 303, 379, 380, 381
Moir, David Macbeth, 53-57, 76, 94, 401; *Mansie Wauch*, 53-57, 90, 401
Monro, Alexander, 5
Montgomerie, William, 239
Montrose, James Graham, Marquess, 172, 177, 188

Morris, William, 179, 343

Muir, Edwin, 207, 210-213, 373, 393n.; 394, 399, 401, 402, 405, 407; *Autobiography*, 209n.; *Essays in Literature and Society*, 209n.; *The Labyrinth*, 209n.; *Poor Tom*, 210, 212-213, 401, 402; *Scott and Scotland*, 2, 209n., 407; *The Structure of the Novel*, 209n.; *The Three Brothers*, 210-212, 213, 401, 405; *The Voyage*, 209n.

Muir, Willa, 208-210, 399, 405; *Belonging*, 208, 210; *Imagined Corners*, 208-210, 405; *Living with Ballads*, 209n.; *Mrs. Grundy in Scotland*, 209n.

Munro, Ian S., 236-237, 239

Munro, Neil, 134, 144, 164-169, 214, 325-326, 375-376, 399, 405; *The Brave Days*, 376; *The Daft Days*, 165n.; *Doom Castle*, 165-166; *Fancy Farm*, 165n.; *Gilian the Dreamer*, 128, 134, 165n., 166, 211, 376; *John Splendid*, 52, 166-167, 168, 376; *The Lost Pibroch*, 164-165n.; *The New Road*, 165, 167-169, 376; *Para Handy Tales*, 164n., 165, 375-376

Nairn, Tom, 145, 146

Napoleon, 266, 327

National Party of Scotland, 202

Newman, J. H., 300

Nicoll, W. Robertson, 99, 120n.

Noctes Ambrosianae, 55, 73, 80n., 89

Novalis, 398

Oliphant, Margaret, 89, 92, 93-101, 399, 401, 403, 404; *Adam Graeme of Mossgray*, 94; *Annals of a Publishing House*, 93n.; *Autobiography*, 93-94; *The Beleaguerd City*, 100; Carlingford Chronicles, 94, 97; *Harry Muir*, 94; *Katie Stewart*, 94; *The Laird of Norlaw*, 94; *Margaret Maitland*, 94, 95-97, 100, 401, 403; *Merkland*, 92, 94; *The Perpetual Curate*, 94, 98; *The Rector*, 98; *Salem Chapel*, 94, 97, 98-100, 404; Stories of the Seen and Unseen, 95, 100-101; biographies of Thomas

Chalmers and Edward Irving, 93n.

Oliver Jane: *Alexander the Glorious*, 192; *The Lion and the Rose*, 192; *The Lion Is Gone*, 192

Oppenheim, E. Phillips, 175

Oral tradition, 2, 25, 26, 27, 30, 34, 37, 44, 77, 91, 123, 146-147, 152, 190-191, 326, 327, 334, 339, 340, 344, 359-360, 369, 375, 390, 392, 398, 403, 405

Orkneyinga Saga, 250-251, 396

Ortega y Gassett, Jose, 114

Orwell, George: *1984*, 361

Ouida (Maria Louise de la Ramée), 194

Paine, Tom, 82

Pastoral idyll, 20, 80-81, 83-84, 87, 88, 90, 111, 118, 119, 121-123, 129, 136, 138, 217, 236, 261, 272, 274, 275, 280, 282-283, 286, 308, 311, 346, 357, 371, 373, 379, 382, 386, 401, 405, 406, 407

Pater, Walter, 71, 186, 210, 229-30, 340, 343, 398; *Marius the Epicurean*, 71, 186, 210; *Studies in the Renaissance*, 398

Paterson, Neil: *Behold Thy Daughter*, 358

Peacock, Thomas Love, 248, 255

Phillipson, N. T., 10

Plaidy, Jean (Eleanor Hibbert), 192-193; *The Captive Queen of Scots*, 193; *The Royal Road to Fotheringay*, 193

Plato: *The Republic*, 183, 189, 232

Pliny the Elder, 263

Poe, Edgar Allan, 17

Porter, Katherine Anne: "Flowering Judas," 279

Power, William, 103, 114-115

Prévost, Abbé: *Manon Lescaut*, 79

Price, Martin, 10

Pritchett, V. S., 17, 48, 91, 131

Proust, Marcel, 375

Provinciality, 1-2, 3, 31-52 passim, 53-57, 58, 61, 65, 71, 72, 206, 209, 237, 239, 246, 269, 360, 388, 399, 401, 402

Rabelais, Francois, 211, 243, 244, 245, 248

Radcliffe, Ann, 15, 22
Raeburn, Henry, 5
Ramsay, Alen, 4
Ramsay, Dean, 80, 89, 115
Reid, Alexander, 273
Reid, Alastair, 204
Reid, J. M., 89, 206
Richardson, Samuel, 3, 7, 62, 326
Robertson, William, 5
Romance, 19, 29, 30, 52, 68, 84, 101-
    102, 107, 109, 129-130, 139, 143-197,
    224-225, 249, 263-264, 325, 326, 338-
    339, 345, 358, 399, 400, 404-405,
    406, 408
Rosa, Salvator, 19
Ross, William, 203
Rossetti, D. G., 340
Rousseau, Jean Jacques: *Confessions*,
    226; *Julie*, 8
Ruskin, John, 337, 340

Sabatini, Rafael, 194
Schools and schoolmasters, 10, 89,
    102, 112-113, 204, 267, 275, 277,
    319-320, 367, 404
Scott, Alexander, 182n., 288, 317
Scott, Alexander John, 116
Scott, J. D., 116
Scott, Sir Walter, 2, 5, 6, 8-9, 10, 13,
    15, 18-22, 24, 25, 31, 43, 49, 50, 52,
    57, 70, 88, 90, 103, 109, 125, 143,
    144, 146, 148-150, 151, 152, 155,
    157, 159, 162, 164, 165, 167, 170,
    171, 175, 179, 186, 188, 190, 191,
    194, 291, 325, 326, 398, 400, 401,
    403, 404, 405; *The Abbot*, 148, 149;
    Anne of Geierstein, 148; *The Anti-
    quary*, 81, 150; *The Black Dwarf*,
    149; *The Bride of Lammermoor*, 8,
    19-20, 21-22, 111, 149, 150, 163, 339;
    Count Robert of Paris, 148, 150; *The
    Fortunes of Nigel*, 19, 148, 149, 150;
    Guy Mannering, 94, 148, 149, 149-
    150; *The Heart of Midlothian*, 90,
    103; *Ivanhoe*, 148, 149, 227; *Kenil-
    worth*, 148; *The Lady of the Lake*,
    19n; *The Lay of the Last Minstrel*,
    19n.; *A Legend of Montrose*, 150;
    Marmion, 19n.; *The Minstrelsy of
    the Scottish Border*, 19n.; *The Mona-*

stery, 211; *Old Mortality*, 7, 20, 21-
    22, 25, 49-50, 122, 133, 148, 150,
    171, 173; *Peveril of the Peak*, 148,
    150; *The Pirate*, 150; *Quentin Dur-
    ward*, 19, 148, 149, 150; *Redgauntlet*,
    20, 21-22, 148, 163, 191; *Rob Roy*,
    111, 150, 153; *St. Ronan's Well*, 8,
    62, 150, 291; *The Surgeon's Daugh-
    ter*, 150, 277; *The Talisman*, 148;
    Waverley, 8-9, 19, 128, 146, 147,
    148, 149, 167, 175; *Woodstock*, 148,
    150; biographies of Dryden and
    Swift, 19n.
Scottish Covenant, 203
Scottish Home Rule Association, 202-
    203
Scottish National Convention, 202
Scottish nationalism, 10, 105, 152, 182,
    201, 202-203, 224, 252, 380, 399,
    406
Scottish National Party, 202-203, 205-
    206
Sellar, Patrick, 327, 328, 329, 330
Shakespeare, William, 48, 160, 361,
    362; *All's Well That Ends Well*, 309;
    Hamlet, 160, 312-313, 314, 351;
    Henry IV, 381, 382; *King Lear*, 75;
    Measure for Measure, 361; *The
    Tempest*, 224, 362; *Twelfth Night*,
    382-383
Sharp, Alan, 118, 119, 136, 270, 311-
    312, 400, 402; *A Green Tree in
    Gedde*, 311n., 311-312; *The Wind
    Shifts*, 312
Shaw, George Bernard: *Man and
    Superman*, 226, 228
Shelley, Mary: *Frankenstein*, 23, 163
Shorthouse, J. H., 210
Shroder, Maurice Z., 144
Slesser, Malcolm, 205
Small-nation consciousness, 205-206,
    224, 246, 259, 282, 399, 402
Smith, Adam, 5
Smith, Iain Crichton, 134-135, 206,
    319, 320-321, 327, 328-329, 330, 332,
    334, 394, 403, 404; *Biobuill Is Sana-
    san Reice*, 327n.; *Consider the Lilies*,
    327, 328-329, 330, 332, 334, 403;
    Deer on the High Hills, 327n.; *The
    Last Summer*, 327n.; *My Last*

Duchess, 206, 319, 320-321, 327n.; *Thistles and Roses*, 327n.

Smith, J. A., 10

Smith, Sydney Goodsir, 115, 241, 243-245, 250; *Carotid Cornucopius*, 241, 243-245, 250; *Short Introduction to Scottish Literature*, 243n.; *Skail Wind*, 243n.; *The Stick-up*, 243n.; *Under the Eildon Tree*, 243n.; *The Wallace*, 243n.

Smollett, Tobias George, 3, 5, 13-19, 24, 30, 31, 38, 56, 74, 136, 284, 378, 398; *Adventures of Ferdinand Count Fathom*, 14-16; *History of England*, 14n.; *Humphry Clinker*, 16, 33, 34, 377; *Peregrine Pickle*, 17-18, 36, 60; *Roderick Random*, 16-17; *Travels through France and Italy*, 14n., 378

Smout, T. C., 2, 9

Spark, Muriel, 3, 62, 79, 270, 284, 287, 294-310, 400, 401, 402, 404, 405; *The Abbess of Crewe*, 295, 297, 300, 302, 303, 309; *The Bachelors*, 295, 297-298, 301, 305-306; *The Ballad of Peckham Rye*, 295, 297, 305; *The Comforters*, 294n., 295, 297, 301, 303-304; *The Driver's Seat*, 295, 299, 307-308; *The Girls of Slender Means*, 295, 298, 307, 309, 402; *The Hothouse by the East River*, 295, 299-300, 309-310; *The Mandelbaum Gate*, 295, 298-299, 301-302, 307, 309; *Memento Mori*, 295, 297, 303, 305; *Not to Disturb*, 295, 299, 308-309; *The Prime of Miss Jean Brodie*, 204, 270, 294, 295, 302, 306-307, 308, 309, 401, 402, 404; *The Public Image*, 295, 307; *Robinson*, 295, 297, 304; *The Takeover*, 294n.; "What Images Return," 296-297

Spector, Robert, 14-15

Speirs, John, 136

Spence, Lewis, 207

Stanford, Derek, 295, 302-303

Stendhal, 21

Sterne, Laurence, 3, 6-7, 34; *Tristram Shandy*, 228, 244

Stevenson, Robert Louis, 23, 46, 132-134, 144, 146, 151, 152, 153, 154-164, 169, 170, 171, 172-173, 185, 194, 325, 399, 400, 401, 404, 408; *The Black Arrow*, 159-160; *A Child's Garden of Verses*, 154n.; *David Balfour*, 159, 160-161, 168; *Dr. Jekyll and Mr. Hyde*, 311; *Familiar Studies of Men and Books*, 154n.; "A Gossip on Romance," 155-156, 160; "A Humble Remonstrance," 155-156, 160; *Kidnapped*, 52, 152, 153, 154, 157-159, 160, 161-162, 163, 167, 168, 173, 269-270; *The Master of Ballantrae*, 154n., 160, 161, 162-164, 166, 172, 401; *St. Ives*, 161-162; *Travels with a Donkey*, 154n.; *Treasure Island*, 152, 154n., 156-157, 173; *Underwoods*, 154n.; "Victor Hugo's Romances," 154-155; *Virginibus Puerisque*, 154n.; *Weir of Hermiston*, 132-134, 160, 161, 162, 403

Strauss, Albrecht, 14

Survival, 1, 4, 28, 38, 157, 159, 160, 176, 188, 206, 214, 215, 222, 246-286 *passim*, 325, 342, 346-347, 350-351, 399, 405, 407, 408

Swinnerton, Frank, 223

Tennyson, Alfred, 80

Thackeray, William Makepeace, 59, 87, 91, 92, 96, 151; *Henry Esmond*, 59, 226; *Vanity Fair*, 79, 96

Thomas, Dylan, 293, 317, 396

Thompson, Alistair, 277

Topography and sense of place, 19, 26-27, 52, 70, 72, 81, 126, 151-152, 155, 158, 170, 171, 173, 176, 178-179, 185, 186, 188, 217, 224-225, 236, 242, 249, 279, 280, 294, 295, 297-298, 299-300, 312, 319, 337-338, 345, 346-347, 349, 350, 352, 353-354, 355, 363, 370-371, 388-389, 391, 397, 402

Tranter, Nigel: *The Path of the Hero King*, 193; *The Price of the King's Peace*, 193; *The Steps to the Empty Throne*, 193; Master of Gray trilogy, 193n.

Trollope, Anthony, 44, 73, 87, 90, 91, 96, 97, 98, 379

Tulloch, Principal, 110

Turner, J. M. W., 337

Twain, Mark: *Huckleberry Finn*, 119

Tytler, Sarah (Henrietta Keddie), 109-113, 114, 399, 402; *Logie Town*, 109, 110, 112-113; *St. Mungo's City*, 109-113, 402; *Three Generations*, 109-110

Union (1707), 2, 3-4, 10, 44, 150, 202, 399

Urquhart, Sir Thomas, of Cromarty, 243

Voltaire, 259

Walpole, Horace, 22

Watson, James, 4

Watt, Ian, 9

Watt, James, 5

Webb, Mary, 385

Webster, John: *The Duchess of Malfi*, 79, 309

Welsh, Alexander, 147

Williams, Gordon: *From Scenes like These*, 316, 317; *The Last Day of Lincoln Charles*, 316; *The Siege of Trencher's Farm*, 316n.; *Walk Don't Walk*, 316-317, 318

Wilson, John: *The City of the Plague*, 80n.; *The Foresters*, 80-83; *The Isle of Palms*, 80n.; *Lights and Shadows of Scottish Life*, 80; *Margaret Lyndsay*, 80-84; *Noctes Ambrosianae*, 80n.

Winner, Anthony, 20

Wittig, Kurt, 15, 89-90, 134, 152, 233-234

Woman, images of, 48-49, 58, 62-63, 79, 83-84, 94-97, 104, 107, 118, 126-127, 133, 139, 160, 189, 196, 209-210, 218, 219, 221-222, 234, 236, 237, 238, 240, 241-242, 291-292, 328-329, 332-333, 338, 340n., 359, 403

Woolcott, Alexander, 120-121

Woolf, Virginia, 293

Wordsworth, William, 79, 80, 81, 83, 87, 103, 266

Yeats, William Butler, 340, 341, 343, 400

Young, Douglas, 1, 203

Zabel, Morton D., 164

Zamiatin, Eugene: *We*, 361

Zweig, Paul, 144-145

OKALOOSA-WALTON COLLEGE

1000016968

RARY
IN JUNIOR COLLEGE